Благодарности:

В подготовке и апробации данной книги нимали участие наши американские колл преподаватели языковой школы Lingua Progres Plus (Казань).
Особую благодарность авторы выражают директору школы Lingua Progress Plus Джошу Херрингу и его жене Эми Херринг за внимательное и вдумчивое чтение книги, корректировку ключей к заданиям и лингвокультурных реалий. Большое спасибо Джеймсу и Ханне Хансон за возможность апробации грамматических заданий. Неоценимую помощь в финальной вычитке, а также в корректировке курса фонетики нам оказал преподаватель английского языка школы филолог Даг Элдерс.
Большое спасибо, коллеги! Совместная работа с вами имела очень большое значение для этой книги и была необычайно приятна и продуктивна для её авторов.

Acknowledgement:

Our American colleagues, teachers of the language school “Lingua Progress Plus” (Kazan) took part in preparation and approbation of assignments and the plot of this book.
The authors express special gratitude to the director of the school “Lingua Progress Plus” Josh Herring and his wife Amy Herring for attentive and thoughtful reading of the book, correcting tasks and exercises and linguacultural realities. Many thanks to James and Hannah Hanson for the possibility of approbation of grammar tasks. An invaluable help in the final proofreading, as well as in adjusting the phonetics course, was provided by the English language teacher, philologist Doug Elders.
Many thanks, colleagues! Working together with you was very important for the publication of this book and was extremely enjoyable and productive for authors.

Lada Moskaleva,
Tatiana Shakhmatova,
Dina Murtazina

Russian Journey

Intensive Russian language course
in the form of an adventure novel

St. Petersburg
«Zlatoust»

2020

Лада Москалева,
Татьяна Шахматова,
Дина Муртазина

Вояж по-русски

Интенсивный курс русского языка
в форме приключенческого романа

Санкт-Петербург
«Златоуст»

2020

УДК 811.161.1

Москалева, Л., Шахматова, Т., Муртазина, Д.
Вояж по-русски : интенсивный курс русского языка в форме приключенческого романа. — СПб. : Златоуст, 2020. — 352 с.

Moskaleva, L., Chakhmatova, T., Murtazina, D.
Travel like a Russian : intensive Russian language course in the form of an adventure novel. — St. Petersburg : Zlatoust, 2020. — 352 p.

ISBN 978-5-86547-925-3

Зав. редакцией: к. ф. н. *А.В. Голубева*
Редактор: *М.О. Насонкина*
Корректор: *О.С. Капполь*
Иллюстрации: *С. Шахматов*
Концепция иллюстраций: *Л. Москалёва*
Оригинал-макет: *Л.О. Пащук*
Обложка:
ООО «Авторская творческая мастерская» («АТМ Книга»)

This is a self-instruction book in the form of the game novel, with the original detective-adventure plot and tasks built into the course of the narrative. It allows you to easily and naturally master the grammar of the Russian language, as well as get acquainted with the realities of Russian life.

The textbook is a full-fledged reference book on the Russian language of the level A1-A2. It presents detailed grammatical tables with detailed explanations. A sufficient number of exercises allows not only to understand the grammatical theme, but to work it out on exercises, dialogues and texts for reading. Phonetic themes are processed using audio tasks. At the end of the book you will find answer key for self-assessment.

В этой книге вашему вниманию предлагается интенсивный курс русского языка для начинающих (уровень А1–А2). Благодаря своему уникальному формату книга может быть использована в качестве как самостоятельного учебника или самоучителя для изучения русского языка, так и дополнительного пособия для аудиторных занятий.

Книга предназначена для англоговорящих читателей, которые хотят в непринуждённой и увлекательной форме овладеть основами грамматики и лексики русского языка и познакомиться с русской культурой. Этот учебник также рекомендуется преподавателям русского языка как иностранного, которые хотят разнообразить и расширить свои методические подходы.

Послушать или скачать аудиозапись к заданию можно по QR-коду рядом с заданием.

Подготовка оригинал-макета: издательство «Златоуст».
Подписано в печать 06.11.19. Формат 84×108/16. Печ. л. 22. Печать офсетная. Тираж 1000 экз. Заказ № 1023.
Код продукции: ОК 005-93-953005.

Санитарно-эпидемиологическое заключение на продукцию издательства Государственной СЭС РФ № 78.01.07.953.П.011312.06.10 от 30.06.2010 г.

Издательство «Златоуст»: 197101, Санкт-Петербург, Каменноостровский пр., д. 24, оф. 24.
Тел.: (+7-812) 346-06-68; факс: (+7-812) 703-11-79; e-mail: sales@zlat.spb.ru; http://www.zlat.spb.ru.

Отпечатано в ООО «Аллегро».
196084, Санкт-Петербург, ул. К. Томчака, д. 28. Тел.: (+7-812) 388-90-00.

Сайт издательства

CONTENTS

INTRODUCTION

The book you are holding in your hands is a kind of generalization, the result of many years' work with foreign students who have studied the Russian language. It was conceived, first of all, as a self-instruction book, for a slow and thoughtful reading. The form of the game novel, with the original detective-adventure plot and tasks built into the course of the narrative allows you to easily and naturally master the grammar of the Russian language, as well as get acquainted with the realities of Russian life.

However, the entertaining form here is not an end in itself. The game approach is combined with traditional communicative methods of teaching Russian as a foreign language (RFL), accepted in leading Russian universities. The textbook corresponds to the state educational standard of elementary and pre-intermediate levels of RFL (A1-A2). Therefore, the quality of mastering the material and your language level can be checked with help of practice tests[1].

The game novel is designed with an orientation to the simultaneous development of all types of speech activity. During the course of acquaintance with the book you will be actively involved in the process of learning the language: the development of the plot provides for reading, writing, responding to questions and situational tasks along with the characters of the book. Together with the heroes you will have to navigate in speech situations in Russian, get into funny situations of misunderstanding (linguistic and cultural), understand the dialogues and stories of characters, create your own texts in Russian. While reading a book you will not even notice how gradually the English text will give way to Russian. At the same time, you will be less likely to use the dictionary.

The lexical, grammatical and country specific material is assembled into thematic blocks in order to immediately provide the reader with the necessary material for full communication, depending on the situation of communication. Thus, mastering the book chapter by chapter, you master the basics of the Russian language at a comfortable pace and get acquainted with Russian culture. The book does not require an indispensable memorization of grammar and words, a tedious paging in search of the right word. All Russian words appearing for the first time are provided with a translation where they appear. You will master them, having met many times in the dialogues of the heroes. In addition, all words are listed alphabetically in the dictionary at the end of the book and are pronounced.

Speech situation of the book is modeled taking into account ethnocultural traditions and realities of Russia, in other words, the game novel puts the characters of the book in situations that can really happen to a foreigner in the conditions of another country and another language (confusion due to inability to introduce or disassemble the speech of the interlocutor correctly, examples of typical language errors and their consequences, incidents due to incorrect understanding of the language game, Russian traditions and customs, comic, and sometimes tragic misunderstandings, etc.).

Unlike another textbook which is oriented to significant additions on the part of the teacher, this book is a full-fledged reference book on the Russian language of the declared level. The textbook presents detailed grammatical tables with detailed explanations. A sufficient number of exercises allows not only to understand the grammatical theme, but to work it out on exercises, dialogues and texts for reading. Phonetic themes are processed using audio tasks. At the end of the book you will find answer key for self-assessment.

Assignments of the game novel have also been tested during classroom sessions with students of different ages (from adolescence to adulthood) and it can be recommended as both a primary and an additional textbook in the classroom with the teacher. In addition, the game novel gives excellent results when using as the correction course for students who have already studied the language at home. The book will be interesting for both teenagers and adults.

The events, characters, episodes and dialogues described in the book are pure fictitious. Any resemblance to real events or people is accidental. The exception is Nicholas II and his family (including the two Grand Dukes Nicholas Mikhailovich Romanov and George Mikhailovich Romanov), Grigory Rasputin and other historical figures mentioned in the text of the book (baker Filippov, poet A.S. Pushkin, scientist M.V. Lomonosov, writer A.P. Chekhov and others) are all part of the Russian history. The authors adhered to the chronology of historical events, but this book is not a history textbook. A quest game with a plot involves the study of the Russian language, as well as acquaintance with linguistic and regional peculiarities and some historical events and personalities.

Track 1 — audio   — key

[1] Типовые тесты по русскому языку как иностранному. Базовый уровень. Общее владение. Варианты / В.Е. Антонова и др. — 2-е изд. — СПб. : Златоуст, 2012. — 124 с.; Открытые тесты по русскому языку как иностранному / И. Ильичёва и др. — СПб.: Златоуст, 2020.

ПРЕДИСЛОВИЕ ДЛЯ ПРЕПОДАВАТЕЛЕЙ

Книга, которую вы держите в руках, — это своеобразное обобщение, итог многолетней работы авторов с иностранными студентами, изучавшими русский язык. Она задумывалась в первую очередь как самоучитель, книга для неспешного и вдумчивого чтения. Форма романа-игры с оригинальным детективно-приключенческим сюжетом и заданиями, встроенными в ход повествования, позволяет легко и непринуждённо освоить грамматику русского языка, а также познакомиться с реалиями русской жизни.

Однако занимательная форма здесь не самоцель. Игровой подход совмещён с традиционными коммуникативными методиками обучения русскому языку как иностранному (РКИ), принятыми в ведущих российских вузах. Учебное пособие соответствует требованиям к элементарному и базовому уровням РКИ. Поэтому качество усвоения материала и языковой уровень учащихся можно проверить по типовым тестам (А2)[1].

Роман-игра разработан с ориентацией на одновременное развитие всех видов речевой деятельности. В ходе знакомства с книгой учащиеся будут активно вовлечены в процесс освоения языка: развитие сюжета предусматривает чтение, письмо, реагирование на вопросы и решение ситуативных задач вместе с героями книги. Им предстоит ориентироваться в сложных и неоднозначных ситуациях, понимать диалоги и рассказы героев, создавать собственные тексты на русском языке. Читая книгу, учащиеся даже не заметят, как постепенно английский текст уступит место русскому. При этом к помощи словаря они будут обращаться всё реже.

Лексический, грамматический и страноведческий материал собран в тематические блоки, чтобы сразу предоставить читателю необходимую базу для полноценной коммуникации в той или иной ситуации общения. Таким образом, осваивая книгу глава за главой, учащиеся в комфортном для них темпе овладеют основами русского языка и познакомятся с русской культурой. Книга не требует непременного заучивания грамматики и лексики, утомительного листания в поисках нужного слова. Все русские слова, появляющиеся впервые, снабжены переводом. Учащиеся освоят их, встретив много раз в диалогах героев. Кроме того, все слова в алфавитном порядке вынесены в словарь в конце книги, а их произношение можно услышать в аудиоприложении.

Речевые ситуации книги смоделированы с учётом этнокультурных традиций и реалий российской действительности, иными словами, они действительно могут произойти с иностранцем в условиях другой страны и другого языка (путаница из-за неумения правильно представиться или понять речь собеседника; типичные языковые ошибки и их последствия; казусы вследствие неверного понимания языковой игры, русских традиций и обычаев; комические, а порой и трагические недоразумения и мн. др.).

В отличие от обычного учебника, ориентированного на значительные дополнения со стороны преподавателя, данная книга является полноценным справочником по русскому языку заявленного уровня. В ней представлены развёрнутые грамматические таблицы с подробными объяснениями. Достаточное количество упражнений позволяет не только понять грамматическую тему, но и отработать её в упражнениях, диалогах и текстах для чтения. Фонетические темы отрабатываются при помощи аудиоприложения. В конце книги учащиеся найдут ответы к заданиям для самопроверки.

Упражнения романа-игры прошли апробирование в ходе классных занятий с учащимися различных возрастов (от подросткового до зрелого возраста), и он может быть рекомендован в качестве как основного, так и дополнительного пособия на занятиях с педагогом. Кроме того, роман-игра даёт отличные результаты при использовании в курсе коррекции для студентов, уже изучавших язык у себя на родине. Сюжет книги будет интересен и подросткам, и взрослым.

Авторы будут признательны за высказанные замечания. Отзывы можно направлять по адресу: editor@zlat.spb.ru.

Track 1 — аудиоприложение — имеется ключ

Список сокращений

sg. — singular (единственное число)
pl. — plural (множественное число)
IPF — Imperfect (несовершенный вид)
PF — Perfect (совершенный вид)
n. — noun (существительное)
adv. — adverb (наречие)
adj. — adjective (прилагательное)
fem. — female form of a noun
офиц. — официальное
∅ — знак нулевого окончания

[1] Типовые тесты по русскому языку как иностранному. Базовый уровень. Общее владение. Варианты / В.Е. Антонова и др. — 2-е изд. — СПб. : Златоуст, 2012. — 124 с.; Открытые тесты по русскому языку как иностранному / И. Ильичёва и др. — СПб.: Златоуст, 2020.

Chapter 1

У ка́ждого есть в душе́ свой **skeletons**, как говоря́т англича́не.

Л.Н. Толсто́й. А́нна Каре́нина

Every heart has its own skeletons, as the English say.

— L. Tolstoy, "Anna Karenina"

"A good joke I should say! Granddad loved having fun!", the man burst out laughing. He was about thirty-six, very handsome, slim and well-built.

"I am afraid you are mistaken, this is not a joke," his companion replied immediately. He was a self-respectful elderly man sitting in a chair at an antique table with green cloth. The whole interior of the study — bookcases, maps on the walls, old-fashioned leather armchairs, a small spinning globe and a malachite ink set in which, of course, there was no ink for a long time, — all this gave the owner away as one who loved antiques and comfort.

"Father, what you told me is not even Stevenson or Swift, it's a cheap paperback adventure story! A fairy-tale for romantic young men! It's acceptable for me, a computer specialist, to believe in such stories, but you, a historian, professor…"

"The only reason why I think the story might be true is that I am a historian". He sipped some wine from his glass looking meaningfully at his son.

"Right," said the young man, "supposing that wasn't one of granddad's tricks and he was very serious about it, why then was he silent all those years? Why did he wit to tell you about what he had found just before his death?"

The senior man theatrically rolled his eyes, "John, I have a feeling that computers have destroyed the imaginative part of your brain. Think about it, everything started in 1918 in Russia, there was the revolution, then the civil war, World War II, then the USSR, the Iron Curtain and almighty KGB, then Perestroika in the 80s and putsch in the 90s..."

"Exactly! And the last thing to be there now is you and me!"

"The situation has changed", the middle-aged man answered evasively. His name was Alexander Young, he was a professor of History and a Londoner, retired, if it is possible to apply this word to a scientist. Sometimes he consults hiscollegnes at the University.

"Can you imagine how important it is for our family!" the professor exclaimed, "and for the science!"

"Oh," John understood, that his father had started this conversation about the family secret for a reason, and he decided to clarify everything once and for all. "Ok, what do you want me to do? You have a plan, don't you?"

Alexander Young put the half-full glass of wine aside and smiled.

"The plan is simple. First, it would be nice if you learned Russian..."

The young man's eyes widened a little, but nothing else gave away his extreme surprise.

Having noticed this reaction, the man explained, "Of course, I don't mean to learn it to the level of your native language, but to the extent of coming to Moscow without an interpreter or any other assistance, going to the local library, finding the archive there and taking photos of some documents for me."

"So 'the treasure' that my granddad told you about is a document?" John looked surprised.

"What do you think it is, gold and diamonds?"

"Well, when you hear the word 'treasure' you imagine something like a trunk with maps, gold and rings with hidden poison," the young man shrugged his shoulders. "Wait, dad, why are they in a library then? You told me that my granddad Benjamin Young hid what he had found in a cache... in a house... I forgot already... in Moscow, when he escaped from Russia in 1918".

"That's right, but in the Soviet times during the reconstruction work these hidden documents were found. However, even Russian historians didn't have a clue of how valuable these papers were, and they simply archived them. I talked to my colleagues: they think these are diaries and drafts of two royal Romanov family members, which in itself makes the discovery historically important, though it is not the point. I think your granddad gave me the clue to this secret. To solve it I need the whole pile of documents from that house. I have to make sure this story is real. Your granddad loved to joke too much."

John sighed, showing that in this very last point lay the clue to the 'secret'. His father pretended not noticing it and only said, "You know that my health doesn't allow me to go myself."

"Why don't you ask your Russian colleagues to take photos of these documents?", John argued mildly. He realized that his father was pulling out the big guns and to win this battle he needed all his wit and strategic thinking. "I am not a specialist, you know. Even in an English archive it would be difficult for me to find anything not to mention in a library where every single text is in Russian."

"I don't want my colleagues to know about the research," Alexander sighed, "neither Russian nor English. I want to sort everything out myself. This is our family business, and it could be quite profitable. I want to keep it a secret for a while. It shouldn't take long, I promise. I will teach you some rules of the Russian language, and contrary to popular belief it isn't so difficult. I wish you had shown some interest in it — your granddad mastered his Russian language skills and due to this I am now a well-known historian and an expert in Slavic history. After my two-week intensive course you will be able to fly to Moscow and explain everything necessary in Russian."

"Two weeks?" John couldn't believe his ears.

"Only two weeks. Imagine what we can get in case of success: scientific recognition and a lot of money, I guess."

Father's eyes were burning with childlike excitement. John began to imagine pros and cons of the proposed activities. On the one hand, searching for some century-old secret was probably the last thing that could happen to a modern Londoner working for an international IT company. On the other hand, quite by chance John Young had recently been offered a business trip to the office in Moscow in order to evaluate the possibilities of expanding the business. It meant that he could easily combine useful with useless and the trip was becoming more and more attractive in his eyes. Besides, for the first time in the last couple of months John saw his father so excited. Learning Russian and searching for treasure didn't seem to be a high price to pay when it came to improving the morale and health of the Young Senior.

Having thought about all the pros and cons, John said, "Well, if it is so important to you, then I'm ready."

A few seconds later Alexander Young suddenly started making weird sounds — a combination of roaring, hissing and whistling. John heard something like this:

"Drrrrsshzzshsszssz". He already regretted having let his dad persuade him so easily as he realized that those funny noises were nothing else but the sound of Russian speech.

"What is that you have just said?" John was getting a bit desperate.

"Дорого́й мой сын! Я знал, что ты согласи́шься! Здра́вствуй, ру́сский язы́к![1]," his father repeated slowly, and John could recognize the final phrase. "Здра́вствуй[2], ру́сский язы́к[3]! Hello, Russian language!" he translated.

"Say it in Russian," asked his father.

[Zdravstvooy roosskiy yazuik] they repeated this phrase several times together.

Then something incredible started.

"Russian is not difficult. It's a myth," his father started the first lesson, "Look, this is Russian alphabet, or Cyrillic as it is usually called here."

Ру́сский алфави́т

At first glance John thought the Russian alphabet was like the mysterious Russian soul — everything was different and weird. But his father asked him to look carefully and find the similarities between Russian and English letters.

[1] My dearest son! I knew you would agree! Hello Russian language!

[2] Hello

[3] ру́сский язы́к: the Russian language

Аа	Кк	Хх
Бб	Лл	Цц
Вв	Мм	Чч
Гг	Нн	Шш
Дд	Оо	Щщ
Ее	Пп	ъ
Ёё	Рр	Ыы
Жж	Сс	ь
Зз	Тт	Ээ
Ии	Уу	Юю
Йй	Фф	Яя

***Exercise 1.* What letters look similar to letters of the English alphabet?**

Alexander Young read the letters so that John could check those he had guessed correctly.

***Exercise 2.* Write down the sounds using English alphabet and compare your result.**

Track 1

Answer check:

Of all the letters John had matched his father approved: А, а, О, о; К, к, М, м.

Letter В, в represents the sound [v], and the sound [b] is represented by the letter Б, б which goes right before В, в.

The letter И, и represents the sound [ee] and not [u] or [oo], which is represented by the letter У, у which John has matched to Y, y.

The letter Й, й which looks like И is a consonant [y (j)].

The letter Н, н represents the sound [n] and not [kh], and the sound [kh] is represented by the letter Х, х.

The letter С, с stands for the sound [s].

The letter Р, р indicates [r] and not [p]. This sound was different from the English sound [r] and was pronounced with roaring and vibration. John doubted if he could ever pronounce it right.

And the letter П, п represents the sound [p].

The letter Е, е sounds as [ye] and the familiar sound [e] without soft [y] sound in front is represented by the letter Э, э. Thus the letters Э and Е can be coupled — the sound [e] with the sound [y] in front and without it. Е, е [ye] — Э, э [e].

There were also similar letters representing combined sounds with [y] in front — Ё, ё [yoh], Ю, ю [yoo], Я, я [yah]. These are so-called soft pair for the sounds without [y]: Ё, ё [yoh] — О, о [oh]; Ю, ю [yoo], — У, у [oo]; Я, я [yah] — А, а [ah]. Attention! Ё is always stressed!

The letter Ы, ы is the most mysterious of all and it seems to be a weird pair for the sound [ee]: Ы — И which is pronounced somewhere at the back of the mouth.

Alexander Young thought it could be a good idea to "translate" the Russian letters into English*:

А, а	ah	К, к	k	Х, х	kh
Б, б	b	Л, л	l	Ц, ц	ts
В, в	v	М, м	m	Ч, ч	ch
Г, г	g	Н, н	n	Ш, ш	sh
Д, д	d	О, о	oh	Щ, щ	shch
Е, е	ye	П, п	p	ъ	hard sign (")
Ё, ё	yo	Р, с	r	Ы, ы	special Russian sound, like *y'*
Ж, ж	zh (zsh), like *treasure*	С, с	s	ь	soft sign (')
З, з	z	Т, т	t	Э, э	e (eh)
И, и	ee (ē)	У, у	oo	Ю, ю	yoo
Й, й	y (j)	Ф, ф	f	Я, я	ya

It was getting clearer.

John could even write his name with Russian letters.

And here is what he wrote — Джон.

* You can use special service for example: transliteonline.com.

Exercise 3. **Try to write your name using the letters from the Russian Alphabet. Use "translated" letters to help you.**

Then father asked his son to pronounce all these sounds.

Exercise 4. **Listen and repeat.**

Track 2

А — О — У — Э

Russian vowels in an isolated position, under stress or at the beginning of a word are longer than English ones. It sounds somewhere in between a monophthong and a diphthong. For example, А, а may sound more like [ah] and О, о as [oh].

The sound [у] is different from the English [u] in such words as 'good': The sound is a bit longer and you need to fold your lips and pull the tongue back.

Russian sound [о] is similar to the English [o], be aware of diphthongs when sound [о] finishes with overtones of [u].

1. Say : О, о, then fold your lips and say У, у. Repeat several times.

Making the sound [э] you need to stretch the lips into a smile. Do not pull your tongue, relax it and put it down like a shovel. Do the same when you pronounce the words *red*, *Fred*, *net*, *bread*.

2. Say: О, о — Э, э.

3. Pronounce all vowel sound and monitor how you move your lips:

1.	2.	3.
а — о	а — э	а — о — у — о — а
о — а	э — а	а — э — о — э — а
о — у	о — э	а — э — о — у
у — о	э — о	у — о — э — а
а — о — у	а — э — а	
	э — а — э	
	о — э — о	
	э — о — э	

4. Say the chain of vowels:

аэ, эа, ао, оа, уо, оу, эу, ау, ао, уо, эо, аэ, уэ, оэ

5. Express your emotions:

Surprise — О!

Understanding — А!

Question — А?

Disappointment — У!

Warning — Э!

"I am exhausted," said John wiping his wet forehead with his handkerchief.

"Я устáл," translated his father and wrote it on a piece of paper — [ya oostal] — John managed to read it using knowledge of Cyrillic letters he had just received.

"Хорошó[1]. Сегóдня[2] всё[3]," his father smiled.

[1] very well
[2] today
[3] that's all

"Хорошо́…?" repeated John.

"Russians say so when they are happy about something. I am very happy with our first lesson. That's why it's ХОРОШО́. "Сего́дня всё" means "That's all for today".

All these Russian sounds and words seemed to John deliberately bright, too expressive and too loud. Listening to his father he suddenly remembered a program about Russia he had seen the previous week. A professor of Slavic languages was telling that despite the complexity of the grammar, Russian, as well as all Slavic languages — Polish, Czech, and Bulgarian are easy to remember. "Maybe because of the sound?", John thought and sighed with hope. The skeleton having fallen out of the family closet gave John the task that was not easy to perform.

Chapter 2

2

Учéнье — свет, а неучéнье — тьма.

А.В. Сувóров, рýсский полковóдец

Learning is light and ignorance is darkness.

A. Suvorov, Russian military leader

Granddad Benjamin's story was known to all the members of the Young family. Benjamin Young came to Russia with his mother who gave lessons of English to noble children. Those were the times when Russia was one of the most powerful and richest countries in the world. However, it was not the best time for foreign teachers like John's great-grandmother.

During the end of the 19th and early 20th centuries Russian replaced French and English, the languages of the 19th century's noble people. Russian became the only language for the whole empire, as both peasants and nobility spoke it. While in the 19th century even an English coachman could become a teacher in a provincial noble family, in the early 1900s one should have recommendations and good pedagogical experience to get a similar position.

John's great-grandmother was not a professional teacher, the intricacies of fate led her to Moscow with little Benjamin in her hands. At that time he was only one and a half years old. The woman could find a position in a noble, but not very rich family. She could hardly make ends meet, which is why Benjamin Young was ten when he started working in a bakery — a very nice and warm place. The little Englishman spoke two languages and could find his place under the sun.

During the revolution in 1917 granddad Benjamin escaped from Russia, managed to get to Europe and traveled all the way to native England. Granddad told his family a lot about Russia and Europe in the early 1900s, about the bloody Russian revolution and about his lucky escape. But as it turned out he didn't tell them the most important thing. Amazing person he was, granddad Benjamin.

The next day Alexander Young started a lesson even more energetically.

1. М — П — Б — В — Ф

Track 3

***Exercise 1.* Listen and repeat.**

"These sounds are called labial and labiodental," he started. "They are similar to the English sounds."

1. Say:

ма — мо — му — мэ: мáма[1]

па — по — пу — пэ: пáпа[2]

[1] a mother

[2] a father

The first words showed John that stress in Russian as it is in English could fall on any syllable: мáма, рýсский, язы́к, хорошó.

"And how…?" John started.
"Only learning. Or looking up in dictionaries," his father guessed his question.
"All the words?"
"Yes, at first. For your convenience we will start working with schemes: —́ — ма́ма.

2. Say:

A) ба — бо — бу — бэ
ва — во — ву — вэ
фа — фо — фу — фэ

B)

ма — ам	мо — ом	му — ум	мэ — эм
па — ап	по — оп	пу — уп	пэ — эп
ба — аба	бо — обо	бу — убу	бэ — эбэ
ва — ава	во — ово	ву — уву	вэ — эвэ
фа — аф	фо — оф	фу — уф	фэ — эф

C) ма — вма
па — фпа
бо — вбо
фу — фпу

D) мам, пап, баб, вав, фаф
ма́ма, па́па, ба́ба, ва́ва, фа́фа

3. Imitate the sounds and express emotions:
Tiredness — Уф!
American surprise — Ва́у!
Getting somebody startled — Бу!
Biting something off — Ам!
Taking rabbit out of the hat — Ап! Оп!
Bell rings — Бам! Бом! Бум!
It's disgusting! — Фу!
Shooting — Паф!

2. Т — Д — Н — Л

***Exercise 2.* Listen and repeat.**

Professor Young warned his son that these sounds have two characteristic features:

1. When pronouncing these sounds you have to put the tip of your tongue at the back part of your upper teeth as if you want to pull them out of your mouth; if you compare English *T*, *D*, *N*, *L* to Russian Т, Д, Н, Л, it becomes clear that the difference is in the position of your tongue: when pronouncing English sounds the tongue is on the teeth ridge while Russian sounds are pronounced with the tongue placed on the back part of your teeth. Imagine that your teeth are gates and your tongue is a ram.

2. These sounds are harder than the English ones.

1. Say:
та — то — ту — тэ
ат — от — ут — эт

2. Say:

—	тут[1], там[2], Том
⌐́ —	Тáта, фóто[3], э́то[4]
— ⌐́	автó[5], томáт[6]
— — ⌐́	тет-а-тéт[7]

[1] here
[2] there
[3] a photo
[4] this, it
[5] an auto
[6] a tomato
[7] тет-а-тéт [тэ]: tete-a-tete
[8] and; but

Alexander showed his son a family photo, "Э́то фóто. Тут пáпа. **А**[8] э́то мáма."

"This is a photo. Here is dad. This is mom," translated John. "Хорошó?"

"Хорошó".

"Then I have two questions: where is the verb 'to be' and why is 'a photo' written without an article?"

"In such stative sentences in the Present tense, Russians don't use the verb 'to be'. However, this verb appears in Past and Future. We will talk about it later. As far as the second question is concerned, there are no articles in Russian. They decide if the object is definite or indefinite according to the context."

"I see… If there are no articles, then what is А? Тут пáпа. **А** э́то мáма".

"А is a conjunction."

"Хорошó. Here is dad. **And** this is mom," John improved his translation.

Professor Young was about to approve it, but didn't. He knew Russian almost as a native speaker that's why he couldn't have thought he would face such a difficult pedagogical problem at the very first lesson. He couldn't say exactly how to translate this little word in English.

Alexander asked his son to wait and looked in textbooks. There were a lot of sentences with the conjunction а from the very first pages, but nowhere could he find the explanation of its meaning.

"Sorry, son. I'd like to make a call," said John's father, opening skype. "Здрáвствуйте, Вéра!" heard John in a minute.

"Здрáвствуйте, профéссор[9] Янг!" a good-looking woman in her forties smiled from the screen of the monitor. A colleague from Russia, as John understood from the conversation in the language which was unknown to him so far. "Профéссор" — that's how colleagues and students called his father in England: professor.

[9] a professor

As John listened, trying to identify some familiar words, Alexander Young was writing something quickly on a piece of paper.

"Done! Obvious things are usually very difficult to systemize, but Doctor Vera and I will give it a try," said his father dramatically.

So, in English the conjunction '**and**' expresses addition while the conjunction '**but**' is used to show opposition.

1. In Russian 'and' corresponds to и:

Conjunction **и** means addition of logically similar statements:

A) addition in simple sentences;

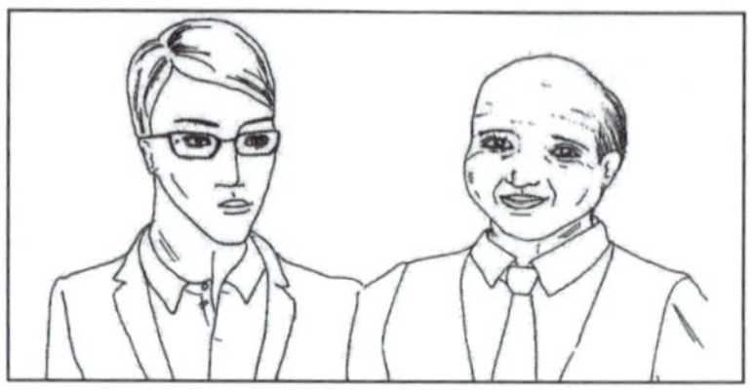

Джон и Алекса́ндр.
Студе́нт[1] и профе́ссор.

Э́то А́нна и А́лла.

[1] a student

B) combines two simple sentences into a composite one;

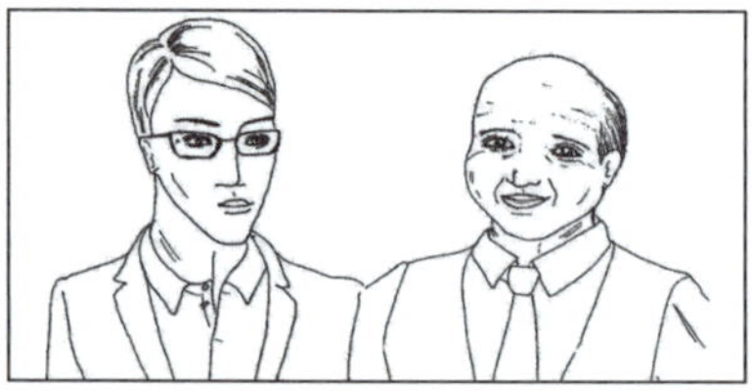

Тут фо́то, и тут фо́то.

[2] a poet

C) indicates homogeneity of objects

Э́то Джон, и э́то Джон.

Профе́ссор
Алекса́ндр Янг.

Ру́сский поэ́т[2]
Алекса́ндр Пу́шкин.

Э́то Алекса́ндр, и э́то Алекса́ндр.

2. Conjunction 'but' corresponds to Russian но:

It has the meaning of contrasting. The presence of one object or characteristic denies the presence of the other one.

Джон **не**[3] ребёнок, **но** студе́нт.

[3] not

Э́то А́нна.

Но э́то **не** А́нна. Э́то Э́лла.

Thus, in the English language there is an opposition: addition — contrast (and — but). It can be easily paralleled with Russian opposition и — но.

3. Also, in Russian there is the third component of a paradigm — conjunction а indicating juxtaposition:

Э́то А́нна, а э́то А́лла.

Э́то А́нна, а э́то Э́лла.

We can identify two different girls in the photos. We suggest comparing them without emphasizing the significant difference between them.

Э́то па́па, а э́то ма́ма.
It is the same in the initial position:
Тут па́па. А тут ма́ма.

To sum up, in Russian there are two conjunctions и and но, which correlate in meaning with English conjunctions 'and' and 'but'. And there is one more conjunction which stands somewhere in between и and но and has intermediate meaning: а. It means juxtaposition but not contrasting two objects or characteristics and is used quite often.

Э́то стол и стул. Э́то ру́чка и каранда́ш. Э́то стол, стул и ноутбу́к. These are a table and a chair. These are a pen and a pencil. These are a table, a chair and a laptop.	+	 
Э́то стол. Но э́то **не** стол. Э́то стул. Э́то ру́чка. Но э́то **не** ру́чка. Э́то каранда́ш. This is a table. But this is not a table. This is a chair. This is a pen. But this is not a pen. This is a pencil.		 
Э́то стол, а э́то стул. Э́то ру́чка, а э́то каранда́ш. This is a table, and/but this is a chair. This is a pen, and/but this is a pencil.		 

***Exercise 3*. Fill in the gaps with И, А, НО.**

Example: стол + стул: Э́то стол и стул.
каранда́ш ≠ ру́чка: Э́то каранда́ш. Но э́то не каранда́ш. Э́то ру́чка. (Но э́то не каранда́ш, а ру́чка.)
ма́ма ↔ па́па: Э́то ма́ма, а э́то па́па.

1. ноутбу́к + каранда́ш: Э́то ноутбу́к и каранда́ш
2. студе́нт ≠ поэ́т: Это студент, но не это поэт
3. студе́нт ↔ профе́ссор: Это студент а это профессор

Alexander thanked his colleague from Moscow University. Never he had been so close to pedagogical failure. "There is nothing more deceptive than an obvious fact," Arthur Conan Doyle put these words into his famous character's mouth. It turned out that the same rule could be applied to the language.

"Now, when we have managed to translate it, please, read the whole phrase," Alexander asked his son, "Listen and repeat".

Intonation was rather unusual, and John listened carefully to the interesting 'pattern' of the foreign speech, drawing 'ups' and 'downs'* (ИК-1).

***Exercise 4*. Listen and repeat.**

Track 5

1. Say:

Э́то фо́то. Тут па́па. А э́то ма́ма.

Having drawn the scheme John repeated everything according to it:
"Э́то фо́то. Тут па́па. А э́то ма́ма".
"А э́то Джон," he added pointing at himself.

А э́то Джон.

"Perfect! Go on!" his father exclaimed.

2. Say:

да — до — ду — дэ
ад — од — уд — эд

3. Say:

— да[1], дом[2]
—́ — до́ма[3], мо́да[4]
— —́ Эде́м[5]

[1] yes
[2] a house
[3] at home
[4] fashion
[5] Эде́м [дэ]: Eden

4. Say:

на — но — ну — нэ
ан — он — ун — эн

---

* Read more about intonation in Russian inside back cover.

5. Say:

—́ — На́та, А́нна

— —́ Анто́н, бана́н[1], фонта́н[2]

[1] a banana
[2] a fountain

6. Say:

ла — ло — лу — лэ

ал — ол — ул — эл

7. Say:

— пол[3]

—́ — ла́мпа[4], А́лла, Э́лла, Бэ́лла

— —́ луна́[5]

[3] a floor (of a room)
[4] a lamp
[5] the moon

8. Say:

A)

та — ат	то — от	ту — ут	тэ — эт
да — ада	до — одо	ду — уду	дэ — эдэ
на — ан	но — он	ну — ун	нэ — эн
ла — ал	ло — ол	лу — ул	лэ — эл

B) дна — дно — дну — днэ
тна — тно — тну — тнэ
нла — нло — нлу — нлэ
тва — тво — тву — твэ
фта — фто — фту — фтэ
вна — вно — вну — внэ

C) фан — фон — фун — фэн
вал — вол — вул — вэл

9. Imitate the sounds and express emotions:

Surprise! — Та-да́!
I agree — Да.
A song — Ла-ла-ла́!
Objection — Но…
Encouragement — Ну!

"What sentences can you make now?" asked Alexander.
"Э́то дом. Па́па тут. Джон тут. А фонта́н там."
"Хорошо́!"
"And now listen to a question. The intonation is different, listen carefully. Э́то па́па?"
John drew a pattern (ИК-3):

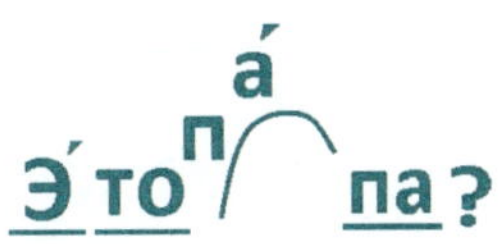

Э́то па́па?

"Э́то па́па?" his father repeated the question.
"Да, э́то па́па." John answered using the answer intonation (ИК-1).
"Э́то Джон?"
"Да, э́то Джон."
"Э́то дом?"
"Да, э́то дом."

3. З — С

Exercise 5. Listen and repeat.

Track 6

The sounds that are represented by the letters З [z] и С [s] are more or less similar to the English ones. While pronouncing them in Russian the tongue doesn't touch the back part of upper teeth but only aims to do it. In English pronunciation the tongue touches teethridge, which constitutes the main difference.

The sound represented by the letter З is similar to the English sound [z] in such words as *zebra*, *visit*.

The letter С in Russian always only represents the sound [s]. The sound is similar to the English [s] in such words as *less*, *some*, *start*, *center*, *city*.

1. Say:

	A)		B)
	за — зо — зу — зэ		ста — сто — сту — стэ
	аз — оз — уз — эз		аст — ост — уст — эст
	са — со — су — сэ		сла — сло — слу — слэ
	ас — ос — ус — эс		асл — осл — усл — эсл

2. Say:

—	зал[1]
—́ —	ва́за[2], Те́мза[3]
—	Сэм, суп[4], стол[5], стул[6]
—́ —	пу́сто[7], Сте́лла [тэ], сло́во[8], ма́сло[9].

[1] a hall
[2] a vase
[3] Те́мза [тэ]: the Thames
[4] soup
[5] a table
[6] a chair
[7] it's empty
[8] a word
[9] butter, oil

"Could you describe the pictures using the words that you already know?" asked Alexander.

"Э́то стол. Тут ва́за и ла́мпа," John showed at the first picture.
"Э́то стол. Тут суп и ма́сло," it's the second one.
"Э́то стол. Тут пу́сто," and the third one.
"Great! You have added enumeration. The intonation corresponds to ИК-3, listen:
ИК-3: Тут стол, стул, ла́мпа.
Э́то ла́мпа, стол, стул.
John drew this intonation pattern.

***Exercise 6.* Listen and repeat.**

Say:

A

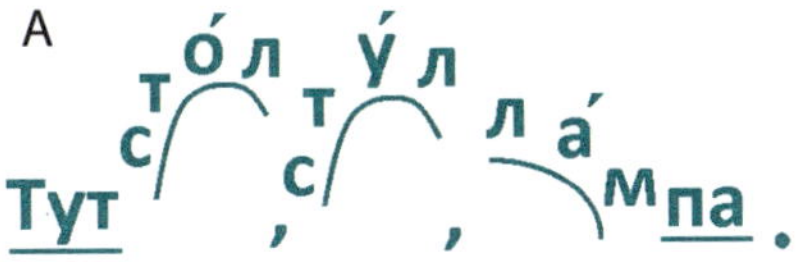

Тут стол, стул, ла́мпа.

B

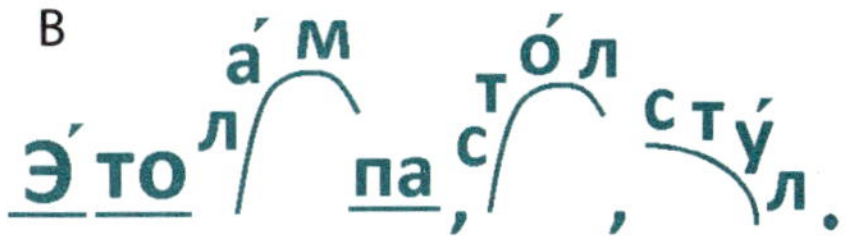

Э́то ла́мпа, стол, стул.

It turns out that we can express enumeration in narrative sentences in the following way: ИК-3 + ИК-3 + ИК-1.

"Could you enumerate Russian words that you know using this intonation pattern," asked John's father.

— Э́то ма́ма, па́па, фо́то, А́нна, Джон, Алекса́ндр…

***Exercise 7.* Complete this task with John, using all the nouns that you now know.**

Э́то __________, __________, __________, __________, __________, __________.

4. Ж — Ш

The sound represented by the letter Ж is close to the English [zh] in such words as *treasure*, *pleasure*.
The sound represented by the letter Ш is close to the English [sh] in such words as *ship*, *show*, *finish*.
Letters Ж and Ш are always pronounced hard in Russian.

***Exercise 8.* Listen and repeat.**

1. Say:

жа — жо — жу — жэ
аж — ож — уж — эж

2. Say:

жна — жно — жну — жнэ
жда — ждо — жду — ждэ
жла — жло — жлу — жлэ

3. Say:

—	Джон, муж[1]
—́ —	то́же[2]
— —́	жена́[3], журна́л[4]

[1] муж (pl. мужья́): a husband
[2] also, too
[3] жена́ (pl. жёны): a wife
[4] a magazine

"Let's use the word то́же," Alexander was inspired by his son's success. "Russians almost don't use the verb есть *(to be)* in the Present tense, so forget about it for now.

John said, "Э́то стол. Э́то то́же стол. Стол тут. Стул то́же тут."

"Хорошо́! You've started speaking Russian!"

4. Say:

ша — шо — шу — шэ
аш — ош — уш — эш
шна — шно — шну — шнэ

шта — што — шту — штэ
шла — шло — шлу — шлэ

5. Say:

´— —	Ма́ша, Са́ша
— ´—	шоссе́[1], планше́т[2]

! эта́ж[3] [эта**ш**]

! что[4] [**ш**то]

[1] шоссе́ [сэ́]: a highway
[2] планше́т (планше́тный компью́тер): a tablet PC
[3] a floor (level of a building)
[4] what;
что э́то?: what's this?

So John could make up new phrases, "Э́то наш дом. Тут па́па. Джон то́же тут".

6. Say:

ша — аш   шо — ош   шу — уш   ше — эш

жа — ажа   жо — ожо   жу — ужу   жэ — эже

7. Say:

зба — збо — збу — збэ

спа — спо — спу — спэ

жба — жбо — жбу — жбэ

шпа — шпо — шпу — шпэ

John got used to hissing and buzzing but the growling sound which his father suddenly made took him by surprise.

"Rrrrrrrrrrr," pronounced his father smiling and showing his teeth.

"I never thought that studying Russian phonetics was so… unusual," said John and tried to make the same sound. But he failed, the sound was similar to the 'round' English [r].

5. Р

"Place your tongue on the teethridge (tubercles of the upper teeth). Open your teeth a little bit and let the air go through your teeth so that the tongue vibrated," prompted Alexander.

Exercise 9. **Listen and repeat.**

Track 9

1. Say:

Ррррррррррррррррр!

"There is a very effective exercise which is called "the old engine," said Alexander trying to help his son.

2. Say:

Тра-тра-тра-тра-тра-тра-тра-тра-тра-тра-тра.

Дра-дра-дра-дра-дра-дра-дра-дра-дра-дра-дра.

Surprising though, it helped — the combination of [д], [т] and [р] is easier to pronounce.

3. Say:

тра — тро — тру — трэ

ра — ро — ру — рэ

ара — оро — уру — эрэ

ар — ор — ур — эр

арт — орт — урт — эрт

ара — ора — ура — эра

ра — ар — ро — ор — ру — ур — рэ — эр

4. Say:

—	шарф[1], спорт[2], торт[3]
—́ —	здра́вствуй, тру́дно[4]
— —́	страна́[5]
—́ — —	Та́уэр[6]
— —́ —	рабо́та[7]
— — —́	Алекса́ндр, тротуа́р[8]
— — — —́	аэропо́рт[9]

[1] a scarf
[2] sport
[3] a cake
[4] it's difficult
[5] a country
[6] the Tower
[7] work
[8] a pavement
[9] an airport

5. Imitate the sounds and express emotions:

"I won!" — Ура́!
"I am a cat" — Мур-мур-му́р!
"I am a tiger" — Ррррррр!

6. К — Г — Х

The sounds represented by the letters К [k] — Г [g] — Х [kh] are called 'velar' (from Lat. velum — veil) because when pronouncing them, the back part of the tongue touches the soft palate. The difference is only in the participation of the vocal cords.

***Exercise 10.* Listen and repeat.**

Track 10

1. Say:

ка — ко — ку — кэ
ак — ок — ук — эк

2. Say:

—	кто[10], как[11], знак[12], звук[13], фрукт[14], шкаф[15]
—́ —	ка́рта[16], ко́фе[17], бу́ква[18], па́пка[19], по́лка[20], жа́рко[21]
— —́	окно́[22], ноутбу́к[23], Москва́[24]
—́ — —	ко́мната[25]
— — —́	каранда́ш[26], потоло́к[27]

3. Imitate the sounds and express emotions:

"Cuckoo" — Ку-ку́!
"Crow" — Кар-кар-ка́р!
"Knock on the door" — Тук-тук-ту́к!

[10] who; кто э́то?: who's this?
[11] how; как э́то?: how come?
[12] a sign
[13] a sound
[14] a fruit
[15] a closet
[16] a map
[17] coffee
[18] a letter
[19] a file
[20] a shelf
[21] it's hot
[22] a window
[23] a laptop
[24] Moscow
[25] a room
[26] a pencil
[27] a ceiling

Pay attention to the sound Х: unlike the English [h] as in words *he*, *home*, Russian letter Х indicates the harder sound, more like К with exhale instead of explosion.

Alexander picked up his glasses and pronounced English [h].

"You see, glasses are not steamed. When pronouncing Russian Х air ejection force is stronger. They should be steamed."

"I remember professor Higgins teaching Eliza Doolittle — he sought just the opposite, to make the light of the candle barely wave while pronouncing [h]," said John.

Professor Young roared with laughter.

"If you pronounce Russian Х in the English manner, it won't change the meaning, but your speech will have a strong accent. Though in the times of Bernard Shaw in England it was unforgivable, I can't say the same about modern Russia. Nevertheless, try to pronounce the Russian sound [kh] properly.

4. Say:

ка — ко — ку — кэ
ха — хо — ху — хэ
ах — ох — ух — эх
кха — кхо — кху — кхэ

ка — кха — ха: ха — ха— ха
ко — кхо — хо: хо — хо — хо
ку — кху — ху: ху — ху — ху
кэ — кхэ — хэ: хэ — хэ — хэ

5. Say:

ка — ак ко — ок ку — ук кэ — эк
ха — ах хо — ох ху — ух хэ — эх

6. Say:

—́ — плóхо[1]
—́ — — хóлодно[2]
— — —́ хорошó

[1] it's bad
[2] it's cold

7. Imitate the sounds and express emotions:

Russians laughing — Ха-ха-хá!
Santa Claus laughing — Хо-хо-хó!
Admiration — Ах!
Surprise with admiration — Ух!
Regret with surprise — Ох!
Regret with reproach — Эх…
Reproach with regret — О-хо-хó…
Disappointment — Э-хэ-хэ́…

8. Say:

ка — ко — ку — кэ
га — го — гу — гэ
ка — га — ко — го
ку — гу — кэ — гэ

ак — ок — ук — эк
аг — ог — уг — эг
ага — ога — уга — эга

9. Say:

— друг[3]
—́ — гóрод[4], Гáрвард[5]
— —́ — дорóга[6], подрýга[7], бумáга[8]
— — —́ Вашингтóн[9]

[3] a friend
[4] a city
[5] Harvard
[6] a road
[7] a girlfriend
[8] paper
[9] Washington

10. Imitate the sounds and express emotions:

Agreement (= Да) — Агá…
Grim agreement (= Да) — Угý…
Amusement — Огó!
Big size (+ showing with your hands that the size is big) — О-го-гó! (You've caught a big fish, о-го-гó!)
You drive fast and you are excited — Э-гэ-гэ́!!!

Model*: Э́то кто.

Example: Э́то па́па. Э́то ма́ма. Э́то Джон.

Question: Кто э́то?

"Кто э́то?" John's father puzzled him with another question, pointing at himself.
"Э́то па́па," John didn't hesitate.
Getting used to Russian speech John noticed that the intonation was different.
"Dad, could you repeat it please, I'll draw it".
"Кто э́то? Джон, кто э́то?"

John drew the phrases (ИК-2) both with addressing to someone and without it. His dad approved the result.

Кто э́то?

Джон, кто э́то?

Father and son had a small talk looking at family pictures:
— Э́то Ло́ра. (ИК-1) Кто э́то? (ИК-2)
— Э́то ма́ма. (ИК-1)
— Э́то А́нна. (ИК-1) Кто она́[1]? (ИК-2)
— Э́то ба́бушка[2]. (ИК-1)
— Э́то ми́стер Па́уэрс. (ИК-1) Кто э́то? (ИК-2)
— Э́то друг. (ИК-1)
— Э́то Марк. (ИК-1) Кто он[3]? (ИК-2)
— Он то́же друг. (ИК-1)
— Э́то Ма́рта. (ИК-1) Кто э́то? (ИК-2)
— Она́ подру́га. (ИК-1)

[1] she
[2] a grandmother
[3] he

7. Ц — Ч — Щ

No sooner had John wondered how in just one lesson he was able to maintain a conversation in Russian, though a very simple one, his father surprised him again. This time Alexander hissed and clicked in even more sophisticated way.

"Ц, ц [ts], Ч, ч [ch], Щ, щ [shch]. These are the most "Russian" letters and sounds," professor introduced three new letters.

The letter Ц represents the sound [ts] which is pronounced as a very quick combination of sounds [t+s]. You need to close the front teeth together. Smile, but not too much, not as for a ceremonial family photo. And then press the tongue to the junction of the teeth, just like for the Russian sound [t]. Then you need to quickly and dramatically push back the tongue from the teeth at the same time revealing your teeth.

John followed the instructions and he managed to pronounce it the right way.

"Great! Combine them in one sound! Sharper! Quicker!" his father encouraged him.

* Hereinafter 'model' is a typical sentence pattern, and 'question' is a question form to a given model.

***Exercise 11*. Listen and repeat.**

Track 11

1. Say:

ца — цо — цу — цэ
ац — оц — уц — эц

2. Say:

— царь[1], центр[2]

[1] You will meet letter ь in the next chapter. Now try to pronounce the sound before this letter softly: [tsar'].
[2] a centre

"Nice, Ц sounds nice! Now let's turn to Ч and the sound [ch]. The tongue to the starting position!" Alexander was definitely enjoying the process.

"You should have become a general, dad," John spoke ironically.

"Да-да́, Че́рчилль[3], Че Гева́ра[4] и Чемберле́н[5]".

"I don't hear the difference with the English sound represented by letters ch," said John.

"That's right, it sounds like [ch] as in the words *cheese*, *reach* or in the name *Winston Churchill*.

[3] Churchill
[4] Che Guevara
[5] Chamberlain

3. Say:

ча — чо — чу — че
ач — оч — уч — эч

ача — очо — учу — эче
чач — чоч — чуч — чеч

4. Say:

—́ — ча́сто[6]
чка — шка
ру́чка[7], то́чка[8] — ча́шка[9]

[6] often
[7] a pen
[8] a point
[9] a cup

In order to pronounce Щ the initial position of the tongue should be the same as in pronouncing Ч. The difference is that air goes through the slot between the tongue and the teeth. Like Ч the sound Щ is soft.

5. Say:

ща — що — щу — ще
ащ — ощ — ущ — эщ

ча — ща	ач — ащ	чащ	щач
чо — що	оч — ощ	чощ	щоч
чу — щу	уч — ущ	чущ	щуч

6. Say:

—́ — о́вощ[10]
— —́ щека́[11]
ща — ша — щу — шу — ще — ше
щека́ — шу́тка[12]

[10] a vegetable
[11] a cheek
[12] a joke

Model:	**Э́то как**
Question:	**Как э́то?**

"Russian winter. Как э́то?" John was puzzled again by professor Young's question. Professor himself was waiting for the answer with his hands crossed on the chest. His entire appearance demonstrated that the question was too easy for John not to answer it.

John found both words in his notes.

Exercise 12. **Find the translation of the words как and э́то and try to guess the meaning of the question Как э́то?**

John had to think logically. He looked it up in the dictionary: the question Как? is 'how' in English.

"That's right," he told his father, "I often hear you say Как дела́? or 'How are you?' when you talk to your Russian colleagues Как дела ? — Хорошо!".

"The auxiliary verb in the question Как дела́? is omitted because it is the Present tense. 'Winter' is the English for зима́. And it means that Зима́. Как э́то? is a question about how winter is doing. Am I right?"

Having heard his son's arguments Alexander Young understood that in this case the English language logic does not correspond to the Russian one. He explained, "Your translation of the question Как? is right: in what condition, in what manner, by what means.

Зима́. Как э́то? — Winter. What is it like?

Зима́. Э́то хо́лодно. — Winter. It is cold.

The question Как? always involves an adverb as a response.

Как дела́? — Хорошо́.

Зима́. Э́то как? — Хо́лодно.

Very often we use adverbs in Russian instead of adjectives in English. It's good. — Э́то хорошо́. It's comfortable. — Э́то комфо́ртно. It's beautiful. — Э́то краси́во.

For example:

Авто́. Как э́то? Э́то комфо́ртно.

Москва́. Как э́то? Э́то краси́во.

In the Russian language we use adverbs when we talk about our subjective feeling or evaluation. An adverb always answers the question Как?, it is invariable and it often ends in О, so it is easy to recognise it. An adjective, on the contrary, indicates an object's constant characteristic. The difference will be obvious when we elaborate on adjectives."

"The question Как? implies quality or mode of action," speculated John. "We would say "What is it like?" in English, so the answer will be an adverb."

***Exercise 13.* Find all five Russian adverbs in this chapter and write them down.**

__________ __________ __________ __________ __________

(often bad good cold hot)

— Зима́. Как э́то? — Alexander Young repeated the question.
— Э́то хо́лодно, — answered John.
— Хорошо́! — his father clapped his hands with joy.

— To have a rest. Как э́то?
— Э́то хорошо́.

***Exercise 14.* Help John to answer professor Young's questions using new words or the ones you already know.**

Хо́лодно.	Жа́рко.	Хорошо́.	Пло́хо.	Тру́дно.	Тепло́.
It is cold.	It is hot.	It is good.	It is bad.	It is difficult.	It is warm.

— А́фрика[1]. Как э́то?
— __________________
— Боле́ть[2]. Как э́то?
— __________________
— Рабо́та. Как э́то?
— __________________
— Антаркти́да[3]. Как э́то?
— __________________

[1] Africa
[2] to be ill
[3] Antarctica

Questions: Что э́то? Кто э́то?

"The last thing we are going to learn today is the question Что э́то?" Alexander was inspired by his son's success. "This question is related to things. When we talk about living creatures we say Кто э́то? By the way, remember, that in Russian we say кто about all animals. A creature is animate if it can move and goes beyond Botany. For example, when we talk about larvae of butterflies we ask Что э́то? while if we ask about butterflies we say кто. We also say кто about lizzards, snakes, insects and other creatures."

"Do I really have to remember Biology and Botany to speak Russian?" thought John.

Кто э́то?

Кто э́то?
Э́то кот.

А кто э́то?
А э́то Альбе́рт Эйнште́йн.

John noticed the similarity between patterns and the same intonation of the questions (ИК-2).

His father pointed at a pen:

— Что э́то?

— Э́то ру́чка.

"And what's this?" he pointed at a lamp.

"This is a lamp." Э́то ла́мпа.

2

Exercise 15. **Help John to answer professor Young's questions using the words in brackets.**

— Что э́то?
— (chair) ________________

— Что э́то?
— (vase) ________________

— Что э́то?
— (cup) ________________

The easiest model of the sentence in Russian is Что — э́то что. With its help you can characterize different things. Note that there is no verb 'to be' here as this is the Present tense. Let's take the word шоссе́ (highway) for instance, which was borrowed from French, and the word автоба́н (autobahn) which was borrowed from German.

Шоссе́ — э́то доро́га.

Автоба́н — э́то то́же доро́га.

Using the words from this lesson John built phrases with the help of this model.

«А» — э́то бу́ква.

Бу́ква — э́то знак.

То́чка — э́то то́же знак.

«Ва́за» — э́то сло́во.

Тома́т — э́то о́вощ.

Бана́н — э́то фрукт.

Model: Кто — э́то кто

"Can we build a model Кто — э́то кто?" asked John.

"Yes, of course."

"OK, then Ло́ра — э́то ма́ма. А́нна — э́то ба́бушка. Ми́стер Па́уэрс — э́то друг. Алекса́ндр — э́то па́па."

Models: Что — э́то как
Где[1] как

"Try the model: Что — э́то как," suggested professor. And John could easily make phrases with the words he already knew:

"Рабо́та — э́то тру́дно.

Спорт — э́то тру́дно."

"And now let's try the model Где как, and remember, the answer for the question Как? is an adverb":

"Э́то дом. Здесь[2] как? Здесь тепло́.

Э́то А́фрика. Там как? Там жа́рко.

Э́то Росси́я. Там как? Там хо́лодно."

"Now, if you look at the map, you can make a text. For example, Э́то ка́рта. Тут Росси́я. Росси́я — э́то страна́. Там хо́лодно. А э́то Москва́. Москва́ — э́то го́род."

[1] where
[2] here

Exercise 16. **Look at the map and make up a text as in the example.**

Exercise 17. **Say where you are from. Answer the question Как там? Хóлодно? Жáрко? Хорошó? Нормáльно[1]?**

"It's wonderful, John! And now I have a surprise for you! The play is called «Гу́си»." His father gave John a piece of paper with some text in it.

— Гу́си[2], гу́си!

— Га-га-гá![3]

— Есть хоти́те?[4]

— Да-да-дá!

"What's гу́си?" asked John.

"A goose is the main Christmas dish, long before it was replaced by turkey, of course."

"Does гусь mean *goose*?"

"That's right."

"Do Russians eat goose for Christmas as well?"

"No, John, goose for Christmas is a purely English tradition."

John and his father role-played the play.

"Entr'acte!" said John as his throat started to ache — it was unusual for him to strain the back part of his throat while pronouncing [g], [k] and [kh].

"Антрáкт! Sounds the same in Russian, English and French. By the way, it's lunchtime. Есть хоти́те?"

"Нет-нет-нéт[5]. I have a lot to do today, dad. Thanks for the lesson, I have to go. Oh, sorry. Спаси́бо![6]"

[1] fine
[2] гусь (pl. гуси): a goose (pl. geese)
[3] English geese say "honk-honk-honk", Russian geese say "ga-ga-ga".
[4] Are you hungry?
[5] no, no, no
[6] thanks

Exercise 18. **As the Youngs are busy, practice expressing emotions in Russian. Here are the situations:**

1. You have read the chapter carefully and you are a bit tired.
2. You have pronounced all the sounds correctly and you feel fantastic about that!
3. Have you done a great job today?
4. Is the job you've done really impressing?
5. You've decided to impress your friends with your knowledge of Russian. It's a surprise.
6. You've demonstrated to your friends "The bell", "Cuckoo-clock", "I'm shooting", "Knock on the door", "Russians love driving fast".
7. You've shown your friends your skills in Russian. Your friends' reaction is…
8. They try to pronounce it the same way but they fail. They regret that.

Chapter 3

Два сéрдца Росси́и.
Two hearts of Russia.

3

John's lessons with his father continued. Professor Young hissed like a snake imitating sounds [sh] Ш and [shch] Щ, growled like a pre-revolutionary engine [trtrtrtrdrdrdrdr] ТР — ДР, snorted like a cat [f] and put his hands on his hips showing that it was not usual Latin *F*, but special Cyrillic Ф. He buzzed like a bee and imitated the sound of cicades, claiming that the sound [ts] is very similar, and the letter Ц which represents that sound looks like a heron and stands on one leg too.

Teaching his son Professor looked younger. He probably remembered the time when he was lecturing at the university. Having noticed that, John was about to admit that even in the absence of any other benefit from the lessons, such a result is also quite satisfactory. This was really worth 'bending' his tongue.

1. Й — И

On the next lesson John had to literally bend his tongue when his father introduced the sound Й.

John remembered from the alphabet that it was a consonant [y].

"This sound is very important, John. While pronouncing Й your lips are forming a smile, teeth are visible, the tip of the tongue touches the lower teeth row, and the middle of the tongue is curved towards the hard part of your palate. You have to feel the outcoming air. Your vocal cords are vibrating (it is a voiced sound)."

"The sound Й is very close to the short English [ĭ] or Russian И [ee]," John noticed after completing the exercise. "It is not by chance are these letters similar in writing, isn't it?"

"Exactly, while pronouncing the vowel И the glottis is in the same position as in the pronunciation of the consonant Й, the only exception is that when you produce the vowel the air coming out of your mouth doesn't meet any obstructions, and while producing the consonant the palate touches the tongue, and the air has to overcome it."

Track 12

***Exercise 1*. Listen and repeat.**

1. Say:

и — ий — й
ай — ой — уй — эй
май — мой — муй — мэй
тай — той — туй — тэй
вай — вой — вуй — вэй

2. Say:

ои — ой   тои — той   мои — мой   вои — вой

3. Say:

— май[1], чай[2]
— —́ сейча́с[3]
—́ —́ Гайд-па́рк[4], Нью-Йо́рк[5], Йо́ркшир[6]

[1] May
[2] tea
[3] now
[4] Hyde Park
[5] New York
[6] Yorkshire

4. Imitate the sounds and express emotions:

I didn't expect that — Ой!
I have hit my arm. It hurts! — Ой-ой- óй!
I'm attracting attention — Эй!
I have pricked my finger with a pin — Ай!
Let's do it — Давáй![1]

— Каравáй, каравáй
Шúре рот открывáй![2] —

Dad started singing unexpectedly.

"This is how your granny Anna sang to me when I was a little boy. And here there is something useful," Alexander explained.

«Каравáй — что э́то?» — asked John.

[1] Let's…!
[2] [Karavaj, karavaj, sheeree rot atkryivaj] — Karavay, Karavay, open your mouth wider!

INTERESTING INFORMATION!

In Russia, bread is not only food, it is also a sympol. For centuries bread has been associated with wealth, prosperity, and home. Russian people welcome guests and bless newlyweds with bread. They do not have a meal without bread. 'Karavay' is a traditional round rye bread, it is a symbol of the Sun.

John understood that it was nothing more than another methodological trick for practicing the new sound, and sang this poem in 'Happy Birthday' manner to please his father.

2. Ы — И

"And now listen to this sound," John's father pushed the lower jaw forward and pronounced with a devilish smile: Ы-ы-ы-ы-ы.

"It looks… weird," John commented.

"I could hardly meet any students who liked this sound. I guess it is the hardest part of Russian phonetics. There is nothing like this in English. I also heard that to pronounce this sound you have to imagine that someone has hit you in the stomach."

"With all respect to you and the methods you apply, we will not practice that," said John very slowly and distinctly.

"As you wish," Professor smiled mysteriously. "Then simply try to say У and stretch your lips in a smile. And put your hand on the chest, you will feel vibration."

"You are kidding."

"I am not. Do it: Ы-ы-ы-ы-ы."

John followed all the instructions and pronounced SOMETHING. His father was dissatisfied, and John had to admit that he didn't hear the difference between Ы and И. But Alexander didn't want to give up:

Exercise 2. Listen and repeat.

Track 13

1. Say:

ы — и   и — ы   и — ы — и

ры́ба[1] — рис[2]

[1] fish
[2] rice

3

"The sound [ы] is a 'hard' version of [и]," John's father went on explaining. He understood that it was difficult for his son.

"Let's try another way," said father after several unsuccessful attempts. "Take a pencil and hold it with your teeth."

"What?" John wanted to make sure that he heard it right.

"Hold it with your teeth, like a dog holding a bone."

"A punch in the stomach sounds better now," grinned John.

"Yes, like this! And now, hold the pencil, say И. Do you hear it? What does it sound like?"

"Well, in your terms, it sounds like someone has been hit by a football in solar plexus."

"Right, and now put the pencil aside and say again И. Now say it again with a pencil. And now say it without it. Do you hear the difference?

In spite of his skepticism regarding his father's teaching methods, John suddenly realized that now he really hears the difference between ы and И.

"Now you have to practice the pronunciation of these sounds without a pencil," Professor Young concluded with a victorious smile.

2. Say:

у — ы — у — ы — и — ы   о — ы — у — ы — и — ы

о — ы — о — ы — и — ы   у — ы — о — ы — и — ы

3. Say:

1.	2.	3.
то — ты — ту	му — мы — мо	во — вы — ву
ту — ты — то	мо — мы — му	ву — вы — во
тур — тыр — тор	мур — мыр — мор	вос — выс — вус
рут — рыт — рот	рум — рым — ром	рос — рыс — рус

4. Say:

—   и, сын[3]

— —́   часы́[4]

— —́ —   откры́тка[5], улы́бка[6]

[3] a son
[4] a watch
[5] a postcard
[6] a smile

3. Я, Ё, Ю, Е

"These vowels can be called 'soft pairs' for the sounds [а, о, у, э]. The softness is provided by the sound [y] at the beginning (go back to the Russian alphabet in Chapter 1 if necessary, see p.14). The sound [y] is always soft.

Track 14

Exercise 3. **Listen and repeat.**

1. Say:

'hard' vowels	а	о	у	э
'soft' vowels	я	ё	ю	е

At the beginning of a word and after the vowels the letters Я, Ё, Ю, Е sound like a compination of [y] and a 'hard' vowel:

2. Say:

Я = Й + А [yah]: я[1], я́блоко[2], Янг, язы́к
Ё = Й + О [yoh]: ёлка[3]
Ю = Й + У [yoo]: Ю́ра
Е = Й + Э [ye]: Еле́на

[1] I
[2] an apple
[3] a fir-tree

"Let's add the pair И [ee] and Ы [ui] which is also defined by its 'hardness' and 'softness' to this list. The letter И like the other 'soft' vowel starting with [y] softens the preceding consonant. And now we have the full list of 'hard' (not softening) and 'soft' (softening) vowels."

'hard' vowels	а	о	у	э	и
'soft' vowels	я	ё	ю	е	ы

"Я is not only a letter of the alphabet," said Professor Young, "я is a pronoun which means 'I'. Perhaps this is the word in the light of which every person looks at the world. The same can be said about the mentality of a people: its view of the world is reflected in the system of pronouns. It is obvious that attitudes to this pronoun in English and in Russian are different. First of all, English speakers always write 'I' with the capital letter. In Russian the letter я is neither right nor desired. The letter я is always small[4]. Russians have a saying, «Я — после́дняя бу́ква в алфави́те» ("Я is the last letter of the alphabet"), which not only shows the real sequence of the letters in the alphabet, but also indicates the attitude to personality in this culture. It is known that European cultures including the English one and the relevant American and Australian ones are the cultures of individualism; Russian culture, on the contrary, is the culture of collectivism. In general, however, it is clear that within the framework of both there are a lot of intermediate forms.

[4] if it is not the first letter in a sentence

While the English culture prioritizes personality, the Russian culture is focused on group, collective interest: 'we' is more important than 'I'. This belief is reflected in the Russian proverb: «Один в по́ле не во́ин», «Одна́ голова́ хорошо́, а две — лу́чше», «В кулаке́ все па́льцы равны́»[5] and others.

In collectivist cultures personal space distance is traditionally shorter. In average Russians physically prefer standing 10–20 cm closer to each other than Englishmen or Americans, be it a private conversation or a talk of colleagues at work. It is easy to get used to it especially

[5] "One is not the warrior in the battlefield" ("There is safety in numbers"), "One head is good, but two heads are better" (two people co-operating are more efficient than one), "Teeth are all friends among each other."

when you know that such behavior is not due to rudeness or a desire to interfere with your private space (by the way, the word 'privacy' doesn't have a direct translation in Russian and requires explanation and some comments), but due to the peculiarities of the world view and the role of a personality in this world. By the way, most Russians perceive the 'English' distance as a display of indifference and secrecy in communication."

"And what if I wrote я with the capital letter? Would it mean that I belong to a different culture and that I want everyone to respect my privacy?" asked John.

"No, it would just be weird," his father shrugged his shoulders.

"I see. And what about the other pronouns? Are there any Russian soul mysteries here?"

"Everything is the same as in English," Alexander Young assured his son.

3

3. Say:

Еди́нственное число́ (Singular)		Мно́жественное число́ (Plural)	
я	I	мы	we
ты (Вы)	you	вы	you
он, она́, оно́	he, she, it	они́	they

"I can see another difference," said John after studying the table. "One English 'you' corresponds to three Russian forms — ты, Вы and вы.

"It is not the difference. I told you the truth when I said that all the Russian pronouns are the same as the English ones. There is a little difference in time though," his father said innocently. "Not long ago there were two forms in the second person Singular in English as well which corresponded to informal ты and respectful Вы with the capital letter. For example, in Shakespeare's plays there are pronouns *thou*, *thy*, *thine*, *thee* (the equivalent of ты in Russian), which were later replaced by more formal *you*: "If thou hast any sound or use of voice speak to me" — Horatio turns to the ghost of the king, and his addressing doesn't sound respectful as to the royal person ("Hamlet", Act 1 Scene 1). Polonius refers to Ophelia with *you*, and to Laertes with *thou*, which means that his son is closer to him than his daughter."

"Wait, Dad! I know that you will get away with it, but let's omit the time travel," John said.

"We can do that. When you turn to anyone in English nowadays you use the only form *you*. In the Russian language this system is like the Old English: ты is used when addressing close relatives, friends or a younger person; Вы is used when addressing one person if one is older, occupies the higher position in society, or a stranger — in all cases when you need to create a distance or to show your respect. In official correspondence such respectful tone is expressed by a capital letter: Вы. And if you write вы with a small letter it means that you address several people."

John was surprised. "Why do Russians need so many pronouns?"

"The clue is in the type of culture again. In our culture it is not acceptable to emphasize the differences between higher and lower positions, older and younger people. Courteous behavior strategy is to demonstrate equality of interlocutors. That is why pronouns reflecting this difference were lost. In Russia if you address your boss or the older person with ты (if быть на ты[1] is not discussed in advance) it means that you are ill-bred. You should address a new acquaintance with Вы as well until you have arranged to use ты when addressing each other."

[1] To address a person using ты.

"I think I can remember that."

"I am glad you think positively," Alexander smiled and pointed at his son:

— Кто э́то?
— Э́то я, — said John.
Then Alexander pointed at himself:
— А э́то кто?
— А э́то ты, па́па. «На ты», хорошо́? — John smiled.
— Да, «на ты» — хорошо́! Ты и я, кто э́то?
— Э́то мы. Мы па́па и сын.
The Professor showed his son a photo on the table:
— А там кто?
— Там па́па и ма́ма. Э́то вы. И я — Джон.

Exercise 4. **Write down personal pronouns that John named to answer Alexander's questions.**

1) — Кто Алекса́ндр?
— ______________________.

2) — Кто Джон?
— ______________________.

3) — Кто Алекса́ндр и Джон?
— ______________________.

4) — Кто Ло́ра?
— ______________________.

Exercise 5. **Complete Alexander's story about his family using the corresponding pronouns.**

1. Алекса́ндр — э́то __________ . Джон — э́то ___________ . Ло́ра — э́то ___________ .

Now it is John's turn to tell the story. Fill in the necessary pronouns:

2. Алекса́ндр — э́то ___________ . Джон — э́то ___________ . Ло́ра — э́то ___________ .

"Pay attention to the third person pronouns," said Alexander. "Он, она́, оно́. They identify the category of gender."

"I guess the difference between Russians and us is not so different in this aspect to identify gender with the help of pronouns."

"I have to disappoint you, my friend, it is not only French and Spanish inanimate nouns have gender. All Russian nouns have the category of gender as well. It is quite easy to remember it in Russian though."

ОН — zero word ending — male gender.

ОНА́ — ending -а, it means that it is female gender.

ОНО́ — ending -о or -е, it means that it is neuter gender.

"What cultural characteristics explain this?" asked John.

"None. It is a purely formal category.

ОН_	ОН**А́**	ОН**О́**
стол_	ла́мп**а**	окн**о́**
Джон_	Ло́р**а**	
Ло́ндон_[1]	Москв**а́**	

[1] London
[2] a man

"What about the word па́па? Is it female?" John was surprised.

"There are some exceptions. These are the words ending in -а but having male gender: па́па, мужчи́на[2]. Some male names especially their short forms end in -а, for example, Алекса́ндр has a shortened form Са́ша, Ю́рий — Ю́ра, Григо́рий — Гри́ша. If a name is male the word has male gender."

Exercise 6. Define the gender and complete the sentences with necessary pronouns.

Example: Ма́ма — э́то … . → Ма́ма — э́то **она́**.

1. Я́блоко — э́то ________ .
2. Ю́ра — э́то ________ .
3. Еле́на — э́то ________ .
4. Сыр — э́то ________ .
5. Сло́во — э́то ________ .
6. Дом — э́то ________ .
7. Ры́ба — э́то ________ .
8. Ма́сло — э́то ________ .
9. Фонта́н — э́то ________ .
10. Окно́ — э́то ________ .
11. Спорт — э́то ________ .
12. Фо́то — э́то ________ .
13. Москва́ — э́то ________ .
14. Авто́ — э́то ________ .

3

Exercise 7. You have met these words in the previous lessons. Remember their meaning, define the gender and fill in the table.

авто́, ма́ма, па́па, фо́то, го́род, дом, бана́н, шарф, ла́мпа, Москва́, стол, стул, ва́за, ба́бушка, суп, тома́т, друг, знак, Ло́ндон, Пари́ж[1], подру́га, рабо́та, то́чка, спорт, фрукт, о́вощ, сло́во, доро́га, ка́рта, ру́чка, бу́ква, жена́, муж, звук, сын, улы́бка, луна́

[1] Paris

ОН	ОНА́	ОНО́
1.	1.	1.
2.	2.	2.
3.	3.	3.
4.	4.	
5.	5.	
6.	6.	
7.	7.	
8.	8.	
9.	9.	
10.	10.	
11.	11.	
12.	12.	
13.	13.	
14.	14.	
15.	15.	
16.		
17.		
18.		
19.		

Model: Чей э́то?

— Possessive pronouns agree in gender, number and case with the noun. They answer the questions: Чей? Чья? Чьё? Чьи? (Whose?)

***Exercise 8.* Listen and repeat.**

Track 15

Притяжа́тельные местоиме́ния — Possessive Pronouns

кто?	чей?		чья?		чьё?		чьи?	
я →	мой	my	моя́[1]	my	моё[2]	my	мои́	my
ты →	твой	your	твоя́	your	твоё	your	твои́	your
мы →	наш	our	на́ша	our	на́ше	our	на́ши	our
вы →	ваш	your	ва́ша	your	ва́ше	your	ва́ши	your
он (оно́) →	его́				his			
она́ →	её				her			
они́ →	их				their			

[1] Я [yah] is a 'soft' variant of the female ending -a. It is used after a vowel or a 'soft' consonant.

[2] Ё [yoh] is a 'soft' variant of the neuter ending -o. It is used after a vowel or a 'soft' consonant.

Alexander Young drew his son's attention to the following aspects:

1. After vowels (моя́, моё) the vowels Е, Ё, Ю, Я sound like Й + vowel [ye, yoh, yoo, yah].

2. Pronounciation is different: sg. мой [moy] — pl. мои́ [moee], sg. твой [tvoy] — pl. твои́ [tvoee].

3. These pronouns are easy to learn in pairs: мой — твой, наш — ваш.

4. The pronouns мой — моя́ — моё — мои́, твой — твоя́ — твоё — твои́, наш — на́ша — на́ше — на́ши, ваш — ва́ша — ва́ше — ва́ши have the same gender as corresponding nouns:

- Э́то я. Э́то мой стол, моя́ ла́мпа, моё окно́. — This is me. This is my table, my lamp, my window.
- Э́то ты. Э́то твой стол, твоя́ ла́мпа, твоё окно́. — This is you. This is your table, your lamp, your window.
- Э́то мы. Э́то наш стол, на́ша ла́мпа, на́ше окно́. — This is us. This is our table, our lamp, our window (several people have 1 table, 1 lamp and 1 window).
- Э́то вы. Э́то ваш стол, ва́ша ла́мпа, ва́ше окно́. — This is you. This is your table, your lamp, your window.
- Э́то Вы. Э́то Ваш стол, Ва́ша ла́мпа, Ва́ше окно́. — This is you. This is your table, your lamp, your window (one respected man has 1 table, 1 lamp and 1 window).

5. Pronouns его́, её, их are used for nouns of all genders:

- Э́то он. Э́то его́ стол, его́ ла́мпа, его́ окно́. — This is him. This is his table, his lamp, his window.
- Э́то она́. Э́то её стол, её ла́мпа, её окно́. — This is her. This is her table, her lamp, her window.
- Э́то они́. Э́то их стол, их ла́мпа, их окно́ (several people have 1 table, 1 lamp, 1 window). — This is them. This is their table, their lamp, their window.

Alexander Young, who was hurrying to make his student apply his new knowledge, started to name all things in the house: Э́то мой дом. Э́то моя́ ко́мната. Э́то мой стол. Э́то моё окно́.

— А э́то чьё? — asked Alexander pointing at the photo of John.

— Э́то моё фото, — answered John.

"And now imagine that I have presented these things to you."

***Exercise 9.* Help John to make a list of his new things:**

A) авто́, бума́га, ва́за, журна́л, каранда́ш, ка́рта, ла́мпа, ноутбу́к, па́пка, Ло́ндон, пол, по́лка, потоло́к, ру́чка, Санкт-Петербу́рг, стол, стул, улы́бка, ча́шка, шкаф

Example: Э́то моё авто́.

"Now these things are not mine but yours," Professor Young went on. "How can I say it in Russian?"

B) *Example:* Э́то ты. Э́то твой стол.

Э́то ты. Э́то _____ стол, _____ стул, _____ ручка, _____ ва́за, _____ окно́.

"And now let's present everything to your mother."

C) *Example:* Э́то её авто́.

Э́то она́. Э́то _____ стол, _____ стул, _____ ру́чка, _____ ва́за, _____ окно́.

"And now let's present it to Mr. Smith."

D) Э́то он. Э́то _____ стол, _____ стул, _____ ру́чка, _____ ва́за, _____ окно́.

— Мы семья́[1], — Alexander said in Russian. — Алекса́ндр, Ло́ра и Джон — э́то мы. Алекса́ндр, Ло́ра и Джон — э́то семья́. Мы — э́то семья́. Мы семья́.

[1] a family

E) Now say that these things are ours.

— Э́то мы. Э́то _____ стол, _____ стул, _____ ру́чка, _____ ва́за, _____ окно́.

— Э́то мой сын! — exclaimed Alexander who hadn't hoped to hear a word in Russian from John in spite of the fact that one fourth of his blood was Russian.

— Ру́сский язы́к — мой язы́к, — answered John, deeply moving his father.

4. Russian consonants. Pairs: voiceless-voiced, hard-soft

CONSONANTS

While talking to his father John noticed that some Russian consonant sounds can differ from the letter they are represented by. For example, although the word друг has the letter Г at the end it is pronounced as [druk]. And the word го́род is pronounced as [gorat].

John asked his father about it, and his father told him about the phonetic rule which is applied to all Russian consonants.

Most Russian consonant sounds form pairs according to the characteristic of being voiceless or voiced.

There are two main rules:

- At the end of the word a voiced sound is replaced by a voiceless pair.
- If a voiced sound is followed by a voiceless one, it is also replaced by its voiceless pair.

Voiced consonants	б	в	д	з	ж	г	й
Voiceless consonants	п	ф	т	с	ш	к	
	улы́бка [ooluipka]	Ивано́в [eevanof]	го́род [gorat] во́дка[1] [votka]	глаз[2] [glas] АвтоВА́З[3] [aftavas]	эта́ж [ehtash] Пари́ж [parish]	друг [drook]	йод [jod]

The rest of the consonants don't have pairs:

Always voiced	м	н	л	р
Always voiceless	х	ц	ч	щ

[1] vodka
[2] an eye
[3] Avtovaz (a factory that produces cars in Russia)

Professor Young also introduced another system of consonant pairs — the Russian consonants form pairs according to their hardness and softness.

Exercise 10. **Listen and repeat. Pay attention to the difference of hard and soft sounds.** Track 16

Hard consonants	б	п	в	ф	д	т	з	с	м	н	л	р	к	г	х
Soft consonants	б'	п'	в'	ф'	д'	т'	з'	с'	м'	н'	л'	р'	к'	г'	х'

Pairless consonants:

Always hard	ж	ш	ц
Always soft	щ	ч	й

This is very important because it is not only about pronunciation, it also concerns noun and adjective declension. There are certain spelling rules concerning hard and soft consonants followed by different vowels, that is why there are soft and a hard variants of noun declension in the Russian language.

К, Г, Х are never followed by Ы in nouns and adjectives.

Ж, Ч, Ш, Щ are never followed by Я and Ю. In case with У and О if the word stress falls on a syllable with Ж, Ч, Ш, Щ, you write О, if it doesn't, — you write Е.

So,

ДА	НЕТ
КИ, ГИ, ХИ	~~КЫ, ГЫ, ХЫ~~
ЖА, ЧА, ША, ЩА	~~ЖЯ, ЧЯ, ШЯ, ЩЯ~~
ЖУ, ЧУ, ШУ, ЩУ	~~ЖЮ, ЧЮ, ШЮ, ЩЮ~~

3

PAIRS IN THE SYSTEM OF VOWELS

"The idea of twoness pervades the whole Russian phonetic system and is applied to the vowels as well," explained Professor Young. "Firstly, vowels also form the so-called 'hard' and 'soft' pairs. Such name is, of course, figurative, as philologists would argue that a vowel can't be soft or hard, although as 'hard' vowels follow 'hard' consonants and 'soft' vowels follow 'soft' consonants I don't see any problems in naming them this way."

'Hard' vowels	а	о	у	э	ы
'Soft' vowels	я	ё	ю	е	и

Hard consonants + 'hard' vowels: ма́ма [mama], па́па, дом.

Soft consonants + 'soft' vowels: ня́ня[1] [nyanya] , тётя[2], дя́дя[3].

[1] a nanny
[2] an aunt
[3] an uncle

ATTENTION! Sounds Ж, Ш, Ц are always hard, so in combinations like ЦЕ, ЖЕ, ШЕ the vowel sound is a 'hard' [eh]: ЦЕ [tse], ЖЕ [zhe], ШЕ [she]). For example, you have met the word центр [tsentr] in the previous chapter. Or the words жена́ [zhena], шесть[4] [shest'] can be good examples, too.

Sounds Ч и Щ in Russian are always soft, that is why you will never meet such combinations as ЧЭ, ЧЫ, ЩЭ, ЩЫ.

[4] six

Exceptions: pairless and always hard consonants (Ж, Ш, Ц) as pairless and always soft ones (Щ, Ч) are always followed by 'hard' vowels А, У and never Я, Ю: ча́шка, шу́тка.

The second very important rule is about when the pairs of vowels appear in the unstressed position. Russians pronounce:

А instead of О: спаси́бо [spasiba], фонта́н[5] [fantan], э́то [eta]

И instead of Е: телефо́н[6] [tilifon], телеви́зор[7] [tilivizar].

"Why on earth can't Russians simply read what they write!" John sighed.

[5] a fountain
[6] a telephone
[7] a TV

"I guess that can't be applied to any of the European languages. The difference between spelling and pronunciation in Russian is much less than in English or French. Anyway, the next rule is the last in the short list of peculiar features of Russian phonetics." Alexander Young calmed his son down.

5. Softening of consonants and letters ь and ъ

"In spelling the softness of a consonant is denoted by either 'soft' vowels which are pronounced without a sound [й], or a special letter ь."

Exercise 11. **Listen and repeat.**

Track 17

1. Say:

да — дя́дя
на — ня́ня
ма — мяч[1]
то — тётя

вы — телеви́зор
луна́ — жалюзи́[2]
тет-а-те́т — тетра́дь[3]

2. Say:

пол — Поль
по́лка — по́лька[4]
стул — пульт[5]

центр — царь
бар[6] — слова́рь[7]
тома́т — крова́ть[8]

[1] a ball
[2] blinds
[3] a notebook
[4] polka
[5] a remote
[6] a bar
[7] a dictionary
[8] a bed

John asked what the letter Ъ was for.

In Russian these two letters are called 'signs'. The signs Ъ — Ь look similar and seem to be a pair, a hard and a soft variant. After Professor Young's explanation it became clear that these signs' function in the middle of a word is to separate the sounds. This function is common for both signs and this can explain why they look so similar. The difference between them is in the following:

Ъ (hard sign) only separates a hard consonant from a soft vowel which is pronounced with the sound [j]. In this case if we place ъ between them the vowel will not lose the sound [j] in pronunciation: объём[9] [abjom], объе́кт[10] [abjekt].

Ь (soft sign) has two functions:

1. it has already been demonstrated that it can soften the preceding consonant: Поль, по́лька, О́льга, пульт, слова́рь [slavar'].

2. it separates the sounds in order to make the vowels Я, Ё, Ю, Е sound like combinations of Й + А, Й + О, Й + У, Й +Э: Сью, компью́тер[11] [kampyooter], семья́[12] [simyah].

[9] volume
[10] an object
[11] a computer
[12] a family

3. Say:

объём, объе́кт, компью́тер, семья́

"So, speaking about articulation, we can make a consonant soft if we raise the back of the tongue towards the hard palate. You should feel the back teeth with your tongue from both sides, and the tongue itself should be flat and touch the palate with its entire surface. When you are speaking Russian your tongue should always go up a little."

Exercise 12. **Listen and repeat.**

Track 18

1. Say:

м — ма — мо — му — мэ — мы
мь — мя — мё — мю — ме — ми
п — па — по — пу — пэ — пы
пь — пя — пё — пю — пе — пи

б — ба — бо — бу — бэ — бы
бь — бя — бё — бю — бе — би

2. Say:

в — ва — во — ву — вэ — вы
вь — вя — вё — вю — ве — ви

ф — фа — фо — фу — фэ — фы
фь — фя — фё — фю — фе — фи

3. Say:

т — та — то — ту — тэ — ты
ть — тя — тё — тю — те — ти
д — да — до — ду — дэ — ды
дь — дя — дё — дю — де — ди

н — на — но — ну — нэ — ны
нь — ня — нё — ню — не — ни
л — ла — ло — лу — лэ — лы
ль — ля — лё — лю — ле — ли

4. Say:

з — за — зо — зу — зэ — зы
зь — зя — зё — зю — зе — зи

с — са — со — су — сэ — сы
сь — ся — сё — сю — се — си

5. Say:

р — ра — ро — ру — рэ — ры
рь — ря — ре — рю — ре — ри

6. Say:

к — ка — ко — ку — кэ — кы
кь — кя — кё — кю — ке — ки

г — га — го — гу — гэ — гы
гь — гя — гё — гю — ге — ги

х — ха — хо — ху — хэ — хы
хь — хя — хё — хю — хе — хи

7. Say:

ма — мя — мья
мо — мё — мьё
му — мю — мью
мэ — ме — мье
мы — ми — мьи

па — пя — пья
по — пё — пьё
пу — пю — пью
пэ — пе — пье
пы — пи — пьи

ба — бя — бья
бо — бё — бьё
бу — бю — бью
бэ — бе — бье
бы — би — бьи

ва — вя — вья
во — вё — вьё
ву — вю — вью
вэ — ве — вье
вы — ви — вьи

фа — фя — фья
фо — фё — фьё
фу — фю — фью
фэ — фе — фье
фы — фи — фьи

та — тя — тья
то — тё — тьё
ту — тю — тью
тэ — те — тье
ты — ти — тьи

да — дя — дья
до — дё — дьё
ду — дю — дью
дэ — де — дье
ды — ди — дьи

на — ня — нья
но — нё — ньё
ну — ню — нью
нэ — не — нье
ны — ни — ньи

ла — ля — лья
ло — лё — льё
лу — лю — лью
лэ — ле — лье
лы — ли — льи

са — ся — сья
со — сё — сьё
су — сю — сью
сэ — се — сье
сы — си — сьи

за — зя — зья
зо — зё — зьё
зу — зю — зью
зэ — зе — зье
зы — зи — зьи

ра — ря — рья
ро — рё — рьё
ру — рю — рью
рэ — ре — рье
ры — ри — рьи

ка — кя — кья	га — гя — гья	ха — хя — хья
ко — кё — кьё	го — гё — гьё	хо — хё — хьё
ку — кю — кью	гу — гю — гью	ху — хю — хью
кэ — ке — кье	гэ — ге — гье	хэ — хе — хье
ки — кьи	ги — гьи	хи — хьи

ча — чья	ша — шья	жа — жья	ща — щья
чо — чьё	шо — шьё	жо — жьё	що — щьё
чу — чью	шу — шью	жу — жью	щу — щью
че — чье	ше — шье	же — жье	ще — щье
чи — чьи	ши — шьи	жи — жьи	щи — щьи

8. Say it right:

тётя, семья́, ма́ма, мяч, пульт, объём, телеви́зор, …

9. Imitate the sounds and express emotions:

To spit over the left shoulder (a superstition, it protects you from the evil eye and bad intentions [t'foo]) — Тьфу-тьфу-тьфу́.

Prohibition (shake the index finger) — Ни-ни́! Ты э́то ни-ни́!

Surprise — Ну́ и ну́!

Let's sing — Ля-ля-ля́. Тра-ля-ля́.

Let's sing a traditional Russian song "Берёзка" — Ай, люли-люли-люли!

Sly laughter — Хи-хи-хи́!

Exercise 13. **Listen and repeat. Say the soft sounds in the following words:**

Track 19

1. газе́та	a newspaper	12. кре́сло	armchair
2. дверь	a door	13. мо́ре	a sea
3. дива́н	a sofa	14. не	not
4. занаве́ска	a curtain	15. нет	no
5. зе́ркало	a mirror	16. они́	they
6. кабине́т	a study	17. отли́чно	excellent
7. карти́на	a picture	18. письмо́	a letter
8. кварти́ра	a flat	19. стена́	a wall
9. кни́га	a book	20. столи́ца	a capital
10. ковёр	a carpet	21. телефо́н	a telephone
11. конве́рт	an envelope		

"Ну и ну!" John was very surprised. "Either you are a great teacher, or I am a smart student! I never thought I would know all the rules to be able to read in Russian on the third lesson."

"As I have told you spelling rules in Russian have much less exceptions than in English and especially in French. A lot of starters are confused by Cyrillic letters, but after you get used to them everything falls into place. And now back to business! Let's practice in identifying gender. Он, она́, оно́ — it is easy. There is only one difficulty — the words that end in ь.

> The words ending in ь, like слова́рь or тетра́дь, can be referred to either male or female gender. You have to look these words up in the dictionary. For example, слова́рь is male gender, and тетра́дь is female one.

Pay attention to hard and soft variants of the endings in female and neuter gender:

ОНА́: -а (hard variant) ма́ма
-я (soft variant) семья́

ОНО́: -о (hard variant) окно́
-е (soft variant) мо́ре

***Exercise 14.* Define the gender and put the words into the corresponding lines:**

газе́та, дверь, дива́н, зе́ркало, кабине́т, карти́на, кни́га, ковёр, компью́тер, конве́рт, кре́сло, крова́ть, письмо́, семья́, слова́рь, стена́, телеви́зор, телефо́н, тетра́дь, мо́ре

Э́то мой ________________________________

Э́то моя́ ________________________________

Э́то моё ________________________________

Мно́жественное число́ существи́тельных — Plural form of nouns

1) Most nouns of male and female gender with hard stem (the letter and sound preceding the ending) in plural end in -Ы.

2) Nouns with soft stem or ending in -Ь (both male and female gender) in plural end in -И.

3) Nouns of neuter gender ending in -О in plural have -А ending. A soft stem requires 'soft' ending -Е and in this case the plural ending will be soft too, it is -Я.

4) There are some exceptions and you have to remember them, and also due to historical reasons the stems ending in backlingual К, Г, Х and all sibilant consonants require ending -И, and not -Ы.

он →	стол — стол**ы́** ча**й** — ча**и** слова́р**ь** — слова**ри́**	-Ø → -Ы -Й → -И -Ь → -И
она́ →	ва́за — ва́зы тётя — тёти дверь — две́ри	-А → -Ы -Я → -И -Ь → -И
оно́ →	окно́ — о́кна мо́ре — моря́	-О → -А -Е → -Я
!!!	знак — зна́ки ёлка — ёлки кни́га — кни́ги мяч — мячи́ о́вощ — о́вощи эта́ж — этажи́	К, Г, Х + И ~~КЫ, ГЫ, ХЫ~~ Ч, Ш, Ж, Щ + И ~~ЧЫ, ШЫ, ЖЫ, ЩЫ~~
!!! Exceptions!	сын — сын**овья́** друг — дру**зья́** муж — муж**ья́** стул — сту́**лья** дом — дом**а́** го́род — город**а́** ковёр — ков**ры́**	
! These nouns don't change their form	авто́ (one form for sg. and pl.) фо́то (one form for sg. and pl.) ко́фе (always sg.) жалюзи́ (always pl.) часы́ (always pl.)	(моё авто́ — мои́ авто́) (моё фо́то — мои́ фо́то) (! мой ко́фе) (мои́ жалюзи́) (мои́ часы́)

***Exercise 15.* Make the plural form of the words:**

авто́, ба́бушка, бана́н, бу́ква, ва́за, газе́та, го́род, дверь, дива́н, дом, доро́га, друг, жалюзи́, жена́, занаве́ска, звук, зе́ркало, знак, кабине́т, ка́рта, карти́на, кварти́ра, кни́га, ковёр, компью́тер, конве́рт, кре́сло, крова́ть, ла́мпа, ма́ма, мо́ре, муж, о́вощ, па́па, письмо́, подру́га, рабо́та, ру́чка, семья́, слова́рь, сло́во, стена́, стол, стул, суп, сын, телеви́зор, телефо́н, тетра́дь, тома́т, то́чка, улы́бка, фонта́н, фо́то, фрукт

Они́: ______________________________

"Хорошо́! And now let's talk about property," John's father said unexpectedly.

Knowing his father's ability of being utterly impractical, John looked at him with surprise. However, by saying 'property' Alexander implied nothing by grammar.

— Что э́то? (ИК-2), — Alexander looked around.

— Э́то кабине́т. (ИК-1) — answered John. — Э́то твой кабине́т.

— Хорошо́. (ИК-1) Кабине́т — э́то что? (ИК-1 + ИК-2)

— Э́то ко́мната. (ИК-1)

— Хорошо́. (ИК-1) Э́то ва́за? (ИК-2)

— Да, э́то ва́за. (ИК-1)

— А э́то?

John could recognize a new intonation pattern and asked his father to repeat it one more time. He added this pattern to his 'collection' (ИК-4).

***Exercise 16.* Listen and repeat.**

Track 20

Say:

А э́то? Стол?

— А э́то? — repeated Professor Young, pointing at the lamp.

— А э́то ла́мпа.

— Ла́мпа?

John took a pen, but then checked his intonation pattern and realized that it is the same ИК-4.

— Да, э́то ла́мпа, — he said.

Exercise 17. **Read. Remember the main types of questions and answers in Russian. Listen and repeat, follow the intonation.**

Track 21

Models:	Examples:
QUESTIONS	
Special question	
Что э́то?	
General question (or Yes/No question)	
Э́то … ?	Э́то стол?
Specifying question	
А э́то? А э́то …? … ?	А э́то? А э́то стол? Стол?
ANSWERS	
Ascertaining	
Э́то … .	Э́то стол.
Affirmation	
Да, э́то … .	Да, э́то стол.
Negation	
Нет, э́то не … .	Нет, э́то не стол.
The same objects	
Э́то … . Э́то то́же … . Э́то …, и э́то … .	Э́то стол. Э́то то́же стол. Э́то стол, и э́то стол.
Different object	
Э́то …, а э́то … .	Э́то стол, а э́то стул.
Object characteristics through negation	
Нет, э́то не …, а … . Нет, э́то …, а не … .	Нет, э́то не стол, а стул. Нет, э́то стул, а не стол.
Enumeration	
Э́то … и … . Э́то …, … и … .	Э́то стол и стул. Э́то стол, стул и шкаф.
The answer to the part-question «А э́то?»	
А э́то … .	А э́то стол.

Exercise 18. Then there was a conversation in Russian between Professor Young and his son. Look at the pictures кабине́т and стол and complete the dialogue.

— Что э́то?
— Э́то (1) __________.
— Э́то ва́за?
— Да, э́то (2) __________.
— А э́то?
— Э́то то́же (3) __________.
— А э́то?
— А э́то (4) __________.
— Что э́то и э́то?
— Э́то (5) __________ и (6) __________.
— А что э́то, э́то и э́то?
— А э́то (7) __________, (8) __________ и (9) __________.
— А э́то стол?
— Нет, э́то не стол, а (10) __________.
— А э́то пол?
— Нет, э́то не пол, а (11) __________.
— Что э́то, а что э́то?
— Э́то (12) __________, а э́то (13) __________.
— А э́то твой шкаф?
— ______, э́то мой (14) _______.
— А э́то твоя́ ла́мпа?
— Нет, э́то не моя́ ла́мпа, э́то мой (15) __________.
— А э́то?
— А э́то мой (16) __________.
— А э́то чьё (17)__________?
— Тут я, Алекса́ндр Янг. Э́то _____ (17)__________.

КАБИНЕ́Т

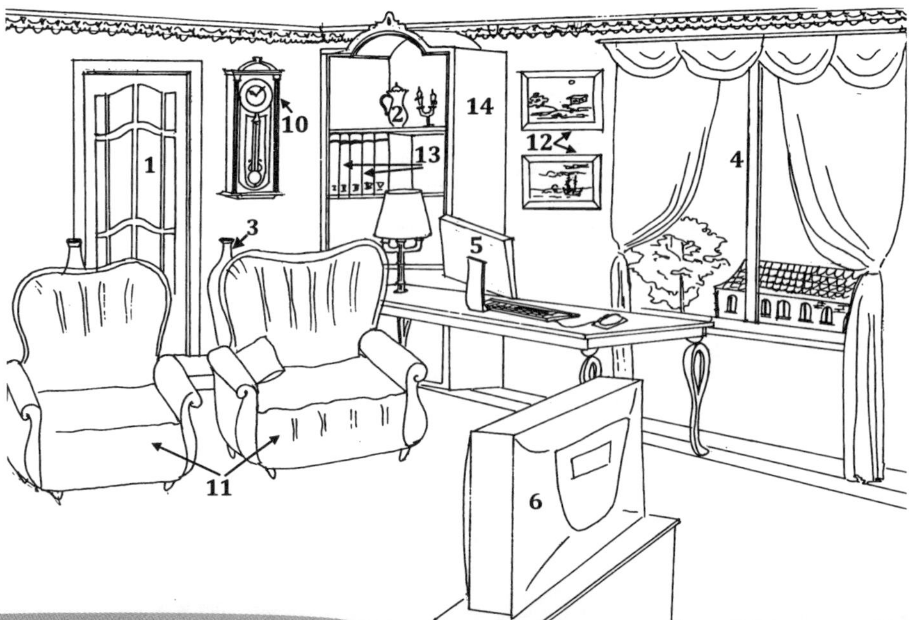

СТОЛ

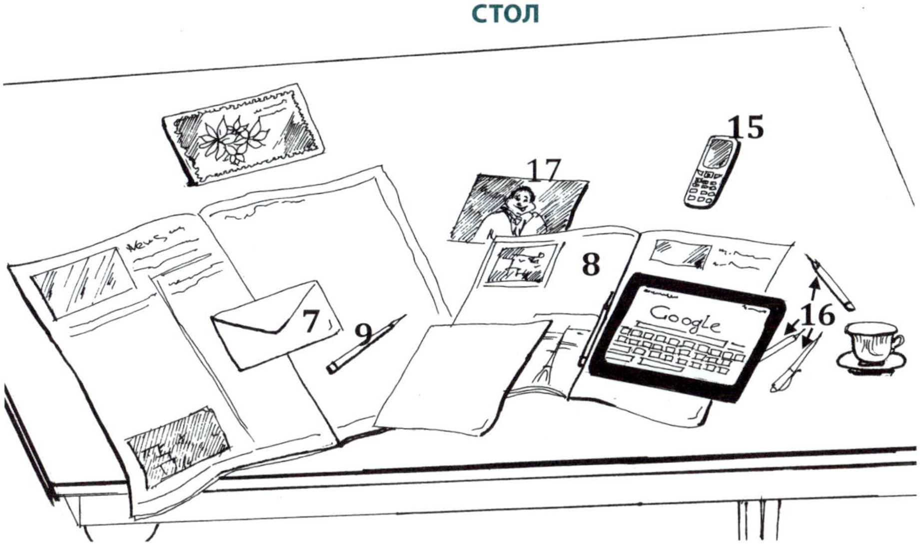

Exercise 19. **Identify the objects in John's room.**

КО́МНАТА

Exercise 20. **Name the objects in your room. Write a small text «Мой стол» using the models, words and pronouns that you already know.**

Example: Э́то моя́ ко́мната. Э́то мой стол. Тут ..., ... и ... . А э́то ... .

"And now let's add some colours and volume," suggested Professor Young.

Прилага́тельное — Adjective

Stem	**он**	**она́**	**оно́**	**они́**	
	како́й?	**кака́я?**	**како́е?**	**каки́е?**	**Choice of ending**
Hard stem	но́вый	но́вая	но́вое	но́вые	Ы/и/о, А/я, О/е, Ы/и
Hard stem with stressed ending	прямо́й	пряма́я	прямо́е	прямы́е	ы/и/О, А/я, О/е, Ы/и
Soft stem **-ний**	си́ний	си́няя	си́нее	си́ние	ы/И/о, а/Я, о/Е, ы/И
Stem **к, г, х**	ма́ленький	ма́ленькая	ма́ленькое	ма́ленькие	ы/И/о, А/я, О/е, ы/И
Stem **к, г, х** with stressed ending	плохо́й	плоха́я	плохо́е	плохи́е	ы/и/О, А/я, О/е, ы/И
Stem **ж, ч, ш, щ**	хоро́ший	хоро́шая	хоро́шее	хоро́шие	ы/И/о, А/я, о/Е, ы/И
Stem **ж, ч, ш, щ** with stressed ending	большо́й	больша́я	большо́е	больши́е	ы/и/О, А/я, О/е, ы/И
	-ЫЙ, -ИЙ, -ОЙ	-АЯ, -ЯЯ	-ОЕ, -ЕЕ	-ЫЕ, -ИЕ	

"If you don't want to learn every new word by heart, think logically only once," suggested professor.

Pay attention to the endings — there are only a few of them, three forms for male gender, two forms for female and neuter genders correspondingly, and two forms for plural. All endings are subject to phonetic rules.

There are certain variants for adjectives: ы/и/о, а/я, о/е, ы/и.

ATTENTION!

Ending form -ОЙ occurs when there is a stressed ending, and forms -ИЙ, -ЫЙ occur in unstressed position.

In the Russian language adjectives, as possessive pronouns, agree with nouns in gender and number.

— Что э́то?
— Э́то мой больш**о́й** дом.

— Что э́то?
— Э́то мо**я́** больш**а́я** ко́мнат**а**.

— Что э́то?
— Э́то мо**ё** больш**о́е** окн**о́**.

Exercise 21. **Read and learn the initial adjective form (sg. masculine — он).**

	он	она́	оно́	они́
Which?	**како́й?**	**кака́я?**	**како́е?**	**каки́е?**
new	но́в*ый*	но́в*ая*	но́в*ое*	но́в*ые*
old	ста́рый	ста́р___	ста́р___	ста́р___
young	молод**о́**й			
beautiful	краси́вый			
ugly	некраси́вый			
interesting	интере́сный			
boring	ску́чный			
light/bright	све́тлый			
dark	тёмный			
right	пра́вый			
left	ле́вый			
direct/straight	прямо́й			
red	кра́сный			
white	бе́лый			
black	чёрный			
blue	си́**ний**			
light-blue	голубо́й			
pink	ро́зовый			
long	дли́нный			
short	коро́т**к**ий			
small, little	ма́лень**к**ий			
big	боль**ш**о́й			
wide	широ́**к**ий			
narrow	у́з**к**ий			
high/tall	высо́**к**ий			
low	ни́з**к**ий			
bad	пло**х**о́й			
good	хоро́**ш**ий			

Exercise 22. **Complete the table with adjectives you have just learned. Write down the endings using the ones you have in the table. The table on the p. 54 will help you.**

Exercise 23. **Find equivalents.**

1. шкаф	а) кра́сная
2. ко́мната	б) ма́ленький
3. ру́чка	в) большо́е
4. окно́	г) си́няя
5. стол	д) но́вая
6. занаве́ска	е) ста́рый

Exercise 24. **Write down the endings.**

Кра́сн___ я́блоко, больш___ дом, но́в___ компью́тер, ста́р___ кре́сло, си́н___ ва́за, кра́сн___ ру́чка, коро́тк___ доро́га, интере́сн___ газе́та, больш___ окно́.

Exercise 25. **Read and define the difference between an adverb and an adjective.**

1. — Кака́я Москва́?
   — Москва́ краси́вая.
2. — Москва́. Как э́то?
   — Э́то краси́во.
3. — Како́й сви́тер?
   — Сви́тер широ́кий. (It's the style of the sweater.)
4. — Как сви́тер?
   — Широко́. (This sweater doesn't fit me.)
5. — Кака́я кни́га?
   — Интере́сная кни́га.
6. — Как кни́га? (The question is about a person's opinion about this book.)
   — Интере́сно!
7. — Э́то Росси́я. Кака́я здесь зима́?
   — Здесь зима́ холо́дная. (objective reality).
8. — Э́то ко́мната. Как здесь?
   — Здесь хо́лодно.
   — Нет, здесь жа́рко!

Указа́тельные местоиме́ния — Demonstrative pronouns

Which kind?	он	она́	оно́	они́
	како́й?	кака́я?	како́е?	каки́е?
sg. this / pl. these	э́тот	э́та	э́то	э́ти
sg. that / pl. those	тот	та	то	те

Э́тот стол но́вый, а тот стол ста́рый. — This table is new, and that table is old.
Э́та кни́га интере́сная, а та кни́га ску́чная. — This book is interesting, and that book is boring.

Exercise 26. **Complete the sentences using the adjectives from the table.**

Example: Э́тот дом но́вый, а тот дом …
Э́тот дом но́вый, а тот дом **ста́рый**.

1. Та по́лка у́зкая, а э́та по́лка ________________________.
2. Э́тот дом высо́кий, а тот дом ________________________.
3. Те компью́теры но́вые, а э́ти компью́теры ________________________.
4. Э́то окно́ ма́ленькое, а то окно́ ________________________.
5. Э́та дверь бе́лая, а та дверь ________________________.
6. Э́то шоссе́ широ́кое, а то шоссе́ ________________________.
7. Э́ти слова́ дли́нные, а те слова́ ________________________.
8. Та шу́тка ску́чная, а э́та шу́тка ________________________.

"Па́па," John addressed his father having noticed that he was eager to give him another exercise. "I have been thinking about granddad Benjamin's story. He was 14 or maybe 15 years old when he escaped from Russia after he had hidden some valuable documents. But our granddad worked as a courier in a bakery — he delivered bread. How could he have these secret documents? Something is wrong here. I think we should check everything one more time before going to Moscow."

"You are right, granddad Benjamin was only a courier," answered father. "And he delivered bread. But I never mentioned his clients."

"Who were they?" John was intrigued, and besides, after the exercises with adjectives he wasn't so enthusiastic about the idea of going to Russia.

"I couldn't believe it myself at first. But your grandfather delivered bread to the Russian Emperor."

"How could that happen?" John didn't know how to react.

"I checked everything. That bakery was famous and fashionable all over Russia. The baker Phillipov and his sons were the only people who had those unique recipes. Bread and cakes from Philippov's bakery were delivered to the noblest Russians and the Russian Emperor himself! Granddad Benjamin worked in this bakery and often went to the Emperor's palace, and he could describe everything in detail. So I tend to believe him."

"And so what?" John was surprised. "I bet he could hardly go far from the gates."

"Spies say that information travels around the world," objected Alexander.

During the conversation John was surfing the net, and then he approached the map on the wall and pointed at two places there.

"Dad, I am not a professor of history and I know nothing about the bakery business in Russia at the beginning of the last century. But Google says that Russian Tzar Peter I made St. Petersburg the capital of Russian instead of Moscow in 1712. And it remained the capital till 1918 when Bolsheviks overthrew the throne of the last Tsar Nicholas II. In other words the emperor lived in St. Petersburg and our granddad Benjamin lived and worked, according to his history, in Moscow. Besides, there is information about Philippov's bakery on the Moscow site: the bakery itself was in Moscow, too, on Tverskaya Street. These days a bakery in the house on Tverskaya street opened again, and it bakes bread following Filippov's recipes. It means that there is something wrong in granddad's story, unless the Russian tzar liked stale bread."

"Everything is right," Professor Young wasn't confused at all. "But it is also true that bread indeed was delivered from Moscow to St. Petersburg."

"You are joking!" John couldn't believe it because he was too pragmatic for that.

"It was impossible to make bread of good quality in St. Petersburg because of the poor quality of local water. The city was built on swamps, and people couldn't purify water those days. That's why every day couriers delivered bread by train from Moscow to St. Petersburg. Philippov knew how to deliver it fresh and crispy to the tzar's table."

"I think I am confused," John looked at the map again. "It turns out that there are two capitals in Russia — Moscow and St. Petersburg, isn't it?"

Alexander Young stood up and approached the map as well.

— Э́то ка́рта. Э́то Росси́я. Э́то Москва́ — э́то **столи́ца**. А тут — Санкт-Петербу́рг. Сейча́с Санкт-Петербу́рг не столи́ца.

"I understand that не столи́ца means that St. Petersburg is not a capital," commented John reminding himself that the verb быть (*to be*) is not used in the Present.

"Nevertheless, Russia has two hearts," his father went on. "Russians say that warmth comes from Moscow and light comes from St. Petersburg. I hope you will see it with your eyes and understand what it means."

John thought that a man judges everything by himself: Moscow is a heart. St. Petersburg seems to be a head. If we go on with this analogy, the Siberian cities are hands, and Ural is a spine. The Professor liked such allegories. John looked at an old anatomical atlas — a rare edition in Russian. The young man opened the book on the page with the picture of a human body and made up the sentences:

Э́то Росси́я. Москва́ — э́то столи́ца. Э́то её се́рдце.

Э́то А́нглия. Ло́ндон — э́то столи́ца. Э́то на́ше се́рдце.

— О́чень хорошо́! — Professor Young was pleased. And John went on.

***Exercise 27*. Read, translate and match the words with the parts of the body.**

___ голова́: a head
___ грудь: a chest
___ живо́т: a stomach
___ нога́: a leg
___ па́лец (pl. па́льцы): a finger (pl. fingers)
___ рука́: an arm
___ се́рдце: a heart
___ те́ло: a body

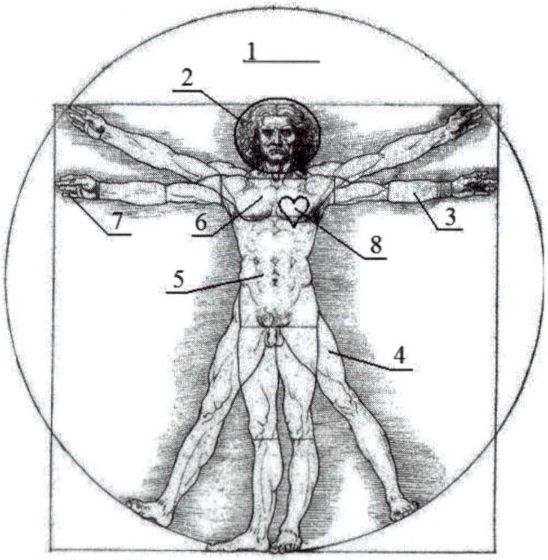

— Москва́ — э́то се́рдце. Санкт-Петербу́рг — э́то голова́. Сиби́рь — э́то ру́ки и но́ги.

— Отли́чно! Here are some more words for you to be able to support any anthropomorphic conversations.

___ во́лосы: hair
___ глаз (pl. глаза́): an eye (pl. eyes)
___ голова́: a head
___ го́рло: a throat
___ губа́ (pl. гу́бы): a lip (pl. lips)
___ лоб: a forehead
___ нос: a nose
___ рот: a mouth
___ у́хо (pl. у́ши): an ear (pl. ears)
___ ше́я: a neck

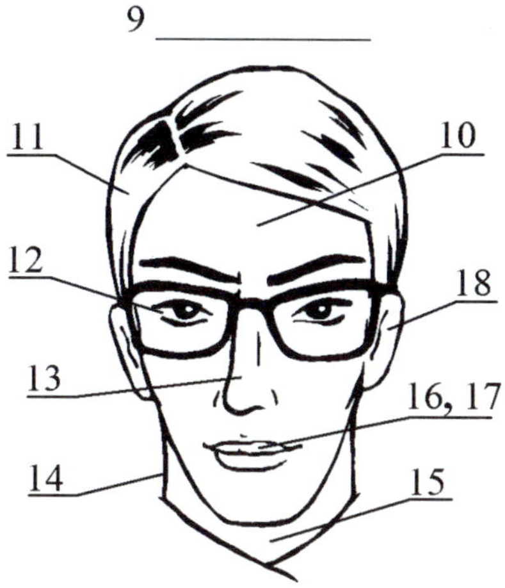

Exercise 28. **Find the adjectives in the table that can describe a man and describe yourself.**

Example: Э́то я. Я высо́кий. Мои́ глаза́ си́ние. Мои́ во́лосы тёмные и коро́ткие. Моё лицо́ молодо́е, у́зкое, све́тлое. Мой нос прямо́й. Мой лоб высо́кий. Мои́ гу́бы то́нкие. Я краси́вый.

Describe a man you know.
Describe a woman you know.
Describe a child you know.

Exercise 29. **Read the proverbs, then read their translation and guess their meaning. Are there any equivalents in your language?**

Глаза́ — зе́ркало души́[1].
Хлеб всему́ голова́[2].

[1] Eyes are the mirror of one's soul.
[2] Bread is everything's head.

Chapter 4

Поéхал зá море телёнком, а вернýлся бычкóм.

Рýсская послóвица

Going overseas as a calf – coming back as a bull.

— Russian proverb

"At the beginning of the 19th century even a French or English coachman could become a tutor in Russia and get a good salary. Russian nobility spoke Russian, French and English and there was always a lack of native-speaking teachers," this was how Alexander Young started his next lesson. "But in the late 1890s a great writer and dramatist Anton Chekhov wasn't ashamed by his ignorance in the sphere of foreign languages. "I speak all languages but the foreign ones, and getting from one railway station to another in Paris is the same for me as playing hide-and-seek" he wrote playfully. What changed? The fact is that by the end of the 19th century, the Russian Empire had strengthened its position in the world, and when in 1894 Nicholas II, the last Russian tsar, came to the throne, Russia was one of the most powerful countries: the biggest army and navy. Russian science and art were recognized in the whole civilized world. The status of the Russian language rose as it became the main language of Russian nobility and peasants and all people who lived in Russia those days (Belarusians, peoples of Caucasus, Tatars, Ukrainians, Finns and many others)."

"I wonder if I can speak the Russian language anywhere else but Russia," John remembered that there was a discussion at work about opening a branch office in Kazakhstan.

***Exercise 1.* Compare the names of the countries and continents in Russian and in English.**

Австрáлия — Australia
Азербайджáн — Azerbaijan
Амéрика (США)[1] — America (The USA)
Áнглия (Великобритáния) — England (Great Britain)
Аргентíна — Argentina
Армéния — Armenia
Белорýссия (Беларýсь)[2] — Belorussia
Бéльгия — Belgium
Бразíлия — Brazil
Грéция — Greece
Гермáния — Germany
Грýзия — Georgia
Дáния — Denmark
Егíпет — Egypt
Изрáиль — Israel
Íндия — India

[1] [se she ah]

[2] In speech there are two variants of the names of former soviet republics. In official documents: Республика Беларусь, Республика Кыргызстан, Республика Молдова, Республика Туркменистан. In informal speech: Белоруссия, Киргизия, Молдавия, Туркмения. In informal speech when referring to the modern period the first variant is preferrable (even without the word Республика), when referring to the period of the Soviet Union — the second variant is preferrable.

Испа́ния — Spain
Ита́лия — Italy
Казахста́н — Kazakhstan
Кана́да — Canada
Кита́й — China
Кирги́зия (Кыргызста́н) — Kyrgyzstan
Ла́твия — Latvia
Литва́ — Lithuania
Ме́ксика — Mexico
Молда́вия (Молдо́ва) — Moldavia
По́льша — Poland
Португа́лия — Portugal
Росси́я — Russia
Сау́довская Ара́вия — Saudi Arabia
Таджикиста́н — Tajikistan
Туркме́ния (Туркмениста́н) — Turkmenistan
Ту́рция — Turkey
Узбекиста́н — Uzbekistan
Украи́на — Ukraine
Финля́ндия — Finland
Фра́нция — France
Швейца́рия — Switzerland
Шве́ция — Sweden
Эквадо́р — Ecuador
Эсто́ния — Estonia
Япо́ния — Japan

Евро́па — Europe
А́зия — Asia
А́фрика — Africa

INTERESTING INFORMATION

Russian is the language of the Russian nation, international and interethnic communication, one of the UN official languages (along with English, Arabic, Spanish, Chinese and French) and one of the working languages of other international organizations such as UNESCO, WHO, OSCE, IAEA and others.

Russian is considered to be their native language by more than 200 million people, and about 360 million people know Russian. It is 6th among the major languages in the world. 114 million people learn Russian as a foreign language. According to the 2010 census in Russia, the Russian language is spoken by 99.4 % of the population.

The Russian language is the state language of the Russian Federation, one of the official languages in the Republic of Belarus, Kazakhstan, Kyrgyzstan, the partially recognized republic of South Ossetia, and Abkhazia.

In the countries of the former Soviet republics: Georgia, Tajikistan, Uzbekistan, Ukraine, and parts of Moldova, the Russian language is not an official government language, though it is the second most spoken language of people living in them. The debate on the status of the Russian language is still under way in the Baltic States (Latvia, Lithuania, Estonia), and in the Ukraine. In Tajikistan, the Russian language is used in the legislation as a language of international communication. In New York, official published documents include Russian.

Russian is learned in China, Israel, Canada, Finland and many other countries where there is a lot of Russian people and active economic interaction between the countries.

Exercise 2. **Look at the map of Russia and the former Soviet Union. Find the countries which were discussed in the commentary.**

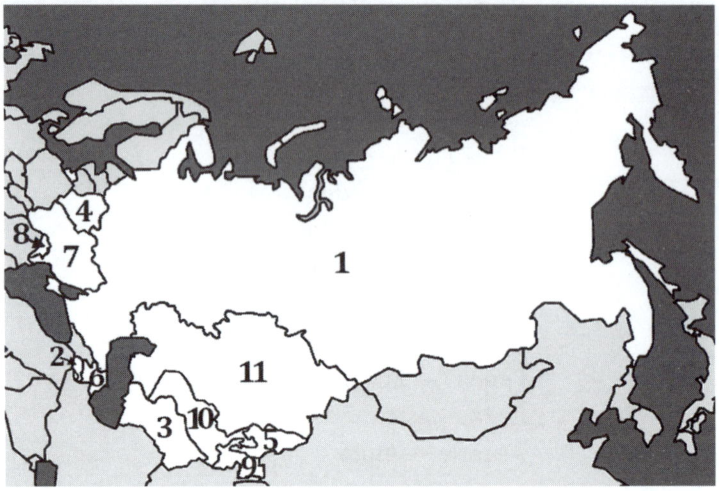

Росси́я — 1,
Арме́ния — 2
Туркмениста́н — 3
Белору́ссия (офиц. Респу́блика Белару́сь) — 4
Кирги́зия — 5
Азербайджа́н — 6
Украи́на — 7
Молда́вия (офиц. Респу́блика Молдо́ва) — 8
Таджикиста́н — 9
Узбекиста́н — 10
Казахста́н — 11

Exercise 3. **Look at the formation of nationality names and complete the table (note that nationality names come from everyday names of the countries, not from official ones).**

Страна́ (контине́нт)	**Национа́льность**		
	они́	**он**	**она́**
	-АНЕ/-ЯНЕ	**-АНИН/-ЯНИН**	**-АНКА/-ЯНКА**
А́нглия	англич**а́не**	англич**а́нин**	англич**а́нка**
Да́ния	датч**а́не**	датч**а́нин**	датч**а́нка**
Молда́вия	молдав**а́не**	молдав**а́**______	молдав**а́**______
Росси́я	росси**я́не**	росси**я́**______	росси**я́**______
Арме́ния	арм**я́не**	арм**я́**______	арм**я́**______
Изра́иль	израильт**я́не**	израильт**я́**______	израильт**я́**______
Еги́пет	египт**я́не**	египт**я́**______	египт**я́**______
	-ЦЫ	**-ЕЦ**	**-КА**
Аме́рика (США)	! америка́н**цы**	америка́н**ец**	америка́н**ка**
Великобрита́ния	! брита́н**цы**	брита́н**ец**	брита́н**ка**
Азербайджа́н	азербайджа́н**цы**	азербайджа́н**ец**	азербайджа́н**ка**
Испа́ния	испа́н**цы**		
Ме́ксика	мексика́н**цы**		
Эсто́ния	эсто́н**цы**		
Япо́ния	япо́н**цы**		
Аргенти́на	аргенти́н**цы**		
Украи́на	украи́н**цы**		
Швейца́рия	швейца́р**цы**		
Эквадо́р	эквадо́р**цы**		
Кана́да	кана́д**цы**		

Литва́	! лито́в**цы**		
Австра́лия	австрали́й**цы**		
Бе́льгия	бельги́й**цы**		
Ита́лия	! итальян́**цы**		
И́ндия	инди́й**цы**		
Герма́ния	!! не́м**цы**		
А́фрика	африка́н**цы**		
	-Ы **-И**	**—**	**-КА**
Белору́ссия	белору́с**ы**	белору́с	белору́с**ка**
Кирги́зия	кирги́з**ы**	кирги́з	кирги́з_____
Туркме́ния	туркме́н**ы**		
Шве́ция	! шве́д**ы**		
Сау́довская Ара́вия	! ара́б**ы**		
Гру́зия	! грузи́н**ы**		
Ла́твия	! латыш**и́**		
	-ХИ **-КИ**	**-Х** **-К**	**-ШКА** **-ЧКА**
Казахста́н	каза́**хи**	каза́**х**	каза́**шка**
Таджикиста́н	таджи́**ки**	таджи́**к**	таджи́**чка**
Узбекиста́н	узбе́**ки**	узбе́**к**	узбе́_____
Remember! (irregular patterns)			
Фра́нция	францу́**зы**	францу́**з**	францу́**женка**
Гре́ция	гре́**ки**	гре**к**	гре**ча́нка**
Кита́й	кита́й**цы**	кита́**ец**	кита**я́нка**
Ту́рция	ту́р**ки**	ту́р**ок**	тур**ча́нка**
Брази́лия	брази́**льцы**	брази́**лец**	бразиль**я́нка**
По́льша	поля́**ки**	поля́**к**	по́л**ька**
Португа́лия	португа́**льцы**	португа́**лец**	португа́**лка**
Финля́ндия	фи́**нны**	фи́**нн**	фи́н**ка**
Евро́па	европ**е́йцы**	европ**е́ец**	европ**е́йка**
А́зия	ази**а́ты**	ази**а́т**	ази**а́тка**

☞ **ATTENTION!**

Ру́сские, ру́сский and ру́сская are adjectives. It is the only nationality indicated by such pattern. Ру́сские is a nationality, россия́не are citizens of Russia.

Do not confuse ☺

И́ндия ≠ Аме́рика
инди́йцы ≠ инде́йцы

***Exercise 4.* Analyze the formation of adjectives**

ру́сские = ру́сск + **ие** ~~ИЕ~~ ру́с~~СК~~ + СКИЙ = ру́с**ский** (язы́к)
францу́зы = францу́з + **ы** ~~Ы~~ францу́з + СКИЙ = францу́з**ский** (язы́к)
белору́сы = белору́с + **ы** ~~Ы~~ белору́с + СКИЙ = белору́с**ский** (язы́к)
латы́ш = латыш + **й** ~~И~~ латы́ш + СКИЙ = латы́ш**ский** (язы́к)
шве́ды = шве́д + **ы** ~~Ы~~ шве́д + СКИЙ = шве́д**ский** (язы́к)

If there is a letter Ц preceding the ending it is omitted together with the ending.

испа́нцы = испа́н + **цы** ~~ЦЫ~~ испа́н + СКИЙ = испа́н**ский**
италья́нцы = италья́н + **цы** ~~ЦЫ~~ италья́н + СКИЙ = италья́н**ский**
швейца́рцы = швейца́р + **цы** ~~ЦЫ~~ швейца́р + СКИЙ = швейца́р**ский**

Exceptions:
не́мцы + **ский** = нем**е́цкий**
ту́рки + **ский** = тур**е́цкий**
поля́ки + **ский** = по́л**ьский**
англича́не + **ский** = англи́**йский**
датча́не + **ский** = да́т**ский**
фи́нны + **ский** = фи́н**ский**

***Exercise 5.* Make a pair "Nationality — language".**

Example: не́мцы — неме́цкий язы́к

францу́зы — ____________________
фи́нны — ____________________
шве́ды — ____________________
азербайджа́нцы — ____________________
испа́нцы — ____________________
португа́льцы — ____________________
япо́нцы — ____________________
англича́не — ____________________

***Exercise 6.* Make a pair "country — language".**

Example: Австра́лия — англи́йский язы́к

Аме́рика — ____________________
Аргенти́на — ____________________
Бе́льгия — ____________________
Брази́лия — ____________________
Еги́пет — ____________________
Кана́да — ____________________
Ме́ксика — ____________________
Сау́довская Ара́вия — ____________________
Эквадо́р — ____________________

***Exercise 7.* What pair is here?**

Изра́иль — ____________________
И́ндия — ____________________
Ира́н — ____________________

"According to the map there are a lot of places in the world where Russian is spoken," said John.

"Today we will speak Russian here in London," Professor Young stressed the word 'speak'. "Говори́ть по-ру́сски. What do we need for it?"

"Разгово́рник?" suggested John pointing at his tab: there were not less than ten English-Russian phrase-books on the Internet.

"[Wazgovownik] won't help here," by saying this, Professor Young dropped his son a hint that Russian Р [r] pronunciation requires further practice. "It is possible to start speaking a language rather soon if you know how a VERB 'works' in this language. In Russian it is ГЛАГО́Л. It concerns not only Russian but any other language as well. In order to speak a foreign language in everyday life you have to know only 300–400 words, 50–70 out of them are verbs, because it explains what is going on. 100–200 of them are nouns, and the rest of them are adjectives and adverbs. If you know them you can easily communicate in another country — you can ask the directions, buy food, ask the time, take a taxi and so on."

"It is more than enough," John thought.

Глаго́л. Настоя́щее вре́мя — Verb. Present Tense

Russian verbs can be divided into 2 basic groups according to their endings: I group and II group. The first group can be named «Е»-model, because there is a letter Е in the ending, and the second group can be named «И»-model, because it has the letter И in the ending.

Almost all Russian verbs are formed this way. There are some exceptions that we will speak about later.

The most common representatives of these groups are the verbs знать[1] and говори́ть[2].

[1] to know
[2] to speak

Exercise 8. **Learn the verbs знать (I group «Е»-model), говори́ть (II group «И»-model) in the Present Tense:**

I group (Е)				**II group (И)**			
я	зна́**ю**	мы	зна́**ем**	я	говор**ю́**	мы	говор**и́м**
ты	зна́**ешь**	вы	зна́**ете**	ты	говор**и́шь**	вы	говор**и́те**
он	зна́**ет**	они́	зна́**ют**	он	говор**и́т**	они́	говор**я́т**

— Мы говори́м по-ру́сски, — suggested father. — For example, let's talk about countries, people and languages.

Model: **Кто говори́т как / Как говори́т кто**
Questions: **Как он говори́т? Он говори́т как?**
Как они́ говоря́т? Они́ говоря́т как?

Model: **како́й язы́к — как говори́ть (говори́ть как)**
ру́сский язы́к — говори́ть **по**-ру́сск**и**
англи́йский язы́к — говори́ть **по**-англи́йск**и**
францу́зский язы́к — говори́ть **по**-францу́зск**и**

неме́цкий —
испа́нский —
япо́нский —
португа́льский —
ара́бский —

!!! Говори́ть по-ру́сски, по-англи́йски, по-кита́йски. But НА иври́те, НА хи́нди, НА фарси́.

— Джон, как ты говори́шь? (Ты говори́шь как?)

John translated: How… you… speak… It is very unusual that Russians don't use the auxiliary, but the meaning is clear. How do you speak? It is the second intonation pattern with the tone going down on the word как. It means that it is a special question which requires a specific answer and not only 'yes' or 'no'. The question word как (how) requires an adverb for an answer. Англи́йский is an adjective, по-англи́йски is an adverb. The answer was ready:

— Я говорю́ по-англи́йски, — said John.

— Хорошо́! А ты говори́шь по-ру́сски?

— Нет, не говорю́.

— Не говори́шь? — his father was surprised. — But I hear Russian speech!

John smiled, he knew that this pedagogical genius was preparing some kind of a trap again.

— All right, another question. Как ты говори́шь по-ру́сски? — Professor squinted slyly.

— Nonsense! Как ты говори́шь? Как ты говори́шь по-ру́сски? — John was surprised at first, but then he realized that these two questions have different meanings.

— Как ты говори́шь по-ру́сски? — repeated his father.

— Я говорю́ по-ру́сски пло́хо, — answered John.

"Отли́чно!" said Professor Young. "I take back my words about the impact of modern computers on the brain. Your brain is perfectly fine."

— А как ты говори́шь по-англи́йски?

— Я говорю́ по-англи́йски отли́чно. Э́то мой язы́к.

— А ты говори́шь по-испа́нски?

— Я не говорю́ по-испа́нски.

— А ты говори́шь по-италья́нски?

— Не говорю́.

— А по-неме́цки?

— Не говорю́.

— А каки́е языки́ ты зна́ешь?

John started to think as a man whose brain was not spoiled by a computer. The question word каки́е (plural form of како́й — which) is logically connected with an adjective and not with an adverb. Англи́йский is an adjective, по-англи́йски is an adverb. So he should choose англи́йский.

— Я зна́ю англи́йский и францу́зский языки́, — answered John.

— Хорошо́! Како́й язы́к ты не зна́ешь?

— Я не зна́ю япо́нский язы́к.

— Отли́чно, Джон! Ты говори́шь по-ру́сски!

☞ REMEMBER!

говори́ть *как*	**знать *что***
	знать *како́й язы́к*
говори́ть + (adverb)	**знать** + (adjective + noun)
по-ру́сски	ру́сский язы́к
по-англи́йски	англи́йский язы́к
по-неме́цки	неме́цкий язы́к
по-кита́йски	кита́йский язы́к

Exercise 9. Using the table from exercise 3, make phrases as in the examples:

A) *Example:* Э́то Росси́я. Тут (кто?) ру́сские.
Тут **говоря́т** (как?) по-ру́сски.

Э́то Фра́нция ______________________________

Э́то Аме́рика ______________________________

Э́то Герма́ния ______________________________

Э́то Испа́ния ______________________________

Э́то Япо́ния ______________________________

Э́то Сау́довская Ара́вия ______________________________

Э́то Казахста́н ______________________________

B) *Example:* Э́то ру́сские.
Они́ **говоря́т** (как?) по-ру́сски.
Они́ **зна́ют** (что? како́й язы́к?) ру́сский язы́к.

Э́то англича́не. Они́ говоря́т по-англи́йски. Они́ зна́ют англи́йский язы́к.

Э́то америка́нцы. ______________________________

Э́то францу́зы. ______________________________

Э́то не́мцы. ______________________________

Э́то испа́нцы. ______________________________

Э́то ара́бы. ______________________________

Э́то япо́нцы. ______________________________

Model: **Кто живёт где / Где живёт кто**
Questions: **Где? — Where?**
Где он живёт? — Where does he live?
Где они́ живу́т? — Where do they live?

— You have to learn the verb жить[1]. It is irregular. (жи → жив-) «е» → «ё».

Group I («E»-model)			
я	жив**у́**	мы	жив**ём**
ты	жив**ёшь**	вы	жив**ёте**
он, она́, оно́	жив**ёт**	они́	жив**у́т**

[1] to live

Э́то А́нглия. Джо́н и Алекса́ндр Я́нги живу́т тут.
О́льга и Анто́н Ивано́вы **не живу́т тут**.
Дэ́вид Бе́кхэм то́же живёт тут.
А Вы то́же живёте тут?

Да, ______________________________

Нет, ______________________________

Глаго́л. Проше́дшее вре́мя — Verb. Past tense

Infinitive	Formation of the Past ть → л : зна-~~ть~~ → зна + л → знал	
знать →	он она́ оно́ они́	зна**л** зна́**ла** зна́**ло** зна́**ли**
говори́ть →	он она́ оно́ они́	говори́**л** говори́**ла** говори́**ло** говори́**ли**
жить →	он она́ оно́ они́	жи**л** жила́ жи́**ло** жи́**ли**

Э́то А́нглия. Дэ́вид Бе́кхэм живёт тут. Уи́нстон Че́рчилль жил тут.
Э́то Аме́рика. Бара́к Оба́ма живёт тут. Джордж Ва́шингтон жил тут.

Exercise 10. **A) Read and analyze. Pay attention to the connection between of the verb tense and the words ра́ньше[1], сейча́с.**

[1] earlier

Model 1. **Ра́ньше** я зна**л** англи́йский язы́к. **Сейча́с** я зна́**ю** англи́йский и ру́сский языки́.

Model 2. **Сейча́с** я зна́ю англи́йский и ру́сский языки́, **а ра́ньше** знал англи́йский язык.

Model 3. **Ра́ньше** я не знал ру́сский язы́к, **а сейча́с** зна́ю.

B) Replace the verb знать with the verb говори́ть:

Model 1. Ра́ньше я говори́л по-англи́йски. Сейча́с я ______________________________

____

Model 2. ____

____

Model 3. ____

____

C) Write what languages you speak and what languages John speaks.

____

____

____

____

____

____

____

Exercise 11. **Look at the pictures of famous writers. Make stories about them as in the example, using the verbs in Present and in Past tenses:**

Example: Э́то Лев Толсто́й. Он ру́сский. Росси́я — э́то его́ страна́. Толсто́й жил там. Он говори́л по-ру́сски и по-францу́зски. Он знал ру́сский и францу́зский языки́.

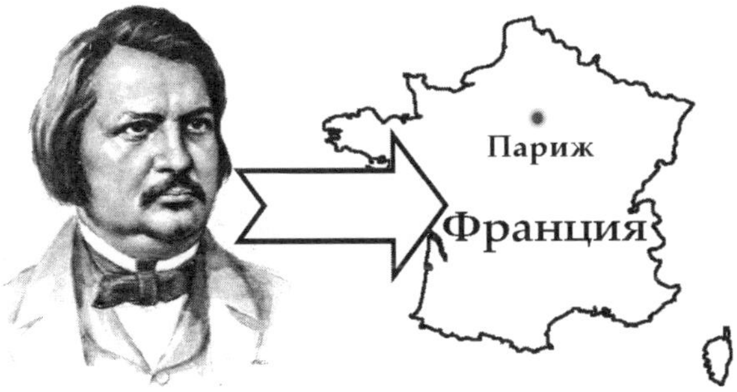

Э́то Оноре́ де Бальза́к ____________________

____

____

____

____

____

Э́то Марк Твен. ____________________

____

____

____

____

____

____

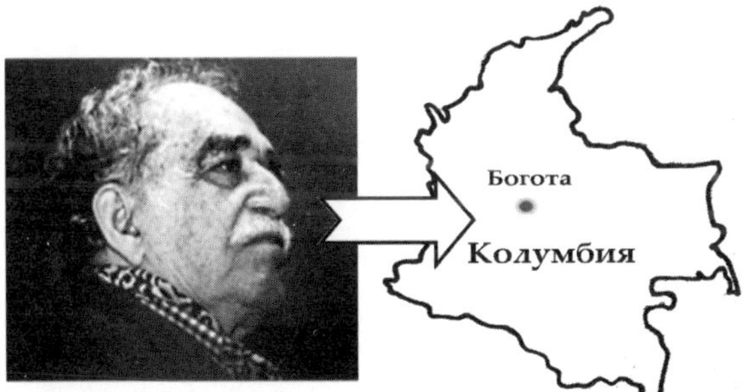

Э́то Габриэ́ль Гарси́а Ма́ркес. ____________________

____

____

____

____

____

____

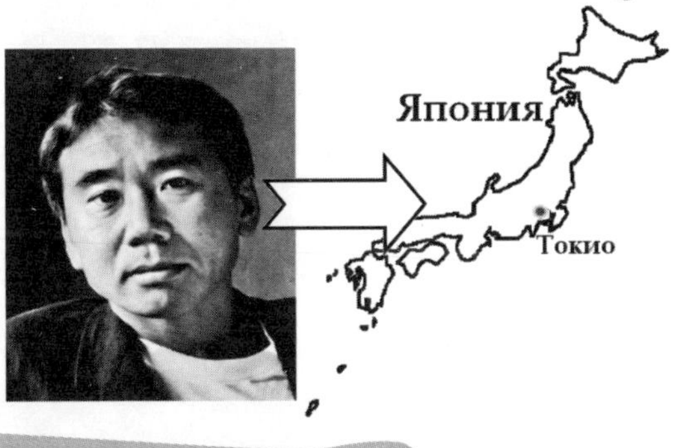

Э́то Хару́ки Мурака́ми.____________________

____

____

____

____

____

____

Э́то Ага́та Кри́сти. ______________________________

____

____

____

____

____

____

____

Exercise 12. **Remember who these people are, when they lived and choose the right form of the Present or the Past tense: живёт/ живу́т or жил/жила́/жи́ли.**

Example: Э́то А́нглия. Ше́рлок Холмс ________ здесь.
Э́то А́нглия. Ше́рлок Холмс **жил** здесь.

Э́то США. Кве́нтин Таранти́но ________ здесь.
Э́то США. Кве́нтин Таранти́но **живёт** здесь.

Э́то А́нглия. Бенеди́кт Камбербэ́тч ________________ здесь.
Э́то США. Бара́к Оба́ма ________________ здесь.
Э́то Росси́я. Пётр Ильи́ч Чайко́вский ________________ здесь.
Э́то Росси́я. Анто́н Па́влович Че́хов ________________ здесь.
Э́то Ме́ксика. Фри́да Ка́ло ________________ здесь.
Э́то США. Мэ́рилин Монро́ ________________ здесь.
Э́то Кана́да. Сели́н Дио́н ________________ здесь.
Э́то Росси́я. Ма́йя Плисе́цкая ________________ здесь.
Э́то Герма́ния. А́нгела Ме́ркель ________________ здесь.
Э́то США. Ме́рил Стрип ________________ здесь.
Э́то Ита́лия. Роме́о и Джулье́тта ________________ здесь.
Э́то Фра́нция. Наполео́н и Жозефи́на ________________ здесь.
Э́то Гре́ция. Одиссе́й и аргона́вты ________________ здесь.
Э́то Великобрита́ния. Кейт Ми́ддлтон и принц Уи́льям ________________ здесь.
Э́то США. Брэд Питт и Анджели́на Джоли́ ________________ здесь.
Э́то Средизе́мье. Хо́ббит Би́льбо и драко́н[1] Сма́уг ________________ здесь.

[1] a dragon

Model: Я зна́ю, что…[1]
Questions: Что ты зна́ешь?
Ты зна́ешь, что…?

— Я зна́ю, что э́то мой дом, — said Alexander. — А что ты зна́ешь?
— Я зна́ю, что Толсто́й ру́сский, — said John.
— А я зна́ю, что мой сын Джон говори́т по-ру́сски.
— Ты зна́ешь, что я говорю́ по-ру́сски?
— Да, я хорошо́ э́то зна́ю. А сейча́с и ты э́то зна́ешь!

[1] что (сою́з): that (conjunction). Я зна́ю, что…: I know that

4

The Professor complicated the task:

"We have been talking about famous writers, and now you can summarize it. Say, Что ты сейча́с знае́шь?" asked professor.

John's story: Э́то Лев Толсто́й. Я зна́ю, что он ру́сский писа́тель[2]. Я зна́ю, что он говори́л по-ру́сски и по-францу́зски. Я зна́ю, что Росси́я — э́то его́ страна́. Я зна́ю, что он жил там.

[2] a writer

Exercise 13. **Talk about the writers from exercise 11. Then write down your story.**

Что Вы зна́ете?

Э́то Оноре́ де Бальза́к. Я зна́ю, что он ______________________________

____

____

Э́то Марк Твен. ______________________________

____

____

Э́то Габриэ́ль Гарси́а Ма́ркес. ______________________________

____

____

Э́то Ага́та Кри́сти. ______________________________

____

____

Э́то Хару́ки Мурака́ми. ______________________________

____

____

Exercise 14. **Write a story about your favourite writer, musician, actor or someone else.**

Э́то ______________________________

____

____

____

____

____

"With the verbs жить and быть we use the question Где? (Where?). The Present form есть[1] is omitted."

— Джон, где я живу́?

— Ты живёшь тут, па́па. Э́то твой дом.

— А где ты сейча́с? (literally А где ты есть сейча́с?)

— Я сейча́с тут. (literally Я есть сейча́с тут.)

John had already learned some adverbs indicating spatial relations: тут, там, до́ма. Alexander Young added more adverbs to this list:

Здесь, бли́зко[2] (ря́дом[3]), далеко́[4], о́чень[5] бли́зко, о́чень далеко́.

After that their conversation acquired some conventional features. John could easily support the discussion about geography.

[1] to be
[2] close
[3] near
[4] far
[5] very

Exercise 15. Say what the distance is from London to these places:

Example: Э́то Ло́ндон. Джон здесь. А э́то Москва́. Москва́ **далеко́**.

Э́то Ло́ндон. Джон здесь. А э́то Луна́[6]. Луна́ о́чень ______________________ .

Э́то Ло́ндон. Джон здесь. Э́то Пари́ж. Пари́ж ______________________ .

Э́то Ло́ндон. Мы здесь. Э́то Ке́мбридж. Ке́мбридж ______________________ .

Э́то Амстерда́м. Мы здесь. Э́то Нью-Йо́рк. Нью-Йо́рк ______________________ .

Э́то Нью-Йо́рк. Вы здесь. А э́то Вашингто́н. Вашингто́н ______________________ .

Э́то Росси́я. Вы здесь. А э́то Украи́на. Украи́на ______________________ .

Э́то Москва́. Вы здесь. А э́то Пеки́н, Кита́й. Пеки́н ______________________ .

[6] the Moon

Shishkin's "Rye"

Tkachev's "In the Field"

Levitan's "Over Eternal Peace"

Kustodiev's "Summer"

INTERESTING INFORMATION!

Pay attention to the fact that the attitude to the distances is special in Russia. For example, Vladivostok is, of course, далеко́ from Moscow (7 days by train and 10 hours by plane). Kazan is не о́чень далеко́ from Moscow (800 km — a night by train). The distance of 300–400 km is often thought of as ря́дом.

Linguists say that Russians' world view is formed by the words characterizing Russian distances: широ́кий (wide), далёкий (far), просто́р (vast), раздо́лье, приво́лье (expanse), свобо́да (freedom). On the one hand these words make a Russian-speaking person feel elated, but on the other hand this infinity creates anxiety, discouragement and sadness — a state which is reflected in the word тоска́ and which is integral part of a Russian soul (ру́сская душа́).

"The first fact about Russian history is Russian fields and its boundlessness <...> from which comes the untranslatability of the word просто́р, accompanied by the feeling that for a foreigner is hardly understandable", writes V. Veidle, an art critic. Philosopher Berdyaev noticed that while a European concentrates on small space, a Russian's mind is occupied by the infinity of Russian lands. This wideness forms a special world view, and you will come across it while learning the language.

Russian painters made Russian landscape painting famous, depicting the beauty of the vast spaces.

Model: **Что там, где что**
Example: **Стул там, где стол**[1]

John made up the following sentences on this model:

Я там, где ты. Ло́ндон там, где А́нглия. Ма́ма там, где сын. Москва́ там, где Росси́я. На́ши докуме́нты там, где Москва́.

[1] Literally, without omitting the verb "*to be*": Что есть там, где что есть: X is in the place where Y is.

Exercise 16. **Make your own sentences with the words you know Что там, где что.**

____

____

____

"It is time we answered the question Где? in Russian," Alexander Young concluded. "For this purpose Russians use the prepositional case (or case № 6) with prepositions В and НА. Let's see how it works."

We can say:
Э́то Ло́ндон. Биг-Бе́н там. — This is London. Big Ben is there.
Э́то стол. Кни́га тут. — This is a table. The book is here.
Э́то мой дом. Я до́ма. — This is my home. I am at home.
It is understandable, but it is better to say like this:
Биг-Бе́н в Ло́ндоне. — Big Ben is in London.
Кни́га на столе́. — The book is on the table.
Я в моём до́ме. = Я до́ма. — I am at home.

ПАДЕ́Ж — CASE

There are six cases in Russian. This language doesn't have a fixed word order, and that is why the case is so important: it shows the function of a noun in a sentence. Each case has its own meaning (subject, object, destination, location and so on). The noun case is transferred to adjectives and pronouns.

Имени́тельный (case № 1) — Nominative

Роди́тельный (case № 2) — Genitive

Да́тельный (case № 3) — Dative

Вини́тельный (case № 4) — Accusative

Твори́тельный (case № 5) — Instrumental

Предло́жный (case № 6) — Prepositional

We will study cases not in the 'right' order, but in the order which will help you to start speaking sooner.

Up till now we have been using only case № 1. This is when a noun is in the position of a subject in a sentence.

We will start with case № 6, which is called the prepositional because it needs a prepostion. Case № 6 answers the question Где?

Предло́жный паде́ж (паде́ж № 6) — Prepositional case (case № 6)
Где? (В чём? На чём?)

	case №1				case № 6					
		чей? чьё? чья?	како́й? како́е? кака́я?	что?		в/на чьём? чьей?	в/на како́м? како́й?	в/на чём?		
он	э́тот, тот	мо**й** тво**й** наш ваш **его́**, **её**, **их**	но́в**ый** больш**о́й** хоро́ш**ий** си́н**ий** ру́сск**ий**	стол слова́р**ь** музе́**й**[1] санато́р**ий**[2]	э́**том**, **том**	мо**ём** тво**ём** на́ш**ем** ва́ш**ем** **его́**, **её**, **их**	но́в**ом** больш**о́м** хоро́ш**ем** си́н**ем** ру́сск**ом**	стол**е́** словар**е́** музе́**е** санато́р**ии**	**-ОМ /** **-ЕМ**	**-Е /** **-ИИ**
оно́	э́то, то	мо**ё** тво**ё** на́ш**е** ва́ш**е** **его́**, **её**, **их**	но́в**ое** больш**о́е** хоро́ш**ее** си́н**ее** ру́сск**ое**	письм**о́** мо́р**е** зда́н**ие**[3]	э́**том**, **том**	мо**ём** тво**ём** на́ш**ем** ва́ш**ем** **его́**, **её**, **их**	но́в**ом** больш**о́м** хоро́ш**ем** си́н**ем** ру́сск**ом**	письм**е́** мо́р**е** зда́н**ии**	**-ОМ /** **-ЕМ**	**-Е /** **-ИИ**
она́	э́та, та	мо**я́** тво**я́** на́ш**а** ва́ш**а** **его́**, **её**, **их**	но́в**ая** больш**а́я** хоро́ш**ая** си́н**яя** ру́сск**ая**	ко́мнат**а** дере́вн**я**[4] тетра́д**ь** аудито́р**ия**[5]	э́**той**, **той**	мо**е́й** тво**е́й** на́ш**ей** ва́ш**ей** **его́**, **её**, **их**	но́в**ой** больш**о́й** хоро́ш**ей** си́н**ей** ру́сск**ой**	ко́мнат**е** дере́вн**е** тетра́д**и** аудито́р**ии**	**-ОЙ /** **-ЕЙ**	**-Е /** **-И /** **-ИИ**

	case № 1				case № 6					
		чьи?	каки́е?	что?		в/на чьих?	в/на каки́х?	в/на чём?		
они́ (он, она́, оно́)	э́**ти**, **те**	мо**и́** тво**и́** на́ш**и** ва́ш**и** **его́**, **её**, **их**	но́в**ые** больш**и́е** хоро́ш**ие** си́н**ие** ру́сск**ие**	стол**ы́** словар**и́** музе́**и** санато́р**ии** пи́сьм**а** мор**я́** зда́н**ия** ко́мнат**ы** дере́вн**и** тетра́д**и** аудито́р**ии**	э́**тих**, **тех**	мо**и́х** тво**и́х** на́ш**их** ва́ш**их** **его́**, **её**, **их**	но́в**ых** больш**и́х** хоро́ш**их** си́н**их** ру́сск**их**	стол**а́х** словар**я́х** музе́**ях** санато́р**иях** пи́сьм**ах** мор**я́х** зда́н**иях** ко́мнат**ах** деревн**я́х** тетра́д**ях** аудито́р**иях**	**-ЫХ / -ИХ**	**-АХ / -ЯХ / -ИЯХ**

In order to express the meaning of a location we change the ending and add prepositions в (in) and на (on).

Джон живёт **в[6] А́нглии, в Ло́ндоне**. — John lives in England in London.

Джон живёт **в но́вой кварти́ре**. — John lives in a new flat .

Иммануи́л Кант жил **в дере́вне**. — Immanuel Kant lived in the village.

Ле́том мы живём **в санато́рии на мо́ре**. — In the summer we live in a sanatorium near the sea.

Э́та карти́на сейча́с **в Ру́сском музе́е в Санкт-Петербу́рге**. — This painting is in the Russian Museum in St. Petersburg now.

Exercise 17. Puzzle:

Но́вые слова́ в словаре́. Слова́рь на столе́. Стол в аудито́рии. Аудито́рия в зда́нии. Зда́ние в Москве́. Что э́то?

Э́то МГУ (Моско́вский госуда́рственный университе́т).

Professor Young formulated the task in Russian:

— Докуме́нты в библиоте́ке[7]. Библиоте́ка в Москве́.

— Я зна́ю, что докуме́нты в библиоте́ке. Я зна́ю, что библиоте́ка в Москве́, — answered John.

— Отли́чно!

[1] a museum
[2] a sanatorium
[3] a building
[4] a village
[5] a lecture hall
[6] When the word following the preposition в starts with the sounds В or Ф, the preposition в turns to во, facilitating pronunciation: во Фра́нции.
[7] a library

The meaning of the prepositions В and НА

В	НА
1. Closed space: в столе́[1], в ко́мнате, в кни́ге	1. Open space or event: на столе́, на по́лке, на стене́, на этаже́, на рабо́те, на ле́кции[2], на конце́рте[3]
2. Building, city, village: в до́ме, в гости́нице (оте́ле)[4], в кварти́ре, в ко́мнате, в но́мере[5], в общежи́тии[6], в го́роде, в дере́вне, в Москве́	2. Street, square, avenue: на у́лице[7], на пло́щади[8], на проспе́кте[9]
3. Countries and regions: в Росси́и, в Евро́пе, в Татарста́не	3. Water objects, mountains, islands, cardinal direction[10]: на Во́лге, на реке́[11], на мо́ре, на океа́не[12], на о́зере[13], на о́строве[14], на Ура́ле, на горе́[15], на ю́ге

[1] in the table
[2] a lecture
[3] a concert
[4] a hotel
[5] a hotel room
[6] a dormitory
[7] a street
[8] a square
[9] an avenue
[10] Forms на реке́, на о́зере, на мо́ре mean "on the bank of the river, lake, sea". To talk about diving in the water use preposition в: в реке́, в о́зере, в мо́ре.
[11] a river
[12] an ocean
[13] a lake
[14] an island
[15] a mountain

Exercise 18. **Make one sentence out of two.**

Example: Э́то по́лка. Кни́га тут. — Кни́га **на по́лке**.
Э́то ва́за. Фру́кты тут. — Фру́кты **в ва́зе**.

1. Э́то кни́га. Текст здесь. ______________________________
2. Э́то стол. Ва́за тут. ______________________________
3. Э́то ко́мната. Кре́сло там. ______________________________
4. Э́то стена́. Карти́на там. ______________________________
5. Э́то гости́ница. Джон там. ______________________________
6. Э́то у́лица. Мой сын там. ______________________________
7. Э́то река́ Во́лга. Мой го́род здесь. ______________________________
8. Э́то Мадри́д. Его́ дом там. ______________________________
9. Э́то Росси́я. Моё се́рдце здесь. ______________________________
10. Э́то Эквадо́р. Бана́ны там. ______________________________

Exercise 19. **Describe the geographical position of your country.**

Example: Э́то Росси́я. Казахста́н **на** ю́го-за́пад**е**. Монго́лия **на** ю́го-восто́к**е**.
Финля́ндия и Шве́ция **на** се́веро-за́пад**е**.

____
____
____
____
____
____
____
____

	Что?	Где?
он	Казахста́**н** Эквадо́**р** Еги́п<u>е</u>**т** Санкт-Петербу́р**г** Ло́ндо**н** Пари́**ж**	в Казахста́н**е** в Эквадо́р**е** в Еги́<u>пт</u>**е**[1] в Санкт-Петербу́рг**е** в Ло́ндон**е** в Пари́ж**е**
	Изра́ил**ь** Акро́пол**ь**	в Изра́ил**е** в Акро́пол**е**
	Кита́**й**	в Кита́**е**
она́	Евро́п**а** Аме́рик**а** Кана́д**а** Ме́ксик**а** Москв**а́**	в Евро́п**е** в Аме́рик**е** в Кана́д**е** в Ме́ксик**е** в Москв**е́**
	Росс**и́я** Великобрита́н**ия** А́нгл**ия** Япо́н**ия** Белору́сс**ия**	в Росс**и́и** в Великобрита́н**ии** в А́нгл**ии** в Япо́н**ии** в Белору́сс**ии**
	НО! Белару́с**ь**	в Белару́с**и**

[1] **Attention**, altering vowel!

4

Exercise 20. **Make sentences as in the model Где есть что. Use places from point 1 and sights from point 2 as in the example:**

Example: (1): Росси́я

(2): Кра́сная пло́щадь.

В Росси́и есть Кра́сная пло́щадь.

1: Росси́я, Фра́нция, Еги́пет, Гре́ция, А́нглия, Ме́ксика.

2: Лувр, Акро́поль, сфинкс, Эрмита́ж, Ло́ндонский глаз, Кремль, пирами́ды ма́йя.

***Exercise 21.* What cities are these sights situated in? Say according to the model что (есть) где. Use the sights from point 1 and cities from point 2.**

1: Фра́нция, Еги́пет, Гре́ция, А́нглия, Ме́ксика.
2: Лувр, Акро́поль, сфинкс, Ло́ндонский глаз, пирами́ды ма́йя.

Example: Кра́сная пло́щадь — в Росси́и.

***Exercise 22.* Explain where these famous people lived.**

Example: Майкл Фараде́й (А́нглия, Ло́ндон)
Майкл Фараде́й жил в А́нглии, в Ло́ндоне.

1. Алекса́ндр Пу́шкин (Росси́я, Санкт-Петербу́рг)
___
2. Стив Джобс (Аме́рика, Сан-Франци́ско)
___
3. Леона́рдо да Ви́нчи (Ита́лия, Флоре́нция)
___
4. Наполео́н Бонапа́рт (Ко́рсика, Ая́ччо)
___
5. Сокра́т (Гре́ция, Афи́ны)
___
6. Короле́ва Викто́рия (Великобрита́ния, Ло́ндон)
___
7. Мо́царт (А́встрия, Ве́на)
___

REMEMBER!

The name of the objects originated not in the Russian language with endings -о, -е, -и, -у DO NOT change: Перу́, Чи́ли, Бордо́, О́сло, Толья́тти, Торо́нто, Гла́зго, Мона́ко, Хе́льсинки, Пуатье́, Душанбе́, о́стров Тенери́фе, etc.

Олимпиа́да-2014 была́ в Со́чи.
Мы бы́ли на Тенери́фе.
Я был в Перу́.
Мой друг живёт в Хе́льсинки.

Model: А́дрес — Address

Я живу́ в Росси́и, в Москве́, на у́лице Поля́рная, в до́ме 8, в кварти́ре 10.
(в до́ме 8 — в до́ме № 8 — в до́ме но́мер 8)
Моя́ кварти́ра на этаже́ 5.

Exercise 23. **Listen and repeat. Russian numerals.**

Track 22

Ско́лько? — How many/much?

1. оди́н
2. два
3. три
4. четы́ре
5. пять
6. шесть
7. семь
8. во́семь
9. де́вять
10. де́сять
11. оди́н**надцать**
12. две**на́дцать**
13. три**на́дцать**
14. четы́р**надцать**
15. пят**на́дцать**
16. шест**на́дцать**
17. сем**на́дцать**
18. восем**на́дцать**
19. девят**на́дцать**
20. два́**дцать**
21. два́дцать оди́н
22. два́дцать два
23. два́дцать три
24. два́дцать четы́ре
25. два́дцать пять
26. два́дцать шесть
27. два́дцать семь
28. два́дцать во́семь
29. два́дцать де́вять
30. три́дцать

10 — де́сять
20 — два́**дцать**
30 — три́**дцать**
40 — **со́рок** !!!
50 — пять**деся́т**
60 — шесть**деся́т**
70 — се́мь**десят**
80 — во́семь**десят**
90 — девяно́**сто** !!!

100 — **сто**
200 — две́**сти**
300 — три́**ста**
400 — четы́ре**ста**
500 — пять**со́т**
600 — шесть**со́т**
700 — семь**со́т**
800 — восемь**со́т**
900 — девять**со́т**

1000 — ты́сяч**а**
2000 — дв**е** ты́сяч**и**
3000 — три ты́сяч**и**
4000 — четы́ре ты́сяч**и**

5000 — пять ты́с**яч**
6000 — шесть ты́с**яч**

0 — ноль (нуль)

Exercise 24. **Say the numbers[1] using the table.**

Example: 23 — два́дцать три

22, 123, 467, 1976, 87, 258, 300, 450, 11, 81, 2012, 9999.

[1] ци́фра: figure, чи́сло: number (notion from maths expressing quantity, e.g. Pi): но́мер: number (= №).

Exercise 25. **Say the address where people live as in the example.**

Example: Анто́н. Москва́, у́лица Строи́телей, дом 10, кварти́ра 12.
Анто́н живёт в Москве́, на у́лице Строи́телей, в до́ме 10, в кварти́ре 12.

1. Майкл Фри́мен. Москва́, Ле́нинский проспе́кт, дом 38, кварти́ра 34.
2. Ари́на и Никола́й Ивано́вы. Каза́нь, у́лица Толсто́го, дом 56, кварти́ра 78.
3. Ва́ся Никола́ев. Ни́жний Но́вгород, Медици́нская у́лица, общежи́тие № 1, дом 5, эта́ж 4, ко́мната 45.
4. А́нна Петро́ва. О́мск, пло́щадь Серо́ва, дом 18, кварти́ра 145.
5. Ива́н Пло́тников. Дере́вня Оси́новка, дом 27.

REMEMBER!

1. Names of Russian cities have gender.

The name has a masculine gender if its ending corresponds to the masculine gender endings (Ло́ндон, Омск, Пари́ж, Санкт-Петербу́рг).

If there is a feminine ending than a city is a female (Москва́, Оде́сса).

If it ends in -ь, you should remember the gender.

For example: **Она́:** Каза́нь, Ряза́нь, Тверь (в Каза́ни, в Ряза́ни, в Твери́);
Он: Су́здаль (в Су́здале).

2. The name preceding the words у́лица, проспе́кт, пло́щадь has declension: Садо́вая у́лица — на Садо́вой (case № 6) у́лице (case № 6).

But the name following the words у́лица, проспе́кт, пло́щадь has no declension: пло́щадь Свобо́ды — на пло́щади Свобо́ды, у́лица Ми́ра, на у́лице Ми́ра.

Exercise 26. **Say about yourself or your friend answering the following questions.**

1. Кто Вы (он, она́)?
2. Како́й язы́к Вы (он, она́) зна́ете (зна́ет)?
3. Как Вы (он, она́) говори́те (говори́т)?
4. В како́й стране́, в како́м го́роде Вы (он, она́) живёте?
5. Что там есть?
6. Ваш (его́, её) а́дрес?

Exercise 27. **Say about John's granddad Benjamin Young answering the questions:**

1. Кто он был?
2. В каки́х стра́нах он жил?
3. В каки́х города́х он жил?
4. Каки́е языки́ он знал?

"Dad, now please tell me, no matter in Russian or in English, but it is very important that I understand, what document should I take a photo of for you в Росси́и, в Москве́, в библиоте́ке?"

"Still, all these new technologies have no good effect on the brain," grumbled the professor. "If it was a single document and I knew exactly what it was, I would have sent a request to the archive, not you."

It was a new twist: John got worried.

"As far as I am concerned," the professor went on, "In 1916 the Russian Tsar Nicholas II did not believe in the revolution. In Tsarskoye Selo it was calm and quiet, except for the fact that the beautiful noble duchesses, which his grandfather had often seen walking in the park, had measles. Of course, we know from the history books, that the political life at the beginning of the last century was in full swing in Russia. Parties struggled for power: the Cadets, essers, the Bolsheviks, the Mensheviks... But outwardly the country seemed stable, especially compared to Europe, where there was the First World War. So, Granddad was doing his job: bread was delivered from Moscow to St. Petersburg, to Tsarskoye Selo, to Alexander Palace where Nicholas II and his family lived. Neither the Russian Tsar nor our grandfather did not think to leave Russia.

On February 27, 1917, while granddad was unloading trunks with bread, he suddenly was called by one of the senior officers of the guard and given a packet with orders to hide it at the bottom of a special bread coffer, which helped keep the bread fresh for days.

In Moscow, Benjamin was supposed to meet someone and give him the package."

"What was in the package?"

"At first he did not look inside. He was going to deliver the package, but it didn't happen. The red proletarian revolution, which changed the whole course of Russian and world history, started exactly the same day. It was February 27, 1917, the year when riots in St. Petersburg started because of the lack of bread, and the station where grandfather Benjamin's train was stopped was captured by the strikers. Granddad threw the saddlebags which only attracted attention of hungry dwellers of St. Petersburg, and took a package to deliver it to Moscow on his own. But he was unlucky again: on the way to Moscow it was very cold and he caught a terrible cold and had to stop in one of the small towns. He arrived in Moscow only a few months later, in early April, when everyone stopped waiting and looking for the messenger. By that time the Emperor Nicholas II had abdicated, and the provisional government was ruling in Russia. The state's fate was not clear and grandfather decided to come back to his historical homeland in England to his mother, who at that time was no longer alive."

"So, granddad Benjamin just took the package with him?"

"No, he left it in a hiding place in the wall of Philippov's bakery where he worked. It was too dangerous to travel with the former royal family possessions."

"Right. But then the bakery was reconstructed and the package was found, wasn't it?"

"It was."

"And what was in it?"

"That's what I want to know with your help. That is, you need to take inventory of the finds in the archive and copy everything for me."

"But what does it all mean? Of course, the documents have already been studied and if there was some kind of information, where to look for the possessions of the royal family, everything must have been found long time ago..."

"Well, firstly, they weren't found, otherwise I would have known. And secondly, I'm afraid that they could not find anything, because I seem to have a key."

"Sorry, what did you just say?!" John could not believe it, and he felt as if his father was playing with him again. However, Professor Young opened one of the drawers of his malachite writing set and pulled out a sheet of yellow porous paper similar to the one which was used to print books in the late XIX — early XX century. On a sheet of this paper something was written in a column with fine handwriting.

На берегу́ пусты́нныхъ во́лнъ
Стоя́лъ онъ, думъ вели́кихъ по́лнъ.
И ду́малъ: «Все мое — и Бо́га!»
Но да́льше насъ ведетъ доро́га.
Тамъ ска́зочный стои́тъ дворе́цъ.
Но въ немъ не человѣкъ жиле́цъ.
Съ друзья́ми ча́сто здѣсь гуля́лъ,
Сейча́съ друзе́й я потеря́лъ.
Вста́нь въ кругъ, клади́ моне́ты въ рядъ.
Шага́й навстрѣчу лошадя́мъ.

"And what does it say here?" John asked looking at the paper with a strange feeling.

"Quite a strange poem, it sounds absurd. But this is clearly a cipher. A common way to code messages. Especially when it comes to members of one family. Literary allusions, a reference to the places known only to a certain number of people. If you get the inventory list, I think we will be able to decode all that is written here."

"Oh, but this is unbelievable!" The young man couldn't but say that. "If you didn't make up the whole story and faked the paper so that I finally took the Russian language, it is something that I can't understand!"

"Now, I hope you understand that this is an interesting case!"

"Yes, I think now I understand why you are not sorry to send your only son to perish in the expanses of Russia as someone like Magellan."

"If you perish, you will not do it like Magellan, but like Aphanasy Nikitin. By the way, here's the case № 6, it's time to practice," with an imperturbable smile retorted Professor Young.

Exercise 28. **Read two short stories and answer the questions.**

Магелла́н был португа́лец, он жил в Португа́л**ии**. Он был в Атланти́ческ**ом** океа́н**е**. Он был в Ю́жн**ой** Аме́рик**е**, на юг**е**. Там сейча́с Магелла́нов проли́в[1]. Магелла́н был в Ти́х**ом** океа́н**е**. Пото́м[2] он был на остров**а́х** Филиппи́ны (на Филиппи́н**ах**).

На како́м языке́ говори́л Магелла́н? ______________________

В како́й стране́ он жил? ______________________

[1] a strait
[2] then

John couldn't remember exactly what Aphanasy Nikitin did and waited for his father's story.

Афана́сий Ники́тин был ру́сский, он жил в Росс**ии**, в го́род**е** Тверь (в Твер**и́**). Он был на рек**е́** Во́лг**е** (на Во́лг**е**), на Каспи́йск**ом** мо́р**е**, в Ира́н**е**, в И́нд**ии**, в А́фрик**е**, на Арави́йск**ом** полуо́стров**е**[3], на Чёрн**ом** мо́р**е**.

Кто был Афана́сий Ники́тин? ______________________

В како́й стране́ он жил? ______________________

Где он был? ______________________

[3] a peninsula

Now John remembered that it was a Russian traveller who opened India to Europe in the 15 century, but died on his way back a few hours away from his hometown.

"Great sense of humour, dad!"

— Да! Спаси́бо, сын! By the way, I don't want you to get lost in Moscow, so I have arranged a training excursion for you, as Russians say, "Good advice is better than money."

***Exercise 29.* Listen to the text and complete the exercises.**

Track 23

Экску́рсия по Москве́ — Excursion to Moscow

A) Listen and repeat:

1. ГУМ (Госуда́рственный универса́льный магази́н) — GUM (State Department Store)
2. Истори́ческий музе́й — Historical Museum
3. Кра́сная пло́щадь — the Red Square
4. Кремлёвская стена́ — the Kremlin Wall
5. Кремль — the Kremlin
6. Кура́нты (часы́) — Chimes (clock)
7. Мавзоле́й — Mausoleum
8. Москва́-река́ — The Moscow River
9. Собо́р Васи́лия Блаже́нного — St. Basil's Cathedral
10. Спа́сская ба́шня — The Spasskaya Tower

B) Listen to the audio. Place the Moscow sights in the order you hear them. Listen twice if necessary.

1. Госуда́рственный универса́льный магази́н (ГУМ) — №__
2. Истори́ческий музе́й — №__
3. Кра́сная пло́щадь — №__
4. Кремлёвская стена́ — №__
5. Кремль — №__
6. Кура́нты (часы́) — №__
7. Мавзоле́й — №__
8. Москва́-река́ — №__
9. Собо́р Васи́лия Блаже́нного — №__
10. Спа́сская ба́шня — №__

C) Answer the questions using case № 6.

1. Где Кремль? (Кра́сная пло́щадь) ______________________________
2. Где кура́нты? (Спа́сская ба́шня[1]) ______________________________
3. Где Ле́нин? (Мавзоле́й) ______________________________

[1] Use preposition на.

Chapter 5

Но панталóны, фрак, жилéт,
Всех э́тих слов на рýсском нет.

А.С. Пýшкин. Евгений Онегин

But pantaloons, tail-coat, vest —
there're not such words in Russian, yet.

A. Pushkin, "Eugene Onegin"

"I met a Russian girl," said John to his dad the following day.

"Oh! А Мáрта?" asked Alexander.

"Мáрта — э́то подрýга!" John smiled and explained, "We chat online in "Chat with native speakers." A Russian girl is teaching me Russian."

"Онá говори́т по-англи́йски?"

"Да, онá говори́т по-англи́йски… Не плóхо и не отли́чно… Нормáльно…"

John looked at his laptop and saw that МАРИ́Я СКВОРЦÓВА is online. Then he called her.

"Мари́я Скорцóва — э́то рýсский… Нет, э́то онá… рýсская… girl".

"Дéвушка," said his father looking at the photo.

"Мари́я Скворцóва — э́то рýсская дéвушка."

Джон Янг: Привéт, Мари́я!

Мари́я Скворцóва: Привéт, Джон! Как делá?

Джон Янг: Хорошó! Как делá?

Мари́я Скворцóва: Отли́чно!

John turned his laptop so that she could see his father.

Джон Янг: Познакóмьтесь, пожáлуйста! Э́то Алексáндр Янг. Он мой пáпа. Он профéссор. А э́то Мари́я. Онá студéнтка.

Алексáндр Янг: Здрáвствуйте, Мáша!

Мари́я Скворцóва: Здрáвствуйте! Óчень прия́тно!

Алексáндр Янг: Мне тóже óчень прия́тно.

Exercise 1. **Listen. Read the phrases and say what Masha, John and Alexander talk about.** Track 24

Разговóрник — The phrasebook

Saying "Hello":	
Здрáвствуй(-те)!	Hello!
Привéт!	Hi!
Дóброе ýтро!	Good morning!
Дóбрый день!	Good afternoon!
Дóбрый вéчер!	Good evening!

Getting acquainted:	
Дава́й(-те) познако́мимся	Let's get acquainted
Разреши́те предста́виться	Let me introduce myself
Name and surname:	
Как тебя́ зову́т? Как е́го зову́т? Как её зову́т?	What's your name? What's his name? What's her name?
Меня́ зову́т… Его́ зову́т… Её зову́т…	My name is… His name is… Her name is…
Как твоё и́мя?	What's your name?
Моё и́мя…	My name is…
Как твоя́ фами́лия?	What's your surname?
Моя фами́лия…	My surname is…
Как Ва́ше и́мя и о́тчество?	What's your patronymic (middle name)?
А как Вас зову́т?	And what's your name?
А Вас?	And yours?
Как Ва́ша фами́лия?	What's your surname?
А Ва́ша?	And yours?
Кто ты? Кто Вы? Кто он? Кто она́?	Who are you? Who are you? Who is he? Who is she?
Я… (Я Майкл. Я студе́нт)	I'm…
Introducing someone:	
Познако́мьтесь, пожа́луйста, э́то…	Please, meet…
Разреши́те (Вам) предста́вить. Э́то…	Let me introduce you. This is…
Разреши́те вас познако́мить.	Let me introduce you.
Phrases after saying "Hello":	
О́чень рад(-а) Вас ви́деть	I'm very glad to see you!
Как дела́? А как твои́ (Ва́ши) дела́?	How are you? And how are you doing?
Как (твоё, Ва́ше) здоро́вье?	How are you getting on?
Answers:	
Спаси́бо, хорошо́	Good, thanks
Отли́чно	Great!
Непло́хо	Not bad
Всё в поря́дке	I'm fine
Норма́льно	I'm OK
Так себе́	So so
Ни хорошо́ ни пло́хо	Not too bad
Всё по-ста́рому	The same old day
Nice to meet you!	
О́чень прия́тно (познако́миться)!	I'm very glad to meet you!
Ра́д(-а) познако́миться!	Nice to meet you!
Взаи́мно.	Me too.

Polite refusal:	
К сожале́нию, я не могу́… + verb (говори́ть, вспо́мнить, ждать, etc.)	Sorry, I can't + verb (talk, remember, wait, etc.)
С удово́льствием, но я не могу́… (говори́ть, вспо́мнить, ждать, etc.)	I'd love to, but I can't + verb (talk, remember, wait, etc.)
Inconclusive response:	
Мо́жет быть	Maybe
Возмо́жно	Probably so
Наве́рное	I guess so
Saying "sorry":	
Извини́(-те)	I'm sorry
Saying "good bye":	
До свида́ния!	Good bye!
Пока́!	Bye!
До встре́чи!	See you!
Счастли́во!	Good luck!
До за́втра!	Till tomorrow!
До ве́чера!	See you in the evening!
Споко́йной но́чи!	Good night!

"Почему́ Ма́ша, а не Мари́я?" asked John after going offline.

"Ма́ша is short for Мари́я," his father told him. Every Russian name has a full and a short variation. There is only one full name, but there can be lots of short variations. Ма́ша is a neutral form of the name Мари́я. There is also Ма́шенька, Ма́ня, Машу́ля, Маню́ня and so on. This is what her family and friend may call her, they are all very emotional. There are also forms with the suffix -к(а), like Ма́шка. It is impolite a bit. It seems strange at first but then you get used to it. These name forms can express your attitude and relationship to a person.

"What's your shortened name?"

"Алекса́ндр is Са́ша. Or Са́шка if you know me very well."

"And what's my name in Russia?"

"Foreign names don't have shortened forms in Russian. John is John, Kevin is Kevin, Monica is Monica."

Exercise 2. **Look at the most common Russian names and their shortened forms.**

Ру́сские мужски́е имена́		**Ру́сские же́нские имена́**	
Дли́нное и́мя	**Коро́ткое и́мя**[1]	**Дли́нное и́мя**	**Коро́ткое и́мя**
Алексе́й	Алёша (Лёша)	А́нна	А́ня
Алекса́ндр	Са́ша	Алекса́ндра	Са́ша
Валенти́н	Ва́ля	Валенти́на	Ва́ля
Ви́ктор	Ви́тя	Викто́рия	Ви́ка
Влади́мир	Воло́дя (Во́ва)	Гали́на	Га́ля
Генна́дий	Ге́на	Екатери́на	Ка́тя
Дми́трий	Ди́ма	Еле́на	Ле́на
Евге́ний	Же́ня	Евге́ния	Же́ня
Ива́н	Ва́ня	Ири́на	И́ра
Константи́н	Ко́стя	Мари́я	Ма́ша
Михаи́л	Ми́ша	Наде́жда	На́дя
Никола́й	Ко́ля	Ната́лья	Ната́ша
Леони́д	Лёня	О́льга	О́ля
Серге́й	Серёжа	Светла́на	Све́та
Станисла́в	Сла́ва	Татья́на	Та́ня
Ю́рий	Ю́ра	Ю́лия	Ю́ля

John chatted not only with Maria, but also with a Russian journalist. They talked about his coming to Russia.

Exercise 3. **Read and translate the conversation.**

Журнали́ст[2]: Hello! I know you are going to come to Russia to start a Russian-English business.

Джон: Здра́вствуйте! Как Вас зову́т?

Журнали́ст: О, Вы говори́те по-ру́сски!

Джон: Да, я говорю́ по-ру́сски.

Журнали́ст: Разреши́те предста́виться. Я журнали́ст. Газе́та «Москва́ и би́знес[3]». Меня́ зову́т Никола́й. Моя́ фами́лия Красно́в.

Джон: Никола́й — э́то Ко́ля?

Журнали́ст: Да!

Джон: О́чень прия́тно.

Журнали́ст: Взаимно. Где Вы живёте в Москве́?

Джон: В гости́нице. В це́нтре.

Журнали́ст: Хорошо́. До встре́чи в Москве́!

Джон: До свида́ния.

[1] Most shortened male names are declined as female ones, like the words мужчи́на, дя́дя. The shortened forms of the female and male names Алекса́ндр(а), Валенти́н(а) and Евге́ний(я) are the same: Са́ша, Ва́ля, Же́ня. Their gender is defined from the context, and their declension is female.

[2] журнали́ст(-ка): a journalist (a female form is with the suffix -к(а))

[3] би́знес [нэ]: business

Exercise 4. **Listen to the conversation between John and the representatives of a Russian company Oleg, Nina and Igor.**

Track 25

Джон Янг — экономи́ст: an economist
Серге́й Кузнецо́в — дире́ктор: a director
Ни́на Вави́лова — секрета́рь: a secretary
И́горь Попо́в — перево́дчик: a translator

Серге́й: До́брый день!
Джон: Здра́вствуйте! Меня́ зову́т Джон Янг. Я экономи́ст.
Серге́й: О́чень прия́тно. Меня́ зову́т Серге́й Кузнецо́в. Я дире́ктор.
Джон: Рад познако́миться!
Серге́й: Познако́мьтесь, пожа́луйста, э́то мой секрета́рь. Её зову́т Ни́на Вави́лова.
Джон: Прия́тно познако́миться, Ни́на.
Ни́на: Взаи́мно.
Серге́й: А э́то наш перево́дчик. Его́ зову́т И́горь Попо́в.
И́горь: Рад познако́миться!
Джон: Я то́же рад познако́миться.

In the evening John was online again. Maria wasn't there. So he talked to another Russian girl.

Викто́рия: Приве́т! Дава́й познако́мимся. Меня́ зову́т Викто́рия!
Джон: До́брый ве́чер! Я Джон.
Викто́рия: Ты англича́нин?
Джон: Да, я англича́нин.
Викто́рия: Ты живёшь в А́нглии?
Джон: Да, я живу́ в А́нглии.
Викто́рия: Э́то отли́чно! А где в А́нглии ты живёшь?
Джон: В Ло́ндоне.
Викто́рия: Э́то отли́чно! А где в Ло́ндоне? В це́нтре?
Джон: Нет.
Викто́рия: В хоро́шем райо́не[1]?
Джон: М-м-м… нет.
Викто́рия: Хорошо́. Пока́!
Джон: Пока́.

[1] a district

While he was waiting for Masha he talked to some other people.

(Mikhail 13 y.o.)
Михайл: Приве́т!
Джон: Приве́т! Как тебя́ зову́т?
Михайл: Михайл. А как Вас зову́т?
Джон: Меня́ зову́т Джон. А како́е твоё коро́ткое и́мя?
Михайл: Ми́ша.
Джон: О́чень прия́тно.
Михайл: Мне то́же. Вы не ру́сский?

Джон: Я англича́нин.
Михаи́л: Вы хорошо́ говори́те по-ру́сски!
Джон: Спаси́бо! Как дела́?
Михаи́л: Ничего́.

(Olga Pavlovna, 70 y.o.)
О́льга: До́брый день! Как дела́?
Джон: До́брый день! Отли́чно! Как Ва́ши дела́?
О́льга: Сего́дня так себе́.
Джон: Как Ва́ше здоро́вье?
О́льга: Ни хорошо́ ни пло́хо!

Then a girl called. She didn't have a video, and there was a question mark instead of a photo. It was much more difficult to talk that way.

Де́вушка: Здра́вствуйте. Я зна́ю, что Вы Джон Янг.
Джон: Здра́вствуйте. Извини́те, кто Вы? Как Вас зову́т?
Де́вушка: Я зна́ю, что Ваш оте́ц — профе́ссор Алекса́ндр Янг. Ваш оте́ц — мой профе́ссор. Я студе́нтка! Меня́ зову́т Ле́на.
Джон: О! Хорошо́! О́чень прия́тно!
Де́вушка: Я живу́ в Москве́. Вы живёте в Москве́ в гости́нице?
Джон: Да.
Де́вушка: Кака́я гости́ница?
Джон: Я не зна́ю. Наве́рное, э́то хоро́шая гости́ница.
Де́вушка: Ха-ха-ха́! ☺ Да, коне́чно, э́то хоро́шая гости́ница! Как она́ называ́ется?[1]
Джон: Моя́ гости́ница называ́ется «Ко́смос».
Де́вушка: О́чень хорошо́! Спаси́бо! Вы хорошо́ говори́те по-ру́сски.
Джон: Спаси́бо. А как Ва́ша фами́лия?
Де́вушка: ...

[1] Compare «Как Вас зову́т?» and «Как э́то называ́ется?». The first one refers to animate objects (people and animals), the second one is applied to inanimate objects. Как Вас зову́т? — Джон.
Как э́то называ́ется? (pointing at a table) — Э́то называ́ется «стол».

John wanted to tell his dad about his student's call, but something happened and she was disconnected. Maybe she wanted to give something to him if she tried to find out where he would stay. John tried to call her again but he couldn't get connected. John waited a while and answered another incoming call.

***Exercise 5.* Read the dialogue and pay attention to the ways of ending a conversation if one cannot talk any more.**

Ната́лья: Приве́т, Джон! Я Ната́лья!
Джон: Приве́т! О́чень прия́тно! Как дела́?
Ната́лья: Ничего́! Я сейча́с на рабо́те. Я журнали́ст...
Джон: Извини́, Ната́ша... К сожале́нию, я не могу́ говори́ть сейча́с, — said John when he saw that Maria Skvortsova was online. — Сейча́с уро́к. Ру́сский язы́к.
Ната́лья: Коне́чно![2] Счастли́во![3]
Джон: Пока́!

[2] a form of agreement = OK, of course, certainly
[3] Good luck! (don't confuse it with сча́стливо: happily)

5

Мари́я Скворцо́ва: Приве́т, Джон!

Джон: Приве́т, Ма́шенька!

Мари́я: Что, извини́? Ма́шенька?!!!

Джон: О, извини́! Мой оте́ц говори́т — э́то коро́ткое и́мя…

Мари́я: ☺☺☺

Джон: Я не понима́ю.

Мари́я: Ма́ша, Мари́я — так говоря́т на рабо́те, так говоря́т друзья́. Ма́шенька, Машу́ня, Ма́ня — так говоря́т до́ма.

Джон: А́-а-а, извини́!

Мари́я: Всё хорошо́! ☺☺☺

"I need to get used to it," thought John. "Five different names at home and at work, that's too much!" He decided to use only those names that Russians say when they indroduce themselves.

Мари́я Скворцо́ва: Джон, как дела́?

Джон: Хорошо́! Я говори́л по-ру́сски.

Мари́я: Отли́чно! Всё хорошо́?

Джон: Да, всё хорошо́! Но есть оди́н вопро́с[1].

Мари́я: Како́й вопро́с?

[1] a question

John could hardly make a question in Russian, and asked in his native language.

"If I get it right, the question Как дела́? is the same as the English 'How are you?'"

"Of course," said Masha.

"But people are often so sad when they answer this question. Some even started to tell me about their day or even complain of their health problems. Is it OK?"

"Oh, I know what you mean," Maria laughed. "Yes, it's OK. In English the question 'How are you?' is another polite way of saying 'hello'. In Russian the question Как дела́? has also its direct purpose, when you ask it you are actually expressing interest in a person's life. That's why when you ask Как дела́? be ready to hear a full answer. It depends on circumstances, though. You can also hear так себе́, всё по-ста́рому, ни хорошо́ ни плохо́, норма́льно, отли́чно, прекра́сно."

John remembered one answer that surprised him:

— Как дела́?

— Ничего́!

"This is a truly Russian answer," Masha smiled. "Ничего́ (nothing) means that nothing bad has happened. It means that everything's fine."

"Ничего́! = Хорошо́!" John looked surprised.

"Да."

"And people don't think it's impolite?"

"What?"

"Being so negative all the time."

"No. Being impolite means being insincerely cheerful. Of course sometimes it's easier to say «Всё отли́чно» even if it's not true, especially with people you don't know well. In big cities it's OK to say «Как дела́?» — «Отли́чно! Всё су́пер! Хорошо́!»."

John remembered about "individualist" (Western) and "collectivist" (Eastern) cultures from the course of history in college. It turned out that for English-speaking people it was very important not to interfere in somebody's privacy, not to get them involved in their problems. For those who speak Russian, though, being sincere, expressing sympathy is what they call being polite.

"As far as Russians' pessimism is concerned… In our country, if you look too positive and optimistic and say something like «Отли́чно!», «Прекра́сно!» too often, it may be regarded as boldness or even boastfulness."

"Oh, now I see, that's why Russians are famous for not smiling at all."

"Да-да!" Masha smiled. "Etiquette smile in Russia is uncommon. You see the widest smile in an expensive shop or in a bank when the percentage rate is increadibly high. Everyone knows it. Russians themselves often don't understand this form of etiquette. Besides, it's sometimes unpleasant to smile when it's cold. That's why Russians seem too serious, but it's not always true."

"It's neither western nor eastern. Russian culture is a mixture of both," thought John.

5

Compare Russian and English sayings:
About laughing and smiling:
— Laugh and the world laughs with you: weep and you weep alone.
— Смех без причи́ны — при́знак дурачи́ны. (Laugh without reason is a sign of foolishness.)
— Смешки́ смешка́ми, а де́ло — де́лом. (Laugh is laugh, business is business.)
About friendship and distance:
— A hedge between keeps friendship green.
— Friends are like fiddle-strings and they must not be screwed too tightly.
— Two is company, three — is a crowd.
— Не име́й сто рубле́й, а име́й сто друзе́й. (It is better to have a hundred friends than a hundred rubles.)
— Сам погиба́й, а това́рища выруча́й. (Die yourself but help a friend.)
— Одино́кое де́рево ве́тер ле́гче ва́лит. (A lonely tree is bent more easily.)
— Оди́н в по́ле не во́ин. (One is not a warrior in a field.)
— В тесноте́, да не в оби́де. (In a crowd but not offended.)

"Englishmen have a proverb "They are rich who have true friends," John was surprised by this overgeneralization.

"That's right, true friendship is valuable in every culture, but there are no sayings about a hedge and fiddle-strings in Russian. It's not easy to keep privacy in our climate, especially when the distances are so great. Some years ago it was literally dangerous. Trust me, this is useful information."

Talking to Masha was interesting, as if she encouraged him to look at the world from a different angle.

"Let's start with something in common."

— Я твой инстру́ктор, а ты мой инстру́ктор, — said Masha and texted these words to John.

— Инстру́ктор — э́то англи́йское сло́во, instructor? — guessed John.

— Да! Англи́йский — э́то прилага́тельное. Англи́йский язы́к, англи́йская грамма́тика, англи́йское сло́во.

— Да, спаси́бо, я зна́ю, что э́то прилага́тельное. Англи́ский язы́к — э́то мужско́й род, англи́йская грамма́тика — же́нский род, англи́йское сло́во — сре́дний род.

— Отли́чно!

— Мой оте́ц — мой инстру́ктор. Он говори́т по-ру́сски.

— Су́пер! Есть ру́сское сло́во «учи́тель» — teacher.

— В ру́сском языке́ есть англи́йские слова́? — said John timidly. But Masha understood him very well.

"Мно́го[1]!" — answered the girl. "English has influence on all the languages in the world. There are lots of English words in the spheres of computer technology, business, sports, advertising, politics. Компью́тер, ска́нер, при́нтер, сайт, веб-ка́мера, пост, CD (сиди́), френд (only on the net, in real life a friend is called друг, so friendship on the net and 'live' friendship are strictly distinguished), се́лфи. Би́знес, бизнесме́н, ме́неджер, ди́лер, офшо́р, дедла́йн, интервью́, ко́фе-бре́йк, тест. Футбо́л, волейбо́л, баскетбо́л (and other sport games), спортсме́н, фана́т. Топ-моде́ль, эксклюзи́вный, и́мидж, прайс-ли́ст. Мини́стр, мэр, премье́р-мини́стр, парла́мент.

[1] a lot

A lot of words in fashion, theatre and cooking come from French. These words are often similar in English and in Russian, too: бюро́ (bureau), премье́ра (premiere), софа́ (sofa), пантало́ны (pantaloons), кашне́ (cachenez), фрак (tailcoat, frock coat), кастрю́ля (saucepan), салат (salad), желе́ (jelly); актёр (actor), балéт (ballet)."

«Не зна́ю, как перевести́»[2], — a great Russian poet Alexander Pushkin once complained about being incapable of translating adequately lots of French words. Now we have the same situation with English words."

[2] I don't know how to translate it

Masha started to pronounce the words.

In spite of Russian pronunciation, John could recognize them.

Exercise 6. **Listen and repeat. Do you recognize these words? Match Russian words with English or French ones. Then check.**

Track 26

Ру́сские слова́	Put the right number of an English word here	Англи́йские слова́
1. актёр		1. test
2. компью́тер		2. manager
3. теа́тр		3. deadline
4. при́нтер		4. interview
5. ко́фе-бре́йк		5. fan
6. премье́ра		6. premiere
7. би́знес		7. auto
8. бизнесме́н		8. coffee break
9. ме́неджер		9. theatre
10. дедла́йн		10. printer
11. интервью́		11. parliament
12. пост		12. actor
13. тест		13. computer
14. спортсме́н		14. businessman
15. фана́т		15. sportsman
16. и́мидж		16. chocolate
17. мини́стр		17. post
18. парла́мент		18. business
19. желе́		19. jelly
20. шокола́д		20. image

21. автомоби́ль		21. camera
22. авто́		22. video
23. ра́дио		23. basketball
24. видеока́мера		24. football
25. ви́део		25. minister
26. футбо́л		26. radio
27. баскетбо́л		27. automobile, car

☞ REMEMBER ABOUT FALSE FRIENDS!

Magazine — in Russian журна́л (compare: журнали́ст (journalist), магази́н — shop, store).
Stress — стресс[1] (a state of physical and emotional exhaustion, a feeling that one cannot cope with a difficult problem or situation). It is not used in Russian in the meaning of 'word stress'.
Medicine — медици́на (the science of human health).
Medicine in the meaning of "drug, pill" — лека́рство.
Tablet — по-ру́сски планше́т, and табле́тка — pill.
Class — уро́к. Класс — classroom.
Cabinet — ку́хонный шкаф and кабине́т — private office, etc.

[1] стресс [рэ]

— В англи́йском языке́ то́же есть ру́сские слова́, — remembered John.

— Ма́ло[2], — answered Masha, showing it putting her palms together so that only a tiny mouse could fit between them.

— Спу́тник, космона́вт (astronaut), ко́смос, балала́йка, борщ, да́ча, гла́сность, кала́шников, сте́рлядь (starlet), ру́сский сала́т, — remembered John.

— Матрёшка, во́дка, квас, царь, самова́р, тро́йка, сове́тский, перестро́йка, колхо́з, совхо́з, — said Masha.

— Я зна́ю, что сове́тский, перестро́йка, гла́сность, колхо́з, совхо́з — э́ти слова́ бы́ли в СССРе, — replied John.

— В СССР[3] (эсэсэсэ́р), — said Masha. — Сове́тские слова́.

[2] few, little

[3] Remember: abbreviations in the Russian language do not have cases. ООН — Где? В ООН; США (the USA) — Где? В США; СССР — Где? — В СССР. Exceptions: ГУМ — Где? В ГУ́Ме. АВТОВА́З — Где? На АВТОВА́Зе. КАМА́З — Где? На КАМА́Зе. That is, if we can replace an abbreviation with one word, it has case declension: В ГУ́Ме = в магази́не. На АВТОВА́Зе, на КАМА́Зе = на заво́де.

Exercise 7. **Listen to the pronunciation of these words. Write their transcription.** Track 27

спу́тник ____________________

борщ ____________________

сове́тский ____________________

балала́йка ____________________

матрёшка ____________________

во́дка ____________________

квас ____________________

царь ____________________

тро́йка ____________________

да́ча ____________________

самова́р ____________________

перестро́йка ____________________

гла́сность ____________________

колхо́з ____________________

совхо́з ____________________

***Exercise 8.* Check yourself. Revise the lessons on phonetics.**

Слова **колхóз**, **совхóз**.

Russians pronounce them as [kalkhos, safkhos]. According to the rule from Chapter 3 (p. 44) we write колхóЗ and say [kalkhoS], we write соВхóЗ and say [saFkhoS], we write вóДка but say [voTka].

In the Russian language the letter Л can be both hard and soft. The word балалáйка has a hard sound [balaláyka] while in the word стéрлядь there is [l'] [st'erl'ad'].

Совéтский is pronounced as [sov'etskiy]. The wrong pronunciation is [sovetskiy] and [sov'yetskiy] — in Russian the sound [v] can also be either hard or soft.

According to the rule of vowel reduction in an unstressed position (Chapter 3, p. 45) we write космонáвт and say [kasmanaft], we write самовáр and say [samavar].

Remember, the farther the sounds [a] и [o] from the stressed position, the less tensed they are. For example, in the word космонáвт the first sound [a] is similar to the reduced [ă]. The same sound is pronounced in the word хорошó instead of the first sound [o] — [khărasho].

Listen to the words again, pay attention to the peculiarities of pronunciation.

Masha kept talking. John could hear the words мáма, пáпа, семья́, му́зыка, Чéхов, Булгáков, теáтр and thought she was talking about herself and her interests. John was disappointed: when Masha started talking only in Russian he understood almost nothing.

— Не понимáешь? — Masha reacted to her student's frowning face.

— Э-э, извини́, что ты говори́шь?

— Понимáть — to understand.

— Не понимáю, — John shrugged his shoulders but then remembered that his flight to Moscow was the next day and changed a frown for a smile.

— Пожáлуйста! — He read the translation of the word "please" in the dictionary.

— Пожáлуйста! — Masha smiled demonstrating that the Russian word пожáлуйста has the meaning of request and reply to request, so it can mean "please" и "you are welcome".

***Exercise 9.* Read the text that Masha wrote to John and try to understand the general meaning. Then we will decode it together.**

ПИСЬМÓ. Я И МОЯ́ СЕМЬЯ́

Меня́ зову́т Мáша. Мне 24 гóда. Я аспирáнтка[1], пишу́ диссертáцию[2]. Я живу́ в Москвé и учу́сь в Москóвском госудáрственном университéте[3] (МГУ) на биологи́ческом факультéте[4]. Там я изучáю биолóгию, эколóгию и хи́мию. Я óчень люблю́ прирóду[5]. Я знáю, что э́то óчень вáжно[6].

Моя́ семья́ большáя.

Э́то мой пáпа. Егó зову́т Ви́ктор. Ему́ 55 лет. Он инженéр, он рабóтает на завóде. Он мнóго знáет о маши́нах[7].

Э́то моя́ мáма. Её зову́т И́нна. Ей 50 лет. Онá касси́р, онá рабóтает в бáнке. Онá мнóго знáет о деньгáх[8].

Э́то мой брат и сестрá.

Мой стáрший брат Дми́трий — IT-инженéр[9]. Он рабóтает в фи́рме. Он мнóго знáет о компью́терах и Интернéте[10]. Ему́ 30 лет. Он женáт[11].

[1] аспирáнт(-ка): a postgraduate (a female form is with the suffix -к(а))
[2] a thesis
[3] a university
[4] Biology faculty
[5] nature
[6] important
[7] a car
[8] money
[9] [ay-tee-inzhener]
[10] Интернéт [нэ]: Internet
[11] married (for a man)

Его́ жена́ О́льга — домохозя́йка[1]. Ей 28 лет.

Их сын Пётр у́чится в шко́ле[2]. Он шко́льник. Ему́ 8 лет. Он хорошо́ игра́ет в футбо́л[3].

Моя́ мла́дшая сестра́ Мари́на — студе́нтка, она́ у́чится в консервато́рии[4]. Там она́ изуча́ет му́зыку и у́чится игра́ть на скри́пке и на роя́ле. Ей 21 год. Она́ не за́мужем[5].

Я и Мари́на — хоро́шие подру́ги. Мы лю́бим му́зыку и теа́тр. Ещё[6] мы чита́ем кни́ги. Я люблю́ чита́ть Анто́на Че́хова, а Мари́на лю́бит чита́ть Михаи́ла Булга́кова. Мы вме́сте мно́го говори́м о кни́гах, о му́зыке, о теа́тре, о приро́де.

Мои́ ба́бушки́ и де́душки — пенсионе́ры. Ра́ньше они́ мно́го рабо́тали, а сейча́с отдыха́ют до́ма и в дере́вне. Они́ лю́бят расска́зывать о жи́зни[7], о рабо́те, о семье́.

1 a housewife
2 a school
3 football
4 a conservatoire
5 married (for a woman)
6 also
7 life
8 a scientist (in Russian it is declined as an adjective)
9 a canteen (it is decline as an adjective)
10 a plane
11 a voyage
12 together
13 chess

Де́душка Ива́н был учёный[8]. Он рабо́тал в университе́те. Сейча́с ему́ 80 лет.

Ба́бушка Ната́лия — его́ жена́. Она́ по́вар. Она́ рабо́тала в столо́вой[9]. Сейча́с ей 73 го́да. Мой па́па — их сын.

Ещё есть де́душка Па́вел и ба́бушка Еле́на. Сейча́с им 76 лет. Моя́ ма́ма — их до́чка. Де́душка Па́вел был пило́т. Он служи́л в авиа́ции и лета́л на самолёте[10]. Он мно́го расска́зывает о самолётах, о путеше́ствиях[11] и о стра́нах. А его́ жена́ Еле́на была́ учи́тельница и рабо́тала в шко́ле. Там она́ учи́ла шко́льников чита́ть и писа́ть. Она́ лю́бит расска́зывать о шко́ле и ученика́х.

Ещё есть дя́дя Васи́лий, его́ жена́ Джейн и их сын Майкл. Они́ живу́т в Аме́рике.

Я о́чень люблю́ мою́ большу́ю семью́. Мы лю́бим отдыха́ть вме́сте[12].

А ещё я люблю́ гуля́ть в лесу́ и́ли в па́рке. Я рису́ю и танцу́ю. До́ма я люблю́ игра́ть в ша́хматы[13].

Having received the longest letter in his life, John regretted asking Masha to write it. But that was a letter from a girl, so he didn't want to turn to his father for help. So, he opened a phrasebook, a dictionary and a book of grammar and started reading.

Exercise 10. **Take highlighters of different colours, a pencil and a rubber and follow John's method of the text analysis.**

I

First of all John looked at the names.
He knew the model Меня́ (его́, её, нас, вас, их) зову́т, so he highlighted it with one colour.

Я Ма́ша	Меня́ зову́т Ма́ша.
Ты Ма́ша?	Тебя́ зову́т Ма́ша?
Он Джон.	Его́ зову́т Джон.
Она́ Ма́ша.	Её зову́т Ма́ша.
Мы Джон и Ма́ша.	Нас зову́т Джон и Ма́ша.
Вы Джон и Ма́ша?	Вас зову́т Джон и Ма́ша?
Они́ Джон и Ма́ша.	Их зову́т Джон и Ма́ша.

Exercise 11. **Find the models with the names in the text and highlight them with one colour.**

Exercise 12. **Find and underline the phrases with the word зовут. Rewrite the phrases with the names without the word зовут like this:**

Example: Мой ста́рший брат Дми́трий — IT-инжене́р. → Э́то брат. Его́ **зову́т** Дми́трий.

Exercise 13. **Fill in the table "Masha's Family". Write the names in empty boxes.**

♂	♀
па́па — dad	ма́ма — mom
сын — son	до́чка (дочь) — daughter
муж — husband	жена́ — wife
брат — brother	сестра́ — sister
ста́рший — elder	ста́ршая — elder
мла́дший — younger	мла́дшая — younger
родно́й брат — sibling	родна́я сестра́ — sibling
кузе́н = двою́родный брат — cousin	кузи́на = двою́родная сестра́ — cousin
де́душка — grandpa	ба́бушка — grandma
внук — grandson	вну́чка — granddaughter
дя́дя — uncle	тётя — aunt
племя́нник — nephew	племя́нница — niece

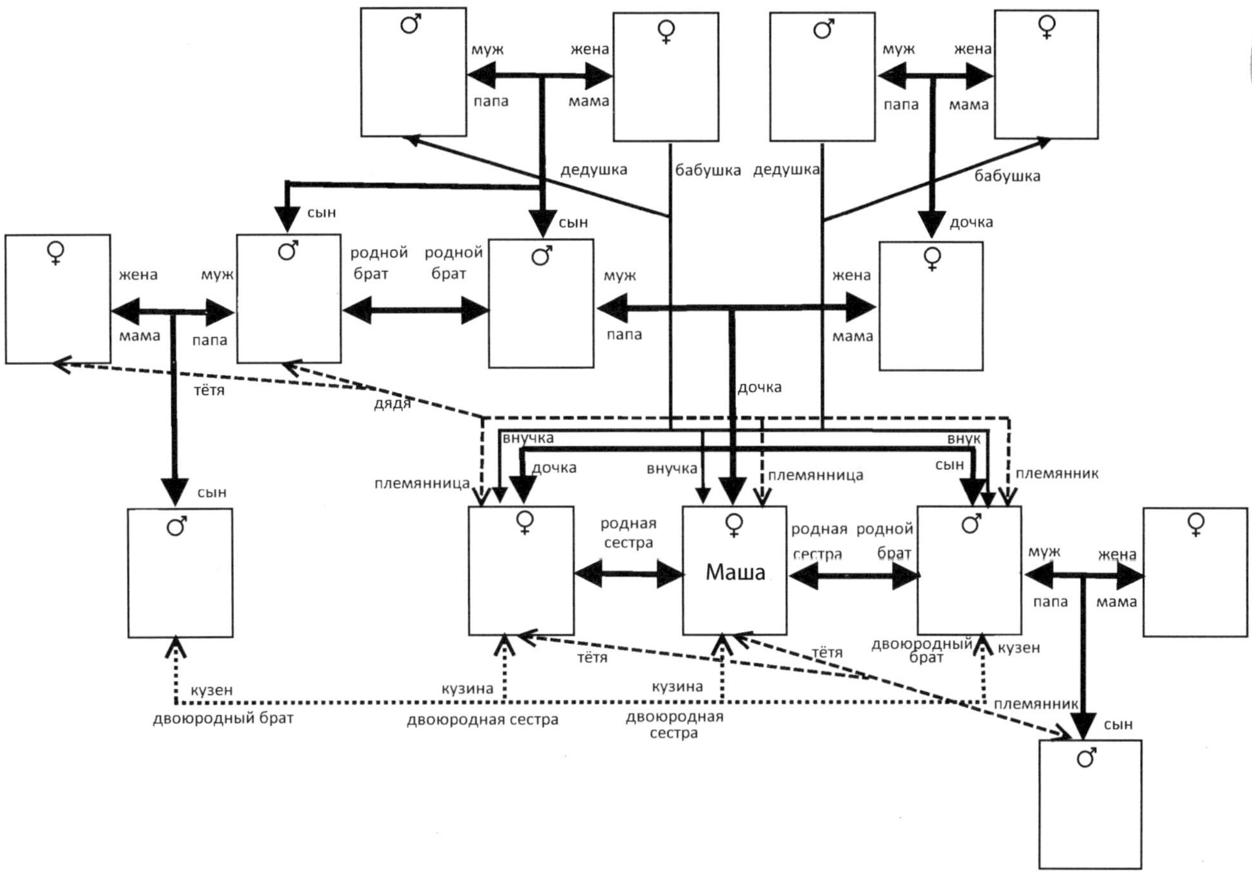

Exercise 14. **Make a table «Моя́ семья́» taking Masha's family as an example.**

II

The next stage was understanding how old the members of the family are.

Model: Ско́лько Вам лет? — How old are you?

Мне 20 лет. Мне 21 год. Мне 22 го́да.

John preferred not to think about the case, he just tried to remember the pronouns.

Я Ма́ша.	Мне	
Ты Ма́ша?	Тебе́	
Он Джон	Ему́	21 год.
Она́ Ма́ша.	Ей	22 го́да.
Мы Джон и Ма́ша.	Нам	20 лет.
Вы Джон и Ма́ша.	Вам	
Они́ Джон и Ма́ша.	Им	

☞ **REMEMBER!**

ГОД — ГО́ДА — ЛЕТ[1]

Rule:	**Examples:**
1 → оди́н **год**	1, 21, 31, 41, 51, 61, 71, 81, 91, 101, 1251 год
2, 3, 4 → два, три, четы́ре **го́да**	2, 3, 4, 22, 33, 44, 52, 63, 74, 153, 672, 1604 го́да
5 — ∞ → пять **лет**	5, 6, 7, 8, 9, 10, 20, 30, 47, 55, 68, 79, 88, 95, 105, 1528 лет

[1] год (pl. case № 2 лет): a year (pl. years)

Exercise 15. **Write the sentences as in the example (don't forget the pronouns and the words год — го́да — лет). Write the questions to these sentences.**

Example: Она́ — 23. → Ей 23 года. Ско́лько ей лет?

1. Я — 25. ______
2. Она́ — 31. ______
3. Он — 58. ______
4. Они́ — 44 и 38. ______
5. Мы — 18 и 20. ______
6. Ты — 36. ______
7. Вы — 21 и 29. ______

Exercise 16. **Write how old you and members of your family are.**

Example: Э́то мой па́па. Ему́ … .

Exercise 17. **Read and translate the text «Did you know...?».**

А Вы зна́ете, что?

Джулье́тта. Ей бы́ло 13 лет.
Её ма́ма — синьо́ра Капуле́тти. Ей бы́ло 26 лет.
Роме́о. Ему́ бы́ло 16 лет.
А́нна Каре́нина (Л. Толсто́й, «А́нна Каре́нина»). Ей бы́ло 28 лет.
Кардина́л Ришелье́ (А. Дюма́, «Три мушкетёра»). Ему́ бы́ло 42 го́да.
Дон Кихо́т (М. Серва́нтес, «Дон Кихо́т»). Ему́ бы́ло 50 лет.
Ше́рлок Холмс. В 1882 году́ ему́ бы́ло 28 лет.

Exercise 18. **Pay attention to the names of different ages in Russia:**

Who?	Кто?	**Age**	Кто?	**Who?**
A little girl	де́вочка	1–15	ма́льчик	A little boy
A girl	де́вушка	16–30	ю́ноша / молодо́й челове́к	A young man
A woman	же́нщина	31 — ∞	мужчи́на	A man

John highlighted the "age" model with a different colour.

III

John remembered that the main word in a sentence is a **verb**. He found all the verbs in the letter and highlighted them.

Exercise 19. **Highlight all the verbs in Masha's letter with a different colour. First do it yourself. Then check your answers (see next exercise).**

As you can see, the verbs have the ending that you already know.

Exercise 20. **Look at their infinitive forms:**

быть	to be	лета́ть	to fly	служи́ть	to serve
говори́ть	to talk	люби́ть	to love	танцева́ть	to dance
гуля́ть	to walk	отдыха́ть	to have a rest	учи́ть	to learn
жить	to live	писа́ть	to write	учи́ться	to study
знать	to know	рабо́тать	to work	чита́ть	to read
игра́ть	to play	расска́зывать	to tell		
изуча́ть	to study	рисова́ть	to draw		

You know how to turn the infinitive into the past form (: -ть + -л (-ла, -ло, -ли)).

Exercise 21. **Find the sentences with verbs in the past, change the past forms to the infinitive forms according to the table, translate them.**

In Russian, the same as in English sometimes an infinitive follows the main verb. For example:
Она́ учи́ла шко́льников **чита́ть** и **писа́ть**. — She taught pupils to read and to write.
Она́ лю́бит **расска́зывать**. — She likes **to tell** stories.
Мы лю́бим **отдыха́ть**. — We like **to have a rest**.
Я люблю́ **гуля́ть**. — I like **to walk**.
Я люблю́ **игра́ть**. — I like **to play**.

Exercise 22. **What do you like to do? — А что Вы лю́бите де́лать?**

Я люблю́ отдыха́ть.
Я люблю́ ____ .
Я ____ .

You should know that you can make the past form of the verb from the infinitive stem (infinitive without -ть). The present form of the verb has its own stem.

5

Exercise 23. **Fill in the table. Add the endings of I or II group to the underlined stem.**

	I group (1.R.VOW)						II group (2.R.CONS.1)
	зна**ть**	рабо́та**ть**	расска́зыва**ть**	гуля́**ть**	чита́**ть**	игра́**ть**	говор**и́ть**
я	зна́**ю**	рабо́та**ю**	расска́зыва**ю**	гуля́___			говор**ю́**
ты		рабо́та___	расска́зыва___	гуля́___			
он(а́, о́)		рабо́та___	расска́зыва___	гуля́___			
мы		рабо́та___	расска́зыва___	гуля́___			
вы		рабо́та___	расска́зыва___	гуля́___			
они́		рабо́та___	расска́зыва___	гуля́___			говор**я́т**

While you were working with these verbs, John found how they change.

All the verbs in their infinitive form answer the question **Что де́лать[1]?** You can change this question according to the person to whom it is addressed:

Что я де́лаю? Я рабо́таю (I group) / Я говорю́ (II group)
Что ты де́лаешь? Ты рабо́та**е**шь / Ты говори́шь
Что он де́лает? Он рабо́та**е**т / Он говори́т
Что она́ де́лает? Она́ рабо́та**е**т / Она́ говори́т
Что оно́ де́лает? :) Оно́ не рабо́та**е**т и не говори́т. Оно́ не челове́к[2]
Что мы де́лаем? Мы рабо́та**е**м / Мы говори́м
Что вы / Вы де́лаете? Вы рабо́та**е**те / Вы говори́те
Что они́ де́лают? Они́ рабо́та**ю**т / Они́ говоря́т

[1] to do
[2] челове́к (pl. лю́ди): a person (pl. people)

Exercise 24. **Answer the questions using the verbs in brackets.**

Example: Что ты де́лаешь? Я (говори́ть). → Я говорю́.

1. Что он де́лает? Он (чита́ть) ______
2. Что она́ де́лает? Она́ (расска́зывать) ______
3. Что мы де́лаем? Мы (гуля́ть) ______
4. Что они́ де́лают? Они́ (игра́ть) ______
5. Что Вы де́лаете? Я (отдыха́ть) ______
6. Что вы де́лаете? Мы (отдыха́ть) ______

Exercise 25. **Ask questions for the sentences.**

Example: О́льга игра́ет на роя́ле. → Что она́ де́лает?

1. Анто́н чита́ет кни́гу. ______
2. О́льга и Ната́ша гуля́ют в па́рке. ______
3. Ка́тя игра́ет. ______
4. Па́па рабо́тает сего́дня. ______
5. Мы отдыха́ем в а́вгусте. ______

In Masha's letter John met some special forms of the verbs.

When Professor Young was telling John about the verb system in the Russian language he suggested that his son should use a special table of his. When John saw this 'skyscraper' he thought that he could never solve it and lost it somewhere. And now no matter how hard he tried to find the answer in google, it was impossible to understand. When the chaos in John's head overcame everything else, he remembered that his father told him that the table included all the changes of the Russian verb in Present and Past tenses. The table would help to find any necessary form of any Russian verb, as the Bradis table helps to find cosine of any angle.

"Let's see," thought John having finally found the table and comments about it.

RUSSIAN VERB

I group (-Е) **-ю/-у, -ешь, -ет,** **-ем, -ете, -ют/-ут**		**SPECIAL** **есть,** **дать,** **хотéть,** etc.	**II group (-И)** **-ю/-у, -ишь, -ит,** **-им, -ите, -ят/-ат**	
Regular	**Irregular**		**Regular**	**Irregular**
1.R.VOW **дéлать** **1.R.CONS** **брать**	**1.IR** **жить** **писáть** **etc.**		**2.R.CONS.1** **говори́ть** **2.R.CONS.2** **учи́ть** **2.R.VOW** **стрóить**	**2.IR** **люби́ть,** **ви́деть,** **etc.**

A verb group shows the type of an ending (-Е/-И).

An Index shows the type of changes in a stem or a suffix.

I group (-Е)

1.R.VOW (дéлать): Regular model with stem ending in a vowel is basic one.

1.R.CONS (брать): Regular model with stem ending in a consonant differs only in the endings -у, -ут instead of -ю, -ют.

1.IR (жить, писáть, etc.): Irregular models have alternations in a root or last sounds of the stem right before the ending.

II group (-И)

2.R.CONS.1 (говори́ть): Regular model with the vowel stem is basic one.

2.R.CONS.2 (учи́ть): Regular model with the stem ending in consonants Ж, Ч, Ш, Щ differs only in the endings -у, -ат instead of -ю, -ят.

2.R.VOW (стрóить): Regular model ending in the vowel stem has no differences with **2.R.CONS.1.** except for the stem.

2.IR (люби́ть, ви́деть, etc.): Irregular models have alternations in the last sounds of the stem before the ending. After the sounds ж, ч, ш, щ, ц you write -у, -ат instead of -ю, -ят.

SPECIAL (есть, дать, хотéть, петь, бежáть, мочь, сесть, идти́, éхать): This group is very small, it has a unique system of alterations.

Good news! At the end of the book at page 351–352 you can find the table of verb conjugations of all the types demonstrated. This table has all the basic types of Russian verbs. If you learn to work with it you will be able to use any verb.

This table will help you to conjugate any Russian verb. And while you are learning along with this book, verbs will be marked with indexes, which will help you to find the type of conjugation you want.

Verbs ending in -СЯ: These verbs **do not differ** from regular verbs of the corresponding type, except for the ending which places **between** the stem and -СЯ. The particle -СЯ indicates the reflexive nature of the verb, so the action is directed towards the subject.

Example:

учи́ТЬ — to learn		**учи́ТЬся — to study**	
я	учУ́	я	учУ́**сь**
ты	у́чИШЬ	ты	у́чИШЬ**ся**
он, она́	у́чИТ	он, она́	у́чИТ**ся**
мы	у́чИМ	мы	у́чИМ**ся**
вы	у́чИТЕ	вы	у́чИТЕ**сь**
они́	у́чАТ	они́	у́чАТ**ся**
я, ты, он	учи́Л	я, ты, он	учи́Л**ся**
я, ты, она́	учи́ЛА	я, ты, она́	учи́ЛА**сь**
мы, вы, они́	учи́ЛИ	мы, вы, они́	учи́ЛИ**сь**

This time John saved the table to write down new verbs there. You can see this table at the end of the book.

Then John looked at all the unusual verbs in the text and compared them with the verbs in the table.

***Exercise 26.* Change the verbs according to the person, pay attention to the table at page 351–352, check your answers.**

Infinitive		sg.		pl.
писа́ть (1.IR С-Ш)	я	пишу́	мы	
	ты	пи́шешь	вы	
	он/она́		они́	

Infinitive		sg.		pl.
рисова́ть (1.IR ОВА-У)	я		мы	
	ты	рису́ешь	вы	
	он/она́	рису́ет	они́	

Infinitive		sg.		pl.
танцева́ть (1.IR ЕВА-У)	я		мы	танцу́ем
	ты		вы	
	он/она́		они́	

Infinitive		sg.		pl.
люби́ть	я	люблю́	мы	
(2.IR Б, П, М, В + Л)	ты		вы	
	он/она́		они́	лю́бят

To contrast the verb люби́ть John added the verb ненави́деть[1]. It also had alternation.

[1] ненави́деть (2.IR Д-Ж): to hate

Infinitive		sg.		pl.
ненави́деть	я		мы	
(2.IR Д-Ж / ЗД-ЗЖ)	ты		вы	
	он/она́		они́	

Infinitive		sg.		pl.
учи́ть	я		мы	
(2.R.CONS.2)	ты		вы	
	он/она́		они́	

Infinitive		sg.		pl.
учи́ться	я	уч______**сь**	мы	у́ч______**ся**
(2.R.CONS.2)	ты	у́ч______**ся**	вы	у́ч______**ся**
	он/она́	у́ч______**ся**	они́	у́ч______**ся**

Exercise 27. **Fill in the table.**

A) Present tense:		B) Past tense:
1. Я (писа́ть)	Я пишу́	Я писа́л (писа́ла)
2. Ты (рисова́ть)	Ты рису́ешь	
3. Он (фотографи́ровать)		
4. Мы (учи́ться[2])		
5. Они́ (учи́ть)		
6. Она́ (танцева́ть)		
7. Вы (люби́ть)		
8. Мы (чита́ть)		
9. Ты (изуча́ть)		
10. Он (лета́ть)		
11. Вы (рабо́тать)		
12. Она́ (расска́зывать)		

[2] -СЯ is placed after Л in Past tense.

IV

In the Russian language every verb is followed by a noun in a certain case.

1. For example the verbs жить (1.IR+B), быть (SPECIAL), рабо́тать (1.R.VOW), отдыха́ть (1.R.VOW), учи́ться (2.R.CONS.2), служи́ть (2.R.CONS.2), гуля́ть (1.R.VOW) require case № 6.

жить (где?) в Аме́рике, в го́роде
рабо́тать (где?) на заво́де
учи́ться (где?) в университе́те

!!! Remember prepositions В and НА

В	НА
1. For buildings, rooms and other closed spaces: институ́т: an institute — в институ́те теа́тр: a theatre — в теа́тре музе́й: a museum — в музе́е парк: a park — в па́рке о́фис: an office — в о́фисе университе́т: an university — в университе́те шко́ла: a school — в шко́ле банк: a bank — в ба́нке фи́рма: a company — в фи́рме	**1. For the events:** заня́тие: a class — на заня́тии конце́рт: a concert — на конце́рте вы́ставка: an exhibition — на вы́ставке экску́рсия: an excursion — на экску́рсии рабо́та: a work — на рабо́те
2. With the verb служи́ть: а́рмия: an army — в а́рмии авиа́ция: aviation — в авиа́ции поли́ция: a police — в поли́ции	**2. With the verb служи́ть:** флот: navy — на фло́те
	3. Remember! по́чта: a post office — на по́чте заво́д: a factory — на заво́де вокза́л: a railway station — на вокза́ле ста́нция: a station — на ста́нции ро́дина: a homeland — на ро́дине факульте́т: a faculty — на факульте́те ры́нок: a market — на ры́нке стадио́н: a stadium — на стадио́не

Exceptions:

	case № 1		case № 6
forest airport garden	лес аэропо́рт сад	в	лесу́ аэропорту́ саду́
corner wardrobe eye nose	у́гол шкаф глаз нос	в/на[1]	углу́ шкафу́ глазу́ носу́
bridge floor	мост пол	на	мосту́ полу́

[1] In these cases, the preposition В indicates the inside of the object, while the preposition НА indicates the surface of the object: В углу́ ва́за (the vase is located in the corner of the room). Э́то стол, а на углу́ ру́чка (pen is placed on the corner of the table).

5

Exercise 28. **Answer the questions using the verbs you know and a noun in case № 6. Don't forget prepositions В and НА.**

Example: Где у́чится Ма́ша? → Ма́ша у́чится **в** университе́т**е**.

1. Где у́чится её сестра́? ____________________
2. Где у́чится Пётр? ____________________
3. Где рабо́тает её па́па? ____________________
4. А где рабо́тает её брат? ____________________
5. Где отдыха́ют ба́бушки и де́душки? ____________________
6. Где рабо́тала ба́бушка Еле́на? ____________________
7. А где служи́л де́душка Па́вел? ____________________
8. Где Ма́ша лю́бит гуля́ть? ____________________
9. Где живу́т Васи́лий и Дже́йн? ____________________
10. Где Вы у́читесь и́ли рабо́таете? ____________________
11. Где живёте Вы и Ва́ша семья́? ____________________

Exercise 29. **Where do they work? Say in Russian.**

Example: Профе́ссор. Рабо́тает. Институ́т. → Профе́ссор рабо́тает **в** институ́т**е**.

an actor	актёр		стадио́н
a director	дире́ктор		теа́тр
an engineer	инжене́р		сад
a cashier	касси́р		о́фис
a postman	почтальо́н	рабо́тает	заво́д
a gardener	садо́вник		музе́й
a secretary	секрета́рь		фи́рма
a sportsman	спортсме́н		банк
a guide	экскурсово́д		по́чта

Exercise 30. **Where does this person слу́жит / у́чится / рабо́тает / отдыха́ет?**

Example: Офице́р. А́рмия. → Офице́р слу́жит в а́рмии.

	кто?	что де́лает?	где?
an officer	офице́р	слу́жит	в а́рмии (а́рмия)
a policeman	полице́йский	____________	поли́ция
a chef	по́вар	____________	столо́вая
		____________	кафе́[1]
a pensioner	пенсионе́р	____________	санато́рий
a pilot	пило́т	____________	авиа́ция
a schoolboy	шко́льник	____________	шко́ла
a student	студе́нтка	____________	институ́т
		____________	университе́т
a housewife	домохозя́йка	____________	дом
a teacher	учи́тель	____________	шко́ла
a postgraduate	аспира́нт	____________	аспиранту́ра[2]
a professor	преподава́тель	____________	институ́т
		____________	университе́т
a tourist	тури́ст	____________	дом

[1] a café
[2] a graduate school

Exercise 31. **You have been called, but you can't talk now. Say sorry and explain where you are.**

Example: институ́т. заня́тие. → Извини́, я сейча́с не могу́[3] говори́ть. Я сейча́с в институ́те на заня́тии.

[3] не могу́ (мочь) (SPECIAL): I can't (to be able)

1. теа́тр. конце́рт.

____

2. музе́й. вы́ставка.

____

3. парк. экску́рсия.

____

4. о́фис. рабо́та.

____

Exercise 32. **Write something about yourself.**

1. Вы у́читесь, рабо́таете и́ли[4] слу́жите? ____________
2. Где Вы у́читесь / рабо́таете / слу́жите сейча́с? ____________
3. Где Вы учи́лись / рабо́тали / служи́ли ра́ньше? ____________
4. Где Вы лю́бите отдыха́ть? ____________
5. Где Вы не лю́бите быть? ____________

[4] the coordinating conjunction или introduces an alternative here: you must choose one of the proposals. ИК-3.

2. The verb летáть (1.R.VOW) operates case № 6, too. Летáть (**на** чём?) на самолёте.

Я летáю на самолёте. Но я не пилóт, а турúст.

3. The verb игрáть (1.R.VOW) with preposition НА means playing a musical instrument. Игрáть (на чём?) на балалáйке.

— На чём игрáет Марúна?
— Онá игрáет на ______________________________

Exercise 33. **Write something about yourself: Вы игрáете на музыкáльных инструмéнтах?**

Да, ______________________________
Нет, ______________________________
На чём Вы игрáете? ______________________________

Dictionary:

музыкáльный инструмéнт	musical instrument
рóяль (он)	a grand piano
скрúпка	a violin
гитáра	a guitar
балалáйка	a balalaika
аккордеóн	an accordion

INTERESTING INFORMATION!

The following idioms are popular in Russian:

игрáть на нéрвах — to play on one's nerves
игрáть на чýвствах — to play on one's feelings
игрáть на привы́чках — to play on one's habits

In all these idioms the verb has the meaning 'to manipulate' with the object in the 6th case as an instrument. Are there any similar idioms in English?

4. In Masha's letter John met the verbs indicating speech and thought producing activity: говорúть (2.R.CONS.1), знать (1.R.VOW), расскáзывать (1.R.VOW). All of them can also have object in case № 6.

Пáпа Вúктор мнóго знáет о машинáх.
Брат Дмúтрий мнóго знáет о компьютерах и Интернéте.
Бáбушка Елéна лю́бит расскáзывать о рабóте.

This is the second and the last meaning of the case № 6.
This meaning is connected with the preposition О.
As soon as John looked this preposition up in the dictionary, the meaning of the phrase became clear to him.

расскáзывать о рабóте — to talk about work
знать о машúнах — to know about cars

Exercise 34. **Highlight all the phrases like Verb + О + noun in case № 6 with the highlighter of different colour in Masha's letter. Translate these sentences to English.**

Exercise 35. **Without looking at the letter make up sentences about Masha's family. Then look at the**

letter and check your answers.

Who	What they do	What about
па́па Ви́ктор		маши́ны
ба́бушка Еле́на	знать	де́ньги
ба́бушки и де́душки		самолёты, путеше́ствия и стра́ны
брат Дми́трий	говори́ть	рабо́та
де́душка Па́вел		компью́теры и Интерне́т
ма́ма И́нна	расска́зывать	кни́ги, му́зыка, теа́тр, приро́да
Ма́ша и Мари́на		жизнь, рабо́та, семья́

Exercise 36. **Study personal pronouns in case № 6. Translate them to your language.**

Ли́чные местоиме́ния (паде́ж № 6) — Personal pronouns (case № 6)

case № 1	кто?	я	ты	он, оно́	она́	мы	вы	они́
case № 6	о ком?	обо мне́	о тебе́	о нём	о ней	о нас	о вас	о них

Exercise 37. **Complete the sentences using pronouns in case № 6. Don't forget about the preposition О.**

Example: Э́то кни́ги. А́нна расска́зывает __________.
Э́то кни́ги. А́нна расска́зывает **о них**.

1. Э́то му́зыка. Ма́ша лю́бит говори́ть ______________.
2. Э́то маши́ны. Па́па Ви́ктор мно́го зна́ет ______________.
3. Э́то самолёт. Де́душка расска́зывает ______________.
4. Э́то я. Мой друг расска́зывает ______________.
5. Э́то мы. Па́па и ма́ма ча́сто говоря́т ______________.
6. Э́то ты? Я сейча́с говори́л ______________.

Exercise 38. **Say it in Russian. Use the words in brackets in case № 6 and prepositions В, НА or О.**

Example: Я расска́зываю __________ (Ло́ндон). — Я расска́зываю о Ло́ндоне.

1. Я говорю́ _________________________ (университе́т).
2. Я рабо́таю ______________ (банк).
3. Я отдыха́ю ____________________________ (ру́сская дере́вня).
4. Я зна́ю всё ____ (стра́ны и путеше́ствия).
5. Я живу́ ____________________________ (Великобрита́ния).
6. Я говорю́ ________________________________ (интере́сные кни́ги).
7. Я учу́сь ____ (Моско́вский госуда́рственный университе́т).
8. Я был ____________________________ (э́ти стра́ны).
9. Я расска́зываю ______________ (Лувр).
10. Я был ______________ (музе́й).
11. Я гуля́л _______________________________ (восто́чный ры́нок[1]).

[1] In this noun, О is a mobile vowel, it appears only in case № 1.

V.

John knew that he had almost finished his translation. He only hadn't highlighted the verbs followed by infinitives and nouns.

The grammarbook said: "As in the English language, there are many verbs in Russian which are called transitive. These verbs are used

1. with verbs in the infinitive form. For example, Я люблю́ чита́ть. Он у́чит писа́ть.

2. with nouns in case № 4 without a preposition. A noun has a meaning of a direct object. For example, Я люблю́ кни́ги. Студе́нт изуча́ет биоло́гию. Учи́тель у́чит шко́льников."

John highlighted both variants with a highlighter of different colour.

ATTENTION! Verbs учи́ться, учи́ть and изуча́ть work with different cases:
Учи́ться (где? case № 6) в институ́те. — study (where?) at the university
Учи́ть (кого́? case № 4) студе́нтов. — teach (who?) students
Изуча́ть (что? case № 4) биоло́гию. — study (what?) biology

"The only illogical phrase was игра́ть в ша́хматы." John remembered that he had just read about игра́ть **на** + case № 6: игра́ть на фортепиа́но, игра́ть на скри́пке.

"The preposition В and a noun in case № 4 used with the verb игра́ть means «to play a game»: игра́ть в ша́хматы, игра́ть в футбо́л, игра́ть в те́ннис[1], игра́ть в волейбо́л[2]." John highlighted this model with another colour.

He knew then what Masha and her family liked to do. А Вы зна́ете?

[1] те́ннис [тэ]
[2] Play chess, play football, play tennis, play volleyball.

ATTENTION! The endings of animate and inanimate nouns in case № 4 are different.

5

Вини́тельный паде́ж (паде́ж № 4) — Accusative (case № 4)

Что? (inanimate nouns) Masculine and neuter genders are the same as case № 1, except for the words in feminine gender

	case № 1				case № 4					
		чей? чьё? чья?	какóй? какóе? какáя?	что?		чей? чьё? **чью?**	какóй? какóй? **какýю?**	что?		
он	э́тот, тот	мо**й** тво**й** наш ваш **его́**, **её**, **их**	но́в**ый** больш**о́й** хоро́ш**ий** си́н**ий** ру́сск**ий**	стол слова́р**ь** музе́**й** санато́р**ий**	э́т**от**, **тот**	мо**й** тво**й** наш ваш **его́**, **её**, **их**	но́в**ый** больш**о́й** хоро́ш**ий** си́н**ий** ру́сск**ий**	стол слова́р**ь** музе́**й** санато́р**ий**	case № 4 = case № 1	
оно́	э́то, то	мо**ё** тво**ё** на́ш**е** ва́ш**е** **его́**, **её**, **их**	но́в**ое** больш**о́е** хоро́ш**ее** си́н**ее** ру́сск**ое**	письм**о́** мо́р**е** зда́н**ие**	э́то, то	мо**ё** тво**ё** на́ш**е** ва́ш**е** **его́**, **её**, **их**	но́в**ое** больш**о́е** хоро́ш**ее** си́н**ее** ру́сск**ое**	письм**о́** мо́р**е** зда́н**ие**	case № 4 = case № 1	
она́	э́та, та	мо**я́** тво**я́** на́ш**а** ва́ш**а** **его́**, **её**, **их**	но́в**ая** больш**а́я** хоро́ш**ая** си́н**яя** ру́сск**ая**	ко́мнат**а** дере́вн**я** тетра́д**ь** аудито́р**ия**	э́т**у**, т**у**	мо**ю́** тво**ю́** на́ш**у** ва́ш**у** **его́**, **её**, **их**	но́в**ую** больш**у́ю** хоро́ш**ую** си́н**юю** ру́сск**ую**	ко́мнат**у** дере́вн**ю** тетра́д**ь** аудито́р**ию**	**-УЮ /** **-ЮЮ**	**-У /** **-Ю /** **-Ь /** **-ИЮ**

	case № 1				case № 4				
		чьи?	каки́е?	что?		чьи?	каки́е?	что?	
они́ **(он,** **она́,** **оно́)**	э́т**и**, т**е**	мо**и́** тво**и́** на́ш**и** ва́ш**и** **его́**, **её**, **их**	но́в**ые** больш**и́е** хоро́ш**ие** си́н**ие** ру́сск**ие**	стол**ы́** словар**и́** музе́**и** санато́р**ии** пи́сьм**а** мор**я́** зда́н**ия** ко́мнат**ы** дере́вн**и** тетра́д**и** аудито́р**ии**	э́т**и**, т**е**	мо**и́** тво**и́** на́ш**и** ва́ш**и** **его́**, **её**, **их**	но́в**ые** больш**и́е** хоро́ш**ие** си́н**ие** ру́сск**ие**	стол**ы́** словар**и́** музе́**и** санато́р**ии** пи́сьм**а** мор**я́** зда́н**ия** ко́мнат**ы** дере́вн**и** тетра́д**и** аудито́р**ии**	case № 4 = case № 1

Что ты чита́ешь? Я чита́ю но́вый журна́л. Я чита́ю но́вую кни́гу.
Что ты зна́ешь? Я зна́ю но́вые слова́.

Кого́? (animate nouns)
Feminine gender singular has the same endings for both animate and inanimate nouns

	case № 1				case № 4					
		чей? чья?	како́й? кака́я?	кто?		чьего? **чью?**	како́го? **каку́ю?**	кого́?		
он	э́тот, тот	мо**й** тво**й** наш ваш **его́**, **её**, **их**	но́в**ый** больш**о́й** хоро́ш**ий** ру́сск**ий**	друг фи́зик студе́нт писа́тел**ь** Андре́**й** Анато́л**ий**	э́т**ого,** т**ого́**	мо**его́** тво**его́** на́ш**его** ва́ш**его** **его́**, **её**, **их**	но́в**ого** больш**о́го** хоро́ш**его** ру́сск**ого**	дру́г**а** фи́зик**а** студе́нт**а** писа́тел**я** Андре́**я** Анато́л**ия**	**-ОГО /** **-ЕГО**	**-А /** **-Я /** **-ИЯ**
она́	э́та, та	мо**я́** тво**я́** на́ш**а** ва́ш**а** **его́**, **её**, **их**	но́в**ая** больш**а́я** хоро́ш**ая** ру́сск**ая**	подру́г**а** ба́бушк**а** А́н**я** Аде́л**ь** Мар**и́я**	э́т**у**, т**у**	мо**ю́** тво**ю́** на́ш**у** ва́ш**у** **его́**, **её**, **их**	но́в**ую** больш**у́ю** хоро́ш**ую** ру́сск**ую**	подру́г**у** ба́бушк**у** А́н**ю** Аде́ль Мар**и́ю**	**-УЮ /** **-ЮЮ**	**-У /** **-Ю /** **-Ь /** **-ИЮ**

	case № 1				case № 4					
		чьи?	каки́е?	кто?		чьих?	каки́х?	кого́?		
они́ **(он,** **она́,** **оно́)**	э́т**и**, т**е**	мо**и́** тво**и́** на́ш**и** ва́ш**и** **его́**, **её**, **их**	но́в**ые** больш**и́е** хоро́ш**ие** ру́сск**ие**	друзь**я́** фи́зик**и** студе́нт**ы** писа́тел**и** Андре́**и** Анато́л**ии** подру́г**и** ба́бушк**и** А́н**и** Аде́л**и** Мар**и́и**	э́т**их**, т**ех**	мо**и́х** тво**и́х** на́ш**их** ва́ш**их** **его́**, **её**, **их**	но́в**ых** больш**и́х** хоро́ш**их** ру́сск**их**	друз**е́й** фи́зик**ов** студе́нт**ов** писа́тел**ей** Андре́**ев** Анато́л**иев** подру́г ба́бушек Ан**ь** Аде́л**ей** Мар**и́й**	**-ЫХ /** **-ИХ**	**-ОВ /** **-ЕВ /** **-ЕЙ /** **-Ь /** **Ø**

Кого́ ты зна́ешь (Вы зна́ете)? Я зна́ю Джо́на и Ма́шу.
Кого́ ты лю́бишь (Вы лю́бите)? Я люблю́ моего́ бра́та и мою́ сестру́.

5

Exercise 39. Choose matching words and make up phrases, paying attention to the endings.

A) Приро́да, Вади́м, го́род, му́зыка, ма́ма, роди́тели[1], матрёшка, сад, Алекса́ндр, Ма́ша, спу́тник, мо́ре, би́знес, шокола́д, брат, де́ньги.

[1] роди́тели (pl.): parents

Я люблю́ что? Я люблю́ **приро́ду**. ______________________________

____

____

Я люблю́ кого́? Я люблю́ **Вади́ма**. ______________________________

____

____

B) Краси́вая приро́да, высо́кий Вади́м, но́вый го́род, ста́рая му́зыка, ру́сская ма́ма, хоро́шие роди́тели, ма́ленькая матрёшка, зелёный сад, ску́чный Алекса́ндр, краси́вая Ма́ша, америка́нский спу́тник, си́нее мо́ре, большо́й би́знес, тёмный шокола́д, родно́й брат, францу́зские де́ньги.

Ты зна́ешь что? Ты зна́ешь ______________________________

____

____

Ты зна́ешь кого́? Ты зна́ешь ______________________________

____

____

C) На́ша краси́вая приро́да, ваш высо́кий Вади́м, э́тот но́вый го́род, на́ша ста́рая му́зыка, твоя́ ру́сская ма́ма, его́ хоро́шие роди́тели, её ма́ленькая матрёшка, наш зелёный сад, мой ску́чный Алекса́ндр, их краси́вая Ма́ша, наш америка́нский спу́тник, ва́ше си́нее мо́ре, твой большо́й би́знес, её тёмный шокола́д, мой родно́й брат, их францу́зские де́ньги.

Я рису́ю что? Я рису́ю ______________________________

____

____

____

Я рису́ю кого́? Я рису́ю ______________________________

____

____

____

Exercise 40. Read and compare.

Inanimate (Что?)	**Animate** (Кого́?)
Я чита́ю журна́л. — I'm reading a magazine. Я чита́ю кни́г**у**. — I'm reading a book.	Я чита́ю Анто́н**а** Че́хов**а**[2]. — I'm reading Anton Chekhov. Я чита́ю Ага́т**у** Кри́сти. — I'm reading Agatha Christie.
Я люблю́ мой дом и мою́ ко́мнат**у**. — I love my house and my room.	Я люблю́ моего́ бра́т**а** и мою́ сестр**у́**. — I love my brother and my sister.

[2] Meaning books by Anton Chekhov.

The endings of animate nouns in case № 4 plural

Masculine	Hard stem + -ОВ →	студе́нт**ы** — студе́нт**ов**
	Soft stem + -ЕВ →	Андре́**и** — Андре́**ев**
	Soft stem (-Ь / -ТЕЛЬ) + -ЕЙ →	писа́тел**и** — писа́тел**ей**
Feminine and masculine ending in -а / -я	Hard stem (zero ending) →	подру́г**и** — подру́г
	Hard stem + КА (zero ending + mobile vowel) →	ба́бушк**и** — ~~бабушк~~ — ба́бушек
	Soft stem (-Я) + -Ь / -ЕЙ →	тёт**и** – тёт**ь** / тёт**ей**
Feminine ending in -ь	Soft stem (-Ь) + -ЕЙ →	ло́шад**и**[1] — лошад**е́й**
All genders	Stem on Ж/Ч/Ш + -ЕЙ →	малыш**и́**[2] — малыш**е́й** мы́ш**и**[3] — мыш**е́й**
Nouns that are always plural	Stem + -ЕЙ	де́т**и**[4] — дет**е́й** роди́тел**и** — роди́тел**ей**

[1] a horse
[2] a baby
[3] a mouse
[4] де́ти (pl.): children (sg. ребёнок)

***Exercise 41.* Using the table with case № 4 write down in Russian who you know.**

Example: шко́льник — Я зна́ю шко́льника (sg.). Я зна́ю шко́льников (pl.).

Шко́льница, царь, секрета́рь, вну́чка, журнали́ст, Али́на, А́ня, аспира́нтка, пило́т, почтальо́н, мужчи́на, преподава́тель, тётя, дя́дя, де́вочка.

Я зна́ю ______________________________

____

____

____

____

____

____

____

____

____

____

____

____

____

____

***Exercise 42.* Look at Masha's letter again and find sentences about her relatives' professions. Work with the table.**

Models for forming words indicating professions and occupations

Suffix -ИК	
фи́зИК[1] хи́мИК[2] исто́рИК[3]	Но! Он: шко́льнИК, худо́жнИК[4] Она́: шко́льнИЦА, худо́жнИЦА
Suffix -ИСТ	
экономИ́СТ[5] юрИ́СТ[6]	Но! Он: журналИ́СТ Она́: журналИ́СТКА
Suffix -ТЕЛЬ	
учи́ТЕЛЬ преподава́ТЕЛЬ строи́ТЕЛЬ	
Others	
инжене́р спортсме́н — (она́) спортсме́нКА по́вар	

[1] a physicist
[2] a chemist
[3] a historian
[4] худо́жник (-ица): a painter

[5] an economist
[6] a lawyer

***Exercise 43.* These are the models of forming adjectives.**

	-ИК-А / -И-Я	-И́ЧЕСК-ИЙ (-АЯ, -ОЕ)	
physics	фи́з**ика**	физ**и́ческий** физ**и́ческая** физ**и́ческое**	physical physical physical
biology	биоло́г**ия**	биолог**и́ческий**	biological
economy	эконо́м**ика**	эконом**и́ческий**	economic
chemistry	хи́м**ия**	хим**и́ческий**	chemical
ecology	эколо́г**ия**	эколог**и́ческий**	ecological
history	исто́р**ия**	истор**и́ческий**	historical
mathematics	матема́т**ика**	математ**и́ческий**	mathematical

***Exercise 44.* Translate the phrases.**

Example: a physical institute — физи́ческий институ́т

1. A physical object ______________________
2. A biological magazine ______________________
3. A chemical factory ______________________
4. An economic map ______________________
5. A historical museum ______________________
6. An ecological problem ______________________
7. A mathematical faculty ______________________

***Exercise 45.* Answer the questions:**

A) Кто у́чится где? Кто изуча́ет что?

Example: Студе́нт-хи́мик у́чится на хими́ческом факульте́те, он изуча́ет хи́мию.

Студе́нт-исто́рик ____________________
Студе́нт-матема́тик ____________________
Аспира́нт-экономи́ст ____________________

B) Кто игра́ет во что?

Example: Футбол**и́ст**[1] игра́ет в футбо́л.

[1] a footballer

теннис**и́ст**: tennis player ____________________
волейбол**и́ст**: volleyball player ____________________
хокке**и́ст**: hockey player ____________________

5

Ли́чные местоиме́ния (паде́ж № 4) — Personal pronouns (case № 4)

case № 1	кто?	я	ты	он, оно́	она́	мы	вы	они́
case № 4	кого́?	меня́	тебя́	его́	её	нас	вас	их

After learning pronouns in case № 4 John remembered the model: Как **тебя́** зову́т? — **Меня́** зову́т Джон.

Remember: my name is, your name is, his…

***Exercise 46.* Analyse the sentences. Work with tables with case № 4.**

Э́то мой брат.	**Его́** зову́т Кен. ↓	**Бра́та** зову́т Кен. ↓	**Моего́ брата** зову́т Кен. ↓
case №1	case № 4	case № 4	case № 4
Э́то моя́ подру́га.	**Её** зову́т О́ля.	**Подру́гу** зову́т О́ля.	**Мою́ подру́гу** зову́т О́ля.
Э́то сёстры.	**Их** зову́т Ма́ша и Мари́на.	**Сестёр** зову́т Ма́ша и Мари́на.	**Мои́х сестёр** зову́т Ма́ша и Мари́на.

***Exercise 47.* Have you got a photo of your family? What are their names?**

Model: кого́ (case № 4) зову́т как (case № 1)

Example: Э́то мой па́па. Его́ зову́т Алекса́ндр. Моего́ па́пу зову́т Алекса́ндр.
Э́то моя́ ма́ма. Мою́ ма́му зову́т…

At last John had translated Maria Skvortsova's letter. According to his translation Masha had a wonderful family. But he decided to check himself. Masha was online and he called her.

ЗВОНО́К — A CALL

Джон: Приве́т, Ма́ша, что ты де́лаешь?

Ма́ша: Я отдыха́ю. А ты что де́лаешь?

Джон: А я учу́ ру́сский язы́к. Я чита́л твоё письмо́.

Ма́ша: О чём я писа́ла?

Джон: Ты писа́ла о твое́й семье́.

Ма́ша: Да. Пра́вильно. А что я писа́ла?

Джон: Твоя́ семья́ больша́я и о́чень хоро́шая.

Ма́ша: Спаси́бо! А кака́я твоя́ семья́?

Джон: Моя́ семья́ небольша́я: я, па́па, ма́ма и брат.

Ма́ша: А что ты лю́бишь де́лать?

Джон: Я люблю́ рабо́тать и чита́ть.

Ма́ша: А что ты ненави́дишь?

Джон: Ненави́жу?... М-м-м... Я ненави́жу плохи́е ба́нки и плохи́е... auto.

Ма́ша: Да, по-ру́сски auto то́же авто́ и́ли маши́на.

Джон: О, я зна́ю, что ты лю́бишь, но я не зна́ю, что ты ненави́дишь.

Ма́ша: Я ненави́жу неинтере́сных люде́й[1]. А что ты чита́ешь?

Джон: Я чита́ю кни́ги об эконо́мике, о больши́х деньга́х и люблю́ кни́ги об исто́рии Росси́и.

Ма́ша: Об эконо́мике и об исто́рии?

Джон: Да, в мое́й семье́ э́то норма́льно[2]. Я экономи́ст, а па́па — исто́рик. Я учи́лся в гуманита́рном[3] ко́лледже[4], пото́м в университе́те на экономи́ческом факульте́те.

Ма́ша: А я чита́ю кни́ги о любви́[5]. И кни́ги о биоло́гии и об эколо́гии.

Джон: Да, ты у́чишься на биологи́ческом факульте́те, и ты де́вушка. Э́то норма́льно.

[1] I hate uninteresting people.
[2] normal
[3] a humanitarian
[4] a college
[5] любо́вь: love (О is a mobile vowel, it appears only in case № 1)

So, now John knew enough to write her back. He could test his knowledge writing a letter about his family.

***Exercise 48.* Help John to write a letter. Open the brackets.**

МОЯ́ СЕМЬЯ́

(Я) зову́т Джон. (Я) 36 (год–го́да–лет). (Я) экономи́ст. Я (жить) в (Ло́ндон).

(Мой па́па) зову́т Алекса́ндр. (Он) 72 (год–го́да–лет), он исто́рик, профе́ссор. Он (рабо́тать) (в/на) (университе́т) (в/на) (истори́ческий факульте́т). Он (учи́ть) (студе́нты).

(Моя́ ма́ма) зову́т Ло́ра. (Она́) 68 (год–го́да–лет). (Она́) худо́жница и фото́граф[6]. Она́ (писа́ть[7]) (карти́ны) и (фотографи́ровать[8]). Она́ (люби́ть) (писа́ть) (карти́ны) (в/на) (го́род) и (в/на) (приро́да).

(Мой ста́рший брат) Кен — врач. Он (рабо́тать) (в/на) (Кра́сный Крест[9]). Он (жить) (в/на) (А́фрика).

(Мой де́душка) зва́ли Бенджами́н. Он (рабо́тать) (в/на) (шко́ла). Он (быть) дире́ктор.

(Моя́ ба́бушка) зва́ли А́нна. Она́ (быть) домохозя́йка. Она́ (люби́ть) (игра́ть) (роя́ль[10]).

[6] a photographer
[7] Painters don't paint, but «write» their paintings.
[8] (1. IR ОВА-У): to take pictures
[9] "Red Cross"
[10] a grand piano

Exercise 49. **Write a letter about your family. Give it to your Russian friends to check or show it to somebody you chat with online. Are there many mistakes? Correct the mistakes.**

Alexander Young took a book from the shelf. It was in Russian and called «Дом Рома́новых». According to the two-headed eagle and formal portraits, demonstrating the courtly fashion of the Middle Ages and the beginning of the XX century, John realized that the word дом in this case means семья́ — the imperial house.

— Э́то кни́га о ца́рской семье́, — Alexander confirmed his guess. — There was information about two grand dukes — Nicholas Mikhailovich and George Mikhailovich. We know almost nothing about them. Both brothers were scientists. As the last Russian tsar Nicholas II said, they were the most talented people of all the Romanovs. He meant their scientific talents.

— Why do I need to know about them? Are they connected with the documents in Moscow? — John began to worry.

— Yes, and soon you will know how. And now read what скоро поймёшь как. In the meantime, read about them, what position they had at the court. Accordingly, assess the possibilities that these people had.

Exercise 50. **Read a story about the tsar family. You already know how to analyse texts. Good luck!**

The Romanovs after Nicholas I

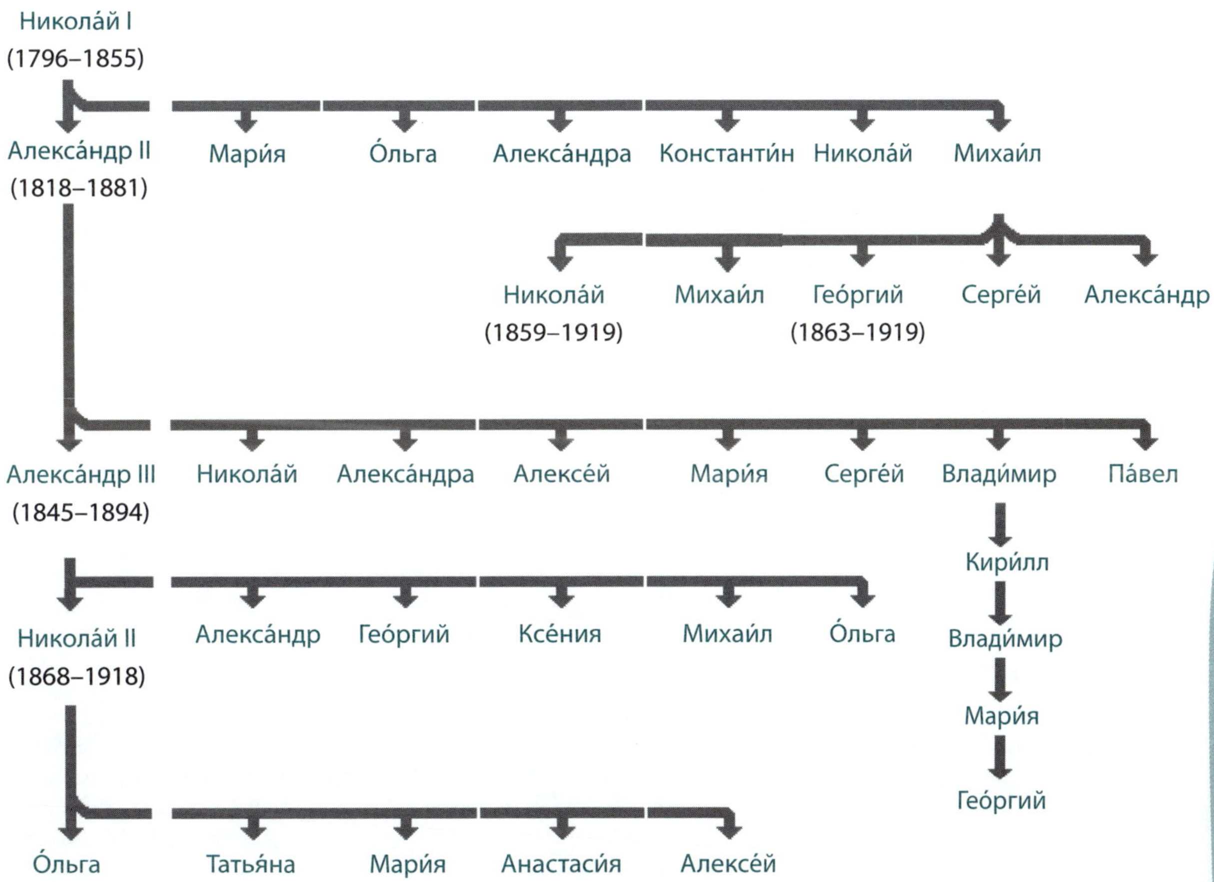

Вели́кий князь[1] Никола́й Миха́йлович и царь Никола́й I — внук и де́душка.

Вели́кий князь Гео́ргий Миха́йлович и царь Никола́й I то́же внук и де́душка.

Вели́кий князь Никола́й Миха́йлович и вели́кий князь Гео́ргий Миха́йлович — бра́тья.

Вели́кие князья́ Никола́й и Гео́ргий и царь Алекса́ндр II — племя́нники и дя́дя.

Вели́кие князья́ Никола́й и Гео́ргий и царь Алекса́ндр III — двою́родные бра́тья.

Вели́кие князья́ Никола́й и Гео́ргий и царь Никола́й II — двою́родные дя́ди и племя́нник.

[1] a title of the direct descendants of the tsar

Георгий Михайлович

Здесь на фо́то вели́кий князь Гео́ргий Миха́йлович. Князь Гео́ргий люби́л лошаде́й, мно́го занима́лся[2] в мане́же[3]. Ещё он изуча́л ста́рые де́ньги. Он был учёный-нумизма́т[4]. Его́ колле́кция[5] сейча́с в Санкт-Петербу́рге, в музе́е Эрмита́ж.

Э́то его́ брат — вели́кий князь Никола́й Миха́йлович. Он жил в Росси́и и во Фра́нции, в Пари́же. Он был учёный-исто́рик. В Пари́же он жил в ста́рой гости́нице «Вандо́м» и занима́лся в библиоте́ке[6]. Никола́й Миха́йлович изуча́л истори́ческие та́йны[7]. Князь Гео́ргий и князь Никола́й служи́ли в ру́сской а́рмии. Они́ офице́ры.

[2] (1.R.VOW) — *here* to practise
[3] a manege (the place where we train horses)
[4] a numismatist (specialist in the study of coins and medals)
[5] a collection
[6] a library (национальная библиотека: a national library)
[7] a mystery

Николай Михайлович

Вели́кий князь Влади́мир Кири́ллович и царь Никола́й II — двою́родные дя́дя и племя́нник.

Царь Никола́й II люби́л лошаде́й, люби́л фотографи́ровать и о́чень люби́л свою́ семью́[8].

Здесь на фо́то Никола́й II, его́ жена́ Али́са Ге́ссен-Дармшта́дтская и их де́ти.

Али́са жила́ в Герма́нии и А́нглии и в Росси́и. Её ба́бушка — англи́йская короле́ва[9] Викто́рия. Али́са Ге́ссен-Дармшта́дтская изуча́ла рели́гию[10] и филосо́фию[11] в университе́те в Ке́мбридже. В Росси́и Али́су зва́ли Алекса́ндра Фёдоровна.

[8] Now Nicholas II and his family are canonized by the Orthodox Church as the martyrs because of their tragic death of the hands of the Bolsheviks. However, the attitude to Nicholas II as a historical figure is difficult and ambiguous. Some consider him to be the most intelligent Russian monarch, who had to rule in catastrophic times for Russia and all of Europe. Others consider him to be a weak politician who was occupied by his family affairs more than affairs of state, who foolishly squandered the political, industrial and economic power of Russia at that time, plunging the country into a senseless First World War, thus pushing it to the bloody 1917 revolution.
[9] a queen
[10] religion
[11] philosophy

Э́то де́ти. Их зову́т О́льга, Татья́на, Мари́я, Анастаси́я и Алексе́й. Они́ мно́го учи́лись. Де́вушки и де́вочки люби́ли чита́ть, гуля́ть и танцева́ть. Ма́льчик люби́л гуля́ть и игра́ть, и ещё он о́чень хорошо́ учи́лся.

(Based on the book "The mystery of the Romanov house" by V.A. Balyazin)

Exercise 51. **Tell us about Nicholas II's family.**

1. Кто любúл что?
2. Кто изуча́л что?
3. Где мно́го занима́лся князь Гео́ргий Миха́йлович?
4. Где мно́го занима́лся князь Никола́й Миха́йлович?
5. Как учи́лся Алексе́й?

Exercise 52. **Tell us about yourself.**

1. Что Вы лю́бите?
2. Что Вы не лю́бите?
3. Что Вы лю́бите де́лать?
4. Что Вы не люби́те делать?

Chapter 6

Никогда́ не разгова́ривайте с неизве́стными.

М.А. Булга́ков. Ма́стер и Маргари́та

Never talk to strangers.

— M. Bulgakov, "Master and Margarita"

— Что у тебя́ есть?
— Я не понима́ю, о чём ты говори́шь.
— «Что у тебя́ есть» = «что ты име́ешь».
Alexander Young explained, "I mean the things that you have in your suitcase".

Model: У кого́ (case № 2) есть[1] что/кто (case № 1)[2]
У кого́ есть что. — Who has what

У меня́ есть сестра́. — I have a sister.

У него́ есть маши́на. — he has a car.

я	У **меня́** есть кни́га.	мы	У **нас** есть кни́га.
ты	У **тебя́** есть кни́га.	вы	У **вас** есть кни́га.
он, оно́	У **него́** есть кни́га.	они́	У **них** есть кни́га.
она́	У **неё** есть кни́га.		

Compare:

Case № 4	!	Case № 2
Я люблю́ **меня́**[3].	=	У **меня́** есть кни́га.
Я люблю́ **тебя́**.	=	У **тебя́** есть кни́га.
Я люблю́ **его́**.	+ Н	У **него́** есть кни́га.
Я люблю́ **её**.	+ Н	У **неё** есть кни́га.
Я люблю́ **нас**.	=	У **нас** есть кни́га.
Я люблю́ **вас**.	=	У **вас** есть кни́га.
Я люблю́ **их**.	+ Н	У **них** есть кни́га.

[1] есть (у меня́ есть, у тебя́ есть): to have (I have, you have)

[2] There is a model in Russian which perfectly corresponds to the English one with the verb **to have** (I have, you have...): it is a construction with the verb **име́ть** (Я име́ю семью́. — I have a family. Я име́ю кни́гу. — I have a book). But in spoken Russian in the meaning of 'to have' we use passive construction **у меня́ есть**: У меня́ есть сестра́. У меня́ есть кни́га. The verb **име́ть** is often used in official speech and forms and has possessive meaning: Я име́ю би́знес. Я име́ю рестора́н (= I own a business, a restaurant), Я жена́т/за́мужем. Име́ю сы́на и дочь (I am married. I have a son and a daughter.)
У кого́ (case № 2) есть что (case № 1): У меня́ есть кни́га.
Кто (case № 1) име́ет что (case № 4): Я име́ю маши́ну.

[3] Such construction is possible but it is not used. It is used here only for demonstration. You can say that you love yourself in the following way: я люблю́ себя́. You will learn more about reflexive pronoun себя́ in Chapter 10.

— У меня́ есть **балала́йка**, **ша́пка-уша́нка**, **шу́ба и ва́ленки**, — joked John.

— Да, балала́йка, ва́ленки, шу́ба и ша́пка-уша́нка — э́то о́чень по-ру́сски! Ру́сские всегда́ игра́ют на балала́йке. Ру́сские всегда́ **но́сят ша́пку**, **шу́бу и ва́ленки**.

— Э́то пра́вда?!

— Коне́чно, нет!

Model: Кто (case № 1) но́сит[1] что (case № 4)

Infinitive		Singular (sg.)		Plural (pl.)
носи́ть (2.IR **с** → **ш**)	я	но<u>ш</u>**у́**	мы	но́с**им**
	ты	но́с**ишь**	вы	но́с**ите**
	он	но́с**ит**	они́	но́с**ят**
Past		**Singular (sg.)**		**Plural (pl.)**
носи́ть	он	носи́**л**	мы	носи́**ли**
	она́	носи́**ла**	вы	
	оно́	носи́**ло**	они́	

[1] (2.IR С-Ш): to wear

НАЦИОНА́ЛЬНЫЕ СТЕРЕОТИ́ПЫ — NATIONAL STEREOTYPES

ЧТО ОНИ́ НО́СЯТ?

Э́то ба́бушки. Они́ живу́т в Росси́и. Они́ но́сят сарафа́н и ла́пти.
Кто они́?
Где они́ живу́т?
Что они́ но́сят?

Э́то Саю́ри. Она́ живёт в Япо́нии. Она́ япо́нка. Она́ но́сит япо́нское кимоно́.
Кто она́?
Где она́ живёт?
Что она́ но́сит?

Э́то Клод Моне́. Он жил во Фра́нции. Он францу́з[2]. Он носи́л францу́зский бере́т.
Кто он?
Где он жил?
Что он носи́л?

[2] Present simple tense

Э́то Уи́льям Уо́ллес. Он жил в Шотла́ндии. Он шотла́ндец. Он носи́л шотла́ндский килт.

Кто он?

Где он жил?

Что он носи́л?

Э́тот челове́к но́сит америка́нские джи́нсы и ковбо́йскую[1] шля́пу. Он америка́нец?

Кто он?

Где он живёт?

Что он но́сит?

[1] ковбо́й: a cowboy. The model of adjective formation: ковбо́й + ский

After John named the things he had packed, Professor Young understood that his son wasn't joking about ша́пка-уша́нка and ва́ленки. "People wear this in Siberia at the beginning of September, but not in Moscow," thought the Professor. He had to help his son to prepare for Russia.

Exercise 1. **Look at the list of things and think what things you would take.**

1. в тёплую страну́ (case № 1 тёплая страна́): to a hot country
2. в холо́дную страну́ (case № 1 холо́дная страна́): to a cold country
3. в делову́ю пое́здку (case № 1 делова́я пое́здка): to a business trip
4. на о́тдых (case № 1 о́тдых): on holidays

вещь	a thing	кроссо́вки	trainers
оде́жда	clothes	сапоги́	boots
компью́тер	a computer	реме́нь	a belt
па́спорт	a passport	га́лстук	a tie
часы́	a watch	шарф	a scarf
бума́жник	a wallet	перча́тки	gloves
зонт	an umbrella	шля́па	a hat
костю́м	a suit	ша́пка	a cap
пиджа́к	a jacket	ку́ртка	a jacket
руба́шка	a shirt	пальто́	a coat
сви́тер	a sweater	плащ	a raincoat
футбо́лка	a T-shirt	шу́ба	a fur-coat
пла́тье	a dress	чемода́н	a suitcase
ко́фта	a cardigan, a sweater	су́мка	a bag
брю́ки	trousers	мы́ло	soap
джи́нсы	jeans	зубна́я щётка	a toothbrush
шо́рты	shorts	зубна́я па́ста	toothpaste
ю́бка	a skirt	бри́тва	a razor
колго́тки	tights	пома́да	a lipstick
ту́фли мужски́е	men's shoes	расчёска	a brush
ту́фли же́нские	women's shoes	салфе́тки	tissues

Exercise 2. **Do a crossword and find out what John decided to take on his trip to Russia. Use the words from the table in Exercise 1.**

1. Э́то но́сят на те́ле[1].
2. Э́то но́сят на те́ле.
3. Э́то но́сят на нога́х.
4. Э́то но́сят на голове́.
5. Э́то но́сят на те́ле.
6. Э́то но́сят на ше́е.
7. Э́то но́сят на рука́х.

A prompt: you can revise parts of the body looking at Chapter 3 (p. 58) Где но́сят? — На те́ле (case № 1 те́ло).

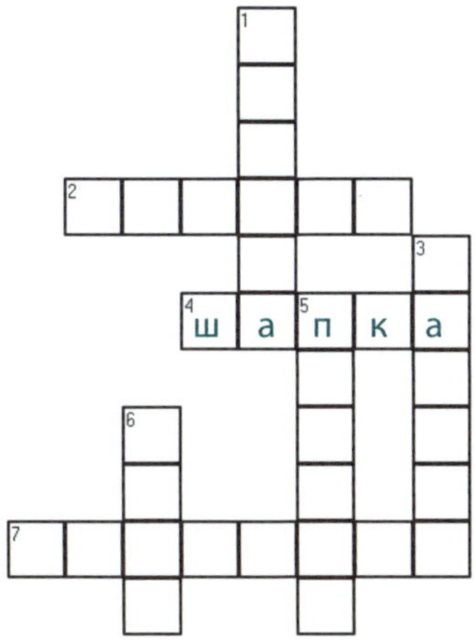

[1] In the Russian language it is possible to omit the subject of the sentence if it is not important, for example if we talk about all people or most people. In English we say such sentences with the subject "they": Э́то но́сят на те́ле. = Они́ (лю́ди) но́сят э́то на те́ле. (They (people) wear it on their bodies.)

— О! У тебя́ есть **зи́мняя** ку́ртка?! — Alexander Young took a warm hooded jacket from the suitcase.

— Коне́чно! В Росси́и хо́лодно!

— Э́то Москва́, э́то не Сиби́рь! Сейча́с в Москве́ о́сень. Сейча́с сентя́брь. В Москве́ сейча́с но́сят **ле́тние** и **осе́нние** ве́щи.

— Каки́е ве́щи? — John didn't understand.

Exercise 3. **Analyse the table and answer the question: what clothes does John's father recommend him to take to Russia?**

Model: Word formation of adjectives from words with the meaning "season"

	что?	како́й?	кака́я?	како́е?	каки́е?	
winter	**зим**а́ →	зи́м**н**ий	зи́м**н**яя	зи́м**н**ее	зи́м**н**ие	winter
summer	**ле́т**о →	ле́т**н**ий	ле́т**н**яя	ле́т**н**ее	ле́т**н**ие	summer
autumn	**о́сень** →	осе́н**н**ий	осе́н**н**яя	осе́н**н**ее	осе́н**н**ие	autumn
spring	**весн**а́ →	весе́н**н**ий	весе́н**н**яя	весе́н**н**ее	весе́н**н**ие	spring

Model: Word formation of adverbs from words with the meaning "season"

о́сень → о́сен**ью**: in autumn
ле́то → ле́т**ом**: in summer
зима́ → зим**о́й**: in winter
весна́ → весн**о́й**:

Когда́ хо́лодно? Хо́лодно **зимо́й**. Хо́лодно **в январе́**.
Когда́ жа́рко? Жа́рко **ле́том**. Жа́рко **в ию́ле**.
Когда́ тепло́?[2] Тепло́ **весно́й**. Тепло́ **в ма́е**.
А о́сенью? **О́сенью** тепло́ и́ли хо́лодно. **В сентябре́** тепло́ и хо́лодно.

[2] warm (adv.)

СЕЗО́НЫ[1] И МЕ́СЯЦЫ[2]:

Зима́:
дека́брь
янва́рь
февра́ль

Весна́:
март
апре́ль
май

Ле́то:
ию́нь
ию́ль
а́вгуст

О́сень:
сентя́брь
октя́брь
ноя́брь

Что?

Зимо́й:
в декабре́
в январе́
в феврале́

Весно́й:
в ма́рте
в апре́ле
в ма́е

Ле́том:
в ию́не
в ию́ле
в а́вгусте

О́сенью:
в сентябре́
в октябре́
в ноябре́

Когда?

[1] a season
[2] ме́сяц: a month (янва́рь, февра́ль, март, апре́ль, май, ию́нь, ию́ль, а́вгуст, сентя́брь, октя́брь, ноя́брь, дека́брь): January, February, March, April, May, June, July, August, September, October, November, December

— А в Росси́и о́сенью тепло́ и́ли хо́лодно? — asked John and then added: — Тепло́, хо́лодно и́ли о́чень хо́лодно?

— В Москве́ в сентябре́ ещё тепло́, в октябре́ уже́ не о́чень тепло́, а в ноябре́ — хо́лодно.

☞ ATTENTION!

You know the adverb ещё in the meaning of 'in addition'. Ещё is a synonym of то́же.

ТО́ЖЕ = ЕЩЁ: Э́то кни́га. Э́то то́же кни́га. = Э́то кни́га. Вот ещё кни́га. (кни́га + кни́га)
This is a book. And this is a book, too. It is also a book.
Э́то Ма́ша, у неё есть брат. Ещё у неё есть сестра́. (брат + сестра́)
This is Masha, she has a brother. She also has a sister.

The word ещё has a second meaning 'yet'. In this meaning it is an antonym of the word уже́ ('already'), and they are often used in a pair.

УЖЕ́ ≠ ЕЩЁ: Вы уже́ бы́ли в ка́ссе[3]? — Нет, я ещё не́ был.
Лау́ра уже́ говори́т по-ру́сски? — Нет, она́ ещё не говори́т по-ру́сски.

— Како́й сейча́с сезо́н? — asked professor Young and pointed at the calendar.

— Сейча́с ле́то, — answered John.

— А за́втра[4]?

— За́втра о́сень.

— Сего́дня **ещё** ле́то, а за́втра **уже́** о́сень. Сейча́с ещё а́вгуст, а за́втра **уже́** сентя́брь.

— Сего́дня в Росси́и **ещё** тепло́, а за́втра **уже́** хо́лодно? — asked John.

— Нет. В сентябре́ в Росси́и **ещё** тепло́. В сентябре́ в Росси́и ба́бье ле́то[5].

[3] a ticket office
[4] tomorrow
[5] Germans call it 'old summer', Italians — 'St. Martin's summer', Czechs — 'gipsies' summer' and French people — 'St. Deni's summer' or 'Indian summer'. Ба́ба is a folk name of a woman. The name ба́бье ле́то also comes from folklore. Russian people compare warm autumn days after the first cold ones to late love, when an elderly woman looks young and beautiful again. It is sad a little, because young age is short, the same as warm days in September.

Exercise 4. **А в ва́шей стране́ когда́ жа́рко, когда́ тепло́, когда́ хо́лодно?**

Exercise 5. **Do the crossword using the words Вещи (Things), and you'll know what thing you need in Russia at the beginning of autumn.**

1. Э́то но́сят на нога́х.
2. Э́то но́сят в су́мке.
3. Э́то но́сят на те́ле.
4. Э́то но́сят на те́ле.
5. Э́то но́сят в карма́не.
6. Э́то докуме́нт. Его́ но́сят в су́мке и́ли в карма́не.
7. ↓ — Э́то но́сят на те́ле.
8. Э́то но́сят в су́мке и́ли в руке́.
9. Э́то но́сят в руке́.

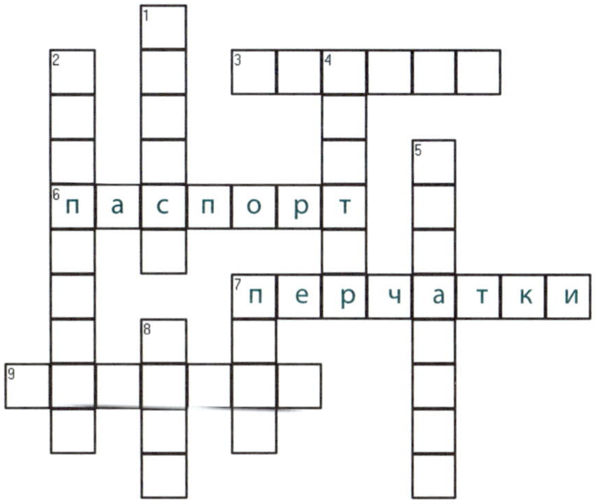

Exercise 6. **John packed the suitcase with the help of his father. Answer the question Что у него́ есть сейча́с?**

Example: Сейча́с у него́ есть перча́тки, ____________________ , ____________________.

Exercise 7. **What thing that John packed himself was approved by his father?**

A prompt: Э́то но́сят на рука́х.

"By the way," Alexander remembered, "in Russia, especially in Moscow, a lot of people speak English. Nevertheless a little advice will help you to look around and not to get confused. When you go through customs in the airport you'll have to answer the questions where you come from and where you are going, and also where you are going to stay in Russia.

This is a rule of directions of the rule 2 — 4 — 6."

— A code? — John was curious.

— In a language everything is a code. And the language itself, too. The numbers are the numbers of the cases which together with the necessary prepositions help to indicate the right direction.

Cases № 4 and № 6 were familiar to John. But there was a new one — case № 2 — genitive (роди́тельный паде́ж).

Пра́вило 2 — 4 — 6 — Rule 2 — 4 — 6

Места́ и направле́ния
Places and directions

Отку́да? (Where from?)
Куда́? (Where to?)
Где? (Where?)

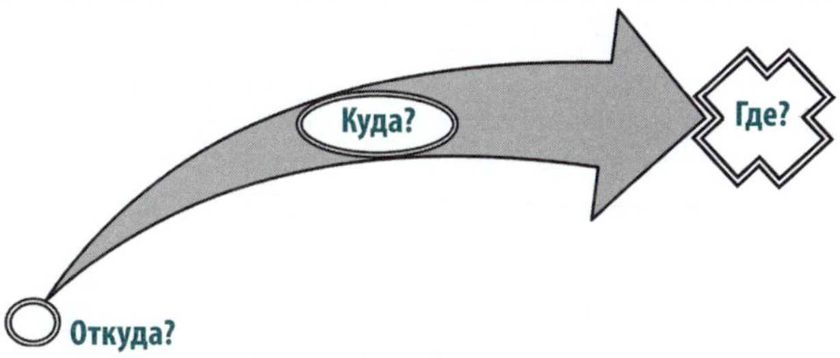

PREPOSITIONS:
ИЗ → В → В
С → НА → НА

	case № 2 Откýда?			case № 4 Кудá? (direction)		case № 6 Где? (localisation)	
он	Парúж —	**из**	Парúж**а**	**в**	Парúж__	**в**	Парúж**е**
онó	Китáй —	**из**	Китá**я**	**в**	Китáй__	**в**	Китá**е**
	Лóндон —	**из**	Лóндон**а**	**в**	Лóндон__	**в**	Лóндон**е**
	Израúль —	**из**	Израúл**я**	**в**	Израúль__	**в**	Израúл**е**
	окнó —	**из**	окн**á**	**в**	окн**ó**	**в**	окн**é**
!!![1]	юг —	**с**	ю́г**а**	**на**	юг__	**на**	ю́г**е**
	сéвер —	**с**	сéвер**а**	**на**	сéвер__	**на**	сéвер**е**
	мóре —	**с**	мóр**я**	**на**	мóр**е**	**на**	мóр**е**
	Кипр —	**с**	Кúпр**а**	**на**	Кипр__	**на**	Кúпр**е**
	Мадагаскáр —	**с**	Мадагаскáр**а**	**на**	Мадагаскáр__	**на**	Мадагаскáр**е**
онá	Россúя —	**из**	Россú**и**	**в**	Россú**ю**	**в**	Россú**и**
	Фрáнция —	**из**	Фрáнци**и**	**во**	Фрáнци**ю**	**во**	Фрáнци**и**
	Москвá —	**из**	Москв**ы́**	**в**	Москв**ý**	**в**	Москв**é**
	дерéвня —	**из**	дерéвн**и**	**в**	дерéвн**ю**	**в**	дерéвн**е**
!!!	Кýба —	**с**	Кýб**ы**	**на**	Кýб**у**	**на**	Кýб**е**
	Ямáйка —	**с**	Ямáйк**и**	**на**	Ямáйк**у**	**на**	Ямáйк**е**

[1] With the names of cardinal directions, islands, water objects we use prepostions С, НА. In other cases we use В or НА according to the rule we studied in Chapter 4. Do you remember the difference: в столé / на столé? **Pay attention to the fact that preposition В has a connection with preposition ИЗ**: Я живý **В** Лóндоне. — Я **ИЗ** Лóндона. And preposition **НА** has a connection with **С**: Я живý **НА** Кúпре. — Я **С** Кúпра.

Стандáртные вопрóсы на тамóжне[2] — Common questions at customs:

Офицéр: Откýда Вы?
Турúст: Я из Áнглии. Я из Лóндона.
Офицéр: Кудá Вы **летúте**?
Турúст: Я лечý в Россúю, в Москвý.
Офицéр: Где Вы живёте в Москвé?
Турúст: Я живý в гостúнице.

[2] customs

летéть (2.IR Т–Ч): to fly			
я	ле**чý**	мы	лет**úм**
ты	лет**úшь**	вы	лет**úте**
он, онá, онó	лет**úт**	онú	лет**я́т**

éхать (Special): to go, ride (+ kind of transport)			
я	éд**у**	мы	éд**ем**
ты	éд**ешь**	вы	éд**ете**
он, онá, онó	éд**ет**	онú	éд**ут**

Exercise 8. **Read and translate the dialogues.**

НА ТАМО́ЖНЕ

Добро́ пожа́ловать! — Welcome!

Счастли́вого пути́! — Have a good trip!

1.
— Здра́вствуйте! Отку́да Вы?
— Здра́вствуйте! Я из Испа́нии. Из Барсело́ны.
— Куда́ Вы лети́те?
— Я лечу́ в Еги́пет.
— Отдыха́ть?
— Да, отдыха́ть.
— Вы живёте в гости́нице?
— Да.
— О́чень хорошо́! Счастли́вого пути́!

2.
— До́брый день!
— До́брый день!
— Отку́да вы?
— Мы из Брази́лии.
— Куда́ вы лети́те?
— Мы лети́м в Росси́ю.
— Где Вы живёте в Росси́и?
— В Санкт-Петербу́рге.
— В гости́нице?
— Да, в гости́нице.
— Счастли́вого пути́!

3.
— До́брое у́тро!
— Здра́вствуйте!
— Отку́да вы е́дете?
— Я е́ду из Казахста́на, а мой друг е́дет из Кита́я.
— Куда́ вы е́дете?
— Мы е́дем в Росси́ю.
— Добро́ пожа́ловать в Росси́ю!

Exercise 9. **Complete the dialogues. Pay attention to the following: Вы or вы (one person or a lot of people), е́хать и́ли лете́ть.**

1.
Офице́р: До́брый день!
Пассажи́р[1]**:** ______________________________
Офице́р: Отку́да (Вы) ______________?
Пассажи́р: ______________________ (И́ндия)
Офице́р: Куда́ ________________ (лете́ть)?
Пассажи́р: ___________________ (Герма́ния)
Офице́р: Где ___________________________?
Пассажи́р: ______________________ (Берли́н)
Офице́р: В гости́нице?
Пассажи́р: Да, ___________________________

2.
Офице́р: ________________________________
Пассажи́ры: До́брое у́тро!
Офице́р: Отку́да вы ______________________?
Пассажи́ры: _______________________ (Бе́льгия)
Офице́р: Куда́ _________________________ (е́хать)?
Пассажи́ры: _______________________ (Фра́нция)
Офице́р: Где ________________________________?
— _____________________________ (Орлеа́н)
— В гости́нице?
— Да, _______________________________________

[1] a passenger

6

Exercise 10. Where do these people come from?

A) _Example:_ Бе́лла — Ита́лия → Бе́лла **из** Ита́ли**и**

1. Хосе́ — Испа́ния ______________________
2. Никола́й — Белору́ссия ______________________
3. Пьер — Фра́нция ______________________
4. Грэ́тхен — Герма́ния ______________________
5. Джон — А́нглия ______________________
6. Ро́за — Португа́лия ______________________

B) _Example:_ Мари́на — Санкт-Петербу́рг. → Мари́на **из** Санкт-Петербу́рг**а**

1. Са́ша — Влади́мир ______________________
2. Ван — Пеки́н ______________________
3. Ната́ша — Ки́ев ______________________
4. Лючи́я — Мила́н ______________________
5. Муха́ммед — Ира́н ______________________
6. Дави́д — Изра́иль ______________________
7. Алексе́й — Су́здаль ______________________
8. Жера́р — Брюссе́ль ______________________

C) _Example:_ Билл — Аме́рика → Билл **из** Аме́рик**и**

1. Ферна́ндо — Ме́ксика ______________________
2. Ла́ура — Аргенти́на ______________________
3. Джейн — Кана́да ______________________
4. Па́вел — Литва́ ______________________
5. Ли́ля — Каза́нь ______________________
6. Вади́м — А́страхань ______________________

Exercise 11. Read and translate the document «Приглаше́ние на въезд в Росси́йскую Федера́цию» (Invitation to enter the Russian Federation). Answer the questions after the text.

A) Приглаше́ние на въезд в Росси́йскую Федера́цию

Гражда́нство / Citizenship —	Великобрита́ния
Госуда́рство / Country —	Великобрита́ния
Да́ты пребыва́ния (въе́зд — вы́езд) Dates of stay (entry — departure)	1.09.2016 — 10.09.2016
На срок (дней) / For a period of (days) —	10 дней
Фами́лия / First name —	Янг
И́мя / Last name —	Джон
О́тчество / Middle name —	
Пол / Sex —	мужско́й
Да́та рожде́ния / Date of birth —	15.03.1980
Страна́ рожде́ния / Country of birth —	Великобрита́ния

Профе́ссия / Profession —	экономи́ст
Цель поéздки / Purpose of visit —	делова́я[1]
Приглаша́ющая организа́ция и её а́дрес / The host organization and its address —	Фи́рма «Бы́стро е́дем»[2], го́род Москва́, у́лица Тополи́ная, дом 53, о́фис 12

[1] business (adj.)
[2] The «Travel fast» company

1. Как его́ зову́т?
2. Где он живёт?
3. Кака́я его́ профе́ссия?
4. Отку́да он лети́т?
5. Куда́ он лети́т?
6. В каку́ю страну́ он лети́т?
7. В како́й го́род он лети́т?

B) Приглаше́ние на въезд в Росси́йскую Федера́цию

Гражда́нство / Citizenship —	Испа́ния
Госуда́рство / Country —	Герма́ния
Да́ты пребыва́ния (въе́зд — вы́езд) Dates of stay (entry — departure)	10.09.2016 — 10.10.2016
На срок (дней) / For a period of (days) —	30 дней
Фами́лия / First name —	Родри́гес
И́мя / Last name —	Габриэ́ла
О́тчество / Middle name —	
Пол / Sex —	же́нский
Да́та рожде́ния / Date of birth —	24.02.1991
Страна́ рожде́ния / Country of birth —	Испа́ния
Профе́ссия / Profession —	актри́са
Цель поéздки / Purpose of visit —	делова́я
Приглаша́ющая организа́ция и её а́дрес / The host organization and its address —	Драмати́ческий теа́тр[3], г. Каза́нь, у́лица Ба́умана, дом 48

[3] a drama theatre

1. Как её зову́т?
2. Где она́ живёт?
3. Кака́я её профе́ссия?
4. Отку́да она́ лети́т?
5. Куда́ она́ лети́т?
6. В каку́ю страну́ она́ лети́т?
7. В како́й го́род она́ лети́т?

John took his suitcase and headed to taxi when he suddenly put his hand into his pocket.

— Ой! А где мой биле́т[4]?!
— Твой биле́т в бума́жнике.
— «Вбума́жнике»?
— В бума́жнике.
— Что э́то? «Вбума́жнике»?
— Бума́жник — э́то **wallet**. Ты говори́шь: «Где биле́т?» Я говорю́: «В бума́жнике».
— А́-а-а! Бума́жник — в бума́жнике. Паде́ж № 6.
— Пра́вильно.
— И ты зна́ешь, что биле́т — в бума́жнике…
— Да.

[4] a ticket

— А где мой бума́жник?
— Твой бума́жник в пиджаке́.
— Здесь нет.
— В су́мке?
— В су́мке то́же нет.
— В чемода́не?
— Нет... Извини́, па́па, вот мой бума́жник. Он был в брю́ках. А вот мой биле́т.
— А вот твоё такси́! Счастли́вого пути́!

While waiting for the flight registration Ло́ндон — Москва́ John decided to plan his trip to Moscow. He wrote something in Russian in his diary to practice.

ЕЖЕДНЕ́ВНИК[1]

01.09. Пе́рвое сентября́
10 часо́в 15 мину́т: я в аэропорту́ в Москве́.
10 часо́в 20 мину́т: я встреча́ю[2] Ма́шу.
11 часо́в 30 мину́т: экску́рсия в Москве́.
14 часо́в: мы в рестора́не[3].
15 часо́в: мы гуля́ем в Кремле́ и на Кра́сной пло́щади.
18 часо́в: я в гости́нице.
19 часо́в: я отдыха́ю.

[1] a diary, a daily planner
[2] (1.R.VOW): to meet
[3] a restaurant

02.09. Второ́е сентября́
10 часо́в 15 мину́т: я на встре́че[4] в фи́рме «Бы́стро е́дем»
11 часо́в: ко́фе-бре́йк.
11 часо́в 30 мину́т: я на заво́де говорю́ о догово́ре[5].
14 часо́в: мы в рестора́не.
16 часо́в: ру́сская ба́ня[6] (The Russian cultural program!))

[4] a meeting
[5] a contract
[6] a banya (Russian sauna)

03.09. Тре́тье сентября́
12 часо́в: я рабо́таю в библиоте́ке.

Exercise 12. **Learn ways to tell the time to better understand John's schedule. In the course of the study, go back to the diary and highlight the studied.**

Каки́е пла́ны? (What are the plans?)
In order to answer the question what plans John has or what plans you have it is important to answer the question Когда́?, because plans cannot exist without timing. When you answer the question Когда́? (When?), use cases № 4 or № 6 and adverbs or time.

Days of the week with the question Когда? are used in case № 4 or case № 6

A week	! неде́ля (она́)	! на неде́ле (case № 6)
Monday	понеде́льник (он)	в понеде́льник (case № 4)
Tuesday	вто́рник (он)	во вто́рник (case № 4)
Wednesday	среда́ (она́)	в сре́ду (case № 4)
Thursday	четве́рг (он)	в четве́рг (case № 4)
Friday	пя́тница (она́)	в пя́тницу (case № 4)
Saturday	суббо́та (она́)	в суббо́ту (case № 4)
Sunday	воскресе́нье (оно́)	в воскресе́нье (case № 4)

case № 1

Что?

понеде́льник → вто́рник → среда́ → четве́рг → пя́тница → суббо́та → воскресе́нье

case № 6

Когда́?

в понеде́льник → во вто́рник → в сре́ду → в четве́рг → в пя́тницу → в суббо́ту → в воскресе́нье

Names of months (and the word неде́ля) with the question Когда́? are used in case № 6.

СЕЗО́НЫ И МЕ́СЯЦЫ:

case № 1

Что?

Зима́:
дека́брь
янва́рь
февра́ль

Весна́:
март
апре́ль
май

Ле́то:
ию́нь
ию́ль
а́вгуст

О́сень:
сентя́брь
октя́брь
ноя́брь

неде́ля

case № 6

Когда?

Зимо́й:
в декабре́
в январе́
в феврале́

Весно́й:
в ма́рте
в апре́ле
в ма́е

Ле́том:
в ию́не
в ию́ле
в а́вгусте

О́сенью:
в сентябре́
в октябре́
в ноябре́

на неде́ле

6

COMPARE AND REMEMBER:

Когда́? — (case № 6)	Когда́? — (case № 4)	Когда́? — (adv. — doesn't change)
в сентябре́	в понеде́льник	о́сенью
в ма́е	в сре́ду	весно́й
в ию́не	в воскресе́нье	ле́том
		зимо́й
в э́том ме́сяце		
в э́том году́ (! Exception !)		
на э́той неде́ле (! Exception !)		

Когда́? О́сенью. / В сентябре́.
На э́той неде́ле. / На про́шлой[1] неде́ле. / На бу́дущей[2] неде́ле.
This week. / Last week. / Next week.
Когда́ то́чно[3]? В пя́тницу. / На э́той неде́ле в пя́тницу.
On Friday. / On Friday this week.

[1] last, past
[2] next, future
[3] exactly

Exercise 13. **Read and translate the dialogues. Write your own dialogues.**

1. — Когда́ Вы лети́те в Росси́ю?
   — Я лечу́ в Росси́ю в сентябре́.
2. — Когда́ вы е́дете в Ни́ццу?
   — Мы е́дем в Ни́ццу ле́том. В ию́не и́ли в ию́ле.
3. — Когда́ вы отдыха́ете?
   — Мы отдыха́ем в суббо́ту и в воскресе́нье.
4. — Когда́ в Кана́де но́сят зи́мние ве́щи?
   — В Кана́де зи́мние ве́щи но́сят в декабре́, в январе́ и феврале́.
5. — Когда́ Джон лети́т в Росси́ю?
   — ______________________________
6. — А Вы лети́те в Росси́ю? Когда́?
   — ______________________________

никогда́ ≠ всегда́
never ≠ always

Exercise 14. **Answer the questions. Use никогда́ or всегда́.**

1. — Когда́ в И́ндии но́сят зи́мние ве́щи?
   — Никогда́.
2. — Когда́ на Таи́ти но́сят зи́мние ве́щи?
   — Никогда́.
3. — Когда́ на Таи́ти но́сят ле́тние ве́щи?
   — Всегда́.
4. Когда́ в Майа́ми хо́лодно? ______________________________
5. Когда́ в Антаркти́де хо́лодно? ______________________________
6. Когда́ Ваш друг лети́т в ко́смос? А Вы? ______________________________

☞ ATTENTION!

In the full question use double negation никогда́ не.

Когда́ в И́ндии но́сят зи́мние ве́щи?

Никогда́ = В И́ндии **никогда́ не** но́сят зи́мние ве́щи.

Когда́ на Таи́ти но́сят зи́мние ве́щи?

Никогда́ = На Таи́ти **никогда́ не** но́сят зи́мние ве́щи.

***Exercise 15.* Answer the questions, use никогда́ не.**

Когда́ в Майа́ми хо́лодно?

Когда́ в Антаркти́де жа́рко?

While John was waiting for the flight he heard skype calling.

Ма́ша: Приве́т, Джон!

Джон: Приве́т, Ма́ша!

Ма́ша: Ты лети́шь в Росси́ю?

Джон: Да, я уже́ в аэропорту́.

Ма́ша: Каки́е у тебя́ пла́ны сего́дня в Москве́?

Джон: В 10:20 я встреча́ю тебя́, мы гуля́ем.

Ма́ша: А каки́е пла́ны второ́го сентября́?

Джон: Второ́го сентября́ я рабо́таю. Но в 16:00 я уже́ отдыха́ю.

Ма́ша: А тре́тьего сентября́?

Джон: Тре́тьего сентября́ я рабо́таю, пото́м немно́го гуля́ю. Пото́м лечу́ в Ло́ндон. Мой самолёт в 19:30.

Ма́ша: Хорошо́! Экску́рсия по Москве́ сего́дня и, мо́жет быть, тре́тьего сентября́.

Джон: Хорошо́, спаси́бо!

***Exercise 16.* In order to understand what Masha and John were talking about, look at how we indicate time in Russian.**

ВРЕ́МЯ — TIME

Remember what cases and prepositions we use in these constructions.

Когда́? Сего́дня (adv.).
О́сенью (adv.).
В сентябре́ (case № 6).
На э́той неде́ле (case № 6). (На про́шлой неде́ле. На бу́дущей неде́ле)

Когда́ то́чно? В пя́тницу (case № 4).
На э́той неде́ле (case № 6) в пя́тницу (case № 4).

В како́е вре́мя? (What time?)

Во ско́лько? (case № 4 = case № 1)
В 8:00 (в во́семь ноль ноль)
В 9:15 (в де́вять пятна́дцать)
В 9:30 (в де́вять три́дцать)
В 9:45 (в де́вять со́рок пять)

Ско́лько сейча́с вре́мени[1]? (What time is it?) 9:30. (Сейча́с де́вять три́дцать.)

[1] вре́мя: cases 1, 4 — вре́мя, all other cases = the same form — вре́мени

ДА́ТА — A DATE

Како́е сего́дня числó? Сегóдня трéтье сентября́.
(We put a date in nominative case № 1, and a month in genitive case № 2.)

Поря́дковые числи́тельные — Ordinal numerals

first	пéрв**ый** (-ая, -ое, -ые)	tenth	деся́т**ый** (-ая, -ое, -ые)
second	втор**óй** (-áя, -óе, -ы́е)	twentieth	двадцáт**ый** (-ая, -ое, -ые)
third	трéт**ий (-ья, -ье, -ьи)**	thirtieth	тридцáт**ый** (-ая, -ое, -ые)
fourth	четвёрт**ый** (-ая, -ое, -ые)	fourtieth	сороков**óй** (-áя, -óе, -ы́е)
fifth	пя́т**ый** (-ая, -ое, -ые)	fiftieth	пятидеся́т**ый** (-ая, -ое, -ые)
sixth	шест**óй** (-áя, -óе, -ы́е)	sixtieth	шестидеся́т**ый** (-ая, -ое, -ые)
seventh	седьм**óй** (-áя, -óе, -ы́е)	seventieth	семидеся́т**ый** (-ая, -ое, -ые)
eighth	восьм**óй** (-áя, -óе, -ы́е)	eightieth	восьмидеся́т**ый** (-ая, -ое, -ые)
ninth	девя́т**ый** (-ая, -ое, -ые)	ninetieth	девянóст**ый** (-ая, -ое, -ые)
		hundredth	сóт**ый** (-ая, -ое, -ые)
eleventh	оди́ннадцат**ый** (-ая, -ое, -ые)	thousandth	ты́сячн**ый** (-ая, -ое, -ые)
twenty-first	двáдцать пéрв**ый** (-ая, -ое, -ые)	one hundred-and-first	сто пéрв**ый** (-ая, -ое, -ые)
twenty-second	двáдцать втор**óй** (-áя, -óе, -ы́е)	one thousand-tenth	ты́сяча деся́т**ый** (-ая, -ое, -ые)
twenty-fifth	двáдцать пя́т**ый** (-ая, -ое, -ые)	two thousandth	двухты́сячн**ый**

! PAY ATTENTION that трéтье (сентября́), вторóе (апрéля), двáдцать пéрвое (ию́ня) are the ordinal numerals in neuter gender!

Exercise 17. **Write the dates in Russian.**

Example: 02.01 → янвáрь — января́ — вторóе января́

02.01 — ____________________

05.02 — ____________________

08.03 — восьмóе мáрта

10.04 — ____________________

01.05 — ____________________

03.09 — ____________________

Роди́тельный паде́ж (паде́ж № 2) — Genitive (case № 2)
Кого́? Чего́?

	case № 1				**case № 2**					
		чей? чьё? чья?	како́й? како́е? кака́я?	что?		чьего́? чьей?	како́го? како́й?	кого́? чего́?		
он	э́тот, тот	мо**й** тво**й** наш ваш **его́**, **её**, **их**	но́в**ый** больш**о́й** хоро́ш**ий** бу́дущ**ий** си́н**ий** ру́сск**ий**	стол слова́р**ь** музе́**й** санато́р**ий** друг фи́зик студе́нт писа́тел**ь** Андре́**й** Анато́л**ий**	э́т**ого**, т**ого́**	мо**его́** тво**его́** на́ш**его** ва́ш**его** **его́**, **её**, **их**	но́в**ого** больш**о́го** хоро́ш**его** бу́дущ**его** си́н**его** ру́сск**ого**	стол**а́** словар**я́** музе́**я** санато́р**ия** дру́г**а** фи́зик**а** студе́нт**а** писа́тел**я** Андре́**я** Анато́л**ия**	**-ОГО /** **-ЕГО**	**-А /** **-Я /** **-ИЯ**
оно́	э́то, то	мо**ё** тво**ё** на́ш**е** ва́ш**е** **его́**, **её**, **их**	но́в**ое** больш**о́е** хоро́ш**ее** си́н**ее** ру́сск**ое**	письм**о́** мо́р**е** зда́н**ие**	э́т**ого**, т**ого́**	мо**его́** тво**его́** на́ш**его** ва́ш**его** **его́**, **её**, **их**	но́в**ого** больш**о́го** хоро́ш**его** си́н**его** ру́сск**ого**	письм**а́** мо́р**я** зда́н**ия**	**-ОГО /** **-ЕГО**	**-А /** **-Я /** **-ИЯ**
она́	э́та, та	мо**я́** тво**я́** на́ш**а** ва́ш**а** **его́**, **её**, **их**	но́в**ая** больш**а́я** хоро́ш**ая** си́н**яя** ру́сск**ая**	ко́мнат**а** дере́вн**я** тетра́д**ь** аудито́р**ия** подру́г**а** ба́бушк**а** А́н**я** Аде́л**ь** Мари́**я**	э́т**ой**, т**ой**	мо**е́й** тво**е́й** на́ш**ей** ва́ш**ей** **его́**, **её**, **их**	но́в**ой** больш**о́й** хоро́ш**ей** си́н**ей** ру́сск**ой**	ко́мнат**ы** дере́вн**и** тетра́д**и** аудито́р**ии** подру́г**и** ба́бушк**и** А́н**и** Аде́л**и** Мари́**и**	**-ОЙ /** **-ЕЙ**	**-Ы /** **-И /** **-ИИ**

	case № 1				case № 2					
		чьи?	каки́е?	что?		чьей?	каки́х?	кого́? чего́?		
они́	э́т**и**,	мо**й**	но́в**ые**	стол**ы́**	э́т**их**,	мо**и́х**	но́в**ых**	стол**о́в**	**-ЫХ /**	**-ОВ /**
	те	тво**й**	больш**и́е**	словар**и́**	**тех**	тво**и́х**	больш**и́х**	словар**е́й**	**-ИХ**	**-ЕВ /**
		на́ш**и**	хоро́ш**ие**	музе́**и**		на́ш**их**	хоро́ш**их**	музе́**ев**		**-ЕЙ /**
		ва́ш**и**	си́н**ие**	пи́сьм**а**		ва́ш**их**	си́н**их**	пи́с**ем**		**-ИЙ /**
		его́,	ру́сск**ие**	мор**я́**		**его́**,	ру́сск**их**	мор**е́й**		**Ø**
		её,		зда́н**ия**		**её**,		зда́н**ий**		
		их		ко́мнат**ы**		**их**		ко́мнат		
				дере́вн**и**				дереве́н**ь**		
				тетра́д**и**				тетра́д**ей**		
				аудито́р**ии**				аудито́р**ий**		
				друз**ья́**				друз**е́й**		
				фи́зик**и**				фи́зик**ов**		
				студе́нт**ы**				студе́нт**ов**		
				писа́тел**и**				писа́тел**ей**		
				Андре́**и**				Андре́**ев**		
				Анато́л**ии**				Анато́л**иев**		
				подру́г**и**				подру́г		
				ба́бушк**и**				ба́бушек		
				А́н**и**				Ан**ь**		
				Аде́л**и**				Аде́л**ей**		
				Мари́**и**				Мар**и́й**		

ДА́ТА — A DATE

When we answer the question When? with the exact date we use case № 2 for ordinal numbers as well Когда́? Тре́тьего сентября́ (a date and a month are in case № 2).

***Exercise 18.* Answer the questions.**

New Year	Когда́ Но́вый год в Евро́пе? (31.12 / 01.01)
	Когда́ Но́вый год в Росси́и? (31.12 / 01.01)
	Когда́ Но́вый год в Ва́шей стране́?
Christmas	Когда́ Рождество́ в Евро́пе? (25.12)
	Когда́ Рождество́ в Росси́и? (7.01)
Halloween	Когда́ Хеллоуи́н? (31.10)
Labour Day	Когда́ в Росси́и день труда́? (1.05)
	Когда́ в Ва́шей стране́ День труда́?
Birthday	Когда у Вас день рожде́ния?

[1] (1.IR OBA-У): to celebrate

***Exercise 19.* Како́й пра́здник Вы лю́бите? Почему́? Когда́ его́ пра́зднуют[1] (зимо́й, весно́й, ле́том, о́сенью, днём, но́чью)? Како́го числа́ его́ пра́зднуют?**

ДА́ТА — A DATE **A question about a date has three variations, depending on degree of accuracy.** **Pay attention to the difference of the questions Како́й (Како́е)? and Когда́?**		
1.	**Како́й сейча́с год?** (year — case № 1) Сейча́с две ты́сячи трина́дцат**ый** год.	**Когда́?** (only year — case № 6) В две ты́сячи трина́дцат**ом** год**у́**. Я прие́хал в Росси́ю в две ты́сячи трина́дцат**ом** году́ (case № 6).
2.	**Како́й сейча́с ме́сяц?** (month — case № 1, year — case № 2) Сейча́с **янва́рь** (case № 1). Сейча́с **янва́рь** (case № 1) две ты́сячи трина́дцатого го́да (case № 2).	**Когда́?** (month — case № 6 and year — case № 2) **В сентябре́** (case № 6) две ты́сячи трина́дцат**ого** го́д**а** (case № 2). Я прие́хал в Росси́ю в сентябре́ (case № 6) две ты́сячи трина́дцат**ого** го́д**а** (case № 2).
3.	**Како́е сего́дня число́?** (date — case № 1, month — case № 2, year — case № 2) 1.09.2013 — Пе́рвое сентябр**я́** две ты́сячи трина́дцат**ого** го́д**а**.	**Когда́? / Како́го числа́?** (date — case № 2, month — case № 2, year — case № 2) Пе́рв**ого** сентябр**я́** две ты́сячи трина́дцат**ого** го́д**а**. Я прие́хал в Росси́ю пе́рв**ого** (case № 2) сентябр**я́** (case № 2) две ты́сячи трина́дцат**ого** го́д**а** (case № 2).

Exercise 20. **Answer the question Когда́?, look at the table.**

Я роди́лся (родила́сь) 08.11.1994
Я роди́лся (родила́сь) в ты́сяча девятьсо́т девяно́сто четвёртом году́.
Я роди́лся (родила́сь) в ноябре́ ты́сяча девятьсо́т девяно́сто четвёртого го́да.
Я роди́лся (родила́сь) восьмо́го ноября́ ты́сяча девятьсо́т девяно́сто четвёртого го́да.

1. Когда́ Вы родили́сь?
2. Когда́ родили́сь Ва́ши роди́тели?
3. Когда́ бы́ли Олимпи́йские и́гры в Со́чи? А в Ло́ндоне?

Exercise 21. **Using the information from the document «Приглаше́ние на въезд в Росси́йскую Федера́цию» (p. 128), answer the quesitons.**

1. Когда́ Джон бу́дет в Москве́?
2. Когда́ Джон пра́зднует день рожде́ния?
3. Когда́ Вы пра́зднуете день рожде́ния?
4. Когда́ Вы бу́дете в Москве́?
5. Когда́ (в како́м году́) де́душка Бенджами́н прие́хал в Росси́ю в пе́рвый раз?

ВРЕ́МЯ: ЧАС[1], МИНУ́ТА[2]

The full answer to the question with case № 2:

Сейча́с де́вять **часо́в** (case № 2) три́дцать **мину́т** (case № 2).

All numbers except 1, 21, 31... numbers ending in 1 (go with the words that indicate **units** in genitive case (case № 2)).

1 + час — ОДИ́Н ЧАС (case № 1, sg.)
2, 3, 4 + час**а́** — ДВА ЧАС**А́** (case № 2, sg.)
5, 6, 7 etc. + час**о́в** — ПЯТЬ ЧАС**О́В** (case № 2, pl.)

1 + мину́та — ОДНА́ МИНУ́ТА (case № 1, sg.)
2, 3, 4 + мину́т**ы** — ДВ**Е** МИНУ́Т**Ы** (case № 2, sg.)
5, 6, 7 etc. + мину́т — ПЯТЬ МИНУ́Т (case № 2, pl.)

[1] an hour
[2] a minute

Exercise 22. **Answer the questions. Use the words час and мину́та.**

1. У Вас до́ма в э́то вре́мя ско́лько вре́мени?
2. What's the difference between Moscow time and your time?

Example: В Москве́ 12:00, а в Нью-Йо́рке 5:00. Ра́зница — 7 часо́в.

In Russia a day is traditionally divided into four parts.

4:00 — 11:00 → у́тро: morning.
12:00 — 16:00 → день: day.
17:00 — 22:00 → ве́чер: evening.
23:00 — 3:00 → ночь: night.

5:00 — пять часо́в утра́ (case № 2)
13:00 — час дня (case № 2)
17:00 — пять часо́в ве́чера (case № 2)
1:00 — час но́чи (case № 2)

According to this we specify the time.

— Ско́лько сейча́с вре́мени?

— Сейча́с де́вять часо́в **утра́**.
— Сейча́с де́вять часо́в **ве́чера**.
— Двена́дцать часо́в **дня**.
— Два часа́ **но́чи**.

Exercise 23. **Answer the questions using adverbs of time у́тром, днём, ве́чером, но́чью.**

Example: Когда́ лю́ди обе́дают? — Днём.

1. Когда́ студе́нты у́чатся?
2. Когда́ лю́ди спят?
3. Когда́ лю́ди гуля́ют?
4. Когда́ Вы отдыха́ете?
5. Когда́ Вы рабо́таете?

что?	когда́?	When?
у́тро	у́тро**м**	in the morning
день	**днём**	in the afternoon
ве́чер	ве́чер**ом**	in the evening
ночь	но́чь**ю**	at night

You can hear another answer to the question Ско́лько вре́мени?:

5:00 — пять часо́в ро́вно or пять ноль-но́ль
5:05 — пять мину́т шесто́го or пять ноль пять
5:10 — де́сять мину́т шесто́го or пять де́сять
5:15 — пятна́дцать мину́т шесто́го or пять пятна́дцать
5:30 — полови́на шесто́го (полшесто́го) or пять три́дцать
5:40 — без двадцати́ мину́т шесть (без двадцати́ шесть) or пять со́рок
5:45 — без пятна́дцати мину́т шесть (без пятна́дцати шесть) or пять со́рок пять
5:50 — без десяти́ мину́т шесть (без десяти́ шесть) or пять пятьдеся́т
5:55 — без пяти́ мину́т шесть (без пяти́ шесть) or пять пятьдеся́т пять

Де́сять. Деся́тый (case № 1) — деся́того (case № 2).
Три́дцать три мину́ты **деся́того**.

Четы́ре. Четвёртый (case № 1) — четвёртого (case № 2).
Две мину́ты **четвёртого**.

Exercise 24. **Дайте полные и краткие варианты ответа на вопрос «Ско́лько вре́мени?».**

A)

B)

C) А на Ва́ших часа́х ско́лько сейча́с вре́мени?

Сло́жное бу́дущее вре́мя глаго́ла — Complex Future tense of the verb

Infinitive		Singular (sg.)		Plural (pl.)
быть	я	бу́д**у** де́лать	мы	бу́д**ем** де́лать
+	ты	бу́д**ешь** де́лать	вы	бу́д**ете** де́лать
де́лать	он, она́, оно́	бу́д**ет** де́лать	они́	бу́д**ут** де́лать

Example: — Что ты **бу́дешь де́лать** за́втра?
— За́втра я **бу́ду отдыха́ть**.
— А я **бу́ду писа́ть** письмо́. Анто́н **бу́дет изуча́ть** францу́зский язы́к.

Exercise 25. **Say what these people did yesterday, what they do today and what they will do tomorrow.**

Example: Говори́ть → **Вчера́**[1] я говори́л. **Сего́дня** я говорю́.
За́втра я бу́ду говори́ть.

[1] yesterday

1. **писа́ть** → Вчера́ я ______________ . Сего́дня я ______________ . За́втра я ______________ .
2. **фотографи́ровать** → Вчера́ они́ ______________ . Сего́дня они́ ______________ .
За́втра они́ ______________.
3. **гуля́ть** → Вчера́ мы ______________ . Сего́дня мы ______________ . За́втра мы ______________ .
4. **отдыха́ть** → Вчера́ я ______________ . Сего́дня я ______________ . За́втра я ______________ .

Exercise 26. **Read John and Masha's dialogue about the meeting again and tell us about John's plans using the Future tense. Pay attention to the fact that in Russian like in English it is possible to express Future with the form of the Present.**

Example: За́втра в 18:00 я встреча́юсь[2] с друзья́ми. =
За́втра в 18:00 я бу́ду встреча́ться с друзья́ми.
Tomorrow at 6.00 I'm meeting my friends. = Tomorrow at 6.00 I will meet my friends.

[2] (1.R.VOW): to meet

Exercise 27. **Look at your calendar and explain why you can't meet at a particular date.**

Example: — Что ты бу́дешь де́лать тре́тьего апре́ля?
— Извини́, тре́тьего апре́ля я бу́ду рабо́тать (бу́ду лете́ть в Москву́ / бу́ду на конце́рте / бу́ду в университе́те на ле́кции…).

Exercise 28. **Look at John and Masha's dialogue in skype again. What did they decide? How many times are they going to meet in Moscow? What dates? Now fill in John's calendar, using the information from the dialogue. Now you can write down John's plans and add the information using different verb forms.**

Example:

Ма́ша бу́дет встреча́ть Джо́на в 10:15 (в де́сять часо́в пятна́дцать мину́т и́ли в де́сять пятна́дцать) в понеде́льник пе́рвого сентября́.

Ма́ша бу́дет встреча́ть Джо́на в пятна́дцать мину́т оди́ннадцатого в понеде́льник пе́рвого сентября́.
Джон бу́дет в Москве́ ______________________________
Джон бу́дет рабо́тать ______________________________
Джон бу́дет отдыха́ть ______________________________
Его́ самолёт бу́дет в 19:30. ______________________________
Экску́рсия бу́дет ______________________________

1 Понеде́льник Monday	2 Вто́рник Tuesday	3 Среда́ Wednesday
8	8	8
9	9	9
10	10	10
11	11	11
12	12	12
13	13	13
14	14	14
15	15	15
16	16	16
17	17	17
18	18	18
19	19	19
20	20	20

4 Четве́рг Thursday	5 Пя́тница Friday	6 Суббо́та Saturday
8	8	
9	9	
10	10	7 Воскресе́нье Sunday
11	11	
12	12	
13	13	
14	14	
15	15	
16	16	
17	17	
18	18	
19	19	Неделя **Week**
20	20	Сентя́брь September

6

***Exercise 29.* Look at your diary. Imagine the plans in detail.**

Having filled in the calendar John turned to Internet to find out what weather is going to be in Moscow.

Погóда — Weather

	Сегóдня **какáя** погóда?	Сегóдня на ýлице **как**?	Сегóдня на ýлице **что**?
	Сегóдня я́сная погóда. The weather is clear today.	Сегóдня я́сно. Today it is clear.	Сегóдня сóлнце. Today it is sunny.
	вéтреная погóда The weather is windy.	вéтрено It is windy.	вéтер There's wind.
	óблачная погóда The weather is cloudy.	óблачно It is cloudy.	—
	—	—	перемéнная óблачность It is partly cloudy.
	—	—	снег It is snowy.
	дождли́вая погóда The weather is rainy.	дождли́во It is rainy.	дождь Rain.
	жáркая погóда The weather is hot.	жáрко It is hot.	—
	тёплая погóда The weather is warm.	теплó It is warm.	—
	холóдная погóда The weather is cold.	хóлодно It is cold.	—

Exercise 30. **Look at the window and answer the question: Какáя сегóдня погóда?**

Model: Како́й → Как?

Exercise 31. **Study the model of forming qualitative adverbs (Как?), complete the table as in the example.**

како́й?	**как?**
я́сн**ый**	я́сн**о**
ве́трен**ый**	ве́трен**о**
си́н**ий**	си́н**е**
но́в**ый**	но́в**о**
широ́к**ий**	широк**о́**
жа́рк**ий**	жа́рк**о**
ста́р**ый**	________

интере́сн**ый**	________
ску́чн**ый**	________
кра́сн**ый**	________
све́тл**ый**	________
тёмн**ый**	________
прям**о́й**	________
высо́к**ий**	________

Exercise 32. **Paraphrase it.**

Example: Сего́дня тепло́. → Сего́дня **тёплая** пого́да.

Сего́дня жа́рко. → Сего́дня ________ пого́да.
Сего́дня хо́лодно. → Сего́дня ________ пого́да.
Э́то интере́сно. → Э́то ____________ журна́л.
Э́то ску́чно. → Э́то ____________ кни́га.

Model: Ско́лько гра́дусов[1]? — What temperature is it?

1 гра́дус (case № 1, sg.)
2, 3, 4 + ДВА гра́дуса (case № 2, sg.)
5, 6, 7 etc. + гра́дусов (case № 2, pl.)
Question Ско́лько? + гра́дусов (case № 2, pl.)

[1] a degree

	+25	плюс два́дцать пять гра́дусов plus twenty-five degrees
	+5	плюс пять гра́дусов plus five degrees плюс пять plus five
	0	
	–10	ми́нус де́сять гра́дусов minus ten degrees ми́нус де́сять minus ten

In the airside of the airport John began to examine passengers who were also waiting for their flights. His mother was a painter, so she taught him to watch people in his early childhood. Sometimes she took him to the classes, sometimes they were just sitting at a street café, looking around and playing "who is who?" for hours. His mother understood people perfectly, she could identify their character by the folds on the face, she could tell someone's biography after watching them move, dress, hold a cigarette or drink coffee. Very often people that they had discussed appeared in her paintings. John realized that unfortunately he didn't have his mother's intuition, but the habit to observe people served him right in everyday life and in his work. To practice he tried to think in Russian.

— Вот больша́я гру́ппа[1]. Оде́жда неофициа́льная[2]: шо́рты, футбо́лки, ле́тние пла́тья, джи́нсы. Они́ отдыха́ли тут, в А́нглии.

[1] a group
[2] unofficial

— Кто они́? — John asked questions from the game "Who is who?" («Кто есть кто?»).

— Они́ тури́сты.

— Отку́да они́?

John knew that only Russian and Chinese tourists travel in such big groups. And they definitely did not look like Chinese.

— Они́ из Росси́и? Мо́жет быть.

— Куда́ они́ летя́т?

— Они́ летя́т домо́й — в Росси́ю.

— Э́то наш самолёт! — heard John from one of the members of this group.

— Хорошо́!

— Прекра́сно!

— Ура́!

— Э́то муж и жена́. Их оде́жда краси́вая. Она́ то́же неофициа́льная, но она́ не ле́тняя, она́ осе́нняя, тёплая. На же́нщине пла́тье и сапоги́, на мужчи́не — пальто́, брю́ки, га́лстук, боти́нки[3]. Они́ элега́нтные[4].

[3] боти́нок (pl. боти́нки): a shoe (pl. shoes)
[4] elegant

— Отку́да они́?

— Мо́жет быть, э́ти лю́ди из А́нглии и́ли Фра́нции?

— Куда́ они́ летя́т?

— Они́ летя́т на се́вер. В Росси́ю и́ли в Норве́гию, и́ли в Кана́ду.

Э́то де́вушка. На де́вушке костю́м. Её оде́жда официа́льная.

— Отку́да она́?

— Её во́лосы све́тлые. Её глаза́ то́же све́тлые. Она́ высо́кая. Мо́жет быть, она́ из Ла́твии, из Литвы́ и́ли из Эсто́нии.

— Куда́ она́ лети́т?

— Она́ то́же лети́т домо́й. В Ла́твию, в Литву́ и́ли в Эсто́нию.

There was a man with an aquiline nose and dark curly hair sitting not far from John.

— Он из Ита́лии.

— Э́тот мужчи́на лети́т в Ита́лию.

There was a couple with four girls running and playing around, plumpy, with smooth oily skin and mischievous black eyes. The girls were wearing traditional bright Indian saris.

— Они́ из И́ндии. Мо́жет быть, э́та семья́ из Де́ли.

— Э́та семья́ лети́т домо́й в И́ндию. В Де́ли.

***Exercise 33.* Read and translate the dialogues.**

1. — Ты зна́ешь, отку́да я лечу́?
   — Да. Я зна́ю, отку́да ты лети́шь. Из Фра́нции.
   — А ты зна́ешь, куда́ я лечу́?
   — Да. Зна́ю. Ты лети́шь в И́ндию.
2. — Испа́ния — э́то ме́сто, куда́ я лечу́ сейча́с.
   — Э́то страна́, куда́ я лета́л в про́шлом году́.
3. — Таи́ти — э́то ме́сто, где я отдыха́л.
   — Да, э́то ме́сто, где всегда́ о́чень тепло́.
4. — Там, куда́ ты е́дешь, есть хоро́шая гости́ница?
   — Я не зна́ю, что там есть. Но там, где я был в про́шлом году́, была́ отли́чная гости́ница.

While John was spending his time that way, his flight was announced. Before the registration a stout intelligent-looking man approached him. Англича́нин, — thought John at once. — Оде́жда официа́льная[1]: костю́м, га́лстук. Лети́т из А́нглии в Росси́ю. Мо́жет быть, у него́ есть би́знес в Росси́и. О́чень типи́чный[2].

[1] official
[2] typical

John knew the word 'typical' in many languages from his mother. "The most important thing is to see typical and individual features in a person, — these are the outlines of a portrait," she liked to say.

"Excuse me," the stout man interrupted his thoughts. Overall he looked ordinary except for the red folder he was holding in his hands. "You are flying to Moscow, would you mind passing this folder to my partners in Russia? They will meet you at the airport. Just hold this folder in your hand when you enter the landside and they will understand that you are there instead of me. I would love to fly myself, but… my daughter is ill… everything happened so quickly…," said the man.

The individual feature of a worried father flashed in this typical businessman, and John couldn't refuse him. However, the procedure of passing the documents seemed too dramatic to him.

"Why do I need to hold the folder? Can you phone your partners and tell them my name and describe me to them? They could write my name on the table…"

"Of course, I will phone them," said the man after saying the words of appreciation a thousand times. "But you hold a folder, it is bright and red, just to be on the safe side…"

John took the folder, although he didn't quite understand what this 'to be on the safe side' really meant.

Having received the stamp of the customs control, John honestly raised a folder in his outstretched hand, and stepped out of the neutral zone on the Russian land: «Зо́на прилёта», that is how "arrival area" was written in the table. However, no one was interested in him and the folder. Then he saw a table «Вы́ход в го́род». Что э́то? — asked John to himself. — Вы́ход (as we say, exit) Куда́? (case № 4 with preposition 'to') в го́род. That's right, there was a translation in English, but John could understand it without any translation: somewhere near the exit, at the taxi rank, Masha was waiting for him. John headed to the table «Вы́ход в го́род», but he didn't reach it.

— Здра́вствуйте! Вы Джон Янг? — a tall strong man with fair hair, light-blue eyes and big mouth, with a little flat face and wide cheekbones, approached him. "A real Russian hero from the Vasnetsov's painting," thought John.

— Здра́вствуйте, да, я Джон, — John could demonstrate his poor knowledge of Russian. This was the maximum of the conscious speech he could utter. The young hero burst with a great number of whistling sounds as if he was shouting at the crows. John was ready for this as he had heard his father speaking Russian many times, but now the Russian language seemed tougher and more energetic. The new acquaintance tried to look friendly and smiled, but the effect was just the opposite. John remembered that they had discussed it with Masha — Russians are frowning and they can't have a friendly face. But now John also noticed that the problem is not only in the fact that Russians can only smile when they mean it. It was also difficult to speak Russian and smile at the same time! "It's not only the mentality, it's phonetics as well!" thought the Englishman.

— Рома́н Харито́нов! — a strong man roared and held out his hand. "He told me his name," understood John.

— Рома́н Харито́нов, — repeated John and held out his hand too. — Джон Янг.

Chapter 7

Щи да ка́ша — пи́ща на́ша.

Ру́сская посло́вица

Shchi and kasha are our food.

— Russian proverb

John did not immediately realize what name to give to the blond's behaviour: rudeness, disgust, violence, or treacherous robbery plan. It was terrible. That strange man didn't speak any language but Russian, he didn't understand anything (or pretended not to understand), he didn't want to wait for his interlocutor to find the required words in a phrasebook, but persistently led him out of the airport without letting him get lost in the crowd or stop. John didn't feel at ease. When they approached the car, which was waiting, as it turned out, for him and the Russian, John shook his head.

— Нет, извини́те, — John said politely but firmly. And then something absolutely incredible happened. The blond joyfully cried something unintelligible, and suddenly fell on John with all his dense body, hugged and kissed him three times, first on the left cheek, then on the right, then deftly twisted and again pressed his lips to the guest's left cheek ... John felt totally unhappy. He almost fell into the open front door of the car and got frozen on the seat, completely bewildered.

ABOUT RUSSIAN CULTURE

The triple kissing seems to be an exclusively Slavic tradition.

Even in pagan legends and fairy tales there is a mention of "magical" number three: three-headed dragons, three-eyed giants, three magic travellers, three brothers. In the pre-Christian Russian representation of the world it was believed that the world is made up of three elements, three dimensions, three spaces. Unless you pass the first two, you will not get to the third.

In times of Christianity, Slavic love of this number only increased due to the special veneration of the Trinity and the Easter holiday, when people traditionally kissed three times.

The triple kissing is an expression of special joy and trust. But be careful: this sign of friendliness is unlikely to be appropriate at business meetings. Usually it is used in casual conversation, during religious holidays or to impress foreign guests. ☺

In this case, a new acquaintance deliberately simulates hospitality in the Russian manner. Later you will find out the reason of such behaviour.

— Говори́шь! Ты говори́шь! Ты понима́ешь по-ру́сски! — John could understand from the blond's speech flow.

Apparently, the Russian phrase «нет, извини́те» that John uttered while trying to explain that he wouldn't go anywhere with the stranger, provoked such a reaction.

— Я немно́го говорю́ по-ру́сски, — John could say finally. — Извини́те. У меня́ сейча́с встре́ча.

John tried to get out of the car, but at this point the car abruptly moved. Roman Kharitonov managed to jump in the back seat.

— Да, да, встре́ча! — Kharitonov agreed.

John suddenly clearly realised the tragedy of the life around them. Something horrible, Kafkaesque looked at him as soon as he stepped off the plane in Moscow — something crazy, strange, what can not be managed. At high speed the car had already taken him somewhere for five or ten minutes — John lost the feeling of time. He only knew that he had got into some trouble, but he could not figure out what to do. Surprisingly, the decision came naturally: the phone rang. It was Masha. "Masha is still waiting for me at the airport! — John thought — and there are police at the airport. My companions, they don't understand English, so if I call for help, they won't react. Great." John put his hand in his pocket, found the phone, but Masha didn't answer hers. This time the car pulled up smoothly and John looked out the window with horror.

— Рестора́н?! — the young Englishman was very surprised to see the building when their car stopped opposite it.

— Рестора́н! Пожа́луйста, — Roman Kharitonov pointed at the huge glass doors and the doorman in front of them.

This unexpected turn made John forget about the phone and the fact that a moment ago he was going to call the police. He got out of the car, with his hands still holding a red folder, which he had been handed over by the man in the London airport. "Apparently, there has been a misunderstanding," John thought. The man at the airport only talked about handing over the folder, but Roman Kharitonov, who met him in Moscow, didn't seem to know that that man could not come. "I must try to explain that there has been a confusion."

— Спаси́бо! — Roman said, smiling and gently taking the folder from John's hands.

— Пожа́луйста! — answered John automatically.

— Пожа́луйста! — said the doorman letting the guests in.

***Exercise 1*. Listen, read the examples, follow the intonation.** Track 28

1. Responding for gratitude:

— Спаси́бо!

— **Пожа́луйста**!

2. Asking politely:

— Я хорошо́ зна́ю ру́сский язы́к. Говори́те, **пожа́луйста**, по-ру́сски!

3. I'm doing this for you:

— Говори́те, пожа́луйста, по-ру́сски!

— **Пожа́луйста**!

In the restaurant there were two people waiting at a table.

— Разреши́те предста́вить, э́то Оле́г Петро́в, — said Kharitonov, and John remembered the note in a phrasebook: the phrases разреши́те предста́вить and разреши́те предста́виться (if a person introduces himself) are used in business conversations. "That's interesting," he thought, "why so formally?"

— Оле́г Петро́в — дире́ктор, — Roman said, pointing at the high clean-shaven man in a suit and tie. "The director of what?" — John thought.

— О́чень рад. Джон, — diligently uttered Young, too, holding out his hand. He realised that there was some misunderstanding. If they wanted to do something bad to him, it is unlikely that they brought him to a crowded place.

— Я то́же о́чень рад! — the director Oleg shook his hand.

— А э́то Све́та, наш ме́неджер, — Roman introduced a girl.

REMEMBER!

In Russian some verbs have the suffix -ся (-сь), which means that the action is directed to the doer of this action.

учи́ть — учи́ться (2.R.CONS.2)

Учи́тель у́чит, а шко́льник у́чит**ся**. (A teacher teaches, a student studies)

умыва́ть — умыва́ться (1.R.VOW)

Ма́ма умыва́ет О́лю. Ма́ша умыва́ется. (Mother washes Olya. Masha washes (herself))

представля́ть — представля́ть**ся** (1.R.VOW)

Разреши́те предста́вить: мой друг Ива́н. Разреши́те предста́вить**ся**. Меня́ зову́т Джон.

(Let me introduce my friend Ivan. Let me introduce myself: my name is John.)

— Све́та — э́то Светла́на? — asked John.

— О, Вы отли́чно зна́ете ру́сский язы́к! — Oleg exclaimed.

— Спаси́бо!

— Пожа́луйста, Джон, — Oleg pointed at a spare chair, asking John to sit down.

Finding that John wanted to say something, but he did not have the words, Oleg turned to Roman:

— Рома́н, а где перево́дчик?

— Да, перево́дчик! Пожа́луйста! — John cheered up, hoping finally to fix this stupid situation. Probably, he was taken for a gentleman who had stayed in London and handed him a folder.

7

— Перево́дчик до́ма. Он сего́дня отдыха́ет, — Kharitonov said, and under the strict director's look reached into his pocket for his phone.

While Roman Kharitonov was negotiating with the interpreter, John was offered Russian food. The restaurant was recommended as the most Russian restaurant in the whole of Russia. John was already hungry and so he decided to have lunch here.

Fortunately, there was a menu in English.

Track 29

Меню́ — Menu

Сала́ты:	**Salads:**
овощно́й сала́т (све́жие о́вощи)	vegetable salad (Fresh vegetables)
мясно́й сала́т	meat salad
селёдка под шу́бой	herring under a fur coat (dressed herring)
винегре́т	beetroot salad
оливье́	russian salad
Пе́рвые блю́да: **Супы́:**	**Entree:** **Soups:**
борщ	borshch (beetroot soup)
щи	shchi (cabbage soup)
лапша́ грибна́я	mushroom noodles
бульо́н	bouillon
соля́нка	solyanka

Втори́е блю́да:	Main course:
ка́ша гу́рьевская (ма́нная ка́ша с изю́мом, с оре́хами и мёдом) сла́дкая	guryev porridge (semolina with raisins, nuts and honey) — sweet
ка́ша гре́чневая с мя́сом	buckwheat porridge with meat
пельме́ни (с ма́слом, со смета́ной)	russian ravioli (with butter, sour cream)
ку́рица варёная	boiled chicken
мя́со варёное	boiled meat
яйцо́ варёное	boiled egg
ку́рица жа́реная	fried chicken
ры́ба жа́реная	fried fish
мя́со жа́реное	fried meat
карто́фель варёный	boiled potatoes
карто́фель жа́реный	fried potatoes
о́вощи варёные	boiled vegetables
макаро́ны	pasta
Горя́чие заку́ски:	**Hot appetizers:**
Пироги́:	**Pies:**
пиро́г с мя́сом	meat pie
пиро́г с ры́бой	fish pie
пиро́г с ку́рицей	chicken pie
пиро́г с яйцо́м и лу́ком	egg and onion pie
Пирожки́:	**Small pies:**
пирожки́ с варе́ньем	jam pies
пирожки́ с мя́сом	meat pies
пирожки́ с капу́стой	cabbage pies
Блины́:	**Blini:**
блины́ с кра́сной икро́й	blini with red caviar
блины́ с мёдом	blini with honey
блины́ с варе́ньем	blini with jam
Холо́дные заку́ски:	**Cold appetizers:**
солёные огурцы́	salted cucumbers
солёные грибы́	salted mushrooms
солёная кра́сная ры́ба	salted red fish
ква́шеная капу́ста	sauerkraut
кра́сная икра́	red caviar
чёрная икра́	black caviar
сыр	cheese
Десе́рты:	**Desserts:**
торт (шокола́дный, медо́вый, фрукто́вый, оре́ховый, смета́нный, сли́вочный)	cakes (chocolate cake, honey cake, fruit cake, nut cake, sour cream cake, cream cake)

пиро́жное (фрукто́вое, я́годное, оре́ховое)	pastries (fruit pastrie, berry pastrie, nut pastrie)
моро́женое (фрукто́вое, сли́вочное, шокола́дное)	ice cream (fruit, cream, chocolate)
све́жие фру́кты	fresh fruit
фру́кты в са́харе	fruit in sugar
фрукто́вый сала́т	fruit salad
варе́нье	jam
све́жие я́годы	fresh berries
мёд с оре́хами	honey with nuts
мёд с изю́мом	honey with raisin
изю́м в шокола́де	raisin in chocolate
Напи́тки безалкого́льные:	**Soft drinks:**
чай (чёрный, зелёный, фрукто́вый)	tea (black, green, fruit)
ко́фе (чёрный, экспре́ссо, капучи́но, америка́но, латте́)	coffee (blak, espresso, cappuccino, americano, latte)
сок	juice
квас (хле́бный, медо́вый)	kvas (made from bread, honey)
молоко́ (горя́чее, холо́дное)	milk (hot, cold)
вода́ (без га́за, с га́зом)	water (still, sparkling)
Алкого́ль:	**Alcohol:**
вино́	wine
пи́во	beer
во́дка	vodka
шампа́нское	champagne
Со́усы и припра́вы:	**Sauces and condiments:**
майоне́з	mayonnaise
смета́на	sour cream
лук	onion
чесно́к	garlic
горчи́ца	mustard
соль	salt
пе́рец	pepper
са́хар	sugar
хрен	horseradish
ке́тчуп	ketchup
ма́сло	butter
сли́вки	cream
Хлеб:	**Bread:**
хлеб чёрный	black (rye) bread
хлеб бе́лый (бу́лка)	white (wheat) bread

***Exercise 2.* Help John: find nouns and adjectives with the same root.**

Example 1: хлеб — хле́бный

Example 2: фру́кты — фрукто́вый

мёд ______________________

мя́со ______________________

о́вощ (о́вощи) ______________________

шокола́д ______________________

соль ______________________

гриб (грибы́) ______________________

оре́х (оре́хи) ______________________

фрукт (фру́кты) ______________________

я́года (я́годы) ______________________

сли́вки ______________________

смета́на ______________________

— Официа́нт[1], здесь есть стейк и крем-су́п[2]? — asked John after looking through the whole menu.

— Извини́те, но э́то ру́сский рестора́н. У нас есть то́лько[3] традицио́нные[4] ру́сские блю́да. Э́то о́чень вку́сно[5]! — answered the waiter.

John chose those dishes which were familiar to him: овощно́й сала́т, бульо́н, мя́со жа́реное, карто́фель варёный, сыр, све́жие фру́кты и францу́зское вино́.

When he announced his choice to the waiter, the company at the table revived:

— Нет, Джон, не э́ти блю́да!

— Здесь о́чень вку́сный[6] борщ и пельме́ни! Вку́сная ка́ша гу́рьевская. А како́й вку́сный тут медо́вый квас! — Oleg recommended.

— Ру́сские пироги́ — э́то то́же о́чень вку́сно, — added Sveta.

— Э́то пра́вда[7], — the waiter agreed.

In the end, John's new friends made an order for him.

[1] a waiter
[2] cream soup
[3] only
[4] traditional
[5] tasty, delicious (adv.)
[6] tasty, delicious (adj.)
[7] it's true

***Exercise 3.* What dishes you think have the new John's friends chosen? What would you choose?**

Зака́з[8]:

Сала́т ______________________

Пе́рвое блю́до: ______________________

Второ́е блю́до: ______________________

Горя́чие заку́ски: ______________________

Холо́дные заку́ски: ______________________

Напи́тки: ______________________

Десе́рт: ______________________

Со́ус: ______________________

[8] an order

John voiced his order to the waiter, implying that he was going to pay for himself.

About Russian hospitality, or Who's going to pay the bill

Hospitality has always been a feature of the Russian people. A guest in the old days was supposed to get drunk and fed to satiety. The custom was to almost force guests to wine and dine. Traditionally they offered the dish three times, and twice it was rejected. Only after the third failure the guest was left in peace. Therefore, today the inviting party (be it a man, business partners, a birthday party, just a friend) usually pays the bill at a restaurant or in a café. But, of course, there may be other agreements, it is better to discuss it in advance.

Russians willingly invite guests into their houses. If you visit a Russian family, be prepared for the fact that you will be offered very tasty food. A generous table and exclusive recipes is the pride of the hostess.

While they were waiting for the order, John drew attention to the remarkable stone tool near the wall. He asked the Russians: «Что э́то?»

Э́то ру́сская пе́чка[1]. Ра́ньше э́то бы́ло гла́вное[2] ме́сто[3] в ру́сском до́ме. Там ру́сские лю́ди гото́вили[4] еду́: вари́ли[5] ка́шу и суп, жа́рили[6] мя́со и карто́фель.

[1] a stove
[2] main
[3] a place
[4] (2.IR Б, П, М, В + Л) : to cook
[5] (2.R.CONS.1): to boil
[6] (2.R.CONS.1): to fry
[7] (1.IR Ч–К–Ч): to bake

Svetlana added to the Oleg's story:

А ещё в ру́сской пе́чке пекли́[7] хлеб, пироги́ и пирожки́.

While Oleg was telling all this, John used the dictionary which recognized the voice on the phone, and translated.

***Exercise 4.* Translate the text.**

***Exercise 5.* Say the infinitives of the verbs гото́вили, вари́ли, жа́рили. Remember that the past form is derived from the infinitive.**

Infinitive — ~~ть~~ + л(-а, -о, -и)
чита́~~ть~~ → чита́ + л → чита́л(-а, -о, -и)
говори́~~ть~~ → говори́ + л → говори́л(-а, -о, -и)

гото́вили — гото́вить
вари́ли — ____________
жа́рили — ____________

***Exercise 6.* Fill in the table.**

они́	гото́вили	вари́ли	жа́рили
он	гото́вил	________	________
она́	________	вари́ла	________

Remember the conjugation of verbs in the Present tense:

вари́ть (2.R.CONS.1): to boil			
я	вар**ю́**	мы	ва́р**им**
ты	ва́р**ишь**	вы	ва́р**ите**
он(а́, о́)	ва́р**ит**	они́	ва́р**ят**

жа́рить (2.R.CONS.1): to fry			
я	жа́р**ю**	мы	жа́р**им**
ты	жа́р**ишь**	вы	жа́р**ите**
он(а́, о́)	жа́р**ит**	они́	жа́р**ят**

гото́вить (2.IR Б, П, М, В + Л): to cook			
я	гото́в**лю**	мы	гото́в**им**
ты	гото́в**ишь**	вы	гото́в**ите**
он(а́, о́)	гото́в**ит**	они́	гото́в**ят**

ATTENTION! You should remember how the verb 'to bake' is declined:

Infinitive	**печь (1.IR Ч–К–Ч)**			
Present	я	пеку́	мы	печём
	ты	печёшь	вы	печёте
	он(á, ó)	печёт	они́	пеку́т
Past		**! пёк (пеклá, пеклó)**		**! пекли́**

Exercise 7. **Now you can find root words for these verbs in the menu:**

вари́ть ______________________________

жа́рить ______________________________

Exercise 8. **Rewrite the story about the Russian stove in the Present tense.**

Э́то ру́сская пе́чка. Сейча́с ______________________________

____

____

____

____

____

____

____

____

Exercise 9. **Read the story about the stove in the Past tense, and then in the Present tense. Where, you think, can you see the stoves nowadays? Где сейча́с есть ру́сские пе́чки?**

These words will help you to answer this question:

я ду́маю, я зна́ю, в го́роде, в дере́вне, в ру́сском кафе́ и́ли рестора́не

Exercise 10. **Write the sentences which you think are true in the column «Пра́вда», and false sentences in the column «Непра́вда».**

Example: **Пра́вда:** Э́то пе́чка. Ра́ньше э́то бы́ло гла́вное ме́сто в ру́сском до́ме.
Непра́вда: Э́то пе́чка. Сейча́с э́то гла́вное ме́сто в ру́сском до́ме.

	Пра́вда	Непра́вда
1. Ра́ньше в ру́сской пе́чке гото́вили еду́.	________	________
2. Сейча́с в города́х то́же гото́вят еду́ в ру́сской пе́чке.	________	________
3. В ру́сской пе́чке жа́рят суп.	________	________
4. Ра́ньше в ру́сской пе́чке жа́рили мя́со и карто́фель.	________	________
5. Сейча́с телеви́зор — э́то гла́вное ме́сто в до́ме.	________	________
6. У бизнесме́на гла́вное ме́сто в до́ме — э́то кабине́т.	________	________
7. В ру́сском рестора́не хлеб пеку́т в ру́сской пе́чке.	________	________

Exercise 11. Где пра́вда, а где непра́вда?

	Пра́вда	Непра́вда
1. Ра́ньше англича́не и францу́зы пекли́ хлеб в ру́сской пе́чке.	________	________
2. Сейча́с япо́нцы жа́рят мя́со и карто́шку в ру́сской пе́чке.	________	________
3. Ра́ньше ру́сские вари́ли суп в ру́сской пе́чке.	________	________
4. Ра́ньше англича́не не вари́ли ка́шу в ру́сской пе́чке.	________	________
5. Сейча́с францу́зы не гото́вят еду́ в ру́сской пе́чке.	________	________
6. Сейча́с не́мцы пеку́т пироги́ в ру́сской пе́чке.	________	________

Exercise 12. Answer the question using the words: ку́хня[1], плита́[2], микроволно́вая пе́чка[3]. Use case № 6.

ку́хня + НА чём
плита́ + НА чём
пе́чка + В чём

[1] a kitchen
[2] a cooker
[3] (микроволно́вка): a microwave oven

1. Где есть плита́ и микроволно́вая пе́чка? (ку́хня)
2. Где сейча́с гото́вят еду́ ру́сские? (плита́ и микроволно́вая пе́чка)
3. Где нахо́дится Ваш телеви́зор: на ку́хне и́ли в ко́мнате?
4. Каки́е традицио́нные блю́да Вы гото́вите на плите́?
5. Что Вы гото́вите в микроволно́вой пе́чке?

Exercise 13. Како́е Ва́ше гла́вное ме́сто в до́ме? Use the dictionary to find out the meaning of the words.

Кабине́т? Крова́ть? Телеви́зор? Ва́нная ко́мната? Бассе́йн? Гара́ж? Ку́хня? Холоди́льник? Спа́льня? Коридо́р? Сад?

John got used to the Russian speech and began to understand what they were talking about.

Finally the dinner was served.

Све́та: Джон, э́то Ва́ша лапша́ грибна́я?
Рома́н: Нет, э́то моя́ лапша́. У Джо́на борщ.
Све́та: Чей сала́т?
Рома́н: Э́то сала́т Джо́на.
Све́та: Чьё францу́зское вино́?
Рома́н: Джо́на.
Све́та: Чьи щи?
Рома́н: Щи мои́.
Све́та: Чей пиро́г с яйцо́м и лу́ком?
Рома́н: Джо́на.
Све́та: Чья ка́ша?
Рома́н: Джо́на.

"That's strange," John thought. If these people take me for someone else, it is still unlikely to confuse me with a woman. Meanwhile, why do they call me a female name "Johna"? What kind of a name is it? John pointed at his chest and clearly said:

— Меня́ зову́т Джон. Я — ДжоН.

— Да-да, — his companions nodded and continued as if nothing had happened.

Све́та: Чьи пирожки́ с мя́сом?

Рома́н: Джо́на.

Джон: Я Джон. Я не Джо́нА.

Sveta smiled and tried to understand:

Све́та: Вас зову́т Джон. Я зна́ю э́то. Но… **Чей пирожо́к?** Э́то **Ваш** пирожо́к. **У Джо́на есть пирожо́к. Э́то пирожо́к Джо́на.** Понима́ете?

Джон: Не понима́ю.

Then Sveta took her handbag and pointed at it.

Све́та: Э́то **я**. **У меня́** есть су́мка. Э́то **моя́** су́мка.

Э́то **Све́та**. **У Све́ты** есть су́мка. Э́то су́мка **Све́ты**.

Then she took Roman's phone from the table.

Све́та: А э́то **Рома́н**. **У Рома́на** есть телефо́н. Э́то телефо́н **Рома́на**.

Э́то **он**. **У него́** есть телефо́н. Э́то **его́** телефо́н.

Then she pointed at the newly brought food on the table and quickly wrote on a napkin:

Све́та: Э́то **мы**. = Э́то **Оле́г, Джон, Рома́н и Све́та**.

У нас есть зака́з. = **У Оле́га, у Джо́на, у Рома́на и у Све́ты** есть зака́з.

Э́то **наш** зака́з. = Э́то зака́з **Оле́га, Джо́на, Рома́на и Све́ты**.

Понима́ете?

«Понима́ю!» — John finally got that. He understood that Джо́н**а**, Оле́г**а**, Рома́н**а** were not female names, it was a certain form (case) from the names Джо́н, Оле́г, Рома́н.

Све́т**ы** is a form of the feminine noun Све́та.

Apparently, it was about possessiveness: сала́т Джо́на, су́мка Све́ты, i.e. the salad is John's, the bag is Sveta's.

To verify the guess and prevent further confusion, John consulted his pocket grammar book. **Possessiveness** in the Russian language is expressed by the **genitive case**. It is possible to say that something or someone belongs to someone in two ways:

Model: У кого́ (case № 2) есть что (case № 1). =
Э́то что (case № 1) кого́ (case № 2) / чей.

У меня́ есть пирожо́к. = Э́то мой пирожо́к.

↓ ↓

У Джо́на есть пирожо́к. = Э́то пирожо́к Джо́на.

To say that something or someone belongs to someone we can use:

- possessive pronoun (мой),
- the personal pronoun in the genitive case with the preposition у (у меня́),
- the noun in the genitive case with or without preposition (у Джо́на, Джо́на).

All these constructions are interchangeable:

у	Джóна Свéты Ромáна Харитóнова дирéктора	есть	суп кáша я́блоко пирогú

Э́то	(есть)	суп кáша я́блоко пирогú	Джóна Свéты Ромáна Харитóнова дирéктора

"Exactly!," John remembered the phrase he had learned from the phrasebook: «Аллó[1], э́то квартúра Ивановá?» Ивáнов is a man. And квартúра Ивановá means that the flat belongs to Mr. Ivanov. It means that **фúрма** Смирнóва is a firm that belongs to Smirnov, «Ресторáн Кáти Семёновой» means that the owner of the restaurant is Katya Semenova. It is a common Russian name, but it may seem that it is a French girl Kati with male Polish surname. Amazing Russian grammar!

[1] hello

Exercise 14. **Answer the question using the words in brackets in genitive case (see Chapter 6, p. 135 for the genitive case table).**

A) *Example:* Чья э́то машúна? (дирéктор) → Э́то машúна дирéктора.

[2] a president

1. Чей э́то журнáл? (сестрá) ____________________
2. Чьи э́то кнúги? (профéссор) ____________________
3. Чей э́то самолёт? (президéнт[2]) ____________________
4. Чья э́то квартúра? (актрúса) ____________________
5. Чьи э́то дéньги? (подрýги) ____________________
6. Чьё э́то я́блоко? (брат) ____________________

B) *Example:* Чья э́то машúна? (наш нóвый дирéктор) → Э́то машúна нáшего нóвого дирéктора.

1. Чей э́то журнáл? (моя́ стáршая сестрá) ____________________
2. Чьи э́то кнúги? (извéстные[3] профессорá) ____________________
3. Чей э́то самолёт? (росси́йский президéнт) ____________________
4. Чья э́то квартúра? (извéстная францýзская актрúса) ____________________
5. Чьи э́то дéньги? (егó хорóшие подрýги) ____________________
6. Чьё э́то я́блоко? (млáдший брат) ____________________

[3] famous

C) Replace the constructions from part B for the construction У кого́ есть что.

Example: Э́то маши́на на́шего но́вого дире́ктора. →
У на́шего но́вого дире́ктора есть маши́на. → У него́ есть маши́на.

1. ______________________________
2. ______________________________
3. ______________________________
4. ______________________________
5. ______________________________
6. ______________________________

REMEMBER!

Type 1. Чья э́то кни́га? — Э́то кни́га моего́ дру́га Са́ши Кузнецо́ва. (Sasha Kuznetsov is the owner of the book.)
Type 2. Чья э́то кни́га? — Э́то кни́га изве́стного ру́сского писа́теля Анто́на Че́хова. (Anton Chekhov is the author of the book/)
! Only the first type can be replaced by the construction У кого́ есть что.

Some examples of the surnames declension in case № 2:

	case № 1	case № 2
он ♂	Кузнецо́в Ко́нев Толсто́й Рожде́ственский Ле́тний Бетхо́вен[1]_	Кузнецо́ва Ко́нева Толсто́го Рожде́ственского Ле́тнего Бетхо́вена
она́ ♀	Кузнецо́ва Ко́нева Толста́я Рожде́ственская Ле́тняя ! Бетхо́вен_	Кузнецо́вой Ко́невой Толсто́й Рожде́ственской Ле́тней ! Бетхо́вен_
они́ ♂ + ♀	Кузнецо́вы Ко́невы Толсты́е Рожде́ственские Ле́тние ! Бетхо́вены	Кузнецо́вых Ко́невых Толсты́х Рожде́ственских Ле́тних ! Бетхо́венов

[1] About foreign surnames: 1) Foreign surnames ending in a consonant like Бетхо́вен are declined as nouns. Female versions of these surnames do not decline. 2) Surnames ending in -ко, -о, -ец, -и do not decline.

***Exercise 15.* Name the authors of these works using case № 2.**

Example: Му́зыка. Бетхо́вен. → Му́зыка Бетхо́вена.
О́пера[1]. Компози́тор[2] Пётр Ильи́ч Чайко́вский. → О́пера компози́тора Петра́ Ильича́ Чайко́вского.

[1] an opera
[2] a composer
[3] a song
[4] a novel
[5] an architect
[6] a story

1. Карти́на. Марк Шага́л. ______________________________
2. Пе́сня[3]. Э́лтон Джон. ______________________________
3. Рома́н[4] «Кра́сное и чёрное». Писа́тель Стенда́ль. ______________________________
4. Рома́н «Войн́а и мир». Лев Толсто́й. ______________________________
5. Дом. Архите́ктор[5] Га́уди. ______________________________
6. Расска́зы[6]. Ага́та Кри́сти. ______________________________
7. Карти́на. Казими́р Мале́вич. ______________________________
8. Карти́на. Поль Гоге́н. ______________________________
9. Расска́з. Анто́н Че́хов. ______________________________

— Вот сала́т, вот пироги́ Све́ты, вот суп Рома́на. **У вас есть зака́з. А у меня́ нет моего́ зака́за!** — Oleg said.

— Пра́вда? — Sveta was surprised, and looked at the dishes.

— Пра́вда-пра́вда. У вас есть суп, а у меня́ нет су́па. У вас есть сала́т, а у меня́ нет сала́та. У вас есть пироги́, а у меня́ нет пирого́в.

A note in John's notebook:

Model: НЕТ + case № 2 describes the absence of the object.
У МЕНЯ́ ЕСТЬ что (case № 1) ≠ У МЕНЯ́ НЕТ чего́ (case № 2) —

For example:

У меня́ есть суп. У меня́ нет су́па.
У меня́ есть пироги́. У меня́ нет пирого́в.

Роди́тельный паде́ж (паде́ж № 2). Мно́жественное число́.
Genitive forms (case № 2) plural

Genitive forms (case № 2) plural (pl.) are similar to the forms of accusative (case № 4) plural for animate nouns.

Use the same rule to form genitive case plural

		Паде́ж № 1. Еди́нственное число́ case № 1, sg.		**Паде́ж № 2. Мно́жественное число́ case № 2, pl. СКО́ЛЬКО? МНО́ГО...; 5, 10, 11, 125...; НЕТ...**
ОН	__ + ОВ	стол го́род час банк	a table a city an hour a bank	столо́в городо́в часо́в ба́нков
	Исключе́ния	стул (сту́лья) брат (бра́тья) сын (сыновья́) друг (друзья́) челове́к (лю́ди) ребёнок (де́ти) иностра́нец (иностра́нцы) граждани́н (гра́ждане) год раз	a chair (chairs) a brother (brothers) a son (sons) a friend (friends) a person (people) a child (children) a foreigner (foreigners) a citizen (citizens) a year a time	сту́льев бра́тьев сынове́й друзе́й люде́й (мно́го люде́й) / челове́к (Ско́лько? 5, 10... челове́к) дете́й иностра́нцев гра́ждан лет раз
	Ж Ч + ЕЙ Ш Щ	эта́ж ключ каранда́ш това́рищ	a floor a key a pencil a comrade	этаже́й ключе́й карандаше́й това́рищей
	Й → ЕВ	трамва́й музе́й	a tram a museum	трамва́ев музе́ев
	Ь → ЕЙ	слова́рь преподава́тель ру́бль	a dictionary a teacher a rouble	словаре́й преподава́телей рубле́й
	Исключе́ния	па́рень день	a young man, a guy a day	парне́й дней

		Паде́ж № 1. Еди́нственное число́ case № 1, sg.		Паде́ж № 2. Мно́жественное число́ case № 2, pl. СКО́ЛЬКО? МНО́ГО...; 5, 10, 11, 125...; НЕТ...
ОНА́	А → ∅	ма́ма ка́рта кни́га подру́га страни́ца	a mom a map a book a friend (female) a page	мам карт книг подру́г страни́ц
	Исключе́ния	сестра́ (сёстры)	a sister (sisters)	сест**ё**р
	МКА → МОК ПКА → ПОК ШКА → ШЕК ЧКА → ЧЕК ЖКА → ЖЕК ЙКА → ЕК	су́мка ша́пка ча́шка ру́чка ло́жка ма́йка лине́йка копе́йка	a bag a hat a cup a pen a spoon a shirt a ruler a coin	су́мок ша́пок ча́шек ру́чек ло́жек ма́ек лине́ек копе́ек
	Я → Ь	тётя неде́ля	an aunt a week	тёть / тётей неде́ль
	Ь → ЕЙ	ло́шадь дверь	a horse a door	лошаде́й двере́й
	Исключе́ния	мать дочь	a mother a daughter	матере́й дочере́й
	ИЯ → ИЙ	ста́нция аудито́рия	a station a lecture hall	ста́нций аудито́рий
ОНО́	О → ∅	сло́во ме́сто я́блоко окно́ кольцо́ число́	a word a place an apple a window a ring a number	слов мест я́блок о́к**о**н кол**е́**ц чи́с**е**л
	Исключе́ния	о́зеро (озёра) де́рево (дере́вья)	a lake (lakes) a tree (trees)	озёр дере́вь**ев**
	Е → ЕЙ	мо́ре	a sea	море́й
	ИЕ → ИЙ	зда́ние	a building	зда́ний
ОНИ́		де́ньги сли́вки	money cream	де́нег сли́вок

Exercise 16. **A) Say what these people don't have:**

Example: Антóн. Маши́на. → У Антóна нет маши́ны.

1. Мари́на. Нóвое плáтье. ______________________________
2. Пéтя. Совремéнный[1] компью́тер. ______________________________
3. Дирéктор. Врéмя[2]. ______________________________
4. Секретáрь. Докумéнты. ______________________________
5. Студéнт. Подру́га. ______________________________
6. А чегó нет у Вас? ______________________________

[1] contemporary, modern

[2] врéмя (and all nouns ending in -мя) have irregular declension (cases № 1 and № 4 врéмя, other cases врéмени). Remember the phrases: У меня́ есть (свобóдное) врéмя. — I have free time. У меня́ нет (свобóдного) врéмени. — I don't have free time.

B) Say what these people have:

Example: Антóн. Маши́на. → У Антóна есть маши́на.

1. Студéнт лéтом. Врéмя. ______________________________
2. Áнна. Дорогóе[3] пальтó. ______________________________
3. Дми́трий. Áнгло-ру́сский словáрь. ______________________________
4. Сестрá. Нóвая су́мка. ______________________________
5. Перевóдчик. Большóй текст. ______________________________
6. А у Вас есть дорогóе автó? ______________________________

[3] expensive

Exercise 17. **Как Вы ду́маете, каки́е вéщи и докумéнты есть сейчáс у Джóна?**

1. Пальтó?
2. Шу́ба?
3. Телефóн?
4. Регистрáция?
5. Ви́за?
6. Паспорт?
7. Страхóвка?
8. Крáсная пáпка?
9. Разговóрник?
10. Словáрь?
11. Кáрта?
12. Шáпка?
13. Ру́сские дéньги (рубли́, копéйки)?
14. Чемодáн?
15. Билéты в Лóндон?
16. Пи́сьма?
17. Ру́чки, карандаши́, тетрáди?
18. Истори́ческие кни́ги?

Exercise 18. **Remember how the models У кого́ есть что and У кого́ нет чего́ are changed in the Present and the Past.**

Model: У кого́ есть что — БЫТЬ + case № 1

In the Past tense the verb **быть** agrees with the noun in gender:

У меня́ был суп, была́ ка́ша, бы́ло я́блоко, бы́ли пироги́.

In the Future tense the verb **быть** agrees with the noun in number:

У меня́ бу́дет суп / ка́ша / я́блоко; у меня́ бу́дут пироги́.

У	Джо́на Све́ты Рома́на Харито́нова дире́ктора	есть был(-а́, -о, -и) бу́дет (бу́дут)	суп. ка́ша. я́блоко. пироги́.

Model: У кого́ нет чего́ — БЫТЬ + НЕТ + case № 2

If we need to say that there is no something, there was no something or there will be no something we use impersonal form of the verb 'be' with the genitive case:

нет су́па, нет ка́ши, нет я́блока, нет пирого́в;

не́ было су́па, не́ было ка́ши, не́ было я́блока, не́ было пирого́в;

не бу́дет су́па, не бу́дет ка́ши, не бу́дет я́блока, не бу́дет пирого́в.

У	Джо́на Све́ты Рома́на Харито́нова дире́ктора	нет (~~есть~~) не́ был**о** не бу́д**ет**	су́па. ка́ши. я́блока. пирого́в.

Exercise 19. **Transform the sentences in the past and the future.**

Example: У меня́ есть ку́ртка. → У меня́ была́ ку́ртка. У меня́ бу́дет ку́ртка.
У меня́ нет ку́ртки. → У меня́ не́ было ку́ртки. У меня́ не бу́дет ку́ртки.

1. У Анто́на есть хоро́ший друг. ______________________________
   У Анто́на нет хоро́шего дру́га. ______________________________
2. У студе́нта сего́дня есть заня́тия. ______________________________
   У студе́нта сего́дня нет заня́тий. ______________________________
3. У дире́ктора есть вре́мя. ______________________________
   У дире́ктора нет вре́мени. ______________________________

***Exercise 20.* Read the text. Answer the questions.**

ЧТО ГДЕ ЕСТЬ? ЧЕГÓ ГДЕ НЕТ?

В рýсской кýхне есть квас, а в европéйской кýхне нет кваса.
В англи́йской кýхне есть пýдинг, а в рýсской кýхне нет пýдинга.
В америкáнской кýхне есть стейк, а в рýсской кýхне нет стéйка.
В рýсской кýхне есть борщ, а в япóнской кýхне нет борщá.

В какой кýхне есть пельмéни?
В какой кýхне есть пéрец?
Чегó нет в кýхне Фрáнции?
В какóй кýхне нет мя́са?

***Exercise 21.* Look at the menu and say:**

Каки́е блю́да рýсские вáрят, жáрят, пекýт?
Каки́е блю́да рýсские едя́т[1] свéжие?
Каки́е блю́да рýсские едя́т солёные (use case № 4)?

[1] есть (SPECIAL): to eat (кýшать)

Example: Рýсские вáрят **ры́бу**.

Они́ вáрят: ____________________
Они́ жáрят: ____________________
Они́ пекýт: ____________________
Они́ едя́т свéжие: ____________________
Они́ едя́т солёные: ____________________

In the Russian language the infinitives of the verbs 'eat' (есть) and 'have' (be) (есть) correspond. The verb 'have' (be) doesn't alter in person in the Present, and the verb 'eat' does alter.

***Exercise 22.* Есть и есть. Find the verb 'eat' in the table at page 352. Write it down and remember.**

Infinitive	**Есть (Special): to eat**			
Present	я		мы	
	ты		вы	
	он(-á, -ó)		они́	
Past				

***Exercise 23.* Answer the questions.**

Что Вы еди́те ýтром? ____________________
Вы еди́те пóсле шести́ часóв вéчера? ____________________
Что мы все еди́м лéтом, когдá жáрко? ____________________
Ваш кот мнóго ест? ____________________
А что ест Вáша собáка? ____________________
Дéти плóхо едя́т. Что дéлать? ____________________
— У меня́ нет моегó закáза! — Oleg told the waiter.

— Извини́те. Сейча́с смотрю́. Борщ есть?

— Борща́ нет.

— А жа́реное мя́со есть?

— Жа́реного мя́са то́же нет.

— А блины́ есть?

— И блино́в то́же нет.

— Извини́те! Сейча́с Ваш зака́з бу́дет!

— О́чень мно́го вре́мени! — Oleg was surprised. — Почему́[1]?

— Потому́ что[2] Ваш зака́з ещё гото́вят на ку́хне, — said the waiter politely and went to the kitchen.

[1] why
[2] because

Model: — Почему́? — Потому́ что
(a question about the reason — the explanation of the reason)

— **Почему́** нет зака́за?

— **Потому́ что** зака́з ещё гото́вят на ку́хне.

Нет зака́за, **потому́ что** его́ ещё гото́вят на ку́хне.

7

***Exercise 24.* Open the brackets.**

Example: Я не бу́ду отдыха́ть в А́фрике (я не люблю́ жа́ркую пого́ду). — Я не бу́ду отдыха́ть в А́фрике, потому́ что я не люблю́ жа́ркую пого́ду.

1. Я спортсме́н (я люблю́ спорт)
2. Я не говорю́ по-испа́нски (не зна́ю испа́нский язы́к)
3. Я не́ был в теа́тре (в моём го́роде нет теа́тра)
4. Я изуча́ю матема́тику и фи́зику (моя́ профе́ссия — инжене́р)
5. Ле́том нет сне́га (ле́том жа́рко)
6. Я не гото́влю до́ма (у меня́ до́ма нет ку́хни)
7. Ка́тя не жа́рит мя́со (она́ вегетариа́нка[3])

[3] вегетариа́нец(-анка): a vegetarian

***Exercise 25.* A) Listen to the dialogues.**

Track 30

1. — Почему́ Вы не еди́те лапшу́?
   — Потому́ что у меня́ нет со́ли.
   — О, извини́те, вот соль.
   — Спаси́бо!
2. — Дава́йте говори́ть по-ру́сски!
   — У меня́ нет перево́дчика.
3. — Почему́ Вы не еди́те жа́реное мя́со?
   — Потому́ что я вегетариа́нец.
   — Вот сала́т, здесь нет мя́са. Прия́тного аппети́та!
   — Спаси́бо большо́е!
4. — Почему́ ты не де́лаешь зака́з?
   — Потому́ что у меня́ нет де́нег.
   — Нет де́нег? Э́то не пробле́ма[4]. У меня́ есть де́ньги!

[4] a problem

5. — Дава́йте рисова́ть!
   — У меня́ нет карандаша́ и бума́ги.
6. — Дава́йте писа́ть стихи́ по-япо́нски!
   — А я не зна́ю япо́нские слова́.
   — Э́то не пробле́ма! Слова́ есть в словаре́.
   — У нас нет словаря́.
   — А э́то пробле́ма!
7. — Дава́йте говори́ть по-кита́йски[1]!
   — Дава́йте!

[1] in Chinese

B) Make your own dialogues.

— Почему́ так до́лго[2]? — asked Oleg when the waiter brought only a glass of juice.

— Потому́ что блины́ пеку́т 40 мину́т, борщ ва́рят 30 мину́т и мя́со жа́рят 30 мину́т.

— У Вас есть пробле́ма? — asked John. He wanted to participate, but didn't know what else to say.

— У меня́ нет пробле́мы. А у по́вара сейча́с бу́дет пробле́ма.

They could hear Oleg's voice from the kitchen:

— У мои́х друзе́й есть пироги́, суп, мя́со и ры́ба. А у меня́ нет пирого́в, нет блино́в, нет су́па и нет мя́са! Почему́?!

— Извини́те, пожа́луйста, мы гото́вим! Ваш зака́з бу́дет о́чень бы́стро[3].

[2] long (adv.)
[3] quickly

Exercise 26. **Make one sentence with потому́ что out of two.**

Example: — Почему́ Вы не еди́те мя́со?
— Потому́ что я вегетариа́нец.
Я не ем мя́со, **потому́ что** я вегетариа́нец.

1. — Почему́ в Росси́и не едя́т крем-су́п?
   — В Росси́и э́то не традицио́нное блю́до.

   ____

2. — Почему́ Вы не еди́те в рестора́не?
   — У меня́ нет де́нег.

   ____

3. — Ни́на гото́вит до́ма?
   — Нет, у неё нет плиты́.

   ____

4. — Мы бу́дем сейча́с пить чай?
   — Нет, у нас нет вре́мени.

   ____

Model: Поэ́тому[1] (explanation of the consequence)[2]

(Я не ем мя́со, **потому́ что** я вегетариа́нец)

Я вегетариа́нец, **поэ́тому** я не ем мя́со.

Я вегетариа́нец, **поэ́тому** я не ем мя́со.

Я не ем мя́со, **потому́ что** я вегетариа́нец.

[1] so; that's why

[2] The sentences with conjunctions of cause and effect Потому́ что — Поэ́тому are inverted.

Exercise 27. **Reread the sentences that in the previous exercise. Change them according to the model.**

Example: Я не ем мя́со, потому́ что я вегетариа́нец. → Я вегетариа́нец, поэ́тому я не ем мя́со.

1. ____________________
2. ____________________
3. ____________________
4. ____________________

7

The interpreter did not come. John remembered that he had not called back to Masha. What a shame! How to explain his disappearance from the airport now? That he was captured by the hospitable Russians? As in a bad comedy?

By the way, cinematic stereotypes about Russians seemed to come true. On the table there was a jug of vodka, which Oleg had ordered. John suddenly remembered a paragraph from a textbook on the history: in some ancient times, it seemed, in the 11th century, Prince Vladimir, choosing a religion for Russia, said the famous phrase[3]:

[3] Весе́лие на Руси́ есть пи́ти не мо́жем без того́ бы́ти ("Drinking in Russia is fun, we can't exist without it")

Весѣлиє Роуси єсть пити не можемъ безъ того бꙑти

The story says that this argument was decisive in the choice of Christianity, which was loyal to wine, unlike, for example, Islam. "And maybe, Masha, being a Russian girl, would have perceived the situation as normal, — John thought. — They confused a man wih someone else, then drank vodka and everything was fine?" However, John put the phone back into his pocket again, deciding to postpone the call until he made up a more profound explanation. John found the verb 'drink' in the dictionary, its modern form was пить.

Exercise 28. **Find the verb пить in the table at page 351. Write it down and remember.**

Infinitive	**пить (Special): to drink**			
Present	я		мы	
	ты		вы	
	он(á, ó)		они́	
Past				

***Exercise 29.* Answer the questions.**

1. Что Вы пьёте у́тром, чай и́ли ко́фе? ___
2. Вы пьёте на рабо́те пи́во?___
3. Вы пьёте ко́ка-ко́лу? ___
4. Что пьют в Ва́шей семье́, когда́ жа́рко? ___
5. Ле́том в Росси́и лю́ди пьют квас. Э́то пра́вда? ___
6. Ва́ш друг пьёт алкого́ль? ___

To be on the safe side John refused the Russian vodka and ordered wine.

— Одна́ рю́мка во́дки! — Oleg was persuasive.

It was clear: «рю́мка во́дки». As in the English language "a shot of vodka" means a part of something and is indicated by the preposition 'of'. In Russian it is the genitive case.

All numbers except 1, 21, 31 and all others ending in 1 agree with the words that denote units in genitive case (case № 2)

sg. РУБЛЬ — pl. РУБЛИ́

Do not decline! Е́ВРО: 1 Е́ВРО, 7 Е́ВРО, 100 Е́ВРО

1 РУБЛЬ
2, 3, 4 + ДВА РУБЛ**Я́** (genitive sg.)
5, 6, 7 etc. + РУБЛ**Е́Й** (genitive pl.)

Compare: Ско́лько Вам лет? — Мне 21 год.
Мне 23 го́д**а**.
Мне 27 **лет**.

***Exercise 30.* Study the table, pay attention to how the rule works.**

1	он →	**оди́н**	оди́н час, оди́н **день**, оди́н ме́сяц, оди́н год
	оно́ →	**одно́**	одно́ число́
	она́ →	**одна́**	одна́ мину́та, одна́ секу́нда[1], одна́ неде́ля
2,	он →	**два**	два часа́, два дня, два ме́сяца, два го́да
	оно́ →	**два**	два числа́
	она́ →	**две**	две мину́ты, две секу́нды, две неде́ли
3, 4	он →	**три,**	три часа́
	оно́ →	**четы́ре**	три числа́
	она́ →		три мину́ты
5–...	он →	**пять,**	пять часо́в, шесть дней, оди́ннадцать лет
	оно́ →	**шесть,**	пять чи́сел
	она́ →	**...**	пять мину́т, три́дцать секу́нд

[1] a second

21, 31, **…**	он → онó → онá →	**оди́н** **однó** **однá**	двáдцать оди́н год сóрок однó числó три́дцать однá мину́та
22, 32,	он → онó → онá →	**два** **два** **две**	двáдцать два гóда двáдцать два числá двáдцать две мину́ты
23, 24, **33, 34,** **…**	он → онó → онá →	**три,** **четы́ре**	двáдцать три часá двáдцать три числá двáдцать три мину́ты

Exercise 31. **A) Look at the names of the dishes and containers.**

бáнка	a jar	пакéт	a plastic bag
бокáл	a glass (of wine)	пáчка	a packet
буты́лка	bottle	рю́мка	a shot
блю́до	a plate	сковородá	a frying pan
блю́дце	a saucer	стакáн	a glass (of water)
кастрю́ля	a saucepan	тарéлка	a plate
корóбка	a box	чáшка	a cup
лóжка	a spoon		

B) Using the table above and genitive plural, translate the phrases into Russian.

1 plastic bag ____________________
33 glasses (of water) ____________________
5 glasses (of wine) ____________________
21 spoon ____________________
2 frying pans ____________________
12 plates ____________________
1 saucepan ____________________
2 packets ____________________
2 plates ____________________
10 plastic bags ____________________
3 shots ____________________
8 jars ____________________
7 cups ____________________
4 boxes ____________________

REMEMBER!

Quantity + Container (case № 2) + Content (case № 2)

Оди́н стакáн молокá. Однá чáшка чáя. Однá кастрю́ля су́па

Content nouns in such phrases can be used in case № 2 sg (молокó, водá, суп, мáсло, винó, вóдка и др.)

оди́н стакáн молокá

однá тарéлка су́па

or in genitive pl. if a noun does not have the form of sg. (сли́вки, пельмéни, макарóны, духи́)

оди́н стакáн сли́вок

однá тарéлка пельмéней

Exercise 32. Match the words from the first column with the words from the second column and say it in Russian.

Example: однá чáшка воды́

чáшка	водá	______
лóжка	сли́вки	______
стакáн	чай	______
рю́мка	вóдка	______
бокáл	винó	______
кастрю́ля	суп	______
бáнка	варéнье	______
пакéт	пирожки́	______
буты́лка	молокó	______
корóбка	сáхар	______
пáчка	соль	______
тарéлка	кáша	______
сковородá	жáреный картóфель	______

Exercise 33. Correct the mistakes in the text.

У Áнна большóй семья́, поэ́тому онá готóвить оди́н большóй кастрю́ля суп, оди́н мáленький кастрю́ля кáша, два сковородá блины́, три́ пакéт сок.

______

______

______

______

— Однá рю́мка вóдки! — Oleg repeated and passed a shot to John.

— Спаси́бо! У меня́ есть оди́н бокáл винá! — answered John having looked at the table.

John noticed that his answer satisfied his new friends and each of them was drinking what they had ordered for themselves.

— У меня́ тóже оди́н бокáл винá! — Sveta smiled. — За здорóвье всех![1]

— За здорóвье!

— Я бýду пить вóдку оди́н? — Oleg got disappointed.

— Я тóже бýду пить вóдку, — said Roman.

John paid attention to the fact that he needed genitive case not only to stay sober but also to deal with his order and the bill.

[1] Cheers. A traditional Russian saying before drinking which foreigners often confused with На здорóвье. На здорóвье is a traditional response to the words 'thank you' Спаси́бо! — На здорóвье! (you are welcome). If Russians say За здорóвье they mean that they drink to health. They also drink to love, health, peace, you: За любóвь!, За здорóвье!, За мир!, За Вас!.

***Exercise 34.* A) Compare the two bills:**

Заќаз 1:	Заќаз 2:
Суп. Таре́лка (× 1) — 100 руб.[1] Ка́ша. Таре́лка (× 1) — 50 руб. Пирожо́к (× 1) — 35 руб. Чай. Ча́шка (× 1) — 20 руб.	Ка́ша. Таре́лка (× 4) — 200 руб. Сок. Стака́н (× 4) — 100 руб. Жа́реный карто́фель. Сковорода́ (×1) — 150 руб. Пельме́ни. Таре́лка (× 2) — 300 руб. Вино́. Буты́лка (× 1) — 2000 руб.
Счёт[2] 1 = 205 руб.	Счёт 2 = 2750 руб.

[1] руб. and коп. — abbreviations of рубль and копе́йка
[2] a bill

B) Compare the two bills and answer why the first one is small and the second one is so big:

1. Счёт 1 ма́ленький, потому́ что там одна́ таре́лка су́па, ____________________
2. Счёт 2 большо́й, потому́ что ____________________

C) Transform the sentences to the model Поэ́тому:

1. В зака́зе 1 есть одна́ таре́лка супа, __________, __________, поэ́тому счёт ма́ленький.
2. В зака́зе 2 есть __________, __________, __________, поэ́тому счёт большо́й.

7

Despite the fact that Roman supported the director and also began to drink vodka, Oleg was somehow upset by the fact that the guest refused to try strong drinks.

— В ру́сском рестора́не он пьёт францу́зское вино́! Эх, англича́не, англича́не! — said Oleg.

Although this remark was said with a smile, it really surprised John. By the other Russians' reaction he noticed that the criticism was perceived as a joke.

***Exercise 35.* Listen and repeat: the construction of doubling and its meanings.**

Track 31

A) Regret:

Эх, Ми́ша, Ми́ша!
Ох, ру́сский футбо́л, ру́сский футбо́л!

B) Cheering up, consent, confirmation:

Хорошо́-хорошо́!
Да-да́!
Говори́те-говори́те!

— Эх, Джон, Джон! — Oleg repeated, sincerely believing that there was a lot to lose. — Дава́йте, Джон, пе́йте! Дава́йте е́шьте!

Communicating with Russians, John noticed that they were very fond of the phrase "come on". If they invited each other to do something, they used the words дава́й or дава́йте. They invited each other to take joint action whenever it was possible.

Повели́тельное наклоне́ние — Imperative

It is quite convenient to form imperatives from the verbs in the third person ending in -ут/-ют, -ат/-ят (for imperfective verbs — the form of the Present tense, for perfective verbs — the form of the simple Future tense).
Они́ говоря́т. Они́ фотографи́руют.
The endings -ут, -ют, -ат, -ят are omitted.
Add to the stem:
Й (ты) и ЙТЕ (вы) if the stem ends in a vowel,
И (ты) и ИТЕ (вы) if the stem ends in a consonant.
Они́ говоря́т. — Говори́! Говори́те!
Они́ фотографи́руют. — Фотографи́руй! Фотографи́руйте!

Exercise 36. **Fill in the table using the rule of forming the imperative. Check it at the table at the end of the book (pp. 351–352).**

Infinitive	они́	ты	вы
де́лать	де́ла**ют**	де́ла**й**	де́ла**йте**
говори́ть	говор**я́т**	говор**и́**	говор**и́те**
учи́ться	у́ч**ат**ся	уч**и́**сь	уч**и́те**сь
танцева́ть	танцу́**ют**	танцу́**й**	танцу́**йте**
печь	пек**у́т**	пек**и́**	пек**и́те**
знать			
учи́ть			
отдыха́ть			
расска́зывать			
рисова́ть			
вари́ть			

Pay attention to the imperative forms of the following verbs:

Infinitive	они́	ты	вы
пить	пьют	пей	пе́йте
есть	едя́т	ешь	е́шьте
гото́вить	гото́вят	гото́вь	гото́вьте
жа́рить	жа́рят	жарь	жа́рьте

INTERESTING!

Etiquette: advice, request, command, criticism

Speaking in Russian, you will notice that the imperative form of the verb is used in the Russian language more often than in English. In the English language it is not accepted to voice requests and advice directly. To express request, English-speaking people prefer to use modal phrases (would you, should you, rarely ought to), questions or allegories: It seems to me it is a good (bad) thing to do, etc. In Russian, instead of these phrases you are more likely to hear Imperatives. Russian-speaking people often use Imperatives without special means of making them more polite in situations of caring, request or giving advice (by the way, to give advice in Russia is not considered to be impolite: advice is not perceived as an invasion, but rather as evidence that people care about the speaker. According to the poll 75% of Russians are ready to listen to unsolicited advice if it is useful and offers a good solution to the problem). Foreigners often perceive this behavior as rude, but it's not. Such verbal behaviour is associated with a weaker value of Imperative, and on the other hand, a stronger meaning of words such as пожа́луйста, спаси́бо and other words of politeness in Russian.

The word пожа́луйста in the Russian language has a much stronger emotional burden than the English 'please'. It has not lost its connection with the words жале́ть ('to sympathize' or 'to regret'), пожале́ть and is not simply the designation of request, but a request as such. Phrases Пиши́те, пожа́луйста!, Ду́майте, пожа́луйста!, Пожа́луйста, не де́лайте / де́лайте э́то! you can hear throughout the lessons with a teacher. Пожа́луйста, е́шьте!, Пожа́луйста, пе́йте! are polite invitations to the table, the advice to try food and drinks, and the words are perceived that way.

As the words дава́й, дава́йте: Дава́йте е́шьте, Дава́йте пейте, which Oleg used inviting John and his friends to do it together. A tone also plays an important role in the expression of polite requests.

You will notice that a lot of signs in the city are made with the negative Imperative form.

Не фотографи́ровать! (No photos)

Не сто́йте у кра́я платфо́рмы! (Mind the gap)

Не кури́ть! (No smoking) etc.

Russian advice is more expressive, insistent. However, it is not perceived by the Russian-speaking people as rude.

The words извини́те and прости́те still retained the connection with the words вина́ (guilt) and проще́ние (forgiveness), that is a Russian will apologize only if he really feels guilty. In most of the situations when American and European people feel that they have to say «sorry», a resident of Russia simply does not perceive that he is obliged to apologize. It especially concerns violations of the borders of personal space, when a person is getting too close, almost to the face, or touches you accidentally. These situations are not perceived as a reason for an apology, because they have no malice, and private space for Russian people as members of collectivist culture is of much smaller value than for the Europeans or Americans whose culture often can be viewed as an individualist one.

It is strongly not recommended to apologize for the apology! Neither извини́те nor прости́те is purely ritual form like 'sorry', both of those words suggest that you do not only regret about the incident, but ask for forgiveness. Responding to an apology, you can say: Ниче́го! (nothing

7

(meaning 'it's nothing serious')), Ничегó стрáшного! (nothing terrible (has happened)), Всё хорошó! (it's all right).

Russian спасибо is also stronger than the English 'thank you'. If you want to thank in Russian, reduce twice what you were going to say in English.

Thank you! = Спасибо!

Thank you very much! = Спасибо!

Thank you so much! = Спасибо!

Thank you so much! You are so kind! = Большóе спасибо!

Thank you so much! That's absolutely fantastic! = Большóе спасибо!

(See: Larina, T.V. Englishmen and Russians. Language. Culture. Communication. — M.: Languages of Slavic cultures, 2013. — 360 p.; Lauren, Anna-Lena. There is something wrong with their Russian heads. — M.: Publisher "Fluid", 2011. — 192 p.)

Request or command?

The degree of persistence of a request is determined not only by the presence of the word «пожáлуйста» but also by the tone.

ИК-3 — request: Учите, пожáлуйста, словá!

ИК-2 — command: Учите словá!

For an ultimate command use the Infinitive — Учить словá!!! Не курить!!!

***Exercise 37.* Transform a command to a request. Say these phrases, paying attention to the intonation.**

Example: Учите слóва! → Учите, пожáлуйста, словá.

1. Пéйте сок! ____________________
2. Читáйте книгу! ____________________
3. Говорите по-рýсски! ____________________
4. Бы́стро лети в Москвý! ____________________
5. Дéлайте салáт! ____________________

Asking to do something together: Давáй(те) + Infinitive

Давáй читáть! Давáй есть! Давáй(те) говорить по-францýзски!

The new friends started to treat John:

— Давáйте éшьте!

— Кладите, пожáлуйста, салáт!

— Берите, пожáлуйста, вот э́тот пирóг!

— Кладите кáшу! Э́то гýрьевская кáша. Традициóнное рýсское блю́до.

— Кладите-кладите, э́то óчень вкýсно!

— Берите, пожáлуйста, хлеб!

John heard two new verbs. In the form of Imperative they sounded like that: кладите and берите. Their meaning was generally clear: a guest is suggested to take something. But it was important to understand the difference.

Exercise 38. **Help John: find in the table how the verbs класть and брать are changed.**

Infinitive	кла**сть** (1.IR СТ–Д): to put				бра**ть** (1.R.CONS ! БР–БЕР): to take			
Present	я	клад**у́**	мы	клад**ём**	я	бер**у́**	мы	_____**ём**
	ты	_____**ёшь**	вы	_____**ёте**	ты	____**ёшь**	вы	_____**ёте**
	он, она́, оно́	_____**ёт**	они́	_____**ут**	он, она́, оно́	____**ёт**	они́	беру́т
Past	он	клал	они́	_____**ли**	он	брал	они́	_____**ли**
	она́	____**ла**			она́	____**ла́**		
	оно́	____**ло**			оно́	____**ло**		
Imperative	ты	Клад**и́**!	вы	____**и́те**!	ты	____**и́**!	вы	Бер**и́те**!

Exercise 39. **Read these small texts and answer the questions.**

A) *Model:* Брать что (case № 4) где (case № 6)

1. Мари́я Петро́вна берёт молоко́ на ры́нке. В магази́не она́ молоко́ не берёт. Она́ говори́т, что в магази́не молоко́ несве́жее.
   А где Вы берёте проду́кты?

2. Макси́м берёт де́ньги в ба́нке.
   А где Вы берёте де́ньги? А Ваш друг?
   Когда́ вам на́до е́хать бы́стро, Вы берёте такси́?
   Где молоды́е лю́ди беру́т кни́ги? А немолоды́е лю́ди где беру́т кни́ги?

B) *Model:* Брать что (case № 4) для[1] чего́ (case № 2)

1. Для бутербро́да Джон берёт бе́лый хлеб. Пото́м кладёт хлеб в то́стер[2] и немно́го печёт. Пото́м на хлеб он кладёт ма́сло и джем.
   А что Вы берёте для бутербро́да?

[1] for
[2] то́стер [тэ]: a toaster

C) *Model:* Класть что (case № 4) куда́ / во что (case № 4)

1. Ру́сские кладу́т в чай са́хар и лимо́н. А кита́йцы что кладу́т в чай? А англича́не?
2. Монго́лы и калмы́ки кладу́т в чай ма́сло и соль. Э́то пра́вда?
3. В Еги́пте в ко́фе кладу́т соль и пе́рец. А Вы кладёте соль в ко́фе? А пе́рец?
4. В Росси́и о́чень лю́бят сала́ты винегре́т и оливье́. А в Ва́шей стране́ како́й сала́т де́лают ча́сто? Что туда́ кладу́т?

Suddenly Oleg looked at the guest, pointed at his chest and said:
— Я ем.
— Да, — John agreed. It was obvious. The director demonstrated a good appetite.
Then Oleg pointed at Roman and Sveta.
— Он ест. Она́ ест. Мы еди́м.
— Да, коне́чно.
— А вы, Джон, не еди́те!
— Почему́? Я то́же ем.
— Вы еди́те о́чень ма́ло.
— Не понима́ю, — said John.

Oleg pointed at his chest again.

— Я пью.

— Да, — John nodded.

— Роман пьёт, Свéта пьёт. Мы пьём. А Вы не пьёте.

— Почемý? Я тóже пью! — John was surprised.

— Вы пьёте óчень мáло.

— Что э́то — мáло? — asked John.

***Exercise 40.* A) Read Oleg's story about himself and try to understand what the words мнóго, мáло mean.**

Я дирéктор. Я мнóго рабóтаю и мáло отдыхáю. У меня́ есть фи́рма. Там рабóтает мнóго людéй. В 8 часóв утрá мы ужé рабóтаем в óфисе. Мы рабóтаем нéсколько часóв. У нас обéд[1] в час дня. Но обы́чно у меня́ нет обéда, потомý что я дирéктор. И у меня́ мáло врéмени. У меня́ мнóго друзéй, но нет врéмени отдыхáть.

[1] lunch (у нас обéд = we are having lunch)

B) Using the table find and underline all the phrases with the words мнóго, мáло.

1. *Example:* Я **мнóго** рабóтаю.
   Question: **Скóлько** Вы рабóтаете?

2. *Example:* У меня́ **мнóго** друзéй.
   Question: **Скóлько** у Вас друзéй?

	Model:			**Examples:**
Few/little	Мáло	+	case № 2 (plural)	Здесь мáло людéй.
Many/much	Мнóго			У меня́ мнóго друзéй.
Some/a few/a little	Нéсколько			Я знáю нéсколько слов по-рýсски.

***Exercise 41.* Answer the questions using the words мнóго, мáло, нéсколько.**

1. Скóлько языкóв Вы знáете?
2. В скóльких стрáнах Вы бы́ли? В каки́х?
3. Скóлько в ми́ре хорóших писáтелей?
4. Скóлько в ми́ре извéстных спортсмéнов?
5. А скóлько хорóших людéй, как дýмаете?
6. У Вас обы́чно мнóго врéмени и́ли мáло?
7. Скóлько у Вас брáтьев и сестёр? А двоюрóдных брáтьев и сестёр?
8. Мнóго дéнег — э́то скóлько? А мáло дéнег?

***Exercise 42.* Say if something is few, little, many, much in your country (мнóго or мáло):**

Example: музéй → В моéй странé мнóго музéев.

1. гóрод ____________________
2. лес ____________________
3. рекá ____________________
4. óзеро ____________________
5. горá ____________________

6. совреме́нный худо́жник ______________________________

7. изве́стный писа́тель ______________________________

8. интере́сное ме́сто ______________________________

— А чего́ в А́нглии мно́го? — asked Sveta.

— В А́нглии мно́го хоро́шего ви́ски и банки́ров, — John smiled. — А ещё в А́нглии мно́го дожде́й.

— А я из Белору́ссии, — said Roman Kharitonov. — В Белору́ссии мно́го карто́феля. У нас о́чень вку́сный карто́фель.

— А я с Се́вера Росси́и, — said Sveta. — На Се́вере мно́го кра́сной ры́бы и кра́сной икры́. Джон, Вы лю́бите кра́сную икру́?

— Да, э́то о́чень вку́сно!

— А блины́ лю́бите? Мы кладём кра́сную икру́ в блины́.

— О, э́то о́чень интере́сно.

— Приглаша́ю[1] всех вас за́втра **в мой дом** на блины́[2].

[1] (1.R.VOW): to invite

[2] приглаша́ть на блины́ — invite to eat blini. Compare: приглаша́ть на день рожде́ния: invite to a birthday party; приглаша́ть на пра́здник: invite to a party; приглаша́ть на вы́ставку: invite to see an exhibition.

Exercise 43. **Make phrases using the model.**

Model: Кто (case № 1) приглаша́ет кого́ (case № 4) куда́ (case № 4)

Example: Анто́н. Мари́на. парк. → Анто́н приглаша́ет Мари́ну в парк.

1. Све́та. Джон. Теа́тр. ______________________________
2. Рома́н Харито́нов. Джон. Спорти́вный[3] клуб[4]. ______________________________
3. Оле́г. Джон. Ба́ня и стадио́н. ______________________________
4. Я. Ты. Рестора́н. ______________________________
5. Я. Вы. День рожде́ния. ______________________________
6. Худо́жник. Друзья́. Вы́ставка. ______________________________

ГОТО́ВИМ БЛИНЫ́

(реце́пт[5])

Берём большу́ю кастрю́лю. Кладём в кастрю́лю три яйца́, одну́ ло́жку са́хара, соль и ма́сло.

Берём четы́ре стака́на муки́[6], четы́ре стака́на молока́ (и́ли два стака́на молока́ и два стака́на воды́).

Гото́вим те́сто[7]: меша́ем[8] молоко́, муку́ и я́йца.

Пото́м берём сковороду́. Ста́вим её на плиту́. Жа́рим блины́ на ма́сле, на горя́чей[9] сковороде́.

Пото́м берём кра́сную икру́, варе́нье, мёд, я́годы, фру́кты, ры́бу, грибы́ и мно́го смета́ны. Кладём их на стол.

Пото́м приглаша́ем друзе́й и́ли семью́ на блины́.

Прия́тного аппети́та![10]

[3] sport (adj.)
[4] a club
[5] a recipe
[6] flour
[7] batter
[8] (1.R.VOW): to mix
[9] hot
[10] Enjoy your meal!

Exercise 44. **How are pancakes made in your country?**
Use the example of the recipe «Блины́» and write a recipe of your favourite meal.

Model: Что (case № 1) для чего́ (case № 2) — What for what

РУ́ССКИЙ ЭТИКЕ́Т. СЕРВИРО́ВКА СТОЛА́
RUSSIAN ETIQUETTE. SERVING THE TABLE

1. нож[1] для ма́сла
2. таре́лка для хле́ба и ма́сла
3. ло́жка[2] для пе́рвого блю́да[3]
4. ви́лка для холо́дных заку́сок
5. нож для заку́сок
6. ви́лка для мя́са и сала́тов
7. нож для вторы́х блюд
8. декорати́вная[5] таре́лка
9. таре́лка для су́па
10. ло́жка для десе́рта
11. ви́лка[4] для десе́рта
12. стака́н для воды́
13. бока́л для шампа́нского
14. бока́л для кра́сного вина́
15. бока́л для бе́лого вина́
16. салфе́тка

[1] a knife
[2] a spoon
[3] пе́рвое блю́до: a first course (soup)
[4] a fork
[5] decorative

John had already eaten everything and since the translator had not yet arrived, he decided to explain the situation:

— Я был в аэропорту́. Там был мужчи́на. Англича́нин. Ваш колле́га[1]. Я лете́л в Москву́... он — не лете́л, — said John, but after looking at his new friends' confused faces, he decided to let them deal with this situation themselves.

[1] a colleague

— Гости́ница, — he said. — Я е́ду в гости́ницу.

— Дава́йте ещё! — said Oleg pointing at John's bottle of wine and his jug of vodka.

— Нет-не́т, большо́е спаси́бо, но я е́ду отдыха́ть.

John was ready for the fact that the offer would be three times repeated and he had to reject it three times too. And that really happened! After the third rejection the waiter brought the bill. Despite all John's protests the Director Oleg grabbed all the checks. The waiter understood John's intention to pay for himself and brought two separate bills, but Oleg didn't allow the guest to pay. John remembered a book that his father had given him to read before the trip, it was an informal guide to Russia by a girl from Europe, who wrote that in Russia she learned two things: to appreciate, when you are being treated, and treat. Russians believe that these small pleasures make life better. If you are treated in Russia, talking about the sum of the restaurant bill is considered indecent. John relaxed and let himself accept this situation.

— Споко́йной но́чи! До свида́ния! До за́втра! — said Oleg, Roman and Sveta while John was getting into the taxi.

«До за́втра? До свида́ния? No no, проща́йте![2]» — John thought, settling on the seat. Oddly enough, he was not angry at these strange people, because of whom he had to stay in the Russian capital for at least one day longer. However, he didn't mean to meet them again and in his thought he said goodbye to them forever.

[2] adieu!

INTERESTING!

Russia and alcohol

The words пить, пи́во, пир[3] have the same root. Russians ate much and drank even more at feasts. The word пи́во, which now designates 'beer' used to name any drink from water to alcoholic beverage.

By the way, во́дка appeared in Russia relatively late. Grape alcohol in Russia was brought from Genoa in the 15th century, but it was used only as a medicine. Strong 40 % alcohol became popular in the 16th–17th centuries, when the government announced a monopoly on the production of vodka and established каба́к (a Russian name for inn or pub).

Traditionally, Russians drank beverages of natural fermentation, which had a small percentage of alcohol. Медову́ха (from the word мёд) is a drink infused with honey, квас is a drink produced from the fermentation of bread and yeast, сби́тень is a drink prepared by boiling honey and molasses (and, later, sugar) with hops and spices: cloves, cinnamon, ginger, pepper, bay leaf. Nowadays these drinks are served in restaurants with Russian cuisine.

[3] a feast

Exercise 45. Translate and guess! Ру́сские зага́дки о еде́ (Russian puzzles about food).

1. Бе́лый сла́дкий ка́мень[1]
   В на́шей ча́шке та́ет[2]
   А солёный ка́мень
   В на́шем су́пе та́ет.

2. Ба́нка — дом.
   Кто живёт в нём?
   Не лягу́шки[3], но зелёные,
   Не из мо́ря, но солёные?

3. Я́ркий[4], сла́дкий, молодо́й,
   Он в оде́жде золото́й.
   Он не конфе́та[5] с фа́брики[6],
   Он фрукт из жа́ркой А́фрики.

4. В те́сте
   Есть мно́го ме́ста,
   В нём не пу́сто —
   Там мя́со и капу́ста.

5. Не снег, но бе́лое всегда́.
   Ты пьёшь, но э́то не вода́.

6. Капу́ста, мя́со, о́вощи.
   Вари́ла до́ма ма́ма…

7. В печи́ пеку́т,
   На стол кладу́т.

8. Тётя в шля́пе на плите́
   Суп гото́вит в животе́.

9. Зу́бы есть, но она́ не ест.

[1] a stone
[2] (1.R.VOW): to melt
[3] a frog
[4] bright
[5] a sweet
[6] a factory

Chapter 8

Москва́... как мно́го в э́том зву́ке
Для се́рдца ру́сского слило́сь!
Как мно́го в нём отозвало́сь!

А.С. Пу́шкин. Евге́ний Оне́гин

Moscow... how much within that sound there lies
To make a Russian's heart awake,
How many echoes does it give and take…

— A. Pushkin, "Eugene Onegin"

Ве́чером в гости́нице...

***Exercise 1.* Listen to the dialogue between John and the receptionist.**

A) Here are some words and phrases that can be useful in a hotel:

Model: Для кого́ (case № 2) / Для чего́ (case № 2)

Preposition для + noun in case № 2 = addressee, receiver, purpose of something:

таре́лка для су́па (Chapter 7) — a bowl for soup

су́мка для рабо́ты — a bag for work

письмо́ для Анто́на — a letter for Anton

блины́ для друзе́й — blini for friends

«Одну́ мину́ту» («Одну́ секу́нду», «Пять мину́т»)[1] — asking to wait for a while.

[1] One minute! (One second! Five minutes!)

Model: Кто за́нят[2] (занята́, за́нято, за́няты)
Кто свобо́ден[3] (свобо́дна, свобо́дно, свобо́дны)

In order to form a shortened adjective one should omit the full form ending. In a sentence a shortened adjective serves as a predicate. You have already seen a shortened form of an adjective in the phrase: я рад.

To express past or future tense in a sentence with a shortened adjective, add the verb быть in the right form.

[2] to be busy (shortened form of the adj.)
[3] to be free (not busy) (shortened form of the adj.)

Извини́те, я сейча́с **за́нят**. Я рабо́таю.	Дом **за́нят**. Там живу́т Ивано́вы.
Вчера́ ве́чером А́нна **была́ занята́**. Она́ гото́вила суп.	Ра́ньше э́та кварти́ра **была́ занята́**. Там жи́ли Ивано́вы.
О́сенью де́ти **бу́дут за́няты**. Они́ бу́дут учи́ться.	Ко́мнаты **бу́дут за́няты**. О́сенью тут бу́дут жить но́вые студе́нты.
	Э́то ме́сто **за́нято**. Вот мой биле́т.

Synonyms: **брони́ровать**[1] (1.IR ОВА-У) (что? case № 4) **но́мер**[2]
резерви́ровать[3] (1.IR ОВА-У) (что? case № 4) **гости́ницу**

[1] to book
[2] number
[3] to reserve

B) Answer the questions:

1. Како́й но́мер резерви́ровали для Джо́на?
2. Како́й но́мер взял Джон?
3. Почему́?

C) Check your answers.

Track 32

— Здра́вствуйте! Меня́ зову́т Джон Янг. Для меня́ резерви́ровали но́мер?

— До́брый ве́чер! Да, для Вас резерви́ровали но́мер трина́дцать.

— Извини́те, мо́жет быть, у вас есть друго́й[4] но́мер? Трина́дцатый но́мер — э́то не о́чень хорошо́ для меня́.

— О, я понима́ю. Одну́ мину́ту... Есть но́мер два́дцать два. Э́то то́же люкс[5]. Ой... извини́те, но́мер два́дцать два сейча́с за́нят. Но есть но́мер три́дцать пять. Он свобо́ден.

— Да, но́мер три́дцать пять — э́то отли́чно!

— Добро́ пожа́ловать!

— Спаси́бо!

[4] another
[5] luxe

INTERESTING!

Did you know?

In Russia, as in many Christian countries, it is believed that the number 13 is unlucky. It is called "the devil's dozen". We can trace the Scandinavian idea of the 13th god Loki, god of war and death and the Christian symbolism of the thirteenth follower — traitor Judas. Number 7 is usually considered to be a happy alternative to the number 13.

У́тром в гости́нице...

John woke up late and saw a text message from Masha.

Exercise 2. **Read the Masha's and John's text messages. Answer the questions and underline the necessary information.**

1. Куда́ е́дет Ма́ша?
2. Как далеко́ от Москвы нахо́дится э́тот го́род?
3. Как до́лго Ма́ша бу́дет там?
4. Ма́ша обижа́ется[6] на Джо́на?

[6] обижа́ться (1.R.VOW): to be offended (на кого? case № 4 на что? case № 4) обижа́ться на роди́телей / обижа́ться на жизнь

Ма́ша, пожа́луйста, извини́! Я прилете́л в Москву́, но не мог встре́тить тебя́ в аэропорту́. Э́то о́чень стра́нная исто́рия. Я понима́ю. Ты свобо́дна за́втра?

Извини́, Джон, за́втра я занята́.

Ты обижа́ешься?

Нет, всё хорошо́. Я пра́вда занята́ за́втра. Уже́ сентя́брь. За́втра я е́ду на пра́ктику[1].

Куда́ ты е́дешь?

В Каза́нь.

Э́то го́род?

Да.

Каза́нь — э́то о́чень далеко́? Э́то в Казахста́не?

Нет, э́то бли́зко. Э́то в Татарста́не.

Где э́то?

900 киломе́тров[2] — одна́ ночь в по́езде.

Да, э́то о-о-о́чень бли́зко ☺.

Хорошо́, что я не е́ду во Владивосто́к!

Э́то далеко́?

Э́то шесть ноче́й в по́езде и́ли во́семь часо́в в самолёте.

Да, хорошо́, что ты не е́дешь во Владивосто́к! А Каза́нь — краси́вый го́род?

Каза́нь — о́чень краси́вый и интере́сный го́род.

Ско́лько вре́мени ты бу́дешь в Каза́ни?

Оди́н ме́сяц.

Как до́лго! Уда́чи[3], Ма́ша!

Спаси́бо! Пиши́!

Я бу́ду писа́ть. До свида́ния!

[1] traineeship
[2] киломе́тр (case № 2 киломе́тров): kilometre
[3] good luck!
[4] breakfast

After the conversation John ordered breakfast.

— Я ем мой за́втрак[4], — he said to himself when the waiter brought a plate of scrambled eggs and coffee.

— Я **съ**ел мой за́втрак, — he said, when the waiter took away the empty plate. Well, it can be sorted out. Есть is a process, съесть is a result. «Ты пил, но не **вы**пил», Roman told him yesterday at lunch. Hence, the notion of perfect and imperfect in the Russian language is solved by a prefix.

Exercise 3. **Look at the table of the category of Aspect of the most common Russian verbs. Analyze the table. Answer the question: Was the conclusion made by the hero about the formation of Aspect in the Russian language right?**

Образова́ние ви́дов глаго́ла — The Aspect of the verb: formation

	Imperfect (IPF) Что де́лать?	Perfect (PF) Что сде́лать?	Translation
prefixes с- по- вы- за- при-	де́лать (1.R.VOW)	**с**де́лать (1.R.VOW)	to do
	вари́ть (2.R.CONS.1)	**с**вари́ть (2.R.CONS.1)	to cook
	фотографи́ровать (1.IR ОВА-У)	**с**фотографи́ровать (1.IR ОВА-У)	to take photos
	чита́ть (1.R.VOW)	**про**чита́ть (1.R.VOW)	to read
	знать (1.R.VOW)	**у**зна́ть (1.R.VOW)	to know / to learn
	писа́ть (1.IR С-Ш)	**на**писа́ть (1.IR С-Ш)	to write
	рисова́ть (1.IR ОВА-У)	**на**рисова́ть (1.IR ОВА-У)	to draw
	рабо́тать (1.R.VOW)	**по**рабо́тать (1.R.VOW)	to work
	ду́мать (1.R.VOW)	**по**ду́мать (1.R.VOW)	to think
	смотре́ть (2.R.CONS.1)	**по**смотре́ть (2.R.CONS.1)	to look
	звони́ть (2.R.CONS.1)	**по**звони́ть (2.R.CONS.1)	to phone
	слу́шать (1.R.VOW)	**по**слу́шать (1.R.VOW)	to listen
	учи́ть (2.R.CONS.2)	**вы́**учить (2.R.CONS.2)	to learn
	гото́вить (2.IR Б, П, М, В + Л)	**при**гото́вить (2.IR Б, П, М, В + Л)	to prepare
	печь (1.IR Ч-К-Ч)	**ис**пе́чь (1.IR Ч-К-Ч)	to bake
	хоте́ть (SPECIAL)	**за**хоте́ть (SPECIAL)	to want
	брони́ровать (1.IR ОВА-У)	**за**брони́ровать (1.IR ОВА-У)	to book
	резерви́ровать (1.IR ОВА-У)	**за**резерви́ровать (1.IR ОВА-У)	to reserve
	ненави́деть (2.IR Д-Ж)	**воз**ненави́деть (2.IR Д-Ж)	to hate
	та́ять (1.R.VOW)	**рас**та́ять (1.R.VOW)	to melt
suffixes -а-/-и- -я-/-и-	изуч**а́**ть (1.R.VOW)	изуч**и́**ть (2.R.CONS.2)	to study
	реш**а́**ть (1.R.VOW)	реш**и́**ть (2.R.CONS.2)	to decide
	повтор**я́**ть (1.R.VOW)	повтор**и́**ть (2.R.CONS.1)	to repeat
	объясн**я́**ть (1.R.VOW)	объясн**и́**ть (2.R.CONS.1)	to explain
	отвеч**а́**ть (1.R.VOW)	отве́т**ить** (2.IR Т-Ч)	to answer
	провер**я́**ть (1.R.VOW)	прове́р**ить** (2.R.CONS.1)	to check
	вспомин**а́**ть (1.R.VOW)	вспо́мн**ить** (2.R.CONS.1)	to remember
	исправл**я́**ть (1.R.VOW)	испра́в**ить** (2.IR Б, П, М, В + Л)	to correct
-ыва-/-а- -ива-/-и- -ыва-/-ы- -ва-/-а-	расска́з**ыва**ть (1.R.VOW)	рассказ**а́**ть (1.IR З-Ж)	to tell
	зака́з**ыва**ть (1.R.VOW)	заказ**а́**ть (1.IR З-Ж)	to order
	спра́ш**ива**ть (1.R.VOW)	спрос**и́**ть (2.IR С-Ш)	to ask
	забы**ва́**ть (1.R.VOW)	заб**ы́**ть (SPECIAL)	to forget
	да**ва́**ть (1.IR ВА-Ø)	д**а**ть (SPECIAL)	to give
	прода**ва́**ть (1.IR ВА-Ø)	прод**а́**ть (SPECIAL)	to sell

-а-/-ну-	отдыха́ть (1.R.VOW)	отдохну́ть (1.IR НУ)	to relax / to have a rest
по-...-а-/ -и-	**по**купа́ть (1.R.VOW)	купи́ть (2.IR Б, П, М, В + Л)	to buy
suppletive pairs: one verb but two different forms	говори́ть (2.R.CONS.1)	сказа́ть (1.IR З-Ж)	to tell / to say
	переводи́ть (2.IR Д-Ж)	перевести́ (1.IR СТ-Д)	to translate
	понима́ть (1.R.VOW)	поня́ть (1.IR НЯ-ЙМУ)	to understand
	брать (1.R.CONS ! БР-БЕР)	взять (1.IR Я-МУ)	to take
	класть (1.IR СТ-Д)	положи́ть (2.R.CONS.2)	to put

По- is very frequent. Many of the verbs you know form the perfect with the help of this prefix:

по- + танцева́ть, за́втракать, обе́дать, у́жинать, жа́рить, носи́ть, жить, гуля́ть, игра́ть, учи́ться, люби́ть, занима́ться.

***Exercise 4.* Compare:**

танцева́ть — потанцева́ть, за́втракать — поза́втракать…

REMEMBER!

The prefix not only creates the perfect form, but also adds its own meaning. Do not be surprised if you find one verb with different prefixes. See the meanings in the dictionary.
For example: **с**вари́ть, **за**вари́ть, **от**вари́ть (1— result: Ма́ма свари́ла суп, семья села есть. 2 — put in boiling water for infusion: завари́ть чай, 3 — make boiled: Отвари́те рис, положи́те его́ в сала́т); сде́лать — переде́лать (1 — the action is completed: Оте́ц сде́лал но́вый стол; 2 — the action is redone: Студе́нт переде́лал зада́ние, потому́ что снача́ла сде́лал его́ непра́вильно.

John realized that he had to learn pairs of verbs together and then practice the use and conjugation. Having taken a small list of verbs familiar to him and found their perfect couple in a dictionary, he began to practice.

While doing something he commented his actions in Russian.

— **Проце́сс**… Сейча́с… Что я де́лаю сейча́с? Сейча́с я де́лаю предложе́ние. Сейча́с я пишу́ предложе́ние в блокно́те. Сейча́с я чита́ю разгово́рник. Сейча́с я ду́маю о ру́сском языке́. Я о́чень до́лго ду́маю о ру́сском языке́. А сейча́с я де́лаю оши́бку, но бы́стро исправля́ю её. О, я вспомина́ю слова́! А сейча́с я хочу́ яи́чницу, и я ем яи́чницу. А сейча́с я хочу́ ко́фе и пью ко́фе.

Я весь день ду́маю о ру́сском языке́. Я всё у́тро де́лаю предложе́ния по-ру́сски.

— **Преде́л (Результа́т)**… Что я уже́ сде́лал неда́вно? Я сде́лал предложе́ние. Я написа́л предложе́ние в блокно́те. Я прочита́л весь разгово́рник. Я поду́мал о ру́сском языке́ (а сейча́с я не ду́маю о нём). Я то́лько что сде́лал оши́бку, но сра́зу испра́вил её. Я вспо́мнил все слова́. Я захоте́л яи́чницу и съел её. Я захоте́л ко́фе и вы́пил его́. Я молоде́ц! Я вы́учил э́ту грамма́тику!

***Exercise 5.* Compare the use of verbs in imperfect (IPF) and perfect forms (PF). Find which of the items of the table are each of John's arguments refer to.**

Значе́ния ви́дов глаго́ла — The meaning of the verb aspect

<table>
<tr><th>Imperfect (IPF)</th><th>Perfect (PF)</th></tr>
<tr><td>

1. A CONTINUOUS ACTION

(⟶)

1. "an action in progress"

Markers: весь (вс**ю**, всё, все)[1], 1 час, 2 часа́, мно́го часо́в.

Он весь ве́чер **чита́л**. — He has been reading for the whole evening.

Он **рабо́тал** мно́го часо́в. — He has been working for many hours.

2. "the accent on the duration of the action, not on the result"

— Что Вы **де́лали** вчера́? — What were you doing yesterday?

— **Чита́л** текст, **писа́л** и **учи́л** слова́. — I was reading a text, writing and learning the words.

</td><td rowspan="2">

3. A COMPLETED ACTION

(∨)

1. "a period of time which is completed"

markers: наконе́ц[7], уже, ещё не, весь (вс**ю**, всё, все) торт, 2 письма́.

Он **поéл торт**, но **съел** не весь торт, а то́лько 2 куска́. — He ate a cake, but he didn't eat all the cake, only two pieces.

Я зна́ю, что вчера́ ве́чером Вы отли́чно **позанима́лись**. — I know that yesterday evening you studied well.

2. "the focus on the presence on the action"

— Вчера́ **пришли́** мои́ друзья́. Они́ **принесли́** но́вый фильм, мы его́ **посмотре́ли**, **попи́ли** чай, пото́м они́ **ушли́**.

— Что Вы **сде́лали**?

— **Прочита́л** текст, **написа́л** упражне́ние[8], **вы́учил** слова́.

3. "a single fact"

markers: а сего́дня, но вчера́[9], одна́жды[10], и сего́дня (вчера́) то́же.

Обы́чно я пью чай, **а сего́дня вы́пил** ко́фе. — Usually I drink tea, but today I have drunk coffee.

[1] all (the whole)
[2] usually
[3] regularly
[4] rarely
[5] sometimes
[6] every
[7] at last
[8] exercise
[9] yesterday
[10] once, one day

</td></tr>
<tr><td>

2. THE ACTION WHICH HAPPENS REGULARLY

(=∨=∨=∨)

1. "regularly"

markers: всегда́, обы́чно[2], регуля́рно[3], ча́сто, ре́дко[4], иногда́[5], никогда́ (negation); ка́ждый (ка́жд**ую**, ка́ждое, ка́ждые)[6].

Ве́чером он **обы́чно** смо́трит телеви́зор. — In the evening he usually watches TV.

О́льга никогда́ не лета́ла на самолёте. — Olga has never flown by plane.

(⟶ ⟶ ⟶)

2. Я преподава́тель и рабо́таю в шко́ле. — I am a teacher and I work at school.

Ра́ньше я де́лал маши́ны, а сейча́с де́лаю велосипе́ды. — I used to make cars, now I make bicycles.

</td></tr>
</table>

Meanwhile, John continued to study the Aspect pairs of the Russian verb: if I did something yesterday, how to identify where there was a process, an action with the result, or the limit?

Я чита́л кни́гу, но не **про**чита́л её. (there was a process but not a result)

Вчера́ я вари́л суп, но не свари́л его́ и поу́жинал в рестора́не.

For convenience, John invented the system:

Paragraph 1.2 (IPF) — as if we scanned the list in the calendar and remembered their details and circumstances.

(Action in the past has the form of a line and has length in time (⟶).)

Paragraph 3.2 (PF) — as if we scanned the list of things we did yesterday and ticked what has already been done. Action has the form of a point, it is important to tick only the very existence of the action (∨).

— Что ты **де́лал** вчера́? (——➤)

— Я **чита́л** кни́гу. (——➤)

— Ты **прочита́л** её? (∨)

— Нет ещё не **прочита́л**. (∨)

— А что ты **сде́лал** ещё? (∨)

— Ещё я **пообе́дал** (∨) в рестора́не, **послу́шал** (∨) диало́ги, **написа́л** (∨) СМС[1], **поговори́л**. (∨)

[1] [эс эм эс]: sms

(2.1) If you think about the frequency of the action, it is, in the logic of Russians, a process consisting of a number of completed actions (=∨=∨=∨). Phrases can be joined on the contrast in pairs.

Я **ка́ждый день пишу́** план в ежедне́внике. (=∨=∨=∨) **А сего́дня** я **написа́л** в ежедне́внике стихи́. (∨)

Я **всегда́ пишу́** план в ежедне́внике. (=∨=∨=∨) **И сего́дня то́же написа́л** план. (∨)

(2.2) My current job is that what I do on a regular basis in the Present, it is true now, and past work is what was true at one time, what I was doing on a regular basis.

Я **рабо́таю** на фи́рме. Я **де́лаю** прое́кты. (——➤——➤——➤)

Ра́ньше я **рабо́тал** в о́фисе в Ло́ндоне, а **сейча́с рабо́таю** в Москве́.

***Exercise 6.* Read and explain the phrases, match the actions with the the symbols (——➤, =∨=∨=∨, ——➤——➤——➤, ∨), then check the answers:**

(1.1. vs 3.1.) Он весь день чита́л кни́гу и наконе́ц прочита́л её.

(1.2. vs 3.2.) Что Джон де́лал ве́чером и у́тром? Заброни́ровал гости́ницу, прочита́л СМС, написа́л отве́т, поза́втракал, изуча́л грамма́тику.

(2.1. vs 3.3.) Ра́ньше он никогда́ не вари́л ко́фе, но сего́дня свари́л.

Обы́чно он не кладёт де́ньги в карма́н, но сего́дня положи́л.

Он всегда́ чита́ет СМС и сего́дня то́же прочита́л.

(1.1. vs 1.1.) Сейча́с он изуча́ет ру́сский язы́к, а ра́ньше он изуча́л францу́зский.

***Exercise 7.* Read the sentences. Look at the table and say the Aspect of the verb.**

1. Мой друг **учи́л** но́вые слова́. — Он **вы́учил** но́вые слова́.
2. Студе́нт **обе́дал** в кафе́. Он **пообе́дал** в кафе́.
3. Дире́ктор **покупа́л** кни́ги. Дире́ктор **купи́л** кни́ги.

***Exercise 8.* Say that you have already done it.**

Example: — Андре́й чита́ет рома́н «Война́ и мир».
— А я **уже́** прочита́л его́.

[2] a film, a movie

1. Ви́ктор смо́трит фильм[2] «Тита́ник». А Вы? ____________________
2. А́нна пи́шет письмо́. А Ве́ра? ____________________
3. Русла́н у́чит грамма́тику. А его́ друг? ____________________
4. Ива́н реша́ет пробле́му. А Анто́н? ____________________
5. Мари́на смо́трит футбо́л. А Джон? ____________________

***Exercise 9.* Answer the questions using the model потому́ что.**

Example: Почему́ ты не у́чишь текст? → Я не учу́ текст, потому́ что я уже́ вы́учил его́.

1. Почему́ ты не пи́шешь письмо́? ______________________
2. Почему́ ты не звони́шь домо́й? ______________________
3. Почему́ ты не покупа́ешь хлеб? ______________________
4. Почему́ не реша́ешь зада́чу? ______________________
5. Почему́ ты не смо́тришь кино́? ______________________

An indication of time in the Aspect (markers): time (process of the action)

Model 1: **Ско́лько вре́мени** ты рабо́тал? / **Как до́лго** ты рабо́тал?
Я рабо́тал 5 часо́в (я учи́л слова́ мно́го дней, я слу́шал му́зыку не́сколько часо́в)

Я рабо́тал 5 часо́в.

5 часо́в

6:00 **9:00** **14:00** **18:00**

не рабо́тал **рабо́тал** **не рабо́тал**

REMEMBER!

That the phrases "how long" with the words оди́н, одна́, одно́ are in the case № 4): оди́н день (ме́сяц, год); одну́ неде́лю (мину́ту, суббо́ту, ночь); одно́ у́тро (воскресе́нье, ле́то).

***Exercise 10.* Do you remember what case you should use after the number? Write how long you have been doing it.**

1. Ско́лько вре́мени Вы чита́ли э́ту кни́гу? (2, день) ______________________
2. Ско́лько вре́мени Вы изуча́ли грамма́тику? (8, неде́ля) ______________________
3. Ско́лько вре́мени Вы живёте в Росси́и? (1, ме́сяц) ______________________
4. Как до́лго он де́лал э́то упражне́ние? (1, мину́та) ______________________

Model 2: **Ско́лько вре́мени** ты рабо́тал? / **Как до́лго** ты рабо́тал?
Я рабо́тал весь день, всю неде́лю, всё ле́то, все выходны́е[1].

[1] выходно́й: a day off (a noun in the form of an adjective, declines as an adjective)

Я рабо́тал всё ле́то.

весна́ **ле́то** **о́сень**

рабо́тал

REMEMBER!

That the phrases "how long" with the words весь, вся, всё, все are in case № 4):
Весь день (ве́чер, понеде́льник, вто́рник, четве́рг, ме́сяц, янва́рь, Но́вый год, час).
Всю неде́**лю** (сре́ду, пя́тницу, суббо́ту, ночь, мину́ту, секу́нду, весну́, зи́му, о́сень).
Всё у́тро (воскресе́нье, ле́то, Рождество́, 1-ое ма́я, вре́мя).
Все выходны́е (кани́кулы, пра́здники).

Sequence (Action repetition)

Model 3: Как ча́сто ты рабо́тал?
Я рабо́тал ка́ждый день (ка́ждую неде́лю, ка́ждое ле́то, ка́ждые выходны́е)

Я рабо́тал ка́ждый день, всю неде́лю.

Понеде́льник	Вто́рник	Среда́	Четве́рг	Пя́тница	Суббо́та
рабо́тал	**рабо́тал**	**рабо́тал**	**рабо́тал**	**рабо́тал**	**рабо́тал**

REMEMBER!

That ка́ждый, ка́ждая, ка́ждое, ка́ждые are in case № 4):
Ка́ждый день (ве́чер, понеде́льник, вто́рник, четве́рг, ме́сяц, янва́рь, Но́вый год, час).
Ка́ждую неде́**лю** (сре́ду, пя́тницу, суббо́ту, ночь, мину́ту, секу́нду, весну́, зи́му, о́сень).
Ка́ждое у́тро (воскресе́нье, ле́то, Рождество́, 1-ое ма́я).
Ка́ждые выходны́е (кани́кулы, пра́здники).

Model 4: Как ча́сто ты рабо́тал?
Я рабо́тал всегда́.

The most frequent adverbs: всегда́, обы́чно, регуля́рно, ча́сто, ре́дко, иногда́ (when the action is in the past we add ра́ньше, в про́шлом, давно́, мно́го лет (1 год, 2, 3, 4 го́да) наза́д[1], в про́шлом году́, на про́шлой неде́ле.

[1] before, in the past, long ago, many years ago (1, 2, 3, 4 years) ago

Exercise 11. **Determine if this is the process or the repetition of the action.**

1. Я чита́ю э́ту кни́гу весь день. — Я чита́ю э́ту кни́гу ка́ждый день.
2. Я изуча́л матема́тику весь год. — Я изуча́л матема́тику ка́ждый год.
3. Я отдыха́ю на ю́ге всё ле́то. — Я отдыха́ю на ю́ге ка́ждое ле́то.
4. Я учу́ ру́сский язы́к весь день. — Я учу́ ру́сский язы́к ка́ждый день.
5. Мы бы́ли в Пари́же мно́го дней. — Мы бы́ли в Пари́же ка́ждый год.

Exercise 12. **How do you understand these expressions?**

Все лю́ди — Ка́ждый челове́к

Exercise 13. Complete the phrases:

Example: Я ду́маю[1], что все лю́ди лю́бят отдыха́ть, но не ка́ждый челове́к лю́бит рабо́тать.
Я ду́маю, что все лю́ди бра́тья.

> [1] ду́мать/поду́мать (1.R.VOW): to think

1. Я ду́маю, что все де́ти ____________________
2. Я ду́маю, что ка́ждый ребёнок ____________________
3. Я ду́маю, что все мужчи́ны ____________________
4. Я ду́маю, что ка́ждый мужчи́на ____________________
5. Я ду́маю, что все же́нщины ____________________
6. Я ду́маю, что ка́ждая же́нщина ____________________

Exercise 14. Say how often you do these things Как ча́сто? (Use adverbs in _Model 4_, p. 189.)

Example: чита́ть журна́лы. → Как ча́сто Вы чита́ете журна́лы? — Иногда́ я чита́ю журна́лы.

1. смотре́ть телеви́зор
2. писа́ть пи́сьма домо́й[2]
3. отдыха́ть в тёплых стра́нах
4. спать днём
5. рабо́тать в воскресе́нье
6. переводи́ть но́вые слова́
7. повторя́ть оши́бки[3]
8. забыва́ть хоро́ших люде́й
9. гото́вить традицио́нные блю́да
10. брать кни́ги в библиоте́ке
11. та́ять от комплиме́нтов[4]
12. объясня́ть просты́е ве́щи
13. понима́ть рома́нтиков[5]
14. говори́ть пра́вду
15. класть де́ньги в банк
16. ду́мать о семье́
17. смотре́ть в бу́дущее[6]
18. слу́шать друго́го челове́ка

> [2] домо́й (куда?): home (where?)
> [3] a mistake
> [4] a compliment
> [5] a romantic person
> [6] future

Exercise 15. Say everything above in the negative using the word никогда́ не. Pay attention to the double negation!

Example: Иногда́ я чита́ю журна́лы. — Я **никогда́ не** чита́ю журна́лы.

Exercise 16. Find the Perfect pair to the verbs in exercise 14.

Example: Я смотрю́ телеви́зор ка́ждый день. — Вчера́ я посмотре́л но́вый фильм.

Я ре́дко пишу́ пи́сьма домо́й. — Вчера́ я написа́л большо́е письмо́ домо́й.
Я никогда́ не сплю днём. — А вчера́ я поспа́л днём це́лый час.

Exercise 17. Read the dialogues. Look at the table and indicate the Aspect. Explain the meaning using the table of Aspect meanings.

1. — Мари́я, что ты **де́лала** вчера́?
   — У́тром я **учи́лась**, днём **гото́вила** обе́д, а ве́чером **чита́ла** журна́л.
2. — Что ты уже́ **сде́лала**?
   — Я **сде́лала** мно́го. Я **прочита́ла** текст, **повтори́ла** слова́ и **вы́учила** стихи́[7].
3. — Где Вы **купи́ли** э́ту кни́гу?
   — Я **купи́л** э́ту кни́гу в кни́жном магази́не, в це́нтре. Я **ча́сто покупа́ю** кни́ги в э́том магази́не.

> [7] (pl.): verse (poems)

4. — Вы чита́ли газе́ту «Спорт»?
— Да, я чита́л э́ту газе́ту.
— А Вы прочита́ли статью́[1] о футбо́ле?
— Коне́чно, прочита́л.
— Мо́жно мне посмотре́ть э́ту статью́?
— Пожа́луйста.

5. — Где Вы бы́ли вчера́ днём?
— Я был в магази́не «Кни́ги».
— Что Вы там де́лали?
— Я покупа́л учёбники[2] по ру́сскому языку́.
— Вы что́-нибудь купи́ли?
— Да, я купи́л ру́сско-францу́зский слова́рь.

[1] an article
[2] a textbook (manual)

ATTENTION!

ру́сск**ий** + францу́зский	ру́сск**о**-францу́зский слова́рь ру́сск**о**-францу́зская фи́рма
францу́зск**ий** + ру́сский	францу́зск**о**-ру́сский
япо́нский + францу́зский	япо́нск**о**-францу́зский
НО! английйский + ру́сский	**а́нгло**-ру́сский
английйский + япо́нский	**а́нгло**-япо́нский

Exercise 18. **Study the conjugation of the verb чита́ть.**

REMEMBER!

1. The Simple Future tense differs from the Present tense by the prefix.
   Prefix + Present tense = Simple Future tense
2. Complex Future tense: Я бу́ду чита́ть рома́н Толсто́го (I will be reading the novel but I don't know if I'll read it to the end).
3. Simple Future tense: Я прочита́ю рома́н Толсто́го (I'm sure I'll read it till the end).

Useful tips: the endings of the verbs in the Future tense of the Perfect Aspect coincide with the endings of the verbs in the Present tense of the Imperfect Aspect.
Чита́ю — прочита́ю, слу́шаю — послу́шаю, ду́маю — поду́маю, зна́ю — узна́ю.
It only can be applied to those verbs which form the Aspect pairs with the help of the prefixes.
Imperfective verbs have Complex Future tense and Simple Future tense (to emphasize the development of the action or its frequency and relevance in the future — see the meaning in the Aspect table, p. 184).
Perfective verbs have only Simple Future tense (the meaning of the limit).

Verb forms	IPF		PF	
Infinitive	**чита́ть**		**прочита́ть**	
Past	я, ты, он	чита́л	я, ты, он	прочита́л
	я, ты, она́	чита́ла	я, ты, она́	прочита́ла
	мы, вы, они́	чита́ли	мы, вы, они́	прочита́ли
Present	я	чита́ю	—	
	ты	чита́ешь		
	он, она́	чита́ет		
	мы	чита́ем		
	вы	чита́ете		
	они́	чита́ют		
Future	я	бу́ду чита́ть	я	прочита́ю
	ты	бу́дешь чита́ть	ты	прочита́ешь
	он, она́	бу́дет чита́ть	он, она́	прочита́ет
	мы	бу́дем чита́ть	мы	прочита́ем
	вы	бу́дете чита́ть	вы	прочита́ете
	они́	бу́дут чита́ть	они́	прочита́ют
Imperative	Чита́й! Чита́йте!		Прочита́й! Прочита́йте!	

What do you think: why do perfective verbs have no present forms?

If the Aspect verb pair is formed by a suffix or another stem, this perfective verb will change differently in Simple Future tense.

***Exercise 19.* Fill in the table of common but difficult verb pairs.**

See conjugations of difficult verbs according to their index in the table at the end of the book p. 351–352 (also see the full conjugation of each verb in the dictionary).

Infinitive		учи́ть — вы́учить	вспомина́ть — вспо́мнить	говори́ть — сказа́ть	забы**ва́**ть — забы́ть	прода**ва́**ть — прода́ть
Past (IPF)	он					
	она́					
	они́					
Past (PF)	он					
	она́					
	они́					
Present (IPF)	я					
	ты					
	он					
	мы					
	вы					
	они́					

Infinitive	IPF — PF	учи́ть — вы́учить	вспомина́ть — вспо́мнить	говори́ть — сказа́ть	забы**ва́**ть — забы́ть	прода**ва́**ть — прода́ть
Future (PF)	я					
	ты					
	он					
	мы					
	вы					
	они́					
Imperative (IPF)	ты					
	вы					
Imperative (PF)	ты					
	вы					

Infinitive	IPF — PF	переводи́ть — перевести́	понима́ть — поня́ть	отдых**а́**ть — отдохну́ть	класть — положи́ть	брать — взять
Past (IPF)	он					
	она́					
	они́					
Past (PF)	он					
	она́					
	они́					
Present (IPF)	я					
	ты					
	он					
	мы					
	вы					
	они́					
Future (PF)	я					
	ты					
	он					
	мы					
	вы					
	они́					
Imperative (IPF)	ты					
	вы					
Imperative (PF)	ты					
	вы					

Exercise 20. **Change the dialogues from Exercise 17 into Future form.**

Exercise 21. **Using the phrases в бу́дущем, в сле́дующем году́, на сле́дующей неде́ле, за́втра, через (день, неде́лю, ме́сяц, год; два дня, две неде́ли, два ме́сяца, два го́да; 5 дней, неде́ль, ме́сяцев, лет) say about your plans for the next 5 years.**

Exercise 22. **Answer the questions, use the Future tense.**

1. Каки́е языки́ Вы бу́дете учи́ть в ближа́йшее вре́мя? Како́й язы́к Вы не вы́учите никогда́?
2. Что Вы бу́дете вспомина́ть на пе́нсии? О ком и́ли о чём Вы не вспо́мните никогда́?
3. О чём Ваш колле́га бу́дет говори́ть за́втра в своём докла́де?
4. Что Вы ска́жете о пого́де в Сиби́ри?
5. Как ча́сто Вы бу́дете забыва́ть тетра́дь до́ма?
6. Вы лети́те в о́тпуск на Средизе́мное мо́ре. Что Вы то́чно не забу́дете?
7. Что Ва́ша страна́ бу́дет продава́ть в следу́ющем году́ други́м стра́нам?
8. У Вас есть би́знес. Вы продади́те его́? Почему́?
9. За́втра Вы бу́дете переводи́ть те́ксты? Вам ну́жен слова́рь? Вы то́чно переведёте э́тот текст? За́втра мы бу́дем его́ обсужда́ть на уро́ке.
10. Где Вы бу́дете отдыха́ть ле́том? (В тураге́нтстве.) Э́то хо́роший санато́рий? Мои́ роди́тели отдохну́т там?
11. Вы хоти́те печь торт ве́чером. Где Вы возьмёте реце́пт: в интерне́те, в кни́ге, позвони́те ма́ме? Вы поло́жите в торт варе́нье и́ли све́жие фру́кты? А что ещё Вы поло́жите в торт?

John dialed his father's London number…

Exercise 23. **Underline the verbs in the dialogue, define their tense and Aspect. Explain why this form is used.**

— Здра́вствуй, па́па! Говори́т Москва́!

— До́брый день! Говори́т Ло́ндон! Как дела́ в Москве́?

— Всё хорошо́. Вчера́ весь ве́чер изуча́л ру́сские тради́ции[1]. Но изучи́л ещё о́чень ма́ло. У́тром учи́л но́вые слова́. И уже́ вы́учил их.

— Ого́, ты вы́учил мно́го но́вых слов! И ты узна́л вид ру́сского глаго́ла!

— Да, я изуча́ю интере́сный и оригина́льный[2] язы́к. Но, ду́маю, бу́ду изуча́ть его́ недо́лго. Сейча́с на́до не реша́ть твой вопро́с о докуме́нтах, а РЕШИ́ТЬ его́.

— Отли́чно говори́шь!

— Спаси́бо! Напиши́, пожа́луйста, а́дрес библиоте́ки. Я бу́ду брать (возьму́) докуме́нты сего́дня. И бу́ду де́лать (сде́лаю) ко́пию[3] для тебя́.

John was going to find a nearby restaurant пообе́дать, and immediately after that go to the address named by his father. Imagine his surprise when he found Roman Kharitonov in the lobby, obviously waiting for him. John couldn't avoid the meeting: Roman joyfully rushed toward the foreign guest...

— Сего́дня ты за́втракаешь[4] со мной! — the blonde stated categorically.

— Спаси́бо, я поза́втракал.

— Ты поза́втракал оди́н[5]. А сейча́с ты бу́дешь за́втракать со мной. Ты и я, и мы с тобо́й! — he sang some cheerful folk tune.

— Мы бу́дем за́втракать вме́сте? — surprised the Englishman.

— Да, ты и я бу́дем за́втракать. Ты бу́дешь за́втракать со[6] мной. А я бу́ду за́втракать с тобо́й. = Мы бу́дем за́втракать вме́сте. О, нет, мы не бу́дем за́втракать, мы бу́дем обе́дать. Сейча́с уже́ 12 часо́в.

[1] a tradition
[2] original
[3] a copy
[4] (1.R.VOW): to have breakfast
[5] alone
[6] with

Твори́тельный паде́ж (паде́ж № 5) — **Instrumental case (case № 5)**

Кем? Чем? С кем? С чем?

	case № 1				case № 5					
		чей? чьё? чья?	како́й? како́е? кака́я?	что? кто?		чьим? чьим? чьей?	каки́м? каки́м? како́й?	чем? кем? с чем? с кем?	adj.	n.
он	э́тот, тот	мо**й** тво**й** наш ваш **его́**, **её**, **их**	но́в**ый** больш**о́й** хоро́ш**ий** бу́дущ**ий** си́н**ий** ру́сск**ий**	стол слова́р**ь** музе́**й** санато́р**ий** друг фи́зик студе́нт писа́тел**ь** Андре́**й** Анато́л**ий** ребён**ок** челове́к	э́**тим,** **тем**	мо**и́м** тво**и́м** на́ш**им** ва́ш**им** **его́**, **её**, **их**	но́в**ым** больш**и́м** хоро́ш**им** бу́дущ**им** си́н**им** ру́сск**им**	стол**о́м** словар**ём** музе́**ем** санато́р**ием** дру́г**ом** фи́зик**ом** студе́нт**ом** писа́тел**ем** Андре́**ем** Анато́л**ием** ребён**к****ом** челове́к**ом**	**-ЫМ /** **-ИМ**	**-ОМ /** **-ЕМ /** **-ЁМ**
оно́	э́то, то	мо**ё** тво**ё** на́ш**е** ва́ш**е** **его́**, **её**, **их**	но́в**ое** больш**о́е** хоро́ш**ее** бу́дущ**ее** си́н**ее** ру́сск**ое**	письм**о́** мо́р**е** зда́н**ие**	э́**тим**, **тем**	мо**и́м** тво**и́м** на́ш**им** ва́ш**им** **его́**, **её**, **их**	но́в**ым** больш**и́м** хоро́ш**им** бу́дущ**им** си́н**им** ру́сск**им**	письм**о́м** мо́р**ем** зда́н**ием**	**-ЫМ /** **-ИМ**	**-ОМ /** **-ЕМ**
она́	э́та, та	мо**я́** тво**я́** на́ш**а** ва́ш**а** **его́**, **её**, **их**	но́в**ая** больш**а́я** хоро́ш**ая** бу́дущ**ая** си́н**яя** ру́сск**ая**	ко́мнат**а** дере́вн**я** тетра́д**ь** аудито́р**ия** подру́г**а** ба́бушк**а** А́н**я** Аде́л**ь** Мари́**я**	э́**той**, **той**	мо**е́й** тво**е́й** на́ш**ей** ва́ш**ей** **его́**, **её**, **их**	но́в**ой** больш**о́й** хоро́ш**ей** бу́дущ**ей** си́н**ей** ру́сск**ой**	ко́мнат**ой** дере́вн**ей** тетра́д**ью** аудито́р**ией** подру́г**ой** ба́бушк**ой** А́н**ей** Аде́л**ью** Мар**и́ей**	**-ОЙ /** **-ЕЙ**	**-ОЙ /** **-ЕЙ /** **-ЁЙ /** **-ЬЮ /** **-ИЕЙ**

8

	case № 1				case № 5					
		чьи?	каки́е?	что? кто?		чьи́ми?	каки́ми?	чем? кем?	adj.	n.
они́	э́**ти**,	мо**й**	но́в**ые**	стол**ы́**	э́**тими**,	мо**ими**	но́в**ыми**	стол**а́ми**	-ЫМИ / -ИМИ	-АМИ / -ЯМИ / -ЬМИ
	те	тво**й**	больш**и́е**	слова**ри́**	**те́ми**	тво**ими**	больш**и́ми**	словар**я́ми**		
		на́ш**и**	хоро́ш**ие**	музе́**и**		на́ш**ими**	хоро́ш**ими**	музе́**ями**		
		ва́ш**и**	бу́дущ**ие**	санато́р**ии**		ва́ш**ими**	бу́дущ**ими**	санато́р**иями**		
		его́,	си́н**ие**	пи́сьм**а**		**его́**,	си́н**ими**	пи́сьм**ами**		
		её,	ру́сск**ие**	мор**я́**		**её**,	ру́сск**ими**	мор**я́ми**		
		их		зда́н**ия**		**их**		зда́н**иями**		
				ко́мнат**ы**				ко́мнат**ами**		
				дере́вн**и**				деревн**я́ми**		
				тетра́д**и**				тетра́д**ями**		
				аудито́р**ии**				аудито́р**иями**		
				де́т**и**				дет**ьми́**		
				лю́д**и**				люд**ьми́**		

Ли́чные местоиме́ния (паде́ж № 5) — Personal pronouns (case № 5)

case № 1	кто	я	ты	он, оно́	она́	мы	вы	они́
case № 5	кем? с кем?	мной со мной	тобо́й с тобо́й	им с ним	ей с ней	на́ми с на́ми	ва́ми с ва́ми	и́ми с ни́ми

Case № 5 has two basic meanings:

1. With preposition **С**, it expresses compatability.
2. Without preposition it denotes a tool, an instrument.

Compatability:

Он обе́дает **с дру́гом**. — He has lunch with his friend.

Мы говори́м **с преподава́телем**. — We are talking to the professor.

На фотогра́фии президе́нт **с жено́й**. — In the photo there is the president with his wife.

Exercise 24. **Make phrases with the help of the model: Кто что де́лает с кем.**

Example: Ива́н. Гуля́ть в па́рке. Мари́я. → Ива́н гуля́ет в па́рке **с Мари́ей**.

1. Анто́н. Рабо́тать на заво́де. Пётр. ____________________
2. Са́ша. Учи́ться в шко́ле. Друг Алекса́ндр. ____________________
3. Рома́н Никола́евич. Отдыха́ть на мо́ре. Жена́ и де́ти. ____________________
4. Татья́на. За́втракать в кафе́. Друзья́. ____________________
5. Е́ва. Е́хать в Ита́лию. До́чка. ____________________

Exercise 25. **Transform the sentences from the previous exercise, replacing the names to personal pronouns as in the example below.**

Example: 1. Ива́н гуля́ет в па́рке **с Мари́ей**. → Э́то Мари́я. Ива́н гуля́ет в па́рке **с ней**.
2. Джон обе́дает **с Рома́ном Харито́новым**. → Э́то Рома́н Харито́нов. Джон обе́дает **с ним**.

Днём в го́роде…

«Дава́й обе́дать здесь! Здесь мно́го ру́сских блюд и о́чень вку́сно!» — Roman stopped the car in front of the restaurant with the red stylized antique signboard ТРАКТИ́Р[1]. The place was called «Жи́ли-бы́ли. Е́ли-пи́ли».

[1] inn, pub

The part «Жи́ли-бы́ли» is a traditional beginning of Russian tales (it means "once upon a time lived…"), and «Е́ли-пи́ли» described a long process of eating and drinking.

Since John was going to have lunch anyway, the company of Roman Kharitonov was even better: Roman said he was a great expert in cafés and restaurants.

The room of that place was not as pompous as the halls of the restaurant the day before, but still it was nice. Everything here was stylized in the atmosphere of pre-war and pre-revolutionary Moscow of the early 20th century.

On the table at which they sat there was a brief description of the original plan which the owners had recreated:

Добро пожа́ловать в наш тракти́р!

В тракти́ре «Жи́ли-бы́ли. Е́ли-пи́ли» стоя́ло мно́го широ́ких деревя́нных[2] столо́в. На сте́нах висе́ли карти́ны и фотогра́фии.

Под нога́ми был деревя́нный пол. На о́кнах стоя́ли ва́зы с цвета́ми[3]. В углу́ находи́лась[4] ру́сская пе́чка. Ря́дом с пе́чкой на стене́ висе́ло зе́ркало и стоя́ли кре́сла: зде́сь отдыха́ли и́ли жда́ли[5] друзе́й. Ме́жду кре́слами на стене́ висе́ли больши́е часы́.

На о́кнах висе́ли занаве́ски. А ме́жду о́кнами стоя́ли шкафы́. В шкафа́х на по́лках стоя́ли традицио́нные ча́шки, таре́лки, ло́жки.

За ба́рной сто́йкой[6] находи́лся официа́нт в национа́льной оде́жде. А на ба́рной сто́йке всегда́ стоя́л самова́р[7]. Самова́р — друг ка́ждого ру́сского челове́ка, генера́л[8] стола́.

Пе́ред ба́рной сто́йкой стоя́ли деревя́нные сту́лья.

На потолке́, над стола́ми, висе́ли ла́мпы.

[2] wooden
[3] pl. цветы́, цвето́к: a flower
[4] (2.IR Д-Ж): to be (to take place)
[5] (1.R.CONS): to wait
[6] a bar
[7] samovar
[8] a general (n.)

Exercise 26. **Study the table and then translate the text «Добро пожа́ловать в наш тракти́р!»**

Preposition + case № 5

ПОД (чем) — under
Мяч (1) лежи́т ПОД СТОЛО́М.

РЯ́ДОМ С (чем) — near
Цветы́ стоя́т РЯ́ДОМ СО СТОЛО́М.

ПЕРЕД (чем) — in front of
Мяч (2) лежи́т ПЕРЕД СТОЛО́М.

НАД (чем) — over
Ла́мпа виси́т НАД СТОЛО́М.

ЗА (чем) — between
Стул стои́т ЗА СТОЛО́М.

МЕ́ЖДУ (чем и чем) — between
Мяч (3) лежи́т МЕ́ЖДУ СТОЛО́М и ЦВЕТА́МИ.

Verbs of being in space:

Находи́ться (2.IR Д-Ж)	Висе́ть (2.IR С-Ш): to hang (the object doesn't have anything under it) Лежа́ть (2.R.CONS.2): to lie (the object is placed horizontally) Стоя́ть (2.R.VOW): to stand (the object is placed vertically)

John looked around: all the objects were placed as it had been described.

Exercise 27. **Place the objects according to the description:**

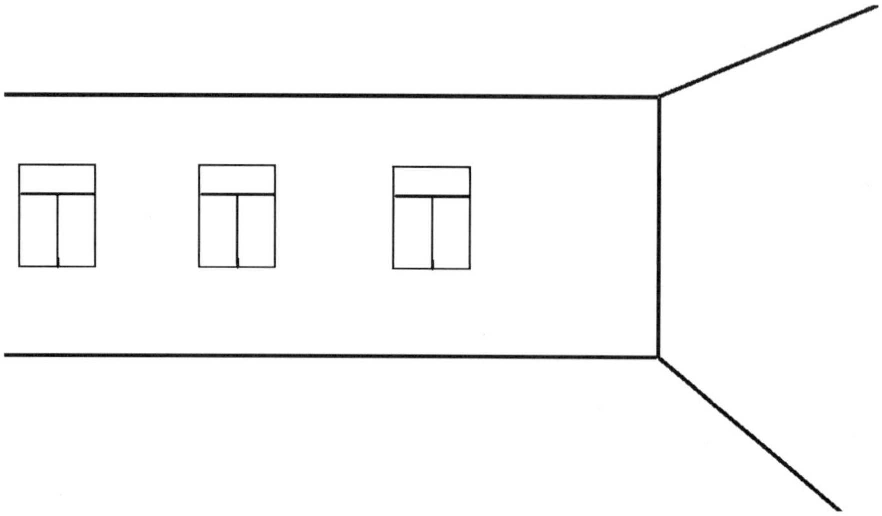

Exercise 28. **Answer the question Где э́то нахо́дится в тракти́ре?**

Example: Где нахо́дится зе́ркало? → Оно́ нахо́дится ря́дом с пе́чкой.

1. Где нахо́дятся ла́мпы? ____________________
2. Где нахо́дятся ча́шки, таре́лки, ло́жки? ____________________
3. Где нахо́дятся ва́зы с цвета́ми? ____________________
4. Где нахо́дится пе́чка? ____________________
5. Где нахо́дится официа́нт? ____________________
6. Где нахо́дятся больши́е часы́? ____________________
7. Где нахо́дятся шкафы́? ____________________
8. Где нахо́дятся занаве́ски? ____________________

Model: Пасси́вное де́йствие — Акти́вное де́йствие
Passive action — active action

висе́ть: to hang	ве́шать / пове́сить (1.R.VOW / 2.IR С-Ш): to hang
стоя́ть: to stand (to be placed vertically)	ста́вить / поста́вить (2.IR Б, П, М, В + Л): to put (to place an object in a vertical position)
лежа́ть: to lie (to be placed in a horizontal position)	класть / положи́ть (1.IR СТ-Д / 2.R.CONS.2): to put (to place an object in a horizontal position)

где? (case № 6)	куда́? (case № 4)
висе́ть (где?) Карти́на виси́т на стене́. Ла́мпа виси́т на потолке́ над столо́м.	**ве́шать / пове́сить** (что? куда́?) Я ве́шаю карти́ну на сте́ну. Я ве́шаю ла́мпу на потоло́к над столо́м.
стоя́ть (где?) Ча́шка стои́т на столе́.	**ста́вить / поста́вить** (что? куда́?) Мы ста́вим ча́шку на стол.
лежа́ть (где?) Кни́га лежи́т на столе́.	**класть / положи́ть** (что? куда́?) Он кладёт кни́гу на стол.

Exercise 29. **You are a designer. You describe a flat you have just finished. Tell the client what you have done.**

Example: Э́то ла́мпы. Они́ вися́т на потолке́ над стола́ми. **Я пове́сил их на потоло́к над стола́ми**.

— Ита́к[1], что ты обы́чно ешь на за́втрак[2]?

John noticed the day before that Roman said ты when he addressed him. But he had some more important things to think over that day.

— Почему́ Вы говори́те мне «ты»?

Roman looked at him in surprise, he obviously didn't expect such a question.

— Извини́… извини́те, — he gave up immediately. — Бу́ду говори́ть «Вы».

— «Ты» — э́то хорошо́. Говори́те «ты». В А́нглии нет ра́зницы: «Ты» и́ли «Вы». Но у меня́ есть вопро́с. Оле́г вчера́ говори́л «Вы», Све́та говори́ла «Вы», а Вы говори́те «ты». Я не понима́ю почему́.

— Извини́те, Джон! Коне́чно, я до́лжен был спроси́ть: мы на «ты» и́ли мы на «Вы»? Но я не **спроси́л**, а э́то неве́жливо. Я ру́сский медве́дь[3], — Roman imitated a bear's walk, he looked confused.

John tried to laugh, but now he felt like an awkward bear himself. Roman was genuinely upset.

— Хорошо́, я по́нял. Дава́й говори́ть «ты». Э́то не пробле́ма!

— Хорошо́, дава́й.

They shook hands, and to smooth over the awkwardness, Roman returned to questions about food:

— Джон, что ты обы́чно ешь на за́втрак?

— Обы́чно я ем на за́втрак я́йца, беко́н[4], тост[5], пью ко́фе… и молоко́.

— Но уже́ по́здно. Сейча́с уже́ не за́втрак, а обе́д. Что ты обы́чно ешь на обе́д?

— Для меня́, пожа́луйста, пельме́ни, — said John to the approaching waiter.

— А мне карто́фель с лу́ком. И пирожки́ с мя́сом.

[1] so, well
[2] есть на за́втрак = за́втракать — eat for breakfast = to have breakfast; есть на обе́д = обе́дать — to have lunch; есть на у́жин = у́жинать — to have dinner
[3] a bear
[4] bacon
[5] a toast

8

Exercise 30. **Go back to the beginning of Chapter 7 (p. 149). Look at the menu of the restaurant where John had dinner with the new Russian friends, find a similar construction with preposition С. You have already guessed what it means.**

Compatibility: X in Y

Он ест суп **с мя́сом**. = В су́пе есть мя́со. — He eats soup with meat. = There is meat in the soup.

Пиро́г **с лу́ком и яйцо́м**. = В пироге́ есть лук и я́йца. — A pie with onions and eggs. = There are onions and eggs in the pie.

Конве́рт **с деньга́ми**. = В конве́рте есть де́ньги. — An envelope with money. = There is money in the envelope.

Самолёт **с росси́йскими гра́жданами**. = В самолёте есть росси́йские гра́ждане. — A plane with Russian citizens. = There are Russian citizens on the plane.

Exercise 31. **Say in Russian:**

1. чай + варе́нье 2. бу́лка + ма́сло 3. пиро́г + ры́ба 4. ко́фе + сли́вки

Model: С чем (case № 5)/ Без чего́ (case № 2)

+	—
с чем? (case № 5)	без[1] чего́? (case № 2)
Я люблю́ ко́фе с са́харом. I like coffee with sugar.	А я люблю́ ко́фе без са́хара. And I like coffee without sugar.
Я ненави́жу ко́фе с молоко́м.	А я ненави́жу ко́фе без молока́.

[1] without

Exercise 32. **Express your attitude (your friends' attitude) to these kinds of food using the model С чем / Без чего́ and the verbs люби́ть / ненави́деть.**

Example: пиро́г, капу́ста / пиро́г, мя́со → Я люблю́ пироги́ с капу́стой.
А моя́ жена́ лю́бит пироги́ с мя́сом.

[2] a lemon

1. чай, лимо́н[2] / чай, молоко́ ______________________________
2. суп, грибы́ / суп, о́вощи ______________________________
3. блины́, сыр / блины́, кра́сная икра́ ______________________________

Exercise 33. **Match the model С чем / Без чего́ to the model С кем / Без кого́. Ответьте на вопросы:**

1. С кем вы лю́бите обе́дать?
2. Без кого́ вы не лю́бите обе́дать?
3. С кем вы лю́бите отдыха́ть?
4. Без кого́ вы не лю́бите отдыха́ть?
5. С кем вы лю́бите рабо́тать?
6. Без кого́ вы лю́бите рабо́тать?
7. Что вы де́лаете оди́н?
8. Что вы де́лаете с друзья́ми?
9. Вы ча́сто у́жинаете с друзья́ми?

— И селёдочку[3] возьми́, — advised Roman.
— Sel'odochkoo?
— Селёдочка — э́то селёдка.
— Селёдка — селёдочка. Во́дка — во́дочка, — said the waiter.
— Нет-не́т, я не зна́ю селёдку. Я не бу́ду э́то есть.
— Селёдка — э́то ры́ба. Ры́ба солёная — о́чень вку́сно, — Roman was upset by the answer.

[3] herring

John looked it up in an online dictionary.

— А́-а-а, селёдочка — ма́ленькая солёная ры́ба. Ры́ба селёдка. Э́то herring.

— Нет-не́т, не ма́ленькая, — explained the waiter. — Норма́льная, о́чень вку́сная солёная селёдка!

— Нет, спаси́бо, я не люблю́ солёную ры́бу.

— А я люблю́! — answered Roman. — Пожа́луйста, селёдочку под шу́бой.

— А во́дку бу́дете? — asked the waiter.

— Да нет, наве́рное[1], — answered Roman.

John didn't know how to interpret an answer that consisted of something affirmative, negative and expressing doubt at the same time. The waiter, on the contrary, seemed to understand everything, nodded and went away.

"Is he going to bring vodka or no?" — thought John.

The waiter didn't bring vodka. So, да нет, наве́рное is negative in meaning. They say нет, не хочу or никогда́ не говори́ никогда́. That's strange, they use double negation as if they don't believe in the only one «нет», but at the same time да нет, наве́рное, is a "no" in meaning but not literally. While John was thinking about Russian linguistic logic, there was one more conversation between Roman and the waiter, and was even more strange from the point of view of an Englishman. As in the case of да нет, наве́рное, John could understand all the words, but not the meaning.

— Есть пить? — asked Roman.

— Во́дка, вино́, — the waiter smiled politely.

— Нет, не вы́пить, а пить.

— А, одну́ мину́ту. Коне́чно, есть сок, есть вода́ минера́льная, есть ру́сский квас.

— Хорошо́. Дава́йте квас.

— А есть что есть?

— Щи, борщ, — offered the waiter not being surprised by the strange question.

— Для меня́ щи, — answered Roman. — А для тебя́? — he turned to John.

— Для меня́ во́ду.

— А вино́? Я ду́мал, все англича́не обе́дают с вино́м.

— Да нет, наве́рное, — John applied the new knowledge and was unexpectedly awarded a respectful and even a little confused glances from Roman and the waiter. "Goal," — John said to himself. Let's say "1:1".

Су́ффиксы уменьши́тельно-ласка́тельные
Diminutive suffixes

селёдка — селёд**очк**а
во́дка — во́д**очк**а
рука́ — ру́ч**к**а (о те́ле челове́ка)
нога́ — но́ж**к**а
глаза́ — гла́з**к**и
нос — но́с**ик**
пиро́г — пирож**о́к**

DID YOU KNOW?

Селёдка под шу́бой is a name of the salad with salted herring as the main ingredient. Herring forms the first lower layer, and all the other salad ingredients are put on top, that is why it is compared to a fur coat. This salad is very good as an appetizer and as a cold dish, so it is often served at the table. There is a lot of beet in this salad, which is what makes it so typically pink.

[1] Да нет, наве́рное: Well, probably no
наве́рное: maybe, probably

***Exercise 34.* Help John understand what the conversation between Roman and the waiter was about.**

ATTENTION! The verb есть = to have
The verb есть = to eat
The verb пить = to drink
The verb вы́пить = 1. to drink alcohol
2. perfective form of the verb пить

DID YOU KNOW?

Roman ate, but asked if there was something to eat. Селёдка под шу́бой is a salad. In Russia, for centuries a salad is not considered to be serious food (in winter in cold weather this food provides little energy). Real food is soup and hot snacks. Therefore, it is possible that after the salad and sandwiches in the Russian house hosts will tell you: «А сейча́с дава́йте есть!» Do not be surprised!

Case № 5. Denoting instrument

Он ест суп **ло́жкой**. — He eats soup with a spoon.

Худо́жник рису́ет **карандашо́м**. — The artist draws in pencil.

Учи́тель пи́шет **кра́сной ру́чкой**. — The teacher writes with a red pen.

Мужчи́ны лю́бят **глаза́ми**. А же́нщины лю́бят **уша́ми**. — Men love with their eyes. And women love with their ears.

Exercise 35. **Connect the words according to the model Кто что де́лает чем.**

Example: **Учи́тель** пи́шет **кра́сной ру́чкой**.

Кто: худо́жник, шко́льник, учи́тель, фото́граф, лю́ди, ка́ждый челове́к, роди́тели.

Что де́лать: писа́ть, рисова́ть, ду́мать, люби́ть, исправля́ть оши́бки, фотографи́ровать, слу́шать.

Что: ру́чка, се́рдце, кра́сная ру́чка, каранда́ш, фотоаппара́т, голова́, у́ши.

Exercise 36. **In the sentences above replace the word denoting one of the participants to the pronoun.**

Example: Учи́тель пи́шет **кра́сной ру́чкой**.
Учи́тель пи́шет **ей**.

РУ́ССКИЕ ПОСЛО́ВИЦЫ — RUSSIAN PROVERBS

Даёшь рука́ми — берёшь нога́ми. — You give with your hands — you take with your feet.

Ду́май голово́й! — Think with your head!

Мы не ла́птем[1] щи хлеба́ем[2]. — We don't eat with our shoe.

[1] ла́поть n.f (pl. лапти): a bast shoe (a kind of traditional folk shoes)
[2] to eat (colloquial)

Do not confuse these meanings! Avoid ambiguences and funny phrases:

Он обе́дал дру́гом. = Он ел дру́га.

Он ест суп с ло́жкой. = Суп гото́вили из ра́зных проду́ктов[3]. Там есть мя́со, карто́фель и ло́жка☺.

[3] different food

Exercise 37. **Answer the questions. Choose all possible correct anwers from the second column.**

С кем ты обе́даешь? С чем ты пьёшь ко́фе? С чем твой чай?	суп, друг, карто́фель, хлеб, ма́сло, де́вушка, па́па, ма́ма, жена́, муж, студе́нт, блины́, молоко́, сли́вки, са́хар

Exercise 38. Read about these people's traditions. Underline the phrases with the words in case № 5.

ЧЕМ МЫ ЕДИ́М?

Сейча́с обы́чно лю́ди едя́т ло́жкой и ви́лкой.

Ло́жку и нож лю́ди зна́ли давно́[1]. Суп е́ли ло́жкой, а мя́со — рука́ми. Но бога́тые[2] лю́ди е́ли ножа́ми. О́дним ножо́м они́ ре́зали[3], а други́м кла́ли еду́[4] в рот. А бе́дные[5] лю́ди е́ли рука́ми.

Ви́лку узна́ли в IX (девя́том) ве́ке в ара́бских стра́нах. Снача́ла у неё бы́ло два зу́ба. Пото́м ви́лку узна́ли в Византи́и, а в XI (оди́ннадцатом) ве́ке — в Ита́лии.

Во всей Евро́пе ви́лкой е́ли уже́ в XIV (четы́рнадцатом) ве́ке.

В Кита́е, Таи́анде, Япо́нии и в други́х стра́нах А́зии едя́т па́лочками[6].

Традицио́нно[7] в Росси́и хлеб беру́т то́лько рука́ми. Ку́рицу едя́т ножо́м и ви́лкой, мо́жно помога́ть рука́ми (ко́нчиками па́льцев). Мя́со, говя́дину и свини́ну, едя́т ножо́м и ви́лкой, а ры́бу не ре́жут ножо́м.

[1] long time ago
[2] rich
[3] (IPF; 1.IR З-Ж): to cut
[4] food
[5] poor
[6] pl. sticks
[7] traditionally

Exercise 39. Read the dialogue. Define the meaning of case № 5.

Джон: Что э́то?
Рома́н: Э́то деревя́нные ло́жки.
Джон: Почему́ здесь едя́т деревя́нными ло́жками?
Рома́н: Потому́ что есть суп деревя́нной ло́жкой — э́то о́чень по-ру́сски.
Джон: Интере́сно! Я ви́жу на ло́жках цветы́.
Рома́н: Э́то хохлома́. Так рису́ют ру́сские наро́дные[8] худо́жники.

[8] folk (adj.)

8

ХОХЛОМА́ — KHOKHLOMA

Khokhloma is an ancient Russian folk craft, born in the 17th century in the area of Nizhny Novgorod.

Khokhloma is a decorative painting of wooden utensils and furniture, made in black and red (rarely green, yellow) colours on golden background. Traditional elements of Khokhloma are red juicy berries of rowanberries and wild strawberries, flowers and twigs. Often there are birds, fish and animals.

Khokhloma is a unique phenomenon not only in Russia but also in the world of national decorative art. Nowadays hereditary painters work in Khokhloma, and they masterfully make this sophisticated ornament with their hands.

While they were eating John was looking at the restaurant and its visitors. His attention was drawn to the lively talking couple.

Case № 5. Subject feature

Рабо́тать учи́телем — work as a teacher
Быть профе́ссором — be a professor
Стать актри́сой — become an actor

Ива́н **рабо́тал**, **рабо́тает** и **бу́дет рабо́тать** **учи́телем**. Он о́чень лю́бит свою́ профе́ссию.
Васи́лий **был** **шко́льником**, **стал** **студе́нтом** и, наве́рное, **бу́дет** **профе́ссором**.
Я **ста́ла** **студе́нткой** театра́льного институ́та, а **ста́ну** **актри́сой** Большо́го теа́тра!

REMEMBER!

Verb быть

Present: Кто — э́то кто? (Что — э́то что?) Past: Кто был кем? (Что бы́ло чем?) Future: Кто бу́дет кем? (Что бу́дет чем?)	Я был инжене́ром. Я инжене́р. Я бу́ду инжене́ром. Москва́ была́ столи́цей Росси́и. Москва́ — столи́ца Росси́и. Москва́ бу́дет столи́цей Росси́и.

***Exercise 40.* Read the dialogue. Explain the humour of the situation.**

Она́: Си́доров? Ты?
Он: О́-о-о! Ивано́ва! Приве́т!
Она́: Приве́т! О́чень ра́да тебя́ ви́деть!
Он: И я то́же рад тебя́ ви́деть!
Она́: Где ты сейча́с живёшь? Где рабо́таешь?
Он: Я живу́ в Москве́. Рабо́таю преподава́телем в университе́те. В про́шлом году́ стал профе́ссором.
Она́: Ты стал профе́ссором! А ведь э́то пра́вильно[1], ты всегда́ был хоро́шим матема́тиком.
Он: Спаси́бо. Ну а ты?
Она́: А я ста́ла актри́сой.
Он: О, я не знал, что у тебя́ есть драмати́ческий тала́нт[2]!
Она́: Я то́же не зна́ла. Но мой муж стал дире́ктором теа́тра.

[1] right, correct
[2] talent

Exercise 41. Choose! Да и́ли нет.

«Быть знамени́тым[3] некраси́во», — said the Russian poet Boris Pasternak. Do you agree? Why or why not? Да и́ли нет?
Быть же́нщиной о́чень интере́сно.
Быть арти́стом — э́то краси́во.
Быть ма́мой — э́то тру́дно, но прия́тно.
Быть мужчи́ной — э́то романти́чно.
Стать студе́нтом — э́то необы́чно[4].
Стать пило́том — э́то интере́сно.
Быть граждани́ном — э́то ва́жно.

[3] знамени́тый = изве́стный. Софи́ Лоре́н — знамени́тая актри́са. Софи́ Лоре́н — изве́стная актри́са: famous = well-known. Sophia Loren is a famous actress. Sophia Loren is a well-known actress.
[4] unusual

John compared the English "I am a director" to the Russian я рабо́таю (явля́юсь) дире́ктором. From the point of view of grammar ем ло́жкой and рабо́таю дире́ктором are the same thing, as if the structure of Russian reminds us that we are only tools, the same as a spoon, a fork or a pen.

— Почему́ ты не ешь? — asked Roman having noticed that John was thinking about something.

— Я ду́маю.

— О чём?

— О ло́жках, ви́лках и о лю́дях.

— О чём?!

— Вот приме́р[1]. Я хо́тел стать пило́том, а стал экономи́стом. А ты кем хоте́л стать?

— А я хоте́л стать космона́втом, коне́чно. А стал… А стал помо́щником[2] дире́ктора.

— Э́то не ва́жно — пило́т, дире́ктор, космона́вт, экономи́ст… Мы все — то́лько фу́нкции[3], то́лько инструме́нты[4].

Roman got interested:

— И́ли англича́не то́же лю́бят филосо́фию за обе́дом[5], и́ли ты стал ру́сским, — joked Roman.

— Да, иногда́ англича́не обе́дают с филосо́фией, — John laughed.

Roman pointed at the declension table in John's phone and said:

— Никогда́ не ду́май о ру́сской грамма́тике за обе́дом! Прия́тного аппети́та!

[1] an example
[2] an assistant
[3] a function
[4] an instrument, a tool
[5] за обе́дом: preposition за followed by a noun expressing a process, takes the meaning of "at the time of". За обе́дом = at lunch. За у́жином = at dinner.

Model: Кто (case № 1) хо́чет быть кем (case № 5)?

Я хочу́ быть **президе́нтом**.

Я хоте́л быть **космона́втом**.

Model: Кто (case № 1) мечта́ет[6] быть[7] кем (case № 5)?

Я мечта́ю быть **президе́нтом**.

Я мечта́л быть **космона́втом**.

[6] (1.R.VOW): to dream
[7] (1.R.VOW): to be

Infinitive		Singular (sg.)		Plural (pl.)
хоте́ть Special	я	! хоч**у́**	мы	! хот**и́м**
	ты	! хо́ч**ешь**	вы	! хот**и́те**
	он	! хо́ч**ет**	они́	! хот**я́т**
Past		**Singular (sg.)**		**Plural (pl.)**
хоте́ть	он	хоте́**л**	мы	хоте́**ли**
	она́	хоте́**ла**	вы	
	оно́	хоте́**ло**	они́	

Model of formal style

Кто явля́ется[1] кем / Что явля́ется чем

Москва́ **явля́ется** столи́цей Росси́и.

Compare: Москва́ — **столи́ца** Росси́и.

[1] (1.R.VOW): to be

Exercise 42. Make the sentences below formal.

Анто́н — инжене́р. ______

Ле́то — хоро́ший сезо́н. ______

Москва́ — столи́ца Росси́и. ______

Вашингто́н — столи́ца Соединённых Шта́тов Аме́рики. ______

______

Exercise 43. Say about yourself, follow the plan:

1. Кто Вы? ______
2. Кем Вы бы́ли в 2010 (две ты́сячи деся́том) году́? ______
3. Кем Вы мечта́ли стать? ______
4. Кем Вы ста́ли? ______
5. Кем Вы рабо́таете сейча́с? Вы не рабо́таете? Кем Вы явля́етесь? ______
______
6. Кем Вы бу́дете рабо́тать в 2030 (две ты́сячи тридца́том) году́? ______
______

Model: Кто занима́ется[2] чем

Ива́н — спортсме́н. **Он** занима́ется **спо́ртом**.
Профе́ссор Петро́в — хи́мик. **Он** занима́ется **хи́мией**.

[2] (1.R.VOW): to be occupied

Exercise 44. Remember the plot of the story and answer the question Кто занима́ется чем?

Example: Джон занима́ется эконо́микой.

Words: исто́рия, карти́ны и фотогра́фии, би́знес, эколо́гия и биоло́гия, компью́теры, маши́ны, му́зыка.

1. Алекса́ндр Янг
2. Ма́ма Джо́на
3. Оле́г
4. Ма́ша
5. Ста́рший брат Ма́ши
6. Па́па Ма́ши
7. Сестра́ Ма́ши

Exercise 45. Answer the questions.

1. Президе́нт Аме́рики занима́ется поли́тикой[3]. А чем занима́етесь Вы?
2. Джон сейча́с занима́ется дела́ми семьи́. А чем сейча́с занима́етесь Вы?

[3] politics (n.)

John realized that he couldn't get rid of Kharitonov politely. He went to the bathroom, its door wasn't visible from the room. John was not going to return. He understood that all Roman's actions were dictated by the most friendly feelings towards him and the desire to show their country from the best side. But John had too little time to continue this ethnic and cultural acquaintance.

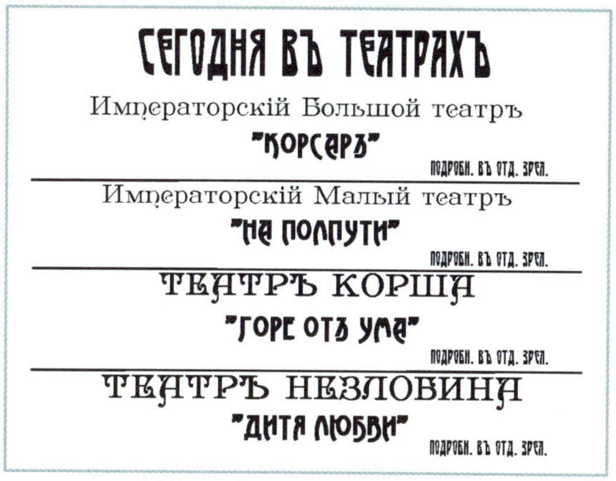

«У́жинать я бу́ду без Рома́на Харито́нова», — thought John heading for the exit.

The restaurant was decorated in the beginning of the twentieth century style. Probably, this was the pre-Revolutionary Moscow, where grandfather Benjamin lived, John thought as he walked down the corridor to the bathroom, in order not to arouse suspicion.

There were photographs of the restaurant of a century ago, old posters and advertisements on the walls.

«Сего́дня в теа́трах», — read John and he caught himself thinking that even though the words had the old spelling with the ъ mark at the end, he could understand almost everything.

Coming out of the bathroom, he stopped involuntarily. A vintage ad on a wall caught his attention.

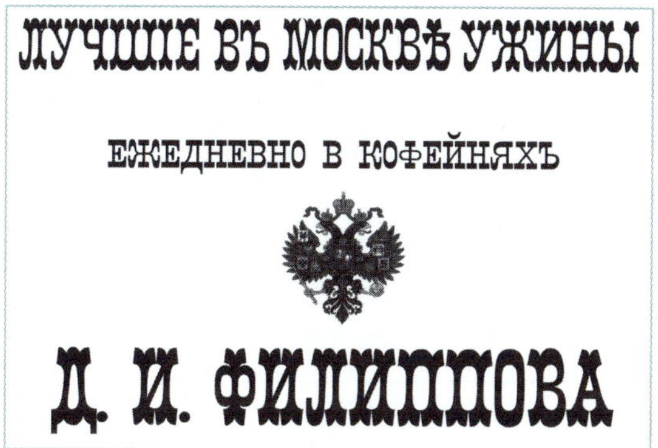

Лу́чшие в Москве́ у́жины. Ежедне́вно в кофе́йнях Д.И. Фили́ппова.

John heard the surname Filippov from his father, and the name was somehow connected with his family's history.

Everything came into the right place:

ежедне́вно[1] → ежедне́вник → ка́ждый день

ко́фе → кофе́йня[2] — ме́сто, где гото́вят ко́фе

Лу́чший = э́то како́й?

[1] daily

[2] a café (coffee shop)

Сте́пени сравне́ния прилага́тельных — Adjectives: degrees of comparison

Superlative	**лу́чший** са́мый[3] хоро́ший	**ху́дший** са́мый плохо́й	вы́сший са́мый высо́кий	тиша́йший[6] са́мый ти́хий	— са́мый молодо́й	краси́вейший са́мый краси́вый
Comparative	**лу́чше** бо́лее[4] (ме́нее[5]) хоро́ший	**ху́же** бо́лее (ме́нее) плохо́й	вы́ше бо́лее (ме́нее) высо́кий	ти́ше бо́лее (ме́нее) ти́хий	моло́же бо́лее (ме́нее) молодо́й	краси́вее бо́лее (ме́нее) краси́вый
0	хоро́ший	плохо́й	высо́кий	ти́хий	молодо́й	краси́вый
Way	**Irregular**	**Irregular**	**Alteration of с — ш**	**Alteration of х — ш, к — ч, г — ж**	**Alteration of д — ж**	**The main model**

[3] the most

[4] more

[5] less

[6] After ш, ж, ч, we add the suffix -е or -айш-. After all other consonants we add the suffix -ее or -ейш-.

Exercise 46. **Fill in the table forming comparatives and superlatives out of these adjectives:**

Superlative						
Comparative						
0	бе́лый	но́вый	вку́сный	большо́й (model ти́хий)	ста́рый	ста́рший

Model: Что лу́чше, чем что — X is better than Y

Тот дом хоро́ший, а э́тот дом лу́чше. → Э́тот дом **лу́чше, чем** тот дом.

Exercise 47. **Make a comparison:**

Example: А́нна. Ива́н. Молодо́й. → А́нна **моло́же, чем** Ива́н.

1. Алекса́ндр. Джон. Ста́рший. ______
2. Ма́ша. Джон. Молодо́й. ______
3. Э́йфелева ба́шня. Лувр. Высо́кий. ______
4. Дере́вня. Го́род. Ти́хий. ______
5. Э́та бума́га. Снег. Бе́лый. ______
6. Америка́нец. Ру́сский. Говори́ть по-англи́йски. Хорошо́. ______
7. Джоа́н Ро́улинг[1]. Певи́ца Аде́ль. Петь. Пло́хо. ______
8. Джоа́н Ро́улинг. Певи́ца Аде́ль. Писа́ть. Хорошо́. ______

[1] Joanne Rowling (а́втор книг о Га́рри По́ттере)

He saw a sign: «Кофе́йня и бу́лочная[2] господи́на[3] Фили́ппова».

Бу́лочная чья? (case № 2) Фили́ппова. = So, the owner of the bakery is Фили́ппов.

[2] a bakery
[3] mister

"Is it the same Philippov?" There was a middle-aged man in a white apron and with lively eyes and hair smoothly brushed towards the parting. Probably in the early 20th century all cooks, barbers, innkeepers and other in the service industry, as we would say today, looked like that all over the world. In the hand of a smiling man there was a loaf of bread with a lot of black specks, similar to raisins.

While John was looking at the signs, Roman Kharitonov approached him. The moment was lost, but it could have been for the best. John suddenly felt that he could not just walk away, without knowing whether his grandfather worked for the same Philippov or not. It seemed that a smiling man was holding out a plump bun directly to him, to a foreigner who was visiting Moscow for the first time.

John stretched out a hand towards the man in the picture.

— Э́то бу́лка с изю́мом, — said Roman.

— Кто? — John didn't understand.

— Не кто, а что. Бу́лка с изю́мом.

— Кто э́то? — asked John pointing at the smiling man.

— Не зна́ю, — Roman shrugged his shoulders and directed him out of the restaurant.

— Кто э́то? — John asked the waiter.

— Одну́ мину́ту, — the waiter disappeared in the inn and suddenly turned up with a booklet. There was a restaurant description and the explanation of those old photos. The waiter bowed politely. — Пожа́луйста, чита́йте!

Despite the desperate attempts of Kharitonov, who suddenly urgently had to go somewhere, John went back to the table.

The brochure was devoted to gastronomic history of Moscow. John got interested in the following text:

И О́ЧЕНЬ ПРО́СТО[1]!

(by В. Гиляровский, «Москва и москвичи[2]»)

Фили́ппов был са́мым изве́стным бу́лочником[3] в Москве́. В бу́лочной Фили́ппова всегда́ бы́ло мно́го покупа́телей[4]. Здесь пекли́ са́мые вку́сные бу́лки в Москве́. В Москве́ бы́ло мо́дно[5] за́втракать здесь. Лю́ди о́чень люби́ли жа́реные пирожки́ с мя́сом, я́йцами, гриба́ми, изю́мом и варе́ньем. Здесь за́втракали и обе́дали бога́тые и бе́дные лю́ди: профессора́, генера́лы, студе́нты, солда́ты. Вся Москва́.

[1] simple
[2] a moscovite
[3] a baker
[4] a customer
[5] fashionable
[6] such
[7] Governor-General
[8] a cockroach
[9] No way! (You must be kidding!)

В бу́лочной Фили́ппова пекли́ вкусне́йший (= са́мый вку́сный) чёрный хлеб.

— Почему́ только у Вас чёрный хлеб тако́й[6] вку́сный? — спра́шивали Фили́ппова.

— И о́чень про́сто! — говори́л Фили́ппов. — Потому́, что я люблю́ хлеб. У меня́ о́чень хоро́шая мука́, о́чень хоро́шее ма́сло и о́чень хоро́шая вода́. А ещё у меня́ о́чень хоро́шие бу́лочники. Поэ́тому мои́ бу́лки са́мые вку́сные.

8

Одна́жды генера́л-губерна́тор[7] Москвы́ ел бу́лку Фили́ппова и уви́дел в бу́лке тарака́на[8].

Генера́л пригласи́л бу́лочника Фили́ппова в свой дом и спроси́л его́:

— Что э́то?

— Э́то изю́м, — сказа́л Фили́ппов.

— Бу́лка с изю́мом? Не мо́жет быть[9]! Э́то бу́лка с тарака́ном!

— Э́то но́вая бу́лка — бу́лка с изю́мом, — сказа́л Фили́ппов, взял бу́лку с тарака́ном и съел её.

Ве́чером в бу́лочной Фили́ппов гото́вил мно́го но́вых бу́лок — э́то бы́ли бу́лки с изю́мом. О но́вой бу́лке в э́тот день зна́ла вся Москва́, а пото́м узна́ла и вся Евро́па.

— Бу́лка с изю́мом — э́то о́чень необы́чно, — говори́ли лю́ди.

— И о́чень про́сто! — говори́л Фили́ппов.

Exercise 48. **Have you understood the text «И о́чень про́сто»? Answer the questions.**

1. Каки́м бу́лочником был Фили́ппов?
2. Ско́лько покупа́телей бы́ло в бу́лочной Фили́ппова? Почему́?
3. Почему́ в Москве́ бы́ло мо́дно здесь за́втракать?
4. Кто здесь за́втракал?

5. Что пекли́ в бу́лочной?
6. Почему́ хлеб Фили́ппова был са́мый вку́сный?
7. Что случи́лось одна́жды?
8. Что сказа́л Фили́ппов о бу́лке с тарака́ном?
9. Что бы́ло ве́чером?
10. О чём узна́ла Москва́ и пото́м Евро́па?
11. Что говори́л об э́том Фили́ппов?

Exercise 49. **Underline the words in case № 5 in the text (p. 209). Do you understand them?**

Exercise 50. **Change the sentences into comparatives and superlatives.**

Example: У меня́ о́чень **хоро́шие** бу́лочники.
У меня́ бу́лочники **лу́чше, чем** в други́х рестора́нах.
У меня́ **лу́чшие** бу́лочники.

У меня́ о́чень хоро́шая мука́, о́чень хоро́шее ма́сло и о́чень хоро́шая вода́.

John found out that the man in the photo is the same man his grandfather worked for.
— Почему́ ты интересу́ешься обы́чным[1] бу́лочником? — Roman was surprised.

Model: Кто интересу́ется[2] чем

Я интересу́юсь **исто́рией**. =
Я люблю́ изуча́ть **исто́рию**.
А́нна интересова́лась **бале́том**. =
Она́ люби́ла смотре́ть **бале́т**.

[1] common, ordinary
[2] (1.IR ОВА-У): to be interested
[3] (2.IR Б, П, М, В + Л): to get acquainted, to meet

— Лу́чше познако́мься[3] с на́шими изве́стнейшими людьми́.

**Model: Кто (по)знако́мится[3] с кем? —
Кто (по)знако́мил кого́ с кем?**

Я познако́мился **с но́вым дру́гом**. — I have met a new friend.
Я познако́мил но́вого дру́га **с мое́й семьёй**. — I introduced my new friend to my family.

**Кто (по)знако́мится с чем? —
Кто (по)знако́мил кого́ с чем?**

В шко́ле я познако́мился **с фи́зикой**. — At school I got acquainted to physics.
Учи́тель знако́мит шко́льников **с фи́зикой**. — The teacher introduces schoolchildren to physics.

Exercise 51. **Answer the questions in Russian.**

1. С кем познако́мился Джон в Росси́и? (Рома́н, Оле́г, Све́та)
2. А с кем он познако́мился ещё в Ло́ндоне? (Ма́ша)
3. С чем познако́мил Джо́на его́ оте́ц? (ру́сский язы́к)
4. А с чем он познако́мился в Москве́? (ру́сские тради́ции, ру́сская еда́)
5. С кем / с чем о́чень ва́жным для Вас Вы познако́мились в э́том году́?

Михаил Васильевич Ломоносов

Антон Павлович Чехов

Александр Данилович Меншиков

— Вот здесь, посмотри́, — Roman turned to the opposite wall, where with the background of high-rise building of the Moscow University, there was a portrait of a man with tight curls.

— Михаи́л Васи́льевич Ломоно́сов был о́чень интере́сным челове́ком. Он роди́лся[1] на се́вере Росси́и, на Бе́лом мо́ре. Его́ оте́ц был рыбако́м[2], а Ломоно́сов стал студе́нтом в Герма́нии, в университе́те го́рода Ма́рбург. Там он познако́мился с европе́йскими[3] нау́ками[4] и со свое́й жено́й Елизаве́той Цильх. В Росси́и, в Петербу́рге, он стал профе́ссором. Ломоно́сов занима́лся нау́ками: фи́зикой, хи́мией, исто́рией, геогра́фией. А ещё он интересова́лся литерату́рой[5] и был изве́стным поэ́том. Ломоно́сов основа́л[6] Моско́вский университе́т — са́мый пе́рвый университе́т в Росси́и. Э́то бы́ло в 1755 (в ты́сяча семьсо́т пятьдеся́т пя́том) году́.

— А э́то Анто́н Па́влович Че́хов. Его́ оте́ц был продавцо́м[7] в Таганро́ге. А Че́хов стал студе́нтом Моско́вского университе́та. Рабо́тал врачо́м[8], а пото́м стал известны́м писа́телем.

— А э́то Алекса́ндр Дани́лович Ме́ншиков. Он был продавцо́м пирого́в в Москве́. А стал вторы́м челове́ком в Росси́и — пра́вой руко́й[9], помо́щником царя́ Петра́ I.

[1] to be born
[2] a fisherman
[3] European
[4] science
[5] literature
[6] осно́вывать (1.R.VOW) / основа́ть: to found
[7] a seller
[8] a doctor
[9] the main assistant (someone's right hand)

Exercise 52. **Underline all the phrases with words in case № 5. Define their meaning.**

John Young gave the walls a closer look: there were merchants, patrons and artists. Feodor Chaliapin, a famous bass of the beginning of the XX century, who was the son of a peasant, was in the image of the demon.

All of these individuals were not from the nobility, they were sons of merchants, farmers, and bourgeois. They all participated in the history of Moscow, the capital of all possibilities. Russians say «Москва́ слеза́м не ве́рит, ей де́ло подава́й» ("Moscow does not believe in tears, give it business").

Passing the portrait of the baker Philippov and following Kharitonov, John smiled and winked at resourceful Russian entrepreneur who employed Benjamin Young a century ago: «Все бу́дет хорошо́! — he thought, interpreting this meeting as a good sign. — И о́чень про́сто!»

Chapter 9

Пу́блика лю́бит театра́льные недоразуме́ния, и е́сли бы вме́сто пьес дава́ли недоразуме́ния, она́ плати́ла бы вдво́е бо́льше.

А.П. Че́хов

The audience loves theatre misunderstandings, and if, instead of plays there were misunderstandings, it would have paid twice as much.

— A. Chekhov

In the end, John did not even have time to see Red Square. He almost could not say anything about Moscow, because he could hardly see anything. But when he saw the huge, magnificent Theatre Square and the Opera House for the first time, he realized that he was in the centre of the Russian capital. The square was beautiful, but it was not the place where he asked Roman to take him.

— Э́то теа́тр? — John asked, looking at a building with columns and a chariot with the god Apollo on the pediment.

— Большо́й теа́тр — лу́чший[1] теа́тр Росси́и!

— Я ду́маю, са́мый изве́стный[2], а не лу́чший, — said John, who always preferred drama to opera and especially ballet, which he could not understand at all.

— Да, в Росси́и мно́го хоро́ших теа́тров. Но Большо́й теа́тр — са́мый изве́стный! — answered Roman approaching the posters.

"Apparently, they have confused me with is a really important person if they have such an extensive cultural program for him," John thought. — "But why hasn't the man from Heathrow airport called to Moscow and clarified the situation? So stupid that it can't be done on purpose."

John looked at the posters.

One was the famous "Swan Lake", he guessed it from the picture. He also recognized the word «о́зеро». John hesitated. On the one hand, it would be great to tell his friends about the famous ру́сский бале́т. On the other hand, it would cost the whole night for that.

— А где библиоте́ка? — asked John anyway.

— Сейча́с полови́на седьмо́го ве́чера. Уже́ по́здно. Библиоте́ка не рабо́тает.

— Библиоте́ка не рабо́тает, а теа́тр рабо́тает. Поэ́тому ты приглаша́ешь[3] меня́ смотре́ть бале́т «Лебеди́ное о́зеро»?

— Нет, — Roman showed him another poster under the rubric called «Сего́дня». John read:

— Что э́то? О́пера и́ли бале́т?

— О́пера! — said Roman solemnly. — Я ду́маю, о́пера — э́то интере́снее[4], чем бале́т.

[1] the best
[2] famous
[3] to invite
[4] comparative интере́снее; superlative са́мый интере́сный (интере́снейший)

Exercise 1. **Read the dialogue in the theatre ticket office. Please note that the majority of theatrical concepts were borrowed from the French language, not only in Russian but also in English, and they should be familiar to you.**

Рома́н: Пожа́луйста, два биле́та в парте́р.
Касси́р: Извини́те, в парте́ре все места́ за́няты.
Роман: А в бельэта́же есть места́?
Касси́р: К сожале́нию, то́же нет. Но есть места́ в ло́же бенуа́р.
Рома́н: Хорошо́. Пожа́луйста, два биле́та в ло́жу бенуа́р.

Exercise 2. **Find what seats Roman and John wanted to have, and what they finally could have.**

Большо́й теа́тр.
Схе́ма зри́тельного за́ла — The scheme of the auditorium

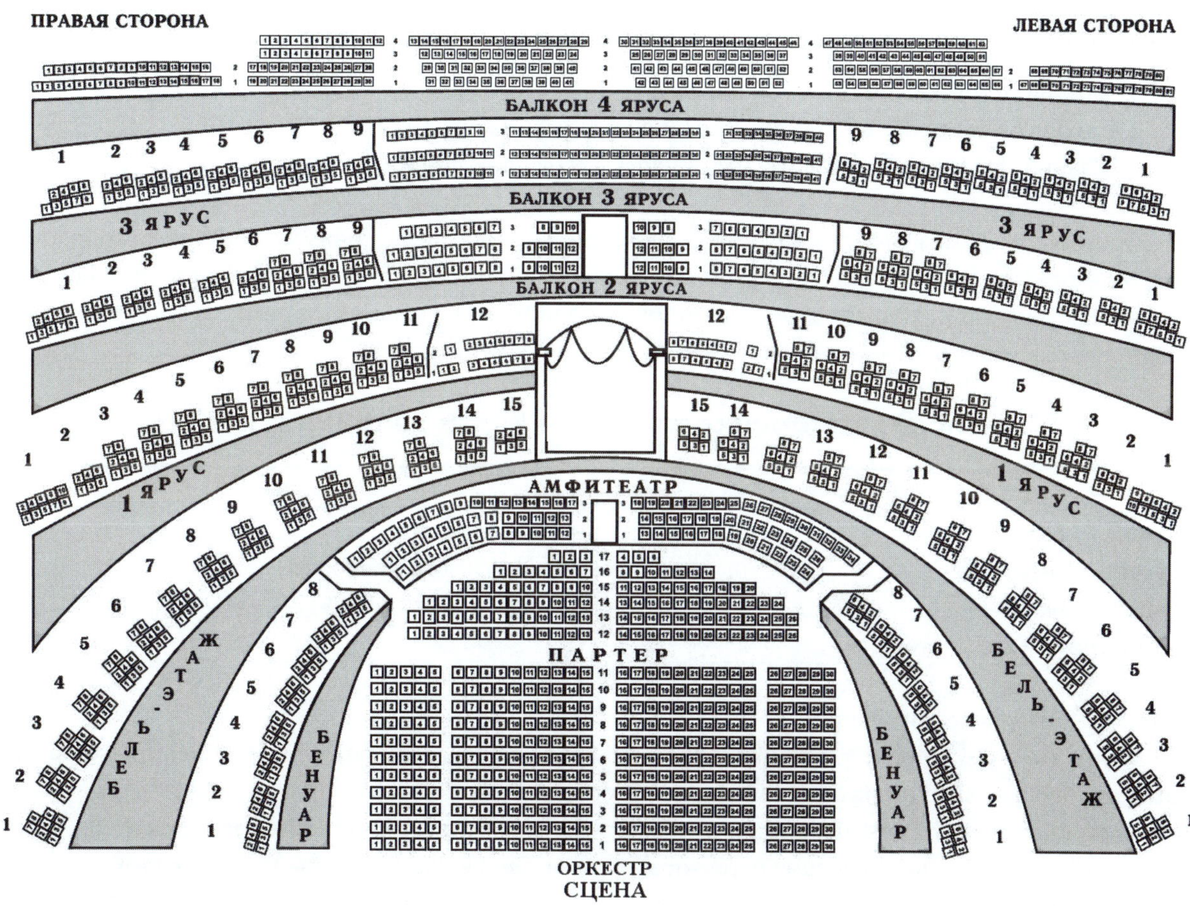

It became clear from the brochure that John couldn't possibly miss that performance if he wanted to get acquainted with Russian culture.

«Евге́ний Оне́гин», рома́н в стиха́х Алекса́ндра Серге́евича Пу́шкина, — э́то энциклопе́дия ру́сской жи́зни.

That's what the brochure said.

By the way, John couldn't understand Russians in that. Dostoevsky, Turgenev, Tolstoy, Chekhov, Bulgakov were outstanding. Everyone knew that. But Pushkin? Well, John read him in translation. "I loved you and my love may still be there, deep in my soul remains to stay aglow". Well, isn't it one of the most trivial lines in the world? Anyway, John defined Russians' love to Pushkin as another mystery of the Russian soul and never opened his translations again.

Unlike the major Russian poet the main Russian theatre made a big impression on him: the auditorium was modelled after the Renaissance style, velvet and gold, crystal and antique molding... However, the opera was in Russian. The music was, of course, beautiful, but John got quickly tired of reading the subtitles. And that was when he decided how to get rid of Roman. He got up from his seat.

— Куда́ ты? — Roman whispered.

— Извини́. Где здесь туале́т? — asked John. The next moment he realized that it was a mistake because Roman who was always willing to help him followed him.

***Exercise 3.* Choose a sentence which suits each situation.**

1. You want somebody to show you the way:
2. You don't want to discuss this question and look for the way yourself:

— Извини́(-те), где здесь туале́т? — Извини́(-те), я на одну́ мину́ту.

Questions with the words где, куда́, во ско́лько, etc. suggest the exact answer with the location, direction, time, or active assistance in finding the way. But if you do not wait for a response or practical help, you can just tell your companion about your intention or condition. The phrases that express condition, mood, desire, etc. will help you.

Слова́ катего́рии состоя́ния — Words denoting states

+	—
мо́жно — can ну́жно — need на́до — have to необходи́мо — it is necessary	нельзя́ — mustn't не ну́жно — don't need to не на́до — don't have to

These adverbs do not change.

If you are a philologist: in a sentence these adverbs perform predicative function in impersonal constructions and are called predicative adverbs or category of state.

The subject in such constructions is indirect (in the form) and marked by dative case (case № 3).

You already know the declination of personal pronouns in the dative (case № 3): Ско́лько **тебе́** (ты) лет? **Мне** (я) 12 лет.

Ско́лько **вам / Вам** (вы / Вы) лет? **Ему́** (он) — 25 лет, **ей** (она́) — 24 го́да, а **им** (они́) — 7 и 8 лет. **Нам** (мы) о́чень мно́го лет.

Model: **Кому́ (case № 3) ну́жно что (case № 4) / куда́**
Кому (case № 3) ну́жно что де́лать / что сде́лать

Извини́те, мне на́до в туале́т. — I'm sorry, I need to go to the bathroom.

Извини́те, я за́нят. Мне ну́жно рабо́тать. — I'm sorry, I'm busy. I need to work.

This is a specific Slavic construction in which the subject is used in a passive form, but in fact is an active subject of action or condition.

Exercise 4. **Study this table and phrases.**

кому́? мне, тебе́, ему́, ей, нам, вам, им	мо́жно ну́жно на́до необходи́мо не ну́жно нельзя́	что? (case № 4)	Мне ну́жно кни́гу.
		что де́лать? что сде́лать?	Мне ну́жно чита́ть кни́гу. Мне ну́жно прочита́ть кни́гу.

1. Вы мно́го рабо́таете, поэ́тому Вам ну́жно бо́льше отдыха́ть.
2. За́втра у неё в Москве́ бу́дет ва́жная делова́я встре́ча[1], поэ́тому ей необходи́мо купи́ть биле́т в Москву́.
3. — У тебя́ температу́ра 38 гра́дусов. Тебе́ не ну́жно сего́дня идти́ в шко́лу.
4. Я вегетариа́нец, поэ́тому мне нельзя́ есть мя́со.
5. — Ма́ма, мо́жно мне взять ещё конфе́ту?
   — Нельзя́. Ты уже́ съел 4 конфе́ты.
6. — Здра́вствуйте! Мне ну́жно купи́ть а́нгло-ру́сский слова́рь. Где мне мо́жно его́ взять?
   — Он нахо́дится на по́лке, где стоя́т все словари́.
7. — Мо́жно мне жа́реную ку́рицу и пиро́г с мя́сом?
   — Да, пожа́луйста.

[1] a business meeting

With the help of the category of state we can express the rules of conduct:

Здесь нельзя́ кури́ть[2]! — No smoking!

С живо́тными[3] нельзя́! — No pets!

Мо́жно сесть[4] ря́дом с Ва́ми? — Can I sit beside you?

Мо́жно мне ме́сто ря́дом с окно́м? — Can I have a seat near the window?

[2] (2.R.CONS.1): to smoke
[3] an animal
[4] сади́ться (2.IR Д-Ж) / сесть (SPECIAL): to sit down

Exercise 5. **Write the rules for these places.**

Example: Библиоте́ка. Гро́мко[5] говори́ть. → В библиоте́ке нельзя́ гро́мко говори́ть.

Place: шко́ла, де́тский парк, па́мятник, истори́ческий музе́й, институ́т, городска́я пло́щадь, шоссе́.

Action: кури́ть, рисова́ть, танцева́ть, гуля́ть с соба́кой[6], есть, пить алкого́льные напи́тки, спать[7].

[5] loudly
[6] a dog
[7] (2.IR Б, П, М, В + Л): to sleep

9

Exercise 6. **Using the sentences from Exercise 5 recommend a place where a person can do something that is prohibited in another place.**

Example: В библиоте́ке нельзя́ гро́мко говори́ть, а на у́лице мо́жно.

Exercise 7. **Give advice in the following situations:**

Example: Она́ сего́дня гру́стная[1] (послу́шать му́зыку) → Ей ну́жно послу́шать му́зыку.

1. За́втра я бу́ду в Москве́, но не зна́ю, где бу́ду жить. (брони́ровать но́мер в гости́нице)
2. Мы забы́ли а́дрес гости́ницы. (позвони́ть в гости́ницу)
3. Они́ мно́го рабо́тали весь год. (отдыха́ть на острова́х в океа́не)
4. Ты не понима́ешь по-францу́зски? (учи́ть францу́зский язы́к)
5. Я не люблю́ го́род. (жить в дере́вне)
6. Он получи́л оце́нку[2] «2»[3] на экза́мене[4]. (мно́го занима́ться)

[1] sad
[2] a mark
[3] a bad school grade in Russia
[4] an exam

Exercise 8. **Add the words мо́жно, ну́жно, на́до, необходи́мо, не ну́жно, нельзя́ to the sentences.**

NOTE: The words ну́жно, на́до and необходи́мо are synonyms, but they differ in style. The word на́до is informal and spoken, the word ну́жно is neutral in style, and необходи́мо is more formal.

Джон в Москве́. Ему́ ______________ встре́титься с партнёрами[4]. Ещё ему́ ______________ узна́ть информа́цию[5] о докуме́нтах семьи́. Ему́ ______________ лете́ть в Ло́ндон без докуме́нтов. Ему́ ______________ встре́титься[6] с Ма́шей, потому́ что она́ на пра́ктике в Каза́ни. Ему́ ______________ в теа́тр, ему́ ______________ в библиоте́ку. Но Рома́н приглаша́ет его́ в теа́тр.

[4] a partner
[5] information
[6] встреча́ться (1.R.WOW) / встре́ти-ться (2.IR Т-Ч): to meet

Exercise 9. **Study the table:**

кому́? мне, тебе́, ему́, ей, нам, вам, им	мо́жно ну́жно на́до необходи́мо не ну́жно нельзя́	**бы́ло** **бу́дет**	что де́лать?	Мне ну́жно **бы́ло** чита́ть кни́гу. Мне ну́жно **бу́дет** чита́ть кни́гу.
			что сде́лать?	Мне ну́жно **бы́ло** прочита́ть кни́гу. Мне ну́жно **бу́дет** прочита́ть кни́гу.

A. Change the text about John's plans in the Future:

Example: Сейча́с Джон в Ло́ндоне. За́втра он бу́дет в Москве́. Ему́ ну́жно бу́дет встре́титься с партнёрами.

B. Change the text about John's plans in the Past:

Example: Джон уже́ в Ло́ндоне. Вчера́ он был в Москве́. Ему́ ну́жно бы́ло встре́титься с партнёрами.

____

____

____

____

John couldn't hesitate. He went to the aisle, pacing himself, but Roman did not lag behind and was explaining something to him, нале́во, напра́во, пря́мо. John opened the door, slipped into the passage, saw another door, the arch, a very tiny door, made his way under metal constructions, jumped into the narrow corridor and looked around — it seemed that Roman finally lost him. Suddenly John felt that he tripped on something and managed to see a staircase flying by... When he opened his eyes, he found himself lying on the floor right in the middle of the passage.

«Осторо́жно!» — there was a gentle voice from above. John looked up and saw a girl in the dress from the 19th century and a hat in the form of a basket with ribbons.

— У Вас боли́т нога́?

— Что Вы сказа́ли?

— У Вас боли́т нога́? Боли́т голова́? — repeated the girl.

— Да, голова́, — John said.

— Пойдёмте со мной, — she replied.

John got up and looked around: apparently, he had landed behind the stage, tripped on part of an iron construction turning over his own head, maybe more than once. Roman was not around.

— Пойдёмте-пойдёмте[1], — she was leading him farther and farther down the hall. People in tailcoats and dresses that were brought into fashion by Napoleon Bonaparte's wife, Josephine, were passing by — light dresses, similar to ancient tunics, strapped under the chest — a fashion of Eugene Onegin time. "Why do they call it 'encyclopedia of Russian life'?" — thought John for some reason.

[1] пойдёмте — imperative of the verb «пойти́» — come on/let's go, — is used when you are invited to follow somebody.

He closed his eyes. It looked like a fairy tale "Alice in Wonderland", all true: Roman Kharitonov as a huge rabbit, the hole, falling down, and here you are — in the 19th century.

In a minute the girl stooped at the door with a sign «Враче́бный кабине́т». John felt the smell of medicine and understood that the word враче́бный is an adjective from the word врач.

— Кабине́т врача́? — John restated, turning to his strange companion.

— Вам ну́жно врача́, — the girl confirmed.

— Нет, спаси́бо! Мне не ну́жно врача́, — John said, but the door opened and the fragile realm of theatrical fairies was disturbed by the imposing woman in a loose white coat.

— Ему́ ну́жно врача́, — the girl explained.

After hearing the girl's story about John falling, the doctor who John had nicknamed Brünnhilde, turned to the Englishman.

— Как Вы? Вам пло́хо?

Here are some words denoting states which express physical or psychic condition: бо́льно, пло́хо, хорошо́.

Model: Кому́ (case № 3) как

Мне хорошо́.

If you are a philologist: from the point of view of the form, these words are similar to adverbs. The difference is that adverbs refer to verbs and characterize actions. The **words** of a category of state characterize the state of a **subject**.

Compare:

Adverb	**Category of state**
Джон **пло́хо** говори́т по-ру́сски.	— Мне **пло́хо**! Где врач?
Окса́на **хорошо́** гото́вит борщ.	— Ле́то, со́лнце, мо́ре. Мне **хорошо́**!
Узна́ть пра́вду — иногда́ э́то **бо́льно**.	— А́-а-а, мне **бо́льно**! Позвони́те 911!

— Нет, мне не пло́хо, — answered John.
— Вам бо́льно?
— Я не понима́ю.
Brünnhilde showed a picture from a Russian cartoon — a suffering lion and a doctor treating him.
— Э́то врач. Э́то лев. Ему́ бо́льно.
John looked it up in the dictionary. Бо́льно was an adverb from the word боль[1].
— Вам бо́льно?
— Нет, мне не бо́льно.
Brünnhilde suddenly bent down and grabbed John's leg:
— Нога́ боли́т?
It became clear that the word боли́т which at first confused John is a verb derived from the word боль.
— Нет, нога́ не боли́т.
— А голова́ боли́т?
— Нет, не боли́т.
— А ру́ки боля́т?
— И они́ не боля́т.
John opened a phrase book and read:
— У меня́ ничего́ не боли́т. Я не бо́лен. Я никогда́ не боле́ю.

[1] pain

Exercise 10. **Look at derivatives from боль. Pay attention to the table:**

боле́ть (1.R.VOW) to be ill	**боле́ть** (2.R.CONS.1) to hurt	**бо́льно** (adverb) it hurts	**бо́лен** (a shortened adjective like за́нят, свобо́ден, рад) to be ill
Я боле́ю. **Он** боле́ет. **Мы** боле́ем.	У меня́ боли́т **рука́**. У них боля́т **но́ги**.	**Мне** бо́льно.	**Я** бо́лен. **Она́** больна́. **Они́** больны́.

ATTENTION!

1. Я болéю and Я бóлен are synonyms.
   Áнна больнá. У неё температýра 39 грáдусов.
   Зимóй Áнна чáсто болéет и сидúт дóма.
2. Shortened adjectives mean temporary feature/state, and full adjectives denote constant feature/state.

Constant	Temporary
Господúн Ивáнов — занятóй человéк. = He is a busy man.	Извинúте, я зáнят. = I'm busy at the moment.
— Почемý Ивáнов не рабóтает? — Он больнóй человéк. (Ivanov has poor health)	— Почемý сегóдня нет студéнта Ивáнова? — Он бóлен. (He is ill at the moment but he will recover soon).

ATTENTION!

The phrase Он / онá больнóй / больнáя can be perceived in a negative way or as a joke, because it has the meaning 'crazy', 'mentally ill person'.
The antonym to the word бóлен is здорóв (здорóва, здорóвы).
— Как Вы?
— Спасúбо, хорошó! Жúв-здорóв!

***Exercise 11.* Complete the sentences paying attention to the highighted words:**

A) 1. Антóн мнóго занимáлся на стадиóне, и **у негó** _______________ нóги.
2. На ýлице бы́ло хóлодно, и сейчáс **я** нахожýсь дóма и _______________.
3. На э́той недéле Марúна не рабóтает. **Онá** _______________.
4. Зимóй **дéти** чáсто _______________.
5. У меня́ _______________ головá. Мне нáдо домóй.
6. Урá! Я ужé не болéю. **Я** _______________!

B) 1. **Мне** óчень _______________. **У меня́** _______________ живóт. Мне нýжно врачá.
2. — Что у Вас _______________?
— Не знáю.
— Здесь Вам _______________?
— Да, здесь _______________.

Brünnhilde and the girl looked doubtfully at each other.
— Шок[1]? — the girl suggested.
— Сегóдня емý не бóльно и не плóхо, а зáвтра емý бýдет бóльно и бýдет óчень плóхо, — said the doctor and took some pills and an injector. — Я **даю́** емý лекáрство.

[1] shock

9

The verb «дава́ть» — «дать» is always followed by the dative (case № 3). You will also notice that the word «dative» (in Russian — да́тельный) is a derivative from this verb. It is said that the verb дава́ть — «дать» 'directs' case № 3.

Дать (кому? case № 3) де́вочке (что? case № 4) мяч.

Verb form	Imperfective		Perfective	
Infinitive	**дава́ть** (1.IR ВА-Ø)		**дать** (SPECIAL)	
Past	он она́ они́	дава́**л** дава́**ла** дава́**ли**	он она́ они́	да**л** да**ла́** да́**ли**
Present	я ты он, она́, оно́ мы вы они	да**ю́** да**ёшь** да**ёт** да**ём** да**ёте** да**ю́т**	—	
Future	я ты он, она́, оно́ мы вы они́	**бу́ду** дава́ть **бу́дешь** дава́ть **бу́дет** дава́ть **бу́дем** дава́ть **бу́дете** дава́ть **бу́дут** дава́ть	я ты он, она́, оно́ мы вы они́	**дам** **дашь** **даст** **дади́м** **дади́те** **даду́т**
Imperative	Дава́**й**! Дава́**йте**!		Да**й**! Да́**йте**!	

Exercise 12. **Put the verbs in brackets into the correct form:**

1. Мы сейча́с боле́ем. Врач (дава́ть) нам лека́рство.
2. Ка́тя — аккура́тная[1] де́вушка, поэ́тому я всегда́ (дава́ть) ей кни́ги и журна́лы.
3. Ма́ма не (дать) нам конфе́ты, потому́ что мы не сде́лали дома́шнее зада́ние.
4. И́горь Влади́мирович, (дать) мне, пожа́луйста, ноутбу́к. Мой ноутбу́к не рабо́тает.
5. Э́то но́вая кни́га Ма́рка Леви́? (Дать), пожа́луйста, почита́ть.
6. Одно́й руко́й (дава́ть), друго́й руко́й берёт (a proverb that describes a greedy man who wants to look generous).

[1] tidy, careful

Exercise 13. **Complete the sentences using the verbs дать — дава́ть, choose the right form of tense and aspect:**

1. Э́то мой друг. Ра́ньше я ча́сто ________________ ему́ маши́ну. И сего́дня я то́же ______________ ему́ маши́ну.
2. Да́рья никогда́ не ____________ но́мер телефо́на. А мне вчера́ ____________.
3. Э́та компа́ния уже́ 10 лет _____________ мне рабо́ту. Мы не мо́жем сейча́с _________________ Вам рабо́ту.
4. Мне пло́хо! Пожа́луйста, ____________________ стака́н воды́!
5. У вас есть де́ти? Никогда́ не __________________ им спи́чки[2]!

[2] (pl.): matches

Да́тельный паде́ж (паде́ж № 3) — Dative (case № 3)

Кому́? Чему́? К кому́? К чему́? По чему́?

	case № 1				case № 3					
		чей? чьё? чья?	како́й? како́е? кака́я?	что? кто?		чьему́? чьему́? чьей?	како́му? како́му? како́й?	чему́? кому́?	adj.	n.
он	э́тот, тот	мо**й** тво**й** наш ваш **его́**, **её**, **их**	но́в**ый** больш**о́й** хоро́ш**ий** бу́дущ**ий** си́н**ий** ру́сск**ий**	стол слова́р**ь** музе́**й** санато́р**ий** друг фи́зик студе́нт писа́тел**ь** Андре́**й** Анато́л**ий** ребёнок челове́к	э́**тому**, **тому́**	мо**ему́** тво**ему́** на́ш**ему** ва́ш**ему** **его́**, **её**, **их**	но́в**ому** больш**о́му** хоро́ш**ему** бу́дущ**ему** си́н**ему** ру́сск**ому**	стол**у́** словар**ю́** музе́**ю** санато́р**ию** дру́г**у** фи́зик**у** студе́нт**у** писа́тел**ю** Андре́**ю** Анато́л**ию** ребё**нку** челове́к**у**	**-ОМУ /** **-ЕМУ**	**-У /** **-Ю /** **-ИЮ**
оно́	э́то, то	мо**ё** тво**ё** на́ш**е** ва́ш**е** **его́**, **её**, **их**	но́в**ое** больш**о́е** хоро́ш**ее** бу́дущ**ее** си́н**ее** ру́сск**ое**	письм**о́** мо́р**е** зда́н**ие**	э́**тому**, **тому**	мо**ему́** тво**ему́** на́ш**ему** ва́ш**ему** **его́**, **её**, **их**	но́в**ому** больш**о́му** хоро́ш**ему** бу́дущ**ему** си́н**ему** ру́сск**ому**	письм**у́** мо́р**ю** зда́н**ию**	**-ОМУ /** **-ЕМУ**	**-У /** **-Ю /** **-ИЮ**
она́	э́та, та	мо**я́** тво**я́** на́ш**а** ва́ш**а** **его́**, **её**, **их**	но́в**ая** больш**а́я** хоро́ш**ая** бу́дущ**ая** си́н**яя** ру́сск**ая**	ко́мнат**а** дере́вн**я** тетра́д**ь** аудито́р**ия** подру́г**а** ба́бушк**а** А́н**я** Аде́л**ь** Мар**и́я**	э́**той**, **той**	мо**е́й** тво**е́й** на́ш**ей** ва́ш**ей** **его́**, **её**, **их**	но́в**ой** больш**о́й** хоро́ш**ей** бу́дущ**ей** си́н**ей** ру́сск**ой**	ко́мнат**е** дере́вн**е** тетра́д**и** аудито́р**ии** подру́г**е** ба́бушк**е** А́н**е** Аде́л**и** Мар**и́и**	**-ОЙ /** **-ЕЙ**	**-Е /** **-И /** **-ИИ**

9

	case № 1				case № 3					
		чьи?	каки́е?	что? кто?		чьим?	каки́м?	чему́? кому́?	adj.	n.
они́	э́т**и**,	мо**и́**	но́в**ые**	стол**ы́**	э́т**им**,	мо**и́м**	но́в**ым**	стол**а́м**	**-ЫМ /**	**-АМ/**
	т**е**	тво**и́**	больш**и́е**	слова**ри́**	т**ем**	тво**и́м**	больш**и́м**	словар**я́м**	**-ИМ**	**-ЯМ/**
		на́ш**и**	хоро́ш**ие**	музе́**и**		на́ш**им**	хоро́ш**им**	музе́**ям**		**-ИЯМ**
		ва́ш**и**	бу́дущ**ие**	санато́р**ии**		ва́ш**им**	бу́дущ**им**	санато́р**иям**		
		его́,	си́н**ие**	пи́сьм**а**		**его́**,	си́н**им**	пи́сьм**ам**		
		её,	ру́сск**ие**	мор**я́**		**её**,	ру́сск**им**	мор**я́м**		
		их		зда́н**ия**		**их**		зда́н**иям**		
				ко́мнат**ы**				ко́мнат**ам**		
				дере́вн**и**				деревн**я́м**		
				тетра́д**и**				тетра́д**ям**		
				аудито́р**ии**				аудито́р**иям**		
				де́т**и**				де́т**ям**		
				лю́д**и**				лю́д**ям**		

Dative (case № 3) denotes the addressee or receiver of the action:

дать / дава́ть — Да́йте **ребёнку** мяч

звони́ть / позвони́ть — Майкл звони́т **бра́ту** в Нью-Йо́рк.

Verbs that direct dative case express:

1. Passing the object to the addressee / receiver: дава́ть/дать, дари́ть/подари́ть[1], отправля́ть/отпра́вить[2]:

Анто́н да́рит цветы́ **А́лле**. Джон отправля́ет письмо́ **отцу́**.

2. Sharing information with an addressee / receiver: писа́ть, звони́ть, говори́ть, чита́ть, расска́зывать, объясня́ть, отвеча́ть, помога́ть[3]:

Преподава́тель объясня́ет **студе́нтам** грамма́тику.

Эже́н расска́зывает **друзья́м** о Пари́же.

Ма́ша пи́шет **дру́гу** письмо́.

[1] (2.R.CONS.1): to present
[2] отправля́ть (1.R.VOW) / отпра́вить (2.IR Б, П, М, В + Л): to send
[3] помога́ть (1.R.VOW) / помо́чь (SPECIAL): to help
[4] a present
[5] an explanation
[6] a response

Nouns formed from these verbs are also used with the dative case: пода́рок[4], письмо́, звоно́к, объясне́ние[5], отве́т[6].

They are often used with the following words: дава́ть (объясне́ние, отве́т), дари́ть (пода́рок), отправля́ть (письмо́, пода́рок), де́лать (зво́нок, пода́рок).

Э́то пода́рок **люби́мой сестре́**.

Мо́жно я сде́лаю звоно́к **дру́гу**?

Я отправля́ю пода́рок **ма́ме** в дере́вню, потому́ что я люблю́ дари́ть **ей** пода́рки.

Плохо́й ме́неджер даёт объясне́ние **дире́ктору**.

Све́та звони́т **дру́гу**.
Она́ пода́рит **ему́** пода́рок.

***Exercise 14.* Choose the appropriate present for John's family and friends:**

У Джóна есть отéц Алексáндр, мáма Лóра и брат Кен. Лóра худóжница, онá лю́бит рисовáть. Алексáндр — истóрик, он лю́бит истори́ческие кни́ги и лю́бит изучáть языки́. Кен лю́бит петь и игрáть на гитáре.

Ещё у Джóна в Лóндоне есть друг Марк и подру́га Мáрта. Марк лю́бит футбóл. А Мáрта лю́бит традициóнную одéжду рáзных нарóдов.

Dictionary: лáпти, сарафáн, вáленки, шарф футбóльного клу́ба «Спартáк», кни́га «Истóрия Москвы́» на ру́сском языкé, балалáйка, карти́на совремéнного ру́сского худóжника.

***Exercise 15.* Read the dialogue. Tell where you can buy presents in your town.**

— Где в Москвé мóжно купи́ть подáрки друзья́м?

— На Арбáте.

— Что такóе Арбáт?

— Арбáт — э́то центрáльная туристи́ческая у́лица Москвы́.

***Exercise 16.* Answer the following questions:**

Кому́ вы пи́шете пи́сьма? Я пишу́ пи́сьма друзья́м

звони́те? Я звоню́

расскáзываете о жи́зни? ________

объясня́ете прáвила? ________

дáрите подáрки? ________

говори́те комплимéнты? ________

читáете стихи́? ________

9

— Что Вы дéлаете? — John asked, pale at the sight of a syringe.

— У Вас шок, — the doctor answered, trying to calm him down. — Э́то обезбóливающее[1]. Анальгéтик. Не бу́дет бóльно.

— Нет-нéт, — John protested again and Brünnhilde put down the syringe and took the phone:

— Я звоню́ перевóдчику.

— Хорошó! — answered John happily.

— Перевóдчик сейчáс зáнят — он рабóтает с америкáнскими актёрами, — said Brünnhilde after she had talked to somebody on the phone. — И он говори́т, что у них нет одногó америкáнского актёра. Поговори́те с переводчиком по телефóну.

[1] a painkiller (in Russian it is declined as an adjective)

! по (чему́?) — communication / transmission facilities

Мне не ну́жно диск. Я ужé ви́дел э́тот фильм по телеви́зору.

говори́ть по телефóну — to talk on the phone

смотрéть по телеви́зору — to watch on tv

отправля́ть по электрóнной пóчте, по фáксу — to send email, fax

слу́шать по рáдио — to listen over the radio

ГОВОРИ́М ПО ТЕЛЕФО́НУ

A talk on the phone is not difficult, especially if you are talking to a friend. Dial the number and wait for the answer: «Да», «Алло́», «У телефо́на», etc.

You can answer — Приве́т, ма́ма. or — Приве́т, Дени́с, мо́жно поговори́ть с О́лей?

And here you are — the conversation has begun.

If you need to talk to someone who you don't know very well, here are some ideas of how to make a conversation effective and to get all necessary information.

You dial the number.

— Секрета́рь (фи́рмы, дире́ктора) слу́шает.

— Здра́вствуйте, говори́т Ивано́в, экономи́ст (инже́нер...) фи́рмы (ба́нка...) Соедини́те[1] меня́, пожа́луйста, с господи́ном Си́доровым.

— Здра́вствуйте. К сожале́нию, сейча́с господи́на Си́дорова нет на ме́сте. Он бу́дет в 14:00.

— Спаси́бо. До свида́ния.

So, you couldn't talk to Sidorov, but you have information when he will be back. When you talk on the phone on business, give your full name — it demonstates your serious intentions.

[1] соединя́ть (1.R.VOW) / соедини́ть (2.R.CONS.1): to connect

"Hello," that was the only thing John could say when he heard, "Go to the stage immediately, Mr. Smith, you have five minutes!" John heard short beeps. John realized that he had been mistaken for someone else again, this time for an American actor.

— Е́сли Вам бу́дет пло́хо, звони́те врачу́ в ско́рую по́мощь[2], — said the doctor.

— Хорошо́-хорошо́. А сейча́с скажи́те, пожа́луйста, где вы́ход?

Having heard the word вы́ход the doctor nodded and said:

— Пойдёмте.

— Э́то америка́нский актёр, — explained Brünnhilde to some people in a dressing room.

— Хорошо́, — the dresser smiled, removing a black coat with a long, narrow tails that made all men look like beetles. She professionally shook John out of his jacket and handed him a suit.

— Нет, — protested the Englishman trying to take his jacket back. — Вы́ход. Где вы́ход?

— Всем актёрам даю́ фра́ки, — the girl understood his words in her own way. — Э́то о́пера. Что тут мо́жно сде́лать? Кла́ссика[3], девятна́дцатый век. Ваш режиссёр хо́чет де́лать совреме́нную о́перу, а наш режиссёр говори́т, что быть же́нщиной в девятна́дцатом ве́ке — э́то носи́ть дли́нные, краси́вые пла́тья. А быть мужчи́ной — э́то носи́ть фрак. И — цили́ндр. Вот, даю́ Вам цили́ндр то́же.

Indeed, there was a black shiny cylinder on John's head.

— О́чень хорошо́, краси́во! — the girl evaluated her work.

— А брю́ки актёрам-мужчи́нам даю́т да́льше[4]. Возьми́те пантало́ны — и Ваш вы́ход, — she gestured down the hall.

[2] по́мощь (она́): aid, help; ско́рая по́мощь: ambulance
[3] classics (n.)
[4] farther

***Exercise 17*. Look at the picture and say what 19th century clothes John put on, and what's left of the modern clothes.**

Pay attention that the meaning of the words га́лстук (German Halstuch — neckcloth), жиле́т (French gilet), фрак (French frac) and трость[5] hasn't changed.

The word цили́ндр, borrowed from ancient Greek (κύλινδρος — roller, cylinder), is applied to a high hat of a certain form. In the meaning of "type of men's hat," the word цили́ндр disappeared from the language with this accessory and fashion. Today this word represents only geometrical figure.

[5] трость (она́): a cane

The word панталóны was also borrowed from the French language, but nowadays this word is used for women's underwear, not for men's trousers.

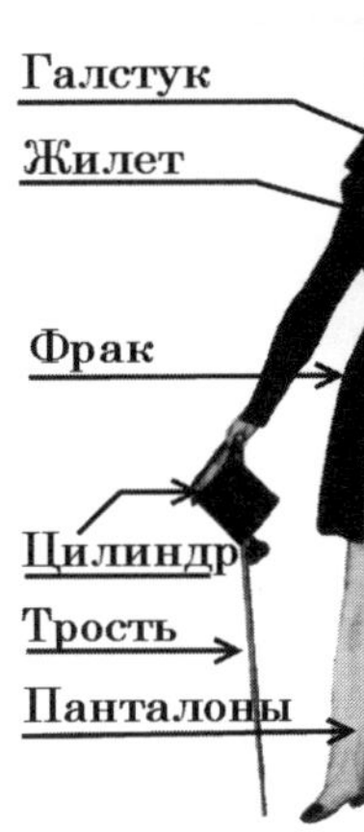

John realized that this strange, inverted world finally gave him freedom of movement. He recognized the word вы́ход, he had seen it at the airport: вы́ход в гóрод.

He decided not to tempt fate any more: he left his jacket at the dressing-room and went quickly down the hall. Just above his head there was a sign saying «вы́ход на сце́ну[1]». He understood it, turned around and went in the opposite direction, away from the Looking Glass, to the street, to freedom.

Слóво «большóй» понимáют на всех языкáх ми́ра, потомý что во всём мире лю́ди знáют Большóй теáтр, — John heard the professional voice of the guide. He took off his hat and held it with his hand. To join a tour to the backstage was a great chance to get out of there without attracting attention.

Большóй теáтр — э́то си́мвол[2] Росси́и. Э́то си́мвол высóких тради́ций в искýсстве[3]. Большóй теáтр — э́то часть[4] рýсской культýры.

Рýсская культýра — что э́то?

Э́то Андре́й Рублёв и егó икóны[5], Казими́р Мале́вич и егó «Чёрный квадрáт»[6], Фёдор Достоéвский, Лев Толстóй и их кни́ги, Сергéй Эйзенштéйн и егó фи́льмы, Константи́н Станислáвский и егó теáтр. Но без óперы Модéста Мýсоргского и Петрá Чайкóвского, без фенóмена Фёдора Шаля́пина, без тáнца Гали́ны Улáновой и Мáйи Плисéцкой нельзя́ познакóмиться с рýсской культýрой.

В ми́ре óчень мнóго пáмятников[7]. Э́то пáмятники знамени́тым лю́дям напримéр, сегóдня вы ви́дели пáмятники Алексáндру Пýшкину, Николáю Гóголю, Льву Толстóму, пáмятники побéдам[8] в вóйнах[9]. Есть пáмятники литератýрным герóям[10]. Большóй теáтр — э́то тóже пáмятник. Пáмятник рýсскому искýсству.

Но э́тот пáмятник не тóлько пóмнит истóрию, он живёт сейчáс. Здесь дéлают новóе искýсство.

John listened without much interest, paying attention only to the names that had already been known to him, since parents had paid very good money for his education.

[1] a stage
[2] a symbol
[3] art
[4] a part
[5] an icon
[6] a square (n.)
[7] a monument
[8] a victory
[9] a war
[10] a hero

9

***Exercise 18.* Do you know these names? What did these people do? Name their profession.**

Андрéй Рублёв — э́то худóжник, он писáл икóны.

Казими́р Малéвич — э́то ____________________ .

Фёдор Достоéвский — э́то ____________________ .

Лев Толстóй — э́то ____________________ .

Сергéй Эйзенштéйн — э́то ____________________ .

Константи́н Станислáвский — э́то ____________________ .

Модéст Мýсоргский — э́то ____________________ .

Пётр Чайкóвский — э́то ____________________ .

Фёдор Шаля́пин — э́то ____________________ .

Гали́на Улáнова — э́то ____________________ .

Мáйя Плисéцкая — э́то ____________________ .

At last the excursion ended. Running out of the stuffy corridors of the theatre to breathe cool Moscow air, John automatically put his hand into his pocket and realized that the only thread that bound this inverted pandemonium world with England and the rest of the world, had been lost. His phone had been left in his jacket in the dressing room. However, John was a careful man, even pedantic, so there was another phone with a copy of all contacts in a suitcase in the hotel. Not much upset by the loss, he approached a passer-by:

— Извини́те, скажи́те, пожа́луйста, где… Где… — and at that moment the English guest got really terrified. No, he had not forgotten the name of his hotel. It was very simple and most importantly, meaningless. John was going to stay at the Cosmos hotel, but unfortunately there were no rooms available in it. Therefore he had to book a room at another hotel. There was a great variety of such small hotels with names like "Palace plus" or "Plus Palace" in Moscow, and locals could hardly know anything about them. The bad thing was that John did not remember the address of the hotel.

— Где гости́ница…? Где у́лица…?

Exercise 19. **Help John to find his way in the city. Find these objects on the map.**

у́лица	a street
пло́щадь	a square
проспе́кт	an avenue
переу́лок	a lane
парк	a park
шоссе́	a highway
перекрёсток	crossroads
остано́вка авто́буса	a bus stop
ста́нция метро́	underground station
подзе́мный перехо́д	subway / pedestrian underpass
пешехо́дный перехо́д	pedestrian crossing

He looked around. Very close to him "Metropol" hotel attracted attention with its beautiful lights, it was pompous, fashionable and elegant at the same time. It seemed that it was the hotel whose pediment was decorated with a mosaic by the great Vrubel. Right. John remembered the famous "Demon" and "Swan Princess" by the Russian artist. "No, the College of Humanities where my father drove me was not in vain. A lot of knowledge, useless though," — John thought irritably. He turned around and went in the opposite direction, where he saw the sign «Метро́».

At the entrance to the underground there was a shopping centre with the sign «Охо́тный ряд». In the morning he saw a map in the underground. It was the centre of Moscow. There was Кремль, just around the corner. He then read: «Ста́нция метро́ "Охо́тный ряд"». He tried to concentrate... The hotel was somewhere in the centre, not far from the Kremlin. Roman Kharitonov got him in a taxi near the hotel. They drove along the embankment of the Moscow River, and immediately saw the Temple of Christ the Savior, which was impossible not to recognize, because, along with the Moscow Kremlin, that temple was shown in all the brochures about Moscow. "So, — thought John, — if I go to the temple and back along the embankment, I'll get to my hotel. This should not be very far away. The question was: where is the temple?"

— Мо́жно фо́то? — asked a thirteen-year-old boy, and put a piece of paper into the cylinder.

— Что Вам на́до? — John was surprised, because the boy put his arm around him and pulled out the phone, ready to make a selfie. — Нет. Нельзя́!

— Ма́ло Вам? — the boy was surprised and put another piece of paper into the hat. — Цили́ндр наде́ньте, пожа́луйста!

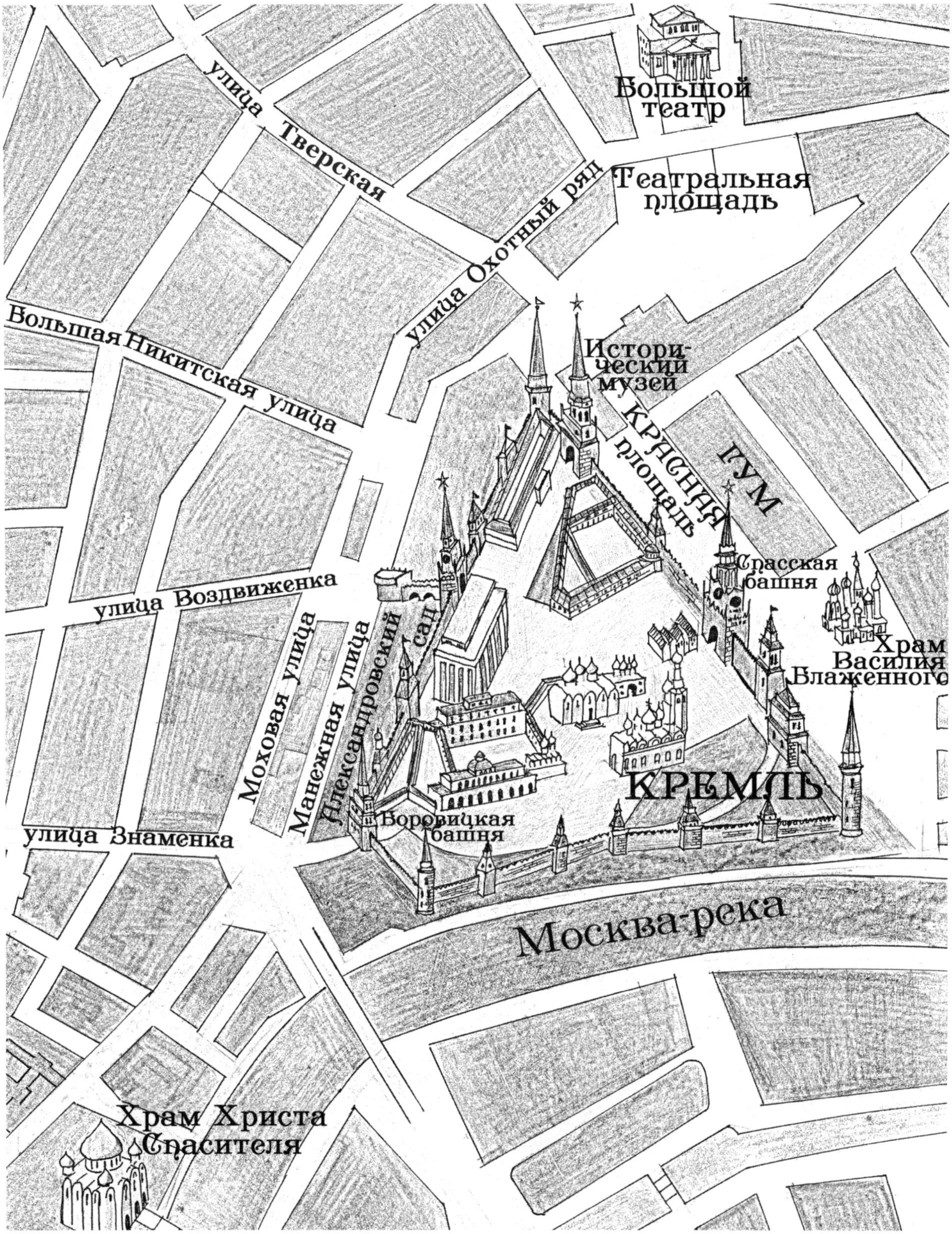
Большой театр
Театральная площадь
улица Тверская
улица Охотный ряд
Большая Никитская улица
Исторический музей
Красная площадь
ГУМ
Спасская башня
Храм Василия Блаженного
улица Воздвиженка
Моховая улица
Манежная улица
Александровский сад
Кремль
Боровицкая башня
улица Знаменка
Москва-река
Храм Христа Спасителя

9

John pulled the pieces out of the cylinder — it was money.

500 и 100 рублей.

John counted — $ 10 for a couple of photos. Not bad. He put on his hat and smiled.

Then John circled the building of Госуда́рственная ду́ма[1] with Soviet style architecture.

— Извини́те, скажи́те, пожа́луйста, где больша́я це́рковь[2]? — He turned to an old man that looked intelligent. Unfortunately, he remembered only that word from the guidebook, but could not remember how the Christ the Savior Cathedral was called in Russian and «церковь» seemed the closest in meaning. The old man stared without any glimpse of understanding in his eyes.

— Це́рковь, це́рковь, больша́я це́рковь, — John repeated and folded his hands over his head, miming the dome. The old man seemed to understand. He patted the young man on the shoulder and said gently, motioning straight then right. — Там Це́рковь Большо́го Вознесе́ния[3]. Здесь Пу́шкин… John couldn't understand what Pushkin was doing in the Great Ascension Church. Why Pushkin again? He understood even less. — Пу́шкин? — John repeated to ensure that they were thinking about the same person. — Пу́шкин, Пу́шкин, — happily nodded the passer-by. John had already heard that the name of the famous poet was mentioned on every occassion in Russia. Apparently, it was such a case again. He thanked the strange old man, took his hat off and walked on.

[1] State Duma (Russian Parliament)
[2] це́рковь (она́): a church
[3] the Great Ascension Church

***Exercise 20.* In the Great Ascension Church, Pushkin got married to his wife — the first beauty Natalia Goncharova — a favourite place of Muscovites and tourists. What do you think, why, looking at John, the old man thought he was looking for that place? What is the difference between the words храм and це́рковь?**

John went down the street and turned where the intelligent old man had shown him. The temple was nowhere in sight. John went on, but his intuition told him that he was going the wrong way. Young Jr. went a little forward and returned back, trying to identify English-speaking people in the crowd.

— Вам нужна́ по́мощь? — somebody asked politely from behind. John turned around and found a middle-aged woman, her head was covered with a scarf, as if she was going to serve in the temple. The cathedral had to be somewhere nearby — John thought.

— Да, по́мощь! Пожа́луйста! Я не по́мню а́дрес гости́ницы.

знать (IPF): know	**по́мнить (IPF): remember**	**забы́ть (PF): forget**	**вспо́мнить (PF): remember**
что? о чём? о ком?	матема́тику о конце́рте о Зида́не	Я по́мню, что конце́рт в 21:00. Я забы́л, что конце́рт в 21:00. Я уже́ вспо́мнил, что в 21:00 бу́дет конце́рт.	

— Поня́тно, — said the woman. — Гостя́м на́шего го́рода ну́жно помога́ть. Ду́маю, что я могу́ Вам помо́чь.

Exercise 21. **The verb помога́ть / помо́чь can help!**

The conjugation of помога́ть is regular (1.R.VOW), but you should learn how to conjugate its perfective form — помо́чь:

Infinitive	**помо́чь (SPECIAL): to help (IPF)**			
Future	я ты он (она́, оно́)	помо**гу́** помо́**жешь** помо́**жет**	мы вы они́	помо́**жем** помо́**жете** помо́**гут**
Past	он (она́, оно́)	помо́**г** (помо**гла́**, помо**гло́**)		помо**гли́**
Impérative	ты	Помо**ги́**!	вы	Помо**ги́те**!

1. Что де́лает сейча́с э́та же́нщина?
2. Как вы ду́маете, она́ помо́жет Джо́ну?
3. А вы ча́сто помога́ете лю́дям?
4. Кто обы́чно помога́ет вам?

— Ско́лько вре́мени Вы уже́ **хо́дите** тут?

— Здесь нельзя́ ходи́ть? — asked John thinking that he had broken a rule again.

Infinitive	**ходи́ть (2.IR. Д-Ж): to go, to walk (IPF)**			
Present	я ты он (она́, оно́)	хо**жу́** хо́**дишь** хо́**дит**	мы вы они́	хо́**дим** хо́**дите** хо́**дят**
Past	он (она́, оно́)	хо**ди́л** (а, о)		хо**ди́ли**
Impérative	ты	Хо**ди́**!	вы	Хо**ди́те**!

— Ходи́ть мо́жно. Но я ду́маю, Вам ну́жно **идти́**, а не **ходи́ть**, — smiled the woman.

— Я не понима́ю.

— Вы хо́дите вперёд-наза́д[1], потому́ что не зна́ете, куда́ Вам на́до идти́[2], — she gestured and John understood what she was talking about.

— Да, мне на́до идти́ в гости́ницу, — John motioned just the same as Lenin in old Soviet posters showing the way to a brighter future.

[1] вперёд: forward; наза́д: backward
[2] идти́ (SPECIAL): to go; to be in process

Exercise 22. **Compare, try to guess what is the difference between the words ходи́ть and идти́.**

Ходи́ть вперёд-наза́д

Идти́ вперёд

John went on.

— Да, Вы всё по́няли пра́вильно. Но я забы́л а́дрес. Я хожу́ вперёд-наза́д, потому́ что я не по́мню а́дрес.

Глаго́лы движе́ния — Verbs of motion

Verbs like **идти́** (moving in a certain direction)	Verbs like **ходи́ть** (moving in different directions)
1. One-way movement, is acted once: У́тром де́ти **иду́т** в шко́лу. На́до **идти́** вперёд, и там бу́дет теа́тр. 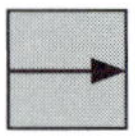	1. Moving "back and forth": Вчера́ мы **ходи́ли** (куда́?) на экску́рсию. = Вчера́ мы бы́ли (где?) на экску́рсии. 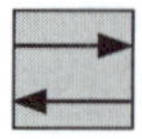
	2. Repeated movement (ча́сто, ка́ждый день, обы́чно, всегда́, ре́дко, иногда́): На рабо́ту обы́чно я **хожу́** пешко́м[1]. 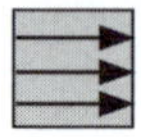 В музе́й я **хожу́** ка́ждый ме́сяц.
	3. Moving without any particular direction / purpose: Мы до́лго **ходи́ли** (гуля́ли). Вы **хо́дите** здесь уже́ час. Вы заблуди́лись[2]? 
	4. The ability to move: Ребёнок уже́ **хо́дит**. 

[1] on foot
[2] (PF; 2.IR Д-Ж): to get lost

Exercise 23. **Fill in the tables with these forms of the verbs идти́ and ходи́ть.**

идти́, хо́дите, шёл, ходи́ть, идёшь, хо́дим, шли, идёт, шло, идём, ходи́, идёте, ходи́те, иду́т, хожу́, иди́, хо́дишь, иди́те, хо́дит, хо́дят, шла.

Note: Вы хо́дите and Ходи́те! Differ only in stress!

Infinitive	**идти́** (SPECIAL)				**ходи́ть** (2.IR. Д-Ж)			
Present	я ты он, она́, оно́		мы вы они́		я ты он, она́, оно́		мы вы они́	
Past	он она́ оно́		они́		он она́ оно́		они́	
Imperative	ты		вы		ты		вы	

Exercise 24. **Explain the use of the verbs идти́ or ходи́ть.**

1. У́тром Анто́н **идёт** в шко́лу, а его́ сестра́ идёт в де́тский сад. 2. Я ча́сто **хожу́** в библиоте́ку, потому́ что я люблю́ чита́ть. 3. Сего́дня Марк **идёт** в библиоте́ку, потому́ что за́втра у него́ экза́мен. 4. В суббо́ту студе́нты **ходи́ли** в клуб. 5. Моя́ мла́дшая сестра́ уже́ **хо́дит**. 6. Я люблю́ **ходи́ть** пешко́м.

Exercise 25. **Complete the sentences with the necessary form of the verbs идти́ or ходи́ть.**

1. Ты ____________ вчера́ в теа́тр на бале́т «Лебеди́ное о́зеро»? 2. Здра́вствуй, Андре́й! Куда́ ты ______________? 3. Я люблю́ __________ пешко́м. 4. Сего́дня Ма́рта ____________ в университе́т пе́рвый раз. 5. Ка́ждый день студе́нты _______________ на заня́тия. 6. У нас ко́нчилось молоко́. И я __________ в магази́н купи́ть молока́. 7. Ка́ждый день я __________ в магази́н.

— Како́е ме́сто Вы по́мните ря́дом с Ва́шей гости́ницей? — asked the woman.

— А ря́дом… э́то… це́рковь.

— Больша́я це́рковь и́ли ма́ленькая?

— Больша́я це́рковь. Са́мая больша́я це́рковь в Москве́.

— А́-а-а, Храм Христа́ Спаси́теля! — guesses the woman. — Вы шли непра́вильно, потому́ что пошли́[1] в другу́ю сто́рону[2].

[1] (SPECIAL): to go
[2] side

Exercise 26. **Study the conjugation of the verb пойти́. It is not difficult: пойти́ is similar идти́, but И is changed to Й.**

Infinitive	**пойти́** (SPECIAL)			
Future	я ты он (она́, оно́)	той**ду́** пой**дёшь** пой**дёт**	мы вы они́	пой**дём** пой**дёте** пой**ду́т**
Past	он она́ оно́	пошёл пошла́ пошло́	они́	пошли́
Imperative	ты	Пойди́!	вы	Пойди́те!

— Вы пошли́ **напра́во**, а на́до бы́ло идти́ **пря́мо**.

John studied all the adverbs associated with movement and the direction very carefully in London. You never know where you could get lost in a foreign country. Now he had only to avoid confusion.

Exercise 27. **Compare adverbs with the meaning of place to adverbs with the meaning of direction.**

где?	**Translation**	куда?	**Translation**
пря́мо	in front of	пря́мо	straight on
спра́в**а**	on the right	**на**пра́в**о**	to the right
сле́в**а**	on the left	**на**ле́в**о**	to the left
впере**ди́**	onward	**в**перёд	ahead
сза́**ди**	behind	**на**за́д	backward
там	there	туда́	there
здесь	here	сюда́	here

— Сейча́с мне куда́ на́до идти́? Пря́мо? Напра́во? И́ли нале́во? — John asked the woman.

— Сейча́с на́до идти́ пря́мо. Пото́м напра́во. И пото́м то́же пря́мо. Э́то у́лица Тверска́я. Сейча́с мы здесь. Вы пойдёте **по** (у́лице) **Тверско́й**. Пото́м напра́во и пойдёте **по у́лице** Охо́тный Ряд. А пото́м пойдёте по (у́лице) Мохово́й, — she explained patiently.

9

— Как э́то **по ули́це**?

The woman shuffled her foot on the ground: идти́ по доро́ге, идти́ по у́лице.

She touched her head with her hand: по голове́.

— Бэ́тмен идёт по стене́, — added John imitating the movements on an imaginary wall to show that he had understood her.

The woman laughed: «Не на́до по стене́! В Москве́ есть доро́ги и у́лицы. Иди́те по у́лице».

Model: По[1] + case № 3 — movement on the surface of the object

— Сейча́с я иду́ по у́лице[2] Тверска́я. Пото́м напра́во. Пото́м по улице Охо́тный Ряд. Пра́вильно?

— Пра́вильно.

— А пото́м куда́?

— Пото́м идёте к Мане́жной пло́щади. Там бу́дет Кремль. Но идти́ к Кремлю́ не на́до. Вам на́до идти́ пря́мо.

[1] on
[2] по у́лице: down the street

It was clear, John imagined the scheme for preposition К which was similar to the one for preposition По.

Model: К[2] + case № 3 — approaching the object

ATTENTION!

Personal pronouns ему́, ей, им change after preposition К.

[2] to

Compare:

case № 1	кто	я	ты	он/оно́	она́	мы	вы	они́
case № 3	кому́? к кому́?	мне ко мне́	тебе́ к тебе́	ему́ к нему́	ей к ней	нам к нам	вам к вам	им к ним

Exercise 28. **A) Using К + case № 3 say that these people are approaching the objects.**

1. Я иду́ (Кремль) ____________________
2. Актёр идёт (Большо́й теа́тр) ____________________
3. Анто́н идёт (Кра́сная пло́щадь) ____________________
4. Мари́на идёт (э́то но́вое зда́ние) ____________________
5. Мы идём (интере́сные па́мятники) ____________________
6. Го́сти иду́т (наш дом) ____________________

B) Change nouns into pronouns.

Exercise 29. **Mark on the scheme John's route and the route that the woman told him about.**

Exercise 30. **Explain to tourists how to go from the Christ the Savior Cathedral to St. Basil's Cathedral.**

When John came to the Manezh Square, he saw in the guidebook what was called Мане́ж. It was a true giant of the Classical period, so wide that its height was not important — it seemed as if Мане́ж crouched closer to the bridge, trying to lay under the feet of passers-by enormous wings of the roof. But it only seemed so. Within this strict classical building with three arches a whole regiment could go through. That is how it was built by Tsar Alexander I.

«Мане́ж — э́то па́мятник войне́ 1812-ого го́да[1]» — the sign at the entrance said. John was surprised: it seemed strange that the monument symbolizing Russian victory over France was called by a French name.

There was a sign over the entrance:

ЦЕНТРА́ЛЬНЫЙ ВЫ́СТАВОЧНЫЙ ЗАЛ[2]

Центра́льный — an adjective derived from the word це́нтр.

Вы́ставочный — an adjective derived from the word вы́ставка. But John couldn't remember what that word meant.

Зал — the same as 'hall', John translated. A useful word, for business as well.

[1] ты́сяча восемьсо́т двена́дцатого го́да

[2] The Central Exposition Hall

Exercise 31. **Look up in the encyclopedia what is in Manege nowadays.**

John was looking at the view of the Kremlin — a huge fortress of red brick, where there was the presidential palace, a cathedral, museums, the famous Царь-пу́шка and Царь-ко́локол and more. John promised himself to come back there later.

Having passed Мане́ж, John sighed with relief. In the distance, behind the houses he saw lighted white walls. Храм Христа́ Спаси́теля — now he remembered. John quickened his pace. Suddenly the crowd that constantly surrounded him on the streets of Moscow, started to become thicker and thicker. At first he did not pay attention, but soon he had to slow down and even almost stop. The view was strange: there were men in exactly the same as John's dress coats and hats. Women were wearing long ball dresses with intricately stacked hairstyles, talking quietly. "Again, through the looking glass," thought John with fear and closed his eyes to make the hallucination disappear. When he opened his eyes, everything was in place: coats, dresses, light-flooded magnificent white house with columns and a belvedere, and the sounds of waltzes from open windows. There was a man in the window. He shouted something and the music became louder. People came to the door of the amazing house. John stopped, but he was taken by the arms: a blonde on one side and a brunette on the other.

«Пе́рвый та́нец за́нят, но второ́й мо́жет быть Ваш», — said the blonde.

Та́нец. John remembered the verb танцева́ть and understood that the blonde had invited him to dance.

— Спасибо, но мне на́до ходи́ть, — answered John confusing the verbs идти́ and ходи́ть.

— Нет, не ходи́ть! Танцева́ть! Сего́дня у нас бал, и все танцу́ют! — the blonde smiled and asked — А Вы иностра́нец?

— Да.

— Отку́да Вы?

— Из Ло́ндона!

— Э́то про́сто великоле́пно! У нас бу́дет междунаро́дный[3] пра́здник! Пойдёмте! — said the girl and John felt that she firmly held his hand.

[3] international. Compare: междунаро́дный аэропо́рт, междунаро́дная конфере́нция.

9

Глава́ 10

На зака́те со́лнца высоко́ над го́родом на ка́менной терра́се одного́ из са́мых краси́вых зда́ний в Москве́... находи́лись дво́е: Во́ланд и Азазе́лло. Они́ не́ были видны́ сни́зу, с у́лицы... Но им го́род был ви́ден почти́ до са́мых краёв.

М.А. Булга́ков. Ма́стер и Маргари́та

At sunset, high above the town, on the stone roof of one of the most beautiful buildings in Moscow... stood two figures — Woland and Azazello. They were invisible from the street below... although they could see almost to the limits of the city.

— M. Bulgakov, "Master and Margarita"

Some time before John could only assume, but then he knew for sure: all Russian women dream to have an Englishman as a husband. Trying to escape from the blonde, he ran across a huge bright room with a checkerboard floor, where the dance was whirling elegant pairs. The staircase where he came led only up — to the balcony above the hall — guessed John. On one of the stairs he started and stopped: in front of him in a pool of blood there was Salome with the head of John the Baptist on a platter. "Through the Looking Glass" — John praised the advantages of installation. The next door led into the classroom. The door next to it — to a room with books. All around was museum purity — walls and arches decorated with stucco and statues in the Empire style. Another room with books. More books. John had already noticed that the most reading country in the world does not skimp on the libraries. While he was going there, he saw a huge library of Lenin, built in the monumental tradition of ancient Egyptian architecture. Several mansions also had a sign «Библиоте́ка». Apparently, that magnificent building served as a library as well.

In one of the distant rooms John stopped, took off his coat and the cylinder — luckily, his trousers and his shirt were quite ordinary. Suddenly, he heard a crunch behind one of the cabinets. John froze and listened. The crunch repeated: a black silhouette slowly appeared from behind the cabinet.

John looked into the darkness, but could see nothing until the silhouette moved forward. Dim light from the street illuminated the thin man, he was not old yet, in jeans and a sweater. The man put his finger to his lips.

— Как Вы вошли́? — whispered the stranger. John did not understand the question and said nothing, looking silently at the thin man.

— Ты что, немо́й[1]? — said the stranger in syllables.

«Коне́чно, не твой», — thought John, he really didn't know how to react.

— Дверь, — the stranger pointed at the door. — Шёл, — the stranger walked in place. — Вошёл, — the man mimed opening the door and coming in. John watched: идти́... шёл... вошёл... Something had already begun to take shape in his head, but the stranger confused him again.

— Вы совсе́м не говори́те?

[1] The man meant немо́й (dumb, mute). In spoken language it sounds the same as «не мой» (not mine).

— Я немно́го говорю́ по-ру́сски, — finally answered Young Jr.

The man recoiled, his face showed discontent:

— Вы из «New York times»? И́ли из «Associated press»? Мо́жет быть, из «Le Monde»?

John remembered: when he was filling in the guest card there was a question there «Отку́да Вы?». He had to answer ИЗ + and the name of the city or country in case № 2.

— Я из Ло́ндона, — said John.

— Из Ло́ндона? — repeated the stranger. — Из «The Independent»?

— Нет.

— «Morning star» и́ли «The Daily Telegraph»?

— Нет-не́т. Я не журнали́ст, — John realised that the man had named the famous newspapers. The man had a professional «Nikon» in his hand, apparently he took him for the colleague from a rival newspaper.

— В тако́м слу́чае, что Вы тут де́лаете? — asked the man in a more friendly way.

John understood the question Что Вы тут де́лаете? He only didn't understand what «в тако́м слу́чае» meant.

— Что э́то — «в тако́м слу́чае»? — he asked.

— «In that case… в тако́м слу́чае — in English» — the man with the camera suddenly translated.

— Вы говори́те по-англи́йски? — John was surprised.

The stranger shrugged his shoulders.

— Я изуча́л англи́йский язы́к в шко́ле. Но э́то бы́ло давно́. И э́то не зна́чит, что я говорю́ по-англи́йски. Я почти́ всё забы́л.

— What are you doing here? — he asked in English.

— And what's wrong? Or only Russian journalists can wait for something in the library at night in total darkness? — John replied, being glad that he could speak his native language. The reaction was not immediate. Apparently the journalist was not too confident in speaking English.

— Не то́лько журнали́сты. Так де́лают ещё шпио́ны, — answered the man seriously.

— Шпио́ны — spies?

— Да. Ме́сто шпио́нов — в КГБ. Э́то ря́дом.

John stared at him surprisingly. The journalist laughed:

— Э́то была́ шу́тка... just a joke. Шу́тка. Понима́ете? Меня́ зову́т Андре́й Григо́рьев.

— Меня́ зову́т Джон Янг, — answered John shaking his hand.

— О́чень прия́тно. Но Вы не отве́тили. Что Вы тут де́лаете?

— Я шёл в гости́ницу.

— Необы́чно.

— Что необы́чно?

— Вы идёте в гости́ницу о́чень необы́чно.

John agreed with that: his way definitely looked very unusual.

— Вам на́до бы́ло ещё в Кремль зайти́, — said Andrey. It was a joke again, apparently.

John understood from the context that зайти́ — is derived from идти́.

Да, на́до бы́ло зайти́ в Кремль: я сего́дня ещё не здоро́вался с ва́шим президе́нтом. Весь мой маршру́т[1] сего́дня — э́то шу́тка! — John smiled for the first time that crazy day.

— Джон, Вы хорошо́ говори́те по-ру́сски! И хорошо́ шу́тите по-ру́сски! Шу́тка — шути́ть. Говори́ть шу́тку = шути́ть. Понима́ете?

— Спаси́бо, — thanked John and made a step towards the door demonstrating that he had to go. — Да, я понима́ю. Андре́й, скажи́те, пожа́луйста, где здесь вы́ход?

[1] route

10

— Вы́ход там, где вход, — answered Andrey watching John. — Но здесь на́до носи́ть фрак.

John remembered that in ordinary clothes he would look unusual at this ball, but he did not want to dress again in a tailcoat and a hat.

— Damn! — he said.

— О, э́то я понима́ю, — replied Andrey immediately. — По-ру́сски мы говори́м: чёрт побери́!

— Мне уже́ не на́до туда́ идти́, — John pointed in the direction of the hall, and added for a more vivid expression. — Чёрт побери́!

— Сади́тесь, — suggested the journalist pointing at the chair. — Почему́ Вы говори́те, что Ваш маршру́т — э́то шу́тка?

John sat down. It was not possible to go out, he had to wait for the end of the party and leave with the crowd. Looking around, the Englishman noticed that library probably also served as a lecture hall. Nearby, he found a board and markers. John drew and said:

Иностра́нец в Москве́. День пе́рвый

У́тром я был в гости́нице.

Мне на́до бы́ло идти́ в библиоте́ку.

Я шёл из гости́ницы, но не в библиоте́ку, а в рестора́н. Пото́м из рестора́на я шёл… в теа́тр. В теа́тре я → кабине́т врача́. Из теа́тра я → э́тот дом.

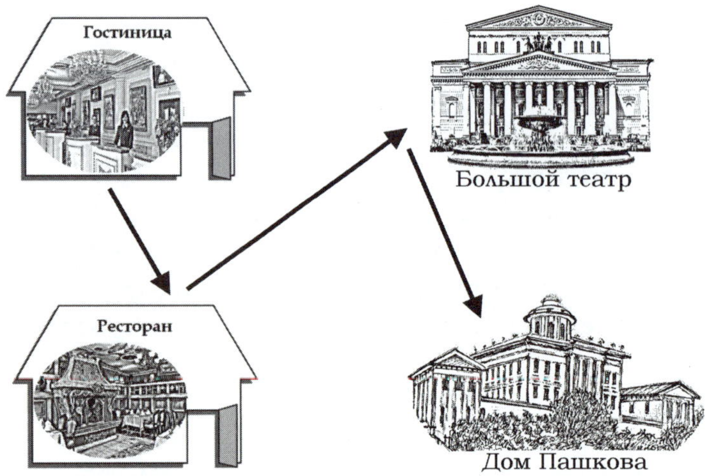

Andrey listened carefully, and when John finished, he translated everything he'd said in Russian, replacing the arrows into words.

Иностра́нец в Москве́. День пе́рвый

У́тром господи́н Джон Янг **вы́шел** из гости́ницы. Ему́ на́до бы́ло идти́ в библиоте́ку, но он **пришёл** в рестора́н. Э́то поня́тно. Быть в рестора́не лу́чше, чем быть в библиоте́ке.

Из рестора́на он ско́ро **ушёл** и **пошёл** в Большо́й теа́тр. Из теа́тра он хоте́л **уйти́**, но **пришёл** в кабине́т врача́. Что там де́лал господи́н Янг? Почему́ ему́ ну́жно бы́ло к врачу́? Э́то не о́чень поня́тно.

Из теа́тра Джон то́же **ушёл**, он хоте́л **пойти́** в гостини́цу, и ему́ ну́жно бы́ло **пойти́** в гости́ницу, но он **шёл ми́мо** э́того до́ма и **зашёл** сюда́. Э́то вообще́[1] непоня́тно.

[1] at all

— Вообще́ непоня́тно, — John complained.

There were too many versions of the verb идти́ in the past: шёл — ушёл, пришёл, пошёл, пришёл, зашёл! With arrows it was better!

— Нет-не́т, — Andrey disagreed. — Вообще́ непоня́тно, потому́ что э́то не маршру́т, а лабири́нт Минота́вра. Понима́ешь… Понима́ете, Джон?

— Да, the Minotaur's labyrinth. Андре́й, говори́те мне «ты». Э́то норма́льно.

— Хорошо́! Зна́ешь, Джон, что са́мое интере́сное в твоём маршру́те?

— Что?

— Ты шёл в библиоте́ку, и ты пришёл в библиоте́ку.

At that point John stopped understanding completely, and Andrey had to use a table.

He began writing a formula on the blackboard.

Глаго́л движе́ния + приста́вка — Verb of movement + prefix

идти́ → -йти́	при+йти́ = прийти́
шёл → -шёл	при+шёл = пришёл
ходи́ть → -ходи́ть	при+ходи́ть = приходи́ть
ходи́л → -ходи́л	при+ходи́л = приходи́л
е́хать → -е́хать	при+е́хать = прие́хать
е́хал → -е́хал	при+е́хал = прие́хал
е́здить → -езжа́ть	при+езжа́ть = приезжа́ть
е́здил → -езжа́л	при+езжа́л = приезжа́л

Group **идти́**	Group **ходи́ть**	Questions and prepositions	Examples
		по-: start of the movement 	
пойти́ **по**е́хать PF	~~походить~~ ~~поезжать~~ IPF	куда́? в, на + case № 4 по чему́? по + case № 3	пойти́ в парк — to go to the park пойти́ по у́лице — to go along the street Он пошёл в теа́тр, пото́м пошёл домо́й. — he went to the theatre, and then he went home. А́нна полете́ла домо́й в Москву́. — Anna flew home to Moscow
		при-: to arrive at a place (often with the indication where from) 	
прийти́ прие́хать PF	приходи́ть приезжа́ть IPF	куда́? в, на + case № 4 отку́да? из, с + case № 2	прийти́ в парк — to come to the park прие́хать из Росси́и — to come from Russia Спортсме́н прибежа́л к фи́нишу пе́рвым. — The sportsman came first.
		у-: to leave 	
уйти́ уе́хать PF	уходи́ть уезжа́ть IPF	отку́да? из, с + case № 2	уходи́ть из шко́лы — to leave school уе́хать из страны́ — to leave the country Он убежа́л от пробле́м на о́стров в Инди́йском океа́не. — He escaped from the problems to the island in the Indian ocean.
		в- / въ- / во-: to enter 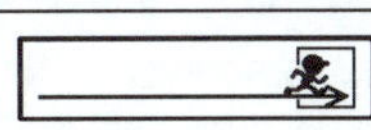	
войти́ въе́хать PF	входи́ть въезжа́ть IPF	куда́? в, на + case № 4	войти́ в дом — to enter the house въе́хать в го́род — to enter the city (on a vehicle)

10

Group **идти́**	Group **ходи́ть**	Questions and prepositions	Examples
вы-: to go out 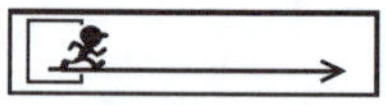			
вы́йти вы́ехать PF	выходи́ть выезжа́ть IPF	отку́да? из, с + case № 2	выходи́ть из до́ма — to go out of the house вы́ехать из го́рода — to leave the city (on a vehicle)
под- / подъ- / подо-: approaching 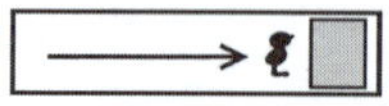			
подойти́ подъе́хать PF	подходи́ть подъезжа́ть IPF	к чему́? к + case № 3	подойти́ к друзья́м на у́лице — to approach friends in the street подъе́хать к до́му — to approach a house
от- / отъ- / ото-: remoteness (at a distance) 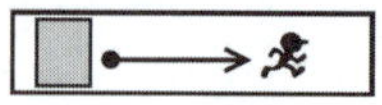			
отойти́ отъе́хать PF	отходи́ть отъезжа́ть IPF	от чего́? от + case № 2 от кого́? от + case № 2	отойти́ от окна́ — get away from the window отойти́ от э́того челове́ка — to move away from this man отъе́хать от остано́вки — to drive away from a stop кора́бль отплы́л от бе́рега — the ship departed from the coast
про-: 1. Passing something; 2. Crossing something 			
пройти́ прое́хать PF	проходи́ть проезжа́ть IPF	ми́мо чего́? ми́мо + case № 2 что? case № 4 через что́? через + case № 4	1. пройти ми́мо до́ма — to go past the house 2. пройти́ весь парк — to go through the park прое́хать через ле́с — to go through the forest (on a vehicle)
пере-: 1. To cross something; 2. To change one place to another 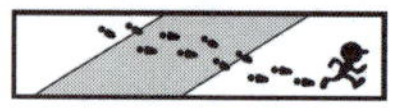			
перейти́ перее́хать PF	переходи́ть переезжа́ть IPF	что? case № 4 через что́? через + case № 4 отку́да? куда́? из + case № 2 в + case № 4	1. перейти́ доро́гу — to cross the street перейти́ через доро́гу — to cross the street 2. перейти́ из кабине́та в зал — to go from the study to the hall перее́хать из Ита́лии в Шве́цию — to move from Italy to Sweden
за-: 1. To go behind something 2. To go inside not for long (usually when you are going somewhere else); 3. To come somewhere in order to take something 			
зайти́ зае́хать PF	заходи́ть заезжа́ть IPF	за что? за + case № 4 куда́? в, на + case № 4 за кем? за + case № 5	1. зайти́ за де́рево = встать за де́ревом — to go behind the tree = to stand behind the tree 2. зайти́ в магази́н — to go to a supermarket зае́хать на автозапра́вку перед рабо́той — to stop by the petrol station before work 3. зае́хать за дру́гом — to pick a friend up

Group идти́	Group ходи́ть	Questions and prepositions	Examples
об- / объ- / обо-: 1. To move around; 2. To move past something 			
обойти́ объе́хать **PF**	обходи́ть объезжа́ть **IPF**	что? case № 4 вокру́г чего́? вокру́г + case № 2	1. обойти́ весь магази́н — to get around the entire store 2. обойти́ лу́жу — to bypass a puddle объе́хать про́бку на доро́ге — to avoid a traffic jam 3. обойти́ вокру́г до́ма — to walk around the house
до-: to reach 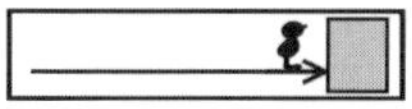			
дойти́ дое́хать **PF**	доходи́ть доезжа́ть **IPF**	до чего́? до + case № 2	дойти́ до до́ма — to get to the house дое́хать до Москвы́ — to come to Moscow

"It looks like a puzzle," — John thought, the movement (walking, running, flying or riding) is shown by the verb, and the direction — by prefixes and preposition.

Take, for example, the words вход and вы́ход. They are formed exactly on the same principle.

Выходи́ть — вы́ход (to exit — exit)

Входи́ть — вход (to enter — entrance)

Переходи́ть — перехо́д (to cross — crossing)

Упражне́ние 1. **Let's turn to Andrey's story «Иностра́нец в Москве. День пе́рвый». Define the meaning of the verb идти́ (шёл) with different prefixes. Use the table.**

To fix the result Andrey illustrated grammar with a poem that he had written and called «Доро́га в магази́н» — "The way to the shop".

Я **из** до́ма у́тром **вы́шел**.
Есть но́вый магази́н — я слы́шал.
Я **от** до́ма **отошёл**
И **по** у́лице **пошёл**.
Я **в** кио́ск[1] **зашёл** на миг[2],
Там касси́р — большо́й шутни́к[3].
Перешёл через доро́гу,
Здесь маши́н сего́дня мно́го.
Через па́рк пото́м **прошёл**,
Там я лу́жу[4] **обошёл**,
Ми́мо Пу́шкина **прошёл**.
Так **дошёл до** магази́на.
Продаве́ц там тётя Зи́на.
Магази́н **весь обошёл**,
Познако́мился, **ушёл**.
Домо́й **пошёл** обра́тно[5] я,
До́ма ждёт меня́ семья́.

Вот я **к** до́му **подошёл**,
Дверь откры́л[6], **в** подъе́зд[7] **вошёл**.
Я по ле́стнице **подня́лся**[8],
Позвони́л. Домо́й **пришёл**!

[1] a kiosk
[2] a moment; на миг = на мину́ту, на секу́нду
[3] a joker (шу́тка, шути́ть, шутни́к)
[4] a puddle
[5] back, backward
[6] открыва́ть (1.R.VOW) / откры́ть (1.IR Ы-О): to open
[7] an entrance hall, an entryway
[8] поднима́ться (1.R.VOW) / подня́ться (1.IR НЯ-ЙМУ): to go up, to escalate (is usually used instead of the verb взойти́)

Упражнéние 2. **Trace the hero's way in the picture.**

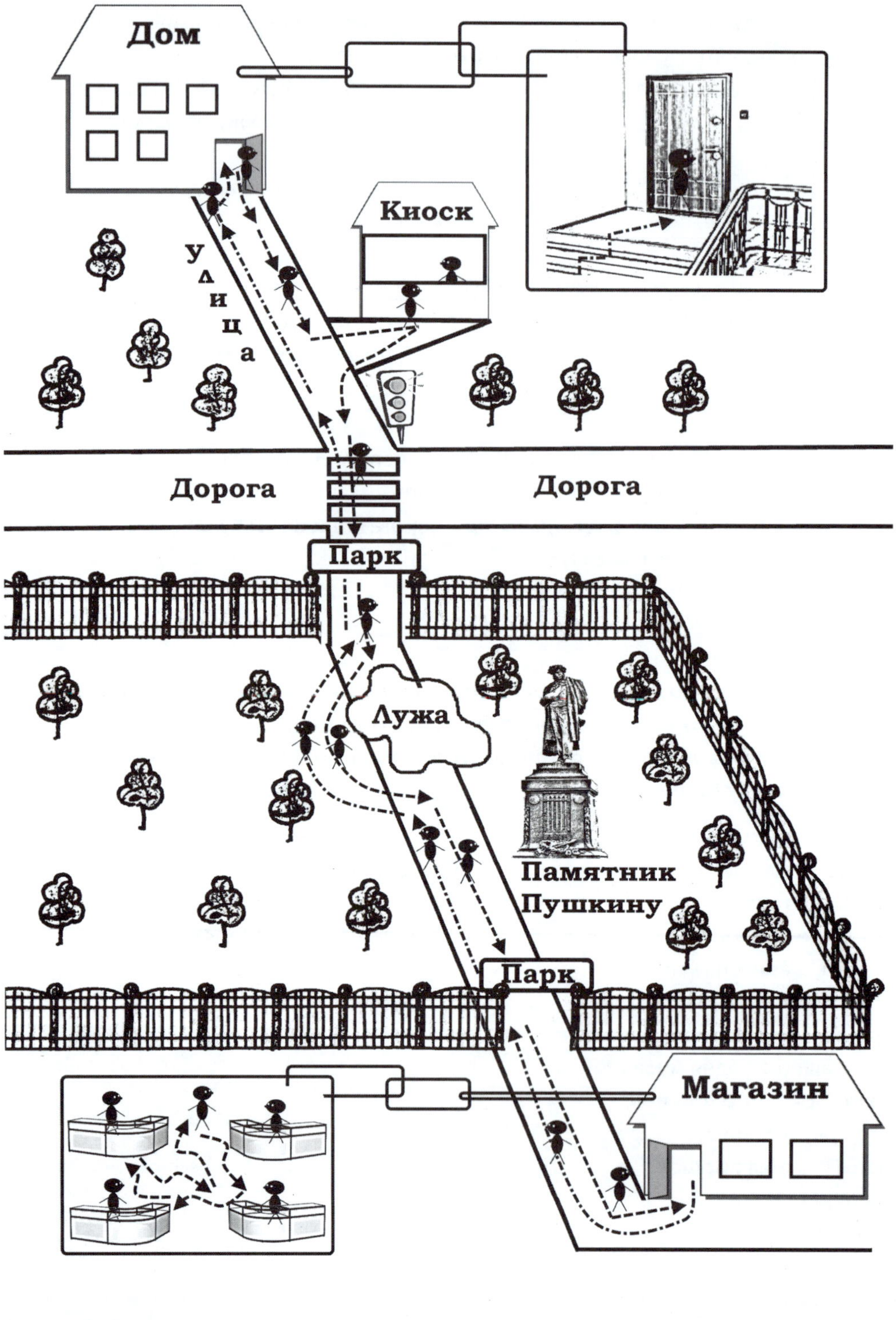

Упражне́ние 3. **Transform the poem «Доро́га в магази́н». Change the verb шёл to the phrase denoting necessity на́до идти́.**

Model: Я из до́ма у́тром **вы́шел**. →
Мне ***на́до вы́йти*** из до́ма у́тром.

Упражне́ние 4. **Following the scheme of «Доро́га в магази́н» tell us about the hero's route from home to the shop, and then back again — from the shop to the house, as if he does it not once, but every day. Instead of the verb идти́ use the verb ходи́ть.**

Он выхо́дит из до́ма, отхо́дит от до́ма, идёт по доро́ге...

After this training Andrey went on to say that they had to wait for a long time, and at least he had something to do. The journalist admitted:

— Я никогда́ не учи́л иностра́нца говори́ть по-ру́сски.

— Ты ру́сский. Э́то нетру́дно для тебя́, — John replied.

— О нет! О́чень тру́дно. Я говорю́ по-ру́сски, но никогда́ не ду́мал, по́чему я так говорю́. Э́то интере́сно!

Andrew drew a table with verbs of motion. As the verbs «идти́» and «ходи́ть» other verbs of motion are divided into two categories: one-directional and multi-directional.

	→	⇆
 как? пешко́м	**идти́ (SPECIAL): to go** я иду́ · мы идём ты идёшь · вы идёте он, она́, оно́ идёт · они́ иду́т **Иди́(те)!** шёл, шла, шло, шли	**ходи́ть (2.IR Д-Ж): to walk** я хожу́ · мы хо́дим ты хо́дишь · вы хо́дите он, она́, оно́ хо́дит · они́ хо́дят **Ходи́(те)!** ходи́л, ходи́ла, ходи́ли
 на чём? на + case № 6 на маши́не, авто́бусе[1]	**е́хать (SPECIAL): to go (by car)** я е́ду · мы е́дем ты е́дешь · вы е́дете он, она́, оно́ е́дет · они́ е́дут **Езжа́й(те)! Поезжа́й(те)!** е́хал, е́хала, е́хали	**е́здить (2.IR ЗД-ЗЖ): to go (regularly by car)** я е́зжу · ты е́здишь ты е́здишь · вы е́здите он, она́, оно́ е́здит · они́ е́здят **Е́зди(те)!** е́здил, е́здила, е́здили
 на чём? на + case № 6 на самолёте	**лете́ть (2.IR Т-Ч): to fly** я лечу́ · мы лети́м ты лети́шь · вы лети́те он, она́, оно́ лети́т · они́ летя́т **Лети́(те)!** лете́л, лете́ла, лете́ли	**лета́ть (1.R.VOW): to fly** я лета́ю · мы лета́ем ты лета́ешь · вы лета́ете он, она́, оно́ лета́ет · они́ лета́ют **Лета́й(те)!** лета́л, лета́ла, лета́ли

[1] a bus

10

	→	⇆
 на чём? на + case № 6 на теплохо́де[1], корабле́[2]	**плыть (1.IR + В): to go (by sea), to sail** я плыву́ ты плывёшь он, она́, оно́ плывёт мы плывём вы плывёте они́ плыву́т **Плыви́(те)!** плыл, плыла́, плы́ли	**пла́вать (1.R.VOW): to go (by sea), to sail** я пла́ваю ты пла́ваешь он, она́, оно́ пла́вает мы пла́ваем вы пла́ваете они́ пла́вают **Пла́вай(те)!** пла́вал, пла́вала, пла́вали
 что? кого́? + case № 4 су́мку, сы́на в / на чём? в + case № 6 в / на рука́х, в су́мке	**нести́ (1.R.CONS): to carry** я несу́ ты несёшь он, она́, оно́ несёт мы несём вы несёте они́ несу́т **Неси́(те)!** нёс, несла́, несли́	**носи́ть (2.IR С-Ш): to carry** я ношу́ ты но́сишь он, она́, оно́ но́сит мы но́сим вы но́сите они́ но́сят **Носи́(те)!** носи́л, носи́ла, носи́ли
 кого́? + case № 4 сы́на как? пешко́м	**вести́ (1.IR СТ-Д): to lead, to take** я веду́ ты ведёшь он, она́, оно́ ведёт мы ведём вы ведёте они́ веду́т **Веди́(-те)!** вёл, вела́, вело́, вели́	**води́ть (2.IR Д-Ж): to lead, to take** я вожу́ ты во́дишь он, она́, оно́ во́дит мы во́дим вы во́дите они́ во́дят **Води́(те)!** води́л, води́ла, води́ли
 что? кого́? + case № 4 кни́гу, сы́на на чём? на + case № 6 на маши́не, авто́бусе, самолёте, корабле́	**везти́ (1.R.CONS): to drive somebody/something** я везу́ ты везёшь он, она́, оно́ везёт мы везём вы везёте они́ везу́т **Вези́(те)!** вёз, везла́, везли́	**вози́ть (2.IR З-Ж): to drive somebody/something** я вожу́ ты во́зишь он, она́, оно́ во́зит мы во́зим вы во́зите они́ во́зят **Вози́(те)!** вози́л, вози́ла, вози́ли

[1] a motor ship
[2] a ship

Упражне́ние 5. **Choose between one-directional and multi-directional motion.**

е́хать — е́здить

1. — Куда́ сейча́с ____________ Оле́г?

— Он ______________ в Истори́ческий музе́й. Он уже́ ______________ туда́ вчера́. Но он бу́дет ________________ туда́ ка́ждый день, потому́ что он экскурсово́д.

2. Сего́дня у́тром Михаи́л ______________ в институ́т, а Ма́ша ________________ в бале́тную шко́лу. Михаи́л ____________________ в институ́т, потому́ что он студе́нт. Ма́ша о́чень лю́бит бале́т, поэ́тому она́ ___________________ в бале́тную шко́лу.

лете́ть — лета́ть

1. В э́том году́ Пётр Ива́нович с жено́й _______________ на юг отдыха́ть. В Со́чи они́ обы́чно ________________ на самолёте.

2. Мой брат бу́дет пило́том и у́чится ___________________ на самолёте. Сего́дня он пе́рвый раз __________________ без инстру́ктора.

нести́ — носи́ть

1. Я ду́маю, э́тот молодо́й челове́к в краси́вом костю́ме идёт на день рожде́ния, потому́ что он _______________ в рука́х цветы́ и торт.

2. Когда́ ребёнок ма́ленький, ма́ма _______________ его́ на рука́х.

вести́ — води́ть

1. Ка́ждое у́тро Ви́ктор Ива́нович ________________ вну́ка в де́тский сад. Но сего́дня Ви́ктор Ива́нович боле́ет, и вну́ка _______________ его́ жена́ А́нна Петро́вна.

2. Ната́ша пе́рвый раз прие́хала в Москву́. Сейча́с сёстры Ве́ра и Ю́лия _______________ её на экску́рсию в Кремль. Ве́ра и Ю́лия бу́дут _________________ её по го́роду всю неде́лю.

везти́ — вози́ть

1. Андре́й рабо́тает в магази́не. Он ________________ проду́кты на маши́не. Сего́дня он ________________ в магази́н со́ки и минера́льную во́ду.

2. Вот аэропо́рт. Смотри́те, э́тот челове́к __________________ сувени́ры из Ло́ндона. А э́та же́нщина _________________ краси́вую ва́зу из А́фрики. А вот железнодоро́жный вокза́л. Тётя Зи́на е́дет из дере́вни в го́род и ______________ пода́рки вну́ку и вну́чке. Тётя Зи́на ____________ пода́рки вну́кам ка́ждую о́сень.

Model: вести́ — води́ть (что? case № 4) маши́ну, мотоци́кл

Я хорошо́ вожу́ маши́ну. — I drive well.

води́тель[1] авто́буса, води́тель маши́ны = шофёр

[1] a driver

Упражне́ние 6. **Try and translate the text yourselves, then look at the translation.**

Я води́тель, я **вожу́** такси́. Мне необходи́мо хорошо́ **води́ть** маши́ну. У меня́ хоро́шая рабо́та, потому́ что лю́ди лю́бят **е́здить на** такси́. Я **веду́** маши́ну и **везу́** пассажи́ров. Мои́ пассажи́ры **е́дут** и **везу́т** ве́щи.

Translation: I am a driver, I drive a taxi. I have to drive well. I have a good job, because people like to take a taxi. I drive a car and I take passengers. My passengers travel and carry things.

Упражнéние 7. **Reread the poem «Дорóга в магази́н».**
Remember that a prefix changes the aspect of the verb (turns imperfective to perfective) only for the verbs of the group идти́. Verbs of the group ходи́ть are imperfectives, regardless of whether they have a prefix or not.

Change the poem:

1. The hero is driving a car
   Сегóдня ýтром он вы́ехал из дóма, он отъéхал от дóма, поéхал по ýлице, заéхал в киóск…
2. The hero drives a car every day
   Кáждое ýтро он выезжáет из дóма, отъезжáет от дóма, éдет по ýлице, заезжáет в киóск…
3. The hero is carrying a bag
   Сегóдня ýтром он вы́нес из дóма большýю сýмку, он отнёс её от дóма, понёс её по ýлице, занёс в киóск…
4. The hero carries a bag every day
   Кáждый день он выносит из дóма большýю сýмку, он относит её от дóма, несёт по ýлице, занóсит в киóск…
5. The hero is taking his brother somewhere
   Сегóдня ýтром он вы́вел брáта из дóма, он отвёл егó от дóма, повёл по ýлице, завёл в киóск…
6. The hero takes his brother somewhere every day
   Кáждый день он вывóдит брáта из дóма, отвóдит егó от дóма, ведёт по ýлице, завóдит в киóск…
7. The hero is taking his bag somewhere by bicycle
   Сегóдня ýтром он вы́вез сýмку из дóма, отвёз её от дóма, повёз по ýлице, завёз в киóск…
8. The hero takes his bag somewhere by bicycle every day
   Кáждый день он вывóзит сýмку из дóма, отвóзит её от дóма, везёт по ýлице, завóзит в киóск…

Упражнéние 8. **Insert the verbs идти́ / éхать using the necessary prefixes.**

В суббóту вéчером мы должны́ бы́ли __________ в теáтр на балéт «Ромéо и Джульéтта». Балéт был в 18:30. Мы ____________ из дóма в 5 часóв, потомý что мы не знáли, скóлько врéмени нýжно __________. Мы ________ к автóбусной остановке и ждáли автóбус. Вот __________ автóбус. Мы сéли[1] и __________. Через 20 минýт мы __________ до стáнции метрó[2]. Мы ________ из автóбуса и __________ в метрó. Когдá мы _________ в вагóн[3], мы уви́дели там друзéй. Они́ тóже _________ в теáтр. Все вмéсте мы __________ до нáшей стáнции, _________ на ýлицу и ____________ к теáтру. Когдá мы __________ к теáтру, мы уви́дели, что óколо теáтра нет людéй. Мы пóняли, что __________ рáно[4]. Но мы ___________ в теáтр, __________ в гардерóб и __________ в театрáльное кафé пить кóфе.

[1] сади́ться (2.IR Д-Ж) / сесть (SPECIAL): to sit down
[2] metro
[3] a wagon, a coach
[4] early

Now John could ask what he had wanted to asked long before.

— Ты говори́шь, что я шёл в библиотéку и я пришёл в библиотéку?

— Да, э́то библиотéка. И ты здесь.

«Плóхо, что э́то другáя библиотéка», — thought John. However, he had already noticed that there were many libraries in Moscow and Moscow itself was huge and it made no sense to hope for success.

Suddenly, the journalist stopped talking and in two jumps closed the distance between John and himself, grabbed him by the waist and carried him away behind a bookcase so that the Englishman did not even have time to rebel. Ти́хо! — Andrey hissed and put his finger to his lips. The door opened, the sounds of the waltz became distinctly audible, and they saw a man's head in the strip of light. The head was there for a second and then disappeared.

— Что э́то бы́ло? — asked John surprisingly.

— Бал зако́нчился.

— Что?

— Бал, — Andrey repeated and suddenly started to sing: Ля-ля-ля. Бал — все танцу́ют, пою́т, знако́мятся, пьют шампа́нское. Вечери́нка. Party.

— Слово «бал» я зна́ю — э́то францу́зское сло́во. Я спроси́л, что случи́лось[1].

— Бал зако́нчился, — he repeated again.

— Не понима́ю. Что бал?

— Зако́нчился.

— У меня́ нет моего́ компью́тера со словарём.

Andrey sighed again and started to explain.

— Когда́ ты шёл в дом Пашко́ва — бал **начина́лся**. Когда́ ты пришёл, он **начался́**. Когда́ мы говори́ли — бал **шёл (был)**. Сейча́с бал **зако́нчился**.

— А, поня́тно! Зако́нчился. Finished, — John realized that it was a guard who had looked into the room to make sure that there was no one left upstairs.

[1] случа́ться (1.R.WOW) / случи́ться (2.R.CONS.2): to happen, to have happened

Phase verbs

	|---|→	|→	→→	---→|	→|
Infinitive	**начина́ться** (1.R.VOW) **to begin to happen (IPF)**	**нача́ться** (1.IR Ø-НУ) **to have started (when something has just started) (PF)**	**идти́** (SPECIAL) **to be in process (IPF)**	**зака́нчиваться** (1.R.VOW) **to start to finish (IPF)**	**зако́нчиться** (2.R.CONS.2) **to have finished (when something has just finished) (PF)**
Present	начина́ется начина́ются	—	идёт иду́т	зака́нчивается зака́нчиваются	—
Past	начина́лся начина́лась начина́лось начина́лись	начался́ начала́сь начало́сь начали́сь	шёл шли	зака́нчивался зака́нчивалась зака́нчивалось зака́нчивались	зако́нчился зако́нчилась зако́нчились
Future	—	начнётся начну́тся	—	—	зако́нчится зако́нчатся

Упражне́ние 9. **Read the examples and translate them.**

6:00 — рабо́чий день начина́ется.

7:00 — я иду́ на рабо́ту. Для меня́ рабо́чий день начался́. А мой мла́дший брат ещё спит. Для него́ рабо́чий день ещё не начался́.

17:00 — мой рабо́чий день зака́нчивается.

18:00 — мой рабо́чий день зако́нчился, я иду́ домо́й. А у моего́ дру́га рабо́чий день зака́нчивается в 20:00. Он о́чень занято́й челове́к.

Упражне́ние 10. **Complete the sentences with appropriate phase verbs: начина́ется, начало́сь, зака́нчивается, зако́нчилось.**

Дире́ктор пришёл в кабине́т. Совеща́ние[1] ________________.

Дире́ктор сказа́л: «Пожа́луйста, внима́ние![2]» Совеща́ние ____________.

Дире́ктор подво́дит ито́ги[3]. Совеща́ние ___________________.

Дире́ктор сказа́л: «Всем спаси́бо, до за́втра!» — и вы́шел. Совеща́ние ________________.

[1] a conference, a meeting
[2] Attention, please!
[3] to summarize

— Бал зако́нчился, — repeated Andrey. — Всё[4], мо́жно идти́!

— Мне на́до идти́, — said John happily. — Спаси́бо! Э́то был поле́зный уро́к. Проща́й, Андре́й! Уда́чи!

[4] The word всё can mean "it has finished" (when the action has been completed).

John took all his things, he wanted to return them to the theatre the next day. He went down the stairs and walked through the hall. The light was gone, as well as the people. There was not even a guard — all the doors were locked and there was only a red alarm light flashing in the dark. John returned to Andrey, who was still sitting by the window on the second floor.

— Что, уже́ закры́то? — asked Andrey surprisingly, pointing at the closed doors.

— Закры́то! — John replied in shock. He had seen that word many times on the shop door, and he knew its meaning: закры́то, откры́то — closed, open, he just did not expect that one could finish the party so fast. Where were all these ladies in long dresses and gentlemen in tailcoats? It all looked mysterious, even devilish.

Ну, ме́сто тако́е, ещё Булга́ков писа́л[5], — said Andrey in a calm voice, but John couldn't understand what he was talking about. And he didn't really want to clarify it.

— Коне́чно, закры́то, — Andrey went on. — Може́т быть, э́то да́же хорошо́. Уже́ ночь. Куда́ ты пойдёшь оди́н но́чью?

— Во ско́лько НЕ закры́то? — said John, he didn't know the right word and tried to explain it as best he could.

— Не закры́то = откры́то, — Andrey wrote it on the board. — За́втра у́тром библиоте́ка бу́дет откры́та.

[5] Andrey means that Pashkov's house, where he and John are located, appears as a scene in one of the most famous Russian mystical novels.

to open	to close
открыва́ть — откры́ть (что?) дверь (1.R.VOW / 1.IR Ы-О) откры́т (-а, -о, -ы): Дверь откры́та.	закрыва́ть — закры́ть (что?) дверь (1.R.VOW / 1.IR Ы-О) закры́т (-а, -о, -ы): Дверь закры́та.

Упражне́ние 11. **Complete the sentences with открыт or закры́т.**

Сейча́с 6:00. Институ́т ________________.

Сейча́с 10:00. Институ́т ________________.

Сейча́с 12:00. Ночно́й клуб ________________.

Сейча́с 23:00. Ночно́й клуб ________________.

Сейча́с 13:00. Вре́мя обе́да. Ка́сса[1] ________________.

Сейча́с 14:00. Обе́д зако́нчился. Ка́сса ________________.

Зима́. Ле́тние дома́ о́тдыха[2] ________________.

Воскресе́нье. Ба́нки ________________.

Э́то круглосу́точный[3] магази́н. Он всегда́ ________________.

Э́то дежу́рная[4] апте́ка. Она́ всегда́ ________________.

[1] ticket office
[2] a resort
[3] 24-h/7-day
[4] on duty (дежу́рная апте́ка: a pharmacy on duty)

— Мне ну́жно телефо́н. Мо́жно взять твой телефо́н?

— Нет, — answered the journalist in a calm voice.

— Почему́?

— Потому́ что я пришёл сюда́ пе́рвый, и пра́вила — мои́. Я де́лаю мою́ рабо́ту. Сейча́с мы сиди́м ти́хо, а у́тром ти́хо ухо́дим.

— В тако́м слу́чае у меня́ то́же есть вопро́с. Что ты тут де́лаешь?

— Молоде́ц! — suddenly exclaimed the journalist.

— «Молоде́ц»? Что э́то? Э́то твоя́ профе́ссия?

— Нет, молоде́ц — э́то good guy (or good job). Ру́сские говоря́т «молоде́ц», когда́ челове́к хорошо́ рабо́тает и́ли де́лает что́-то хорошо́ и́ли он хорошо́, краси́во оде́лся. Сейча́с ты молоде́ц, потому́ что ты хорошо́ говори́шь!..

— Да, я молоде́ц. Но ты не отве́тил, что ты тут де́лаешь?

— Я здесь рабо́таю. Сего́дня но́чью здесь, ря́дом с Кремлём, ря́дом с ба́шней, бу́дет интере́сно.

— Что бу́дет интере́сно? — asked John, watching Andrey's hand pointing in the direction of the Kremlin tower nearest to them.

— Что?... Я ещё не зна́ю. Снача́ла мне на́до сде́лать фотогра́фии изве́стных люде́й, а пото́м я бу́ду писа́ть статью́ и де́лать исто́рию.

— Как исто́рию? Ты де́лаешь исто́рию Росси́и?

— Нет. Не большу́ю исто́рию Росси́и, а ра́зные ма́ленькие исто́рии. Лю́ди их лю́бят.

— Ты paparazzi? — John finally got it.

He was very surprised — such a clever man with such a stupid profession.

— Да, я папара́цци, — Andrey shrugged his shoulders, and John decided not to ask further questions not to offend him.

— А кака́я у тебя́ профе́ссия?

— Я экономи́ст.

— Заче́м ты прие́хал в Росси́ю? — Andrey asked professionally.

— У меня́ здесь есть де́ло.

— Хорошо́. В тако́м слу́чае где твои́ ве́щи?

— В гости́нице.

— А где твой пиджа́к, телефо́н, где бума́жник, докуме́нты?

— В теа́тре, — said John honestly.

— А па́спорт? — asked Andrey.

— Нет, па́спорт тут, — John nervously ran his fingers through his pocket and touched his passport: with his sixth sense he put it into the pocket of his trousers in the theatre.

— Не понима́ю: пиджа́к в теа́тре, фрак и цили́ндр здесь, на тебе́…

— Я то́же не понима́ю, — John's intonation made the journalist stop asking.

John started to look for a toilet. Most of all, after all this bustle with Roman Kharitonov and the blonde, he wanted to wash his face and to drink. However, as soon as he leaned over to tap water, he heard a voice from behind: «Не пей!» John turned around and saw Andrey.

A note in John's diary:
В Росси́и НЕЛЬЗЯ́

- Пить во́ду из кра́на.
- Гуля́ть зимо́й и о́сенью без ша́пки.
- Е́здить зимо́й на маши́не с ле́тними ши́нами.
- Кури́ть в тра́нспорте[1].
- Меня́ть де́ньги на у́лице.
- Игра́ть в по́езде в ка́рты[2].
- Пить вино́, пи́во, во́дку с незнако́мыми людьми́.
- Мно́го говори́ть о пого́де.
- Дари́ть 2, 4, 6, 8… цвето́в.
- Дари́ть пусты́е су́мки, кошельки́.
- Дари́ть ножи́.
- Сли́шком мно́го улыба́ться.

[1] transport
[2] cards

***Упражне́ние 12.* Can you explain the reasons for the prohibition above?**

***Упражне́ние 13.* Check your answers.**

1. Потому́ что вода́ не о́чень чи́стая[3] и Вы мо́жете заболе́ть[4].
2. Потому́ что зимо́й о́чень хо́лодно. Вы бу́дете боле́ть.
3. Потому́ что зимо́й на доро́ге лёд.
4. Потому́ что в тра́нспорте е́дет мно́го люде́й. Лю́дям бу́дет пло́хо.
5. Потому́ что, мо́жет быть, Вас хотя́т обману́ть[5].
6. Потому́ что, мо́жет быть, Вас то́же хотя́т обмануть.
7. Потому́ что э́то опа́сно[6].
8. Потому́ что ру́сские ду́мают, что говори́ть о пого́де — э́то ску́чно.
9. Потому́ что э́то тради́ция: живы́м[7] лю́дям да́рят то́лько 1, 3, 5, 7… цвето́в.
10. Потому́ что в до́ме э́того челове́ка не бу́дет де́нег.
11. Потому́ что Вы с дру́гом ста́нете врага́ми[8].
12. Потому́ что ру́сские мо́гут поду́мать, что Вы нейскренний[9] челове́к.

[3] pure, clean
[4] Perfective of боле́ть: to fall ill, to get sick
[5] обма́нывать (1.R.VOW) / обману́ть (1.IR НУ): to lie, to deceive
[6] dangerous (adv.)
[7] living / alive
[8] стать (PF; 1.IR Ø-НУ) врага́ми: to become enemies
[9] insincere

Упражне́ние 14. **Make recommendations to those who come to Russia using the model е́сли… то:**

Model: Е́сли… то — if… then

Example: Е́сли вы пьёте во́ду из кра́на, то вы мо́жете заболе́ть. — If you drink water from the tap, you can get sick.
Е́сли Вы мно́го говори́те о пого́де, то ру́сские знако́мые бу́дут ду́мать, что Вы ску́чный челове́к. — If you talk a lot about weather, Russians can think of you as a boring person.

Упражне́ние 15. **Make up phrases.**

Example: Е́сли Вы хоти́те пить, то пе́йте во́ду из буты́лки.

Е́сли вы хоти́те пить	то говори́те о семье́, о жи́зни, о литерату́ре, но не о пого́де.
Е́сли хоти́те гуля́ть зимо́й	то положи́те туда́ немно́го де́нег.
Е́сли хоти́те пое́хать зимо́й на маши́не	то дари́те, но возьми́те у него́ немно́го де́нег.
Е́сли хоти́те кури́ть	то иди́те в банк.
Е́сли хоти́те поменя́ть де́ньги	то дари́те 3, 5, 7, 9… цвето́в.
Е́сли хоти́те игра́ть в ка́рты	то вы́йдите из авто́буса.
Е́сли хоти́те вы́пить алкого́ль	то иди́те в рестора́н с друзья́ми.
Е́сли хоти́те хорошо́ поговори́ть с ру́сскими друзья́ми	то поменя́йте[1] ле́тние ши́ны на зи́мние.
Е́сли хоти́те подари́ть цветы́	то улыба́йтесь, когда́ действи́тельно ра́ды.
Е́сли хоти́те подари́ть су́мку и́ли кошелёк[2]	то пе́йте во́ду из буты́лки.
Е́сли хоти́те быть ве́жливым и и́скренним	то носи́те тёплую ша́пку.
Е́сли ду́маете, что нож — э́то лу́чший пода́рок мужчи́не	то игра́йте с друзья́ми.

— Е́сли хо́чешь пить, то скажи́ мне. У меня́ есть вода́ и есть чай, — said Andrey.

— А е́сли я хочу́ есть, то что мне ну́жно де́лать? — John asked sarcastically. He was angry that because of the paparazzi he had to stay there dirty, hungry and sleepy.

— Е́сли хо́чешь есть, то то́же скажи́ мне. У меня́ есть пирожки́ и бутербро́ды[3].

— У тебя́ есть есть, и у тебя́ есть пить, — John remembered his visit to the restaurant with Kharitonov.

— Ах, молоде́ц! — Andrey praised him and added: — Всё своё всегда́ со мно́й!

— Что тако́е всё своё?

— Своё — э́то моё. Но моё — э́то про́сто моё. А своё — э́то о́чень моё. Понима́ешь?

John was already sorry for asking, because pies and sandwiches seemed now much more attractive than linguistic studies. Andrey seemed to guess his thoughts.

— Посмотри́, э́то о́чень краси́во! — John and Andrew were standing at the dark window, eating sausage sandwiches and drinking hot tea from a thermos, and all of Moscow was in front of them. The lights of countless cars created a ghostly haze over the ancient city. The Kremlin walls dissolved in the darkness, as in Impressionist paintings.

— Э́то мой го́род. Я люблю́ свой го́род, — said Andrey.

[1] (1.R.VOW): to change
[2] a wallet
[3] a sandwich

— О́чень краси́во, — John agreed.

— А твой го́род — Ло́ндон?

— Да. Мой го́род — Ло́ндон.

— Ты лю́бишь свой го́род?

— Да, люблю́ мой го́род. Коне́чно. Стра́нный вопро́с.

— На́до сказа́ть: «Я люблю́ свой го́род».

John looked surprisingly at his companion, who seemed to have entered the role of a great educator of foreign people in questions of Russian grammar.

— Почему́ нельзя говори́ть «мой го́род»? Так то́же поня́тно.

— Потому́ что э́то ва́жно.

— Почему́ ва́жно?

Intuitively Andrew knew the answer, but he couldn't explain it, so he gave John his mobile provided that he wouldn't call anywhere, ask anyone to rescue him and thus wouldn't open its beautiful journalist lair.

By the way,

Помоги́те, и́ли Куда́ звони́ть, е́сли…

Е́сли вам ну́жно получи́ть[1] по́мощь, то на́до звони́ть «112». Э́то слу́жба спасе́ния. (the same as 911)

Е́сли вы ви́дите кримина́льную ситуа́цию[2], то на́до звони́ть «02». Э́то поли́ция. Е́сли вы звони́те по моби́льному телефо́ну, то но́мер «102».

Е́сли вам пло́хо, то на́до звони́ть «03». Э́то ско́рая по́мощь. (ambulance) Е́сли вы звони́те по моби́льному телефо́ну, то но́мер «103».

Е́сли вам ну́жно информа́цию о телефо́нах в го́роде, то звони́те «09». Э́то спра́вочная слу́жба. (help-desk)

Е́сли вы звони́те по моби́льному телефо́ну, то но́мер «109».

[1] получа́ть (1.R.VOW) / получи́ть (2.R.CONS.2): to get, to receive
[2] a crime, a criminal situation

Possessive pronoun свой

It is interesting!

According to linguists, the word свой is the key word for the Russian culture, and not all languages of the world have words with exactly the same meaning. Academician Trubachov reconstructed basic words of the Russian culture and found that the word свой is one of the primordial, deep concepts that Russian identity is based on. In the 19th century, F. Dostoevsky and L. Tolstoy spoke of the broad, cosmic, inclusiveness of the Russian soul. But a much earlier understanding of своего́ as something native, right, primordial appeared in people's minds (ancient root -со- means "to give birth"). Perhaps, that is the reason why the Russian soul seems to be mysterious and strange — on the one hand, Russians are open to each other, they are friendly and hospitable, but on the other hand, a Russian never opens his heart to the end, always leaving a hidden place for themselves.

There are a lot of Russian proverbs and sayings built upon the notion of свой: Свой своему́ понево́ле брат (they that are bound must obey; birds of a feather flock together), Своя́ руба́шка бли́же к те́лу (meaning one's own well-being (or the well-being of those dear to one) is more important than other people's interests; self comes first).

You can hear the phrase свои́ лю́ди. For example, the name of Ostrovsky's play about the life and customs of Russian merchants: Свои́ лю́ди — сочтёмся — "We are of the same kind".

Своё is something given by God. There is a part of the root свой in many Russian words: здоро́вье — своё де́рево (the word 'health' in Russian may be interpreted as 'one's own tree' — something given from the family tree); сча́стье — своя́ часть ('happiness' — 'one's own part'), смерть — своя́ ме́ра ('death' — one's own measure).

мой, твой, наш, ваш, его́, её, их = свой
моё, твоё, на́ше, ва́ше, его́, её, их = своё
моя́, твоя́, на́ша, ва́ша, его́, её, их = своя́
мои́, твои́, на́ши, ва́ши, его́, её, их = свои́

The possessive pronoun свой can be used only when there is an object which belongs to the subject.

Э́то я. У меня́ есть кни́га. Э́то моя́ кни́га.
Э́то друг. У дру́га есть мяч. Э́то его́ мяч.
Я даю́ дру́гу **свою́** кни́гу. А **друг берёт мою́** кни́гу.
Друг даёт мне **свой** мяч. А **я беру́ его́** мяч.

Упражне́ние 16. **Read the text which explains the picture.**

Э́то О́ля и Ка́тя. У О́ли есть цвето́к. У Ка́ти то́же есть цвето́к.
У О́ли есть свой (= её) цвето́к, и у Кати есть свой (= её) цвето́к.
Ка́тя берёт цвето́к О́ли. Ка́тя берёт её (не = свой) цвето́к.

Упражне́ние 17. **Read the sentences. Say when we can use the pronoun свой, and when we need pronouns его́, её, их.**

1. Э́то Андре́й. Э́то его́ го́род. Андре́й лю́бит свой го́род. А Джон не лю́бит его́ го́род.
2. Э́то изве́стный писа́тель. Э́то его́ кни́га. Он до́лго писа́л свою́ кни́гу. Я купи́л его́ кни́гу.
3. Э́то Джон. Он потеря́л свой телефо́н. Где его́ телефо́н? Андре́й дал ему́ свой телефо́н.

Reflexive pronoun себя́

Case	Questions	Forms	Examples
№ 1	кто?	—	—
№ 2	кого́?	себя́	Больно́й откры́л глаза́ и уви́дел о́коло[1] себя́ врача́.
№ 3	(к) кому́?	себе́	Мари́я купи́ла себе́ интере́сный журна́л.
№ 4	кого́?	себя́	Э́тот челове́к лю́бит то́лько себя́.
№ 5	(с) кем?	(с) собо́й	А́нна пое́хала в Москву́ и взяла́ с собо́й бра́та.
№ 6	о ком?	о себе́	Эгои́ст[2] ду́мает то́лько о себе́.

[1] near
[2] a selfish man

ATTENTION!

The pronoun себя́ is connected to the doer of an action which is described in a sentence. The action is turned to the person or this person's possession)
Я купи́л слова́рь. Сейча́с э́то мой слова́рь. = Я купи́л слова́рь себе́.
Я купи́л слова́рь. Сейча́с э́то слова́рь дру́га. = Я купи́л слова́рь дру́гу.

10

Упражне́ние 18. **Use the pronoun себя́ in the necessary form.**

1. Э́то дом Ви́ктора. Он рабо́тает тут. У кого́ до́ма он рабо́тает?
2. Анто́н сиди́т на сту́ле. Он поста́вил су́мку ря́дом. Ря́дом с кем он поста́вил су́мку?
3. А́нна в магази́не. Она́ покупа́ет но́вое пла́тье. Э́то бу́дет её пла́тье. Кому́ она́ покупа́ет платье?
4. Пётр лю́бит расска́зывать. Сего́дня он расска́зывает, где он был ле́том. О ком расска́зывает Пётр?
5. Э́то я. Я люблю́ то́лько меня́. Кого́ я люблю?
6. А э́то Мари́на. Она́ лю́бит то́лько Мари́ну. Кого́ лю́бит Мари́на?

Упражне́ние 19. **Complete the sentences using the pronoun себя́ in the appropriate form.**

1. Скро́мный[1] челове́к не лю́бит говори́ть о __________ . 2. Анто́н пришёл к __________ домо́й. 3. Здоро́вый[2] челове́к не говори́т с __________ . 4. Эгои́ст лю́бит то́лько __________ . 5. Анто́н пошёл в теа́тр и пригласи́л с __________ подру́гу. 6. Ве́чером Джон пригото́вил __________ у́жин. 7. Я подари́л __________ но́вый компью́тер.

[1] shy
[2] healthy

Свой is a possessive adjective. It is similar to possessive pronouns (мой, твой, ваш, etc.) and answers the questions како́й? чей? and has case forms.

Себя́ is a reflexive pronoun. It is similar to personal pronouns (меня́, тебя́, вас, etc.) and answers the questions кого́? (case № 2) себя́, о ком? (case № 6) о себе́ etc.

Худо́жник продаёт свою́ карти́ну. — А э́ту карти́ну худо́жник нарисова́л для себя́.

Pay attention to the phrases:

я, ты, он **сам**	Я написа́л э́ту кни́гу сам. — I have written this book myself.
я, ты, она́ **сама́**	Я свари́ла суп сама́. — I cooked soup myself.
оно́ **само́**	Э́то получи́лось само́. — It happened by itself.
мы, вы, они́ **са́ми**	Мы де́лаем свою́ рабо́ту са́ми. — We do our work ourselves.

John looked at the window. The words о́чень краси́во couldn't explain his feelings at that moment.

— Го́род но́чью бо́лее краси́вый, чем го́род днём.

Today's crazy rhythm slowed down in the timeless tranquility of the ancient house. The silence was amazing, it was a different Moscow and a different Russia, solemn and warm.

— Кремль, ря́дом Москва́-река́, Храм Христа́ Спаси́теля, ря́дом парк, — John enumerated what he saw. — А э́тот дом? Что здесь ра́ньше бы́ло?

— Э́тот дом называ́ется дом Пашко́ва, — answered the journalist.

— Пашко́в — э́то изве́стный ру́сский архите́ктор?

— Нет. Дом стро́ил[3] архите́ктор Баже́нов. А Пашко́в — э́то пе́рвый хозя́ин[4] э́того до́ма.

[3] (2.R.VOW): to built, to construct
[4] хозя́ин (fem. хозя́йка, pl. хозя́ева): an owner, a host (fem. a hostess, pl. hosts, owners)

Упражне́ние 20. **Read and translate the Andrey's story about Pashkov's house. What does this house symbolize? What secrets does it hide?**

СА́МОЕ КРАСИ́ВОЕ ЗДА́НИЕ СТА́РОЙ МОСКВЫ́

Э́тот дом постро́ил изве́стный архите́ктор Васи́лий Баже́нов в 1784–1787[1] года́х.

Баже́нов был гениа́льным[2] архите́ктором. Но мно́го свои́х рабо́т он не зако́нчил. С больши́м коли́чеством[3] его́ рабо́т мы мо́жем познако́миться то́лько на бума́ге. Баже́нов занима́лся не то́лько архитекту́рой, но и поли́тикой. Одна́жды императри́ца[4] Екатери́на II (Втора́я) возненави́дела[5] его́, и Баже́нов потеря́л[6] рабо́ту во дворце́[7] императри́цы.

Пашко́в был офице́ром, он пригласи́л Васи́лия Баже́нова стро́ить свой дом, потому́ что Баже́нов был одни́м из лу́чших архите́кторов своего́ вре́мени. И Баже́нов постро́ил дом.

Э́то краси́вейшее зда́ние в сти́ле[8] ру́сского классици́зма[9] нахо́дится на пересече́нии у́лиц Моховóй и Зна́менки, на высо́ком Вага́ньковском холме́[10], ря́дом с Кремлём. Ра́ньше ря́дом с до́мом был парк и фонта́ны. Когда́ Баже́нов зако́нчил стро́ить дом Пашко́ва, жи́тели Москвы́ назва́ли э́тот дом «ска́зочный[11] дом на холме́». Дом Пашко́ва вы́ше, чем Кремль. Говоря́т, что Баже́нов постро́ил не дом, а си́мвол. Э́то са́мое высо́кое и са́мое краси́вое зда́ние ста́рой Москвы́. Э́то си́мвол свобо́ды[12] иску́сства.

О до́ме Пашко́ва расска́зывают мно́го леге́нд[13]. Снача́ла хозя́евами до́ма бы́ли де́ти и вну́ки Пашко́ва. Пото́м хозя́ином до́ма ста́ло госуда́рство. Здесь находи́лся и Дворя́нский[14] университе́т, и музе́й, и библиоте́ка. Но гла́вная та́йна до́ма — его́ ме́сто. Е́сли пойти́ вниз, в подва́л[15], то мо́жно уви́деть та́йный подзе́мный ход[16]. О нём узна́ли, когда́ в до́ме шла реконстру́кция[17]. Э́тот ход идёт в Кремль. Все жи́тели[18] Москвы́ зна́ют, что Кремль то́же стои́т на та́йных и изве́стных подзе́мных хода́х. Е́сли войти́ в ход на за́паде Кремля́, то мо́жно вы́йти на восто́ке и́ли на ю́ге Кремля́. Говоря́т, здесь, под до́мом Пашко́ва, нахо́дится са́мая гла́вная драгоце́нность[19] Кремля́ — библиоте́ка Ива́на Гро́зного.

— Библиоте́ка — под библиоте́кой? — John was surprised. — Здесь о́чень мно́го библиоте́к.

— Я то́же хоте́л знать, леге́нда и́ли пра́вда библиоте́ка Ивана Гро́зного. Вот, здесь, под Борови́цкой ба́шней, — said the journalist pointing at the nearest tower, — есть ход. Когда́ я был студе́нтом, я ходи́л туда́ ка́ждую неде́лю. Когда́ я учи́лся в аспиранту́ре, я писа́л о та́йных хода́х Кремля́.

— Твоя́ профе́ссия — исто́рик? — asked John.

— Ра́ньше я был исто́риком, но сейча́с я журнали́ст.

[1] ты́сяча семьсо́т во́семьдесят четвёртом — ты́сяча семьсо́т во́семьдесят седьмо́м года́х
[2] genius (adj.)
[3] a large amount
[4] an empress
[5] to hate
[6] to lose
[7] a palace
[8] a style; в стиле: in style
[9] В сти́ле (чего? case № 2) класси́зма, рококо́, импрессиони́зма: in Classicism, Rococo, Impressionist style
[10] a hill
[11] dreamlike
[12] freedom
[13] a legend
[14] дворяни́н (дворя́нка): a nobleman. Adj. дворя́нский: noble
[15] a basement
[16] an underground passage
[17] a reconstruction
[18] an inhabitant
[19] a jewel

Упражне́ние 21. **Где пра́вда, а где непра́вда?**

1. Пашко́в — э́то изве́стный ру́сский архите́ктор. ☐
2. Баже́нов жил во вре́мя царя́ Петра́ I (Пе́рвого). ☐
3. Баже́нов занима́лся то́лько архитекту́рой. ☐
4. Дом Пашко́ва — э́то си́мвол свобо́ды иску́сства. ☐
5. Са́мая больша́я та́йна до́ма Пашко́ва — э́то университе́т. ☐
6. Под Кремлём мно́го та́йных ходо́в. ☐
7. Андре́й хоте́л узна́ть, была́ ли в до́ме Пашко́ва библиоте́ка Ива́на Гро́зного. ☐

Упражне́ние 22. **Check the understanding of the text.**

Баже́нов был **одни́м из лу́чших архите́кторов** своего́ вре́мени.

Compare:

Хоро́ший архите́ктор — лу́чший архите́ктор — оди́н из лу́чших архите́кторов.

Мы — оди́н из нас.

Вы — оди́н из вас.

Худо́жники-импрессиони́сты. Моне́ — оди́н из худо́жников-импрессиони́стов.

There was a sentence with the word когда́ in the text:

Когда́ Баже́нов зако́нчил стро́ить дом Пашко́ва, жи́тели Москвы́ назва́ли э́тот дом «ска́зочный дом на холме́».

A sentence with the conjunction когда́ (when)

The conjunction когда́ introduces a time clause. It allows you to set the time relationship between the main clause and the subordinate clause.

Imperfect + imperfect = simultaneous actions

Когда́ ты слу́шаешь му́зыку? Я слу́шаю (IPF) му́зыку, когда́ я иду́ (IPF) домо́й. — When do you listen to music? I listen to music when I go home.

Когда́ идёт (IPF) дождь, стадио́н закры́т. — When it rains, the stadium is closed.

Perfect + perfect = consecutive actions

Когда́ ты вы́учил стихи́? Я вы́учил (PF) стихи́, когда́ пришёл (PF) домо́й. — When did you learn the poems? I learned the poems when I came home.

Пойдёшь (PF) гуля́ть, когда́ помо́ешь (PF) посу́ду. — You will go for a walk after you wash up.

Упражне́ние 23. **Say what scheme the following phrase corresponds: «Когда́ Баже́нов зако́нчил стро́ить дом Пашко́ва, жи́тели Москвы́ назва́ли э́тот дом «ска́зочный дом на холме́». Give the exact translation.**

Упражне́ние 24. **Are these actions simultaneous or consecutive?**

1. Когда́ мой ста́рший брат учи́лся в институ́те, он на́чал писа́ть для журна́ла «Вопро́сы литерату́ры».
2. Мы вы́шли в доро́гу, когда́ дождь зако́нчил идти́.
3. Джон пое́хал в Росси́ю, когда́ оте́ц рассказа́л исто́рию де́да Бенджами́на.
4. Когда́ Джон был в Росси́и, он познако́мился с журнали́стом Андре́ем.

Упражне́ние 25. **Complete the sentences.**

1. Когда́ я отдыха́ю на мо́ре, я ____
____
____
(пла́вать в мо́ре, гуля́ть по пля́жу, мно́го спать, чита́ть, мно́го пить и есть, гото́вить, дума́ть о жи́зни, фотографи́ровать).

2. Когда́ я рабо́таю, я ____
____
____
(пи́ть мно́го ко́фе, гуля́ть по Интерне́ту, ча́сто смотре́ть по́чту, разгова́ривать по телефо́ну, ду́мать об о́тдыхе).

3. Ко́гда пришла́ ма́ма, де́ти уже́ ____
____ (пообе́дать, сде́лать дома́шнее зада́ние).

4. Когда́ мы посмотре́ли фильм «А́нна Каре́нина», мы ______________________________
____ (захоте́ть прочита́ть рома́н Льва Толсто́го).

5. Когда́ худо́жник рису́ет карти́ну, он ____
(ду́мать то́лько о ней).

6. Когда́ Са́ша принёс домо́й соба́ку, роди́тели ____
____ (поня́ть, что начали́сь пробле́мы).

7. Когда́ преподава́тель расска́зывал но́вую те́му, одни́ студе́нты ________________ (слу́шать), други́е студе́нты ______________ (спать), а тре́тьи — ____
(игра́ть в компью́терную игру́).

10

Глава́ 11

Сча́стье зави́сит от пра́вил,
форту́на — от случа́йностей.

А.В. Суво́ров, ру́сский полково́дец

Happiness depends on rules,
luck is unforseen.

— A. Suvorov, Russian military leader

In the morning John went back to the hotel. He had to call his father, find out where the required archive was and contact Moscow colleagues. Those were his plans for the day. However, an unpleasant surprise was waiting for him in his room. At first John did not notice anything, but once opened the suitcase he realized that someone had entered his room.

— В но́мере бы́ли во́ры, — the receptionist explained to the policeman.

— Вор[1] — э́то челове́к, **кото́рый** берёт не свои́ ве́щи, — she tried to explain the word to the stunned guest. However, this was the case when the name of the subject did not change its unpleasant essence. The word "thief" and the word вор sounded equally disgusting in both languages.

[1] a thief

Кото́рый

A subordinate clause with the word кото́рый expresses the meaning of the definition, the characteristics of the object.

The word кото́рый alters in gender and number (кото́рая, кото́рое, кото́рые), and answers the question **како́й?** (кака́я? како́е? каки́е?).

The word кото́рый is used in all types of determining subordinate clauses, regardless of whether it refers to the subject or object, or whether the object is animate or inanimate.

Пётр — э́то **челове́к, кото́рый** (case № 1, subject) о́чень мно́го зна́ет. (Peter is a person who knows a lot.)

Мы прие́хали в **го́род, кото́рый** (case № 4, object) я уви́дел пе́рвый раз. (We arrived at the city, which I saw for the first time.)

Ка́тя — э́то **де́вушка, кото́рую** (case № 4, object) я люблю́. (Kate is the girl I love.)

Худо́жник зако́нчил **карти́ну, кото́рую** (case № 4, object) он рисова́л 5 лет. (The painter finished the picture which he had been painting for 5 years.)

Building such sentences is the same as solving simple mathematical equations:

Э́то дом. Э́тот дом (case № 1) стои́т на у́лице Гага́рина. ↓	Э́то ру́чка. Она́ (case № 1) лежи́т на столе́. ↓
You have two words дом. The second can be replaced with the word кото́рый: masculine (дом), case № 1. We delete the word э́тот. ↓	You have a word ру́чка and a pronoun она́ meaning 'the pen'. We replace the pronoun with the word кото́рая: feminine (она́), case № 1. ↓
Э́то дом, кото́рый стои́т на у́лице Гага́рина.	Э́то ру́чка, кото́рая лежи́т на столе́.

Упражне́ние 1. **Make one sentence out of two using the word кото́рый.**

1. Э́то собо́р. Он стои́т ря́дом с Кремлём.
2. Э́то по́вар. Он гото́вит обе́д в рестора́не.
3. Э́то спортсме́н. Он прибежа́л пе́рвым.
4. Э́то певи́ца. Она́ поёт в Большо́м теа́тре.
5. Э́то вор. Он берёт не свои́ ве́щи.
6. Э́то Джон. Джон — англича́нин. Э́тот англича́нин неда́вно прие́хал в Росси́ю.
7. Алекса́ндр Янг — учёный-исто́рик. Он интересу́ется исто́рией Росси́и.
8. Бенджами́н Янг — де́душка Джо́на. Он вёз докуме́нты из Санкт-Петербу́рга в Москву́.
9. Э́то же́нщина. О́на помогла́ Джо́ну на у́лице.

Кото́рый is changed in the same way as an adjective with firm stem

Паде́ж	он	оно́	она́	они́
№ 1	како́й? -ЫЙ	како́е? -ОЕ	кака́я? -АЯ	каки́е? -ЫЕ
	кото́р**ый**	кото́р**ое**	кото́р**ая**	кото́р**ые**
№ 2	како́го? -ОГО	како́го? -ОГО	како́й? -ОЙ	каки́х? -ЫХ
	кото́р**ого**	кото́р**ого**	кото́р**ой**	кото́р**ых**
№ 3	како́му? -ОМУ	како́му? -ОМУ	како́й? -ОЙ	каки́м? -ЫМ
	кото́р**ому**	кото́р**ому**	кото́р**ой**	кото́р**ым**
№ 4	како́го? -ОГО како́й? -ЫЙ	како́е? -ОЕ	каку́ю? -УЮ	каки́х? -ЫХ каки́е? -ЫЕ
	кото́р**ого** кото́р**ый**	кото́р**ое**	кото́р**ую**	кото́р**ых** кото́р**ые**
№ 5	каки́м? -ЫМ	каки́м? -ЫМ	како́й? -ОЙ	каки́ми? -ЫМИ
	кото́р**ым**	кото́р**ым**	кото́р**ой**	кото́р**ыми**
№ 6	како́м? -ОМ	како́м? -ОМ	како́й? -ОЙ	каки́х? -ЫХ
	кото́р**ом**	кото́р**ом**	кото́р**ой**	кото́р**ых**

11

REMEMBER!

You need to build this type of sentence correctly:

The relative pronoun **кото́рый** will have the same case form as the replaced word in the subordinate clause.

Ка́тя — э́то **де́вушка**. Я люблю́ **э́ту де́вушку** (case № 4).

1. You find the common place in both sentences (де́вушка — э́ту де́вушку)
2. Define the case of the second word (э́ту де́вушку — case № 4)
3. Replace the second word (де́вушку) with the word кото́рый in the same case (case № 4 — кото́рую). You delete the demonstrative pronoun э́тот.
4. Put кото́рый right after the comma. You put other words in the usual order.
   Ка́тя — э́то де́вушка, **кото́рую** (case № 4) я люблю́.
5. The case of the defining word in the main clause doesn't matter!

Э́то мой друг,	
У меня́ нет дру́га,	
Я пишу́ письмо́ дру́гу,	
В аэропорту́ я встре́тил дру́га,	кото́рый живёт в Москве́.
Я встре́тился с дру́гом,	
Я ча́сто вспомина́ю о дру́ге,	

Я говорю́ о краси́вой де́вушке (case № 6). Я познако́мился **с э́той де́вушкой** (case № 5) вчера́.

Я говорю́ о краси́вой де́вушке, **с кото́рой** (case № 5) я познако́мился вчера́.

Упражне́ние 2. **Make one sentence out of two using the word кото́рый in the case required:**

1. Э́то дом Пашко́ва. Джон был в до́ме Пашко́ва.
2. Э́то Андре́й. Джон встре́тил его́ в до́ме Пашко́ва.
3. Джон звони́т Ма́ше. Он познако́мился с Ма́шей в Интерне́те.
4. Э́то докуме́нты де́душки Бенджами́на. О докуме́нтах ду́мают Джон и Алекса́ндр.
5. Э́то буты́лка англи́йского ви́ски. Э́ту буты́лку Джон привёз ру́сским колле́гам.

Упражне́ние 3. **Make two simple sentences out of one:**

Example: Э́то го́род, из кото́рого я уе́хал неда́вно.
Э́то го́род. Я уе́хал из э́того го́рода неда́вно.

1. Э́то ночно́й клуб, в кото́рый я хожу́ ка́ждую суббо́ту.
2. Я зна́ю одного́ челове́ка, кото́рый лю́бит танцева́ть хип-хо́п.
3. Познако́мьтесь с мои́м но́вым дру́гом, о кото́ром я вам расска́зывал вчера́.
4. Я ча́сто звоню́ подру́ге, с кото́рой я познако́мился в Москве́.
5. На́до осторо́жно переходи́ть доро́гу, по кото́рой е́дет мно́го маши́н.
6. Вот тот дом, из кото́рого мы перее́хали в но́вую кварти́ру.
7. Я люблю́ рисова́ть ста́рое о́зеро, вокру́г кото́рого я гуля́ю ле́том.

Relative clauses can help to explain something when you have forgotten a word.

Supposing you have forgotten the word по́вар. So, you can say: Э́то челове́к, кото́рый гото́вит в рестора́не.

Use the words челове́к, вещь, ме́сто.

For example:

Преподава́тель — э́то челове́к, кото́рый чита́ет ле́кции в университе́те.

Студе́нт — челове́к, кото́рый у́чится в университе́те.

Кра́сная пло́щадь — пло́щадь, кото́рая нахо́дится в це́нтре Москвы́.

Упражне́ние 4. **Do the crossword.**

1. Вещь, в кото́рой нахо́дится суп, когда́ мы обе́даем.
2. (→) Ме́сто, в кото́ром мы смо́трим бале́т и слу́шаем о́перу.
2. (↓) Вещь, по кото́рой мы смо́трим фи́льмы и но́вости.
3. Ме́сто, по кото́рому лю́ди перехо́дят доро́гу.
4. Тра́нспорт, на кото́ром е́дет мно́го люде́й на рабо́ту.
5. Вещь, на кото́рой стои́т таре́лка, когда́ мы обе́даем.
6. Францу́зский музе́й, о кото́ром зна́ют во всём ми́ре.
7. Ме́сто, из кото́рого мы у́тром идём на рабо́ту.
8. Вещь, в кото́рой ва́рят суп.
9. Вещь, в кото́рой мы чита́ем но́вости.
10. Ме́сто, по кото́рому мы хо́дим.
11. Тра́нспорт, на кото́ром мы у́тром е́дем на рабо́ту.
12. Ме́сто в Аме́рике, в кото́ром снима́ют фи́льмы.
13. Вещь, по кото́рой мы звони́м друзья́м.
14. Го́род, кото́рый явля́ется столи́цей Росси́и.
15. Тра́нспорт, на кото́ром мы лета́ем.
16. У́лица в Москве́, на кото́рой рабо́тает мно́го худо́жников.

— Пиши́те заявле́ние, — said the policeman.

— Что мне ну́жно писа́ть?

— Заявле́ние[1]. Э́то докуме́нт, кото́рый пи́шут для поли́ции. Напиши́те, что у Вас бы́ло в но́мере, и чего́ тепе́рь нет. Что мы должны́ **иска́ть**?

[1] a declaration, a form

Infinitive	**иска́ть** (1.IR СК-Щ)**: to look for (IPF)**				**найти́** (SPECIAL)**: to find (PF)**			
Present	я	ищ**у́**	мы	и́щ**ем**	—			
	ты	и́щ**ешь**	вы	и́щ**ете**				
	он, она́, оно́	и́щ**ет**	они́	и́щ**ут**				
Imperative	**Ищи́(те)!**				**Найди́(те)!**			
Past	иска́л, иска́ла, иска́ло, иска́ли				нашёл, нашла́, нашло́, нашли́			
Future	бу́ду (бу́дешь…) иска́ть				я	найд**у́**	мы	найд**ём**
					ты	найд**ёшь**	вы	найд**ёте**
					он, она́, оно́	найд**ёт**	они́	найд**ут**

— У меня́ в ко́мнате был компью́тер и бума́жный блокно́т[2], была́ па́пка с докуме́нтами, был догово́р с ру́сской фи́рмой.

Сейча́с здесь нет компью́тера, нет бума́жного блокно́та, нет па́пки с докуме́нтами, нет догово́ра с ру́сской фи́рмой.

Ещё у меня́ был телефо́н.

— Телефо́на то́же нет? — asked the policeman.

— Телефо́н здесь.

— А де́ньги у Вас здесь бы́ли?

— Де́ньги бы́ли. Но они́ сейча́с… то́же здесь. Де́ньги здесь.

— Стра́нно[3], стра́нно, — mumbled the policeman. — Блокно́та нет, а де́ньги есть.

[2] a notebook
[3] strange (adv.)

Упражне́ние 5. **Answer the questions:**

1. Каки́е ве́щи бы́ли в но́мере Джо́на?

____

2. Что сейча́с есть в но́мере?

____

3. Чего́ сейча́с нет в но́мере?

____

Упражне́ние 6. **Fill in the form. Write what things have disappeared from the room.**

☞ **ATTENTION!**

The verbs иска́ть — найти́ are followed by the words in case № 4. Иска́ть (что?), найти́ (что?).

Кому́:	Нача́льнику ОВД[1] го́рода Москвы́ полко́внику поли́ции Ивано́ву Ива́ну Ива́новичу
От кого́:	от Джо́на Я́нга (а́дрес, телефо́н)

ЗАЯВЛЕ́НИЕ

Прошу́ найти́ мои́ ве́щи: *ноутбу́к, па́пку с докуме́нтами*

Да́та По́дпись[2]

If you have to tell somebody about lost things you will also need the verbs теря́ть — потеря́ть.

[1] a local police department
[12] a signature

Упражне́ние 7. **Complete the phrases with the verbs иска́ть — найти́, теря́ть — потеря́ть.**

1. Ура́! Я ________________ кошелёк!
2. Я ________________ свой зонт. Пожа́луйста, помоги́те мне ________________ его́.
3. Архео́логи ________________ дре́вние[3] города́.
4. Я о́чень невнима́тельный[4] челове́к. Я ча́сто ____________ свои́ ве́щи.
5. Хоро́шего дру́га легко́[5] ____________________ , но тру́дно ____________.
6. Мне о́чень нра́вится ______________ отве́ты на тру́дные вопро́сы.

[3] ancient
[4] внима́тельный — (анто́ним) невнима́тельный: attentive — (antonym) inattentive
[5] easily

Упражне́ние 8. **Answer the questions:**

1. Как ча́сто Вы теря́ете Ва́ши ве́щи?
2. Вы находи́ли де́ньги на у́лице? Мно́го? Что Вы с ни́ми сде́лали?
3. Вы хоти́те найти́ клад[6]?
4. Что Вы сде́лаете, е́сли найдёте клад?

[5] treasure
[7] tempest
[8] a needle
[9] стог се́на: a haystack

Упражне́ние 9. **Find the definitions for the phrases:**

Example: Найти́ дру́га — у меня́ не́ было дру́га, а сейча́с есть.

1. Найти́ свою́ втору́ю полови́ну —	а) забы́ть обо всём.
2. Потеря́ть дру́га —	б) найти́ пробле́мы.
3. Е́сли и́щешь ве́тер, то найдёшь бу́рю[7] —	в) реша́ть зада́чу, кото́рую о́чень тру́дно реши́ть.
4. Иска́ть иго́лку[8] в сто́ге се́на[9] —	г) когда́ начина́ешь нехоро́шее де́ло, пробле́ма мо́жет быть бо́льше, чем ты ду́маешь.
5. Потеря́ть го́лову —	д) встре́тить люби́мого челове́ка.
6. Найти́ приключе́ния на свою́ го́лову —	е) у меня́ был друг, а сейча́с его́ нет.

11

John went out into the street. Indian summer rejoiced, shining with the wide sunny, as it seemed to John, the insidious smile of an experienced woman. The Kremlin narrowly squinted through its loopholes.

«Интере́сно, э́то я нашёл пробле́му и́ли пробле́ма нашла́ меня́? — he was so stressed that didn't notice he was thinking in Russian. — Нет, не хочу́ иска́ть приключе́ния на свою́ го́лову. Зака́нчиваю дела́ с ру́сской фи́рмой и е́ду домо́й в А́нглию».

The man activated the phone and suddenly realized that the number of the Russian company was not there: the number was written only in the invitation, and it was carried away by thieves. That was too much. John took out a business card of his only friend in Moscow.

— Алло́, Андре́й, пожа́луйста, мне нужна́ по́мощь.

— Пробле́мы? — asked the sleepy voice on the other side.

— Извини́, пробле́мы, — John was confused, he had just realised that his new friend had been sleeping after a night's work.

РУ́ССКИЙ СО СЛОВАРЁМ

Over the last several years there has been a tendency to use the word пробле́ма where before the word неприя́тность[1] had been more appropriate.

Instead of плохо́й рабо́тник it is now said пробле́мный рабо́тник. Instead of плоха́я ко́жа[2] they now say пробле́мная ко́жа. But when I was telling about this to the "Western" audience, I received the same reaction several times: "On the contrary, it is better not to utter the word "problem" if you don't want to ruin your career. Now we need to say "challenge" instead of "problem". So, there are no problems, only challenges. Even a small problem is viewed as the opportunity to demonstrate how good you are".

In Russia, on the contrary, foreign borrowing пробле́ма for the Russian ear sounds more positive and businesslike than the primordially Russian неприя́тность. After all, неприя́тность is неприя́тное, but пробле́ма is something that can and should be solved. But if you literally translate the word "challenge" by the word вы́зов, then, most likely, you simply will not be understood.

По кни́ге Ири́ны Лево́нтиной «Ру́сский со словарём»

[1] a small problem
[2] skin

— Как в во́ду смотре́л, когда́ телефо́н тебе́ дава́л, — said Andrey.

— Куда́ ты смотре́л?

— Так говоря́т. Смотре́л в во́ду. То есть как знал. Но я, коне́чно, не знал…

The journalist looked at the mess in John's room after the thieves and policemen.

— Я по́нял, — John sighed. — Спаси́бо, что ты смотре́л в во́ду и дал мне телефо́н. Спаси́бо, что прие́хал.

Andrey didn't answer, he was looking at the copy of the form at the table.

— Ты пи́шешь, что во́ры взя́ли блокно́т и компью́тер, но не взя́ли де́ньги? — Andrey was surprised.

— Да, я ду́маю, э́то о́чень стра́нно.

— Стра́нно?

— Полице́йский то́же так сказа́л.

— Пра́вильно он сказа́л. То́лько э́то не стра́нно. Э́то стра́шно[3].

— Почему́ стра́шно? — John guessed what Andrey meant, he also thought that it wasn't just a theft. But could he trust his family secrets to Andrey?

— Потому́ что во́ры беру́т де́ньги. Зна́чит, э́то бы́ли не во́ры!

— А кто?

— Вопро́с — не кто они́, вопро́с — кто ты?

[3] terrifying, scary (adv.)

In no other situation John would not have told the story about grandfather Benjamin and his treasure to a stranger. It seemed to be unreasonable, even unsafe. But he appeared to have no other choice. Andrey listened to John's story very carefully, never interrupting a somewhat uncomfortable story made by using an electronic translator. When John finished, the journalist asked for clarifications.

— Итак, ты говори́шь, что твой дед Бенджами́н рабо́тал в бу́лочной Фили́ппова в Москве́. Не́сколько раз[1] в неде́лю он **е́здил** из Москвы́ в Санкт-Петербу́рг и **вози́л** хлеб и бу́лки для семьи́ импера́тора Никола́я II (Второ́го). 28 января́ 1917 го́да, в день, когда́ петербу́ргские рабо́чие[2] взя́ли под контро́ль[4] железнодоро́жный вокза́л, твой де́душка е́хал обра́тно в Москву́ из Санкт-Петербу́рга и **вёз** докуме́нты. Э́ти докуме́нты ему́ ну́жно бы́ло **привезти́** в Москву́. В Москве́ на вокза́ле его́ ждал челове́к.

— Да, то́чно! Всё пра́вильно! — answered John.

[1] не́сколько раз: several times
[2] a worker
[3] взять под контро́ль (кого́? что? case № 4): to take under control

Упражне́ние 10. **Answer the questions.**

1. Где рабо́тал де́душка Бенджами́н?
2. Отку́да он е́здил ка́ждую неде́лю?
3. Куда́ он е́здил ка́ждую неде́лю?
4. Отку́да и куда́ он е́хал 28 января́ 1917 го́да?
5. Куда́ ему́ ну́жно бы́ло прие́хать с докуме́нтами?

The rule 2–4–6 is applied to the verbs of motion; it is used to talk about location. And if it concerns a person, use rule 2–3–2.

Compare:

Пра́вило 2–4–6 Rule 2–4–6
+ Пра́вило 2–3–2 + Rule 2–3–2

Лю́ди и направле́ния — People and directions

Отку́да? → **От** кого́?
Я иду́ **от дру́га** (= из до́ма дру́га).
— I'm coming from my friend's place.
Куда́? → **К** кому́?
Я пошёл **к дру́гу (= в дом дру́га).**
— I'm going to my friend's place.
Где? → **У** кого́?
Я **у дру́га (= в до́ме дру́га).**
— I'm at my friend's place.
A combined answer is also possible:
Где ты? Я в кварти́ре у дру́га.
Куда́ ты идёшь? Я иду́ в больни́цу к врачу́.

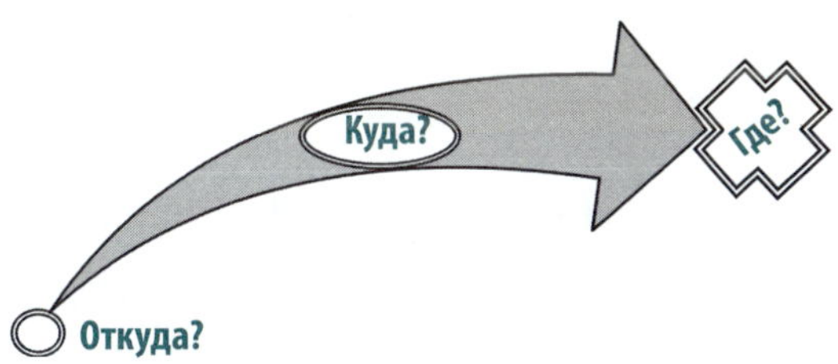

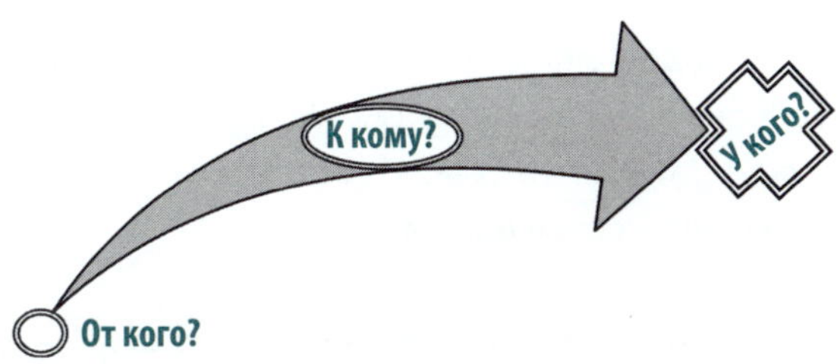

Prepositions:
ОТ → К → У

Case / Gender, number	№ 1	№ 2 **от** кого́?	№ 3 **к** кому́?	№ 2 **у** кого́?
он	друг Андре́й И́горь Анато́лий	**от** дру́г**а** **от** Андре́**я** **от** И́гор**я** **от** Анато́л**ия**	**к** дру́г**у** **к** Андре́**ю** **к** И́гор**ю** **к** Анато́л**ию**	**у** дру́г**а** **у** Андре́**я** **у** И́гор**я** **у** Анато́л**ия**
она́	А́нна подру́га Мари́я	**от** А́нн**ы** **от** подру́г**и** **от** Мар**и́и**	**к** А́нн**е** **к** подру́г**е** **к** Мар**и́и**	**у** А́нн**ы** **у** подру́г**и** **у** Мар**и́и**
они́	подру́ги друзья́	**от** подру́г **от** друз**е́й**	**к** подру́г**ам** **к** друзь**я́м**	**у** подру́г **у** друз**е́й**

Упражне́ние 11. **Read the text about John's grandfather and answer the questions:**

1. У кого́ рабо́тал де́душка Бенджами́н? (Фили́ппов)

   Де́душка Бенджами́н рабо́тал у Фили́ппова

2. К кому́ он е́здил ка́ждую неде́лю? (импера́тор)

   ____

3. От кого́ он е́здил ка́ждую неде́лю? (Фили́ппов)

   ____

4. От кого́ и к кому́ он е́хал 28 января́ 1917 го́да? (импера́тор — челове́к на вокза́ле)

   ____

5. К кому́ он до́лжен был прие́хать с докуме́нтами? (челове́к на вокза́ле)

   ____

Упражне́ние 12. **Read the text, pay attention to the rule 2–3–2 :**

ЕЛЕ́НА И ДРУЗЬЯ́

Меня́ зову́т Еле́на, я студе́нтка. Сего́дня я ходи́ла в го́сти[1]. Я пришла́ к подру́ге Ка́те. У Ка́ти я была́ оди́н час и пошла́ от Ка́ти к подру́ге Жа́нне. У Жа́нны мы смотре́ли фильм. Пото́м мы пошли́ в кафе́, к друзья́м Ко́сте и Се́ве. От Ко́сти и Се́вы Жа́нна пошла́ домо́й к Ка́те, а я пошла́ к себе́ домо́й.

[1] ходи́ть в го́сти — идти́ в го́сти: to visit somebody (usually relatives or friends)

A) Ask questions with words от кого́? — к кому́? — у кого́? (2–3–2).

B) Close your eyes and retell it in your own words.

C) Elena wrote a claim to the police. She should remember every detail of the day. Open the brackets.

Я Еле́на. Сего́дня я ходи́ла в го́сти. Я пришла́ к подру́ге Ка́те (дом № 10, у́лица Ле́нина) ______________ ____.

У Ка́ти (дом № 10, у́лица Ле́нина)______________ ______________________ я была́ оди́н час и пошла́ от Ка́ти (дом № 10, у́лица Ле́нина) ____ к подру́ге Жа́нне (гости́ница, пло́щадь Достое́вского)____.

У Жа́нны (гости́ница, пло́щадь Достое́вского) ____________________ ______________________ мы смотре́ли фильм.

Пото́м мы пошли́ к друзья́м Ко́сте и Се́ве (кафе́ «Рандеву́», проспе́кт Побе́ды) ____________________ ____.

От Ко́сти и Се́вы (кафе́ «Рандеву́», проспе́кт Побе́ды)____________ ____________________________ Жа́нна пошла́ домо́й к Ка́те (дом № 10, у́лица Ле́нина)______________________________________, а я пошла́ к себе́ домо́й.

— Ита́к, де́душка Бенджами́н вёз **каки́е-то** докуме́нты, — Andrey clarified.

— Да. То́лько докуме́нты не **каки́е-то**. Вели́кий князь Гео́ргий Миха́йлович дал докуме́нты де́душке. Гео́ргий Миха́йлович — э́то дя́дя царя́ Никола́я II (Второ́го). Мой оте́ц — исто́рик. Он ду́мает, что э́то докуме́нты бра́тьев Гео́ргия Миха́йловича и Никола́я Миха́йловича. Они́ бы́ли учёными. Никола́й Миха́йлович занима́лся исто́рией Росси́и. Он изуча́л вре́мя царя́ Алекса́ндра I (Пе́рвого). Мно́го жил и рабо́тал в Евро́пе, осо́бенно во Фра́нции, в Пари́же. Мой оте́ц ду́мает, что вели́кий князь Рома́нов иска́л клад Наполео́на.

Неопределённые местоиме́ния и наре́чия — Indefinite pronouns and adverbs

	-ТО	-НИБУДЬ
	The speaker **doesn't know** which object he is talking about	**It doesn't matter** to the speaker which object he is talking about
како́й?	**како́й-то**	**како́й-нибудь**
	Како́й-то журна́л лежа́л на столе́. There was a journal on the table (I don't know what journal it was). **Кака́я-то** кни́га лежи́т на столе́.	Да́йте мне **како́й-нибудь** журна́л. Give me any journal (it doesn't matter which one, choose any). Я хочу́ взять **како́е-нибудь** фо́то.
кто? что?	**кто́-то, что́-то**	**кто́-нибудь, что́-нибудь**
	Вам **кто́-то** звони́л. Somebody called you (a person you don't know). Он хо́чет мне **что́-то** сказа́ть.	Пусть **кто́-нибудь** позвони́т. Let anybody make a call (it doesn't matter who is going to make it). Расскажи́ мне **что́-нибудь** о себе́.
когда́? где? куда́?	**когда́-то, где́-то, куда́-то**	**когда́-нибудь, где́-нибудь, куда́-нибудь**
	Он **когда́-то** был в э́том го́роде. Я **где́-то** ви́дел его́. Его́ нет до́ма, он **куда́-то** ушёл.	Он **когда́-нибудь** прие́дет сюда́. Вы **где́-нибудь** ви́дели его́? Вы **куда́-нибудь** пое́дете ле́том?

ATTENTION!

Како́й, кто, что can be altered.
-то, -нибу́дь is added without alteration:

На столе́ лежи́т кака́я-то кни́га.	В кла́ссе нет кого́-то?
Принесли́ каку́ю-то кни́гу.	Вы с ке́м-то прие́хали?
Расска́зывали о како́й-то кни́ге.	Вы о ко́м-то не рассказа́ли?

Упражне́ние 13. **Fill in the gaps with necessary indefinite pronouns or adverbs.**

A) *Example:* Бенджами́н Янг вёз ____________ докуме́нты. →
Бенджами́н Янг вёз **каки́е-то** докуме́нты.

1. ____________ пришёл и стои́т за две́рью.
2. «Что лежи́т там на по́лке?» — «Э́то ____________ кни́га».
3. Э́то был ____________ мужчи́на. Я не ви́дела его́ лица́.
4. «Где живёт медве́дь?» — «Не зна́ю то́чно. ____________ в лесу́».
5. Вчера́ ____________ забра́л мой слова́рь.
6. Моя́ жена́ вчера́ потеря́ла телефо́н ____________ здесь.

B) *Example:* Гео́ргий Миха́йлович Рома́нов — э́то ____________ ру́сский царь? — Нет, э́то дя́дя ру́сского царя́ Никола́я II (Второ́го). →
Гео́ргий Миха́йлович Рома́нов — э́то **како́й-нибудь** ру́сский царь? — Нет, э́то дя́дя ру́сского царя́ Никола́я II.

1. ____________ зна́ет, где железнодоро́жный вокза́л?
2. Ску́чно. Да́йте почита́ть ____________ журна́л!
3. ____________ из ва́шей гру́ппы занима́ется спо́ртом?
4. В э́том до́ме я ____________ могу́ отдохну́ть?
5. Вы бы́ли ____________ в Аргенти́не?
6. Расскажи́те ____________ о свое́й стране́.
7. Вы ____________ прие́дете в Росси́ю ещё раз?
8. О́льга, ты ви́дела ____________ мой па́спорт?
9. Вы ____________ теря́ли го́лову?

Упражне́ние 14. **Fill in the gaps with кто́-то or что́-то in the case required:**

Example: «Кому́ Вы рассказа́ли э́ту но́вость?» — «Я не по́мню. **Кому́-то** из колле́г».

1. «Кто сейча́с вы́шел из ко́мнаты?» — «Я не ви́дел. ____________ в тёмном костю́ме».
2. «К кому́ Ивано́вы пойду́т сего́дня ве́чером?» — «Я не по́мню. ____________ из свои́х колле́г».
3. «Чего́ здесь нет?» — «____________ о́чень ну́жного».
4. «Э́то вку́сно? Я ещё не поняла́». — «Э́то ____________ солёное».
5. «Чем сейча́с занима́ется профе́ссор Бело́в?» — «Я не зна́ю то́чно. Но ____________ о́чень интере́сным».
6. «О ком спра́шивал преподава́тель?» — « ____________ из студе́нтов».
7. «О чём ду́мает ваш кот?» — «Мой кот всегда́ ду́мает ____________ о́чень ва́жном».

Упражне́ние 15. Fill in the gaps with кто́-нибудь or что́-нибудь in the case required.

1. Вы ду́маете _______________ , когда́ спи́те? 2. Вы пи́шете _________________ пи́сьма на бума́ге? 3. Вы звони́те _________________ в А́фрику? 4. Вы теря́ли __________________ в метро́? 5. Вы говори́ли ________________ ва́жном с Ва́шим дру́гом? 6. Вы ду́маете _________________ , когда́ отдыха́ете на мо́ре? 7. Вы зна́ете __________________ в Олимпи́йском комите́те[1]? 8. Вы зна́ете __________________ стра́шное о Ва́ших друзья́х и́ли колле́гах?

[1] Olympic Committee

— Клад Наполео́на? — Andrey burst out laughing. — Не мо́жет быть! Э́тот клад и́щут уже́ два ве́ка. Иска́ли и ру́сские, и францу́зы, и англича́не, и не́мцы, и испа́нцы. Иска́ли в реке́ Березине́. Иска́ли на Смоле́нской доро́ге, в озёрах и ре́ках, в земле́ и на дере́вьях. Иска́ли в Белору́ссии, в Литве́, в Ла́твии. Иска́ли в города́х: в Ви́льно[2], в Гро́дно, в Ко́вно[3]. Иска́ли в деревня́х и в церквя́х, кото́рые стоя́ли на доро́ге Наполео́на и его́ а́рмии. Иска́ли ря́дом с го́родом Ми́нском и ря́дом с Пона́рской горо́й, где отдыха́л Наполе́он, когда́ бежа́л во Фра́нцию из Росси́и.

Иска́ли, иска́ли, но **ничего́** не нашли́. Я то́же люблю́ истори́ческие та́йны и кла́ды. Но я ду́маю, что **никако́го** кла́да Наполео́на не́ было. Э́то миф.

[2] Сейча́с Ви́льнюс, столи́ца Литвы́.
[3] Сейча́с Ка́унас, второ́й по значе́нию го́род в Литве́.

Отрица́тельные местоиме́ния — Negative pronouns and adverbs

	НИ
	The speaker uses a negation to answer the question
кто? что?	**никто́, ничто́**
	Никто́ не пошёл на конце́рт. Я **никому́ не** звони́л. Он **ничем́ не** занима́лся вчера́. Я **ни о чём** с ним **не** говори́л. Я **ни с кем не** знако́мился вчера́.
како́й?	**никако́й**
	Никако́й челове́к **не** лю́бит непра́вду. **Никака́я** кни́га мне **не** понра́вилась.
когда́? где? куда́?	**никогда́, нигде́, никуда́**
	Я **никогда́ не́** был в э́том го́роде. Я ещё **нигде́ не́** был. Я ещё **никуда́ не** ходи́л.

Pay attention to the double negation! Negative pronouns and adverbs with prefix ни + particle не in front of the verb.

11

Упражне́ние 16. **Answer the questions using negative pronouns or adverbs.**

A) 1. Что его́ интересу́ет?
2. О чём вы говори́ли с ним?
3. Чем Вы занима́лись, кро́ме му́зыки?
4. Что он ви́дел?
5. Что Вы чита́ли ве́чером?
6. Чего́ он бои́тся[1]?

[1] (2.R.VOW): to be afraid

B) 1. В како́й рабо́те Вы уча́ствовали?
2. Кака́я по́мощь нужна́ вам?
3. Каки́е иностра́нные языки́ он зна́ет?
4. Како́й вопро́с был тру́дным для Вас

C) 1. Куда́ Вы пое́дете ле́том?
2. Где Вы отдыха́ли ле́том?
3. Когда́ Вы отдыха́ли в Крыму́?
4. Отку́да Вы получи́ли письмо́?
5. Куда́ Вы пойдёте ве́чером?

— Я то́же ду́маю, что дед рассказа́л отцу́ миф, ска́зку[2], — answered John. — Но оте́ц ду́мает, что э́то пра́вда. Поэ́тому я здесь. Мне ну́жно узна́ть э́то для отца́.

[2] a fairy-tale

— Э́то ну́жно тебе́ и́ли твоему́ отцу́? — asked Andrey.

— Я не могу́ отве́тить отцу́ «нет», — John rolled his eyes.

— Тогда́ э́то друго́е сло́во. Не «ну́жно», а «до́лжен».

— Что? — John was surprised.

— Ты до́лжен найти́ отве́т для твоего́ отца́.

John thought for a second and then opened grammar tables.

Models-synonyms ну́жно / до́лжен / ну́жен

мне ну́жно (на́до) — I need (a person has a need for something).
я до́лжен — I must (a person has an obligation and they realise it).

• Хоро́ший студе́нт: «Мне ну́жно мно́го занима́ться, потому́ что я хочу́ хорошо́ говори́ть по-ру́сски».

• Хоро́ший муж: «Мне ну́жно купи́ть цветы́, потому́ что я хочу́ подари́ть их мое́й жене́».

• Хоро́ший официа́нт: «Я не хочу́ улыба́ться ка́ждую мину́ту. Но я до́лжен: э́то моя́ рабо́та».

• Хоро́ший сын: «Я не хочу́ занима́ться му́зыкой, но я до́лжен. Моя́ ма́ма ду́мает, что у меня́ музыка́льный тала́нт».

А как вы ду́маете, что мо́жет сказа́ть плохо́й студе́нт, плохо́й муж, плохо́й официа́нт и плохо́й сын?

Compare! These models are also synonyms, there is no difference which word to use.

ну́жно	ну́жен
Impersonal sentence where стол, кни́га, я́блоко is an object (case № 4) Кому́ (case № 3) ну́жно что (case № 4)	Simple sentence where стол, кни́га, я́блоко is a subject (case № 1) Кому́ (case № 3) ну́жен (-на́, -но, -ны́) что / кто (case № 1)
Мне **ну́жно** (получи́ть) э́тот стол (case № 4).	Мне **ну́жен** э́тот стол (case № 1).
Мне **ну́жно** (получи́ть) э́ту кни́гу (case № 4).	Мне **нужна́** э́та кни́га (case № 1).
Мне **ну́жно** (получи́ть) э́то я́блоко (case № 4).	Мне **ну́жно** э́то я́блоко (case № 1).
Мне **ну́жно** (получи́ть) э́ти докуме́нты (case № 4).	Мне **нужны́** э́ти докуме́нты (case № 1).
Мне **бу́дет ну́жно** (получи́ть) э́тот стол, э́ту кни́гу, э́то я́блоко, э́ти докуме́нты (case № 4).	Мне **бу́дет ну́жен** э́тот стол (case № 1). Мне **бу́дет нужна́** э́та кни́га (case № 1). Мне **бу́дет ну́жно** э́то я́блоко (case № 1). Мне **бу́дут нужны́** э́ти докуме́нты (case № 1).
Мне бы́ло **ну́жно** (получи́ть) э́тот стол, э́ту кни́гу, э́то я́блоко, э́ти докуме́нты (case № 4).	Мне **бу́дут нужны́** э́ти кни́ги (case № 1).

Models-synonyms мо́жно / могу́

As a rule we can interchange passive and active constructions with little changes in meaning.

Мне мо́жно чита́ть. — I am allowed to read. (= I have a permission!)

Я могу́ чита́ть. — I can read. (= I am able to read.)

Infinitive		Singular (sg)		Plural (pl)
мочь **ч → г → ж** group on -е-	я	мог**у́**	мы	мо́ж**ем**
	ты	мо́ж**ешь**	вы	мо́ж**ете**
	он, она́, оно́	мо́ж**ет**	они́	мо́г**ут**
Past		**Singular (sg)**		**Plural (pl)**
мочь	он	**мог**	мы	мог**ли́**
	она́	мог**ла́**	вы	
	оно́	мог**ло́**	они́	

1. — Здесь мо́жно кури́ть?
   — Да, здесь мо́жно кури́ть = Я могу́ (Вы мо́жете) здесь кури́ть.

2. — Вы уже́ мо́жете ходи́ть?
   — Да, я уже́ могу́ ходи́ть. Нога́ не боли́т.

Упражне́ние 17. **Complete the sentence with one of the following words:**

A) ну́жно / до́лжен / ну́жен

1. Мой сосе́д[1] — студе́нт консервато́рии, поэ́тому он __________ игра́ть класси́ческую му́зыку.
2. Они́ актёры. За́втра им ________________ игра́ть на сце́не. Сего́дня они́ _________________ учи́ть стихи́ всю ночь.
3. Кни́га, кото́рая мне ________________, сто́ит 2000 рубле́й, и я ________________ купи́ть её.
4. Мне ________________ купи́ть э́ту маши́ну, и я ________________ мно́го рабо́тать.
5. Ей бу́дут _____________ но́вые бе́лые ту́фли и пла́тье. Ско́ро у неё бу́дет сва́дьба[2].

[1] a neighbour
[2] a wedding

B) мо́жно / могу́

1. — До́ктор, мне ____________ игра́ть на скри́пке?
   — Да, Ва́ша рука́ уже́ здоро́ва.
2. — Ита́к, Вы хоти́те рабо́тать в орке́стре. На чём Вы _________ игра́ть?
   — Я __________ игра́ть на скри́пке.
3. Здесь ___________ переходи́ть доро́гу. Но мы не _________ перейти́ её, потому́ что здесь мно́го маши́н. Стои́м и ждём уже́ 15 мину́т.

— Да, всё пра́вильно. Я не о́чень хочу́ иска́ть клад, но я до́лжен узна́ть для отца́, — confirmed John.

— Что узна́ть?

— Дед говори́л, что привёз докуме́нты в Москву́ и положи́л их в бу́лочной Фили́ппова… — There was a language difficulty. John could not formulate in Russian that the revolution caught his grandfather by surprise, and when he had the opportunity to escape from Russia to Europe, a heavy bundle of paper wrapped in calfskin appeared not to be the most important item at that time. Therefore, Benjamin hid the documents in a cache in the bakery. It was too difficult to understand all that in English for Andrey who knew English at about the same level as John knew Russian.

As John was typing his answer in Google translator Andrey's erudition helped him to understand.

— Я по́нял! — exclaimed the journalist. — Я слы́шал о докуме́нтах из тайника́ до́ма Фили́ппова. Тайни́к — э́то ме́сто, о кото́ром зна́ет то́лько оди́н и́ли не́сколько челове́к. Понима́ешь? Я чита́л об э́том тайнике́!

John knew the word та́йна (see p. 118): his father mentioned it before he left for Russia: «Вели́кий князь Никола́й Миха́йлович люби́л истори́ческие та́йны». Тайни́к = та́йна + ник.

Model: Word formation with suffix -НИК

This model, as a rule, denotes an object which contains something named in the root:

WORD + -НИК: чай — ча́й**ник** ко́фе — кофе́й**ник** бума́га — бума́ж**ник**

Another option: the model is formed from the verb and denotes an object that performs an action named by a verb:

буди́ть (to wake) — буди́ль**ник** (an alarm clock)
свети́ть (to shine (to give light)) — свети́ль**ник** (a lamp)
холоди́ть (to freeze) — холоди́ль**ник** (a refrigerator)

At that point John thought that perhaps he had done the right thing and told Andrey about the purpose of his visit to Russia. Apparently, Andrey was really a good historian. But why did he work as paparazzi? After the thieves broke into his room, John did not trust anyone. If someone was following him to find out about the search... no, their meeting with the journalist was so absurd and ridiculous that it would not be possible to fine-tune it even for Professor James Moriarty.

— Что бы́ло в тайнике́? — John was very excited.

— Каки́е-то бума́ги и моне́ты[1].

After a brief silence Andrey suddenly said seriously:

— А я ду́маю, что твой оте́ц прав[2]. Исто́рия де́душки Бенджами́на — пра́вда!

— Почему́?

— Как ты ду́маешь, кто до́лжен был встре́тить в Москве́ твоего́ де́да?

— Я не зна́ю — како́й-то «свой челове́к».

— Э́тот како́й-то «свой челове́к» не како́й-то. Я то́лько сейча́с по́нял! Я ду́маю, что э́то был вели́кий князь Никола́й Миха́йлович.

— Сам князь?

— Да. В жи́зни кня́зя для меня́ всегда́ был оди́н стра́нный вопро́с, на кото́рый я не мог отве́тить.

— Како́й вопро́с?

— Все исто́рики зна́ют Никола́я Миха́йловича, потому́ что большевики́[3] уби́ли[4] его́ в 1919 году́. Тогда́ Ле́нин сказа́л изве́стные слова́: «Револю́ции[5] не нужны́ исто́рики».

— Я не знал, что э́ти слова́ Ле́нина о вели́ком кня́зе Никола́е Миха́йловиче Рома́нове.

— Да. Э́ти слова́ о нём. И не то́лько о нём. Револю́ция — э́то всегда́ но́вая исто́рия. Но! Вот тут и вопро́с. Когда́ начала́сь револю́ция 1917 го́да, Никола́й Миха́йлович был о́чень далеко́ от Санкт-Петербу́рга. Он был на ю́ге Росси́и — в Крыму́. Почему́ он прие́хал в Санкт-Петербу́рг 1 ма́рта 1917 го́да?

— Мо́жет быть, ему́ на́до бы́ло ви́деть царя́ Никола́я II. Царь — его́ племя́нник. А тут револю́ция.

— Не мо́жет быть!

— Почему́?

— Ты зна́ешь, кто тако́й Григо́рий Распу́тин?

— Знамени́тый авантюри́ст[6], — John made a mysterious face and waved his hands over the surface of the table imitating a session of magic, because he didn't know words like "prophet" and "healer" in Russian and did not even look for them in the dictionary, because Andrey understood it without translation.

— Распу́тин — э́то... Распу́тин — поня́тно без словаря́.

— Поня́тно?! — exclaimed Andrey. — Ничего́ не поня́тно! Вот, ты говори́шь: Распу́тин — авантюри́ст. Э́то хорошо́ и́ли пло́хо?

— Я ду́маю — пло́хо. Для исто́рии Росси́и — э́то то́чно бы́ло пло́хо.

— Вели́кий князь Никола́й Миха́йлович то́же ду́мал так. Но царь так не ду́мал. И Никола́й II, и его́ жена́ Али́са Ге́ссенская о́чень люби́ли Распу́тина.

In this long dialogue in Russian John began to lose the thread of conversation. What relation did Rasputin have to the arrival of Grand Duke Nicolas Mikhailovich in St. Petersburg in March 1917? Andrey felt that it was difficult for John.

[1] a coin
[2] right
[3] bolshevik
[4] (PF; 1.IR И-Ь): to kill
[5] a revolution
[6] adventurer

11

— Князь Никола́й Миха́йлович хоте́л уби́ть Григо́рия Распу́тина, — Andrey imitated the Duke pouring poison to Rasputin's food, Rasputin eating, and falling on the floor, shaking in agony.

John read about this terrible story — the poison did not affect Rasputin, and despite the fact that he received four bullets, Rasputin was still breathing when he was thrown into the icy water of the Neva River.

— Сам хоте́л уби́ть? Свои́ми рука́ми? — John doubted.

— Коне́чно, не сам, не оди́н. Был це́лый за́говор[1]. Но, когда́ царь Николай II узна́л, что Распу́тина уби́ли, он был в гне́ве[2]. Никола́й Миха́йлович до́лжен был уе́хать в свой дом, кото́рый находи́лся на Чёрном мо́ре, в Крыму́. 1 января́ 1917 го́да вели́кий князь уе́хал из Санкт-Петербу́рга. Но 1 ма́рта он сно́ва прие́хал в Петербу́рг. Исто́рики зна́ют, что князь е́хал через Москву́. Он был в Москве́ не́сколько дней. Заче́м ему́ э́то бы́ло на́до? Дел в Москве́ у кня́зя не́ было. А в Петербу́рге начина́лась револю́ция… Всё э́то говори́т о том, что Никола́й Миха́йлович Рома́нов кого́-то ждал в Москве́. Пото́м он по́нял, что челове́к с докуме́нтами не прие́хал и не прие́дет. И поэ́тому он пое́хал в Санкт-Петербу́рг сам.

[1] conspiracy
[2] гнев: rage; в гне́ве: in rage
[3] the Olympic Games
[4] wonderful; Еле́на Прекра́сная: Helen of Troy

— Мой де́душка вёз что-то о́чень ва́жное для кня́зя?

— Коне́чно, ва́жное! Князь знал, что его́ мо́гут уби́ть. Но он пое́хал в Санкт-Петербу́рг. Ду́маю, он хоте́л найти́ твоего́ де́да и докуме́нты.

Andrey walked around the room, stopped at the window and pointed to the things scattered after the robbery and the visit of the police:

— А всё э́то говори́т о том, что у тебя́, Джон, есть в Росси́и сопе́рник.

— Что у меня́ есть?

— Не что, а кто. Сопе́рник — э́то челове́к, кото́рый хо́чет име́ть то, что хо́чешь име́ть ты. Наприме́р, спортсме́ны на Олимпи́йских и́грах[3] — сопе́рники. И́ли Менела́й и Пари́с, кото́рые люби́ли Прекра́сную[4] Еле́ну. Они́ то́же сопе́рники.

— Да, я по́нял, сопе́рник — э́то как конкуре́нт. Е́сли ты прав и у меня́ есть сопе́рник, то он зна́ет об исто́рии де́душки Бенджами́на. Но э́того не мо́жет быть! Мой оте́ц рассказа́л э́ту исто́рию мне. А отцу́ э́ту исто́рию рассказа́л де́душка. То́лько три челове́ка зна́ют о докуме́нтах!

Andrey shrugged his shoulders and said:

— Мо́жет быть, зна́ет кто́-то ещё.

Andrew started to call all the historians he knew. And in half an hour he found what he was looking for. Andrew exclaimed:

— Ита́к, я зна́ю, куда́ увезли́ докуме́нты из бу́лочной Фили́ппова.

— Куда́?

— В Санкт-Петербу́рг. А моне́ты — в музе́й Эрмита́ж, э́то то́же в Санкт-Петербу́рге.

Everything gradually began to add up. The coins found in the cache were again added to the collection of coins of Grand Duke George Mikhailovich Romanov. This collection remained after the death of Grand Duke George (both Grand Dukes George Mikhailovich and Nicolas Mikhailovich were shot by the Bolsheviks in 1919). Now all the coins from the collection were exhibited in the Hermitage. The curious thing was reason why the princes took only those few coins from the entire collection that grandfather Benjamin was supposed to deliver from St. Petersburg to Moscow. Why did they, according to the plan of the grand dukes, have to be saved and taken out of revolutionary Russia?

— Е́сли ты хо́чешь узна́ть пра́вду, то на́до е́хать в Санкт-Петербу́рг, — заключил Андрей.

— Ты мо́жешь пое́хать со мно́й? — John asked, understanding that either the father overestimated his abilities, or he underestimated Russia. In any case, the assistance of a Russian journalist and historian could be very helpful.

— Ду́маю, что могу́. Но́чью я сде́лал не́сколько фотогра́фий в до́ме Пашко́ва, мне на́до отпра́вить их в реда́кцию мое́й газе́ты и я могу́ е́хать с тобо́й.

— Ско́лько сто́ит[1] твоя́ по́мощь?

Andrey shrugged his shoulders:

— Пе́рвые фотогра́фии и пе́рвые статьи́ о кла́де де́лаю я — э́то раз. Биле́ты на по́езд и самолёт, но́мер в гости́нице, за́втраки, обе́ды, у́жины покупа́ешь ты — э́то два.

— Э́то всё? Ты не хо́чешь де́ньги? — John was surprised.

— Хочу́, — answered the journalist. — Но... е́сли челове́к и́щет клад то́лько для де́нег, то он его́ никогда́ не найдёт. Я э́то то́чно зна́ю!

— Хорошо́, е́сли что́-то найдём, то бу́дем говори́ть о деньга́х.

— Хорошо́, — Andrey agreed at once. — Да, кста́ти[2], о деньга́х. Прочита́й! Э́то ва́жно.

Andrey gave him an article on Russian legislation, which was about how the value of the treasure is distributed. The article was called «ЧЕЙ КЛАД?».

[1] Ско́лько сто́ит...?: How much is it?
[2] by the way

REMEMBER!

цена́:	price	зо́лото:	gold
це́нный:	valuable	золото́й:	gold (adj.)
це́нность:	value	серебро́:	silver
дорого́й:	expensive	сере́бряный:	silver (adj.)
драгоце́нный:	precious	ка́мень:	stone
драгоце́нность:	jewel	зако́н:	law
принадлежа́ть:	to belong	зако́нный:	legal

Упражне́ние 18. **Find the words in the table that have the same root. Write them down according to the model.**

1. Noun + suffix -Н- = adjective ____________________
2. Noun + suffix -ЯН- = adjective ____________________
3. Noun + ending -ОЙ = adjective ____________________
4. Root 1 + Root 2 = new word ____________________
5. Adjective + suffix -ОСТЬ = abstract noun ____________________

11

Упражне́ние 19. **Make words according to the model adjective + suffix -ОСТЬ.**

Example: но́вый + -ОСТЬ = но́вость

зако́нный[3], ва́жный[4], молодо́й, ста́рый, осторо́жный[5]

[3] legal
[4] important
[5] cautious, prudent

Упражне́ние 20. **Translate these sentences to your native language.**

1. Э́тот докуме́нт име́ет большу́ю ва́жность.
2. Э́тот па́мятник име́ет большу́ю це́нность для исто́рии.
3. Я услы́шал интере́сную но́вость.
4. Поли́ция сохраня́ет зако́нность в стране́.
5. Лю́ди быва́ют рома́нтиками в мо́лодости, а в ста́рости они́ уже́ не рома́нтики.
6. Когда́ Вы во́дите маши́ну, Вам необходи́ма осторо́жность.

***Упражне́ние 21*. Read, translate the text.**

ЧЕЙ КЛАД?

В Росси́и кла́ды и́щут и нахо́дят ча́сто. Небольши́е кла́ды нахо́дят в земле́ и в ста́рых дома́х по всей Росси́и. Обы́чно э́то ста́рые моне́ты, золоты́е и серебряные ве́щи, драгоце́нные ка́мни. Есть изве́стные кла́ды, кото́рые и́щут уже́ мно́го лет: э́то библиоте́ка Ива́на Гро́зного, клад Наполео́на, драгоце́нности Каза́нского ха́нства[1] и други́е. Э́ти кла́ды име́ют большу́ю ва́жность для исто́рии. В Моско́вском Кремле́ постоя́нно[2] нахо́дят но́вые кла́ды.

В Росси́и есть зако́н о кла́дах.

1. Е́сли клад не име́ет большо́й це́нности для исто́рии, то:

- 50 % принадлежи́т[3] хозя́ину земли́;
- 50 % принадлежи́т челове́ку, кото́рый нашёл клад.

2. Е́сли клад име́ет большу́ю це́нность для исто́рии, то:

- клад принадлежи́т госуда́рству;
- 50 % цены́ кла́да принадлежи́т хозя́ину земли́ и челове́ку, кото́рый нашёл клад (25 % и 25 %).

[1] The Kazan Khanate (now the Republic of Tatarstan) was conquered by Tsar Ivan the Terrible in 1552. According to legend, numerous treasures belonging to the Khan were hidden from the invaders at the bottom of the lake in the center of the city.
[2] all the time
[3] (2.R.CONS.2): to belong

***Упражне́ние 22*. How much of the value of the treasure will John receive in the first and second cases, if it is known that in both cases he should give half of his profit to Andrey?**

Talks about money and percentage made John return from the romantic mysteries of history to the current moment and remember the main purpose of his visit to Russia:

— Я не могу́ е́хать в Санкт-Петербу́рг! — he said.

— Почему́? — Andrey got very surprised.

— Я прилете́л в Москву́, что́бы рабо́тать с одно́й ру́сской фи́рмой. Я до́лжен е́хать в о́фис э́той фи́рмы. Но я не по́мню а́дрес, не по́мню телефо́н.

— Назва́ние фи́рмы по́мнишь? Как называ́ется фи́рма?

— И́мя фи́рмы? — asked John.

— И́мя — есть у челове́ка, а у фи́рмы — назва́ние.

REMEMBER!

и́мя — name — челове́к	**назва́ние — name** — объе́кт (го́род, фи́рма, кни́га, река́, о́стров)
Как кого́ (case № 2) зову́т	**Как называ́ется что (case № 1)** **What is the name of something** называ́лся (-лась, -лось, -лись)
Э́того челове́ка зову́т Андре́й.	Э́тот аэропо́рт называ́ется Вну́ково.

— Назва́ние фи́рмы — «Бы́стро е́дем».

— Как интере́сно называ́ется э́та фи́рма! Мне бу́дет нетру́дно найти́ её а́дрес и телефо́н.

Andrey surfed the Internet and a few minutes later he already had the number of a Russian partner company. He handed John his mobile with the number dialed on the screen:

— Вот телефо́н. Звони́!

— Э́то кошма́р! — John exclaimed, realizing how many problems there would be with the prolongation of his stay in Moscow, with the payment for the hotel and other things.

— Про́сто позвони́, — Andrey suggested. — Скажи́ о свое́й пробле́ме, я ду́маю, что они́ тебя́ пойму́т.

— Нет-не́т, они́ не пойму́т. Я до́лжен де́лать но́вый контра́кт. Нужна́ моя́ по́дпись.

— По-зво-ни́, — repeated Andrey. — Снача́ла[1] позвони́.

To John's surprise Andrey was right. The call to the director of the office in Moscow was quite enough. He didn't want to see him, didn't ask to send confirmation with his signature by e-mail and didn't even call to London. Although, John didn't know that for sure. The Russian director believed him on his word and agreed to begin work on John's return to Moscow in a few days.

— Он да́же ничего́ не сказа́л о деньга́х за мою́ гости́ницу! — John was surprised.

— Он пове́рил тебе́ на́ слово.

[1] at first

☞ **REMEMBER the following words and phrases**

дава́ть / дать (кому́? case № 3): дава́ть де́ньги де́тям	to give
отдава́ть / отда́ть (что? case № 4): отдава́ть де́ньги	to give
передава́ть / переда́ть (через кого́? case № 4): передава́ть через дру́га	to pass
ве́рить / пове́рить (кому́? чему́? case № 3)	to believe
че́стный	honest
дать че́стное сло́во	to give a word (an honest word)
долг	a debt
дава́ть де́ньги в долг	to lend money
брать де́ньги в долг	to borrow money
отдава́ть долг (долги́)	to repay
де́нежный долг	monetary debt
догово́р (контра́кт)	a contract
догова́риваться / договори́ться	to agree
подписа́ть догово́р (контра́кт)	to sign a contract
по́дпись	signature

11

Упражне́ние 23. **Read the text and answer the questions.**

РЕПУТА́ЦИЯ[2] КУПЦО́В: РУ́ССКИМ ВЕ́РИТЬ
(by V. Medinsky)

Купе́ц — э́то челове́к, кото́рый покупа́ет и продаёт, во́зит ве́щи и проду́кты. Сейча́с э́та профе́ссия называ́ется «предпринима́тель» и́ли «бизнесме́н».

В Сре́дние века́[3] жи́тели Евро́пы зна́ли, что ру́сские купцы́ — о́чень че́стные лю́ди, потому́ что ру́сские купцы́ всегда́ отдава́ли свои́ долги́. Ганзе́йский сою́з[4] никогда́ не **сажа́л** ру́сского купца́ в тюрьму́[5]. Е́сли купе́ц не мог отда́ть долги́, он до́лжен был… пое́хать в Росси́ю. Ру́сский купе́ц до́лжен был дать че́стное сло́во. Все ве́рили

[2] reputation

[3] Middle Ages

[4] From German word *Hanse* — union. The medieval guild of entrepreneurs, which included more than a hundred cities and controlled most of the trade in Europe, they could apply punitive measures to ruined merchants, monitor the observance of trade relations and treaties in Northern Europe.

[5] сажа́ть (1.R.VOW) / посади́ть (2.IR Д-Ж) в тюрьму́: to take someone to prison

ру́сским купца́м. Все зна́ли, что ру́сский бу́дет по́мнить свой долг, привезёт де́ньги из Росси́и и отда́ст долг с проце́нтами[1]. Так и бы́ло.

Э́то типи́чная черта́[2] ру́сского наро́да — догова́риваться у́стно. Ра́ньше, в 18-ом, 19-ом ве́ках, купцы́ догова́ривались в тракти́рах. Э́то ме́сто для еды́, для ча́я и дел[3], недорого́й рестора́н.

И сейча́с в Росси́и ча́сто ве́рят че́стному сло́ву. Друзья́ не подпи́сывают догово́ры. Е́сли друг даёт де́ньги в долг своему́ дру́гу, то они́ не пойду́т к нота́риусу[4]. Друг даст че́стное сло́во: «Я отда́м де́ньги». И друг пове́рит своему́ дру́гу.

Е́сли челове́к бо́лен, то он позвони́т своему́ нача́льнику[5] и не́сколько дней бу́дет боле́ть до́ма. Коне́чно, е́сли челове́к боле́ет до́лго, то ну́жен больни́чный лист[6], но обы́чно э́то не ну́жно и нача́льник ве́рит своему́ сотру́днику.

Сейча́с репута́ция ру́сских бизнесме́нов не всегда́ хоро́шая. Все зна́ют сло́во «олига́рх» (oligarch), кото́рое ча́сто явля́ется сино́нимом сло́ву «вор». Но не все росси́йские бизнесме́ны веду́т себя́ так ужа́сно. Обы́чные предпринима́тели и сейча́с рабо́тают че́стно, ве́рят на́ слово, отдаю́т свой долги́.

[1] проце́нт (pl. проце́нты): percentage
[2] a trait, a feature
[3] business
[4] a notary
[5] a boss
[6] больни́чный лист: a sick leave

Б.М. Кустодиев. Купец

Questions:

1. Купе́ц — кто э́то?
2. Как сейча́с называ́ется э́та профе́ссия?
3. Что зна́ли о ру́сских купца́х европе́йцы (= жи́тели Евро́пы) в Сре́дние века́?
4. Почему́ они́ э́то зна́ли?
5. Что до́лжен был де́лать ру́сский купе́ц, е́сли он не мог отда́ть долги́?
6. Почему́ все ве́рили ру́сским купца́м?
7. Кака́я типи́чная черта́ ру́сского наро́да?
8. Где ра́ньше догова́ривались ру́сские купцы́?
9. Друзья́ в Росси́и пойду́т к нота́риусу?
10. Что сде́лает челове́к, е́сли он бо́лен?
11. Кака́я репута́ция была́ у ру́сских купцо́в?
12. Как сейча́с рабо́тают росси́йские бизнесме́ны?
13. Как вы ду́маете, что лу́чше для би́знеса: ве́рить и́ли внима́тельно чита́ть догово́р?

DID YOU KNOW?

Initially, the word до́лжен meant "to have a monetary debt". But over time, the meaning of the word has been transformed — the word has acquired the meaning of a moral obligation to someone or oneself (John says: «Я до́лжен узна́ть для отца́ о докуме́нтах» — this is his moral duty, his son's duty to his father). The change in meaning of the word до́лжен is connected to the tradition of believing on the word when giving monetary obligations, the violation of which led to a loss of reputation. Now the word до́лжен has two meanings: it can mean either a monetary debt or a moral duty.

Compare:

Я до́лжен (что?) сда́ть экза́мен.

Я до́лжен де́ньги (кому́?) дру́гу.

Догово́р доро́же де́нег! (Russian proverb)

☺ — Дай мне, пожа́луйста, две ты́сячи рубле́й в долг.
— У меня́ есть то́лько одна́ ты́сяча рубле́й.
— Отли́чно! Дай мне ты́сячу рубле́й. А ещё одну́ ты́сячу ты бу́дешь мне до́лжен.

хозя́ин своего́ сло́ва = an honest man (a man of the word)

☺ Я хозя́ин своего́ сло́ва: хочу́ — даю сло́во, а хочу́ — беру́ сло́во наза́д.

While Andrey was on his business at the office, John went to the store.

В магази́не

суперма́ркет: a supermarket
магази́н оде́жды: a clothes shop
сало́н о́буви: a shoe shop
продукто́вый магази́н: a grocery store
проду́кты: food products

Упражне́ние 24. **Choose the right sentence.**

1. Джо́ну на́до купи́ть но́вый пиджа́к.
   Джо́ну на́до купи́ть но́вые шо́рты.
2. Оде́жду лу́чше покупа́ть в суперма́ркете.
   Оде́жду лу́чше покупа́ть в магази́не оде́жды.
3. Джон купи́л молоко́ и но́вый блокно́т в суперма́ркете.
   Джон купи́л молоко́ и но́вый блокно́т в продукто́вом магази́не.
4. Я постоя́нно покупа́ю ту́фли в одно́м сало́не о́буви.
   Я постоя́нно покупа́ю ту́фли в одно́м продукто́вом магази́не.
5. В магази́не мо́жно купи́ть проду́кты и оде́жду.
   В магази́не мо́жно взять в долг проду́кты и оде́жду.

Упражне́ние 25. **Complete the sentences with the words дорого́й, дешёвый, бога́тый, бе́дный. Pay attention to the agreement of adjectives and nouns.**

Цена́ — Price:

дорого́й (до́рого): expensive
дешёвый (дёшево): cheap
бога́тый (бога́то): rich
бе́дный (бе́дно): poor

Example: Маши́на «Ягуа́р» — э́то **дорога́я** маши́на.

1. Карти́на «Джоко́нда» — э́то ______________ карти́на.
2. Клад Наполео́на — э́то ________________ нахо́дка.
3. Купцы́ — э́то ________________ лю́ди.
4. Не рабо́тать и жить хорошо́ мо́гут _________________ лю́ди.
5. Обы́чно худо́жники — э́то ______________________ лю́ди.
6. Де́тская оде́жда — э́то ______________________ ве́щи.

Упражне́ние 26. **Choose the right adverb: до́рого, дёшево, бога́то, бе́дно.**

Example: Ка́ждый год е́здить в Ни́ццу — э́то **дёшево** для меня́.

1. Ка́ждый ме́сяц покупа́ть но́вую маши́ну — э́то ____________ для меня́.
2. Ка́ждый день обе́дать в лу́чшем рестора́не — э́то ____________ для меня́.
3. Лю́ди в А́фрике живу́т ______________________.
4. Име́ть до́ма слона́ — э́то ______________________.
5. Име́ть свой самолёт — э́то ____________ для учи́теля, но __________ для президе́нта.

Узнаём цену — Discover the price

Сто́ить (2.R.VOW): to cost

Ско́лько сто́ит?: How much does it cost? (singular object)

Ско́лько сто́ят?: How much do they cost? (plural objects)

Do not confuse! сто́ит и стои́т

Дире́ктор на совеща́нии: Перед на́ми стои́т вопро́с, ско́лько сто́ит нефть[1] в ми́ре.

[1] oil

Упражне́ние 27. **Put the stress. Make up your own examples.**

1. На по́лке **стоит** ва́за.
2. Ва́за **стоит** 500 рубле́й.
3. Э́та маши́на **стоит** до́рого.
4. Э́та маши́на **стоит** на у́лице весь день.
5. В рестора́не ка́ша **стоит** 200 рубле́й.
6. На плите́ **стоит** ка́ша.
7. Э́ти часы́ **стоят** 3000 рубле́й.
8. Э́ти часы́ **стоят** на столе́ в кабине́те.

____

____

____

Упражне́ние 28. **Choose the right sentence.**

1. Каки́е краси́вые матрёшки!
   a) Ско́лько она́ **сто́ит**?
   b) Ско́лько они́ **сто́ят**?
2. Како́е большо́е я́блоко!
   a) Ско́лько они́ **сто́ят**?
   b) Ско́лько оно́ **сто́ит**?
3. Э́то но́вые пиджаки́.
   a) Ско́лько **сто́ят** э́ти пиджаки́?
   b) Ско́лько **сто́ит** э́тот пиджа́к?
4. Мне нужны́ часы́.
   a) Ско́лько **сто́ят** э́ти часы́?
   b) Ско́лько **сто́ит** э́ти часы́?

Како́й разме́р? — What's the size?

In Russian stores you can find different scales of sizes: English, European, Russian. There are also Chinese sizes. It is better to try a thing on before you buy!

Model: Я хочу́ поме́рить (что? case № 4) пиджа́к, руба́шку и пла́тье. — I want to try on a jacket, a shirt, a dress.

Упражне́ние 29. **Э́ту, э́тот, э́то, э́ти? Fill in the gaps with the necessary form of demonstrative pronoun э́тот (э́та, э́то, э́ти) in case № 4.**

1. Я хочу́ поме́рить ____________ пиджа́к.
2. Я хочу́ поме́рить ____________ ту́фли.
3. Я хочу́ поме́рить ____________ ша́пку.
4. Я хочу́ поме́рить ____________ шу́бу.
5. Я хочу́ поме́рить ____________ перча́тки.

Комфóртно или некомфóртно? — Comfortable or uncomfortable?
Pay attention to the stress in the words малó, великó

Мне (тебé/вам) малó. — It's small to me (you).
Мне (тебé/вам) великó. — It's big (loose).
Мне (тебé/вам) комфóртно / некомфóртно. — It is comfortable for me (you).
Мне (тебé/вам) нýжен размéр бóльше. — I (you) need a bigger size.
Мне (тебé/вам) нýжен размéр мéньше. — I (you) need a smaller size.
Э́то мой размéр! — It's my size!
Мне (тебé/вам) идёт / идýт. — It suits me (you).
Мне (тебé/вам) не идёт. — It doesn't suit me (you).

ATTENTION!
Verbs of motion can have a figurative meaning.
Compare:
Мужчи́на идёт по ýлице. — A man is going along the street.
Э́тот плащ Вам идёт. — This raincoat suits you.

Here are some words which are usually accompanied by the verb идти́: врéмя, часы́, дождь, снег, автóбус, пóезд, корáбль, заня́тие, фильм.

Когдá отдыхáешь, врéмя идёт óчень бы́стро. — When you are on holiday the time passes very fast.

Мой часы́ идýт прáвильно[1]. А у тебя́ — бегýт[2]. — My watch shows the right time. And yours is fast.

Сегóдня в кинó идёт интерéсный фильм. Пойдём? — There is an interesting film at the cinema today. Why don't we go?

[1] correctly
[2] бежáть (SPECIAL): to run; бéгать (1.R.VOW): to run

Упражнéние 30. **Read the dialogue:**

— Здрáвствуйте, я хочý помéрить э́то плáтье.
— Здрáвствуйте! Какóй у Вас размéр?
— У меня́ сóрок шестóй (46-óй) размéр.
— У нас в магази́не одéжда из Фрáнции. Э́то бýдет размéр М.
— Хорошó.
— Вот, пожáлуйста, плáтье.
— Ó-о-о, я ужé сейчáс ви́жу, что онó мне великó.
— Нет-нéт, э́то Ваш размéр!
— Извини́те, мне нýжен размéр мéньше.
— Хорошó, вот размéр S.
— Э́то мой размéр! Мне óчень комфóртно. Скóлько стóит э́то плáтье?
— Двéсти ты́сяч рублéй (200 000 рублéй).
— Двéсти ты́сяч... Ах, я сейчáс понялá, что крáсный цвет мне не идёт.
— Вы бýдете покупáть?
— Нет, спаси́бо!

Упражнéние 31. **Act out dialogues: "Capricious girl in the fitting room" and "A man who doesn't like to go shopping, is buying a suit."**

11

Do not confuse! плати́ть — пла́кать

	плати́ть (2.IR Т-Ч): to pay	**пла́кать (1.IR К-Ч): to cry**
я	плачу́	пла́чу
ты	пла́тишь	пла́чешь
он, она́	пла́тит	пла́чет
мы	пла́тим	пла́чем
вы	пла́тите	пла́чете
они́	пла́тят	пла́чут
	Плати́(те)!	Пла́чь(те)!
	плати́л(-а, -о, -и)	пла́кал(-а, -о, и)

Упражне́ние 32. **Read the stories, then answer the questions.**

Я актёр. Я **игра́ю в** теа́тре и в кино́. Моя́ оде́жда — э́то то́же моя́ рабо́та. Мно́гие мои́ ве́щи сто́ят о́чень до́рого. Наприме́р, э́тот шарф. Он оди́н сто́ил как дорого́й костю́м. Но я зна́ю, что э́тот шарф мне о́чень идёт. На сце́не и на экра́не я до́лжен быть в са́мой лу́чшей оде́жде. Поэ́тому я покупа́ю краси́вые дороги́е ве́щи. Иногда́ я пла́чу, когда́ плачу́.

1. Дороги́е и́ли дешёвые ве́щи покупа́ет э́тот челове́к? Почему́?
2. Почему́ актёр пла́чет, когда́ пла́тит?

Упражне́ние 33. **Fill in the gaps in John's story about going shopping with the words сто́ить, покупа́ть — купи́ть, дорого́й in necessary form.**

Я бизнесме́н. На рабо́те я ношу́ делову́ю оде́жду. Я не смотрю́, ско́лько ____________ вещь. Е́сли мне комфо́ртно, то я ____________ её. Но, коне́чно, е́сли вещь о́чень ___________ , то я не бу́ду ______________ её. Сейча́с мне ну́жно __________ пиджа́к и га́лстук, потому́ что мне ну́жно встре́титься с росси́йскими колле́гами. Я пошёл в магази́н оде́жды для мужчи́н и ___________ не о́чень ___________ , но о́чень комфо́ртный пиджа́к. Га́лстук я то́же ___________ в э́том магази́не.

Глава́ 12

Нет ничего́ лу́чше Не́вского проспе́кта, по кра́йней ме́ре в Петербу́рге; для него́ он составля́ет всё.

Н.В. Го́голь

There is nothing better than Nevsky Prospekt, at least in St. Petersburg; it means everything for this city.

— N. Gogol

St. Petersburg met the travellers in an unfriendly way, with drizzle and icy wind. The great city of Peter I was covered with thick fog.

— Жи́тель[1] Сиби́ри — э́то не тот челове́к, кото́рому не хо́лодно, а тот челове́к, кото́рый но́сит тёплые ве́щи, — said Andrey pulling out his sweater from his miracle-backpack. John only wore a light jacket over his shirt.

— Ты из Сиби́ри? — asked John.

— Нет, но в Росси́и холо́дный кли́мат[2] не то́лько в Сиби́ри. Здесь, в Санкт-Петербу́рге, о́чень мно́го дожде́й, поэ́тому о́сенью и зимо́й дождли́во и хо́лодно. Здесь на́до носи́ть о́чень тёплые ве́щи.

— Норма́льный кли́мат, — John shrugged his shoulders.

— А, ну да, ты живёшь в Ло́ндоне.

— В Ло́ндоне така́я пого́да обы́чная.

— Вот, э́то Санкт-Петербу́рг, — said Andrey when they went out of the railway station. — Э́то гла́вная у́лица — Не́вский проспе́кт. Санкт-Петербу́рг стои́т на реке́ Неве́. Поэ́тому проспе́кт называ́ется Не́вский.

John was pleasantly surprised: the Moscow train brought them to the very center of the second Russian capital.

— Мно́го ви́дел Не́вский проспе́кт, — Andrey said. — Не́вскому проспе́кту 300 лет. Цари́ ушли́, пришли́ коммуни́сты. Пото́м ушли́ коммуни́сты, пришла́ но́вая Росси́я. Исто́рия ка́ждого до́ма здесь — э́то це́лый рома́н. Дворцы́, собо́ры, це́ркви, теа́тры. Здесь гуля́ли дворя́не в XIX ве́ке, здесь шла све́тская[3] и делова́я жизнь.

[1] жи́тель (он): a citizen
[2] a climate

[3] све́тский (-ая, -ое, -ие): social; fashionable (adjective derived from the word свет, see p. 283, ex. 1)

Be careful while talking about the weather

The conversation about the weather in England is ritualistic. This is an opportunity to establish contact, show your disposition to the interlocutor, demonstrate your erudition and education level. Russians often refer to this feature of English conversation with humor. M. Lyubimov, a former Soviet intelligence officer who worked in England, gives an example of such a conversation in Russian interpretation and immediately gives a just explanation for this communicative feature of the English:

— Чуде́сный денёк, пра́вда?
— Про́сто великоле́пный!
— Восхити́тельный, пра́вда?
— Так ми́ло, так тепло́…
— Ли́чно я предпочита́ю жару́.
— Она́ мне всегда́ по се́рдцу. А Вам?
— Коне́чно! Но вчера́ бы́ло па́смурно…
— Ужа́сный был день, пра́вда?
— Про́сто отврати́тельный!
— Ох, э́тот дождь… Я его́ ненави́жу…
— Мне он то́же неприя́тен…
— Предста́вьте тако́й день ле́том. Дождь у́тром. Пото́м на миг вы́глянет со́лнце. И сно́ва дождь!
— Е́сли я пра́вильно по́мню, така́я пого́да была́ ле́том в 1960 году́.
— О, да! Я по́мню!
— И́ли э́то бы́ло в 1950 году́?
— Ка́жется, тогда́ бы́ло плохо́е ле́то.

"It would seem that the whole conversation has a fantastic idiotic character, especially if it occurs between people who know each other well. Oh no, this purely English phenomenon is much more complicated than it seems to the superficial observer: it's not just politeness. <...> The great theme of the weather captures everyone: the plumber who has come to the house to fix the tap, the owner of the sausage shop, the taxi driver who drives you through the London traffic jams."

As for the Russians, they prefer a heart to heart conversation to talking about the weather — a long frank conversation about everything, including the most intimate. A talk about the weather, especially between people who know each other very well, will be perceived with humor or even with resentment. If you talk too much with Russian friends about the weather, they may think that you are hiding something, or you don't want to communicate or speak insincerely. There is even such an expression разгово́р о пого́де which is considered synonymous with an empty conversation, talking about nothing.

(See: Larina, T.V. Englishmen and Russians. Language. Culture. Communication. — M.: Languages of Slavic cultures, 2013. — 360 p.)

Упражне́ние 1. **Study the meaning of the word свет in the Russian language. What meaning of the word свет does the word све́тский have in the phrase све́тская жизнь?**

The word свет in the Russian language has 4 meanings:

1. energy which lights the word and makes it visible, for example, дневно́й свет — daylight;

2. a sourse of light — включи́ть свет — to turn on the light, вы́ключить свет — to turn off the light, кра́сный свет (светофо́ра) — red light (of the traffic lights);

3. свет — the world, the earth with its inhabitants. For example, путеше́ствие вокру́г све́та — travelling around the world;

4. свет — nobility, high society.

Упражне́ние 2. **How do you understand the phrases све́тская жизнь го́рода and делова́я жизнь го́рода? Where can social life and business life take place?**

Examples: клуб, о́фис, теа́тр, фи́рма, магази́н, заво́д, конфере́нция.

— Санкт-Петербу́рг — литерату́рная леге́нда и архитекту́рная симфо́ния[1], — John read in his guidebook.

— «Санкт-Петербу́рг — окно́ в Евро́пу», — так говори́л Пётр I, — Andrey went on.

Through the efforts of his father John was well educated in history and literature, but never showed much interest in these subjects. However, he once read about the Russian Tsar Peter I with pleasure. The carpenter king, who did not disdain to learn from simple Dutch shipbuilders. The king, who tamed nature: despite everything he built a city in the swamp and moved the capital of Russia from Moscow to there. There he built the strongest fleet of that time. An out of the ordinary personality — there are few such rulers in world history.

— А Ле́нин и револю́ция в 1917 году́ — э́то то́же здесь? — asked John.

— Не́вский проспе́кт был гла́вной у́лицей револю́ции.

— Кра́сный Санкт-Петербу́рг, — commented John.

— В 1941, 1942 и 1943 года́х Санкт-Петербу́рг был чёрным. 900 дней неме́цкие солда́ты[2] стоя́ли вокру́г[3] го́рода. Но не смогли́[4] взять его́.

— Чёрный Санкт-Петербу́рг — э́то ужа́сно. Но я зна́ю, что есть и бе́лый Санкт-Петербу́рг.

— Ты говори́шь о бе́лых ноча́х. Да, э́то о́чень краси́во. Э́то когда́ светово́й день о́чень дли́нный, а ночь — о́чень коро́ткая. Но сейча́с мы не уви́дим бе́лые но́чи. Сейча́с сентя́брь, а бе́лые но́чи здесь с 11 (оди́ннадцатого) ию́ня до 2 (второ́го) ию́ля.

[1] a symphony
[2] a soldier
[3] around
[4] мочь / смочь (SPECIAL): to be able, to manage

12

Упражне́ние 3. **What meaning of the word свет does the word светово́й have in the phrase светово́й день?**

INTERESTING INFORMATION!

Each Russian-speaking person uses 30–40 names of colours in speech. Of these, the basic ones are 12. Most European languages use 11 base colours.

	како́й?	**кака́я?**	**како́е?**	**каки́е?**
white	бе́л**ый**	бе́л**ая**	бе́л**ое**	бе́л**ые**
black	чёрн**ый**	чёрн**ая**	чёрн**ое**	чёрн**ые**
red	кра́сн**ый**	кра́сн**ая**	кра́сн**ое**	кра́сн**ые**
pink	ро́зов**ый**	ро́зов**ая**	ро́зов**ое**	ро́зов**ые**
grey	се́р**ый**	се́р**ая**	се́р**ое**	се́р**ые**
blue	си́н**ий**	си́н**яя**	си́н**ее**	си́н**ие**
green	зелён**ый**	зелён**ая**	зелён**ое**	зелён**ые**
yellow	жёлт**ый**	жёлт**ая**	жёлт**ое**	жёлт**ые**
orange	ора́нжев**ый**	ора́нжев**ая**	ора́нжев**ое**	ора́нжев**ые**
violet	фиоле́тов**ый**	фиоле́тов**ая**	фиоле́тов**ое**	фиоле́тов**ые**
brown	кори́чнев**ый**	кори́чнев**ая**	кори́чнев**ое**	кори́чнев**ые**
light blue	голуб**о́й**	голуб**а́я**	голуб**о́е**	голуб**ы́е**

You have already realized that the 12th color is blue. Blue in Ancient Russia was associated with the idea of the devil and death. For example, Ivan the Terrible feared people with blue eyes, believing that they possessed black magic power. However, the colour of the sky — light blue — was assessed positively: light blue were the colours on the icons depicting the cloak of the Virgin, church vaults were painted light blue. There was a need to call this "good blue". So the word голубо́й arose — from the word го́лубь[1], because the feathers of this bird in the bright sunlight have a gentle blue color.

[1] a pigeon

Упражне́ние 4. **Look at the dialogue between John and Andrey again. Write out expressions with the words denoting the colour.**

Think about the symbolism of the colour in Russian, which is manifested in the following expressions, and select the appropriate definition from the list:

1) кра́сное со́лнышко[1]
2) кра́сная де́вица[2]
3) чёрный день
4) чёрная душа́[3]
5) бе́лый день
6) се́рый день
7) се́рый челове́к
8) се́рое лицо́[4]
9) ро́зовые очки́[5]
10) зелёный ма́льчик

а) хоро́ший
б) больно́й
в) ску́чный
г) гру́стный
д) о́чень моло́дой
е) плохо́й
ё) краси́вый
ж) романти́чный

[1] diminutive from the word со́лнце
[2] красна́ де́вица: Phrase from folklore denoting де́вушка
[3] a soul
[4] a face
[5] очки́ (pl.): glasses

Walking along the rich in history Nevsky Prospekt and listening to Andrey, John suddenly thought — earlier this thought never occurred to him — that Russian blood also flowed in his veins.

— Моя́ ба́бушка А́нна о́чень люби́ла Санкт-Петербу́рг.

— Она́ приезжа́ла в Санкт-Петербу́рг как тури́ст? — Andrey asked politely.

— Нет, она́ здесь жила́ ка́ждое ле́то. Моя́ ба́бушка А́нна ру́сская.

Andrey stopped in surprise.

— Ну́ и ну́! Так ты ру́сский?!

— Немно́го ру́сский. 25 проце́нтов. Фами́лия моей ба́бушки Миро́нова. Она́ была́ дворя́нкой.

— Вот э́то сюрпри́з! Твоя́ ба́бушка ру́сская! Ещё и голуба́я кровь!

— Почему́ кровь голуба́я?

— Так называ́ют люде́й, у кото́рых есть дворя́нская кровь. Голуба́я — э́то благоро́дная[6]. Так говоря́т... Но ты сказа́л, что твой де́душка уе́хал из Росси́и в 1917 году́. Ему́ бы́ло 15 лет.

— Пра́вильно. Моей ба́бушке А́нне бы́ло 13 лет. Э́то романти́ческая исто́рия. В 1917 году́ мой де́душка Бенджами́н уе́хал из Росси́и с семьёй ба́бушки А́нны. Бенджами́н жил в семье́ Миро́новых, потому́ что его́ ма́ма (моя праба́бушка) рабо́тала там гуверна́нткой[7]. И он был для них как сын.

— Кака́я необы́чная исто́рия!

The conversation was interrupted because the travelers saw a magnificent view of one of the most beautiful bridges of St. Petersburg — the Anichkov Bridge. Sculptures of famous Klodt "Tamers of the horses" were even more beautiful than in the reference books on art: it seemed that powerful figures were somehow miraculously frozen, tamed by the time. On the right and left of the bridge John saw two beautiful palaces in the classical style. He went to the iron railings.

— Петербу́рг называ́ют Се́верной Вене́цией. Здесь бо́лее девяно́ста (90) рек и кана́лов[8], — recommended Andrey.

— Как здесь краси́во! — exclaimed John in admiration. — Ка́жется, я понима́ю Петра́ Пе́рвого. Мне нра́вится э́тот го́род!

The friends stopped in front of the building in the classical style, and it seemed like it was folded in half, and the second half went to Sadovaya street, perpendicular to Nevsky Prospekt. This turned out to be the right building.

— Мы пришли́. Вот библиоте́ка.

«Росси́йская национа́льная библиоте́ка», — John read the sign on the pediment. — Дава́й ещё немно́го погуля́ем по э́той прекра́сной у́лице! У нас есть вре́мя.

[6] noble
[7] a governess
[8] a canal

12

Andrey agreed:

— С удово́льствием[1]! Вот изве́стный во всём ми́ре Каза́нский собо́р. Архите́ктор Ворони́хин, — Andrey said, pointing to a huge cathedral with a colonnade that looked like the wings of a giant bird.

— Э́тот собо́р и собо́р Петра́ в Ри́ме — сопе́рники, — John smiled. — Каза́нский — э́то как го́род Каза́нь?

— Да. Э́то собо́р в честь[2] Каза́нской ико́ны Бо́жией Ма́тери. Э́то о́чень изве́стная и люби́мая в Росси́и ико́на. Мно́го вре́мени у нас была́ то́лько ко́пия, а сама́ ико́на находи́лась в Ри́ме. Она́ висе́ла на стене́ в кабине́те у па́пы ри́мского. Он говори́л, что ико́на помога́ет ему́ в дела́х. Но не́сколько лет наза́д па́па ри́мский подари́л ико́ну Росси́и. Тепе́рь она́ нахо́дится в Каза́ни. Во всей Росси́и о́чень мно́го хра́мов в честь Каза́нской ико́ны Бо́жией Ма́тери.

— О́чень краси́во, я люблю́ Каза́нский собо́р.

Andrey corrected his English friend:

— Так не говоря́т. Лу́чше сказа́ть: мне нра́вится[3] Каза́нский собо́р.

[1] с удово́льствием — with pleasure
[2] в честь (чего́? case № 2): in the honour of
[3] (2.IR Б, П, М, В + Л): to like / to be liked

Models-synonyms
нра́вится / люблю́

Constructions with words нра́вится and люблю́ are synonyms. The difference is in the intensity of expression. Я люблю́ is stronger. Мне нра́вится reflects more neutral attitude.

Passive model **нра́вится**	**Active model** **люблю́**
Кому́ (case № 3) нра́вится кто / что (case № 1)	Кто (case № 1) лю́бит кого́ / что (case № 4)
Мне **нра́вится** э́тот дом. Мне **нра́вится** э́та кни́га. Мне **нра́вится** э́то мо́ре.	Я **люблю́** э́тот дом. Я **люблю́** э́ту кни́гу. Я **люблю́** э́то мо́ре.
Нам **нра́вится** э́тот дом. Нам **нра́вится** э́та кни́га. Нам **нра́вится** э́то мо́ре.	Мы **лю́бим** э́тот дом. Мы **лю́бим** э́ту кни́гу. Мы **лю́бим** э́то мо́ре.
Мне **нра́вятся** э́ти кни́ги.	Я **люблю́** э́ти кни́ги.
Нам **нра́вился** э́тот дом. Нам **нра́вилась** э́та кни́га. Нам **нра́вилось** э́то мо́ре. Нам **нра́вились** э́ти города́.	Мы **люби́ли** э́тот дом. Мы **люби́ли** э́ту кни́гу. Мы **люби́ли** э́то мо́ре. Мы **люби́ли** э́ти города́.
Мне **бу́дет нра́виться** э́тот дом, э́та кни́га, э́то мо́ре. Мне **бу́дут нра́виться** э́ти города́.	Я **бу́ду люби́ть** э́тот дом, э́ту кни́гу, э́то мо́ре, э́ти города́.

Упражне́ние 5. **Fill in нра́вится or люблю́:**

1. Я о́чень ______________ э́тот ста́рый дом. Я жил в нём, когда́ был ма́ленький.
2. Все де́ти ______________ игру́шки.
3. Мне не ______________ , когда́ лю́ди говоря́т мне непра́вду.
4. Я ______________ свою́ семью́.
5. Им ______________ му́зыка Чайко́вского.
6. Андре́ю ______________ спорти́вные маши́ны.

Упражне́ние 6. **How do you understand the phrase:**

Я люблю́ тебя́, да́же[1] когда́ ты мне не нра́вишься.

[1] even

— Моя́ ба́бушка А́нна люби́ла Санкт-Петербу́рг, потому́ что она́ здесь жила́ ка́ждое ле́то. Она́ хорошо́ зна́ла э́тот го́род. А мне нра́вится Санкт-Петербу́рг, потому́ что я здесь пе́рвый раз, — John formulated the difference between люблю́ and нра́вится.

— То́чно! — Andrey agreed: — Мне нра́вятся все краси́вые де́вушки, но я люблю́ то́лько свою́ жену́.

They were still standing in front of the Kazan Cathedral.

— А Каза́нь — э́то изве́стный го́род? — John asked remembering that it was to the city where his Russian friend Masha went to have practice.

— Да, э́то тре́тья столи́ца Росси́и.

— Тре́тья столи́ца? Ско́лько же у Росси́и столи́ц?

— Одна́ официа́льная столи́ца, одна́ — культу́рная… и ещё одна́… спорти́вная.

REMEMBER!

	number + adjective + noun	adjective + number + noun
он	три но́в**ых** до́ма	но́в**ые** три до́ма
оно́	три больш**и́х** окна́	больш**и́е** три окна́
она́	три но́в**ые** кварти́ры	но́в**ые** три кварти́ры

— Три столи́цы, как три це́нтра: центр полити́ческий[2], центр культу́рный[3], центр спорти́вный[4]. Но ка́ждый большо́й го́род то́же хо́чет быть столи́цей, ведь Росси́я — о́чень больша́я. И вот Екатеринбу́рг называ́ют столи́цей Ура́ла. Новосиби́рск и Ирку́тск — столи́цами Сиби́ри, Владивосто́к — столи́цей Да́льнего Восто́ка.

[2] political
[3] cultural
[4] sport (adj.)

12

It sounded unusual, but there was no reason not to believe Andrey.

Suddenly Andrey stopped in front of a sign «Литерату́рное кафе́».

— Вот здесь! — The journalist said with conviction.

— Что здесь? — John couldn't understand looking at the sign of something between a café and a restaurant.

— Здесь люби́л пить ко́фе Пу́шкин.

The question of the relationship between Russians and Pushkin had long been of interest to John Young. He had been in Russia only a few days, but there was still no day that he did not hear the name of Pushkin. Yes, he was a great writer, but why were they talking about him in the restaurant, on the street, and at the theatre? One of the most popular excursions there was called «Пу́шкинский Санкт-Петербу́рг» — he saw that advertisement as soon as he got off the train at the railway station in St. Petersburg. It was unlikely that many foreigners would go on such an excursion, most likely it was in demand among the Russians themselves.

When Andrey understood what John was asking him about, he suddenly became seriously thoughtful, apparently this question had never occurred to him before.

— О Пу́шкине говоря́т: Пу́шкин — э́то на́ше всё. Я то́же не понима́л, почему́ Пу́шкин но́мер оди́н. В Росси́и мно́го хоро́ших писа́телей и поэ́тов. Но мне ка́жется, сейча́с я по́нял.

ПОЧЕМУ́ ПУ́ШКИН?

(from the book of Dmitry Bykov "Calendar. Disputes about the indisputable")

Не́сколько лет наза́д я ездил в село́[1] Миха́йловское. Э́то небольша́я дере́вня, там был дом и земля́ семьи́ Пу́шкина. Сейча́с там музе́й. Он о́чень необы́чный.

Алекса́ндр Серге́евич Пу́шкин люби́л жить в Санкт-Петербу́рге. Там бы́ли друзья́, све́тское о́бщество. Но Пу́шкин не́ был бога́тым челове́ком. Когда́ у него́ не́ было де́нег, он жил в Миха́йловском. Ещё он жил там, когда́ царь был в гне́ве на него́.

[1] a village
[2] literary a work
[3] a code
[4] a start
[5] a finish

Дом в Миха́йловском — э́то бе́дный дом для дворяни́на. Здесь Пу́шкин ча́сто был оди́н. Но в э́том бе́дном до́ме и в э́том ску́чном ме́сте поэ́т написа́л свои́ лу́чшие произведе́ния[2].

Там, в Миха́йловском, я по́нял, что Пу́шкин узна́л код[3] ру́сского челове́ка: плохо́й старт[4] не всегда́ зака́нчивается плохи́м фи́нишем[5]. Како́й бу́дет фи́ниш — реша́ет сам челове́к.

И ещё в стиха́х Пу́шкина есть отве́т на любо́й вопро́с.

Упражне́ние 7. **Find and underline antonyms in the text.**

Упражне́ние 8. **Make up a plan made of questions from Andrey's story about Pushkin. Retell the main ideas with the help of the plan.**

While Andrey was telling the story John was looking at Pushkin's portrait on the signboard: disobedient curls, sharp eyes. John pointed to the portrait:

— Ты говори́шь, в его́ стиха́х есть отве́т на любо́й вопро́с? Пу́шкин — э́то как ру́сская Би́блия? Тако́й же сло́жный?

— Нет, не Би́блия. Я ду́маю, Пу́шкин — как автома́т Кала́шникова.

— Как автома́т Кала́шникова? — John was surprised. The Kalashnikov did not need a translation, but it did not occur to him that the poet could be compared to a gun.

— Да. Автома́т Кала́шникова о́чень просто́й. Он бу́дет стреля́ть[6] в любы́х усло́виях[7]. Стихи́ Пу́шкина то́же о́чень просты́е — и то́же «стреля́ют» в любы́х усло́виях. Вот э́то, наприме́р, о нас с тобо́й:

Они́ сошли́сь. Волна́[8] и ка́мень,
Стихи́ и про́за, лёд и пла́мень[9]
Не столь[10] разли́чны меж[11] собо́й[12].

[6] (1.R.VOW): to shoot
[7] a condition
[8] a wave
[9] пла́мя (пла́мень) = ого́нь: fire
[10] = так
[11] = между
[12] "They came closer — water and rock, rhymes and prose, ice and fire are less different."

Упражне́ние 9. **Use the words you know to find antonyms to characterize different people.**

Example: интере́сный челове́к — ску́чный челове́к

Andrey went on:

— Да, э́то норма́льно. У англича́н есть Шекспи́р и Ба́йрон, у италья́нцев есть Да́нте, у францу́зов есть Ронса́р, Гюго́, у не́мцев есть Ри́льке и Гёте, у ру́сских — Пу́шкин.

John couldn't agree. It's hard to imagine that in England Byron or Keats would be so often mentioned. But he did not argue.

While they were discussing the phenomenon of Pushkin, Nevsky Prospekt ended and the eyes of the travellers were presented with an absolutely fabulous panorama. Andrey said:

— Спра́ва ты ви́дишь Зи́мний дворе́ц — здесь цари́ жи́ли зимо́й, когда́ хо́лодно. Поэ́тому дворе́ц называ́ется Зи́мний. Э́то Дворцо́вая пло́щадь, здесь коло́нна[1] в честь царя́ Алекса́ндра I (Пе́рвого[2]). Сейча́с в Зи́мнем дворце́ нахо́дится музе́й Эрмита́ж.

[1] a pillar
[2] The ordinal numbers are declined as adjectives

Bypassing the Admiralty they came to the banks of the Neva. On a granite pedestal, or rather on a huge granite rock that served as a pedestal, an unusual monument was erected.

«Петру́ Пе́рвому Екатери́на Втора́я», — John read the sign on the pedestal.

«ПА́МЯТНИК ПЕТРУ́ ВЕЛИ́КОМУ НЕ ДО́ЛЖЕН БЫТЬ ПОРТРЕ́ТОМ — ОН ДО́ЛЖЕН СТАТЬ СИ́МВОЛОМ»

Па́мятник Петру́ I (Пе́рвому) — э́то душа́ Санкт-Петербу́рга. Его́ сде́лал францу́зский ску́льптор[3] Этье́н Фальконе́.

В Росси́ю Фальконе́ пригласи́ла Екатери́на II (Втора́я). Но пе́рвый вариа́нт[4] па́мятника не понра́вился[5] Екатери́не. В пе́рвом вариа́нте па́мятника Пётр I стоя́л на коло́нне. Э́то был царь-оте́ц. Жи́тели должны́ бы́ли уважи́тельно[6] поднима́ть[7] шля́пу, когда́ шли ми́мо па́мятника.

«Па́мятник Петру́ Вели́кому не до́лжен быть портре́том — он до́лжен стать си́мволом», — сказа́ла Екатери́на.

Фальконе́ не мог найти́ о́браз[8] и уже́ хоте́л е́хать домо́й, во Фра́нцию, но одна́жды но́чью он шёл по на́бережной[9] реки́ Невы́ и уви́дел огро́много коня́[10]. На коне́ сиде́л царь Пётр I. Царь кри́кнул[11]: «Всё моё — и всё Бо́га!» В э́ту секу́нду Фальконе́ уви́дел коня́ уже на друго́м берегу́. «Всё моё и всё Бо́га!» — кри́кнул Пётр ещё раз и исче́з[12].

Во́лны на Неве́ бы́ли как на мо́ре. Дождь. Ве́тер. Хо́лодно. Пого́да была́ ужа́сная. И Фальконе́ по́нял: Пётр — э́то не про́сто царь. Э́то челове́к с желе́зным[13] хара́ктером. Он постро́ил го́род там, где никто́ не мог постро́ить. Он победи́л[14] на мо́ре и победи́л на земле́. Он постро́ил но́вую Росси́ю.

У́тром Фальконе́ уже́ знал, что па́мятник бу́дет нетрадицио́нным и необы́чным. Е́сли смотре́ть на па́мятник в плоху́ю пого́ду, когда́ идёт дождь и́ли снег, когда́ си́льный[15] ве́тер, то мо́жно уви́деть живо́го Петра́ I. Па́мятник в э́ти мину́ты как живо́й. Пётр на коне́ — челове́к, кото́рый победи́л саму́ приро́ду.

[3] a sculptor
[4] an option
[5] perfective of нра́виться
[6] with respect
[7] поднима́ть (1.R.VOW) / подня́ть (1.IR НЯ-ИМУ): to lift
[8] an image
[9] embankment (in Russian it is declined as an adjective)
[10] конь (он): a horse
[11] крича́ть (2.R.CONS.2) / кри́кнуть (1.IR НУ): to cry, to shout
[12] исчеза́ть (1.R.VOW) / исче́знуть (1.IR НУ; Past исче́з) : to disappear
[13] желе́зный: iron, here the meaning is figurative. Compare: желе́зная дверь and желе́зная рука́.
[14] побежда́ть (1.R.VOW) / победи́ть (2.IR Д-Ж): to win
[15] strong

Упражне́ние 10. **The following text is a summary of the text about Peter I. Put the sentences in the correct order.**

1. А́втор па́мятника Петру́ I — ску́льптор Э. Фальконе́.
2. Екатери́на II хоте́ла сде́лать э́тот па́мятник си́мволом.
3. Пётр I на коне́ как живо́й.
4. Пётр I постро́ил но́вую Росси́ю.
5. Ску́льптор до́лго иска́л о́браз для па́мятника.
6. Фальконе́ по́нял, каки́м царём и челове́ком был Пётр I.
7. Фальконе́ сде́лал нетрадицио́нный па́мятник.
8. Фальконе́ уви́дел пра́вильный о́браз, когда́ шёл но́чью по на́бережной Невы́.

Упражне́ние 11. **Try not to look at the text and complete the sentences:**

1. Па́мятник Петру́ I — э́то __________ Санкт-Петербу́рга.
2. Па́мятник Петру́ I не до́лжен быть портре́том, он ______________________________________ .
3. В пе́рвом вариа́нте па́мятника Пётр I стоя́л ______________________________________ .
4. Пе́рвый вариа́нт па́мятника ________________________ Екатери́не II.
5. У́тром Фальконе́ уже́ знал, что ______________________________________ .
6. Е́сли смотре́ть на па́мятник в плоху́ю пого́ду, когда́ идёт дождь и́ли снег, когда́ си́льный ве́тер, то мо́жно уви́деть ______________________________________ .
7. Пётр на коне́ — челове́к, кото́рый ______________________________________ .
8. И Фальконе́ по́нял: Пётр — э́то не про́сто царь, э́то челове́к с ______________________________ .
9. Он постро́ил го́род там, где ______________________________________ .
10. Он победи́л на ______________________________________ .

Упражне́ние 12. **Answer the questions using the word кото́рый.**

Example: Э́то па́мятник. **Па́мятник** поста́вила Екатери́на II.
Э́то па́мятник, **кото́рый** поста́вила Екатери́на II.

Како́й э́то па́мятник?
Э́то па́мятник __________________ .

1. Па́мятник сде́лал Этье́н Фальконе́.
2. Па́мятник до́лжен стать си́мволом.
3. Пе́рвый вариа́нт па́мятника не понра́вился Екатери́не II.
4. Фальконе́ до́лго не мог найти́ о́браз для па́мятника.
5. В пе́рвом вариа́нте па́мятника Пётр I стоя́л на коло́нне.
6. Па́мятник бу́дет нетрадицио́нным и необы́чным.
7. В плоху́ю пого́ду па́мятник как живо́й.

After walking along Nevsky Prospekt, John and Andrey returned to the library.

ОТДЕ́Л[1] РУ́КОПИСЕЙ

[1] a department

— Ру́копись = рука́ + писа́ть — something written by hand — answering the constant «Почему́?» and «Что э́то?» of his foreign friend, Andrey realized that the simplest way to explain the meaning of a word is to show what words it consists of or what it is formed from.

Упражне́ние 13. **Complete the sentences. Pay attention to the word structure.**

учи**тель** — э́то челове́к, кото́рый у́чит;

строи**тель** — челове́к, кото́рый ________________ ;

води**тель** — челове́к, кото́рый ______________ маши́ну;

жи**тель** — челове́к, кото́рый где́-то ______________ ;

бу́лоч**ник** — челове́к, кото́рый гото́вит (печёт) ______________ ;

тай**ни́к** — ме́сто, где нахо́дится ________________ ;

шут**ни́к** — челове́к, кото́рый говори́т ______________

— Запо́лните[1] анке́ту, — said the girl in the hall politely, handing the form to John.

— Э́то моя́ ру́копись? — asked John.

But the girl didn't understand and said nothing.

— Ру́копись — э́то ста́рый докуме́нт. И́ли кни́га, кото́рую писа́тель не опубликова́л[2], — explained Andrey.

Having understood that there was a foreigner in front of her the girl smiled and said:

— Е́сли Вы напи́шете мемуа́ры[3] «Как я е́здил в Росси́ю», то Ва́ши мемуа́ры бу́дут называ́ться «ру́копись». Е́сли Вы опублику́ете ру́копись, то ру́копись ста́нет кни́гой, а Вы ста́нете писа́телем. А сейча́с Вы посети́**тель** библиоте́ки.

— Посети́тель — э́то челове́к, кото́рый что́-то посеща́ет и́ли посети́л[4], — understood John.

— Пра́вильно. Ка́ждый посети́тель библиоте́ки до́лжен запо́лнить анке́ту. Э́то Ва́ша анке́та, — the girl smiled again.

[1] заполня́ть (1.R.VOW) / запо́лнить (2.R.CONS.1): to fill in
[2] публикова́ть / опубликова́ть (1.IR ОВА-У): to publish
[3] (pl): memoirs
[4] посеща́ть (1.R.VOW) / посети́ть (2.IR Т-Щ): to visit

АНКЕ́ТА ПОСЕТИ́ТЕЛЯ

И́мя, фами́лия, о́тчество ____________________

____

Страна́ ____________________

Гражда́нство ____________________

Ме́сто рабо́ты ____________________

До́лжность ____________________

А́дрес ____________________

Телефо́н ____________________

All those points no longer aroused questions. However, the following question disconcerted both John and Andrey. It was necessary to attach an official letter to the sending organization.

— Она́ говори́т, что мы не из университе́та, поэ́тому мы должны́ написа́ть заявле́ние, — Andrey simplified the administrator's explanation.

— Заявле́ние? Куда́? Кому́? — asked John who recently wrote a statement to the police.

— Дире́ктору библиоте́ки.

— Ско́лько вре́мени дире́ктор обы́чно чита́ет заявле́ние? — John asked.

— 5–7 дней.

— Почему́ так до́лго?

— Э́то на́ши пра́вила.

— Э́то бюрокра́тия[5], а не пра́вила! — Andrey was indignant, although he understood that it would hardly be easy to get a pass to such a specific department of the library as a department of manuscripts and rare books.

[5] bureaucracy

Model: чтóбы — to (in order to)

Option 1. Чтóбы что дéлать, нáдо что дéлать

Чтóбы посещáть библиотéку, нáдо знать прáвила библиотéки. — In order to visit the library you have to know its rules.

Чтóбы поéхать на пóезде, нáдо купи́ть билéт. — In order to travel by train you have to buy a ticket.

Option 2. Кто дéлает что, чтóбы что дéлать

Я внимáтельно читáю прáвила библиотéки, чтóбы знать их. — I read the library rules carefully to know them well.

Я покупáю билéт, чтóбы éхать на пóезде. — I'm buying the ticket to travel by train.

Option 3. Кто хóчет, чтóбы кто что дéлал

Роди́тели хотя́т, чтóбы дéти стáли хорóшими людьми́. — Parents want their children to become good people.

Attention, if the subject of the two clauses is identical, the following model is used:

Я хочу́, чтóбы я стал арти́стом. = Я хочу́ стать арти́стом.

Я хочу́, чтóбы я получи́л подáрок. = Я хочу́ получи́ть подáрок.

Упражнéние 14. **Make up sentences.**

Example: Чтóбы посещáть библиотéку, нáдо знать прáвила библиотéки.

1. Чтóбы води́ть маши́ну,
2. Чтóбы игрáть в кáрты с незнакóмыми людьми́,
3. Чтóбы быть в свéтском óбществе,
4. Чтóбы купи́ть óстров в океáне,

а) нáдо хорошó знать прáвила игры́ в кáрты.
б) нáдо имéть мнóго дéнег.
в) нáдо знать прáвила дорóжного движéния[1].
г) нáдо знать прáвила этикéта.

[1] rules of the road

Упражнéние 15. **Explain why Andrey and John did the following things:**

Example: читáть прáвила библиотéки — знать прáвила
Я читáю прáвила библиотéки, **чтóбы** знать их.

1. идти́ в библиотéку — узнáть о докумéнтах
2. запóлнить анкéту посети́теля — стать посети́телем библиотéки
3. пришли́ в библиотéку — посмотрéть каталóг[2]

[2] a catalogue

Deciding what to do next, the friends went out into the street. Andrey offered to call John's father and ask him to send the paper from his university. John didn't like that idea, but there seemed to be no other way to get into the library.

Упражне́ние 16. **Explain who wanted what using the option 3 with the word что́бы.**

Example: Кто хо́чет, что́бы кто что де́лал.
Учи́тель → А́нна — прочи́тать кни́гу.
Учи́тель **хо́чет**, **что́бы** А́нна **прочита́ла** кни́гу.

1. Андре́й → Джон — позвони́ть отцу́.
2. Андре́й → Джон — попроси́ть профе́ссорский аттеста́т для Джо́на и Андре́я.
3. Джон → оте́ц — помога́ть сде́лать профе́ссорский аттеста́т для Джо́на и Андре́я.
4. Алекса́ндр → Джон — найти́ информа́цию о докуме́нтах из бу́лочной Фили́ппова.
5. Алекса́ндр → Джон — посети́ть Росси́йскую национа́льную библиоте́ку.

While the companions were discussing the following steps, a girl passed by them, and John thought that he had already seen her before: blonde hair, tall and slim, in a business suit. Thanks to constant training with his mother John had an excellent memory on faces.

— Я ви́дел э́ту де́вушку, — he told Andrey. — Мы жда́ли самолёт в аэропорту́ Хи́троу в А́нглии. Я ду́мал, она́ лети́т в Ла́твию и́ли Эсто́нию, потому́ что у неё о́чень све́тлые во́лосы.

Andrey indifferently looked at the girl: there were lots of blonde girls in the world, similar to each other. The blonde went to the library, showing a university document at the entrance.

John dialed his father's number and less than an hour later they received a document. The girl at the entrance looked at the papers and smiled politely:

— Профе́ссор Янг и профе́ссор Григо́рьев, пожа́луйста, проходи́те!

The hall was enormous.

— Бу́лочная Фили́ппова — бу́ква Б. Э́то в нача́ле[1] за́ла. Фили́ппов — бу́ква Ф, э́то в конце́ за́ла, — explained the librarian. — Ещё посмотри́те в середи́не за́ла — бу́ква Т.

[1] нача́ло — середи́на — коне́ц: beginning — middle — end

Упражне́ние 17. **Turn to Chapter 10 where you learned about the verbs начина́ться, зака́нчиваться. Match them to the nouns нача́ло and коне́ц.**
Explain the following expressions: нача́льная шко́ла, нача́льный у́ровень, коне́чная остано́вка авто́буса.

— Почему́ Т? — asked John and Andrey in surprise.

— Потому́ что бу́лочная находи́лась на Тверско́й у́лице.

Andrey proposed a plan:

— Дава́й так: я иду́ в нача́ло за́ла. Ты идёшь в коне́ц за́ла. Пото́м идём вме́сте в середи́ну за́ла. Э́то бу́дет быстре́е.

Упражне́ние 18. **You read where John and Andrey went. Say where they are.**

Example: Андре́й идёт в нача́ло за́ла. — Сейча́с он нахо́дится в нача́ле за́ла.

Джон ____.
Пото́м они́ вме́сте ________________________________.

12

— Скажи́те, пожа́луйста, — John turned to the librarian, — здесь есть электро́нный катало́г[1]?

— Электро́нный катало́г есть. Но он непо́лный[2]. Там не все докуме́нты. Лу́чше посмотри́те сейча́с обы́чный катало́г.

Approaching the letter Ф John found that the box he needed was being used. Strangely, the letter Ф turned to be in the hands of the elegant blonde he had seen at the airport. There could be no doubt — it was the same girl. "What a strange coincidence," thought John, and walked away a little, so as not to interfere with the girl's work.

[1] an electronic catalogue
[2] по́лный: full, complete. Compare with the words of the same family: запо́лнить. Запо́лните анке́ту = сде́лайте анкету по́лной.
[3] a card
[4] a list

— Что Вы де́лаете?! — John recognised Andrey's voice behind his back, but the journalist addressed the girl and not him. The girl tore several cards from the catalogue, crumpled them, put them in her pocket and rushed down the stairs in the direction of the exit.

— Она́ взяла́ ка́рточки[3]?! — asked Andrey. — Джон, ты ви́дел э́то? Э́то библиоте́чный вор? Заче́м ей нужны́ ка́рточки из катало́га? Эй, де́вушка! Стой!

However, that time John did not look stunned. He went to the catalogue, left by the blonde on the table, flipped through the remaining cards.

— Мне на́до позвони́ть отцу́ — пойдём! — he said heading to the exit.

— А спи́сок[4] веще́й из бу́лочной Фили́ппова?

— Здесь уже́ нет э́того спи́ска, — John pointed to the empty space in the catalogue.

— Ничего́ не понима́ю! — said Andrey.

John's father explained a lot. It turned out that John was not the only person who knew the story. Alexander Young had a talented graduate student, Vanessa. It was her who John had seen at the airport and in the library. It turned out that she flew on the same plane with him. Red folder, a meeting with Roman Kharitonov, a lunch in a restaurant — all this was not accidental. While the next day Roman was showing John Moscow, Vanessa entered his room and stole all the records that were related to the search.

— Мой оте́ц — учёный. Он изуча́ет исто́рию. У него́ есть учени́ца. Её зову́т Ване́сса. Она́ то́же изуча́ет исто́рию. Она́ аспира́нтка и пи́шет диссерта́цию. Оте́ц рассказа́л ей исто́рию о де́душке Бенджами́не... Как бу́дто э́то то́лько на́ша семе́йная леге́нда.

The story was taking an unpleasant turn.

Упражне́ние 19. **Help John to put the events in the right order:**

1. Она́ то́же лете́ла в Росси́ю.
2. В аэропорту́ в Москве́ Джо́на встре́тил Рома́н Харито́нов.
3. Джон ви́дел де́вушку с бе́лыми волоса́ми в аэропорту́ в А́нглии.
4. Джон ду́мал, что она́ лети́т в Ла́твию и́ли Эсто́нию.
5. Джон пло́хо говори́л по-ру́сски.
6. Джон пришёл в гости́ницу и уви́дел, что там нет компью́тера и блокно́та с информа́цией.
7. Пото́м Рома́н повёл Джо́на в тракти́р и в теа́тр.
8. Рома́н повёз Джо́на в рестора́н. Здесь Джон познако́мился с Оле́гом и Све́той.
9. Рома́н узна́л назва́ние гости́ницы и но́мер, где жил Джон.
10. Рома́н, Све́та и Оле́г не говори́ли по-англи́йски.
11. У них не́ было перево́дчика.
12. Но э́то была́ Ване́сса, учени́ца Алекса́ндра Я́нга.
13. Рома́н, Оле́г, Све́та и типи́чный англича́нин с кра́сной па́пкой — э́то бы́ли друзья́ Ване́ссы.
14. Они́ встре́тили Джо́на в аэропорту́, чтобы узна́ть, где он бу́дет жить в Москве́, и укра́ли ноутбу́к и блокно́т.

Упражне́ние 20. **Listen to the story about St. Petersburg and complete the tasks:**

Track 33

A) Listen to the story for the first time. What city sights are mentioned?

1. ______________________________
2. ______________________________
3. ______________________________
4. ______________________________
5. ______________________________

B) Listen again. Fill in the gaps in the text:

САНКТ-ПЕТЕРБУ́РГ

Санкт-Петербу́рг — о́чень __________ го́род. Он не о́чень __________ — ему́ ______ лет, — но о́чень __________.

__________ __________ __________ хоте́л, что́бы э́тот го́род стал но́вой __________ но́вой __________.

Гла́вная __________ Санкт-Петербу́рга — э́то __________ __________. Здесь мно́го прекра́сных __________ и __________. У ка́ждого до́ма своя́ __________. Я ма́ло успе́л уви́деть, но мне о́чень понра́вился __________ __________ — резиде́нция __________ __________. Сейча́с там __________ __________.

Говоря́т, что __________ с Санкт-Петербу́ргом есть __________ __________. Они́ нахо́дятся в музе́йных ко́мплексах «Петерго́ф», «Ораниенба́ум», «Ца́рское Село́» __________. Там о́чень краси́вые __________, __________ и необы́чная __________. Но у меня́ не́ было вре́мени э́то __________, к сожале́нию.

Петербу́рг — э́то __________ __________, здесь бо́лее __________ __________ и __________.

Э́то центр __________ и __________. Здесь нахо́дится оди́н из старе́йший в Росси́и __________.

И да, ещё я по́нял: здесь своя́ атмосфе́ра. Сюда́ __________ тури́сты из ра́зных стран. И любо́му челове́ку здесь __________ и __________. Э́то действи́тельно о́чень __________ го́род. Но не ду́май, что я говорю́ о __________. Пого́да в Санкт-Петербу́рге то́чно как пого́да в __________!

C) Retell the text about St. Petersburg.

12

Упражне́ние 21. **Remember the basic syntactic models and insert the words that are appropriate in meaning: но, что, где, кото́рый, когда́, е́сли, что́бы, потому́ что, по́этому, куда́, отку́да.**

1. Санкт-Петербу́рг — э́то го́род, ________________ зна́ют во всём ми́ре.
2. Санкт-Петербу́рг не ста́рый, ________ о́чень интере́сный го́род.
3. Не́вский проспе́кт — э́то у́лица, ________________ мно́го прекра́сных зда́ний и дворцо́в.
4. Петербу́рг — э́то Се́верная Вене́ция, _______________ здесь бо́лее 90 (девяно́ста) рек и кана́лов.
5. Ря́дом с Санкт-Петербу́ргом есть ца́рские дворцы́, ______________ есть о́чень краси́вые сады́, фонта́ны, необы́чная архитекту́ра.
6. Пётр I хоте́л, ________ Санкт-Петербу́рг стал но́вой столи́цей но́вой Росси́и.
7. ___________ у меня́ бу́дет вре́мя, я посмотрю́ дворцы́ и сады́.
8. Нача́ло ию́ня — э́то сезо́н, ___________ вы мо́жете уви́деть бе́лые но́чи.
9. Ну́жно прие́хать в нача́ле ию́ня, ________________ уви́деть бе́лые но́чи.
10. Здесь нахо́дится старе́йший в Росси́и университе́т, ________________ Санкт-Петербу́рг — центр нау́ки и культу́ры.
11. Я по́нял, __________ здесь своя́ атмосфе́ра.
12. Санкт-Петербу́рг — э́то го́род, _______________ приезжа́ют тури́сты из ра́зных стран.
13. Санкт-Петербу́рг — э́то го́род, _______________ любо́му челове́ку интере́сно и комфо́ртно.

Глава́ 13

Ру́кописи не горя́т.

М.А. Булга́ков

Manuscripts do not burn.

— M. Bulgakov

Alexander Young called back in a few minutes: the young people did not even have time to get far from the library. Alexander was agitated and John realized that not all skeletons had fallen out of the closet of their family history.

— Grandfather Benjamin didn't pick up the whole package handed over to him by the Grand Duke George Romanov. But he did take something from the package with him, — said the father. — There was a document with some strange poems among the papers. Grandfather guessed that that was some kind of a code that the Grand Dukes used to communicate with each other. Benjamin Young took that paper, going to return to Russia someday and unravel the code, which, he was sure, would lead him to the treasure.

— Что он говори́т? — asked Andrey.

John switched on the speakerphone asking his father to speak Russian.

— Здра́вствуйте, Андре́й!

— Здра́вствуйте, Алекса́ндр!

— Андре́й, Вы говори́ли, что в тайнике́ в бу́лочной бы́ли моне́ты и докуме́нты.

— Да, моне́ты и докуме́нты — каки́е-то бума́ги и́ли ру́кописи. Но я не зна́ю, каки́е то́чно моне́ты и о чём э́ти ру́кописи.

Alexander Young went on:

— Я ду́маю, что са́мое гла́вное — э́то моне́ты. Моне́ты — э́то ключ[1]. Э́то пра́вильно по-ру́сски? Мы говори́м «код» и «ключ». A key for code — ключ для ко́да.

— Да-да́, мы то́же так говори́м — код и ключ, — said Andrey.

[1] a key, a clue

Упражне́ние 1. **The word ключ can also be used in figurative meaning:**

1. A tool used to lock something — ключ от чего́ (case № 2): ключ от до́ма, ключ от но́мера.

Ключ от кварти́ры, где де́ньги лежа́т — a saying that became popular due to the famous adventure novel of the early XX century "The Twelve Chairs" by I. Ilf and E. Petrov. The phrase is the answer to the request which the interlocutor considered too overstated.

— Дорого́й, купи́ мне шу́бу!

— А мо́жет быть, тебе́ ещё дать ключ от кварти́ры, где де́ньги лежа́т?!

2. A tool, an opportunity to solve a puzzle, understand something, master something — ключ для чего́ (case № 2): ключ для ши́фра, ключ для ко́да, ключ для зада́чи.

— Стихи́ — э́то код. А моне́ты — э́то ключ, — explained Alexander Young. — Я сам не реши́л э́ту зага́дку, но, мо́жет быть, вы с Андре́ем реши́те.

If Alexander Yang was right, it turned out that those cards with a list of things found in a hiding place in Filippov's bakery that Vanessa had stolen, could not give her a clue. The main document was in the hands of John's father. "It's good that he did not give this document to me in London," John thought.

The father sent a photograph of the old piece of paper on which strange poems were written by the hand of Grand Duke George Romanov:

На берегу́[1] пусты́нныхъ[2] волнъ[3]
Стоя́лъ онъ, думъ[4] вели́кихъ[5] полнъ[6].
И ду́малъ: «Всё мое — и Бо́га[7]!»
Но да́льше насъ ведетъ доро́га.
Тамъ ска́зочный стои́тъ дворе́цъ.
Но въ немъ не человѣкъ жиле́цъ[8].
Съ друзья́ми ча́сто здѣсь гуля́лъ,
Сейча́съ друзе́й я потеря́лъ.
Встань[9] въ кругъ[10], клади́ моне́ты въ рядъ[11].
Шага́й[12] навстрѣчу[13] лошадя́мъ.

— Ничего́ не понима́ю, — said John and turned to Andrey. — А ты понима́ешь?

Alexander attached to the photo a literal translation he had made on the poem:

On the shore of desert waves
He was standing full of great thoughts
And thought, "Everything is mine — and God's!"
But the road leads us further.
There is a fabulous palace.
But it is not a person who lives there.
With friends I often walked here,
Now I lost those friends.
Stand in a circle, put coins in a row.
Walk towards the horses.

[1] a shore, a coast
[2] The word пусты́ня (a desert). A poetic synonym of the noun пустота́ ('emptiness'). *Here* it means that there was nothing on the shore.
[3] a wave (n.)
[4] the process of thinking. An old poetic synonym of the word мысль ('thought'). Compare: Госуда́рственная ду́ма (the State Duma) — parliament, a governmental body where everyone is occupied by the process of thinking (ду́мают).
[5] great
[6] Shortened form of the adj. по́лный (= full): он по́лон, она́ полна́, оно́ полно́, они полны́. Usually it is followed by case № 2: по́лон чего́? Э́тот шкаф по́лон оде́жды (= запо́лнен оде́ждой).
[7] God
[8] an inhabitant
[9] встава́ть (1.IR ВА-Ø) / встать (1.IR Ø-НУ). Here: PF, imperative to stand.
[10] a circle
[11] a row
[12] шага́ть (1.R.VOW): to step. From шаг: a step
[13] towards (adv.)
[14] Attention: they say в музе́е «Эрмита́ж», but в Эрмита́же.

Andrey compared the two texts and made a conclusion:

— Э́то не про́сто слова́. Э́то си́мволы. Я сейча́с то́же не понима́ю. Бу́ду ду́мать. Твой оте́ц ду́мает пра́вильно. Стихи́ — э́то код, а моне́ты — ключ.

In order to decipher the code it is necessary to put together all the elements of the puzzle. It is necessary to understand what kind of coins and what documents were in the cache. Perhaps, then the mysterious poem would also acquire meaning.

— А где сейча́с моне́ты? — asked John.

— Моне́ты сейча́с в музе́е «Эрмита́ж». Там, в Эрмита́же[14], нахо́дится вся колле́кция моне́т кня́зя Гео́ргия Миха́йловича. Моне́ты, кото́рые нашли́ в тайнике́, то́же нахо́дятся в музе́е.

— На́до идти́ в Эрмита́ж и узна́ть, каки́е э́то бы́ли моне́ты, — said John realizing that the more they learned about coins, the faster they would be able to unravel the code.

Alexander Young was still there:

— Я уже́ позвони́л в музе́й «Эрмита́ж». Колле́кция сейча́с на вы́ставке в го́роде Каза́ни.

— Моне́ты в Каза́ни?!

— Да, они́ в Каза́ни.

— Но почему́?

— Там то́же есть музе́й «Эрмита́ж». Э́то филиа́л[1]. Колле́кция там.

John thought that the trip to Kazan also did not arouse his enthusiasm.

— Ты спра́шивал о Каза́ни, — Andrey tried to cheer him up. — Тепе́рь ты уви́дишь го́род Каза́нь свои́ми глаза́ми[2].

— Когда́ вы е́дете в Каза́нь? — asked Alexander as if it had already been planned.

— Сего́дня, — John sighed. — Уже́ идём на вокза́л.

— Е́сли вы полети́те на самолёте, то прилети́те в Каза́нь о́чень бы́стро. От Санкт-Петербу́рга до Каза́ни по́езд е́дет 22 часа́, а самолёт лети́т 2 ча́са 30 мину́т.

— О, я забы́л, что э́то Росси́я и здесь всё далеко́. Хорошо́, па́па, мы е́дем в аэропо́рт, — John agreed.

[1] a branch. Филиа́л (чего́? case № 2) фи́рмы, филиа́л музе́я, филиа́л компа́нии.

[2] ви́деть / уви́деть (чем? case № 5) свои́ми глаза́ми: A fixed expression meaning "to be a witness of something, to be sure of something".

Упражне́ние 2.

A) Define what case is being used in each sentence for the word Каза́нь. Pay attention that this noun is of feminine gender!

1. Паде́ж №_______ Колле́кция сейча́с на вы́ставке в го́роде **Каза́ни**.
2. Паде́ж №_______ Моне́ты **в Каза́ни**?
3. Паде́ж №_______ Ты спра́шивал **о Каза́ни**.
4. Паде́ж №_______ Тепе́рь ты сам уви́дишь **Каза́нь**.
5. Паде́ж №_______ Когда́ вы е́дете **в Каза́нь**?
6. Паде́ж №_______ Вы прилети́те **в Каза́нь** о́чень бы́стро.
7. Паде́ж №_______ От Санкт-Петербу́рга **до Каза́ни** по́езд е́дет 22 часа́.

B) Imagine that the coins are in another city. For example in the ancient city of Ряза́нь (feminine). Replace the word Каза́нь for the word Ряза́нь in these collocations.

C) Imagine that the coins are in England in Ливерпу́ль (masculine). Replace the name of the city for Ливерпу́ль.

D) Imagine that the coins are in Афи́ны (always plural). Replace the name for Афи́ны.

While waiting for landing, John texted a message to Masha, who was supposed to come to Kazan to practice.

— Приве́т, Ма́ша! Как твои́ дела́?

— Спаси́бо, Джон, хорошо́!

— Ты сейча́с в Каза́ни?

— Да, я в Каза́ни. А как твои́ дела́?

— А я е́ду в Каза́нь.

— Вот э́то сюрпри́з[3]! У тебя́ дела́ в Каза́ни?

— Да. А ты о́чень занята́? Я хочу́ встре́титься. Хочу́ пригласи́ть тебя́ в рестора́н. Я хочу́ извини́ться[4] за на́шу пе́рвую встре́чу.

— Ты уже́ извини́лся. Но мо́жно ещё раз!

— Хорошо́, я позвоню́.

[3] a surprise

[4] извиня́ться (1.R.VOW) / извини́ться (2.R.CONS.1) (за что? case № 4): to say sorry about something

13

— Пока́!

— Э́то твоя́ де́вушка и́ли про́сто подру́га? — asked Andrey.

> In Russian the words друг and подру́га stand for friendship rather than romantic relationships.
>
> When people are dating and have romantic relationships they are called па́рень[1] (мой па́рень / мой молодо́й челове́к) and де́вушка (моя́ де́вушка).
>
> When two people are married they are муж and жена́.

— Нет, э́то не моя́ де́вушка и не моя́ подру́га. Э́то мой учи́тель. Когда́ я был в А́нглии, она́ говори́ла со мно́й по-ру́сски. Ма́ша о́чень хоро́шая и у́мная де́вушка.

— Джон, а у тебя́ есть семья́? — asked Andrey.

— Коне́чно: у меня́ есть ма́ма, па́па, брат.

— Жены́, зна́чит, нет?

— Сейча́с нет. А у тебя́?

— У меня́ есть жена́ и сын.

— Твоя́ жена́ то́же журнали́стка?

— Нет, моя́ жена́ рабо́тает в шко́ле, она́ учи́тель исто́рии. Мы познако́мились, когда́ учи́лись в университе́те на истори́ческом факульте́те. Ей не нра́вится моя́ рабо́та в газе́те.

— Почему́?

— Моя́ жена́ говори́т, что моя́ газе́та — э́то са́мая жёлтая газе́та[2] в Москве́. Что э́та газе́та желте́е со́лнца, желте́е оде́жды япо́нского императо́ра. Э́то са́мая жёлтая газе́та в ми́ре[3].

— Е́сли говори́ть пра́вду, то я то́же ду́маю, что быть журнали́стом — э́то не для тебя́. Ты о́чень мно́го зна́ешь об исто́рии. Почему́ ты не рабо́таешь в университе́те? Почему́ ты не занима́ешься нау́кой?

— Э́то жизнь! — Andrey smiled.

[1] a guy, a boyfriend, a young man
[2] жёлтая газе́та: a tabloid
[3] world

Пря́мая речь — Direct speech	**Ко́свенная речь — Indirect speech**
Narrative sentence **что** The tense is the same as in direct speech. All attention should be drawn to personal pronouns.	
Он сказа́л: «**Я** чита́л э́ту кни́гу». He said, "I have read this book". **Он** сказа́л: «**Я** чита́ю э́ту кни́гу». **Он** сказа́л: «**А́нна** была́ тут». **Он** сказа́л **мне**: «**Ты** был тут».	**Он** сказа́л, ***что* он** чита́л э́ту кни́гу. He said he had read that book. **Он** сказа́л, ***что* он** чита́ет э́ту кни́гу. **Он** сказа́л, ***что* А́нна** была́ тут. **Он** сказа́л **мне**, ***что* я** был тут.
Special question (with a question word) The quotation does not change in indirect speech. All attention should be drawn to personal pronouns.	
Он спроси́л **меня́**: «***Что* ты** чита́л?» He asked me, "What have you been reading?" Он спроси́л **меня́**: «***Что* А́нна** чита́ла?» Он спроси́л: «***Когда́* А́нна** была́ тут?» Он спроси́л **нас**: «***Где* вы** бы́ли вчера́?»	Он спроси́л **меня́**, ***что* я** чита́л. He asked me what I had been reading. Он спроси́л **меня́**, ***что* А́нна** чита́ла. Он спроси́л, ***когда́* А́нна** была́ тут. Он спроси́л **нас**, ***где* мы** бы́ли вчера́.

<table>
<tr><th colspan="2">General question (with a question word)
Particle ли
Find what information is required — this part is placed after the comma, then comes particle ли.
The rest of the words are placed in the same order as in the quotation.</th></tr>
<tr><td>Он спроси́л: «Э́то А́нна?»
He asked, “Is it Anna?”
Он спроси́л меня́: «Э́то ты?»
Он спроси́л: «Кни́гу чита́ла А́нна?»
Он спроси́л: «А́нна кни́гу чита́ла?»
Он спроси́л: «А́нна чита́ла кни́гу?»</td><td>Он спроси́л, А́нна ли э́то.
He asked if it was Anna.
Он спроси́л меня́, я ли э́то.
Он спроси́л, А́нна ли чита́ла кни́гу.
Он спроси́л, чита́ла ли А́нна кни́гу.
Он спроси́л, кни́гу ли чита́ла А́нна.</td></tr>
<tr><th colspan="2">Sentences with requests and orders
The word denoting the addressee of the request or order is placed in case № 3.
Option 1. The main verb is in the form of Infinitive.
Option 2. Construction Чтобы кто что делал / сделал
(after чтобы the verb must be in the past).</th></tr>
<tr><td>Он сказа́л мне: «Чита́й кни́гу».
He told me, “Read the book.”

Он попроси́л их: «Купи́те мне, пожа́луйста, кни́гу».</td><td>1. Он сказа́л мне чита́ть кни́гу.
2. Он сказа́л, что́бы я чита́л кни́гу.
He told me to read the book.
1. Он попроси́л их купи́ть ему́ кни́гу.
2. Он попроси́л их, что́бы они́ купи́ли ему́ кни́гу.</td></tr>
</table>

Упражне́ние 3. **Transform John and Andrey’s dialogue into indirect speech.**

It was after midnight when Andrey and John landed at the airport in Kazan.

— Нам нужна́ гости́ница ря́дом с Кремлём, — said Andrey to the taxi driver.

— Есть мно́го гости́ниц ря́дом с Кремлём. Вам нужна́ дорога́я, не о́чень дорога́я и́ли дешёвая гости́ница? — asked the driver.

— Нам нужна́ не о́чень дорога́я гости́ница, — answered John and added: — Не о́чень дорога́я, но хоро́шая.

No wonder Kazan is called “the third capital of Russia”. As they were driving from the airport into the center, John was surprised looking at the city which combined two cultures, two traditions, two religions: Russian and Tatar, Christianity and Islam. Going past the Kremlin, he saw a white stone, bright lighted walls, green-eyed minarets of the central Kul Sharif mosque, blue and golden domes of the ancient Kremlin cathedral.

— Ско́лько лет э́тому го́роду? — John asked the driver.

— 1000 лет, — he answered.

Упражне́ние 4. **Compare the age of the cities:**

Каза́ни 1000 лет.
Москве́ 900 лет.
Санкт-Петербу́ргу 300 лет.

Example: Москва́ ста́рше Санкт-Петербу́рга, но моло́же Каза́ни.

Каза́нь ____

Санкт-Петербу́рг ____________________________________

INTERESTING INFORMATION!
ИНТЕРЕСНАЯ ИНФОРМАЦИЯ!

Moscow was not the first capital of Russian lands.
Initially, the Slavs settled much more south, along the Dnieper and Don rivers. The first capital of Russia wass the city of Kiev (now the capital of Ukraine). This was reflected in the language, the expression from the Russian chronicles is still known: «Ки́ев — мать городо́в ру́сских» ("Kiev is the mother of Russian cities" — although the word "Kiev" is masculine). The saying «Язы́к до Ки́ева доведёт» ("The tongue will bring you to Kiev" means that the knowledge of the language and the ability to use it will help to get to the capital, and in general, anywhere). The history of the city of Kiev is very ancient — it was founded in the 6th century AD. Its Slavic history dates back to 882.
Later the capital of the Russian principalities became the city of Vladimir (in honour of Prince Vladimir Monomakh). Now Vladimir is one of the main cities of the tour "Golden Ring"). Only in the 14th century Moscow became the capital of Russia.

Упражне́ние 5. **Say which of the cities is the oldest and which is the youngest.**

Влади́мир, Каза́нь, Ки́ев, Москва́, Санкт-Петербу́рг

Са́мый ста́рый го́род — э́то ____________________
Са́мый молодо́й го́род — э́то ____________________

In the morning after leaving the hotel John and Andrey saw the Kremlin again. In contrast to the Moscow Kremlin the walls and towers of the Kazan Kremlin were made from white stone. The Kremlin was located on a hill covered with green grass and seemed to hover between the sky and the blue surface of the river.

— Хоро́шее ме́сто для худо́жников, — John said automatically, he thought that his mother would certainly want to paint this place.

— Э́тот кремль ра́ньше был деревя́нный. Каза́нь была́ столи́цей Каза́нского ха́нства[1], — explained Andrey. — В 1552 году́ царь Ива́н Гро́зный взял[2] Каза́нь и постро́ил ка́менный[3] кремль из бе́лого ка́мня. Кре́мль — э́то така́я кре́пость.

Turbulent history left a mark on the modern look of the city. John paid attention to the unusual composition inside the Kazan Kremlin.

— В кремле́ нахо́дится мече́ть[4], и ря́дом с мече́тью нахо́дится це́рковь.

[1] khanate
[2] The verb брать / взять (1.R.CONS! БР-БЕР) can have a meaning 'to conquer'. A special word завоева́ть can also be used in the same meaning, it comes from the word война́ (a war).
[3] made of stone
[4] мече́ть (она́): a mosque

Andrey explained:

— Здесь две гла́вные рели́гии — мусульма́нство[1] и христиа́нство[2]. Э́ти две рели́гии живу́т здесь дру́жно[3]. Каза́нь изве́стна[4] как го́род ра́зных рели́гий.

Кул Шари́ф — э́то одна́ из са́мых изве́стных в Росси́и мече́тей. А ико́на Каза́нской Бо́жией Ма́тери — э́то одна́ из са́мых изве́стных в Росси́и ико́н.

В Каза́ни большо́й университе́т. Э́то оди́н из са́мых ста́рых университе́тов в Росси́и. Он откры́лся в 1804 году́. Здесь учили́сь и рабо́тали изве́стные учёные, писа́тели, поли́тики: фи́зик Е. Заво́йский, хи́мики А. Бу́тлеров, К. Кла́ус, Н. Зи́нин, писа́тели Л. Толсто́й, Е. Шварц, поли́тик В. Ле́нин и други́е. Ре́ктором[6] Каза́нского университе́та был знамени́тый матема́тик Н. Лобаче́вский. Сейча́с здесь у́чатся студе́нты из ра́зных часте́й Росси́и и из ра́зных стран ми́ра.

[1] islam
[2] christianity
[3] in peace
[4] изве́стен (изве́стна, изве́стно, изве́стны): famous for; shortened form of the adjective изве́стный. As a rule it has a function of predicate. It can be seen in such phrase as Каза́нь изве́стна (где? case № 6) в ми́ре — Kazan is famous in the world; Каза́нь изве́стна как (что? Case № 1) тре́тья столи́ца — Kazan is famous as the third capital; Каза́нь изве́стна (чем? case № 5) спо́ртом — Kazan is famous for sport.
[5] постро́ен (-а, -о, -ы): is built (shortened form of the verbal adjective)
[6] a rector

Упражне́ние 6. **Highlight the information in the text which says that Каза́нь — э́то го́род ра́зных рели́гий.**

Near the entrance to the Kremlin John saw a sign with an attractive inscription: ЭКСКУ́РСИИ: все та́йны, кото́рые зна́ют э́ти сте́ны! But they had too little time for such an excursion.

The collection of coins of Grand Duke George Mikhailovich was found at once. There were practically all the coins that were ever produced in Russia. There were also many foreign coins. Andrey was especially surprised to find himself in front of the stand with coins of ancient kingdoms.

— Э́то моне́та царя́ Нимро́да? — with unconcealed astonishment he turned to the museum worker who was watching the hall.

— Да.

— Кто э́то — Нимро́д? — asked John.

— Царь Нимро́д — э́то легенда́рный[7] царь. О нём пи́шут и Би́блия[8], и Кора́н[9]. Э́то царь, кото́рый постро́ил Вавило́нскую ба́шню[10].

John thought that the Tower of Babel was a myth, a biblical allegory. And the king who built it was also part of the legend. He tried to express his perplexity to Andrey:

— Но Вавило́нская ба́шня — э́то леге́нда! И царя́ Нимро́да в исто́рии не́ было.

— Не́ было, — Andrey nodded. He was studying another coin at the moment:

— А э́то что?

— Моне́та го́рода Тарте́сс, — answered the museum worker. — Э́то то́же легенда́рный го́род на ю́ге Испа́нии. Оди́н из городо́в Атланти́ды.

[7] легенда́рный (adjective froms the word леге́нда): legendary
[8] Bible
[9] Coran
[10] The Tower of Babel

13

— Атланти́да[1]? — asked John, he couldn't believe his ears.

— Атланти́да то́же леге́нда, — Andrey nodded again and added: — Я ду́маю, что я то́лько что узна́л об э́тих моне́тах что́-то ва́жное.

The woman smiled and brought Andrey and John to the electronic guide-book stand.

КОЛЛЕКЦИОНЕ́Р[2] И ЕГО́ КОЛЛЕ́КЦИЯ

Колле́кция моне́т вели́кого кня́зя Гео́ргия Миха́йловича Рома́нова — одна́ из са́мых больши́х колле́кций в ми́ре. К сожале́нию, о́чень мно́го моне́т по́сле револю́ции исче́зло: каки́е-то моне́ты потеря́ли, каки́е-то моне́ты про́дали, каки́е-то моне́ты увезли́ из Росси́и.

Вели́кий князь Гео́ргий Миха́йлович не́ был обы́чным коллекционе́ром. Про́сто коллекциони́ровать моне́ты бы́ло для него́ ску́чно. Он был настоя́щим[3] худо́жником. Он создава́л[4] свою́ исто́рию. Он создава́л леге́нды. В его́ исто́рии легенда́рные цари́ начина́ли но́вую жизнь, они́ станови́лись живы́ми.

[1] Atlantide
[2] a collector
[3] real, genuine
[4] создава́ть (1.IR ВА-Ø) / созда́ть (SPECIAL): to create

Е́сли есть моне́та, то бы́ло и госуда́рство. Е́сли бы́ло госуда́рство, то был и царь.

***Упражне́ние 7.* Find the words with the same root in the text above, decide on the model they are built on.**

— Э́то не настоя́щие моне́ты? — asked Andrey at last.

***Упражне́ние 8.* Let's look at the word настоя́щий. How do you understand the phrases: настоя́щий друг, настоя́щий мужчи́на, настоя́щая ле́ди, настоя́щее зо́лото?**

— В колле́кции вели́кого кня́зя есть то́лько две ненастоя́щие моне́ты. Но их це́нность о́чень большá́я. Их це́нность бо́льше, чем це́нность настоя́щих моне́т.

— А где моне́ты из тайника́ бу́лочной Фили́ппова? — asked John realizing how excited he was.

The woman led them to one of the stands.

— Они́ здесь.

— Они́ настоя́щие?

— Да, настоя́щие.

On the stand there were three coins of the time of Nicholas II — contemporaries of the Grand Dukes. Their value was small. These were:

1 ру́бль
2 копе́йки
5 копе́ек

John and Andrey spent a long time examining three coins through the glass — there were no characteristic damages, no special marks, no drilled holes in the coins. Nothing that could point to a secret cipher.

Andrey remembered the text of the poem:

— «Клади́ моне́ты в ряд». Ряд — э́то 125.

— И́ли 521.

They decided that they could figure out the sequence only by unraveling the code. But at least they knew about one component of the cipher. And most importantly — what John Young himself could not believe up to this point in time — the story of grandfather Benjamin really began, as they say, to grow flesh and blood.

At the exit they were handed the newspaper «Каза́нский кремль» on the first page of which John saw very familiar face. The article was called «Алекса́ндр Дюма́ в Каза́ни».

[1] оставля́ть (1.R.VOW) / оста́вить (2.IR Б, П, М, В + Л): to leave
[2] civilisation
[3] urgently

Looking at that reaction the talkative woman started to explain:

— Алекса́ндр Дюма́ прие́хал в Росси́ю, что́бы писа́ть рома́н о Росси́и. В Санкт-Петербу́рге Дюма́ оста́вил[1] свой европе́йский костю́м, потому́ что ду́мал, что в Санкт-Петербу́рге цивилиза́ция[2] зако́нчилась и ему́ не на́до бу́дет носи́ть костю́м. Когда́ Дюма́ прие́хал в Каза́нь, он уви́дел здесь краси́вый го́род, большо́й университе́т и све́тское о́бщество. Дюма́ по́нял, что ему́ на́до сро́чно[3] купи́ть но́вый костю́м. Така́я весёлая исто́рия!

The guide recommended a route outside the Kremlin:

— Посмотри́те университе́т! Посмотри́те собо́р Петра́ и Па́вла в сти́ле баро́кко. Погуля́йте по у́лицам ста́рой Каза́ни! О́чень краси́вая у́лица Кремлёвская. Мы мо́жем помо́чь организова́ть экску́рсию.

All that seemed quite interesting, John even regretted that he had things to do in Moscow, and his father was waiting for information in London and he could not devote sufficient time to Kazan.

Упражне́ние 9. **Repeat the highlighted guide's words in reported speech:**

Экскурсово́д сказа́ла, что́бы мы ______________________________

____

REMEMBER!

Verbs with suffixes -ова-/-ева-
(1.IR ОВА-У / ЕВА-У)

фотографи́ровать: to take pictures	плани́ровать: to plan
танцева́ть: to dance	путеше́ствовать: to travel
рисова́ть: to draw, to paint	сове́товать: to advise
организова́ть: to arrange, to organize	ночева́ть: to stay for a night

We have discussed the conjugation of these verbs in Chapter № 5.
! Suffixes -ова-/-ева- are transformed into -у- (-ю-) when verbs are in the Present, but they stay the same in the Past and the complex Future.

Упражне́ние 10. **Change the verbs with suffixes -ова-/-ева- in the following dialogues:**

Example : коллекциони́р**ОВА**ть

— Я коллекциони́р**У**ю ста́рые кни́ги. А Вы что коллекциони́р**У**ете?

— Ра́ньше я коллекциони́р**ОВАЛ** матрёшки. А сейча́с я ниче́го не коллекциони́р**У**ю.

1. — Вы ____________ (плани́ровать) Ваш о́тдых?
   — Да, я всегда́ ____________ (плани́ровать) о́тдых.
   — А я никогда́ не ____________ (плани́ровать). Но в э́том году́ я реши́л (плани́ровать).

2. — Я ____________ (сове́товать) Вам посмотре́ть университе́т.
   — А что ещё вы ____________ (сове́товать) посмотре́ть в Каза́ни?
   — Вчера́ я ____________ (сове́товать) иностра́нцам посмотре́ть Кремлёвскую у́лицу. Она́ им о́чень понра́вилась.

13

3. Мы ____________________ (организова́ть) экску́рсию.

В про́шлом году́ мы ____________________ (организова́ть) о́чень мно́го экску́рсий для иностра́нцев.

4. Она́ ____________________ (рисова́ть) Каза́нский кремль.

За́втра она́ бу́дет ____________________ (рисова́ть) па́мятник Лобаче́вскому ря́дом с университе́том.

5. На э́той у́лице в Барсело́не лю́ди ____________________ (танцева́ть) ка́ждый ве́чер.

Когда́ мы бы́ли в Барсело́не, мы то́же ____________________ (танцева́ть) там.

6. — Я не ____________________ (сове́товать) смотре́ть э́тот фильм.

— Почему́? Мне вчера́ его́ ____________________ (сове́товать) мой друг. Ему́ фильм о́чень понра́вился.

7. — Вы лю́бите путеше́ствовать?

— Да, я люблю́ ____________________ (путеше́ствовать).

— Где Вы обы́чно ____________________ (путеше́ствовать)? А в э́том году́ Вы ____________________ (плани́ровать) путеше́ствовать?

8. — Где вы ____________________ (ночева́ть) вчера́?

— Мы ____________________ (ночева́ть) в гости́нице.

— А где вы ____________________ (ночева́ть) сего́дня?

— Сего́дня мы ____________________ (ночева́ть) до́ма.

REMEMBER!

расска́зЫВАть

Suffixes -ыва-/-ива- do not change in the Present!

Я расска́зЫВАю о своём о́тдыхе в Росси́и.

Я расска́зЫВАл о своём о́тдыхе в Росси́и.

Я бу́ду расска́зЫВАть о своём о́тдыхе в Росси́и.

REMEMBER!

Untransitional vowels И and Ы	Transitional vowels О and Е
Suffixes -ИК, -НИК, -НИЦ-	Suffixes[1] -ОК, -ЕЦ
фи́з**ик** — нет фи́з**ик**а	потол**о́к** — нет пото<u>лк</u>а́
	зван**о́к** — нет зво<u>нк</u>а́
матема́т**ик** — нет матема́т**ик**а	иностра́н**ец** — нет иностра́<u>нц</u>а
ча́й**ник** — нет ча́й**ник**а	америка́н**ец** — нет америка́<u>нц</u>а
уче**ни́ц**а — нет уче**ни́ц**ы	япо́н**ец** — нет япо́<u>нц</u>а
учи́тель**ниц**а — нет учи́тель**ниц**ы	от**е́ц**[2] — нет о<u>тц</u>а́

[1] Suffixes or those parts of the root that historically were suffixes.
[2] father

Declination of words with transitional vowels

case № 1	потол**о́**к	от**е́**ц
case № 2	потолка́	отца́
case № 3	потолку́	отцу́
case № 4	потоло́к	отца́
case № 5	потолко́м	отцо́м
case № 6	о потолке́	об отце́

Упражне́ние 11. **Decline the word иностра́нец in the following sentences in the case needed and answer the questions:**

Ху́лио Гарси́а Ло́пес — э́то **иностра́нец** в Росси́и.
Мы не ви́дели ни одного́ ________________ (иностра́нец) в Росси́и.
Что мо́жно сове́товать ________________ (иностра́нец) в Росси́и?
Вы встреча́ли ________________ (иностра́нец) в Росси́и?
Тру́дно быть ________________ (иностра́нец) в Росси́и?
Э́та кни́га об ________________ (иностра́нец) в Росси́и.

Of the sights John and Andrey chose the Tatar cuisine. John called Masha to find out which restaurant they should meet in and the girl chose a restaurant of national Tatar cuisine on Bauman Street, one of the central streets of the city. But the girl herself was late. John and Andrey ordered a cup of coffee and opened the code sent by John's father.

— Коне́чно, клад в Санкт-Петербу́рге, — said Andrey.

— Почему́?

— Как почему́? — he asked and read:

На берегу́ пусты́нных волн
Стоя́л он, дум вели́ких полн.

«Бе́рег пусты́нных волн» — э́то Фи́нский зали́в[1].

«Ду́мы вели́кие» — э́то царь Пётр I ду́мает, где стро́ить Санкт-Петербу́рг.

— Почему́? Почему́ како́й-то бе́рег — э́то то́чно Фи́нский зали́в? Почему́ он — э́то Пётр I? Почему́ «ду́мы вели́кие» — э́то Санкт-Петербу́рг? Почему́? — John asked in surprise, because neither St. Petersburg nor Peter I were mentioned in the text.

Andrey explained:

— О, да, извини́. Э́то стихи́ Пу́шкина о Петре́ I (Пе́рвом). Их ка́ждый шко́льник зна́ет. Э́то то́чно Санкт-Петербу́рг.

— «И ду́мал: "Всё моё — и Бо́га!"» — John read the next line and realized that Andrey was not mistaken about the Tsar Peter I and St. Petersburg. Not long ago he read the story about the construction of the monument to Peter the Great by the sculptor Etienne Falconet.

[1] The Gulf of Finland

Упражне́ние 12. **Reread the poem, remember why the author used the words «Всё моё — и Бо́га!» and what they mean.**

«Но да́льше нас ведёт доро́га». Andrey and John had to think about it.

— Куда́ да́льше? — Andrey asked rhetorically. — Санкт-Петербу́рг — э́то коне́чный[1] пункт[2]. Да́льше — мо́ре.

John opened the map of St. Petersburg and suddenly asked:

— Ты говори́шь: Санкт-Петербу́рг — коне́чный пункт?

— Да.

— Нет. Кре́пость[3] Кроншта́дт — вот коне́чный пункт!

— Что ты хо́чешь сказа́ть, Джон?

— Я хочу́ сказа́ть, что ме́жду Санкт-Петербу́ргом и Кроншта́дтом есть доро́га.

[1] final
[2] a point
[3] кре́пость (она): a fortress
[4] strange

Andrey looked at the map, too:

— Э́то знамени́тая Петерго́фская доро́га. И на э́той доро́ге нахо́дятся не́сколько ца́рских дворцо́в.

— Стре́льна, Петерго́ф, Ораниенба́ум, — said John.

«Там ска́зочный стои́т дворе́ц».

The task seemed to have a solution. But which of the palaces? The largest and best known of them was, of course, Peterhof.

— Андре́й, как э́то: «Но в нём не челове́к жиле́ц»? — John asked about the next phrase.

— Жиле́ц, жи́тель — э́то челове́к, кото́рый живёт где́-то. Жиле́ц до́ма — жи́тель до́ма.

«Там ска́зочный стои́т дворе́ц, / Но в нём не челове́к жиле́ц» — в э́том дворце́ живёт не челове́к.

It was serious. Who could live in the palace, in the fairy-tale one? In addition, the horses were confusing: «Иди́ навстре́чу лошадя́м». Going to meet the horses? Starting from an invisible circle? All these interpretations were implausible.

— Я ду́маю, что ло́шади — э́то како́й-то па́мятник.

— Да, мо́жет быть. В Санкт-Петербу́рге о́чень мно́го лошаде́й. Мы ви́дели лошаде́й на мосту́, мы ви́дели Петра́ Пе́рвого на коне́.

At this time Masha came up to the table and they had to interrupt the conversation.

— Кака́я стра́нная[4] жизнь! — said Masha after John introduced her to Andrey. — Мы хоте́ли встре́титься в Москве́, а встре́тились в Каза́ни.

— Жизнь о́чень стра́нная, — John smiled. — Я уже́ был в Москве́, в Санкт-Петербу́рге. Тепе́рь сижу́ в рестора́не в Каза́ни с краси́вой де́вушкой из Москвы́. А е́сли ты узна́ешь, где и как мы познако́мились с Андре́ем, то ты поду́маешь, что э́то шу́тка.

Упражне́ние 13. **Put the words in brackets in the correct form:**

Я пришёл в ________________ (теа́тр). Я был в ______________ (теа́тр). Пото́м я ушёл из ________________ (теа́тр). Я шёл в свою́ ________________ (гости́ница). Я не знал а́дрес ______________ (гости́ница), поэ́тому я до́лго иска́л ______________ (гости́ница). Я уви́дел большо́й краси́вый __________ (дом) и мно́го ______________ (лю́ди). Э́то был ________ (дом) Пашко́ва. Я не хоте́л идти́ в __________ (дом) Пашко́ва, но я зашёл в ______________ (дом). В _____________ (дом) Пашко́ва я познако́мился с Андре́ем. Он сиде́л в ______________ (ко́мната) на ______________________________ (второ́й эта́ж) и ждал, когда́ зако́нчится бал. Андре́й — журнали́ст, он хоте́л фотографи́ровать. Из окна́ ____________ (дом) Пашко́ва мо́жно сде́лать хоро́шее фо́то. Андре́й ча́сто так де́лает. Э́то его́ рабо́та. Мы ночева́ли в _____________ (дом) Пашко́ва. У́тром мы ушли́ из _____________ (дом) Пашко́ва.

In Russian there is a rule of euphony. If the word is repeated in the following sentences, it must be replaced by a synonym or personal pronoun.

Example:

Э́то мой друг **Андре́й**. Я зна́ю **Андре́я** недо́лго. Я познако́мился **с Андре́ем** в Москве́.

Э́то мой друг **Андре́й**. Я зна́ю **его́** недо́лго. Я познако́мился **с ним** в Москве́.

Упражне́ние 14. **Replace the words in brackets in the story above with the pronouns он, она́, оно́, where it is necessary to make it sound better. Do not forget to put these pronouns in the right form!**

Example: Я пришёл в теа́тр. Я был в нём. Пото́м…

Learning that Andrey and John were in the Kremlin, Masha expressed regret that her practice had just ended that day. She had to go back home to Moscow and would not be able to join them in walks around the city. So she just gave them some advice:

— Я сове́тую вам посмотре́ть Каза́нский университе́т. Э́то о́чень краси́вое зда́ние в класси́ческом сти́ле. Ещё Каза́нь — э́то спорт. Здесь мно́го но́вых совреме́нных спорти́вных за́лов и стадио́нов. Я была́ на пра́ктике, на ипподро́ме[1]. Здесь о́чень хоро́ший совреме́нный ипподро́м.

— Пра́ктика на ипподро́ме? — John got very surprised. — Я ду́мал, что ты изуча́ешь биоло́гию в университе́те.

— Да, в э́том году́ я писа́ла рабо́ту о лошадя́х. Поэ́тому моя́ пра́ктика в больни́це для лошаде́й. Э́то на ипподро́ме.

— Тебе́ нра́вятся ло́шади?

— Да, о́чень нра́вятся.

Listening to the conversation between Masha and John, Andrey suddenly exclaimed «Ло́шади!» so loudly that the whole restaurant turned to him.

— Что случи́лось? — Masha was frightened. Andrey raised his eyes and repeated with excitement «Ло́шади, коне́чно!» Just in case, Masha said to John in English:

— Is your friend so worried about the fact that the menu has dishes of horse meat? This is a national Tatar dish. It's very tasty, but we can go to another restaurant.

[1] a hippodrome

13

John also didn't understand and asked:

— Андре́й, почему́ ты крич́ишь? Ма́ша говори́т, что ло́шадь — э́то вку́сно. Э́то национа́льное тата́рское блю́до.

But Andrey only waved his hand and whispered:

— Я по́нял зага́дку! Во дворце́ жил не челове́к. Во дворце́ жи́ли ло́шади!

He repeated meaningfully:

— Ло́шади. Э́то не па́мятник. Э́то настоя́щие живы́е ло́шади!

Masha looked at the young people with horror. According to her expression John realized that he looked in her eyes ambiguously again: he came to Kazan, invited her to the restaurant, brought a crazy friend who shouted something about horses. John didn't understand what Andrey meant. Andrey didn't pay any attention to their stunned faces and continued:

— Вели́кий князь Гео́ргий Миха́йлович люби́л в жи́зни две ве́щи: моне́ты и лошаде́й. Он ка́ждый день занима́лся в мане́же. «Ска́зочный дворе́ц» — э́то мане́ж в Петерго́фе[1]. Его́ постро́ил архите́ктор Бенуа́, и э́то настоя́щий дворе́ц, как в ска́зке. Когда́ я уви́дел э́тот дворе́ц в пе́рвый раз, я не мог пове́рить, что тут живу́т не лю́ди, а ло́шади!

[1] Peterhof — the residence of Peter I which is located on the Peterhof road, on the shore of the Gulf of Finland. In addition to the palace and park ensemble, Peterhof is famous for its fountains and various holidays.

Ло́шади в стихотворе́нии — э́то не па́мятник. Э́то живы́е ло́шади!

John began to understand what Andrey was talking about. The phrase about friends suddenly began to make sense. John asked:

— Друзья́ вели́кого кня́зя Гео́ргия Миха́йловича — э́то ло́шади?

— То́чно, — answered Andrey and cited the poem, — «С друзья́ми ча́сто здесь гуля́л, / Тепе́рь друзе́й я потеря́л».

— Но почему́ князь потеря́л друзе́й?

— В 1917 году́ ца́рская семья́ Рома́новых потеря́ла всё: все свои́ драгоце́нности, страну́ и жизнь. Лошаде́й они́, коне́чно, то́же потеря́ли.

Finally Masha also began to understand something:

— Вы с друго́м разга́дываете зага́дку? — she asked.

— Да, э́то зага́дка. Ста́рая ру́сско-англи́йская зага́дка, — answered John. Andrey went on:

— «Встань в круг» — э́то поня́тно. Круг — э́то мане́ж. На́до встать в центр мане́жа. «Клади́ моне́ты в ряд» — э́то то́же поня́тно: 125.

— И́ли 521, — clarified John.

— Шага́й — э́то сино́ним глаго́ла «иди́»! — explained Andrey.

[2] mews

Петергоф. Фонтаны

Петергоф. Императорские конюшни[2]

— Шага́ть means to step, it comes from the word шаг — a step. Шага́й means make steps, — translated Masha.

[1] ходи́ть по кру́гу: to walk in circles, to circumnavigate
[2] a jockey

Andrey thought a little and said:

— Я не понима́ю «навстре́чу лошадя́м». Ло́шади хо́дят в мане́же по кру́гу[1]. Навстре́чу — э́то куда́?

— Я ду́маю, что навстре́чу — э́то туда́, где вы́ход. Так говоря́т жоке́и[2], — said Masha.

John and Andrey exchanged glances. It turned out that the Grand Duke George Mikhailovich left his treasure to those whom he most trusted — horses.

— Ско́лько на́до шага́ть? — John asked anxiously, although the answer was already clear to him.

— 125 шаго́в.

— Или 521 шаг.

The length of the walk could be identified only on the spot. Andrew looked at the information on the Internet. The building of the royal stables successfully survived the revolution and even World War II (unlike the royal palaces, which the Germans bombarded purposefully). A "fairy-tale palace" used to be a sanatorium for many years.

— А в мане́же сейча́с нахо́дится столо́вая, — said Andrey.

— Что э́то — столо́вая? — asked John.

— Э́то ме́сто, в кото́ром лю́ди едя́т, — explained Andrey.

— Как рестора́н?

— Да, но в рестора́не до́рого, а в столо́вой — дёшево.

— Лю́ди едя́т, а под нога́ми у них тайни́к, — mumbled John. — Как интере́сно!

— О чём вы говори́те? Я ниче́го не понима́ю! Како́й тайни́к? — Masha got excited.

Alexander Young immediately contacted Russian museum curators and historians. To dismantle the old manege in the existing sanatorium was a difficult matter. But apparently they expected to find something very important. Permission to excavate was received. Andrey also demanded not to notify journalists.

— Я ду́маю, что э́то драгоце́нности ца́рской семьи́! — Alexander Young made a statement to his colleagues.

Masha watched all that process with great interest. Everything happened in seconds and it was difficult to understand it at once. Finally John started to explain:

— Мой оте́ц — исто́рик, мы реша́ем истори́ческую зага́дку.

Упражне́ние 15. **Say it in English where the treasure is and how the heroes learned about it. Translate your story into Russian.**

— Как э́то интере́сно! — exclaimed Masha, her eyes were shining with genuine interest. — Когда́ я была́ ма́ленькой де́вочкой, я мечта́ла найти́ клад. Я ду́маю, все де́ти мечта́ют об э́том.

— Все де́ти мечта́ют найти́ клад, но не ка́ждый взро́слый[3] челове́к нахо́дит[4] клад. Мы все о́чень счастли́вые[5] взро́слые лю́ди, — concluded John.

[3] взро́слый (челове́к): an adult (n.)
[4] находи́ть (2.IR Д-Ж) / найти́ (SPECIAL): to find
[5] happy

13

Упражне́ние 16. **Write your own sentences, use the following examples as a model:**

Все лю́ди мечта́ют стать изве́стными, но не ка́ждый челове́к изве́стный.
Все де́ти мечта́ют полете́ть в ко́смос, но не ка́ждый взро́слый челове́к — космона́вт.

So, it was decided to go to St. Petersburg all together. Because the dreams of childhood must be come true.

Глава́ 14

Эпило́г (Epilogue)

When John, Andrey and Masha arrived in Peterhof, Alexander Young and several of other historians were already there.

— Сто два́дцать два, сто два́дцать три, сто два́дцать четы́ре, сто два́дцать пять, — Alexander Young personally counted the number of steps indicated in the code. On the spot, it turned out that 521 steps were far beyond the arena and there could be no cache there. But in any case, modern means were required: colleagues from Moscow brought a metal detector with them and soon the scientists extracted a small stone casket of solid malachite from the cache.

— Что э́то? — the scientists gasped.

— Э́то моне́ты… моне́ты… моне́ты… — said the voices, and everybody approached the table with the treasure on it. For the next few minutes there was a tense silence in the hall, and suddenly someone hesitantly said:

— Но что э́то за моне́ты?

— Моне́ты ненастоя́щие?

— Ненастоя́щие… Ненастоя́щие… Ненастоя́щие…

— Не мо́жет быть! Не мо́жет быть!.. Как э́то? Как ненастоя́щие?

While the scientists were standing in perplexity, Andrey and John exchanged glances — it seemed to them that they had begun to understand what the matter was. After all, they had already seen part of the collection of the Duke in Kazan. Hyperborea, Atlantis, ancient Babylon — it seemed that Grand Duke George Mikhailovich was not just a collector, he also created his own history, real hoaxes. On one of the coins there was the name Кий written in the ancient Slavic letters, which were used long before the arrival of Cyrillic letters to Russia. Andrey managed to read it. He smiled and whispered to John in his ear:

— Леге́нда говори́т, что Кий постро́ил го́род Ки́ев.

John smiled too — they were looking for a real treasure, and they found fakes. Grand Duke George Mikhailovich Romanov did not save the property — he saved his work. Nevertheless, Andrey looked very pleased:

— Я не бу́ду писа́ть статью́ о кла́де. Я напишу́ истори́ческую кни́гу и́ли диссерта́цию. Э́ти моне́ты име́ют о́чень большу́ю це́нность для исто́рии.

Алекса́ндр Янг то́же был сча́стлив:

— Э́то кни́га! А мо́жет быть, две кни́ги!

Alexander took Andrey and John aside from the rest of the scientists and asked:

— В тайнике́ в бу́лочной Фили́ппова лежа́ли докуме́нты и моне́ты, по́мните?

— Коне́чно, — answered Andrey.

— Я зна́ю, что там бы́ло! — said John's father mysteriously.

— Что?

— Князь Гео́ргий Миха́йлович коллекциони́ровал моне́ты. А князь Никола́й Миха́йлович увлека́лся исто́рией. Он был учёным-исто́риком.

— Да, мы зна́ем.

— Никола́й Миха́йлович изуча́л вре́мя ру́сского царя́ Алекса́ндра I, изуча́л вре́мя Наполео́на I и войну́ 1812 го́да. Он мно́го рабо́тал в библиоте́ках в Евро́пе и в Росси́и.

— Да-да́. Э́то я то́же зна́ю, — confirmed Andrey. — Никола́й Миха́йлович написа́л кни́гу «Алекса́ндр I» в 1912 году́.

— Э́то о́чень изве́стная кни́га, — Alexander Young went on. — Но не ка́ждый зна́ет, что Никола́й Миха́йлович Рома́нов написа́л ещё одну́ кни́гу. Она́ называ́ется «Алекса́ндр I и Наполео́н I».

— Вы оши́блись, — said Andrey. — Никола́й Рома́нов писа́л кни́гу об Алекса́ндре I и Наполео́не, но он не написа́л её. Э́та кни́га не существу́ет.

— А я ду́маю, что она́ существу́ет! — whispered Alexander Young joyfully. — Ру́копись в тайнике́ Фили́ппова — э́то кни́га Никола́я Рома́нова. Оста́лось то́лько прове́рить э́то. То́лько поду́майте — исто́рия отдаёт свои́ та́йны ка́ждые 100 лет: 1812 год — 1912 год — 2012 год.

— Никола́й Рома́нов пое́хал из Кры́ма в Санкт-Петербу́рг, что́бы взять свою́ кни́гу?!

— И́менно!

— Но ведь была́ револю́ция…

— Но ведь он был настоя́щий учёный!

— Не ца́рский дом, а настоя́щий университе́т, — John summarized the search results with a laugh.

Masha approached the men who were talking enthusiastically, and Alexander Young smiled at her:

— Здра́вствуйте, прекра́сная Мари́я! Тепе́рь я зна́ю, что Вам нра́вится иска́ть и находи́ть кла́ды! Э́то о́чень хорошо́!

— Почему́ э́то хорошо́? — said Masha with a smile.

— Мо́жет быть, Вы с Джо́ном вме́сте найдёте ещё оди́н клад?!

— Па́па! Что ты говори́шь?! — said John surprisingly.

— Э́то о́чень мо́жет быть! — said Alexander. — Потому что твоя́ ру́сская ба́бушка говори́ла, что привезла́ из Росси́и то́лько 10 проце́нтов свои́х де́нег и драгоце́нностей.

— О нет! — exclaimed John. — Пусть э́тот скеле́т пока́ лежи́т в на́шем семе́йном шкафу́!

14

Check your language skills

1. Как вас зову́т?
2. Ско́лько вам лет?
3. Когда́ у вас день рожде́ния?
4. Кака́я ва́ша профе́ссия?
5. Отку́да вы прие́хали?
6. Каки́е языки́ вы изуча́ли? Каки́е языки́ вы зна́ете?
7. Расскажи́те о ва́шей стране́, го́роде, дере́вне. Чего́ там мно́го, ма́ло?
8. Расскажи́те о стране́, в кото́рой вы живёте сейча́с.
9. Что вы зна́ете о тради́циях и лю́дях э́той страны́?
10. Кем вы рабо́тали ра́ньше?
11. Кем вы хоте́ли рабо́тать?
12. Кем вы ста́ли рабо́тать?
13. Расскажи́те о своём лице́.
14. Каку́ю оде́жду вы но́сите? Кака́я оде́жда вам идёт?
15. Расскажи́те о ва́шей семье́.
16. Расскажи́те о своём хара́ктере.
17. С кем вы отдыха́ете, рабо́таете, гуля́ете?
18. Кому́ и что вы да́рите на день рожде́ния?
19. Чем вы занима́етесь в свобо́дное вре́мя?
20. Где вы у́читесь (учи́лись)?
21. Что вы изуча́ете (изуча́ли)?
22. Чем вы интересу́етесь? О чём вы мечта́ете?
23. Чего́ у вас нет, но вы хоти́те име́ть?
24. Что вам нра́вится де́лать?
25. Что вам не нра́вится де́лать, но что вы должны́ де́лать?
26. Что вы де́лаете, когда́ вам ску́чно?
27. Что вы де́лаете, когда́ вам ве́село?
28. Расскажи́те о ва́шем обы́чном дне.
29. Расскажи́те, что вы сде́лали сего́дня?
30. Что вы бу́дете де́лать на сле́дующей неде́ле?
31. О чём вы лю́бите говори́ть?
32. Кака́я сего́дня пого́да?
33. Куда́ вы лю́бите е́здить?
34. Куда́ вы лю́бите ходи́ть?
35. Куда́ вы пое́дете?
36. Расскажи́те о го́роде, где вы живёте. Что где нахо́дится? Где вы бы́ли сего́дня?
37. Расскажи́те дру́гу, как прийти́ в ваш дом (объясни́те доро́гу).
38. Покажи́те дру́гу ваш дом и расскажи́те о нём. Что где нахо́дится?
39. Что вы лю́бите гото́вить?
40. Расскажи́те реце́пт ва́шего люби́мого блю́да.
41. Расскажи́те ещё о себе́.

Answer Keys

Chapter 2

Exercise 3

1) Э́то ноутбу́к и каранда́ш. 2) Э́то студе́нт, но не поэ́т. 3) Э́то студе́нт, а э́то профе́ссор.

Exercise 7

Э́то язы́к, сын, алфави́т, ма́ма, па́па, фо́то, авто́, тома́т, профе́ссор, студе́нт, поэ́т, каранда́ш, ноутбу́к, ру́чка, дом, мо́да, бана́н, фонта́н, пол, ла́мпа, луна́, зал, ваза, суп, стол, стул, сло́во, ма́сло.

Э́то Джон, Алекса́ндр, Том, Та́та, Ве́ра, А́нна, А́лла, Э́лла, Бэ́лла, Эде́м, Те́мза, Сэм, Сте́лла.

Exercise 13

Ча́сто, пло́хо, хорошо́, хо́лодно, жа́рко.

Exercise 14

Э́то жа́рко. Э́то пло́хо. Э́то тру́дно. Э́то хо́лодно.

Exercise 15

Э́то стул. Э́то ва́за. Э́то ча́шка.

Exercise 16

Э́то ка́рта. Э́то А́фрика. Тут Еги́пет. Еги́пет — э́то страна́. Там жа́рко. А э́то Каир. Каир — э́то го́род.

Exercise 18

1) Уф! 2) Ура! 3) Да (ага). 4) О-го-го́! 5) Та-да́! 6) Бам! Бом! Бум!; Ку-ку́, Паф! Тук-тук-ту́к! Э-гэ-гэ́! 7) Ого́! (Вау! Ах!) 8) Эх…

Chapter 3

Exercise 4

1) ты; 2) я; 3) мы; 4) она́

Exercise 5

1) Алекса́ндр — э́то я. Джон — э́то ты. Ло́ра — э́то она́.
2) Алекса́ндр — э́то ты. Джон — э́то я. Ло́ра — э́то она́.

Exercise 6

1) Я́блоко — э́то оно́. 2) Ю́ра — э́то он. 3) Еле́на — э́то она́. 4) Сыр — э́то он. 5) Сло́во — э́то оно́. 6) Дом — э́то он. 7) Ры́ба — э́то она́. 8) Ма́сло — э́то оно́. 9) Фонта́н — э́то он. 10) Окно́ — э́то оно́. 11) Спорт — э́то он. 12) Фо́то — э́то оно́. 13) Москва́ — э́то она́. 14) Авто́ — э́то оно́.

Exercise 7

ОН: 1) па́па 2) го́род 3) дом 4) бана́н 5) шарф 6) стол 7) стул 8) суп 9) тома́т 10) друг 11) знак 12) Ло́ндон 13) Пари́ж 14) спорт 15) фрукт 16) о́вощ 17) муж 18) звук 19) сын

ОНА́: 1) ма́ма 2) ла́мпа 3) Москва́ 4) ва́за 5) ба́бушка 6) подру́га 7) рабо́та 8) то́чка 9) доро́га 10) ка́рта 11) ру́чка 12) бу́ква 13) жена́ 14) улы́бка 15) луна́

ОНО́: 1) авто́ 2) фо́то 3) сло́во

Exercise 9

A) Э́то моё авто́, моя́ бума́га, моя́ ва́за, мой журна́л, мой каранда́ш, моя́ ка́рта, моя́ ла́мпа, мой ноутбу́к, моя́ па́пка, мой Ло́ндон, мой пол, моя́ по́лка, мой потоло́к, моя ру́чка, мой Санкт-Петербу́рг, мой стол, мой стул, моя́ улы́бка, моя́ ча́шка, мой шкаф.

B) Э́то ты. Э́то твой стол, твой стул, твоя́ ру́чка, твоя́ ва́за, твоё окно́.

C) Э́то она́. Э́то её стол, её стул, её ру́чка, её ва́за, её окно́.

D) Э́то он. Э́то его́ стол, его́ стул, его́ ру́чка, его́ ва́за, его́ окно́.

E) Э́то мы. Э́то наш стол, наш стул, на́ша ру́чка, на́ша ва́за, на́ше окно́.

Exercise 14

Э́то мой дива́н, кабине́т, ковёр, компью́тер, конве́рт, слова́рь, телеви́зор, телефо́н.

Э́то моя́ газе́та, дверь, карти́на, кни́га, крова́ть, семья́, стена́, тетра́дь.

Э́то моё зе́ркало, кре́сло, письмо́, мо́ре.

Exercise 15

Авто́, ба́бушки, бана́ны, бу́квы, ва́зы, газе́ты, города́, две́ри, дива́ны, дома́, доро́ги, друзья́, жалюзи́, жёны, занаве́ски, зву́ки, зеркала́, зна́ки, кабине́ты, ка́рты, карти́ны, кварти́ры, кни́ги, ковры́, компью́теры, конве́рты, кре́сла, крова́ти, ла́мпы, ма́мы, моря́, мужья́, о́вощи, па́пы, пи́сьма, подру́ги, рабо́ты, ру́чки, се́мьи, словари́, слова́, сте́ны, столы́, сту́лья, супы́, сыновья́, телеви́зоры, телефо́ны, тетра́ди, тома́ты, то́чки, улы́бки, фонта́ны, фо́то, фру́кты.

Exercise 22

Молодо́й — молода́я — молодо́е — молоды́е; (не)краси́вый — (не)краси́вая — (не)краси́вое — (не)краси́вые; интере́сный — интере́сная — интере́сное — интере́сные; ску́чный — ску́чная — ску́чное — ску́чные; све́тлый — све́тлая — све́тлое — све́тлые; тёмный — тёмная — тёмное — тёмные ; пра́вый — пра́вая — пра́вое — пра́вые; ле́вый — ле́вая — ле́вое — ле́вые, прямо́й — пряма́я — прямо́е — прямы́е; кра́сный — кра́сная — кра́сное — кра́сные; бе́лый — бе́лая — бе́лое — бе́лые; чёрный — чёрная — чёрное — чёрные; си́ний — си́няя — си́нее — си́ние, голубо́й — голуба́я — голубо́е — голубы́е; ро́зовый — ро́зовая — ро́зовое — ро́зовые; дли́нный — дли́нная — дли́нное — дли́нные; коро́ткий — коро́ткая — коро́ткое — коро́ткие; ма́ленький — ма́ленькая — ма́ленькое — ма́ленькие; большо́й — больша́я — большо́е — больши́е; широ́кий — широ́кая — широ́кое — широ́кие; у́зкий — у́зкая — у́зкое — у́зкие; высо́кий — высо́кая — высо́кое — высо́кие; ни́зкий — ни́зкая — ни́зкое — ни́зкие; плохо́й — плоха́я — плохо́е — плохи́е; хоро́ший — хоро́шая — хоро́шее — хоро́шие.

Exercise 24

Кра́сное я́блоко, большо́й дом, но́вый компью́тер, ста́рое кре́сло, си́няя ва́за, кра́сная ру́чка, коро́ткая доро́га, интере́сная газе́та, большо́е окно́.

Exercise 26

1) широ́кая 2) ни́зкий 3) ста́рые 4) большо́е 5) чёрная 6) у́зкое 7) коро́ткие 8) интере́сная.

Chapter 4

Exercise 3

Молдава́нин, молдава́нка; россия́нин, россия́нка; армяни́н, армя́нка; израильтя́нин, израильтя́нка; египтя́нин, египтя́нка.

Голла́ндец, голла́ндка; инди́ец, индиа́нка; испа́нец, испа́нка; италья́нец, италья́нка; мексика́нец, мексика́нка; эсто́нец, эсто́нка; япо́нец, япо́нка; аргенти́нец, аргенти́нка; украи́нец, украи́нка; швейца́рец, швейца́рка; эквадо́рец, эквадо́рка; не́мец, не́мка; кана́дец, кана́дка; лито́вец, лито́вка; австрали́ец, австрали́йка; бельги́ец, бельги́йка.

Швед, шве́дка; ара́б, ара́бка; туркме́н, туркме́нка; грузи́н, грузи́нка; латы́ш, латы́шка.

Узбе́чка.

Exercise 5

Францу́зский, фи́нский, шве́дский, азербайджа́нский, испа́нский, португа́льский, япо́нский, англи́йский.

Exercise 7

Изра́иль — иври́т. И́ндия — хи́нди. Ира́н — фарси́.

Exercise 9

А) Э́то Фра́нция. Тут францу́зы. Тут говоря́т по-францу́зски.
Э́то Аме́рика. Тут америка́нцы. Тут говоря́т по-англи́йски.
Э́то Герма́ния. Тут не́мцы. Тут говоря́т по-неме́цки.
Э́то Испа́ния. Тут испа́нцы. Тут говоря́т по-испа́нски.
Э́то Япо́ния. Тут япо́нцы. Тут говоря́т по-япо́нски.
Э́то Сау́довская Ара́вия. Тут ара́бы. Тут говоря́т по-ара́бски.
Э́то Казахста́н. Тут каза́хи. Тут говоря́т по-каза́хски и по-ру́сски.

В) Э́то америка́нцы. Они́ говоря́т по-англи́йски, они́ зна́ют англи́йский язы́к.
Э́то францу́зы. Они́ говоря́т по-францу́зски, они́ зна́ют францу́зский язы́к
Э́то не́мцы. Они́ говоря́т по-неме́цки, они́ зна́ют неме́цкий язы́к.
Э́то испа́нцы. Они́ говоря́т по-испа́нски, они́ зна́ют испа́нский язы́к.
Э́то ара́бы. Они́ говоря́т по-ара́бски, они́ зна́ют ара́бский язы́к.
Э́то япо́нцы. Они́ говоря́т по-япо́нски, они́ зна́ют япо́нский язы́к.

Exercise 12

Э́то А́нглия. Бенеди́кт Камберб́этч живёт здесь.
Э́то США. Бара́к Оба́ма живёт здесь.
Э́то Росси́я. Пётр Ильи́ч Чайко́вский жил здесь.
Э́то Росси́я. Анто́н Па́влович Че́хов жил здесь.
Э́то Ме́ксика. Фри́да Ка́ло жила́ здесь.
Э́то США. Мэ́рилин Монро́ жила́ здесь.
Э́то Кана́да. Сели́н Дио́н живёт здесь.
Э́то Росси́я. Ма́йя Плисе́цкая жила́ здесь.
Э́то Герма́ния. А́нгела Ме́ркель живёт здесь.
Э́то США. Ме́рил Стрип живёт здесь.
Э́то Ита́лия. Роме́о и Джулье́тта жи́ли здесь.
Э́то Фра́нция. Наполео́н и Жозефи́на жи́ли здесь.
Э́то Гре́ция. Одиссе́й и аргона́вты жи́ли здесь.
Э́то Великобрита́ния. Кейт Ми́ддлтон и принц Уи́льям живу́т здесь.
Э́то США. Брэд Питт и Анджели́на Джоли́ живу́т здесь.
Э́то Средизе́мье. Хо́ббит Би́льбо и драко́н Сма́уг живу́т здесь.

Exercise 15

1) Э́то Ло́ндон. Джон здесь. А э́то Луна́. Луна́ о́чень далеко́. 2) Э́то Ло́ндон. Джон здесь. Э́то Пари́ж. Пари́ж не о́чень далеко́. 3) Э́то Ло́ндон. Мы здесь. Э́то Ке́мбридж. Ке́мбридж бли́зко. 4) Э́то Амстерда́м. Мы здесь. Э́то Нью-Йо́рк. Нью-Йо́рк о́чень далеко́. 5) Э́то Нью-Йо́рк. Вы здесь. А э́то Вашингто́н. Вашингто́н бли́зко. 6) Э́то Росси́я. Вы здесь. А э́то Украи́на. Украи́на ря́дом. 7) Э́то Москва́. Вы здесь. А э́то Пеки́н, Кита́й. Пеки́н далеко́.

Exercise 18

1) Текст в кни́ге. 2) Ва́за на столе́. 3) Кре́сло в ко́мнате. 4) Карти́на на стене́. 5) Джон в гости́нице. 6) Мой сын на у́лице. 7) Мой го́род на реке́ Во́лге. 8) Его́ дом в Мадри́де. 9) Моё се́рдце в Росси́и. 10) Бана́ны в Эквадо́ре.

Exercise 20

В Росси́и есть Эрмита́ж и Кремль. Во Фра́нции есть Лувр. В Еги́пте есть сфинкс. В Гре́ции есть Акро́поль. В А́нглии есть Ло́ндонский глаз. В Ме́ксике есть пирами́ды ма́йя.

Exercise 21

Лувр — во Фра́нции. Акро́поль — в Гре́ции. Сфинкс — в Еги́пте. Ло́ндонский глаз — в А́нглии. Пирами́ды ма́йя — в Ме́ксике.

Exercise 22

1) Алекса́ндр Пу́шкин жил в Росси́и, в Санкт-Петербу́рге. 2) Стив Джобс жил в Аме́рике, в Сан-Франци́ско. 3) Леона́рдо да Ви́нчи жил в Ита́лии, во Флоре́нции. 4) Наполео́н Бонапа́рт жил на Ко́рсике, в Ая́ччо. 5) Сокра́т жил в Гре́ции, в Афи́нах. 6) Короле́ва Викто́рия жила́ в Великобрита́нии, в Ло́ндоне. 7) Мо́царт жил в А́встрии, в Ве́не.

Exercise 24

Два́дцать два, сто два́дцать три, четы́реста шестьдеся́т семь, одна ты́сяча девятьсо́т се́мьдесят шесть, во́семьдесят семь, две́сти пятьдеся́т во́семь, три́ста, четы́реста пятьдеся́т, оди́ннадцать, во́семьдесят оди́н, две ты́сячи двена́дцать, де́вять ты́сяч девятьсо́т девяно́сто де́вять.

Exercise 25

1) Майкл Фри́мен живёт в Москве́, на Ле́нинском проспе́кте, в до́ме 38, в кварти́ре 34. 2) Ари́на и Никола́й Ивано́вы живу́т в Каза́ни, на у́лице Толсто́го, в до́ме 56, в кварти́ре 78. 3) Ва́ся Никола́ев живёт в Ни́жнем Но́вгороде, на Медици́нской у́лице, в общежи́тии № 1, в до́ме 5, на этаже́ 4, в ко́мнате 45. 4) А́нна Петро́ва живёт в О́мске, на пло́щади Серо́ва, в до́ме 18, в кварти́ре 145. 5) Ива́н Пло́тников живёт в дере́вне Оси́новка, в до́ме 27.

Exercise 27

1) Бенджами́н Янг был англича́нин. 2) Он жил в Росси́и и в А́нглии. 3) Он жил в Москве́ и в Ло́ндоне. 4) Он знал ру́сский и англи́йский языки́.

Exercise 29

B) Э́то Кра́сная пло́щадь (3). Ря́дом Кремль (5) и Кремлёвская стена́ (4). Э́то Спа́сская ба́шня (10). Там кура́нты (6). На Кра́сной пло́щади есть Мавзоле́й (7). Там Ле́нин. На пло́щади есть Госуда́рственный универса́льный магази́н (ГУМ) (1). Ещё там есть Истори́ческий музе́й (2), собо́р Васи́лия Блаже́нного (9). Ря́дом Москва́-река́ (8).

C) 1) Кремль на Кра́сной пло́щади. 2) Кура́нты на Спа́сской ба́шне. 3) Ле́нин в Мавзоле́е.

Chapter 5

Exercise 6

актёр: actor; компью́тер: computer; теа́тр: theatre; при́нтер: printer; ко́фе-брейк: coffee break; премье́ра: premiere; би́знес: business; бизнесме́н: businessman; ме́неджер: manager; дедла́йн: deadline; интервью́: interview; пост: post; тест: test; спортсме́н: sportsman; фана́т: fan; и́мидж: image; мини́стр: minister; парла́мент: parlament; желе́: jelly; шокола́д: chocolate; автомоби́ль: automobile; ра́дио: radio; видеока́мера: video camera; ви́део: video; футбо́л: football; баскетбо́л: basketball.

Exercise 13

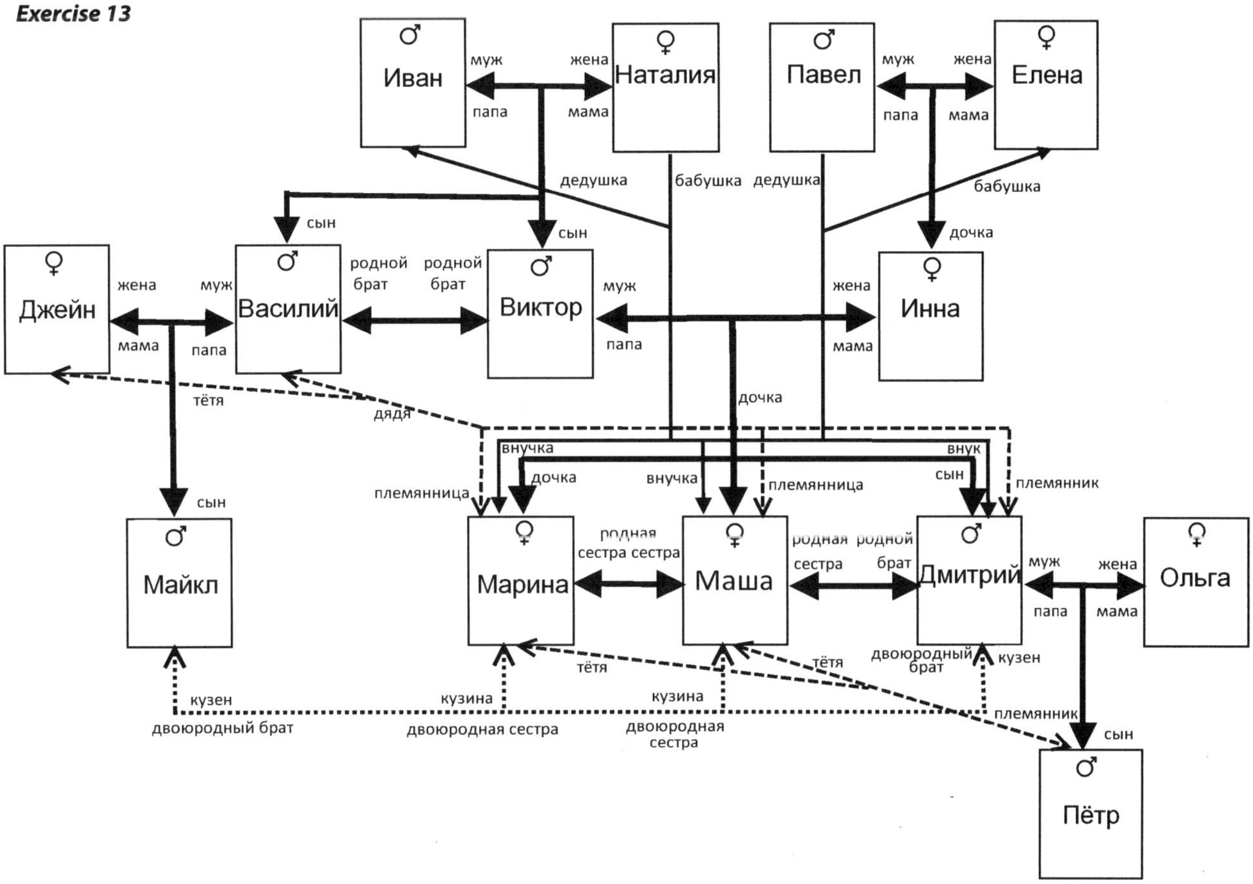

Exercise 15

1) Мне 25 лет. Ско́лько мне лет? 2) Ей 31 год. Ско́лько ей лет? 3) Ему́ 58 лет. Ско́лько ему́ лет? 4) Им 44 го́да и 38 лет. Ско́лько им лет? 5) Нам 18 лет и 20 лет. Ско́лько нам лет? 6) Тебе́ 36 лет. Ско́лько тебе́ лет? 7) Вам 21 год и 29 лет. Ско́лько вам лет?

Exercise 24

1) Он чита́ет. 2) Она́ расска́зывает. 3) Мы гуля́ем. 4) Они́ игра́ют. 5) Я отдыха́ю. 6) Мы отдыха́ем.

Exercise 25

1) Что он де́лает? 2) Что они́ де́лают? 3) Что она́ де́лает? 4) Что он де́лает? 5) Что мы де́лаем в а́вгусте?

Exercise 26

Писа́ть: он/она́ пи́шет, мы пи́шем, вы пи́шете, они́ пи́шут.
Рисова́ть: я рису́ю, мы рису́ем, вы рису́ете, они́ рису́ют.
Танцева́ть: я танцу́ю, ты танцу́ешь, он/она́ танцу́ет, вы танцу́ете, они́ танцу́ют.
Люби́ть: ты лю́бишь, он/она́ лю́бит, мы лю́бим, вы лю́бите.
Ненави́деть: я ненави́жу, ты ненави́дишь, он/она́ ненави́дит, мы ненави́дим, вы ненави́дите, они́ ненави́дят.
Учи́ть: я учу́, ты у́чишь, он/она́ у́чит, мы у́чим, вы у́чите, они́ у́чат.
Учи́ться: я учу́сь, ты у́чишься, он/она́ у́чится, мы у́чимся, вы у́читесь, они́ у́чатся.

Exercise 27

Он фотографи́рует, мы у́чимся, они́ у́чат, она́ танцу́ет, вы лю́бите, мы чита́ем, ты изуча́ешь, он лета́ет, вы рабо́таете, она́ расска́зывает.

Ты рисова́л, он фотографи́ровал, мы учи́лись, они́ учи́ли, она́ танцева́ла, вы люби́ли, мы чита́ли, ты изуча́л, он лета́л, вы рабо́тали, она́ расска́зывала.

Exercise 29

Актёр рабо́тает в теа́тре. Дире́ктор рабо́тает в о́фисе. Инжене́р рабо́тает на заво́де. Касси́р рабо́тает в ба́нке. Почтальо́н рабо́тает на по́чте. Садо́вник рабо́тает в саду́. Секрета́рь рабо́тает в фи́рме. Спортсме́н рабо́тает на стадио́не. Эскурсово́д рабо́тает в музе́е.

Exercise 30

Полице́йский слу́жит в поли́ции. По́вар рабо́тает в столо́вой / в кафе́. Пенсионе́р отдыха́ет в санато́рии. Пило́т слу́жит в авиа́ции. Шко́льник у́чится в шко́ле. Студе́нтка у́чится в институ́те. Домохозя́йка рабо́тает до́ма. Учи́тель рабо́тает в шко́ле. Аспира́нт у́чится в аспиранту́ре. Преподава́тель рабо́тает в институ́те / университе́те. Тури́ст отдыха́ет до́ма.

Exercise 31

Извини́, я сейча́с не могу́ говори́ть. 1) Я сейча́с в теа́тре на конце́рте. 2) Я сейча́с в музе́е на вы́ставке. 3) Я сейча́с в па́рке на экску́рсии. 4) Я сейча́с в о́фисе на рабо́те.

Exercise 37

1) Ма́ша лю́бит говори́ть о ней. 2) Па́па Ви́ктор мно́го зна́ет о них. 3) Де́душка расска́зывает о них. 4) Мой друг расска́зывает обо мне. 5) Па́па и ма́ма ча́сто говоря́т о нас. 6) Я сейча́с говори́л о тебе́.

Exercise 38

1) об университе́те; 2) в ба́нке; 3) в ру́сской дере́вне; 4) о стра́нах и путеше́ствиях; 5) в Великобрита́нии; 6) об интере́сных кни́гах; 7) в Моско́вском госуда́рственном университе́те; 8) в э́тих стра́нах; 9) о Лу́вре 10) в музе́е; 11) на восто́чном ры́нке.

Exercise 39

A) Я люблю́ го́род, му́зыку, матрёшку, сад, мо́ре, би́знес, шокола́д, де́ньги.

Я люблю́ ма́му, роди́телей, Алекса́ндра, Ма́шу, бра́та.

B) Ты зна́ешь но́вый го́род, ста́рую му́зыку, большо́й би́знес.

Ты зна́ешь высо́кого Вади́ма, ру́сскую ма́му, хоро́ших роди́телей, ску́чного Алекса́ндра, краси́вую Ма́шу, родно́го бра́та.

C) Я рису́ю на́шу краси́вую приро́ду, э́тот но́вый го́род, её ма́ленькую матрёшку, наш зелёный сад, наш америка́нский спу́тник, ва́ше си́нее мо́ре, её тёмный шокола́д, их францу́зские де́ньги.

Я рису́ю ва́шего высо́кого Вади́ма, твою́ ру́сскую ма́му, его́ хоро́ших роди́телей, моего́ ску́чного Алекса́ндра, их краси́вую Ма́шу, моего́ родно́го бра́та.

Exercise 41

Я зна́ю шко́льницу, шко́льниц; царя́, царе́й; секретаря́, секретаре́й; вну́чку, вну́чек; журнали́ста, журнали́стов; Али́ну, Али́н; А́ню, Ань; аспира́нтку, аспира́нток; пило́та, пило́тов; почтальо́на, почтальо́нов; мужчи́ну, мужчи́н; преподава́теля, преподава́телей; тётю, тётей / тёть; дя́дю, дя́дей; де́вочку, де́вочек.

Exercise 44

1) физи́ческий объе́кт; 2) биологи́ческий журна́л; 3) хими́ческий заво́д; 4) экономи́ческая ка́рта; 5) истори́ческий музе́й; 6) экологи́ческая пробле́ма; 7) математи́ческий факульте́т.

Exercise 45

1) Студе́нт-исто́рик у́чится на истори́ческом факульте́те, он изуча́ет исто́рию. 2) Студе́нт-матема́тик у́чится на математи́ческом факульте́те, он изуча́ет матема́тику. 3) Аспира́нт-экономи́ст у́чится на экономи́ческом факульте́те, он изуча́ет эконо́мику.

Exercise 48

Моя́ семья́

Меня́ зову́т Джон. Мне 36 лет. Я экономи́ст. Я живу́ в Ло́ндоне.

Моего́ па́пу зову́т Алекса́ндр. Ему́ 72 го́да, он исто́рик, профе́ссор. Он на пе́нсии, но ещё рабо́тает в университе́те на истори́ческом факульте́те. Он у́чит студе́нтов.

Мою́ ма́му зову́т Ло́ра. Ей 68 лет. Она́ худо́жница и фото́граф. Она́ пи́шет карти́ны и фотографи́рует. Она́ лю́бит писа́ть карти́ны в го́роде и на приро́де.

Мой ста́рший брат Кен — врач. Он рабо́тает в Кра́сном Кресте́. Он живёт в А́фрике.

Моего́ де́душку зва́ли Бенджами́н. Он рабо́тал в шко́ле. Он был дире́ктор.

Мою́ ба́бушку зва́ли А́нна. Она́ была́ домохозя́йка. Она́ люби́ла игра́ть на роя́ле.

Exercise 51

1) **Кто лю́бил что?** Вели́кий князь **Гео́ргий Миха́йлович** люби́л лошаде́й и ста́рые де́ньги. Вели́кий князь **Никола́й Миха́йлович** люби́л исто́рию. Царь **Никола́й II** люби́л лошаде́й, люби́л фотографи́ровать и о́чень люби́л свою́ семью́. **О́льга, Татья́на, Мари́я, Анастаси́я** люби́ли чита́ть, гуля́ть и танцева́ть. **Алексе́й** люби́л гуля́ть и игра́ть.

2) **Кто изуча́л что?** Вели́кий князь **Гео́ргий Миха́йлович** изуча́л ста́рые де́ньги. Вели́кий князь **Никола́й Миха́йлович** изуча́л истори́ческие та́йны. **Али́са Ге́ссенская** изуча́ла рели́гию и филосо́фию.

3) **Где мно́го занима́лся князь Гео́ргий Миха́йлович?** Он занима́лся в мане́же.

4) **Где мно́го занима́лся князь Никола́й Миха́йлович?** Он занима́лся в библиоте́ке.

5) **Как учи́лся Алексе́й?** Он учи́лся о́чень хорошо́.

Chapter 6

Exercise 2

1) ку́ртка; 2) сви́тер; 3) сапоги́; 4) ша́пка; 5) пальто́; 6) шарф; 7) перча́тки.

Exercise 5

1) джи́нсы; 2) компью́тер; 3) костю́м; 4) сви́тер; 5) бума́жник; 6) па́спорт; 7) ⟷ перча́тки; 7) ↓ плащ; 8) зонт; 9) чемода́н.

Exercise 7

перча́тки

Exercise 9

1\. — До́брый день!
— До́брый день!
— Отку́да Вы?
— Я из И́ндии.
— Куда́ Вы лети́те?
— Я лечу́ в Герма́нию.
— Где Вы живёте в Герма́нии?
— В Берли́не.
— В гости́нице?
— Да, в гости́нице.

2\. — До́брое у́тро!
— До́брое у́тро!
— Отку́да вы?
— Мы из Бе́льгии.
— Куда вы е́дете?
— Мы е́дем во Фра́нцию.
— Где вы живёте во Фра́нции?
— В Орлеа́не.
— В гости́нице?
— Да, в гости́нице.

Exercise 10

А) 1) Хосе́ из Испа́нии. 2) Никола́й из Белору́ссии. 3) Пьер из Фра́нции. 4) Грэ́тхен из Герма́нии. 5) Джон из А́нглии. 6) Ро́за из Португа́лии.

B) 1) Са́ша из Влади́мира. 2) Ван из Пеки́на. 3) Ната́ша из Ки́ева. 4) Лючи́я из Мила́на. 5) Муха́ммед из Ира́на. 6) Дави́д из Изра́иля. 7) Алексе́й из Су́здаля. 8) Жера́р из Брюссе́ля.

C) 1) Ферна́ндо из Ме́ксики. 2) Ла́ура из Аргенти́ны. 3) Джейн из Кана́ды. 4) Па́вел из Литвы́. 5) Ли́ля из Каза́ни. 6) Вади́м из А́страхани.

Exercise 17

02.01 — второ́е января́
05.02 — пя́тое февраля́
10.04 — деся́тое апре́ля
01.05 — пе́рвое ма́я
03.09 — тре́тье сентября́

Exercise 25

1) **Писа́ть**. Вчера́ я писа́л. Сего́дня я пишу́. За́втра я бу́ду писа́ть. 2) **Фотографи́ровать**. Вчера́ они́ фотографи́ровали. Сего́дня они́ фотографи́руют. За́втра они́ бу́дут фотографи́ровать. 3) **Гуля́ть**. Вчера́ мы гуля́ли. Сего́дня мы гуля́ем. За́втра мы бу́дем гуля́ть. 4) **Отдыха́ть**. Вчера́ я отдыха́л. Сего́дня я отдыха́ю. За́втра я бу́ду отдыха́ть.

Exercise 31

ста́рый → старо́ и ста́ро; интере́сный → интере́сно; ску́чный → ску́чно; кра́сный → красно́ и кра́сно; све́тлый →светло́; тёмный → темно́; прямо́й → пря́мо; высо́кий → высоко́

Exercise 32

жа́ркая; холо́дная; интере́сный; ску́чная

Chapter 7

Exercise 2

мёд — медо́вый; мя́со — мясно́й; о́вощ (о́вощи) — овощно́й; шокола́д — шокола́дный; соль — солёный; гриб (грибы́) — грибно́й; оре́х (оре́хи) — оре́ховый; фрукт (фру́кты) — фрукто́вый; я́года (я́годы) — я́годный; сли́вки — сли́вочный; смета́на — смета́нный

Exercise 5

вари́ть, жа́рить

Exercise 6

Она́ гото́вила, он вари́л, он жа́рил, она́ жа́рила.

Exercise 7

1) Вари́ть. Ку́рица варёная, мя́со варёное, яйцо́ варёное, карто́фель варёный, овощи варёные; пирожки́ / блины́ с варе́ньем (with jam).

2) Жа́рить. Ку́рица жа́реная, ры́ба жа́реная, мя́со жа́реное, карто́фель жа́реный.

Exercise 8

Э́то ру́сская пе́чка. Сейча́с э́то гла́вное ме́сто в ру́сском до́ме. Там ру́сские лю́ди гото́вят еду́: ва́рят ка́шу и суп, жа́рят мя́со и карто́фель.

Exercise 11

1) непра́вда 2) непра́вда 3) пра́вда 4) пра́вда 5) пра́вда 6) непра́вда

Exercise 12

1) на ку́хне 2) на плите́ и в микроволно́вой пе́чке 3) и на ку́хне, и в ко́мнате

Exercise 14

A) 1) Э́то журна́л сестры́. 2) Э́то кни́ги профе́ссора. 3) Э́то самолёт президе́нта. 4) Э́то кварти́ра актри́сы. 5) Э́то де́ньги подру́г. 6) Э́то я́блоко бра́та.

B) 1) Э́то журна́л мое́й ста́ршей сестры́. 2) Э́то кни́ги изве́стных профессоро́в. 3) Э́то самолёт росси́йского президе́нта. 4) Э́то кварти́ра изве́стной францу́зской актри́сы. 5) Э́то де́ньги его́ хоро́ших подру́г. 6) Э́то я́блоко мла́дшего бра́та.

C) 1) У мое́й ста́ршей сестры́ есть журна́л. У неё есть журна́л. 2) У изве́стных профессоро́в есть кни́ги. У них есть кни́ги. 3) У росси́йского президе́нта есть самолёт. У него́ есть самолёт. 4) У изве́стной францу́зской актри́сы есть кварти́ра. У неё есть кварти́ра. 5) У его́ хоро́ших подру́г есть де́ньги. У них есть де́ньги. 6) У мла́дшего бра́та есть я́блоко. У него́ есть я́блоко.

Exercise 15

1) Карти́на Ма́рка Шага́ла. 2) Пе́сня Э́лтона Джо́на. 3) Рома́н «Кра́сное и чёрное» писа́теля Стенда́ля. 4) Рома́н «Война́ и мир» Льва Толсто́го. 5) Дом архите́ктора Га́уди. 6) Расска́зы Ага́ты Кри́сти. 7) Карти́на Казими́ра Мале́вича. 8) Карти́на По́ля Доге́на. 9) Расска́з Анто́на Че́хова.

Exercise 16

A) 1) У Мари́ны нет но́вого пла́тья. 2) У Пе́ти нет совреме́нного компью́тера. 3) У дире́ктора нет вре́мени. 4) У секретаря́ нет докуме́нтов. 5) У студе́нта нет подру́ги.

B) 1) У студе́нта ле́том есть вре́мя. 2) У А́нны есть дорого́е пальто́. 3) У Дми́трия есть а́нгло-ру́сский слова́рь. 4) У сестры́ есть но́вая су́мка. 5) У перево́дчика есть большо́й текст.

Exercise 19

1) У Анто́на был хоро́ший друг. У Анто́на бу́дет хоро́ший друг. У Анто́на не́ было хоро́шего дру́га. У Анто́на не бу́дет хоро́шего дру́га.

2) У студе́нта сего́дня бы́ли заня́тия. У студе́нта сего́дня бу́дут заня́тия. У студе́нта сего́дня нет заня́тий. У студе́нта сего́дня не бу́дет заня́тий.

3) У дире́ктора бы́ло вре́мя. У дире́ктора бу́дет вре́мя. У дире́ктора не́ было вре́мени. У дире́ктора не бу́дет вре́мени.

Exercise 24

1) Я спортсме́н, потому́ что я люблю́ спорт. 2) Я не говорю́ по-испа́нски, потому́ что не зна́ю испа́нский язы́к. 3) Я не́ был в теа́тре, потому́ что в моём го́роде нет теа́тра. 4) Я изуча́ю матема́тику и фи́зику, потому́ что моя́ профе́ссия — инжене́р. 5) Ле́том нет сне́га, потому́ что ле́том жа́рко. 6) Я не гото́влю до́ма, потому́ что у меня́ до́ма нет ку́хни. 7) Ка́тя не жа́рит мя́со, потому́ что она́ вегетариа́нка.

Exercise 26

1) В Росси́и не едя́т крем-су́п, потому́ что в Росси́и э́то не традицио́нное блю́до. 2) Я не ем в рестора́не, потому́ что у меня́ нет де́нег. 3) Ни́на не гото́вит до́ма, потому́ что у неё нет плиты́. 4) Мы не бу́дем сейча́с пить чай, потому́ что у нас нет вре́мени.

Exercise 27

1) Крем-су́п в Росси́и — э́то не традицио́нное блю́до, поэ́тому в Росси́и не едя́т крем-су́п. 2) У меня́ нет де́нег, поэ́тому я не ем в рестора́не. 3) У Ни́ны нет плиты́, поэ́тому она́ не гото́вит до́ма. 4) У нас нет вре́мени, поэ́тому мы не бу́дем сейча́с пить чай.

Exercise 31

B) оди́н паке́т, две па́чки, три́дцать три стака́на воды́, две таре́лки, пять бока́лов вина́, де́сять паке́тов, два́дцать одна́ ло́жка, три рю́мки, две сковороды́, во́семь ба́нок, двена́дцать таре́лок, семь ча́шек, одна́ кастрю́ля, четы́ре коро́бки.

Exercise 32

ча́шка воды́, ло́жка сли́вок, стака́н ча́я, рю́мка во́дки, бока́л вина́, кастрю́ля су́па, ба́нка варе́нья, паке́т пирожко́в, буты́лка молока́, коро́бка са́хара, па́чка со́ли, таре́лка ка́ши, сковорода́ жа́реного карто́феля

Exercise 33

У А́нн**ы** больш**а́я** семья́, поэ́тому она́ гото́ви**т** одн**у́** больш**у́ю** кастрю́л**ю** су́п**а**, одн**у** ма́леньк**ую** кастрю́л**ю** ка́ш**и**, дв**е** сковород**ы́** блин**о́в**, три́ паке́т**а** со́к**а**.

Exercise 34

B) Счёт 1 ма́ленький, потому́ что там одна́ таре́лка су́па, одна́ таре́лка ка́ши, оди́н пирожо́к, одна́ ча́шка ча́я.

Счёт 2 большо́й, потому́ что там четы́ре таре́лки ка́ши, четы́ре стака́на со́ка, одна́ сковорода́ жа́реного карто́феля, две таре́лки пельме́ней и одна́ буты́лка вина́.

C) В зака́зе 1 есть одна́ таре́лка су́па, одна́ таре́лка ка́ши, оди́н пирожо́к, одна́ ча́шка ча́я, поэ́тому счёт ма́ленький.

В зака́зе 2 есть четы́ре таре́лки ка́ши, четы́ре стака́на со́ка, одна́ сковорода́ жа́реного карто́феля, две таре́лки пельме́ней и одна́ буты́лка вина́, поэ́тому счёт большо́й.

Exercise 36

знать	зна́ют	знай	зна́йте
учи́ть	у́чат	учи́	учи́те
отдыха́ть	отдыха́ют	отдыха́й	отдыха́йте
расска́зывать	расска́зывают	расска́зывай	расска́зывайте
рисова́ть	рису́ют	рису́й	рису́йте
вари́ть	ва́рят	вари́	вари́те

Exercise 37

1) Пе́йте, пожа́луйста, сок! *или* Пе́йте сок, пожа́луйста! 2) Чита́йте, пожа́луйста, кни́гу! 3) Говори́те, пожа́луйста, по-ру́сски! 4) Пожа́луйста, лети́ в Москву́! 5) Де́лайте, пожа́луйста, сала́т!

Exercise 38

Infinitive	**класть**				**брать**			
Present	я ты он, она́, оно́	кладу́ кладёшь кладёт	мы вы они́	кладём кладёте кладу́т	я ты он, она́, оно́	беру́ берёшь берёт	мы вы они́	берём берёте беру́т
Past	он она́ оно́	клал кла́ла кла́ло	они́	кла́ли	он она́ оно́	брал брала́ бра́ло	они́	бра́ли
Imperative	ты	Клади́!	вы	Клади́те!	ты	Бери́!	вы	Бери́те!

Exercise 42

1) городо́в; 2) лесо́в; 3) рек; 4) озёр; 5) гор; 6) совреме́нных худо́жников; 7) изве́стных писа́телей; 8) интере́сных мест

Exercise 43

1) Све́та приглаша́ет Джо́на в теа́тр. 2) Рома́н Харито́нов приглаша́ет Джо́на в спорти́вный клуб. 3) Оле́г приглаша́ет Джо́на в ба́ню и на стадио́н. 4) Я приглаша́ю тебя́ в рестора́н. 5) Я приглаша́ю Вас на день рожде́ния. 6) Худо́жник приглаша́ет друзе́й на вы́ставку.

Exercise 45

1) са́хар и соль 2) солёные огурцы́ 3) апельси́н 4) пиро́г 5) молоко́ 6) щи 7) хлеб (и́ли пиро́г) 8) кастрю́ля 9) ви́лка

Chapter 8

Exercise 6

Он весь день чита́л кни́гу (——➤) и наконе́ц прочита́л её (∨).

Что Джон де́лал ве́чером и у́тром? (——➤) Заброни́ровал гости́ницу (∨), прочита́л СМС (∨), написа́л отве́т (∨), поза́втракал (∨), изуча́л грамма́тику (——➤).

Ра́ньше он никогда́ не вари́л ко́фе (=∨ =∨ =∨), но сего́дня свари́л (∨).

Обы́чно он не кладёт де́ньги в карма́н (=∨ =∨ =∨), но сего́дня положи́л (∨).

Он всегда́ чита́ет СМС (=∨ =∨ =∨) и сего́дня то́же прочита́л (∨).

Сейча́с он изуча́ет ру́сский язы́к (——➤), а ра́ньше он изуча́л францу́зский (——➤).

Exercise 8

1) А я уже́ посмотре́л его́. 2) А Ве́ра уже́ написа́ла его́. 3) А его́ друг уже́ вы́учил её. 4) А Анто́н уже́ реши́л её. 5) А Джон уже́ посмотре́л его́.

Exercise 9

1) … потому́ что я уже́ написа́л(а) его́. 2) … потому́ что я уже́ позвони́л(а). 3) … потому́ что я уже́ купи́л(а) его́. 4) потому́ что я уже́ реши́л(а) её. 5) … потому́ что я уже́ посмотре́л(а) его́.

Exercise 10

1) Э́ту кни́гу я чита́л два дня. 2) Грамма́тику мы изуча́ли во́семь неде́ль. 3) Я живу́ в Росси́и оди́н ме́сяц. 4) Он де́лал э́то упражне́ние одну́ мину́ту.

Exercise 19

Infinitive		учи́ть — вы́учить	вспомина́ть — вспо́мнить	говори́ть — сказа́ть	забыва́ть — забы́ть	продава́ть — прода́ть
Past (IPF)	он она́ они́	учи́л учи́ла учи́ли	вспомина́л вспомина́ла вспомина́ли	говори́л говори́ла говори́ли	забыва́л забыва́ла забыва́ли	продава́л продава́ла продава́ли
Past (PF)	он она́ они́	вы́учил вы́учила вы́учили	вспо́мнил вспо́мнила вспо́мнили	сказа́л сказа́ла сказа́ли	забы́л забы́ла забы́ли	про́дал продала́ продали́
Present (IPF)	я ты он мы вы они́	учу́ у́чишь у́чит у́чим у́чите у́чат	вспомина́ю вспомина́ешь вспомина́ет вспомина́ем вспомина́ете вспомина́ют	говорю́ говори́шь говори́т говори́м говори́те говоря́т	забыва́ю забыва́ешь забыва́ет забыва́ем забыва́ете забыва́ют	продаю́ продаёшь продаёт продаём продаёте продаю́т
Future (PF)	я ты он мы вы они́	вы́учу вы́учишь вы́учит вы́учим вы́учите вы́учат	вспо́мню вспо́мнишь вспо́мнит вспо́мним вспо́мните вспо́мнят	скажу́ ска́жешь ска́жет ска́жем ска́жете ска́жут	забу́ду забу́дешь забу́дет забу́дем забу́дете забу́дут	прода́м прода́шь прода́ст продади́м продади́те продаду́т

Imperative (IPF) **Imperative (PF)**	ты вы ты вы	учи́! учи́те! вы́учи! вы́учите!	вспомина́й! вспомина́йте! вспо́мни! вспо́мните!	говори́! говори́те! скажи́! скажи́те!	забыва́й! забыва́йте! забу́дь! забу́дьте!	продава́й! продава́йте! прода́й! прода́йте!

Infinitive		переводи́ть — перевести	понима́ть — поня́ть	отдыха́ть — отдохну́ть	класть — положи́ть	брать — взять
Past (IPF) **Past (PF)**	он она́ они́ он она́ они́	переводи́л переводи́ла переводи́ли перевёл перевела́ перевели́	понима́л понима́ла понима́ли по́нял поняла́ по́няли	отдыха́л отдыха́ла отдыха́ли отдохну́л отдохну́ла отдохну́ли	клал кла́ла кла́ли положи́л положи́ла положи́ли	брал брала́ бра́ли взял взяла́ взя́ли
Present (IPF) **Future (PF)**	я ты он мы вы они́ я ты он мы вы они́	перевожу́ перево́дишь перево́дит перево́дим перево́дите перево́дят переведу́ переведёшь переведёт переведём переведёте переведу́т	понима́ю понима́ешь понима́ет понима́ем понима́ете понима́ют пойму́ поймёшь поймёт поймём поймёте пойму́т	отдыха́ю отдыха́ешь отдыха́ет отдыха́ем отдыха́ете отдыха́ют отдохну́ отдохнёшь отдохнёт отдохнём отдохнёте отдохну́т	кладу́ кладёшь кладёт кладём кладёте кладу́т положу́ поло́жишь поло́жит поло́жим поло́жите поло́жат	беру́ берёшь берёт берём берёте беру́т возьму́ возьмёшь возьмёт возьмём возьмёте возьмут
Imperative (IPF) **Imperative (PF)**	ты вы ты вы	переводи́! переводи́те! переведи́! переведи́те!	понима́й! понима́йте! пойми́! пойми́те!	отдыха́й! отдыха́йте! отдохни́! отдохни́те!	клади́! клади́те! положи́! положи́те!	бери́! бери́те! возьми́! возьми́те!

Exercise 24

1) Анто́н рабо́тает на заво́де с Петро́м. 2) Са́ша у́чится в шко́ле с дру́гом Алекса́ндром. 3) Рома́н Никола́евич отдыха́ет на мо́ре с жено́й и детьми́. 4) Татья́на за́втракает в кафе́ с друзья́ми. 5) Е́ва е́дет в Ита́лию с до́чкой.

Exercise 25

1) Анто́н рабо́тает на заво́де с ним. 2) Са́ша у́чится в шко́ле с ним. 3) Рома́н Никола́евич отдыха́ет на мо́ре с ни́ми. 4) Татья́на у́жинает в кафе́ с ни́ми. 5) Е́ва е́дет в Ита́лию с ней.

Exercise 28

1) Ла́мпы нахо́дятся (вися́т) на потолке́, над стола́ми. 2) Ча́шки, таре́лки, ло́жки нахо́дятся (стоя́т) в шкафа́х, на по́лках. 3) Ва́зы с цвета́ми нахо́дятся (стоя́т) на о́кнах. 4) Пе́чка нахо́дится (стои́т) в углу́. 5) Официа́нт нахо́дится (стои́т) за барно́й сто́йкой. 6) Больши́е часы́ нахо́дятся (вися́т) на стене́ ме́жду кре́слами. 7) Шкафы́ нахо́дятся (стоя́т) ме́жду о́кнами. 8) Занаве́ски нахо́дятся (вися́т) на о́кнах.

Exercise 31

1) чай с варе́ньем 2) бу́лка с ма́слом 3) пиро́г с ры́бой 4) ко́фе со сли́вками

Exercise 35

Худо́жник рису́ет карандашо́м. Шко́льник пи́шет ру́чкой. Учи́тель исправля́ет оши́бки кра́сной ру́чкой. Фото́граф фотографи́рует фотоаппара́том. Лю́ди слу́шают уша́ми. Ка́ждый челове́к ду́мает голово́й. Роди́тели лю́бят се́рдцем.

Exercise 42

1) Анто́н явля́ется инжене́ром. 2) Ле́то явля́ется хоро́шим сезо́ном. 3) Москва́ явля́ется столи́цей Росси́и. 4) Вашингто́н явля́ется столи́цей Соединённых Шта́тов Аме́рики.

Exercise 44

1) Алекса́ндр Янг занима́ется исто́рией. 2) Ма́ма Джо́на занима́ется карти́нами и фотогра́фией. 3) Оле́г занима́ется би́знесом. 4) Ма́ша занима́ется эколо́гией и биоло́гией. 5) Ста́рший брат Ма́ши занима́ется компью́терами. 6) Па́па Ма́ши занима́ется маши́нами. 7) Сестра́ Ма́ши занима́ется му́зыкой.

Exercise 46

Superlative	беле́йший са́мый бе́лый	нове́йший са́мый но́вый	вкусне́йший са́мый вку́сный	____ са́мый большо́й	старе́йший са́мый ста́рый	____
Comparative	беле́е	нове́е	вкусне́е	бо́льше	старе́е	ста́рше
0	бе́лый	но́вый	вку́сный	большо́й	ста́рый	ста́рший

Exercise 47

1) Алекса́ндр ста́рше, чем Джон. 2) Ма́ша моло́же, чем Джон. 3) Э́йфелева ба́шня вы́ше, чем Лувр. 4) Дере́вня ти́ше, чем го́род. 5) Э́та бума́га беле́е, чем снег. 6) Америка́нец говори́т по-англи́йски лу́чше, чем ру́сский. 7) Джоа́н Ро́улинг поёт ху́же, чем Аде́ль. 8) Джоа́н Ро́улинг пи́шет лу́чше, чем Аде́ль.

Exercise 50

1) У меня́ о́чень хоро́шая мука́. У меня́ мука́ лу́чше, чем в други́х рестора́нах. У меня́ лу́чшая мука́. 2) У меня́ о́чень хоро́шее ма́сло. У меня́ ма́сло лу́чше, чем в други́х рестора́нах. У меня́ лу́чшее ма́сло. 3) У меня́ о́чень хоро́шая вода́. У меня́ вода́ лу́чше, чем в други́х рестора́нах. У меня́ лу́чшая вода́.

Exercise 51

1) В Росси́и Джон познако́мился с Рома́ном, Оле́гом и Све́той. 2) Ещё в Ло́ндоне Джон познако́мился с Ма́шей. 3) Алекса́ндр познако́мил Джо́на с ру́сским языко́м. 4) Джон познако́мился в Москве́ с ру́сскими тради́циями, ру́сской едо́й.

Chapter 9

Exercise 5

В шко́ле нельзя́ спать. В де́тском па́рке нельзя́ пить алкого́льные напи́тки. На па́мятнике нельзя́ рисова́ть. В истори́ческом музе́е нельзя́ есть. В институ́те нельзя́ кури́ть. На городско́й пло́щади нельзя́ гуля́ть с соба́кой. На шоссе́ нельзя́ танцева́ть.

Exercise 6

В шко́ле нельзя́ спать, а до́ма мо́жно. В де́тском па́рке нельзя́ пить алкого́льные напи́тки, а в клу́бе мо́жно. На па́мятнике нельзя́ рисова́ть, а в ежедне́внике мо́жно. В истори́ческом музе́е нельзя́ есть, а в рестора́не мо́жно.

В институ́те нельзя́ кури́ть, а на у́лице мо́жно. На городско́й пло́щади нельзя́ гуля́ть с соба́кой, а в лесу́ мо́жно. На шоссе́ нельзя́ танцева́ть, а на конце́рте мо́жно.

Exercise 7

1) Мне на́до брони́ровать но́мер в гости́нице. 2) Нам на́до позвони́ть в гости́ницу. 3) Им необходи́мо отдыха́ть на острова́х в океа́не. 4) Тебе́ ну́жно учи́ть францу́зский язы́к. 5) Мне ну́жно жить в дере́вне. 6) Ему́ на́до мно́го занима́ться.

Exercise 8

Джон в Москве́. Ему́ ну́жно встре́титься с партнёрами. Ещё ему́ необходи́мо узна́ть информа́цию о докуме́нтах семьи́. Ему́ нельзя́ лете́ть в Ло́ндон без докуме́нтов. Ему́ нельзя́ встре́титься с Ма́шей, потому́ что она́ на пра́ктике в Каза́ни. Ему́ не на́до в теа́тр, ему́ на́до в библиоте́ку. Но Рома́н приглаша́ет его́ в теа́тр.

Exercise 9

A) Ещё ему́ необходи́мо бу́дет узна́ть информа́цию о докуме́нтах семьи́. Ему́ нельзя́ бу́дет лете́ть в Ло́ндон без докуме́нтов. Ему́ нельзя́ бу́дет встре́титься с Ма́шей, потому́ что она́ бу́дет на пра́ктике в Каза́ни. Ему́ не на́до бу́дет в теа́тр, ему́ на́до бу́дет в библиоте́ку. Но Рома́н пригласи́т его́ в теа́тр.

B) Ещё ему́ необходи́мо бы́ло узна́ть информа́цию о докуме́нтах семьи́. Ему́ нельзя́ бы́ло лете́ть в Ло́ндон без докуме́нтов. Ему́ нельзя́ бы́ло встре́титься с Ма́шей, потому́ что она́ была́ на пра́ктике в Каза́ни. Ему́ не на́до бы́ло в теа́тр, ему́ на́до бы́ло в библиоте́ку. Но Рома́н пригласи́л его́ в теа́тр.

Exercise 11

A) 1) Анто́н мно́го занима́лся на стадио́не, и **у него́** боля́т **но́ги**. 2) На у́лице бы́ло хо́лодно, и сейча́с **я** нахожу́сь до́ма и боле́ю. 3) На э́той неде́ле Мари́на не рабо́тает. **Она́** боле́ет. 4) Зимо́й **де́ти** ча́сто боле́ют. 5) У меня́ боли́т голова́. Мне на́до домо́й. 6) Ура́! **Я** уже́ не боле́ю. Я здоро́в!

B) 1) **Мне** о́чень бо́льно. **У меня́** боли́т живо́т. Мне ну́жно врача́.

2) — Что у Вас боли́т?
— Не зна́ю.
— Здесь Вам бо́льно?
— Да, здесь бо́льно.

Exercise 12

1) Мы сейча́с боле́ем. Врач даёт нам лека́рство. 2) Ка́тя — аккура́тная де́вушка, поэ́тому я всегда́ даю́ ей кни́ги и журна́лы. 3) Ма́ма не даёт нам конфе́ты, потому́ что мы не сде́лали дома́шнее зада́ние. 4) И́горь Влади́мирович, да́йте мне, пожа́луйста, ноутбу́к! Мой ноутбу́к не рабо́тает. 5) Э́то но́вая кни́га Ма́рка Леви́? Дай, пожа́луйста, почита́ть! 6) Одно́й руко́й даёт, друго́й руко́й берёт.

Exercise 13

1) Э́то мой друг. Ра́ньше я ча́сто дава́л ему́ маши́ну. И сего́дня я то́же дал ему́ маши́ну. 2) Да́рья никогда́ не даёт но́мер телефо́на. А мне вчера́ дала́. 3) Э́та компа́ния уже́ 10 лет даёт мне рабо́ту. Мы не мо́жем сейча́с дать Вам рабо́ту. 4) Мне пло́хо! Пожа́луйста, да́йте стака́н воды́! 5) У Вас есть де́ти? Никогда́ не дава́йте им спи́чки!

Exercise 18

Казими́р Мале́вич — э́то худо́жник, он писа́л карти́ны.
Фёдор Достое́вский — э́то писа́тель, он писа́л рома́ны.
Лев Толсто́й — э́то то́же писа́тель, он то́же писа́л рома́ны.
Серге́й Эйзенште́йн — э́то режиссёр, он снима́л кино́.
Константи́н Станисла́вский — э́то театра́льный режиссёр, он ста́вил спекта́кли.
Моде́ст Му́соргский — э́то компози́тор, он писа́л му́зыку.
Пётр Чайко́вский — э́то то́же компози́тор, он то́же писа́л му́зыку.
Фёдор Шаля́пин — э́то певе́ц, он пел ру́сские наро́дные пе́сни и а́рии из о́пер.

Гали́на Ула́нова — э́то балери́на, она́ танцева́ла на сце́не Большо́го теа́тра.

Ма́йя Плисе́цкая — э́то то́же балери́на, она́ то́же на сце́не Большо́го теа́тра.

Exercise 23

Infinitive	**идти́**				**ходи́ть**			
Present	я ты он, она́, оно́	иду́ идёшь идёт	мы вы они́	идём идёте иду́т	я ты он, она́, оно́	хожу́ хо́дишь хо́дит	мы вы они́	ходи́м хо́дите хо́дят
Past	он она́ оно́	шёл шла шло	они́	шли	он она́ оно́	ходи́л ходи́ла ходи́ло	они́	ходи́ли
Imperative	ты	иди́!	вы	иди́те!	ты	ходи́!	вы	ходи́те!

Exercise 25

1) Ты ходи́л вчера́ в теа́тр на бале́т «Лебеди́ное о́зеро»? 2) Здра́вствуй, Андре́й! Куда́ ты идёшь? 3) Я люблю́ ходи́ть пешко́м. 4) Сего́дня Ма́рта идёт в университе́т пе́рвый раз. 5) Ка́ждый день студе́нты хо́дят на заня́тия. 6) У нас ко́нчилось молоко́. И я иду́ в магази́н купи́ть молока́. 7) Ка́ждый день я хожу́ в магази́н.

Exercise 28

А) 1) Я иду́ к Кремлю́. 2) Актёр идёт к Большо́му теа́тру. 3) Анто́н идёт к Кра́сной пло́щади. 4) Мари́на идёт к э́тому но́вому зда́нию. 5) Мы идём к интере́сным па́мятникам. 6) Го́сти иду́т к на́шему до́му.

В) 1) Я иду́ к нему́. 2) Актёр идёт к нему́. 3) Анто́н идёт к ней. 4) Мари́на идёт к нему́. 5) Мы идём к ним. 6) Го́сти иду́т к нему́.

Глава́ 10

Упражне́ние 3

Я от до́ма отошёл.	Мне **на́до отойти́** от до́ма.
И по у́лице пошёл.	Мне **на́до пойти́** по у́лице.
Я в кио́ск **зашёл** на миг.	Мне **на́до зайти́** в кио́ск на миг.
Перешёл через доро́гу.	Мне **на́до перейти́** через доро́гу.
Через парк пото́м **прошёл**.	Мне **на́до** пото́м **пройти́** через парк.
Там я лу́жу **обошёл**.	Мне **на́до обойти́** там лу́жу.
Ми́мо Пу́шкина **прошёл**.	Мне **на́до пройти́** ми́мо Пу́шкина.
Так **дошёл** до магази́на.	Мне **на́до дойти́** до магази́на.
Магази́н весь **обошёл**.	Мне **на́до обойти́** весь магази́н.
Познако́мился, **ушёл**.	Мне **на́до уйти́**.
Домо́й **пошёл** обра́тно я.	Мне **на́до пойти́** обра́тно домо́й.
Вот я к до́му **подошёл**.	Мне **на́до подойти́** к до́му.
Дверь откры́л, в подъе́зд **вошёл**.	Мне **на́до войти́** в подъе́зд.
Я по ле́стнице **подня́лся**.	Мне **на́до подня́ться** по ле́стнице.
Позвони́л. Домо́й **пришёл**!	Мне **на́до позвони́ть**. Мне **на́до прийти́** домо́й.

Упражне́ние 4

Он **выхо́дит** из до́ма, **отхо́дит** от до́ма, **идёт** по у́лице, он **захо́дит** в кио́ск, **перехо́дит** через доро́гу, **прохо́дит** через парк, там **обхо́дит** лу́жу, **прохо́дит** ми́мо Пу́шкина, **дохо́дит** до магази́на, **обхо́дит** магази́н, **ухо́дит**, **идёт** обра́тно домо́й, **подхо́дит** к до́му, **вхо́дит** в подъе́зд, **прихо́дит** домо́й.

Упражне́ние 5

е́хать — е́здить: 1) Куда́ сейча́с е́дет Оле́г? Он е́дет в Истори́ческий музе́й. Он уже́ е́здил туда́ вчера́. Но он бу́дет е́здить туда́ ка́ждый день, потому́ что он экскурсово́д. 2) Сего́дня у́тром Михаи́л е́дет в институ́т, а Ма́ша е́дет в бале́тную шко́лу. Михаи́л е́здит в институ́т, потому́ что он студе́нт. Ма́ша о́чень лю́бит бале́т, поэ́тому она́ е́здит в бале́тную шко́лу.

лете́ть — лета́ть: 1) В э́том году́ Пётр Ива́нович с жено́й летя́т на юг отдыха́ть. В Со́чи они́ обы́чно лета́ют на самолёте. 2) Мой брат бу́дет пило́том и у́чится лета́ть на самолёте. Сего́дня он пе́рвый раз лета́ет без инстру́ктора.

нести́ — носи́ть: 1) Я ду́маю, э́тот молодо́й челове́к в краси́вом костю́ме идёт на день рожде́ния, потому́ что он несёт в рука́х цветы́ и торт. 2) Когда́ ребёнок ма́ленький, ма́ма но́сит его́ на рука́х.

вести́ — води́ть: 1) Ка́ждое у́тро Ви́ктор Ива́нович во́дит вну́ка в де́тский сад. Но сего́дня Ви́ктор Ива́нович боле́ет, и вну́ка ведёт его́ жена́ А́нна Петро́вна. 2) Ната́ша пе́рвый раз прие́хала в Москву́. Сейча́с сёстры Ве́ра и Ю́лия веду́т её на экску́рсию в Кремль. Ве́ра и Ю́лия бу́дут води́ть её по го́роду всю неде́лю.

везти́ — вози́ть: 1) Андре́й рабо́тает в магази́не. Он во́зит проду́кты на маши́не. Сего́дня он везёт в магази́н со́ки и минера́льную во́ду. 2) Вот аэропо́рт. Смотри́те, э́тот челове́к везёт сувени́ры из Ло́ндона. А э́та же́нщина везёт краси́вую ва́зу из А́фрики. А вот железнодоро́жный вокза́л. Тётя Зи́на е́дет из дере́вни в го́род и везёт пода́рки вну́ку и вну́чке. Тётя Зи́на во́зит пода́рки вну́кам ка́ждую о́сень.

Упражене́ние 7

1. **Сего́дня у́тром** он вы́ехал из до́ма, он отъе́хал от до́ма, пое́хал по у́лице, зае́хал в кио́ск, перее́хал через доро́гу, пото́м прое́хал через парк, там объе́хал лу́жу, прое́хал ми́мо Пу́шкина, дое́хал до магази́на, весь магази́н объе́хал, уе́хал. Он пое́хал обра́тно домо́й. Подъе́хал к до́му, въе́хал в подъезд. Он прие́хал домо́й!

2. **Ка́ждое у́тро** он выезжа́ет из до́ма, отъезжа́ет от до́ма, е́дет по у́лице, заезжа́ет в кио́ск, переезжа́ет через доро́гу, пото́м проезжа́ет через парк, там объезжа́ет лу́жу, проезжа́ет ми́мо Пу́шкина, доезжа́ет до магази́на, весь магази́н объезжа́ет, уезжа́ет. Он е́дет обра́тно домо́й. Подъезжа́ет к до́му, въезжа́ет в подъезд. Он приезжа́ет домо́й!

3. **Сего́дня у́тром** он вы́нес из до́ма большу́ю су́мку, он отнёс её от до́ма, понёс её по у́лице, занёс в кио́ск, перенёс через доро́гу, пото́м пронёс через парк, там обнёс вокруг (!) лу́жи, пронёс ми́мо Пу́шкина, донёс до магази́на, магазин весь — унёс (су́мку из магази́на). Он понёс (су́мку) обра́тно домо́й. Поднёс к до́му, внёс су́мку в подъе́зд. Он принёс су́мку домо́й!

4. **Ка́ждый день** он выно́сит из до́ма большу́ю су́мку, он отно́сит её от до́ма, несёт по у́лице, зано́сит в кио́ск, перено́сит через доро́гу, пото́м проно́сит через парк, там обно́сит су́мку вокру́г лу́жи, проно́сит ми́мо Пу́шкина, доно́сит до магази́на, магази́н весь — уно́сит (су́мку из магази́на). Он несёт (су́мку) обра́тно домо́й. Подно́сит к до́му, вно́сит су́мку в подъе́зд. Он прино́сит су́мку домо́й!

5. **Сего́дня у́тром** он вы́вел бра́та из до́ма, он отвёл его́ от до́ма, повёл по у́лице, завёл в кио́ск, перевёл через доро́гу, пото́м провёл через парк, там обвёл бра́та вокру́г (!) лу́жи, провёл ми́мо Пу́шкина, довёл до магази́на, магази́н весь — увёл (бра́та из магази́на). Он вёл бра́та обра́тно домо́й. Подвёл к до́му, ввёл бра́та в подъе́зд. Он привёл бра́та домо́й!

6. **Ка́ждый день** он выво́дит бра́та из до́ма, отво́дит его́ от до́ма, ведёт по у́лице, заво́дит в кио́ск, переводи́т через доро́гу, пото́м прово́дит через парк, там обво́дит бра́та вокру́г лу́жи (!), прово́дит ми́мо Пу́шкина, дово́дит до магази́на, магази́н весь — уво́дит (бра́та из магази́на). Он ведёт бра́та обра́тно домо́й. Подвёл к до́му, ввёл бра́та в подъе́зд. Он привёл бра́та домо́й!

7. **Сего́дня у́тром** он вы́вез су́мку из до́ма, отвёз её от до́ма, повёз по у́лице, завёз в кио́ск, перевёз через доро́гу, пото́м провёз через парк, там обвёз су́мку вокру́г лу́жи (!), провёз ми́мо Пу́шкина, довёз до магази́на, магази́н весь — увёз (су́мку из магази́на). Он повёз (су́мку) обра́тно домо́й. Подвёз к до́му, ввёз су́мку в подъе́зд. Он привёз су́мку домо́й!

8. **Ка́ждый день** он выво́зит су́мку из до́ма, отво́зит её от до́ма, везёт по у́лице, заво́зит в кио́ск, перево́зит через доро́гу, пото́м прово́зит через парк, там обво́зит су́мку вокру́г лу́жи (!), прово́зит ми́мо Пу́шкина, дово́зит до магази́на, магази́н весь — уво́зит (су́мку из магази́на). Он везёт (су́мку) обра́тно домо́й. Подво́зит к до́му, вво́зит су́мку в подъе́зд. Он приво́зит су́мку домо́й!

Упражне́ние 8

В суббо́ту ве́чером мы должны́ бы́ли идти́ в теа́тр на бале́т «Роме́о и Джулье́тта». Бале́т был в 18:30. Мы вы́шли из до́ма в 5 часо́в, потому́ что мы не зна́ли, ско́лько вре́мени ну́жно е́хать. Мы подошли́ к авто́бусной остано́вке и жда́ли авто́бус. Вот прие́хал авто́бус. Мы се́ли и пое́хали. Через 20 мину́т мы дое́хали до ста́нции метро́. Мы вы́шли из авто́буса и вошли́ в метро́. Когда́ мы вошли́ в ваго́н, мы уви́дели там друзе́й. Они́ то́же е́хали в теа́тр. Все вме́сте мы дое́хали до на́шей ста́нции, вы́шли на у́лицу и пошли́ к теа́тру. Когда́ мы подошли́ к теа́тру, мы уви́дели, что о́коло теа́тра нет люде́й. Мы по́няли, что пришли́ ра́но. Но мы вошли́ в теа́тр, зашли́ в гардеро́б и пошли́ в театра́льное кафе́ пить ко́фе.

Упражне́ние 10

1) Дире́ктор пришёл в кабине́т. Совеща́ние начина́ется. 2) Дире́ктор сказа́л: «Пожа́луйста, внима́ние!» Совеща́ние начало́сь (идёт). 3) Дире́ктор подво́дит ито́ги. Совеща́ние зака́нчивается. 4) Дире́ктор сказа́л: «Всем спаси́бо, до за́втра!» — и вы́шел. Совеща́ние зако́нчилось.

Упражне́ние 11

Сейча́с 6:00. Институ́т закры́т.
Сейча́с 10:00. Институ́т откры́т.
Сейча́с 12:00. Ночно́й клуб закры́т.
Сейча́с 23:00. Ночно́й клуб откры́т.
Сейча́с 13:00. Вре́мя обе́да. Ка́сса закры́та.
Сейча́с 14:00. Обе́д зако́нчился. Ка́сса откры́та.
Зима́. Ле́тние дома́ о́тдыха закры́ты.
Воскресе́нье. Ба́нки закры́ты.
Э́то круглосу́точный магази́н. Он всегда́ откры́т.
Э́то дежу́рная апте́ка. Она́ всегда́ откры́та.

Упражне́ние 18

1) у себя́ до́ма; 2) ря́дом с собо́й; 3) себе́; 4) о себе́; 5) я люблю́ себя́; 6) Мари́на лю́бит себя́.

Упражне́ние 19

1) Скро́мный челове́к не лю́бит говори́ть о себе́. 2) Анто́н пришёл к себе́ домо́й. 3) Здоро́вый челове́к не говори́т с собо́й. 4) Эгои́ст лю́бит то́лько себя́. 5) Анто́н пошёл в теа́тр и пригласи́л с собо́й подру́гу. 6) Ве́чером Джон пригото́вил себе́ (для себя́) у́жин. 7) Я подари́л себе́ но́вый компью́тер.

Упражне́ние 21

1) пра́вда; 2) непра́вда; 3) непра́вда; 4) пра́вда; 5) непра́вда; 6) пра́вда; 7) пра́вда.

Упражне́ние 24

1) simultaneous; 2) consecutive; 3) consecutive; 4) simultaneous.

Упражне́ние 25

1) я пла́ваю в мо́ре, гуля́ю по пля́жу, мно́го сплю, чита́ю, мно́го пью и ем, гото́влю, ду́маю о жи́зни, фотографи́рую; 2) я пью мно́го ко́фе, гуля́ю по Интерне́ту, ча́сто смотрю́ по́чту, разгова́риваю по телефо́ну, ду́маю об о́тдыхе; 3) де́ти уже́ пообе́дали, сде́лали дома́шнее зада́ние; 4) мы захоте́ли прочита́ть рома́н Льва Толсто́го; 5) он ду́мает то́лько о ней; 6) роди́тели по́няли, что начали́сь пробле́мы; 7) одни́ студе́нты слу́шали, други́е студе́нты спа́ли, а тре́тьи — игра́ли в компью́терную игру́.

Глава́ 11

Упражне́ние 1

1) Э́то собо́р, кото́рый стои́т ря́дом с Кремлём. 2) Э́то по́вар, кото́рый гото́вит обе́д в рестора́не. 3) Э́то спортсме́н, кото́рый прибежа́л пе́рвым. 4) Э́то певи́ца, кото́рая поёт в Большо́м теа́тре. 5) Э́то вор, кото́рый берёт не свои́ ве́щи. 6) Э́то Джон, англича́нин, кото́рый неда́вно прие́хал в Росси́ю. 7) Алекса́ндр Янг — учёный-исто́рик,

кото́рый интересу́ется исто́рией Росси́и. 8) Бенджами́н Янг — де́душка Джо́на, кото́рый вёз докуме́нты из Санкт-Петербу́рга в Москву́. 9) Э́то же́нщина, кото́рая помогла́ Джо́ну на у́лице.

Упражне́ние 2

1) Э́то дом Пашко́ва, в кото́ром был Джон. 2) Э́то Андре́й, кото́рого Джон встре́тил в до́ме Пашко́ва. 3) Джон звони́т Ма́ше, с кото́рой он познако́мился в Интерне́те. 4) Э́то докуме́нты де́душки Бенджами́на, о кото́рых ду́мают Джон и Алекса́ндр. 5) Э́то буты́лка англи́йского ви́ски, кото́рую Джон привёз ру́сским колле́гам.

Упражне́ние 3

1) Э́то ночно́й клуб. В э́тот клуб я хожу́ ка́ждую суббо́ту. 2) Я зна́ю одного́ челове́ка. Э́тот челове́к лю́бит танцева́ть хип-хо́п. 3) Познако́мьтесь с мои́м но́вым дру́гом. Об э́том дру́ге я вам расска́зывал вчера́. 4) Я ча́сто звоню́ подру́ге. С э́той подру́гой я познако́мился в Москве́. 5) На́до осторо́жно переходи́ть доро́гу. По э́той доро́ге е́дет мно́го маши́н. 6) Вот тот дом. Из э́того до́ма мы перее́хали в но́вую кварти́ру. 7) Я люблю́ рисова́ть ста́рое о́зеро. Вокру́г э́того о́зера я гуля́ю ле́том.

Упражне́ние 4

1) таре́лка. 2) ↓ телеви́зор. 2) → теа́тр. 3) перехо́д. 4) авто́бус. 5) стол. 6) Лувр. 7) дом. 8) кастрю́ля. 9) газе́та. 10) доро́га. 11) маши́на. 12) Голливу́д. 13) телефо́н. 14) Москва́. 15) самолёт. 16) Арба́т.

Упражне́ние 7

1) Ура́! Я нашёл кошелёк! 2) Я потеря́л свой зонт. Пожа́луйста, помоги́те мне найти́ его́. 3) Архео́логи и́щут дре́вние города́. 4) Я о́чень невнима́тельный челове́к. Я ча́сто теря́ю свои́ ве́щи. 5) Хоро́шего дру́га легко́ потеря́ть, но тру́дно найти́. 6) Мне о́чень нра́вится иска́ть отве́ты на тру́дные вопро́сы.

Упражне́ние 9

1 д); 2 е); 3 г); 4 в); 5 а); 6 б).

Упражне́ние 10

1) В бу́лочной. 2) Из Москвы. 3) В Санкт-Петербу́рг. 4) 28 января́ 1917 го́да он е́хал из Санкт-Петербу́рга в Москву́. 5) Ему́ ну́жно бы́ло прие́хать с докуме́нтами на вокза́л в Москве́.

Упражне́ние 11

2) Он е́здил ка́ждую неде́лю к императору. 3) Он е́здил ка́ждую неде́лю от Фили́ппова. 4) 28 января́ 1917 го́да он е́хал от импера́тора к челове́ку на вокза́ле. 5) Он до́лжен был прие́хать с докуме́нтами к челове́ку на вокза́ле.

Упражне́ние 12

С) Я Еле́на. Сего́дня я ходи́ла в го́сти. Я пришла́ к подру́ге Ка́те, в дом № 10, на у́лицу Ле́нина.

У Ка́ти, в до́ме № 10, на у́лице Ле́нина, я была́ оди́н час и пошла́ от Ка́ти, из до́ма № 10, с у́лицы Ле́нина, к подру́ге Жа́нне, в гости́ницу, на пло́щадь Достое́вского.

У Жа́нны в гости́нице, на пло́щади Достое́вского, мы смотре́ли фильм.

Пото́м мы пошли́ к друзья́м Ко́сте и Се́ве в кафе́ «Рандеву́», на проспе́кт Побе́ды.

От Ко́сти и Се́вы, из кафе́ «Рандеву́», с проспе́кта Побе́ды, Жа́нна пошла́ домо́й к Ка́те, в дом № 10, на у́лицу Ле́нина, а я пошла́ к себе́ домо́й.

Упражне́ние 13

А) 1) Кто́-то пришёл и стои́т за две́рью. 2) «Что лежи́т там на по́лке?» — «Э́то кака́я-то кни́га». 3) Э́то был како́й-то мужчи́на. Я не ви́дела его́ лица́. 4) «Где живёт медве́дь?» — « Не зна́ю то́чно. Где́-то в лесу́». 5) Вчера́ кто́-то забра́л мой слова́рь. 6) Моя жена́ вчера́ потеря́ла телефо́н где́-то здесь.

В) 1) Кто́-нибудь зна́ет, где железнодоро́жный вокза́л? 2) Ску́чно! Да́йте почита́ть како́й-нибудь журна́л. 3) Кто́-нибудь из ва́шей гру́ппы занима́ется спо́ртом? 4) В э́том до́ме я где́-нибудь могу́ отдохну́ть? 5) Вы бы́ли когда́-нибудь в Аргенти́не? 6) Расска́жите что́-нибудь о свое́й стране́. 7) Вы когда́-нибудь прие́дете в Росси́ю ещё раз? 8) О́льга, ты ви́дела где́-нибудь мой па́спорт? 9) Вы когда́-нибудь теря́ли го́лову?

Упражне́ние 14

1) «Кто сейча́с вы́шел из ко́мнаты?» — «Я не ви́дел. Кто́-то в тёмном костю́ме». 2) «К кому́ Ивано́вы пойду́т сего́дня ве́чером?» — «Я не по́мню. К кому́-то из свои́х колле́г». 3) «Чего́ здесь нет?» — «Чего́-то о́чень ну́жного». 4) «Э́то вку́сно?» — «Я ещё не поняла́. Э́то что́-то солёное». 5) «Чем сейча́с занима́ется профе́ссор Бело́в?» — «Я не зна́ю то́чно. Но че́м-то о́чень интере́сным». 6) «О ком спра́шивал преподава́тель?» — «О ко́м-то из студе́нтов». 7) «О чём ду́мает Ваш кот?» — «Мой кот всегда́ ду́мает о чём-то о́чень ва́жном».

Упражне́ние 15

1) Вы ду́маете о чём-нибудь (о ко́м-нибудь), когда́ спи́те? 2) Вы пи́шете кому́-нибудь пи́сьма на бума́ге? 3) Вы звони́те кому́-нибудь в А́фрику? 4) Вы теря́ли что́-нибудь в метро́? 5) Вы говори́ли о чём-нибу́дь ва́жном с Ва́шим дру́гом? 6) Вы ду́маете о чём-нибудь, когда́ отдыха́ете на мо́ре? 7) Вы зна́ете кого́-нибудь в Олимпи́йском комите́те? 8) Вы зна́ете что́-нибудь стра́шное о Ва́ших колле́гах?

Упражне́ние 16

A) 1) ничего́ не интересу́ет; 2) ни о чём не говори́ли; 3) ниче́м не занима́лся; 4) ничего́ не ви́дел; 5) ничего́ не чита́л; 6) ничего́ не бойтся.

B) 1) ни в како́й (!) рабо́те не уча́ствовал; 2) никака́я по́мощь не нужна́; 3) никаки́е иностра́нные языки́ не зна́ет; 4) никако́й вопрос не́ был тру́дным для меня́.

C) 1) никуда́ не пое́ду; 2) нигде́ не отдыха́ли; 3) я никогда́ не отдыха́л в Крыму́; 4) ниотку́да не получи́л; 5) никуда́ не пойдём.

Упражне́ние 17

A) 1) Мой сосе́д — студе́нт консервато́рии, поэ́тому он до́лжен игра́ть класси́ческую му́зыку. 2) Они́ актёры. За́втра им ну́жно (на́до) игра́ть на сце́не. Сего́дня они́ должны́ учи́ть стихи́ всю ночь. 3) Кни́га, кото́рая мне нужна́, сто́ит 2000 рубле́й, и я до́лжен купи́ть её. 4) Мне ну́жно э́ту маши́ну, и я до́лжен мно́го рабо́тать. 5) Ей бу́дут нужны́ но́вые бе́лые ту́фли и пла́тье. Ско́ро у неё бу́дет сва́дьба.

B) 1) «До́ктор, мне мо́жно игра́ть на скри́пке?» — «Да, Ва́ша рука́ уже́ здоро́ва». 2) «Ита́к, Вы хоти́те рабо́тать в орке́стре. На чём Вы мо́жете игра́ть?» — «Я могу́ игра́ть на скри́пке». 3) Здесь мо́жно переходи́ть доро́гу. Но мы не мо́жем перейти её, потому́ что здесь мно́го маши́н. Стои́м и ждём уже́ 15 мину́т.

Упражне́ние 18

1) Noun + suffix -H- = adjective: зако́нный, це́нный; 2) Noun + suffix -ЯН- = adjective: сере́бряный; 3) Noun + ending -ОЙ = adjective: золото́й; 4) Root1 + Root2 = new word: драгоце́нный; 5) Adjective+ suffix -ОСТЬ = abstract noun: це́нность, драгоце́нность.

Упражне́ние 19

зако́нность, ва́жность, мо́лодость, ста́рость, осторо́жность

Упражне́ние 22

1) 25 % Джо́ну, 25 % Андре́ю 2) 12,5 % цены́ кла́да Джо́ну, 12,5 % цены́ кла́да Андре́ю.

Упражне́ние 25

1) Карти́на «Джоко́нда» — э́то дорога́я карти́на. 2) Клад Наполео́на — э́то дорога́я нахо́дка. 3) Купцы́ — э́то бога́тые лю́ди. 4) Не рабо́тать и жить хорошо́ мо́гут бога́тые лю́ди. 5) Обы́чно худо́жники — э́то бе́дные лю́ди. 6) Де́тская оде́жда — э́то дешёвые / дороги́е ве́щи.

Упражне́ние 27

1) На по́лке стои́т ва́за. 2) Ва́за сто́ит 500 рубле́й. 3) Э́та маши́на сто́ит до́рого. 4) Э́та маши́на стои́т на у́лице весь день. 5) В рестора́не ка́ша сто́ит 200 рубле́й. 6) На плите́ стои́т ка́ша. 7) Э́ти часы́ сто́ят 3000 рубле́й. 8) Э́ти часы́ стоя́т на столе́ в кабине́те.

Упражне́ние 28

1) б); 2) б); 3) а); 4) а).

Упражне́ние 29

1) э́тот 2) э́ти 3) э́ту 4) э́ту 5) э́ти

Упражне́ние 33

Я бизнесме́н. На рабо́те я ношу́ делову́ю оде́жду. Я не смотрю́, ско́лько сто́ит вещь. Е́сли мне комфо́ртно, то я покупа́ю её. Но, коне́чно, е́сли вещь о́чень дорога́я, то я не бу́ду покупа́ть её. Сейча́с мне ну́жно купи́ть пиджа́к и га́лстук, потому́ что мне ну́жно встре́титься с росси́йскими колле́гами. Я пошёл в магази́н оде́жды для мужчи́н и купи́л не о́чень дорого́й, но о́чень комфо́ртный пиджа́к. Га́лстук я то́же купи́л в э́том магази́не.

Глава́ 12

Упражне́ние 4

кра́сное со́лнышко — хоро́ший (краси́вый) челове́к; кра́сная де́вица — краси́вая де́вушка; чёрный день — плохо́й день; чёрная душа́ — у челове́ка плоха́я, зла́я душа́; бе́лый день — хоро́ший день; се́рый день — гру́стный (ску́чный) день; се́рый челове́к — ску́чный (гру́стный) челове́к; се́рое лицо́ — больно́е лицо́; ро́зовые очки́ — романти́чный челове́к но́сит ро́зовые очки́; зелёный ма́льчик — о́чень молодо́й челове́к.

Упражне́ние 5

1) люблю́ 2) лю́бят 3) не нра́вится 4) люблю́ 5) нра́вится 6) нра́вятся

Упражне́ние 12

1) Э́то па́мятник, кото́рый сде́лал Этье́н Фальконе́. 2) Э́то па́мятник, кото́рый до́лжен стать си́мволом. 3) Э́то па́мятник, пе́рвый вариа́нт кото́рого не понра́вился Екатери́не II. 4) Э́то па́мятник, для кото́рого Фальконе́ до́лго не мог найти́ о́браз. 5) Э́то па́мятник, в пе́рвом вариа́нте кото́рого Пётр I стоя́л на коло́нне. 6) Э́то па́мятник, кото́рый бу́дет нетрадицио́нным и необы́чным. 7) Э́то па́мятник, кото́рый в плоху́ю пого́ду как живо́й.

Упражне́ние 13

строи́тель — челове́к, кото́рый стро́ит; води́тель — челове́к, кото́рый во́дит маши́ну; жи́тель — челове́к, кото́рый где-то живёт; бу́лочник — челове́к, кото́рый гото́вит (печёт) бу́лки и хлеб; тайни́к — ме́сто, где нахо́дится клад; шутни́к — челове́к, кото́рый говори́т шу́тки.

Упражне́ние 15

1) Они́ иду́т в библиоте́ку, что́бы узна́ть о докуме́нтах. 2) Они́ заполня́ют анке́ту посети́теля, что́бы стать посети́телями библиоте́ки. 3) Они́ пришли́ в библиоте́ку, что́бы посмотре́ть катало́г.

Упражне́ние 16

1) Андре́й хо́чет, что́бы Джон позвони́л отцу́. 2) Андре́й хо́чет, что́бы Джон попроси́л профе́ссорский докуме́нт для Джо́на и Андре́я. 3) Джон хо́чет, что́бы оте́ц помо́г сде́лать профе́ссорский докуме́нт для него́ и Андре́я. 4) Алекса́ндр хо́чет, что́бы Джон нашёл информа́цию о докуме́нтах из бу́лочной Фили́ппова. 5) Алекса́ндр хо́чет, что́бы Джон посети́л Росси́йскую национа́льную библиоте́ку.

Упражне́ние 18

1) Джон идёт в коне́ц за́ла. Сейча́с он нахо́дится в конце́ за́ла. 2) Пото́м они́ вме́сте иду́т в середи́ну за́ла. Сейча́с они́ нахо́дятся в середи́не за́ла.

Упражне́ние 19

3, 4, 12, 1, 2, 8, 5, 10, 11, 9, 7, 6, 13, 14.

Упражне́ние 20

B) **Санкт-Петербу́рг**

Санкт-Петербу́рг — о́чень краси́вый го́род. Он не о́чень ста́рый — ему́ 300 лет, — но о́чень интере́сный.

Царь Пётр I хоте́л, что́бы э́тот го́род стал но́вой столи́цей но́вой Росси́и.

Гла́вная у́лица Санкт-Петербу́рга — э́то Не́вский проспе́кт. Здесь мно́го прекра́сных зда́ний и дворцо́в. У ка́ждого до́ма своя́ исто́рия. Я ма́ло успе́л уви́деть, но мне о́чень понра́вился Зи́мний дворе́ц — резиде́нция ру́сских царе́й. Сейча́с там музе́й Эрмита́ж.

Говоря́т, что ря́дом с Санкт-Петербу́ргом есть ца́рские дворцы́. Они́ нахо́дятся в музе́йных ко́мплексах Петерго́ф, Ораниенба́ум, Ца́рское Село́, Па́вловск. Там о́чень краси́вые сады́ и фонта́ны, необы́чная архитекту́ра. Но у меня́ не́ было вре́мени э́то уви́деть, к сожале́нию.

Петербу́рг — э́то Се́верная Вене́ция, здесь бо́лее 90 (девяно́ста) рек и кана́лов.

Э́то центр нау́ки и культу́ры. Здесь нахо́дится оди́н из старе́йших в Росси́и университе́тов.

И да, ещё я по́нял: здесь своя́ атмосфе́ра. Сюда́ приезжа́ют тури́сты из ра́зных стран. И любо́му челове́ку здесь интере́сно и комфо́ртно. Э́то действи́тельно прекра́сный го́род. Но не ду́май, что я говорю́ о пого́де. Пого́да в Санкт-Петербу́рге така́я же ужа́сная, как пого́да в Ло́ндоне!

Упражне́ние 21

1) Санкт-Петербу́рг — э́то го́род, о кото́ром (кото́рый)* зна́ют во всём ми́ре. 2) Санкт-Петербу́рг не ста́рый, но о́чень интере́сный го́род. 3) Не́вский проспе́кт — э́то у́лица, где (на кото́рой) мно́го прекра́сных зда́ний и дворцо́в. 4) Петербу́рг — э́то Се́верная Вене́ция, потому́ что здесь бо́лее 90 рек и кана́лов. 5) Ря́дом с Санкт-Петербу́ргом есть ца́рские дворцы́, где есть о́чень краси́вые сады́, фонта́ны, необы́чная архитекту́ра. 6) Пётр I хоте́л, что́бы Санкт-Петербу́рг стал но́вой столи́цей но́вой Росси́и. 7) Е́сли у меня́ бу́дет вре́мя, я посмотрю́ дворцы́ и сады́. 8) Нача́ло ию́ня — э́то сезо́н, когда́ вы мо́жете уви́деть бе́лые но́чи. 9) Ну́жно прие́хать в нача́ле ию́ня, что́бы уви́деть бе́лые но́чи. 10) Здесь нахо́дится оди́н их старе́йших в Росси́и университе́тов, поэ́тому Санкт-Петербу́рг — центр нау́ки и культу́ры. 11) Я по́нял, что здесь своя́ атмосфе́ра. 12) Санкт-Петербу́рг — э́то го́род, куда́ (в кото́рый) приезжа́ют тури́сты из ра́зных стран. 13) Санкт-Петербу́рг — э́то город, где (в кото́ром) любо́му челове́ку интере́сно и комфо́ртно.

Глава́ 13

Упражне́ние 2

A) 1) паде́ж № 6; 2) паде́ж № 6; 3) паде́ж № 6; 4) паде́ж № 4; 5) паде́ж № 4; 6) паде́ж № 4; 7) паде́ж № 2.

B) 1) Колле́кция сейча́с на вы́ставке в го́роде Ряза́ни. 2) Моне́ты в Ряза́ни? 3) Ты спра́шивал о Ряза́ни. 4) Тепе́рь ты сам уви́дишь Ряза́нь. 5) Когда́ вы е́дете в Ряза́нь? 6) Вы прилети́те в Ряза́нь о́чень бы́стро. 7) От Санкт-Петербу́рга до Ряза́ни по́езд е́дет 12 часо́в.

C) 1) Колле́кция сейча́с на вы́ставке в го́роде Ливерпу́ль. 2) Моне́ты в Ливерпу́ле? 3) Ты спра́шивал о Ливерпу́ле. 4) Тепе́рь ты сам уви́дишь Ливерпу́ль. 5) Когда́ вы е́дете в Ливерпу́ль? 6) Вы прилети́те в Ливерпу́ль о́чень бы́стро. 7) От Санкт-Петербу́рга до Ливерпу́ля по́езд не е́дет.

D) 1) Колле́кция сейча́с на вы́ставке в го́роде Афи́ны. 2) Моне́ты в Афи́нах? 3) Ты спра́шивал об Афи́нах. 4) Тепе́рь ты сам уви́дишь Афи́ны. 5) Когда́ вы е́дете в Афи́ны? 6) Вы прилети́те в Афи́ны о́чень бы́стро. 7) От Санкт-Петербу́рга до Афи́н по́езд не е́дет.

---

* Знать о Санкт-Петербу́рге *and* знать Санкт-Петербу́рг.

Упражне́ние 3

Андре́й спроси́л, его́ ли э́то де́вушка и́ли про́сто подру́га. Джон отве́тил, что э́то его́ учи́тель.

Андре́й спроси́л, есть ли у Джо́на семья́. Джон отве́тил, что у него́ есть ма́ма, па́па, брат, а жены́ сейча́с нет.

Джон спроси́л, есть ли семья́ у Андре́я. Андре́й отве́тил, что у него́ есть жена́ и сын.

Джон спроси́л, журнали́стка ли жена́ Андре́я. Андре́й отве́тил, что его́ жена́ рабо́тает в шко́ле, она́ учи́тель исто́рии, что они́ познако́мились, когда́ учи́лись в университе́те на истори́ческом факульте́те. И что ей не нра́вится его́ рабо́та в газе́те.

Джон спроси́л почему́. Андре́й отве́тил, что его́ жена́ говори́т, что его́ газе́та — э́то са́мая жёлтая газе́та в Москве́, что э́та газе́та желте́е со́лнца, желте́е оде́жды япо́нского импера́тора, что э́то са́мая жёлтая газе́та в ми́ре.

Джон сказа́л, что он то́же ду́мает, что быть журнали́стом — э́то не для него́ (не для Андре́я). Что Андре́й о́чень мно́го зна́ет об исто́рии.

Джон спроси́л Андре́я, почему́ он не рабо́тает в университе́те и почему́ он не занима́ется нау́кой.

Андре́й отве́тил, что э́то жизнь.

Упражне́ние 4

Каза́нь ста́рше Москвы́ и ста́рше Санкт-Петербу́рга.

Санкт-Петербу́рг моло́же Москвы́ и Каза́ни.

Упражне́ние 5

Са́мый ста́рый го́род — э́то Ки́ев. Са́мый молодо́й го́род — э́то Санкт-Петербу́рг.

Упражне́ние 7

Колле́кция + suffix -ЕР- (-ионЕ́Р-) = коллекционе́р

Коллекционе́р + suffix -ОВА- (-и́рОВА-) = коллекциони́ровать

Упражне́ние 9

Экскурсово́д сказа́ла, что́бы мы посмотре́ли университе́т, посмотре́ли собо́р Петра́ и Па́вла в сти́ле баро́кко, погуля́ли по у́лицам ста́рой Каза́ни. Она́ сказа́ла, что у́лица Кремлёвская о́чень краси́вая и что они́ мо́гут помо́чь организова́ть экску́рсию.

Упражне́ние 10

1) «Вы плани́руете Ваш о́тдых?» — «Да я всегда́ плани́рую о́тдых». — «А я никогда́ не плани́рую. Но в э́том году́ я реши́л плани́ровать».

2) «Я сове́тую Вам посмотре́ть университе́т». — «А что ещё Вы сове́туете посмотре́ть в Каза́ни?» — «Вчера́ я сове́товал(а) иностра́нцам посмотре́ть Кремлёвскую у́лицу. Она́ им о́чень понра́вилась».

3) Мы организу́ем экску́рсию. В про́шлом году́ мы организова́ли о́чень мно́го экску́рсий для иностра́нцев.

4) Она́ рису́ет Каза́нский кремль. За́втра она́ бу́дет рисова́ть па́мятник Лобаче́вскому ря́дом с университе́том.

5) На э́той у́лице в Барсело́не лю́ди танцу́ют ка́ждый ве́чер. Когда́ мы бы́ли в Барсело́не, мы то́же танцева́ли там.

6) «Я не сове́тую смотре́ть э́тот фильм». — «Почему́? Мне вчера́ его́ сове́товал мой друг. Ему́ фильм о́чень понра́вился».

7) «Вы лю́бите путеше́ствовать?» — «Да, я люблю́ путеше́ствовать». — «Где Вы обы́чно путеше́ствуете? А в э́том году́ Вы плани́руете путеше́ствовать?»

8) «Где вы ночева́ли вчера́?» — «Мы ночева́ли в гости́нице». — «А где вы ночу́ете (бу́дете ночева́ть) сего́дня?» — «Сего́дня мы ночу́ем (бу́дем ночева́ть) до́ма».

Упражне́ние 11

Ху́лио Гарси́а Ло́пес — э́то иностра́нец в Росси́и. Мы не ви́дели ни одного́ иностра́нца в Росси́и. Что мо́жно сове́товать иностра́нцу в Росси́и? Вы встреча́ли иностра́нца в Росси́и? Тру́дно быть иностра́нцем в Росси́и? Э́та кни́га об иностра́нце в Росси́и.

Упражне́ние 13

Я пришёл в теа́тр. Я был в теа́тре. Пото́м я ушёл из теа́тра. Я шёл в свою́ гости́ницу. Я не знал а́дрес гости́ницы, поэ́тому я до́лго иска́л гости́ницу. Я уви́дел большо́й краси́вый дом и мно́го люде́й. Э́то был дом Пашко́ва. Я не хоте́л идти́ в дом Пашко́ва, но я зашёл в дом. В до́ме Пашко́ва я познако́мился с Андре́ем. Он сиде́л в ко́мнате на второ́м этаже́ и ждал, когда́ зако́нчится бал. Андре́й — журнали́ст, он хоте́л фотографи́ровать. Из окна́ до́ма Пашко́ва мо́жно сде́лать хоро́шее фо́то. Андре́й ча́сто так де́лает. Э́то его́ рабо́та. Мы ночева́ли в до́ме Пашко́ва. У́тром мы ушли́ из до́ма Пашко́ва.

Упражне́ние 14

Я пришёл в теа́тр. Я был в нём. Пото́м я ушёл из теа́тра (из него́). Я шёл в свою́ гости́ницу. Я не знал её а́дрес, поэ́тому я до́лго иска́л её. Я уви́дел большо́й краси́вый дом и мно́го люде́й. Э́то был дом Пашко́ва. Я не хоте́л идти́ в него́, но я зашёл в него́. В нём я познако́мился с Андре́ем. Он сиде́л в ко́мнате на второ́м этаже́ и ждал, когда́ зако́нчится бал. Андре́й — журнали́ст, он хоте́л фотографи́ровать. Из окна́ до́ма Пашко́ва мо́жно сде́лать хоро́шее фо́то. Андре́й ча́сто так де́лает. Э́то его́ рабо́та. Мы ночева́ли в до́ме (в нём). У́тром мы ушли́ из него́.

Glossary — Слова́рь

А

а: and; but
авантюри́ст: an adventurer
авиа́ция: aviation
авто́: an auto
авто́бус: a bus
автомоби́ль (он): an automobile
а́дрес: an address
аккордео́н: an accordion
аккура́тный (-ая, -ое, -ые): tidy, neat, careful
актёр: an actor
алкого́ль (он): alcohol
алло́: hello
алфави́т: alphabet
а́рмия: army
архите́ктор: an architect
аспира́нт (-ка): a postgraduate (a female form is with the suffix -к(а))
аспиранту́ра: a graduate school
аудито́рия: a lecture hall
афи́ша: a playbill
аэропо́рт: an airport

Б

ба́бушка: a grandmother
балала́йка: a balalaika
бале́т: a ballet
бана́н: a banana
банк: a bank
ба́нка: a jar
ба́ня: bania (Russian sauna)
бар: a bar
ба́рная сто́йка: a bar
баскетбо́л: basketball
ба́шня: a tower
бе́гать (1.R.VOW): to run
бе́дный (-ая, -ое, -ые): poor
бежа́ть (SPECIAL): to run
без: without
безалкого́льный (-ая, -ое, ые): non-alcoholic
беко́н: bacon
бе́лый (-ая, -ое, -ые): white
бе́рег: shore, coast
библиоте́ка: a library (Национа́льная библиоте́ка: National library)
Би́блия: Bible
би́знес: business
бизнесме́н: a businessman
биле́т: a ticket
биологи́ческий (-ая, -ое, -ие): biological; биологи́ческий факульте́т: Biology faculty
биоло́гия: biology
благоро́дный (-ая, -ое, -ые): noble
бли́зко: close (adv.)
блины́ (sg. блин): Blini (sg. blin)
блю́до: a bowl
блю́дце: a saucer
Бог: God
бога́тый (-ая, -ое, -ые): rich
бока́л: a glass (of wine)
бо́лее: more
боле́ть 1: (1.R.VOW): to be ill (Я боле́ю)
боле́ть 2: (2.R.CONS.1): to hurt (У меня́ боли́т рука́)
боль (она): pain
больни́чный лист: sick leave
бо́льно: painfully (adv.); It hurts (Мне бо́льно)
большеви́к: bolshevik
большо́е коли́чество: large amount
большо́й (-а́я, -о́е, -и́е): big
борщ: borshch (beetroot soup)
боти́нок (pl. боти́нки): a shoe (pl. shoes)
боя́ться (2.R.VOW): to be afraid
брат (pl. бра́тья): a brother (pl. brothers)
брать (1.R.CONS! БР-БЕР) / взять (1.IR Я-МУ): to take; бери́те! / возьми́те!: take!; взять под контро́ль (кого? что? case № 4): to take under control
брать де́ньги в долг: to borrow money
бри́тва: a razor
брони́ровать / заброни́ровать (1.IR ОВА-У): to book
брю́ки (pl.): trousers
бу́дущее: future (in Russian it is declined as an adjective)
бу́дущий (-ая, -ее, -ие): next, future
бу́ква: a letter
бу́лка: white (wheat) bread
бу́лочная: a bakery (in Russian it is declined as an adjective)
бу́лочник: a baker
бульо́н: Bouillon
бума́га: paper; бума́ги (pl.): papers, documents
бума́жник: a wallet
бума́жный блокно́т: a notebook
бу́ря: a tempest
бутербро́д: a sandwich
буты́лка: a bottle
бы́стро: quickly
быть (есть) (SPECIAL): to be
бюрокра́тия: bureaucracy

В

в: in
в честь (чего? case № 2): in the honour of
ваго́н: a wagon, a coach
ва́жно: important (adv.)
ва́жный (-ая, -ое, -ые): important
ва́за: a vase
ва́ленки (pl.): felt boots

варе́нье: jam
варёный (-ая, -ое, -ые): boiled
вариа́нт: an option
вари́ть / свари́ть (2.R.CONS.1): to cook, to boil
ваш (ва́ша, ва́ше, ва́ши): your
вегетариа́нец (-а́нка): a vegetarian (a female form is with the suffix -к(а))
везти́ (1.R.CONS): to carry, to drive
вели́кий (-ая, -ое, -ие): great; вели́кий князь: a title of the direct descendants of the tsar
ве́рить / пове́рить (2.R.CONS.1): to believe
весе́нний (-яя, -ее, -ие): spring (adj.)
весна́: spring
весно́й: in spring (adv.)
вести́ (1.IR СТ-Д) / води́ть (2.IR Д-Ж) (что? case № 4) маши́ну, мотоци́кл: to drive (a car), to ride (a motorbike)
весь (вся, всё, все): all (the whole)
ве́тер: wind
ве́трено: windy (adv.)
ве́треный (-ая, -ое, -ые): windy
ве́чер: evening
ве́чером: in the evening (adv.)
ве́шать (1.R.VOW) / пове́сить (2.IR С-Ш): to hang
вещь (она) (pl. ве́щи): a thing (pl. things)
взаимно: mutually
взро́слый (челове́к): an adult (n.) (a noun in the form of an adjective, declines as an adjective)
ви́део: video
видеока́мера: a camera
ви́деть / уви́деть (2.IR Д-Ж): to see
ви́деть / уви́деть (чем? case № 5) свои́ми глаза́ми: a fixed expression meaning "to be a witness of something, to be sure of something"
ви́лка: a fork
винегре́т: salad beetroot
вино́: wine
висе́ть (2.IR С-Ш): to be hung
витра́ж: stained glass
вку́сно: tasty, delicious (adv.)
вку́сный (-ая, -ое, -ые): tasty, delicious
вме́сте: together
Внима́ние!: Attention!
внима́тельный (-ая, -ое, -ые): attentive
внук: a grandson
вну́чка: a granddaughter
вода́ (негазиро́ванная, газиро́ванная): water (still, sparkling)
води́тель (он): a driver
води́ть (2.IR Д-Ж): to drive (a car), to take (somebody to school)
во́дка: vodka
возмо́жно: probably so
война́: a war
вокза́л: a railway station
вокру́г: around
волейболи́ст: a volleyball player
волна́: a wave (n.)
во́лосы (sg. во́лос): hair (sg. a hair)
вообще́: in general
вопро́с: a question
вор: a thief
восто́к: East
вперёд (куда́?): ahead, forward
впереди́ (где?): onward
врач: doctor
вре́мя (оно) (case № 2: вре́мени, pl. времена́): time (pl. times)
всегда́: always
всё: that's all; всё в поря́дке: everything is fine
вспомина́ть (1.R.VOW) / вспо́мнить (2.R.CONS.1): to remember
встава́ть (1.IR ВА-Ø) / встать (1.IR Ø-НУ): to stand (in a circle), to get up
встре́ча: a meeting
встреча́ть (1.R.VOW) / встре́тить (2.IR Т-Ч): to meet
встреча́ться (1.R.VOW) / встре́титься (2.IR Т-Ч): to meet
второ́е блю́до: main course
вход: entrance
входи́ть (2.IR Д-Ж) / войти́ (SPECIAL): to enter
вчера́: yesterday
въе́зд: entrance
вы (Вы): you
вы́езд: exit
высо́кий (-ая, -ое, -ие): high, tall
вы́ставка: exhibition
вы́ход: exit
выходи́ть (2.IR Д-Ж) / вы́йти (SPECIAL): to exit
выходно́й: day off (a noun in the form of an adjective, declines as an adjective)

Г

газе́та: a newspaper
газиро́ванный (-ая, -ое, ые): sparkling
га́лстук: a tie
гардеро́б: wardrobe
где: where
генера́л: général (n.); генера́л-губерна́тор: Governor-General
гениа́льный (-ая, -ое, -ые): genius (adj.)
геро́й: a hero
гита́ра: a guitar
гла́вный (-ая, -ое, -ые): main
глаз (pl. глаза́): an eye (pl. eyes)
гнев: rage; в гне́ве: in rage
говори́ть (2.R.CONS.1) / сказа́ть (1.IR З-Ж): to tell, to say, to speak
год (pl. case № 2: лет): a year
голова́: a head
голубо́й (-а́я, -о́е, -ы́е): light blue
го́лубь (он): pigeon
гора́: a mountain
го́рло: a throat
го́род (pl. города́): a city (pl. cities)
горчи́ца: mustard
горя́чий (-ая, -ее, -ие): hot
господи́н: mister
гости́ница (оте́ль (он)): a hotel

госуда́рственный (-ая, -ое, -ые): national, public, state
госуда́рство: a state
гото́вить / пригото́вить (2.IR Б, П, М, В + Л): to prepare; to cook (food)
гра́дус: degree
граждани́н (pl. гра́ждане): a citizen (pl. citizens)
гражда́нство: citizenship
гриб (pl. грибы́): mushroom (pl. mushrooms)
грибно́й (-а́я, -о́е, -ы́е): mushroom (adj.)
гро́мко: loudly
грудь (она): a chest
гру́ппа: a group
гру́стный (-ая, -ое, -ые): sad
губа́ (pl. гу́бы): a lip (lips)
гуверна́нтка: a governess
гуля́ть / погуля́ть (1.R.VOW): to walk
гуманита́рный (-ая, -ое, -ые): humanitarian
гусь (он) (pl. гу́си): a goose (geese)

Д

да: yes
Дава́й!: Let's…!
дава́ть (1.IR ВА-Ø) / дать (SPECIAL): to give; дава́ть де́ньги в долг: to lend money
давно́: long time ago
да́же: even
далеко́: far (adv.)
да́льше: forward, farther
дари́ть / подари́ть (2.R.CONS.1): to present
да́та: a date; да́та рожде́ния: date of birth
дверь (она): a door
дворе́ц: a palace
дворяни́н: a nobleman (a female form is with the suffix -к(а))
дворя́нский (-ая, -ое, -ие): noble
де́вочка: a little girl
де́вушка: a girl
дед: a grandfather
дедла́йн: a deadline
де́душка: granddad
дежу́рный: on duty (дежу́рная апте́ка: a pharmacy on duty)
декорати́вный (-ая, -ое, -ые): decorative
де́лать / сде́лать (1.R.VOW): to do
де́ло (pl. дела́): affair, business (pl. affairs); Как дела́?: How are you?
делово́й (-а́я, -о́е, -ы́е): business; делова́я встре́ча: business meeting
день (он) (pl. дни): a day (pl. days)
де́ньги (pl.): money
дере́вня: a village
де́рево (pl. дере́вья): a tree (trees)
деревя́нный (-ая, -ое, -ые): wooden
десе́ртное блю́до (десе́рт): dessert
де́ти (sg. ребёнок): children (sg. child)
дешёвый (-ая, -ое, -ые): cheap
дёшево: cheap (adv.)
джи́нсы (pl.): jeans
дива́н: a sofa
дире́ктор: a director
диссерта́ция: thesis
дли́нный (-ая, -ое, -ые): long
для: for
днём: in the afternoon (adv.)
До ве́чера!: See you in the evening!
До встре́чи!: See you!
До за́втра!: Till tomorrow!
До свида́ния!: Good bye!
До́брое у́тро!: Good morning!
До́брый ве́чер!: Good evening!
До́брый день!: Good afternoon!
догова́риваться (1.R.VOW) / договори́ться (2.R.CONS.1): to agree
догово́р (контра́кт): a contract
дождли́во: rainy (adv.)
дождли́вый (-ая, -ое, -ые): rainy
дождь: rain; дождь идёт: it rains
докуме́нт (pl. докуме́нты): a document (pl. documents)
долг: a debt; де́нежный долг: monetary debt
до́лго: long (adv.)
дом (pl. дома́): a house
дом о́тдыха: a resort
до́ма (где?): at home (adv.)
домо́й (куда?): home (where?) (adv.)
домохозя́йка: a housewife
доро́га: a road
дорого́й (-а́я, -о́е, -и́е): expensive
до́чка (дочь; pl. до́чери): daughter
драгоце́нность (она): a jewel
драгоце́нный (-ая, -ое, -ые): precious
драко́н: a dragon
драмати́ческий (-ая, -ое, -ие): dramatic
дре́вний (-яя, -ее, -ие): ancient
друг (pl. друзья́): a friend
друго́й (-а́я, -о́е, -и́е): another
дру́жно: in peace
ду́мать / поду́мать (1.R.VOW): to think
душа́: a soul
дя́дя (он): an uncle

Е

е́вро: euro
европе́йский (-ая, -ое, -ие): european
его́: his
еда́: food
её: her
ежедне́вник: a calendar
ежедне́вно: daily (adv.)
е́здить (2.IR ЗД-ЗЖ): to drive (a vehicle)
е́сли… то: if… then
есть 1: (у меня́ есть, у тебя́ есть): to have (I have, you have)
есть 2: (SPECIAL): to eat (ку́шать)
есть 3: to be
е́хать (SPECIAL): to go, to ride (+ kind of transport)
ещё: also; more; yet

Ё

ёлка: a fir-tree

Ж

жалюзи́ (pl.): blinds
жа́реный (-ая, -ое, -ые): fried
жа́рить / пожа́рить (2.R.CONS.1): to fry
жа́ркий (-ая, -ое, -ие): hot
жа́рко: it's hot (adv.)
ждать (1.R.CONS): to wait
желе́: jelly
желе́зный (-ая, -ое, -ые): iron
жена́ (pl. жёны): a wife (pl. wives)
жена́т: married (for a man) (shortened form of the adjective)
же́нщина: a woman
жёлтый (-ая, -ое, -ые): yellow; жёлтая газе́та: a tabloid
живо́й (-а́я, -о́е, -ы́е): live (adj.)
живо́т: a stomach
живо́тное: an animal (in Russian it is declined as an adjective)
жизнь (она): life
жиле́т: a vest
жиле́ц: inhabitant
жи́тель (он): a citizen; an inhabitant
жить (1.IR +В): to live
жоке́й: a jockey
журна́л: a magazine
журнали́ст (-ка): a journalist (a female form is with the suffix -к(а))

З

за: behind
заблуди́ться (PF; 2.IR Д-Ж): to get lost
забыва́ть (1.R.VOW) / забы́ть (SPECIAL): to forget
заво́д: a factory
за́втра: tomorrow
за́втрак: breakfast
за́втракать / поза́втракать (1.R.VOW): to have breakfast
зака́з: order
зака́зывать (1.R.VOW) / заказа́ть (1.IR З-Ж): to order
зака́нчиваться (1.R.VOW) / зако́нчиться (2.R.CONS.2): to start to finish / to have finished (when something has just finished)
зако́н: a law
зако́нный (-ая, -ое, -ые): legal
закрыва́ть (1.R.VOW) / закры́ть (1.IR Ы-О): to close
заку́ска: an appetizer
заку́сывать (1.R.VOW): to have a snack
зал: a hall
за́мужем: married (for a woman) (adv.)
занаве́ска: a curtain
занима́ться / позанима́ться (1.R.VOW): to be occupied; to practise
за́нят (занята́, за́нято, за́няты): to be busy (shortened form of the adjective)
заня́тие: class
за́пад: West
заполня́ть (1.R.VOW) / запо́лнить (2.R.CONS.1): to fill in
заявле́ние: declaration, form
звать (зову́т): to call; Меня́ зову́т: My name is...; Его́ зову́т: his name is...
звони́ть / позвони́ть (2.R.CONS.1): to phone
звоно́к: a call
звук: a sound
зда́ние: a building
здесь (где?): here
здоро́вье: health
здоро́вый (-ая, -ое, -ые): healthy
Здра́вствуй(-те)!: Hello!
зелёный (-ая, -ое, -ые): green
зе́ркало: a mirror
зима́: winter
зи́мний (-яя, -ее, -ие): winter (adj.)
зимо́й: in winter (adv.)
знак: a sign
знако́миться / познако́миться (2.IR Б, П, М, В + Л): to get acquainted, to meet
знамени́тый (-ая, -ое, -ые): famous, well-known
знать / узна́ть (1.R.VOW): to know / to learn
зо́лото: gold
золото́й (-а́я, -о́е, -ы́е): gold (adj.)
зонт: an umbrella
зубна́я па́ста: toothpaste
зубна́я щётка: a toothbrush

И

и: and
иго́лка: a needle
игра́ть (1.R.VOW): to play
идти́ (SPECIAL): to go, to be in process
из: from
изве́стен (изве́стна, изве́стно, изве́стны): famous for (shortened form of the adjective).
изве́стный (-ая, -ое, -ые): famous, well-known
Извини́(-те)!: I'm sorry!
извиня́ться (1.R.VOW) / извини́ться (2.R.CONS.1): to say sorry for something
изуча́ть (1.R.VOW) / изучи́ть (2.R.CONS.2): to study
изю́м: raisin
ико́на: an icon
икра́: caviar
и́ли: or
и́мидж: image
императри́ца: an empress
и́мя (оно) (pl. имена́): a name (pl. names)
инжене́р: an engineer
иногда́: sometimes
иностра́нец (pl. иностра́нцы): a foreigner (pl. foreigners)
институ́т: an institute
инстру́ктор: an instructor
инструме́нт: an instrument, a tool
интервью́ (оно): an interview
интере́сный (-ая, -ое, -ые): interesting
интересова́ться (1.IR ОВА-У): to be interested
Интерне́т: Internet
информа́ция: information
ипподро́м: a hippodrome
иска́ть (1.IR СК-Щ) / найти́ (SPECIAL): to look for (IPF) / to find (PF)
иску́сство: art

исправля́ть (1.R.VOW) / испра́вить (2.IR Б, П, М ,В + Л): to correct
исто́рик: a historian
истори́ческий (-ая, -ое, -ие): historical
исто́рия: history
исчеза́ть (1.R.VOW) / исче́знуть (1.IR НУ; Past исче́з): to disappear
ита́к: so, well
их: their

К

к: to
к сожале́нию: unfortunately
кабине́т: a study, an office
ка́ждый (-ая, -ое, -ые): every
как: how; Как это?: How come?
Как дела́?: How are you?
Како́й (-а́я, -о́е, -и́е) ...?: What kind ...?
ка́менный (-ая, -ое, -ые): made of stone
ка́мень (он): a stone
кана́л: a canal
капу́ста: cabbage
каранда́ш: a pencil
ка́рта: a map
карти́на: a picture
карто́фель (он): potato
ка́рточка: a card
ка́рты (pl.): cards
ка́сса: ticket office
касси́р: a cashier
кастрю́ля: a saucepan
катало́г: a catalogue
кафе́: a café
ка́ша: porridge
квадра́т: a square (n.)
кварти́ра: a flat
квас: kvas
ква́шеная капу́ста: sauerkraut
ке́тчуп: ketchup
киломе́тр (case № 2: киломе́тров): kilometre
кио́ск: a kiosk
клад: a treasure
класс: classroom
кла́ссика: classics (n.)
класть (1.IR СТ-Д) / положи́ть (2.R.CONS.2): to put (to place an object in a horizontal position); кладите! put down!
кли́мат: a climate
клуб: a club
ключ: a key, a clue
кни́га: a book
ковбо́й: a cowboy
ковёр (pl. ковры́): a carpet (pl. carpets)
код: a code
ко́жа: skin, leather
колго́тки (pl.): tights
колле́га: a colleague
ко́лледж: a college
коллекционе́р: a collector
колле́кция: a collection
коло́нна: pillar
кольцо: a ring
ко́мната: a room
комплиме́нт: a compliment
компози́тор: a composer
компью́тер: a computer
комфо́ртно: comfortably
конве́рт: an envelope
коне́ц: end (E is a mobile vowel, it appears only in cases № 1 and № 4)
коне́чно: a form of agreement = O.K., of course, certainly
коне́чный (-ая, -ое, -ые): final
консервато́рия: conservatoire
конфе́та: a sweet
конце́рт: a concert
конь (он): a horse
копе́йка: a coin
ко́пия: a copy
кора́бль (он): a ship
Кора́н: Coran
кори́чневый (-ая, -ое, -ые): brown
коро́бка: a box
коро́ль (короле́ва): a king (a queen)
коро́ткий (-ая, -ое, -ие): short
костю́м: a suit
кот: a cat
кото́рый (-ая, -ое, -ые): which, who, that
ко́фе: coffee
ко́фе-бре́йк: coffee break
кофе́йня: a café (coffee shop)
ко́фта: a blouse
кошелёк: a wallet
краси́во: beautifully
краси́вый (-ая, -ое, -ые): beautiful
кра́сный (-ая, -ое, -ые): red
крем-су́п: cream soup
кре́пость (она): fortress
кре́сло: an armchair
кримина́льная ситуа́ция: crime situation
крича́ть (2.R.CONS.2) / кри́кнуть (1.IR НУ): to cry, to shout
крова́ть (она): a bed
кровь (она): blood
кроссо́вки (pl.): trainers
круг: circle
кста́ти: by the way
кто: who; Кто это?: Who's this?
куда́?: where to?
кузе́н (двою́родный брат): a cousin
кузи́на (двою́родная сестра́): a cousin
культу́рный (-ая, -ое, -ые): cultural
кури́ть (2.R.CONS.1): to smoke
ку́рица: chicken
ку́ртка: a jacket
ку́хня: a kitchen
ку́хонный шкаф: a cupboard

Л
ла́мпа: a lamp
ла́поть (pl. ла́пти) (он): bast shoe (a kind of traditional folk shoes)
лапша́: noodles
ле́вый (-ая, -ое, -ые): left
леге́нда: a legend
легенда́рный (-ая, -ое, -ые): legendary (adjective from the word леге́нда)
легко́: easily
лежа́ть / полежа́ть (2.R.CONS.2): to lie (to be placed in a horizontal position)
ле́кция: a lecture
лес: a forest
лета́ть (1.R.VOW): to fly
лете́ть (2.IR Т-Ч): to fly
ле́тний (-яя, -ее, -ие): summer (adj.)
ле́то: summer
ле́том: in summer (adv.)
лимо́н: a lemon
лине́йка: a ruler
литерату́ра: literature
лицо́: a face
лоб (pl. лбы): a forehead (pl. foreheads)
ло́жка: a spoon
ло́шадь (она): a horse
лу́жа: a puddle
лу́к: an onion
луна́: the moon
люби́ть (2.IR Б, П, М, В + Л): to love
любо́вь (она): love (О is a mobile vowel, it appears only in cases № 1 and № 4)
люкс: luxe
лягу́шка: a frog

М
магази́н: a shop
ма́йка: a shirt
майоне́з: mayonnaise
макаро́ны (pl.): pasta
ма́ленький (-ая, -ое, -ие): small, little
ма́ло: a few, little
малы́ш: a baby
ма́льчик: a boy
ма́ма (мать): a mom (a mother)
мане́ж: a manege (the place where we train horses)
ма́нная ка́ша: semolina
маршру́т: a route
ма́сло: (сли́вочное) butter, (расти́тельное) oil
матема́тика: mathematics
математи́ческий (-ая, -ое, -ие): mathematical
маши́на: a car
медве́дь (он): a bear
медици́на: medicine
медо́вый (-ая, -ое, -ые): honey (adj.)
ме́жду: between
междунаро́дный (-ая, -ое, -ые): international
мему́ары (pl.): memoirs
ме́неджер: a manager
ме́нее: less
меню́ (оно): menu
меня́ть / поменя́ть (1.R.VOW): to change
ме́сто: a place
ме́сяц: a month (янва́рь: January; февра́ль: February; март: March; апре́ль: April; май: May; ию́нь: June; ию́ль: July; а́вгуст: August; сентя́брь: September; октя́брь: October; ноя́брь: November; дека́брь: December)
метро́: metro
мече́ть (она): a mosque
мечта́ть (1.R.VOW): to dream
меша́ть / помеша́ть (1.R.VOW): to mix, to disturb
мёд: honey
миг: a moment; на миг = на мину́ту, на секу́нду
микроволно́вая пе́чка (микроволно́вка): a microwave oven
мини́стр: a Minister
ми́нус: minus
мину́та: a minute
мир: world, peace
мла́дший (-ая, -ее, -ие): younger
мно́го: a lot
мо́да: fashion
мо́дно: fashionable (adv.)
мо́жет быть: maybe
мо́жно: can
мой (моя́, моё, мои́): my
молодо́й (-а́я, -о́е, -ы́е): young
молоко́: milk
моне́та: a coin
мо́ре: a sea
моро́женое: an ice-cream (in Russian it is declined as an adjective)
москви́ч (-ка): muscovite (a female form is with the suffix -к(а))
мост: a bridge
мочь / смочь (SPECIAL): to be able, to manage
муж (pl. мужья́): a husband (pl. husbands)
мужчи́на (он): a man
музе́й: a museum
му́зыка: music
музыка́льный инструме́нт: a musical instrument
мука́: flour
мусульма́нство: islam
мы: we
мы́ло: a soap
мышь (она): a mouse
мясно́й (-а́я, -о́е, -ы́е): meat
мя́со: meat
мяч: a ball

Н
на: on
на́бережная: embankment (in Russian it is declined as an adjective)
наве́рное: maybe, probably; I guess so

навстре́чу: towards (adv.)
над: over
на́до: need, have to
наза́д (куда́?): backward
наза́д (когда́?): before, in the past, long ago, many years ago (1, 2, 3, 4 years) ago
назва́ние: name (for inanimate objects)
найти́ (PF; SPECIAL): to find
наконе́ц: at last
нале́во (куда?): to the left
напи́ток (pl. напи́тки): a drink (pl. drinks); напи́тки безалкого́льные: soft drinks
напомина́ть (1.R.VOW) / напо́мнить (2.R.CONS.1): to remind
напра́во (куда́?): to the right
наро́дный (-ая, -ое, -ые): folk
настоя́щий (-ая, -ее, -ие): real, genuine
нау́ка: science
находи́ть (2.IR Д-Ж) / найти́ (SPECIAL): to find
находи́ться (2.IR Д-Ж): to be (to take place)
национа́льность (она): a nationality
нача́ло: beginning
нача́льник: a boss
начина́ться (1.R.VOW) / нача́ться (1.IR Ø-НУ): to begin, to happen, to come / to have started (when something has just started)
наш (на́ша, на́ше, на́ши): our
не: not
Не мо́жет быть!: No way! (You must be kidding!)
неде́ля: a week (понеде́льник: Monday; вто́рник: Tuesday; среда́: Wednesday; четве́рг: Thursday; пя́тница: Friday; суббо́та: Saturday; воскресе́нье (оно́): Sunday)
некраси́вый (-ая, -ое, -ые): ugly
нельзя́: mustn't
немо́й (-а́я, -о́е, -ы́е): mute
ненави́деть / возненави́деть (2.IR Д-Ж): to hate
необходи́мо: have to
необы́чно: unusual (adv.)
неофициа́льный (-ая, -ое, -ые): unofficial
неплóхо: not bad
неприя́тность (она́): a small problem
не́сколько: several, some
нести́ (1.IR СТ-С): to carry
нет: no
нефть (она): oil
ни́зкий (-ая, -ое, -ие): low
никогда́: never
ничего́: nothing
но: but
но́вый (-ая, -ое, -ые): new
нога́: a leg
нож: a knife
но́мер: a hotel room; number (= №).
норма́льно: normal; fine (adv.)
нос: a nose
носи́ть (2.IR С-Ш): to wear, to carry
нота́риус: a notary
ноутбу́к: a laptop
ночева́ть (1.IR ЕВА-У): to stay for a night
ночь (она́): a night
но́чью: at night (adv.)
нра́виться / понра́виться (2.IR Б, П, М, В + Л): to like / to be liked
ну́жно: need
нумизма́т: a numismatist (a specialist in the study of coins and medals)
ня́ня: a nanny

О

обе́д: lunch (У нас обе́д = We are having lunch)
обе́дать / пообе́дать (1.R.VOW): to have lunch
обезбо́ливающее: a painkiller (in Russian it is declined as an adjective)
обижа́ться (1.R.VOW) / оби́деться (2.IR Д-Ж): to be offended
о́блачно: it's cloudy
о́блачность (она): cloudiness
о́блачный (-ая, -ое, -ые): cloudy
обма́нывать (1.R.VOW) / обману́ть (1.IR НУ): to lie, to deceive
о́браз: an image
обра́тно (куда?): back, backward
общежи́тие: a dormitory
объе́кт: an object
объём: volume
объясне́ние: an explanation
объясня́ть (1.R.VOW) / объясни́ть (2.R.CONS.1): to explain
обы́чно: usually
обы́чный (-ая, -ое, -ые): common, ordinary
о́вощ (pl. о́вощи): a vegetable (pl. vegetables)
овощно́й (-а́я, -о́е, -ы́е): made from vegetables
огуре́ц (pl. огурцы́): a cucumber (pl. cucumbers) (E is a mobile vowel, it appears only in cases № 1 and № 4)
оде́жда (sg.): clothes
оди́н (одна́, одно́, одни́): alone
одна́жды: once, one day
о́зеро (pl. озёра): a lake (pl. lakes)
океа́н: an ocean
окно́ (pl. о́кна): a window (pl. windows)
о́коло (где?): near
Олимпи́йские и́гры: the Olympic Games
Олимпи́йский комите́т: Olympic Committee
он (она́, оно́, они́): he (she, it, they)
опа́сно: dangerous (adv.)
о́пера: opera
ора́нжевый (-ая, -ое, -ые): orange
организа́ция: organisation
организова́ть (IPF=PF; 1.IR ОВА-У): to arrange, to organize
оре́х (pl. оре́хи): a nut (pl. nuts)
оригина́льный (-ая, -ое, -ые): original
осе́нний (-яя, -ее, -ие): autumn (adj.)
о́сень (она): autumn
о́сенью: in autumn (adv.)
осно́вывать (1.R.VOW) / основа́ть: to found

оставля́ть (1.R.VOW) / оста́вить (2.IR Б, П, М, В + Л): to leave
остано́вка авто́буса: a bus stop
осторо́жный (-ая, -ое, -ые): cautious, prudent
о́стров (pl. острова́): an island (pl. islands)
отве́т: a response, an answer
отвеча́ть (1.R.VOW) / отве́тить (2.IR Т-Ч): to answer
отдава́ть (1.IR ВА-Ø) / отда́ть (SPECIAL): to give / to give away; отдава́ть долг (долги́): to repay
отде́л: department
отдыха́ть (1.R.VOW) / отдохну́ть (1.IR НУ): to relax / to have a rest
оте́ц: a father
открыва́ть (1.R.VOW) / откры́ть (1.IR Ы-О): to open
откры́тка: a postcard
Отку́да?: Where from?
отли́чно: excellent (adv.)
отправля́ть (1.R.VOW) / отпра́вить (2.IR Б, П, М, В + Л): to send
о́тчество: middle name, patronymic
о́фис: an office
офице́р: an officer
официа́льный (-ая, -ое, -ые): official
официа́нт: a waiter
оце́нка: a mark
о́чень: very
очки́ (pl.): glasses
оши́бка: a mistake

П

паке́т: a plastic bag
па́лец (pl. па́льцы): a finger (pl. fingers)
па́лочки (pl.): sticks
пальто́: a coat
па́мятник: a monument
па́па (оте́ц): a dad (a father)
па́пка: a file
па́рень (он): a guy, a boyfriend, a young man
парк: a park
парла́мент: Parliament
партнёр: a partner
па́спорт (pl. паспорта́): a passport (pl. passports)
пассажи́р (-ка): a passenger (a female form is with the suffix -к(а))
па́чка: a packet
пельме́ни (pl.): pelmeni (meat dumplings)
пенсионе́р (-ка): a pensioner (a female form is with the suffix -к(а))
пе́рвое блю́до: a first course
переводи́ть (2.IR Д-Ж) / перевести́ (1.IR СТ-Д): to translate
перево́дчик (-ица): a translator (a female form is with the suffix -ица)
перед: in front of
передава́ть (1.IR ВА-Ø) / переда́ть (SPECIAL): to pass; передава́ть через челове́ка
перекрёсток: crossroads
переу́лок: a lane
перехо́д (подзе́мный, пешехо́дный): a crossing (subway, sub)
переходи́ть (2.IR Д-Ж): to cross
пе́рец: pepper
перча́тки (sg. перча́тка): gloves (sg. a glove)
пе́сня: a song
пе́чка (печь (она́)): a stove
печь / испе́чь (1.IR Ч-К-Ч): to bake
пешко́м: on foot (adv.)
пи́во: beer
пиджа́к: a jacket
пило́т: a pilot
пир: a feast
пиро́г: a pie
пиро́жное: a pastrie (in Russian it is declined as an adjective)
пирожо́к (pl. пирожки́): a small pie (pl. small pies)
писа́тель (-ница): a writer (a female form is with the suffix -ница)
писа́ть / написа́ть (1.IR С-Ш): to write
пистоле́т: a pistol, a gun
письмо́: a letter
пить (1.IR И-Ь): to drink
пла́вать (1.R.VOW): to swim, to sail
пла́кать (1.IR К-Ч): to cry
пла́мя (ого́нь (он)): fire
плани́ровать (1.IR ОВА-У): to plan
планше́т (планше́тный компью́тер): a tablet PC
плати́ть (2.IR Т-Ч): to pay
пла́тье: a dress
плащ: a raincoat
племя́нник: a nephew
племя́нница: a niece
плита́: a cooker
пло́хо: it's bad (adv.)
плохо́й (-а́я, -о́е, -и́е): bad
пло́щадь (она́): a square
плыть (1.IR + В): to swim, to sail
плюс: plus
по: on
побе́да: a victory
побежда́ть (1.R.VOW) / победить (2.IR Д-Ж): to win
по́вар: a chef
повторя́ть (1.R.VOW) / повтори́ть (2.R.CONS.1): to repeat
пого́да (sg.): a weather
под: under
пода́рок (pl. пода́рки): a present (pl. presents) (О is a mobile vowel, it appears only in case № 1/4)
подва́л: basement
подводи́ть (2.IR Д-Ж) / подвести́ (1.IR СТ-Д) ито́ги: to summarize
поднима́ть (1.R.VOW) / подня́ть (1.IR НЯ-ИМУ): to lift
поднима́ться (1.R.VOW) / подня́ться (1.IR НЯ-ИМУ): to go up
подписа́ть догово́р (контра́кт): to sign a contract
по́дпись (она): a signature
подру́га: a friend (female)
подъе́зд: a hall, an entrance

поéздка: a voyage, a trip
пожáлуйста: please, you are welcome
пойти́ (SPECIAL): to go
Покá!: Bye!
покупáтель (-ница): a customer (a female form is with the suffix -ниц-)
покупáть (1.R.VOW) / купи́ть (2.IR Б, П, М, В + Л): to buy
пол 1: a sex
пол 2: floor
поли́тика: politics
полити́ческий (-ая, -ое, -ие): political
полицéйский: a policeman (in Russian it is declined as an adjective)
поли́ция: a police
пóлка: a shelf
пóлный (-ая, -ое, -ые): full, complete
полови́на: a half
полуóстров: a peninsula
получáть (1.R.VOW) / получи́ть (2.R.CONS.2): to get, to receive
пóлька: polka
помáда: a lipstick
пóмнить / вспóмнить (2.R.CONS.1): to remember
помогáть (1.R.VOW) / помóчь (SPECIAL): to help
помóщник (-ница): an assistant (a female form is with the suffix -ница)
пóмощь (она): aid, help; скóрая пóмощь: ambulance
понимáть (1.R.VOW) / поня́ть (1.IR НЯ-ЙМУ): to understand
понрáвиться: perfective of нрáвиться (2.IR Б, П, М, В + Л): to like
посещáть (1.R.VOW) / посети́ть (2.IR Т-Щ): to visit
пост: a post
постоя́нно: all the time (adv.)
пострóен (-а, -о, -ы): is built (shortened form of the verbal adjective)
потолóк (pl. потолки́): a ceiling (O is a mobile vowel, it appears only in case № 1 and № 4)
потóм: then
потомý что: because
почемý: why
пóчта: a post office
почтальóн: a postman
поэ́т: a poet
поэ́тому: that is why
прав (-á, -о, -ы): right (shortened form of the adj.)
прáвая рукá: the main assistant (someone's right hand)
прáвда: truth
прáвила дорóжного движéния: rules of the road
прáвило: a rule
прáвильно: right, correct (adv.)
прáвый (-ая, -ое, -ые): right (adj.)
прáздновать (1.IR ОВА-У): to celebrate
прáктика: a traineeship, a practice
представля́ть (1.R.VOW) / предстáвить (2.IR Б, П, М, В + Л): to present, to introduce
представля́ться (1.R.VOW) / предстáвиться (2.IR Б, П, М, В + Л): to introduce oneself
президéнт: a president
прекрáсный (-ая, -ое, -ые): wonderful
премьéра: a premiere
преподавáтель (-ница): a professor (a female form is with the suffix -ница)
Привéт!: Hi!
приглашáть (1.R.VOW) / пригласи́ть (2.IR С-Ш): to invite
примéр: an example
принадлежáть (2.R.CONS.2): to belong
при́нтер: a printer
припрáва: a condiment
прирóда: nature
прия́тно: nice; Óчень прия́тно (познакóмиться)!: Nice to meet!
Прия́тного аппети́та!: Enjoy your meal!
проблéма: a problem
проверя́ть (1.R.VOW) / провéрить (2.R.CONS.1): to check
продавáть (1.IR ВА-Ø) / продáть (SPECIAL): to sell
продавéц: a seller
продуктóвый магази́н: a grocery store
продýкты (pl.): food products
произведéние: a work
проли́в: a strait
проспéкт: an avenue
прóсто: simple (adv.)
профéссия: a profession
профéссор: a professor
процéнт (pl. процéнты): percentage
прóшлый: last, past
прощáй (прощáйте): adieu!
пря́мо (1. где? 2. куда?): in front of; straight on
прямóй (-áя, -óе, -ые): direct / straight
публиковáть / опубликовáть (1.IR ОВА-У): to publish
пульт: a remote
пункт: a point
пýсто: it's empty (adv.)
путешéствие: voyage
путешéствовать (1.IR ОВА-У): to travel

Р

рабóта: a work
рабóтать / порабóтать (1.R.VOW): to work
рабóчий: a worker (in Russian it is declined as an adjective)
рад (рáда, рáды): glad; Рáд(-а) познакóмиться!: Nice to meet you!
рáдио: a radio
раз: time; нéсколько раз: several times
разговóрник: a phrasebook
рáзный (-ая, -ое, -ые): different
разрешáть (1.R.VOW) / разреши́ть (2.R.CONS.2): to let, to allow
райóн: a district
рáно: early
рáньше: earlier
расскáз: a story
расскáзывать (1.R.VOW) / рассказáть (1.IR З-Ж): to tell
расчёска: a brush

ребёнок (pl. дéти): a child (pl. children)
революция: a revolution
регулярно: regularly
рéдко: rarely
режиссёр: a director
рéзать (IPF; 1.IR З-Ж): to cut
резервировать / зарезервировать (1.IR ОВА-У): to reserve
рекá: a river
реконстрýкция: a reconstruction
рéктор: a rector
религия: a religion
ремéнь (он): a belt
репутáция: a reputation
респýблика: a republic
ресторáн: a restaurant
рецéпт: a recipe
решáть (1.R.VOW) / решить (2.R.CONS.2): to decide
рис: rice
рисовáть / нарисовáть (1.IR ОВА-У): to draw, to paint
рóдина: homeland
родители (pl.): parents
родиться: to be born
роднáя сестрá: a sister; a sibling
роднóй брат: a brother; a sibling
рождéние: birth; странá рождéния: a country of birth; день рождения: a birthday
рóзовый (-ая, -ое, -ые): pink
ромáн: a novel
ромáнтик: a romantic person
рот (pl. рты): a mouth (pl. mouths)
рояль (он): a grand piano
рубáшка: a shirt
рубль (он): a rouble
рукá: an arm
рýсский (-ая, -ое, -ие): Russian
рýчка: a pen
рыба: fish
рыбáк: a fisherman
рынок (pl. рынки): market (O is a mobile vowel, it appears only in cases № 1 and № 4)
рюмка: a shot
ряд: a row
рядом: near

С

с (со): with
с удовóльствием: with pleasure
сад: a garden
садиться (2.IR Д-Ж) / сесть (SPECIAL): to sit down
садóвник: a gardener
сажáть (1.R.VOW) / посадить (2.IR Д-Ж) в тюрьмý: to take someone to prison
салáт: salad
салóн óбуви: a shoe shop
салфéтки (sg. салфéтка): tissues (sg. a tissue)
самовáр: a samovar
самолёт: a plane
сáмый (-ая, -ое, -ые): the most
санатóрий: a sanatorium
сапоги (sg. сапóг): boots (sg. a boot)
сáхар (sg.): sugar
свáдьба: a wedding
свéжий (-ая, -ее, -ие): fresh
свéтлый (-ая, -ое, -ые): light; bright
свéтский (-ая, -ое, -ие): social; fashionable (adjective derived from the word свет)
свитер: a sweater
свобóда: freedom
свобóден (свобóдна, свобóдно, свобóдны): to be free (not busy) (adj.)
свой (своя, своё, свои): one's own (her own, its own, their own)
сéвер: North
сéверо-востóк: northeast
сéверо-зáпад: northwest
сегóдня: today
сезóн: a season
сейчáс: now
секретáрь (он): a secretary
секýнда: a second
селёдка: herring
селó: a village
семья: a family
сéно: hay
сéрдце: a heart
серебрó: silver
серéбряный (-ая, -ое, -ые): silver, made from silver
середина: middle
сéрый (-ая, -ое, -ые): grey
сестрá (pl. сёстры): a sister (pl. sisters)
сзáди (где?): behind
сильный (-ая, -ое, -ые): strong
символ: a symbol
симфóния: a symphony
синий (-яя, -ее, -ие): blue
скáзка: a fairy-tale
скáзочный (-ая, -ое, -ые): dreamlike
сковородá: a frying pan
скóлько: how much; how many; Скóлько стóит?: How much does it cost? (singular object), Скóлько стóят?: How much do they cost? (plural objects)
скрипка: a violin
скрóмный (-ая, -ое, -ые): shy
скýльптор: a sculptor
скýчный (-ая, -ое, -ые): boring
слáдкий (-ая, -ое, -ие): sweet
слéва (где?): on the left
сливки (pl.): cream
словáрь (он): a dictionary
слóво (pl. словá): a word (pl. words)
служить (2.R.CONS.2): to serve
случáться (1.R.VOW) / случиться (2.R.CONS.2): to happen, to have happened
слýшать / послýшать (1.R.VOW): to listen
сметáна (sg.): sour cream

смотре́ть / посмотре́ть (2.R.CONS.1): to look
снача́ла: at first
снег: snow
сно́ва: again
соба́ка: a dog
собо́р: a cathedral
сове́товать / посове́товать (1.IR ОВА-У): to advise
совеща́ние: a conference, a meeting
совреме́нный (-ая, -ое, -ые): contemporary, modern
соединя́ть (1.R.VOW) / соедини́ть (2.R.CONS.1): to unite, to connect
создава́ть (1.IR ВА-Ø) / созда́ть (SPECIAL): to create
сок: juice
солда́т: a soldier
солёный (-ая, -ое, -ые): salty
со́лнце: the Sun
соль (она): salt
сосе́д: a neighbour
соси́ска: a sausage
со́ус: sauce
Спаси́бо!: Thanks!
спать (2.IR Б, П, М, В + Л): to sleep
специали́ст: a specialist
спи́сок: a list
спи́чки (sg. спи́чка): matches (sg. a match)
Споко́йной но́чи!: Good night!
спорт: sport
спорти́вный (-ая, -ое, -ые): sport (adj.)
спортсме́н (-ка): a sportsman (a female form is with the suffix -к(а))
спра́ва (где?): on the right
спра́шивать (1.R.VOW) / спроси́ть (2.IR С-Ш): to ask
Сре́дние века́: Middle Ages
сро́чно: urgently
ста́вить / поста́вить (2.IR Б, П, М, В + Л): to put (to place an object in a vertical position)
стадио́н: a stadium
стака́н: a glass (of water)
ста́нция: a station; ста́нция метро́: an underground station
старт: a start
ста́рший (-ая, -ее, -ие): elder
ста́рый (-ая, -ое, -ые): old
стать (PF; 1.IR Ø-НУ): to become
статья́: an article
стена́: a wall
стиль (он): a style; в сти́ле: in style
стихи́ (pl.): verse (poems)
стог: a haystack
сто́ить (2.R.VOW): to cost
стол: a table
столи́ца: a capital
столо́вая: a canteen (in Russian it is declined as an adjective)
сторона́: side
стоя́ть (2.R.VOW): to stand (to be placed vertically)
страна́: a country
страни́ца: a page
стра́нно: strange (adv.)
стра́нный (-ая, -ое, -ые): strange
стра́шно: terrible (adv.)
стреля́ть (1.R.VOW): to shoot
стро́ить / постро́ить (2.R.VOW): to built, to construct
студе́нт (-ка): a student (a female form is with the suffix -к(а))
стул (pl. сту́лья): a chair (pl. chairs)
су́мка: a bag
суп: soup
су́пер: super
суперма́ркет: a supermarket
сце́на: a stage
Счастли́во!: Good luck! (don't confuse it with сча́стливо)
сча́стливо: happily
счастли́вый (-ая, -ое, -ые): happy
счёт: a bill, an account
сын: a son
сыр: cheese
сюда́ (куда?): here
сюрпри́з: a surprise

Т

табле́тка: a pill
тайна: a mystery
так себе́: so so
тако́й (-а́я, -о́е, -и́е): such
такси́ (оно): a taxi
тала́нт: a talent
там (где?): there
тамо́жня: customs
танцева́ть / потанцева́ть (1.IR ЕВА-У): to dance
育тарака́н: a cockroach
таре́лка: a plate
та́ять / растая́ть (1.R.VOW): to melt
твой (твоя́, твоё, твои́): your
теа́тр: a theatre; драмати́ческий теа́тр: drama theatre
телеви́зор: a TV
телефо́н: a telephone
те́ло: a body
температу́ра: temperature
теннис́ист (-ка): a tennis player (a female form is with the suffix -к(а))
тепло́: warm (adv.)
теплохо́д: a motor ship
теря́ть / потеря́ть (1.R.VOW): to lose
тест: a test
те́сто: dough, batter
тетра́дь (она): a notebook
тёмный (-ая, -ое, -ые): dark
тёплый (-ая, -ое, -ые): warm
тётя: an aunt
типи́чный (-ая, -ое, -ые): typical
ти́хо: quietly
това́рищ: a comrade
то́же: also, too
то́лько: only
тома́т: a tomato

торт: a cake
тост: a toast
то́стер: a toaster
тот (та, то, те): sg. that/pl. those
то́чка: a point
то́чно: precisely, exactly
траге́дия: a tragedy
традицио́нно: traditionally
традицио́нный (-ая, -ое, -ые): traditional
тради́ция: a tradition
тракти́р: an inn
трамва́й: a tram
тра́нспорт (sg.): transport
трость (она): a cane
тротуа́р: a pavement
тру́дно: it's difficult (adv.)
туда́ (куда?): there
тури́ст (-ка): a tourist (a female form is with the suffix -к(а))
тут (где?): here
ту́фли (sg. ту́фля): shoes (sg. a shoe)
ты (Вы): you
тет-а-те́т: tete-a-tete

У

уби́ть (PF; 1.IR И-Ь): to kill
уважи́тельно: with respect (adv.)
у́гол (pl. углы́): a corner (pl. corners)
Уда́чи!: Good luck!
ужа́сно: terribly, awfully
уже́: already
у́жин: a dinner
у́жинать (1.R.VOW): to have dinner
у́зкий (-ая, -ое, -ие): narrow
у́лица: a street
улы́бка: a smile
универса́льный (-ая, -ое, -ые): universal
университе́т: a university
упражне́ние: an exercise
уро́к: a class
усло́вие: a condition
у́тро: morning
у́тром: in the morning (adv.)
у́хо (pl. у́ши): an ear (pl. ears)
уче́бник: a textbook (a manual)
учёный: a scientist (in Russian it is declined as an adjective)
учи́тель (-ница): a teacher (a female form is with the suffix -ница)
учи́ть / вы́учить (2.R.CONS.2): to learn; учи́ть (кого? case № 4) студе́нтов: to teach (who?) students
учи́ться (2.R.CONS.2): to study

Ф

фа́брика: a factory
факульте́т: a faculty
фами́лия: a surname
фана́т (-ка): a fan (a female form is with the suffix -к(а))
фи́зик: a physicist
фи́зика: physics
физи́ческий (-ая, -ое, -ие): physical
филиа́л: a branch; филиа́л (чего́? case № 2) фи́рмы, филиа́л музе́я, филиа́л компа́нии
фило́соф: a philosopher
филосо́фия: philosophy
фильм: a film
фи́ниш: a finish
фиоле́товый (-ая, -ое, -ые): violet
фи́рма: a company
флот: navy
фонта́н: a fountain
фо́то (фотогра́фия): a photo
фото́граф: a photographer
фотографи́ровать / сфотографи́ровать (1.IR ОВА-У): to take pictures
фру́кт (pl. фру́кты): a fruit
фрукто́вый (-ая, -ое, -ые): fruit, made from fruit
фу́нкция: a function
футбо́л: football
футболи́ст: a footballer
футбо́лка: a T-shirt

Х

ха́нство: khanate
хи́мик: a chemist
хими́ческий (-ая, -ое, -ие): chemical
хи́мия: chemistry
хлеб: bread; чёрный хлеб: rye bread; бе́лый хлеб (бу́лка): white (wheat) bread
ход: a passage
ходи́ть (2.IR Д-Ж): to go, to walk; ходи́ть в го́сти / идти́ в го́сти: to visit somebody (usually realtives or friends); ходи́ть по кру́гу: to walk in circles, to circumnavigate
хозя́ин (fem. хозя́йка, pl. хозя́ева): an owner, a host (fem. a hostess, pl. hosts, owners)
хоккеи́ст: a hockey player
холм: a hill
хо́лодно: it's cold (adv.)
холо́дный (-ая, -ое, -ые): cold
хоро́ший (-ая, -ее, -ие): good
хорошо́: very well
хоте́ть / захоте́ть (SPECIAL): to want
христиа́нство: christianity
худо́жник (-ица): a painter (a female form is with the suffix -ица)

Ц

ца́рский (-ая, -ое, -ие): royal, imperial
царь (он): a tsar
цвето́к (pl. цветы́): a flower (pl. flowers)
цель (она): aim, purpose
цена́: price
це́нность (она): value
це́нный (-ая, -ое, -ые): valuable
центр: a centre
це́рковь (она): a church

цивилиза́ция: civilisation
ци́фра: a figure

Ч

чай: tea
час: an hour
ча́сто: often
часть (она): a part
часы́ (pl.): a watch; кура́нты (часы́): chimes (a clock)
ча́шка: a cup
Чей (чья́, чьё, чьи́)?: Whose?
челове́к (pl. лю́ди): a person (pl. people)
Чем?: With what?
чемода́н: a suitcase
черта́: a trait, a feature
чесно́к: garlic
че́стный (-ая, -ое, -ые): honest; че́стное сло́во: an honest word
чёрный (-ая, -ое, -ые): black
число́: a date; a number (notion from maths expressing quantity, e.g. Pi)
чи́стый (-ая, -ое, -ые): pure, clean
чита́ть / прочита́ть (1.R.VOW): to read
что: that (conjunction); я зна́ю, что…: I know that
что: what; Что это?: What's this?
что́бы: to, in order to

Ш

шаг: a step
шага́ть (1.R.VOW): to step
шампа́нское: champagne (in Russian it is declined as an adjective)
ша́пка: a cap
шарф: a scarf
ша́хматы (pl.): chess
шесть: six
ше́я: a neck
широ́кий (-ая, -ое, -ие): wide
шкаф: a closet
шко́ла: a school
шко́льник (-ница): a schoolboy (a schoolgirl)
шля́па: a hat
шок: shock
шокола́д: chocolate
шокола́дный (-ая, -ое, -ые): chocolate, made from chocolate
шо́рты (pl.): shorts
шоссе́ [сэ]: a highway
шу́ба: a fur-coat
шу́тка: a joke
шутни́к (-ница): a joker (a female form is with the suffix -ница)

Щ

щека́ (pl. щёки): a cheek (pl. cheeks)
щи (pl.): shchi (cabbage soup)

Э

эгои́ст: a selfish man
экза́мен: an exam
экологи́ческий (-ая, -ое, -ие): ecological
эколо́гия: ecology
эконо́мика: economy
экономи́ст: an economist
экономи́ческий (-ая, -ое, -ие): economic
экску́рсия: an excursion
экскурсово́д: a guide
элега́нтный (-ая, -ое, -ые): elegant
электро́нный катало́г: an electronic catalogue
энциклопе́дия: an encyclopaedia
эта́ж: a floor
э́то: this, it
э́тот (э́та, э́то, э́ти): sg. this (pl. these)

Ю

ю́бка: a skirt
юг: South
ю́го-восто́к: southeast
ю́го-за́пад: southwest
ю́жный (-ая, -ое, -ые): southern
ю́ноша (молодо́й челове́к): a young man
юри́ст: a lawyer

Я

я: I
я́блоко: an apple
я́блочный (-ая, -ое, -ые): apple, made from apples
явля́ться (1.R.VOW): to be
я́года (pl. я́годы): a berry (pl. berries)
я́годный (-ая, -ое, -ые): berry, made from berries
язы́к 1: a language; ру́сский язы́к: the Russian language;
язы́к 2: a tongue
яйцо́: an egg
я́ркий (-ая, -ое, -ие): bright
я́сно: clearly
я́сный (-ая, -ое, -ые): clear

ОБРАЗОВАНИЯ ФОРМ ГЛАГОЛА

		I group (-E) R		I group (-E) IR						
		1.R. VOW	2.R. CONS	1.IR + В	1.IR И-Ь	1.IR Ы-О	1.IR ОВА-У / ЕВА-У	1.IR С-Ш	1.IR З-Ж	1.IR Т-Ч / К-Ч
Infinitive		**де́лать**	**брать**	**жить**	**пить**	**мыть**	**рисова́ть**	**писа́ть**	**рассказа́ть**	**пря́тать**
Present Tense Imperfect & Future Tense Perfect	я ты он (-á,-ó) мы вы они́	де́лаю де́лаешь де́лает де́лаем де́лаете де́лают	беру́ берёшь берёт берём берёте беру́т	живу́ живёшь живёт живём живёте живу́т	пью́ пьёшь пьёт пьём пьёте пью́т	мо́ю мо́ешь мо́ет мо́ем мо́ете мо́ют	рису́ю рису́ешь рису́ет рису́ем рису́ете рису́ют	пишу́ пи́шешь пи́шет пи́шем пи́шете пи́шут	расскажу́ расска́жешь расска́жет расска́жем расска́жете расска́жут	пря́чу пря́чешь пря́чет пря́чем пря́чете пря́чут
Past Tense	он она́ оно́ они́	**де́лал** де́лала де́лало де́лали	**брал** брала́ бра́ло бра́ли	**жил** жила́ жи́ло жи́ли	**пил** пила́ пи́ло пи́ли	**мыл** мы́ла мы́ло мы́ли	**рисова́л** рисова́ла рисова́ло рисова́ли	**писа́л** писа́ла писа́ло писа́ли	**рассказа́л** рассказа́ла рассказа́ло рассказа́ли	**пря́тал** пря́тала пря́тало пря́тали
Imperative	ты вы	де́лай де́лайте	бери́ бери́те	живи́ живи́те	**! пей** **! пе́йте**	мо́й мо́йте	рису́й рису́йте	пиши́ пиши́те	расскажи́ расскажи́те	пря́чь пря́чьте

		I group (-E) IR								
		1.IR СК-Щ	1.IR Ч-К-Ч	1.IR СТ-Д	1.IR СТ-С/ЗТ-З	1.IR Я-МУ	1.IR ВА-Ø	1.IR НУ	1.IR Ø-НУ	1.IR Ø-НУ
Infinitive		**иска́ть**	**печь**	**класть**	**нести́**	**взять**	**давать**	**пры́гнуть**	**стать**	**нача́ть**
Present Tense Imperfect & Future Tense Perfect	я ты он (-á, ó) мы вы они	ищу́ и́щешь и́щет и́щем и́щете и́щут	пеку́ печёшь печёт печём печёте пеку́т	кладу́ кладёшь кладёт кладём кладёте кладу́т	несу́ несёшь несёт несём несёте несу́т	возьму́ возьмёшь возьмёт возьмём возьмёте возьмут	даю́ даёшь даёт даём даёте даю́т	пры́гну пры́гнешь пры́гнет пры́гнем пры́гнете пры́гнут	ста́ну ста́нешь ста́нет ста́нем ста́нете ста́нут	начну́ начнёшь начнёт начнём начнёте начну́т
Past Tense	он она́ оно́ они́	**иска́л** иска́ла иска́ло иска́ли	**пёк** пекла́ пекло́ пекли́	**клал** кла́ла кла́ло кла́ли	**нёс** несла́ несло́ несли́	**взял** взяла́ взя́ло взя́ли	**дава́л** дава́ла дава́ло дава́ли	**пры́гнул** пры́гнула пры́гнуло пры́гнули	**стал** ста́ла ста́ло ста́ли	**на́чал** начала́ на́чало на́чали
Imperative	ты вы	ищи́ ищи́те	пеки́ пеки́те	клади́ клади́те	неси́ неси́те	возьми́ возьми́те	**! дава́й** **! дава́йте**	пры́гни пры́гните	ста́нь ста́ньте	начни́ начни́те

		II group (-И) R			II group (-И) IR					
		2.R.CONS.1	2.R.CONS.2	2.R.VOW	2.IR Б, П, М, В + Л	2.IR Д-Ж / ЗД-ЗЖ	2.IR С-Ш	2.IR Т-Ч	2.IR З-Ж	2.IR СТ-Щ / Т-Щ
Infinitive		**говори́ть**	**учи́ть**	**стро́ить**	**люби́ть**	**ви́деть**	**носи́ть**	**лете́ть**	**вози́ть**	**чи́стить**
Present Tense Imperfect & Future Tense Perfect	я	говорю́	учу́	стро́ю	люблю́	ви́жу	ношу́	лечу́	вожу́	чи́щу
	ты	говори́шь	у́чишь	стро́ишь	лю́бишь	ви́дишь	но́сишь	лети́шь	во́зишь	чи́стишь
	он (-а́,-о́)	говори́т	у́чит	стро́ит	лю́бит	ви́дит	но́сит	лети́т	во́зит	чи́стит
	мы	говори́м	у́чим	стро́им	лю́бим	ви́дим	но́сим	лети́м	во́зим	чи́стим
	вы	говори́те	у́чите	стро́ите	лю́бите	ви́дите	но́сите	лети́те	во́зите	чи́стите
	они́	говоря́т	у́чат	стро́ят	лю́бят	ви́дят	но́сят	летя́т	во́зят	чи́стят
Past Tense	он	**говори́л**	**учи́л**	**стро́ил**	**люби́л**	**ви́дел**	**носи́л**	**лете́л**	**вози́л**	**чи́стил**
	она́	говори́ла	учи́ла	стро́ила	люби́ла	ви́дела	носи́ла	лете́ла	вози́ла	чи́стила
	оно́	говори́ло	учи́ло	стро́ило	люби́ло	ви́дело	носи́ло	лете́ло	вози́ло	чи́стило
	они́	говори́ли	учи́ли	стро́или	люби́ли	ви́дели	носи́ли	лете́ли	вози́ли	чи́стили
Imperative	ты	говори́	учи́	стро́й	люби́	* видь	носи́	лети́	вози́	чи́сти
	вы	говори́те	учи́те	стро́йте	люби́те	* ви́дьте	носи́те	лети́те	вози́те	чи́стите

		SPECIAL									
Infinitive		**быть** **забы́ть**	**петь**	**есть**	**дать** **прода́ть**	**бежа́ть**	**хоте́ть**	**мочь** **помо́чь***	**сесть**	**идти́** **пойти́** **найти́**	**е́хать**
Present Tense Imperfect & Future Tense Perfect	я	бу́ду	пою́	**ем**	**дам**	бегу́	хочу́	могу́	ся́ду	иду́	е́ду
	ты	бу́дешь	поёшь	**ешь**	**дашь**	бежи́шь	хо́чешь	мо́жешь	ся́дешь	идёшь	е́дешь
	он (-а́, -о́)	бу́дет	поёт	**ест**	**даст**	бежи́т	хо́чет	мо́жет	ся́дет	идёт	е́дет
	мы	бу́дем	поём	**еди́м**	**дади́м**	бежи́м	хоти́м	мо́жем	ся́дем	идём	е́дем
	вы	бу́дете	поёте	**еди́те**	**дадите**	бежи́те	хоти́те	мо́жете	ся́дете	идёте	е́дете
	они	бу́дут	пою́т	**едя́т**	**даду́т**	бегу́т	хотя́т	мо́гут	ся́дут	иду́т	е́дут
Past Tense	он	**был**	**пел**	**ел**	**дал**	**бежа́л**	**хоте́л**	**мог**	**сел**	**шёл**	**е́хал**
	она́	была́	пе́ла	е́ла	дала́	бежа́ла	хоте́ла	могла́	се́ла	**шла**	е́хала
	оно́	бы́ло	пе́ло	е́ло	да́ло	бежа́ло	хоте́ло	могло́	се́ло	**шло**	е́хало
	они́	бы́ли	пе́ли	е́ли	да́ли	бежа́ли	хоте́ли	могли́	се́ли	**шли**	е́хали
Imperative	ты	будь	**! пой**	**! ешь**	дай	беги́	* хоти́	* моги́	ся́дь	иди́	**! езжа́й**
	вы	бу́дьте	**! по́йте**	**! е́шьте**	да́йте	беги́те	* хоти́те	* моги́те	ся́дьте	иди́те	**! езжа́йте**

* Возможно только в приставочных глаголах с этим корнем (Помоги мне!) и в некоторых конструкциях, выражающих условие (Всё твоё, только захоти. = Всё твоё, если ты только захочешь. Только захоти, и получишь. = Если ты только захочешь, ты получишь. Не захоти Джон лететь в Россию, он бы не выучил русский язык = Если бы Джон не захотел ехать в Россию, он бы не выучил русский язык).